Creative
Composition

Creative Composition

PRELIMINARY EDITION

Eileen Pollack
Jeremiah Chamberlin
Natalie Bakopoulos

CENGAGE
Learning·

Australia • Brazil • Japan • Korea • Mexico • Singapore • Spain • United Kingdom • United States

CENGAGE
Learning·

Creative Composition: Preliminary Edition Eileen Pollack, Jeremiah Chamberlin, Natalie Bakopoulos

For product information and technology assistance, contact us at
Cengage Learning Customer & Sales Support, 1-800-354-9706
For permission to use material from this text or product,
submit all requests online at **cengage.com/permissions**
Further permissions questions can be emailed to
permissionrequest@cengage.com

Senior Project Development Manager:
Linda deStefano

Marketing Specialist:
Courtney Sheldon

Senior Production/Manufacturing Manager:
Donna M. Brown

Production Editorial Manager:
Kim Fry

Sr. Rights Acquisition Account Manager:
Todd Osborne

Compilation © 2013 Cengage Learning

ISBN-13: 978-1-285-11727-0

ISBN-10: 1-285-11727-1

Cengage Learning
5191 Natorp Boulevard
Mason, Ohio 45040
USA

Cengage Learning is a leading provider of customized learning solutions with office locations around the globe, including Singapore, the United Kingdom, Australia, Mexico, Brazil, and Japan. Locate your local office at:
international.cengage.com/region.
Cengage Learning products are represented in Canada by Nelson Education, Ltd.
For your lifelong learning solutions, visit **custom.cengage.com.**
Visit our corporate website at **cengage.com.**

TABLE OF CONTENTS

PART II

Narratives

PART III

Portraits

PART V

Alternative Structures

PART VI

Process, Craft, and Revision

PREFACE

Writers write not simply to deliver information but also to discover what they think. As Don DeLillo said in a 1993 *Paris Review* interview, "Writing is an organized way of thinking. I don't know what I think about certain subjects, even today, until I sit down and try to write about them."

At the heart of the writing process, then, is a willingness to ask good questions. Questions guide our research and allow us to uncover new truths about ourselves and the larger world. They are the key to academic inquiry and are fundamental to developing strong critical-thinking skills.

This shift in the way students view writing—*arriving* at a position rather than beginning with one—is perhaps the most significant and exciting change they undergo at college. By reinforcing the philosophy that writing consists of grappling with original ideas and trying to say something new rather than simply repeating what someone else already has proven, students can more fully join the intellectual conversation going on around them and serve as participants and collaborators in their education rather than mere vessels to be filled.

In the many years the three of us have spent teaching composition (Jeremiah and Natalie are former-students-turned-colleagues of Eileen's), we have found few methods more natural, intuitive, or rigorous than centering a class around the materials and techniques of creative nonfiction. Why? Because the central forms of this genre—narratives, portraits, and investigations—are both intuitive and flexible. Because students are more willing to push themselves and ask complex questions about subjects in which they are truly invested. Because there is a natural progression from learning to examine the world through the personal pronoun "I" to honing more objective analytical skills. And because essays written in this genre are so varied in style, strategy, and approach that they provide a more effective way to teach students the fundamentals of style and craft, through modeling and by comparison, than the types of essays traditionally provided in a composition textbook or anthology.

Equally important, the structures or *forms* of creative composition equip students with a means to guide their research and organize their discoveries. For example, by re-creating an event from the past in the form of a reflective narrative, the writer is able to interrogate what took place and make meaning from the evidence, much as a CSI investigator does when reconstructing and analyzing a crime scene. Form becomes a tool to leverage knowledge, whether that knowledge is about the self or society. By using the self as a microcosm of human experience, students can draw larger significance from the evidence of their lives, thereby attempting to answer the "So what?" question all good writing must address. Because creative composition is both grounded in the individual point of view and contextualized within larger notions of human behavior and culture, students discover that they can make meaning from their experience and find connections between themselves and the world, activities that are at the very heart of critical thinking, intellectual inquiry, and argumentation.

The common forms of creative composition not only help a student writer to uncover meaning and depth, these structures are intuitively comprehensible on several levels. Even without a background in writing, a student easily can imagine the structure of a journey or an experiment. And because the unknown is inherent in such forms—we don't undertake quests or carry out experiments whose outcome we already know—the importance of formulating and focusing on a driving central question is reinforced in a natural, organic way.

Unfortunately, when some instructors or program administrators hear the phrase "creative nonfiction," they think only of the memoir or personal essay. As a result, they fear that this type of writing might encourage students to look inward rather than outward, or that the genre lacks the rigor necessary to prepare students to write across the disciplines. Yet the umbrella we call creative nonfiction covers everything from literary journalism to cultural criticism to meditative analysis, encompassing essays by esteemed literary figures such as George Orwell, social theorists such as Malcolm Gladwell, and medical practitioners such as Atul Gawande. The skills inherent in these forms of writing are as transferable to public policy, history, and biology as they are to English, anthropology, and cultural studies. If students can learn to be aware of their audience, to identify and employ a wide variety of rhetorical strategies, to position themselves as authors in relation to their material, and to appreciate language at the level of the paragraph, the sentence, and the word, then these students will be able to adapt and apply their skills to any form of writing. By reaching these goals in the context of creative composition, they will understand that form is a tool, not a container, and that genuine academic inquiry rather than an ability to stitch together sources or a facility with technical jargon or elevated diction defines academic writing.

Luckily, most institutions and writing programs have come to recognize the importance of creative nonfiction as a genre and its benefits for teaching rhetoric and composition. What makes *Creative Composition* (and Eileen's earlier volume, *Creative Nonfiction*) unique is the decision to organize the text not according to subject matter or rhetorical modes—all of which leave students without a natural approach to the writing process—but by structure or form. As Eileen explains in the preface to *Creative Nonfiction*:

> [M]y method is to lay bare the strategies that nonfiction writers actually use to generate their ideas and to write and revise their essays and to introduce students to a

dazzling array of intuitively clear and organic structures that—in combination with a compelling central question—can lend their own essays a dynamic forward motion and a pleasing sense of intentionality. In theory and in practice, the essay's central question keeps the writer focused on what he or she is supposed to be doing with the material while the structure (or *form*) provides a way for the writer to develop, organize, and present his or her line of thinking and research about that question. As a result, students find that they are able to use the strategies and structures presented in this book to generate their own pieces of creative nonfiction, *no matter the material.*

What we have attempted in *Creative Composition* is to couple Eileen's theories about creative nonfiction as a genre with our combined decades of experience teaching rhetoric and composition. A few of the essays in this book have been around for nearly a century, while many others have been published in the last few years. Yet all have proven successful in our classrooms and those of our colleagues. Like Eileen's earlier book, this one builds in complexity, starting with fairly simple structures and progressing to more complicated ones. This organizational method creates a natural progression for a class, as well as providing students with the skills and confidence to tackle each subsequent form.

Creative Composition differs from other first-year writing texts in that we have ordered the readings according to a clear and practical rationale. When a composition textbook divides its readings and assignments based on subject, how do you explain to students why "Body Image" is more complicated than "Immigration," or why the rhetorical skills learned in readings clustered around the theme of "Privacy" might help them write about "The Environment"? Similarly, when students are assigned anthologies organized around "types" of writing, they might be excused for wondering why "Personal" writing is carefully sectioned off from "Argument" when the latter often includes the former and vice-versa.

Here, the skills students learn in the chapter on the reflective narrative—a facility with point of view, chronology, characterization, transitions, causality, etc.—are not discarded but carried forward and built upon in subsequent chapters. Students recognize that they are adding new skills to their repertoire while continually fine-tuning and honing the skills they already have learned, a progression that allows them to feel productive, engaged in a process they can see to be useful and relevant to their academic and personal lives.

THE ORGANIZATION OF *CREATIVE COMPOSITION*

As mentioned previously, this book is organized so that students encounter increasingly complex and analytical forms. Likewise, the readings within each section are structured to introduce new skills with each essay. In this fashion, students learn skill sets that are built upon, stage by stage, in a clear and manageable progression.

Part I covers the essentials of style, content, and form, in addition to addressing the more philosophical questions that emerge from the enterprise of writing. In Chapters 1 through 4, students study the following: (1) fundamental rhetorical strategies of creative composition; (2) how rhetorical strategies can be drawn from the stylistic techniques of fiction, poetry, and drama to engage both reader and writer; (3) the importance of selecting a topic that genuinely interests him or her and the use of a driving question to foster academic inquiry; (4) the process by which a writer uses a specific structure or *form* to guide the search for an answer to the aforementioned question, allowing him or her to arrive at a sophisticated, original, complex position; and (5) the habits of mind necessary to read like a writer and transfer those critical-thinking skills to the student's own work, in English and other disciplines.

Parts II, III, and IV lead the student through an understanding of the three forms of creative nonfiction most pertinent to college writing: the narrative, the portrait, and the investigation. In the same way that the three primary sections have been ordered according to increasing complexity, so, too, have the essays been organized within each section. This versatility allows the book to be adopted at different levels in a given department or used as a single text at institutions that have multiple-semester writing requirements. Further, it offers instructors the flexibility to choose their own paths, depending on the levels and needs of their students.

Part V offers instructors the opportunity to teach a range of exciting alternative structures, such as spatial forms, lists, and diagrams. For example, John McPhee uses a game of Monopoly to organize his material in "The Search for Marvin Gardens," while Michelle Morano shapes her essay according to the rules of the subjunctive mood in Spanish. Because many of these selections incorporate combined elements of narrative, portrait, and investigation, they help illustrate the way sophisticated writers synthesize elements of different forms to create nuanced, subtle work that matters.

Part VI provides support to student and instructor alike in the guise of supplementary essays on craft. Although *Creative Composition* offers textual analysis and guiding questions to accompany each section, comparing how a variety of authors approach craft issues is an invaluable learning tool. And because writing is a process and not simply a product, this section will include extensive strategies for revision: self-directed revision; revision after a group workshop; and the final stages of revision at the global, paragraph, and sentence level. Sample student essays—in various stages of the drafting process—are included as an enrichment tool for the classroom.

KEY FEATURES OF *CREATIVE COMPOSITION*

Unique Approach: *Creative Composition* is the only rhetoric and composition textbook that combines an emphasis on teaching academic writing through the use of driving questions and natural, organic structures or *forms* with a fully integrated reader.

Fresh, Diverse Readings: By introducing students to authors who are interrogating what it means to live in the twenty-first century and encouraging them to use their own research and experience as lenses through which to analyze questions related to sexuality, gender, technology, race, class, and culture, we show students that writing continues to matter. Many of the essays collected here have been published in the last few years, written by a diverse spectrum of authors that includes Eula Biss, Joshua Ferris, Atul Gawande, John Jeremiah Sullivan, and Jesmyn Ward. And because relevancy is not based on publication date alone, we have also selected work by landmark authors such as John Hersey and E.B. White to complement the more contemporary readings, as well as essays by household names in the field of creative nonfiction such as Nora Ephron, Barbara Ehrenreich, Phillip Lopate, and John McPhee.

Student-Centered Approach: The majority of essays in this book have been culled from the hundreds we have collectively taught over the past several decades. First-year writing is a requirement for *all* students at our institution, so we have had the opportunity to test the appeal of these essays, as well as the effectiveness of the accompanying teaching apparatus, for students from a wide variety of educational, social, racial, cultural, and economic backgrounds.

Transfer of Learning: Because many—if not most—of our students will major in fields other than English, the principles we impart must allow students to tackle projects in anthropology, history, geology, biochemistry, and political science, to say nothing of fostering the sort of close-reading and critical-thinking skills they must absorb to succeed in every class at the college level. This is accomplished in many ways: (1) learning to read as writers helps students to develop flexible reading strategies beyond mere content acquisition; (2) studying a genre that is particularly attuned to language at the sentence level helps students to develop clear, concise prose and the ability to articulate their ideas more fluently, precisely, and effectively; (3) becoming aware that writing is a process rather than a product allows students to cultivate individualized, adaptable strategies for all stages of a project—from idea generation and problem solving to research and execution; (4) understanding that content, form, and meaning are inextricable encourages students to grapple with and appreciate complexity; and (5) being exposed to a wide range of subject matter and varied topics reinforces the importance of context, as well as a sophisticated awareness of the relationship between stance and audience, all of which are essential to successful argumentation.

Interest and Curiosity: We use the methods and materials of creative nonfiction not as an *alternative* to teaching rhetoric and composition but because these types of reading and writing assignments are the most effective way to impart the fundamentals of good writing; not because we are trying to entertain our students with contemporary topics that keep their attention but because students who learn to draw meaning from their own lives will approach the complexity of the world with interest and curiosity rather than apathy. And isn't that the key to both academic and personal success?

ACKNOWLEDGMENTS

As Eileen wrote in the acknowledgments to her previous book on this subject, *Creative Nonfiction: A Guide to Form, Content, and Style, with Readings,* her approach to this genre owes much to her apprenticeship with one of its inventors, John Hersey. "Not only was Hersey a brilliant writer and teacher," she recounts, "he was also a kind and generous mentor and friend."

As a graduate student at the University of Iowa in the early 1980s, Eileen was fortunate to study composition theory with Cleo Jones and Dennis Moore, who helped her to apply Hersey's methods to teaching undergraduates how to write.

In this ongoing tradition of apprenticeship, Jeremiah and Natalie were Eileen's students in the early 2000s in the University of Michigan's MFA Program in Creative Writing. The composition classes that Jeremiah and Natalie would later develop would be strongly influenced by Eileen's teaching, blending her philosophies with their own practices. They would like to thank her here for more than a decade of mentorship, collegiality, and friendship.

Likewise, they would like to thank the University of Michigan's English Department Writing Program, particularly Arthur F. Thurnau Professor of English Anne Curzan, who served as the director of this program for seven years and offered them a model of professionalism and excellence in the classroom. She continues to inspire all three authors of this textbook with her enthusiasm for teaching and her dedication to writing as a discipline.

In developing the methods of teaching embodied in *Creative Composition,* the authors profited immeasurably from the suggestions and support offered by their students and colleagues at Tufts, Harvard, Emerson, the Interlochen Arts Academy, and, again, the University of Michigan. They would especially like to acknowledge Paul Barron, Anne Ruggles Gere, Elizabeth Gramm, Nick Harp, Miles Harvey, Michael Hinken, Donovan Hohn, Joseph Horton, Laura Kasischke, Aric Knuth, Alex Ralph, Naomi Silver, Therese Stanton, Elizabeth Staudt, Fritz Swanson, and Keith Taylor for their support, expertise, and ongoing conversations about the use of creative nonfiction in the composition classroom.

Sincere and lasting appreciation goes to the many graduate students at the University of Michigan who have helped to refine this pedagogy over the last several years by teaching and testing the materials in this book in their own classrooms. Their continued feedback has been invaluable in fine-tuning this text. Thanks to Nawaaz Ahmed, Gina Balibrera, Lionel Beasley, Mary Beckman, Nina Buckless, Roohi Choudhry, Sheerah Cole, Monique Daviau, Jaimien Delp, Daniel Distefano, Rachel Farrell, Daniel Frazier, Leigh Gallagher, John Ganiard, Francine J. Harris, Carlus Henderson, Bradford Kammin, Daniel Keane, James Kusher, Henry Leung, Airea Matthews, Eric McDowell, Emily McLaughlin, Kevin Phan, Audra Puchalski, James Redmond, Tina Richardson, Jennifer Riemenschneider, Rocco Samuele, Rebecca Scherm, Ali Shapiro, Anna Sheaffer, Ilana Sichel, Claire Skinner, Franke Varca, Angela Watrous, and Trilbe Wynne.

We are also grateful to the following instructors for their helpful feedback:

Forrest Anderson, Catawba College
Lowell Brower, Harvard University
J.T. Bushnell, Oregon State University
Sabrina Chesne, Northwest Arkansas Community College
Judith Claire Mitchell, University of Wisconsin – Madison
Joe Conway, Towson University
Susan Davis, Arizona State University
Michael Downs, Towson University
Anthony Edgington, University of Toledo
Sarah Frisch, Stanford University
Rebecca Gidjunis, Eastern University
Patricia Gott, University of Wisconsin - Stevens Point
Carol Harrell, Kennesaw State University
Valerie Laken, University of Wisconsin – Milwaukee
Jonathan Liebson, Eugene Lang College – The New School
Benjamin Minor, Arizona State University
Richard Noggle, University of Kansas
Michael Pearson, Old Dominion University
Benjamin Percy, Iowa State University
Patrick Quinn, College of Southern Nevada
Polly Rosenwaike, Eastern Michigan University
Dee Dee Snyder, The Ohio State University Agricultural Technical Institute
Holly Spaulding, Northwestern Michigan College
Beth Stickney, Keene State College
Mary Tripp, University of Central Florida
Joe Wilkins, Waldorf College
Steven Wingate, South Dakota State University

Thanks again to Whitney Stubbs, who contributed many of the author bios and advice along the way, and to Eileen's agent, Maria Massie, for her generous counsel and wise support.

Finally, our deepest thanks and appreciation to everyone at Cengage Learning: Lyn Uhl, Editor-in-Chief, Monica Eckman, Publisher for English Composition, and Michael Rosenberg, Publisher, for having the foresight to appreciate Eileen's innovative approach to the still-emerging field of creative nonfiction and for his gentle prodding to apply that approach to the more traditional field of composition studies; Leslie Taggart, Senior Development Editor, for her advocacy of this book at every stage of its development; Kate Derrick, Acquiring Sponsoring Editor, for her imaginative and far-reaching vision of this book's potential and her steadfast belief in its importance in the field of rhetoric and composition, as well as her encouragement at each step of the process; Stephanie Pelkowski Carpenter, Development Editor, for her friendship, good humor, and the super editing ability that helped us to realize a book even better than the one we originally envisioned; Marjorie Cross, Editorial Assistant, for her able handling of the important details; and James P. Decker, Sales Representative, whose evangelism on our behalf could make anyone a convert.

HOW TO USE THIS BOOK

Many textbooks categorize their readings by subject—"gender," "culture," "nature," and so on. But focusing on what an essay is *about* doesn't give much guidance on where to start or how to construct an insightful essay on the topic. If you were asked to write an essay about technology, where would you begin? Would it help if you were asked to make an argument about an element of digital technology? Most of us still would be left staring at a blank screen. Yet if someone asked you to write a narrative about your relationship with Facebook, you would know immediately where to start: the first time you logged on. Or the first time you heard about Facebook but were too young to have an account. Or the first status update you posted. From there, the path would be clear: tracing your way from that first time to the present. Naturally, you would simultaneously be tracing the ways your feelings toward the technology changed, or how Facebook affected your friendships, or how social networking affected the way you communicate with people who attract you sexually or romantically. Suddenly, the assignment not only has a shape to guide you (i.e., the narrative of your relationship to Facebook), but also an incentive for you to reflect at key points on your material (in this case, analyzing how A might have affected B). Simply by selecting a form to shape your work, you not only have begun writing, you also have developed your critical-thinking skills.

Likewise, you might decide to write a profile of Facebook. Then, instead of using a narrative structure to measure how this new technology has changed a specific aspect of your life, you might define and describe Facebook and examine its collective effect on your family, your circle of friends, or your entire school. In this case, you might use the portrait form to get at the essence of this new technology by examining it from multiple vantage points. Imagine a bicycle wheel, with the subject (Facebook) as the hub and the experiences of your family members, friends, or classmates radiating outward as spokes.

To use yet another form, you might write an investigation of Facebook, perhaps by carrying out an experiment. In this scenario, you might attempt to refrain from logging on for a week. And by chronicling that experience—Day 1, Day 2, Day 3—you would automatically have the structure for your paper as well as the opportunity and incentive to arrive at some greater knowledge of how intertwined the technology is with your daily life, or how many of your relationships are centered around (maybe even exclusively exist in) the virtual realm, or how much of your communication with other people takes place via digital media. This analysis could be supplemented with research from the fields of psychology, communication, cultural studies, and so on.

As should be readily apparent, there are numerous other forms that an essay about Facebook might take. The point here is that a *form*, unlike a subject, gives you both a starting point and a direction for your inquiry. A form allows you to take a certain position in relation to your subject. As we will see in the following sections, in its most basic sense, a reflective narrative looks back at an event or a series of events with the knowledge, wisdom, distance, and insight of the present; a portrait looks at something (a person, place, or thing) straight on, in an attempt to capture its essence; and an investigation looks forward, with the process of investigation often woven into the essay itself. Regardless of your interests or materials, you can use the forms of creative composition to uncover meaning and to gain insight about the world.

Equally important to the philosophy behind this book is that good writing begins with a question rather than with an answer. Look back at the previous Facebook assignment and think about the sorts of questions that would naturally arise to guide your inquiry—questions about communication, about relationships, about how heavily we rely on the new technology. Yet too often, students are asked to start with a thesis statement. How can you know the answer to something before you begin to think or write about it? How can you develop a position on a subject before you have honestly thought about it, let alone researched or interrogated it? And if you *begin* with a position, how likely are you to incorporate evidence that contradicts that point of view? Not likely. You will ignore or discard whatever doesn't fall into line with your reasoning, hoping that your readers never stumble upon anything that might shake their faith in your opinion.

Yet if you begin with an honest question, all sources become equally useful. You will consider alternative viewpoints and not just the token "counter argument" that is tossed in to acknowledge the opposition. If you start with a question, you will honestly interrogate the material—whether an incident from your past, a place that has special significance, or an abstract concept—and eventually arrive at your own unique and original conclusion. Then you can integrate that position (call it a "claim," call it a "thesis") in subsequent drafts of your paper.

Here is another way to think of this method: if form were a car, then the driving question would be the engine that powers your inquiry. Where you steer the vehicle will depend on your interests, background, and needs, as well as what you encounter along the way. At the end of the journey, you can look back to assess where you have been and what you have seen. Best of all: the more you drive, the better driver you will become. And by "better" we don't only mean that you will become more adept at using different rhetorical strategies, but also that you will be more flexible in your ability to adapt these strategies to different styles, modes, and literary or scholarly purposes. In keeping with this metaphor, you will be able to more skillfully operate different vehicles under different conditions and in increasingly difficult terrains.

Using the methods outlined in *Creative Composition* to learn to write may be more natural and enjoyable than other methods, but that doesn't mean you won't find this material challenging. In this genre, there is no "right way" or "right answer," which means you must embrace nuance and complexity in your work. As human beings, we long for answers, definitive facts, and rules. But the world isn't black and white. Politics is about compromise, business is about negotiation, and writing—including as it does analysis and interpretation—is fundamentally about point of view.

The authors of this book view the elements of your life—your background, your experiences, your personality—as assets not detriments. Rather than asking you to strip the "I" from your work, as many students have been taught is a requirement for academic discourse, we recognize that knowledge is based on subjectivity and perspective. By bringing ourselves into our work, we can help readers more readily judge how and why we arrived at our conclusions.

This is not to say that an individual's opinions are sacrosanct. Many of the opinions we grow up with are invalid, misguided, or poorly considered. Again, this is why we bring ourselves into our writing: to shine the light of reflection on our beliefs and our experiences in order that we might hold them up against the beliefs and experiences of others and subject them to critical examination. Writing in this way can be scary. Yet it is equally rewarding because the insights we gain about culture, gender, sexuality, technology, and so forth are derived from and can be applied to our own lives. Seeing that we can make meaning from our own experience is empowering and exhilarating.

Further, by establishing an actual point of view in an essay, you are much less likely to fall into the trap of writing in the passive voice or using elevated language you can't control. Have you ever opened the thesaurus function on Microsoft Word to change a little word to a "big" one, or tried to beef up a perfectly clear and simple sentence with a bunch of professorial-sounding clauses to make your work seem more academic (read: smart)? Yet by inflating your prose or populating it with jargon, you end up sounding like someone you aren't. Sometimes, you don't even know what you are saying. As George Orwell warns in his famous essay "On Politics and the English Language," sloppy language leads to sloppy thinking, one influencing the other in an endless loop. Writing in a straightforward, natural manner highlights the complexity of your thinking instead of the complexity of your language. And few genres of writing are better suited to teaching attention to language than creative nonfiction.

These principles— developing a clear, natural, engaging voice and style; starting with a driving question; and using a variety of natural, organic forms to shape your research and organize your final paper—will be introduced to you in the chapters that immediately follow. Part I covers the essentials of style, content, and form, presenting you with important terminology and key rhetorical strategies. Parts II through V cover some of the most common forms of creative composition, organized by increasing complexity. In this way, the skills you learn while studying the reflective narrative can be built upon and incorporated into, say, the profile. Likewise, elements of both the reflective narrative and profile will come in handy when you work with the forms

...tuation and need. Just as
...rt your arguments, introduce counter
...dered both sides of your position, or
...he choices you make about voice and
...general and successful argumentation
...makes is that imperialism controls and
...e essay exposes the flaws and failings of
...of power that Orwell wields as the sub-
...en he is called to dispatch an elephant on
...st" has passed and the animal is no longer
...ws that what he *should* do is announce to
...g to see and they can go home. Instead, he
...mply out of fear of looking like a fool. Just
...rites:

> ...e to shoot the elephant after all: The people
> ...could feel their two thousand wills pressing
> ...s moment, as I stood there with the rifle in
> ...vness, the futility of the white man's domin-
> ...an with his gun, standing in front of the
> ...e leading actor of the piece; but in reality I was
> ...fro by the will of those yellow faces behind it. I
> ...the white man turns tyrant it is his own freedom
> ...f hollow, posing dummy, the conventionalized
> ...tion of his rule that he shall spend his life in try-
> ...in every crisis he has got to do what the "natives"
> ...d his face grows to fit it.

...and sophisticated analysis. Yet the author's position
...e library, but from Orwell's investigation of his own
...s—its complexity—is made possible by his decision
...d a retrospective point of view. By forcing himself
...on the page, he can more rigorously explore the past,
...ompeting influences of culture that were affecting the

...is the coupling of fact-based research
...of literary fiction: narration, scenic writ-
...e, etc. The goal is to represent what the
...her unique point of view, to create an inti-
...e audience, and, in so doing, to capture the
...ots of this genre go back hundreds of years,
...American writers such as John Hersey, Tom
...Talese, Truman Capote, and Norman Mailer
...as the New Journalism. Only then did nonfic-
...rt form.

...nized was the subjectivity inherent in all writ-
...vriter's duty. The typical reporter's manufactured
...dvantage of the writer's point of view, but also, by
...objective, conveyed a false or incomplete sense
...academic writing. By definition, a thesis must be
...mentation—a process of analyzing and interpreting
...d a claim—lies authorial subjectivity.

...allowed to bend the truth or omit details due to "sub-
...secution in a court case is allowed to lie to the jury or
...ense. In the discipline of creative composition, we hold
...s: the "creative" side of creative composition has noth-
...manipulating facts. What is creative isn't your attitude
...age and stylistic techniques you use to convey that truth
...f a general topic and authentic question that puzzles you
...r selection of a structure or form that guides you as you
...uestion and present your reflections and discoveries to
...ic way.

...e we introduce you to the specific principles and
...tion, let's try to define the genre in more det..."
...erry proposes four essential characteristics:

...documentable subject matter" as on...

2) "exhaustive research," which...
   ibility;

(3) the use of scene as
    multi-dimensional...

6

(4) "a literary prose style."

The key here is that diffe...
proportions and for varying e...
research in her essay "A Few W...
anxiety about growing up boyish...
you sat, crossed your legs, held a c...
these things was absolutely proof of...
Gladwell relies extensively on data to...
of the S.U.V. had less to do with the actu...
tural attitudes brought on by disaster tel...
which led us to believe that accidents are i...
help us survive rather than avoid them. Ho...
elements of research in their work.

In addition to the four characteristics id...
a fifth category: significance. For an essay to ha...
about culture or society that goes beyond a simple...
story. The writer's experience—or the subject matte...
serve as a microcosm of something larger, somethi...
vidual. The work must make claims, whether explici...
writer and reader to some larger insight about the mate...
valid and useful for catharsis or the intimate understand...
we present here, and the work you will be expected to pr...
purely personal, beginning with the individual but by no me...

Creative nonfiction, like any art, is a discipline. As such, i...
attention to detail, and patience. What might surprise you as y...
that the more you learn about the craft, the more you will enj...
writing. Think of a sport you know well. Now compare your exper...
activity to that of someone who knows nothing about its intricacies...
can be amazed watching Michael Phelps swim or Shaun White snow...
are a swimmer or snowboarder yourself, you will understand the incre...
talent needed to make what Phelps or White accomplishes look effortles...

The same is true of writing. As you explore these forms and become a...
of this genre of writing, you will at first find the work demanding. But as y...

for this to happen to me." In addition to immediately...
the writer adopts a tone that is accessible and concise...
choice, to the straightforward rhythm of the sentence...
people hated him, every choice he has made lends a...
ity, in turn, allows us to trust the writer. And trust is...
of the three central Aristotelian appeals, along with...
the span of one line, we already can see the writer d...
strategies.

What's important here is that these choices...
something you are born with, nor does it remain s...
a voice is a rhetorical strategy that you adapt to a...
you may need to include outside sources to suppo...
arguments to demonstrate that you have consi...
organize your sub-claims in a logical manner,...
tone will be foundational for strong writing in...
in particular. In Orwell's case, the argument he...
corrupts the colonizer as well as his subjects;...
English rule in Burma by examining the lac...
divisional police officer of a small village. Wh...
the loose and discovers that its attack of "mu...
a threat to the local inhabitants, Orwell kn...
the gathered thousands that there is nothi...
lifts his rifle and shoots the poor beast si...
before he commits himself to the act, he...

And suddenly I realized that I should ha...
expected it of me and I had got to do it;...
me forward, irresistibly. And it was at th...
my hands, that I first grasped the hollo...
ion in the East. Here was I, the white...
unarmed native crowd—seemingly th...
only an absurd puppet pushed to and...
perceived in this moment that when...
that he destroys. He becomes a sort...
figure of a sahib. For it is the condi...
ing to impress "the natives" and so...
expect of him. He wears a mask, a...

This is complicated thinking...
is derived not from research in th...
life. And the depth of that analys...
to adopt a narrative structure a...
create his time in Burma...
...d illuminating the...

decisions he made all those years ago. In short, the very act of writing leads to discovery and meaning, not the other way around. Despite the central claim not appearing on the first page, Orwell's thesis is hard to miss.

Making an argument from personal experience is challenging, particularly with the sophistication and level of insight Orwell uses. But coming to understand that writing happens *before* you know your position, not afterward, that it is a means to help you *figure out* your position, can be wonderfully liberating.

More than that: if you start with a driving question rather than with a thesis statement, you will be more likely to go out and find and evaluate evidence from both sides of your argument rather than simply snatching up the first few quotes that seem to support your original position. Once human beings decide what they believe, they find it hard not to discard or ignore anything that doesn't back up that belief. But such a process is antithetical to real academic inquiry and legitimate argumentation. As Frank Cioffi argues in "Argumentation in a Culture of Discord" (located in Part VI of this text):

> I propose that we teach students more about how intellectual discourse works, about how it offers something exciting—yet how when it succeeds, it succeeds in only approaching understanding. ... Philosophical and, more generally, argumentative discourse presents no irrefutable proofs, no indelible answers. In fact, the best writing of this kind tends not to answer but to raise questions, ones that the audience hadn't previously considered. Or to put it in terms my college nephew uses, when you're writing an argument, don't go for the slam dunk.

By changing the way we think about academic argumentation—as joining a conversation rather than having the last word—we see that meaning is derived from uncertainty and curiosity rather than from knowing all the answers. Similarly, we can train ourselves to both locate and employ argumentative strategies in a reflective narrative, a portrait, or an investigation just as readily as if we were studying more traditional essays. The difference is that the examples of creative nonfiction included in this book have the questioning process already built into their architecture, effectively and efficiently demonstrating how you can embrace complexity and critical thinking.

CHAPTER 2

An Engaging Voice and Style

CLEAR, NATURAL LANGUAGE

Many students enter college thinking that the more complicated their writing, the better. They craft labyrinthine sentences overpopulated by polysyllabic Latinate words. The only quality these sentences lack is clarity. Why does this happen? As George Orwell lamented more than half a century ago in "Politics and the English Language":

> ... modern writing at its worst does not consist in picking out words for the sake of their meaning and inventing images in order to make the meaning clearer. It consists in gumming together long strips of words which have already been set in order by someone else, and making the results presentable by sheer humbug. The attraction of this way of writing is that it is easy. It is easier—even quicker once you have the habit—to say *In my opinion it is a not unjustifiable assumption that* than to say *I think.*

What is also easier about this style of writing is that the author can hide behind a wall of words. When you write simply and clearly, you can't disguise your position. You put yourself out there, which can be scary, especially if you are still trying to figure out what you truly think.

Fortunately, few activities are better suited to helping you understand what you think than writing itself. How many times have you labored over a sentence, muttering, "No, it's not like that; it's more like *this.*" In the exact moment when you do, finally, describe an action, an emotion, an object, or an experience just right, your fingers are off to the races, clattering across the keyboard. Writing *leads* to thinking, not the other way around. The clearer you allow your language to be, the clearer your thinking will become.

One of the fundamental reasons studying creative nonfiction will help you to write better in any style or academic discipline is that the genre is committed to straightforward, natural language. Not only will you uncover meaning in your work, you will learn to grab and hold your readers' attention. To do so, you will need to write in a voice that is entertaining, moving, memorable, or poetic—or better yet, a voice that is entertaining, moving, memorable, *and* poetic.

Joyce Carol Oates, in her introduction to *The Best American Essays of the Century*, describes the allure of language that is fresh and alive:

> Where in life we sometimes (allegedly, infrequently) fall in love at first sight, in reading we may fall in love with the special, singular qualities of another's voice; we may become mesmerized, haunted; we may be provoked, shocked, illuminated; we may be galvanized into action; we may be enraged, revulsed, and yet!—drawn irresistibly to experience this *voice* again, and again. It's a writer's unique employment of language to which we, as readers, are drawn, though we assume we admire the writer primarily for what he or she "has to say."

While it's more pleasurable to read the work of someone with a facility for language, this doesn't mean a writer needs to show off. "Purple prose," which is what we call writing that is overindulgent, full of verbal acrobatics, and packed with figurative language, is just as bad as the stodgy, jargon-choked style of writing mentioned earlier. This sort of flashy overwriting ends up diluting the power of your language. Imagine going to a basketball game where every player who gets the ball feels the need to dribble between his legs and behind his back, twirl the ball on his finger, and turn cartwheels as he heads toward the basket. At first, you might be delighted. But unless you had bought a ticket to an exhibition match involving the Harlem Globetrotters, you eventually would grow frustrated, or even bored. The point of the game—putting the ball through the hoop—would get lost in all the pointless fireworks. The same happens when a writer packs every sentence with a metaphor, or adds ten details when three would do just fine.

Between these two extremes lies writing at its best: complex but not complicated, artful but not showy, direct but not dull.

A DISTINCTIVE VOICE

In this discussion of clear, natural language, there's been just one missing element: you. As we mentioned earlier, all good writing strives to develop a unique point of view on a subject. (After all, if you aren't saying something new, why write?) One of the easiest ways to establish a point of view is to nurture your distinctive voice. The question is how.

Our advice is to sound like yourself. At first, this recommendation might seem ill-advised or even frightening. *Sound like myself? How could that make me a better writer?* But most of us are fairly talented speakers. We know how to keep the interest of our listeners, how to moderate our tone and vary our diction, how to quote and mimic other people. So why is it that when we sit down to write we pretend to be someone we aren't? Trying to sound like yourself on paper tends to produce your best prose and allows your natural—and naturally unique—voice to come through. Voice is personality; it's like an invisible stamp on your work.

We all have many voices. Think of how you talk to your friends versus how you talk to your mother, how you talk to your kid sister versus how you talk to your grandmother, how you talk to your coach versus how you talk to your teammates. Contrary to what some people think, voice is not an entirely fixed quality. A good writer learns to throw his or her voice—sometimes serious, sometimes funny, sometimes sarcastic, sometimes thoughtful. Like any rhetorical maneuver, how you employ your voice is a strategy. Voice is a tool that helps a writer achieve a desired, deliberate effect. Our voices control how we connect to our audience, how we stay *aware* of our audience, which is a key component of all good writing, regardless of the discipline.

However, in an attempt to connect with that audience, we sometimes fall back on prefabricated language. Before newspapers lost so many of their subscribers and so much of their advertising revenue, Eileen used to travel from paper to paper, helping the reporters improve their writing. At one paper, she worked with a sportswriter who couldn't churn out a sentence without using at least two clichés. His teams *thrashed their opponents* on their way to *garnering trophies*. His freshman quarterbacks *hailed from All-American hometowns, put their noses to the grindstone, gave their teams their all,* and *made their families, friends, teammates, and coaches proud.* When asked why he relied so heavily on expressions that so many sportswriters before him had relied on, the reporter said that he assumed such expressions were a sort of professional lingo he needed to learn if he was going to advance in the field.

At another newspaper, Eileen read a stack of editorials weighed down by hackneyed allusions to football and war (the members of the city council needed *to tackle the issue of unfair taxation,* while the superintendent of the schools was urged *to enter the field and annihilate the disparity in test scores between black and white students*), even though the editorial writer turned out to be a pixieish twentysomething feminist who hadn't attended a single football game in her life or served a day in the military. "What have I done?" she moaned. "I'm the first woman to hold this job, and I guess I thought I needed to sound like one of the guys." Happily, all she needed to do to develop an original voice—and win an award for her editorials—was to stop trying to sound like all the other editorial writers she had ever read.

Not that a reliance on jargon or stale expressions is limited to sports reporters or editorial writers. In some disciplines, earning a PhD can seem like an exercise in stringing together whatever buzzwords are in vogue. Even in daily life, when we sit around talking about our parents or children, our lovers, or our jobs, we often fall back on pop-psychological jargon about families that are dysfunctional, significant others who refuse to commit to a relationship or communicate about their issues, and bosses who have problems with authority and pass along their baggage to their employees. We may think we know what we mean. Maybe we do. But other people might not.

Suppose a writer says: "When I was a child, my father experienced a problem with alcohol that caused him to engage in domestic abuse. This impacted me when I was young, but eventually I learned to deal with the situation." The reality behind this wall of jargon, clichés, and vague or jarring phrases (technically, "impacted" isn't a verb, it's an adjective that means "packed or wedged in," as in "impacted wisdom tooth" or an "impacted bowel") might be that the writer's father was a drunk who would come home from the factory, go through a case of beer, then accuse his wife of cheating on him with everyone from the letter carrier to the clerk at the A&P, after which he would hurl her against the refrigerator and twist her arm behind her back until she confessed to whatever infidelity he wanted her to confess to. The "impact" of this "situation" might be that the writer cowered in his room with his hands over his ears, wishing he were big and strong enough to protect his mother. And his eventual ability to "deal with" his father might mean that when he reached seventh grade, he grew ten inches, put on fifty pounds, and started working out at the gym, with the result that the next time his father tried to stuff his mother's hand down the garbage disposal, he was able to yank him off, throw him outside, and change the locks.

Then again, that "problem with alcohol" might describe a dad who occasionally drank too much bourbon and called the writer a stupid, ugly whore. Maybe, when she was young, the writer believed what he said. But after her mom divorced her father and sent her to see a therapist, she realized she was neither stupid nor ugly nor any more promiscuous than other girls her age. Best of all, her dad eventually joined AA and begged forgiveness for all the terrible names he used to call her.

Whatever the case, you wouldn't really know from the writer's original description.

The real danger of relying on clichés is that in their overuse and familiarity they lose any degree of specificity or significance. Jeremiah calls this the "Mrs. Claus" phenomenon. During a recent fiction-writing workshop, a student presented a story to the class with a grandmother as one of the characters. As the writer described her, the older woman was short and plump, with round glasses and rosy cheeks. Her white hair was styled in close curls, she wore an apron, and she smelled like cookie dough. Sound familiar? All that was missing were the elves! The class liked the story but felt the grandmother was too generic. The student was confused; he thought the point was to create a character with whom readers could identify. Yet connecting to a piece of writing doesn't come through recognition but by *comparison*. To prove this, Jeremiah asked his class to listen to his description of his own grandmother and pay attention to what their brains did as he read:

> Every Thursday my grandmother got her hair set at the nearby salon, and you could be sure that the color of her lipstick always matched her nails. She wasn't exactly prim and proper, but even indoors she wore high-heel shoes with a blouse and skirt. When we sat down to dinner, she'd watch through the pass-through of the kitchen while she had her one cigarette of the day and drank a glass of white wine. She wouldn't join us immediately, making sure we didn't need anything else first. Then, once everyone was done eating, she'd wave us away from the table so that she could begin cleaning up. If you offered to help, she'd laugh and say, "Thank you, hon. You just go and enjoy yourself." Though she didn't seem to consider this work. In fact, I can't remember my grandmother ever not smiling.

While the students couldn't help but envision the woman Jeremiah was describing, they realized they had been comparing their own grandmothers to this description, trying to recall how their own grandmothers dressed, whether or not their grandmothers smoked cigarettes or drank alcohol, how graceful or resentful their grandmothers tended to be about serving others. It's through the specificity of detail rather than the generality of cliché that we engage our readers, keeping their attention while activating the analytical regions of their brains.

Part of developing a distinctive voice, then, involves selecting the details you choose to include in your work. A distinctive voice doesn't only manifest itself in how you structure a sentence or what your language "sounds" like; it's also about what you notice, how you connect one image to another, what significance you ascribe to an encounter with a savage dog, a run-in with a bigoted uncle, or a church service led by an eccentric but inspiring minister. This is why developing a distinctive voice is largely about sounding like yourself, albeit your "best" self, your most aware, most perceptive self. What you choose to relate to the reader says as much about your voice—that is, your personality, your approach, your attitude, your point of view—as the sound and shape of your language.

So whenever you catch yourself using a phrase you have heard before ("black and blue" or "the gym teacher from hell"), ask yourself whether the cliché actually describes what you are trying to capture (your bruises, your gym teacher) in a unique and truthful way or whether you are relying on a generic description because you are writing on auto-pilot. Was that bruise you suffered last week really black and blue, or did you start out with a lump as hard and purple as a plum, after which the bruise faded to a sickly yellowish-green puddle that spread slowly across your skin? Wouldn't you rather provide two horrifying examples of your gym teacher's brutality than dismiss him with a stale generalization? Finding the most specific, accurate words to convey what you saw, heard, smelled, tasted, felt, or thought might seem challenging at first, but eventually you will find more pleasure in selecting the perfect detail than in letting yourself slide by with a hackneyed cliché. By forcing yourself to think about how *you* see the racially charged scuffle that broke out in your high school cafeteria, how *you* would describe the tornado that everyone in your town experienced, you are on your way to developing a distinctive voice and point of view, as well as uncovering the true subject of your essay.

On a practical level, this process will also help you to focus your attention where it belongs: on the sentence. Too often we get so wrapped up in having to finish an essay, or how many pages it needs to be, that we can't generate any real traction to get started. By concentrating on one specific sentence after another, you will have a half a dozen pages before you know it. Why? Because one specific sentence usually leads to a second specific sentence, which leads to a third and a fourth, and so on. As E.L. Doctorow once said, "Writing is like driving at night in the fog. You can only see as far as your headlights, but you can make the whole trip that way."

One exercise the three of us use to illustrate the importance of the specificity of details and why clear writing matters is to ask each student to compose a sentence that conveys something essential about a person who helped to raise them. Then we go around the room and read our sentences aloud. "My mother works from sun up to sun down to buy us the things we need," a student might write. Or: "My aunt always cracks me up." Or: "My father is the most forgiving man in the world." But as is true with any generalization, these examples raise as many questions as they answer. Does the first student's mother wake up at 4 a.m. and take the train to Manhattan, where she shouts herself hoarse on the floor of the Stock Exchange so she can buy the student and her sister thousand-dollar handbags? Or does she spend ten hours a day cleaning houses so she can pay the rent on a shabby bungalow where she lives with the writer and his six siblings on the outskirts of a small Kentucky mining town? Does the writer's aunt tell knock-knock jokes until her nephew chokes on his fried chicken, or does she imitate the sermons delivered by his father, an uptight and not very successful Baptist minister?

As to the assertion that someone's father is the most forgiving man in the world, doesn't it beg you to disagree? Maybe *your* father forgave you for totaling his Porsche and getting expelled from high school—not once but three times. As it turned out, the student who wrote that sentence later told the class that her grandfather used to berate her father for being lazy and beat him so badly he broke both her father's legs, yet her father now worked two jobs so that he could support the old man in a private nursing home rather than let him live out his days in the dilapidated and poorly run institution financed by the state.

The problem is that clichés tend to be abstractions or unproven generalizations. "The most forgiving man in the world" doesn't mean anything unless it's attached to a concrete example that contextualizes what the author has written, giving depth and meaning to the description. Without this specificity, the example is meaningless. The details *prove* the generalization. They also provide the writer with a clearer idea of where to go in the next sentence, and the sentence after that. Don't the specific details about the student's father and grandfather lead you to wonder about the father's deeper motives in working so hard to support a man who beat him and berated him for being lazy?

Most writers don't need long to figure out that a detailed sentence is more memorable and convincing than an unproven generalization. (One student wrote that her father was "an asshole," a vague description that could have meant different things to different readers, until she revised it to convey exactly what she meant: "My mother didn't appreciate my father's habit of showing our dinner guests photos of his mistresses.") But some people become so enamored of using details they don't know when to stop. A simple sentence meant to elicit the fresh smell and silky feel of the spring air on prom night in a small Ohio town might become so overstuffed with sensory detail that the description becomes laughably fussy, slowing us to the point that we never make it to the high school gym for the actual event. As mentioned earlier, you need to find the balance between *overwriting* with purple prose and truly capturing the world or ideas you are describing in a unique, concrete way. This will take practice, but through the process of drafting and revising each essay, as well as getting feedback from a trusted reader or from your peers in workshop, you will slowly become more confident about where to add details and where to eliminate them. For now, let's just say that most such decisions are a matter of asking yourself whether a detail is relevant to what you are trying to do in a given sentence, paragraph, or scene or whether you are putting in so many details that your readers will become impatient to move ahead to find out what happens next. If you can't answer these questions, try coming back to what you have written a day or two later and see if the prose strikes you as cluttered or overwritten. Developing objectivity about your work is one of the hardest but most important skills associated with the art of writing.

In the meantime, one of the best ways to train yourself to understand how details function successfully is to examine how other writers incorporate them into their work. Steve Amick, in the following short essay, "Cold Comfort," captures what his family's summer cottage means to him. He never says, "My favorite place in the world is northern Michigan." Or, "I love spending summers up north." Instead, through his use of clear language and detail, he allows us to *experience* the importance of his family's summer cottage through his point of view. We understand the emotion he is trying to convey through his descriptions and tone of voice. Read the piece once for enjoyment. We call this first read "the content read," which focuses on the "who, what, where, and when" of the essay. Then go back and see if you can identify the passages in which Amick includes significant and telling details, underlining each example and noting *how* and *why* each such detail is significant. We call this second reading "the craft read," which we use to study stylistic technique—not just *what* was said but *how* it was said.

By Steve Amick

COLD COMFORT

WAY back in the 1930's, when spectacular parts of my home state were still dirt cheap, my forward-thinking grandfather purchased a ridiculously large amount of lakefront property on a now highly valued lake up north. (Michigan is shaped a little like a hand: "up north" generally refers to the area represented by your pinky and ring finger.)

The most significant feature of this beautiful and varied land grab was a point—an outcropping of beach that jutted past the unwaveringly windowpane-clear shallows, into "the blue," the Bermudian hue that indicated a sudden drop-off. The water there was more than 60 feet deep. If you entered the lake anywhere else on our beach, say, 20 feet from the point, you could wade out maybe 100 feet before it got deep. Along the way, you could see the rock-lined floor of the lake and spot the sought-after coral fossils called Petoskey stones without even bending closer. But if you entered the lake at the end of the point, the dark-blue water would be well over your head with one small stride.

The point is still there, but it has significantly eroded. (That last sentence is misleadingly passive—to be more precise, jackasses on Jet Skis eroded it.) Originally it was called Lone Elm Point. The elm was long gone before my entry into the family, along with the roots that helped hold all that sand in place. There is some fluctuation to the point, depending on shifting winds and, these days, the wake of watercraft. Sometimes we barely have a beach; sometimes the shifts leave a respectable expanse of sand, a bold reminder of its glory days.

I've heard that before I was born, there were times you could stand on the edge of the beach and dive. One summer, when I was very small, it was out far enough that my cousins—all older than my siblings and I, and therefore, our heroes—dragged out an old diving board (built by my dad in his prolonged bachelor years) and set it up, anchored with rocks, right on the beach, jammed into the sand. I was 3 or 4, so the most I could do was bounce on the board, gripping the hand of a grownup or cousin; take a few brave steps toward the edge and quickly return. Mostly, I squatted in the sand and watched as these long-haired, lanky teenagers hurled themselves unequivocally into the blue.

A few years ago, a rather wealthy woman from a rather wealthy community downstate, hearing of our family's cottage on that lake, told me: "Oh, I was there once. It's so beautiful—but so cold. All we could do, of course, was ride around in a boat and look at the water. I mean, what do you do with it?"

"You enjoy it," I said. "You just…go in."

She looked incredulous. "How?"

I told her you have to be born to it. The lake isn't for riding around and looking at things. It's for jumping in and feeling alive. In that way it's like summer itself.

The water is cold, granted. There are a lot of modifiers one could use here, but if you know the lake I'm talking about, you know what I mean by cold. Because of the clarity of the water, the lack of plant life and silt and because of the depth of the lake, the center being an almost underwater ravine, more than 300 feet at the deepest, the chill of winter lingers long into summer.

When we were children, there was an unspoken competition to be the first one in the lake and the last one in at the end of the year. Mostly my sister and I vied for this title, my brothers typically being more cautious. I think my record on the late end is Oct. 16th and on the early end, maybe a week shy of Memorial Day. As a point of reference, renters—meaning outsiders and neophytes—can be heard screaming and squealing miles away on even a cicada-buzzing white-hot August afternoon. Maybe they go in, say, Independence Day to Labor Day, but they do not go quietly. But if you're born to it, if that's where you learn to swim, if that's where the idea of summer is formed in your head, the cold barely enters into it.

Over the years, there have been girlfriends I've taken up there and introduced to the point; to this geological sudden change of plans. Mostly, they balked, troubled by the abruptness of it, preferring to move down the beach and wade and wince and bathe in their own trepidation. I have photos of these exes, arms folded across their bathing suits, arms goose-pimpled, brows furrowed, glaring back at the camera; at me.

For the most part they loved the beauty and serenity. But it is interesting that anything that wasn't working came to an accelerated conclusion once we'd been up there, once I'd rolled my eyes at their hesitation. (And perhaps that's the true antonym for summer: not winter, but hesitation.)

The last great act of derring-do performed out on the point was perhaps done by my girlfriend at the time, Sharyl, in the summer of 2003. We'd known each other less than a year and I proposed to her out there, in the moonlight, with the waves crashing along the point. It was past midnight, and we were waiting as a cherry pie baked back in the cottage. She was sitting on a bench made of driftwood, both of us covered with flour and sweat, and I knelt in the sand and tried not to drop the ring in the dim light.

She was shaking, but she did it. She said yes to a chaotic bachelor almost 40 years old, betting the long shot on a sudden romance that could have proved fleeting. It was a bold step, taken there at the site of so many bold steps, quick into the deep. Which is probably why I proposed: I knew she was one of us, the hurling-forward kind.

—2005

Learning from Other Writers (Amick)

1. Why does Amick note that the diving board was built by his father "in his prolonged bachelor years"? List other details that are significant and describe why.

2. When noting that he showed the point to other girlfriends, Amick describes that spit of land as a "geological sudden change of plans." How does this description tie in with the larger goal of the essay?

3. Visual details—the shape of Michigan, the "dark-blue" of the water, the Petoskey stones that line the floor of the lake—appear in every paragraph. Find places in which Amick evokes other senses besides sight. How does this multi-sensory experience add richness to his work?

4. Amick makes many comparisons: between past and present, between his earlier girlfriends and Sharyl, between the point that once jutted into the lake and the newly eroded state of the shore. Why are these comparisons significant in terms of the larger meaning or purpose of the essay?

5. Good titles often have more than one layer of meaning. What are some of the connotations of the title "Cold Comfort"?

Adding Your Voice

Think of a ritual that is important to you, the way Amick's ritual of swimming in Lake Michigan is important to him. Now close your eyes and bring to mind a specific time and place this ritual was performed, or imagine a typical occurrence of this ritual. Let the ritual play itself out in your mind until you know where the action is taking place, what sights, sounds, and smells the ritual entails, and who is doing and saying what. Without losing your mental movie of this ritual (you might try to imagine it being projected onto the computer screen or page before you), get the ritual down on paper. Don't worry about grammar or mechanics right now. You don't even need to write in complete sentences. If you want to tell us what you are thinking or feeling as you observe or participate, that's fine, but also remember that good writing conveys what you think or feel about an event through the words you choose to convey it. Be specific and engage as many senses as possible.

OTHER PEOPLE'S VOICES: DIALOGUE

While your language and choice of detail help you to create a distinctive voice on the page, your use of dialogue helps you to reveal the distinctive voices of other people. Dialogue is an extremely effective means to convey the way that people sound, to reveal information, and to bring a scene to life. You don't always need to reproduce the actual words of the people about whom you are writing, but capturing the *way* people talk is an important skill for any writer. In "*Casa*: A Partial Remembrance of a Puerto Rican Childhood," the cautionary tales that the women in Judith Ortiz Cofer's family related in her presence were vital to the lessons those women intended to teach Ortiz Cofer and her cousin about what it is like to be a Puerto Rican woman. As she renders one of her grandmother's favorite *cuentos*, Ortiz Cofer communicates not only the flavor of Mamá's speech (in this case, in translation) and her masterful control of suspense and humor, but also *how* Mamá spoke ("I remember the rise and fall of her voice, the sighs, and her constantly gesturing hands, like two birds swooping through her words"). By more fully grasping Mamá's character through her speech, the reader more clearly understands the significance of the storytelling as both an art and a way to transfer knowledge and wisdom. Later, in the chapter on portraits, we will discuss interviewing techniques and the mechanics of inscribing dialogue on the page. For now, with Ortiz Cofer's essay as a model, use your memories of the best storytellers in your family to develop your ear for the varieties of human speech.

CASA: A PARTIAL REMEMBRANCE OF A PUERTO RICAN CHILDHOOD

At three or four o'clock in the afternoon, the hour of *café con leche*, the women of my family gathered in Mamá's living room to speak of important things and retell familiar stories meant to be overheard by us young girls, their daughters. In Mamá's house (everyone called my grandmother Mamá) was a large parlor built by my grandfather to his wife's exact specifications so that it was always cool, facing away from the sun. The doorway was on the side of the house so no one could walk directly into her living room. First they had to take a little stroll through and around her beautiful garden where prize-winning orchids grew in the trunk of an ancient tree she had hollowed out for that purpose. This room was furnished with several mahogany rocking chairs, acquired at the births of her children, and one intricately carved rocker that had passed down to Mamá at the death of her own mother.

It was on these rockers that my mother, her sisters, and my grandmother sat on these afternoons of my childhood to tell their stories, teaching each other, and my cousin and me, what it was like to be a woman, more specifically, a Puerto Rican woman. They talked about life on the island, and life in *Los Nueva Yores*, their way of referring to the United States from New York City to California: the other place, not home, all the same. They told real-life stories though, as I later learned, always embellishing them with a little or a lot of dramatic detail. And they told *cuentos*, the morality and cautionary tales told by the women in our family for generations: stories that became a part of my subconscious as I grew up in two worlds, the tropical island and the cold city, and that would later surface in my dreams and in my poetry.

One of these tales was about the woman who was left at the altar. Mamá liked to tell that one with histrionic intensity. I remember the rise and fall of her voice, the sighs, and her constantly gesturing hands, like two birds swooping through her words. This particular story usually would come up in a conversation as a result of someone mentioning a forthcoming engagement or wedding. The first time I remember hearing it, I was sitting on the floor at Mamá's feet, pretending to read a comic book. I may have been eleven or twelve years old, at that difficult age when a girl was no longer a child who could be ordered to leave the room if the women wanted freedom to take their talk into forbidden zones, nor really old enough to be considered a part of their conclave. I could only sit quietly, pretending to be in another world, while absorbing it all in a sort of unspoken agreement of my status as silent auditor. On this day, Mamá had taken my long, tangled mane of hair into her ever-busy hands. Without looking down at me and with no interruption of her flow of words, she began braiding my hair, working at it with the quickness and determination that characterized all her actions. My mother was watching us impassively from her rocker across the room. On her lips played a little ironic smile. I would never sit still for *her* ministrations, but even then, I instinctively knew that she did not possess Mamá's matriarchal power to command

and keep everyone's attention. This was never more evident than in the spell she cast when telling a story.

"It is not like it used to be when I was a girl," Mamá announced. "Then, a man could leave a girl standing at the church altar with a bouquet of fresh flowers in her hands and disappear off the face of the earth. No way to track him down if he was from another town. He could be a married man, with maybe even two or three families all over the island. There was no way to know. And there were men who did this. Hombres with the devil in their flesh who would come to a pueblo, like this one, take a job at one of the haciendas, never meaning to stay, only to have a good time and to seduce the women."

The whole time she was speaking, Mamá would be weaving my hair into a flat plait that required pulling apart the two sections of hair with little jerks that made my eyes water; but knowing how grandmother detested whining and *boba* (sissy) tears, as she called them, I just sat up as straight and stiff as I did at La Escuela San Jose, where the nuns enforced good posture with a flexible plastic ruler they bounced off of slumped shoulders and heads. As Mamá's story progressed, I noticed how my young Aunt Laura lowered her eyes, refusing to meet Mamá's meaningful gaze. Laura was seventeen, in her last year of high school, and already engaged to a boy from another town who had staked his claim with a tiny diamond ring, then left for Los Nueva Yores to make his fortune. They were planning to get married in a year. Mamá had expressed serious doubts that the wedding would ever take place. In Mamá's eyes, a man set free without a legal contract was a man lost. She believed that marriage was not something men desired, but simply the price they had to pay for the privilege of children and, of course, for what no decent (synonymous with "smart") woman would give away for free.

"María La Loca was only seventeen when *it* happened to her." I listened closely at the mention of this name. María was a town character, a fat middle-aged woman who lived with her old mother on the outskirts of town. She was to be seen around the pueblo delivering the meat pies the two women made for a living. The most peculiar thing about María, in my eyes, was that she walked and moved like a little girl though she had the thick body and wrinkled face of an old woman. She would swing her hips in an exaggerated, clownish way, and sometimes even hop and skip up to someone's house. She spoke to no one. Even if you asked her a question, she would just look at you and smile, showing her yellow teeth. But I had heard that if you got close enough, you could hear her humming a tune without words. The kids yelled out nasty things at her, calling her *La Loca*, and the men who hung out at the bodega playing dominoes sometimes whistled mockingly as she passed by with her funny, outlandish walk. But María seemed impervious to it all, carrying her basket of *pasteles* like a grotesque Little Red Riding Hood through the forest.

María La Loca interested me, as did all the eccentrics and crazies of our pueblo. Their weirdness was a measuring stick I used in my serious quest for a definition of normal. As a Navy brat shuttling between New Jersey and the pueblo, I was constantly made to feel like an oddball by my peers, who made fun of my two-way accent: a Spanish accent when I spoke English, and when I spoke Spanish I was told that I sounded like a *Gringa*. Being the outsider had already turned my brother and me into cultural chameleons. We developed early on the ability to blend into a crowd, to sit and read quietly in a fifth story apartment building for days and days when it was too bitterly cold to play outside, or, set free, to run wild in Mamá's realm, where she took charge of our lives, releasing Mother for a while from the intense fear for our safety that our father's absences instilled in her. In order to keep us from harm when Father was away, Mother kept us under strict surveillance. She even walked us to and from Public School No. 11, which we attended during the months we lived in Paterson, New Jersey, our home base in the states. Mamá freed all three of us like pigeons from a cage. I saw her as my liberator and my model. Her stories were parables from which to glean the *Truth*.

"María La Loca was once a beautiful girl. Everyone thought she would marry the Méndez boy." As everyone knew, Rogelio Méndez was the richest man in town. "But," Mamá continued, knitting my hair with the same intensity she was putting into her story, "this *macho* made a fool out of her and ruined her life." She paused for the effect of her use of the word "macho," which at that time had not yet become a popular epithet for an unliberated man. This word had for us the crude and comical connotation of "male of the species," stud; a *macho* was what you put in a pen to increase your stock.

I peeked over my comic book at my mother. She too was under Mamá's spell, smiling conspiratorially at this little swipe at men. She was safe from Mamá's contempt in this area. Married at an early age, an unspotted lamb, she had been accepted by a good family of strict Spaniards whose name was old and respected, though their fortune had been lost long before my birth. In a rocker Papá had painted sky blue sat Mamá's oldest child, Aunt Nena. Mother of three children, stepmother of two more, she was a quiet woman who liked books but had married an ignorant and abusive widower whose main interest in life was accumulating wealth. He too was in the mainland working on his dream of returning home rich and triumphant to buy the *finca* of his dreams. She was waiting for him to send for her. She would leave her children with Mamá for several years while the two of them slaved away in factories. He would one day be a rich man, and she a sadder woman. Even now her life-light was dimming. She spoke little, an aberration in Mamá's house, and she read avidly, as if storing up spiritual food for the long winters that awaited her in Los Nueva Yores without her family. But even Aunt Nena came alive to Mamá's words, rocking gently, her hands over a thick book in her lap.

Her daughter, my cousin Sara, played jacks by herself on the tile porch outside the room where we sat. She was a year older than I. We shared a bed and all our family's secrets. Collaborators in search of answers, Sara and I discussed everything we heard the women say, trying to fit it all together like a puzzle that, once assembled, would reveal life's mysteries to us. Though she and I still enjoyed taking part in boys' games—chase, volleyball, and even *vaqueros*, the island version of cowboys and Indians involving capgun battles and violent shoot-outs under the mango tree in Mamá's backyard—we loved best the quiet hours in the afternoon when the men were still at work, and the boys had gone to play serious baseball at the park. Then Mamá's house belonged only to us women. The aroma of coffee perking in the kitchen, the mesmerizing creaks and groans of the rockers, and the women telling their lives in *cuentos* are forever woven into the fabric of my imagination, braided like my hair that day I felt my grandmother's hands teaching me about strength, her voice convincing me of the power of storytelling.

That day Mamá told how the beautiful María had fallen prey to a man whose name was never the same in subsequent versions of the story; it was Juan one time, José, Rafael, Diego, another. We understood that neither the name nor any of the *facts* were important, only that a woman had allowed love to defeat her. Mamá put each of us in María's place by describing her wedding dress in loving detail: how she looked like a princess in her lace as she waited at the altar. Then, as Mamá approached the tragic denouement of her story, I was distracted by the sound of my Aunt Laura's violent rocking. She seemed on the verge of tears. She knew the fable was intended for her. That week she was going to have her wedding gown fitted, though no firm date had been set for the marriage. Mamá ignored Laura's obvious discomfort, digging out a ribbon from the sewing basket she kept by her rocker while describing María's long illness, "a fever that would not break for days." She spoke of a mother's despair: "that woman climbed the church steps on her knees every morning, wore only black as a *promesa* to the Holy Virgin in exchange for her daughter's health." By the time María returned from her honeymoon with death, she was ravished, no longer young or sane. "As you can see, she is almost as old as her mother already," Mamá lamented while tying the ribbon to the ends of my hair, pulling it back with such force that I just knew I would never be able to close my eyes completely again.

"That María's getting crazier every day." Mamá's voice would take a lighter tone now, expressing satisfaction, either for the perfection of my braid, or for a story well told—it was hard to tell. "You know that tune María is always humming?" Carried away by her enthusiasm, I tried to nod, but Mamá still had me pinned between her knees.

"Well that's the wedding march." Surprising us all, Mamá sang out, "Da, da, dara … da, da, dara." Then lifting me off the floor by my skinny shoulders, she would lead me around the room in an impromptu waltz—another session ending with the laughter of women, all of us caught up in the infectious joke of our lives.

—1989

Learning from Other Writers (Ortiz Cofer)

1. How does Ortiz Cofer use the first paragraph to set the stage for what follows?

2. Find instances where Cofer engages each sense: sight, smell, taste, touch, and sound. Why are these details so important?

3. What is the significance of the line that appears toward the end of the essay: "Mamá lamented while tying the ribbon to the ends of my hair, pulling it back with such force that I just knew I would never be able to close my eyes completely again." What does the narrator mean about not being able to close her eyes? How does this connect back with her earlier statement that these stories taught her what it was like to be a Puerto Rican woman?

4. How does Ortiz Cover use the ritual of hair braiding to structure the essay? When does she return to it? When does she move away from it?

5. Examine the way dialogue is presented in the essay. What role does it serve? What does it reveal?

6. Notice the way Ortiz Cofer intersperses the story being told by her mother with her own observations of the other women in the room—Mamá, the narrator's mother, Aunt Laura, Aunt Nena, and the narrator's cousin Sara. How does the author introduce and weave in information about each character who partakes in the ritual?

Adding Your Voice

1. Ask a relative or friend to tell you about his or her most important romance. How did this person meet his or her beloved? Who asked whom out on the first date? What happened on that date? Try to jot down as much of your subject's story as possible, then use your notes to write a monologue that conveys the sense of the speaker's story as well as his or her voice.

2. Think of the best storyteller you know. What makes him or her such a compelling or entertaining speaker? From memory, try to get down this person's most memorable story in his or her own words.

3. Think of the most disturbing, most emotional, or funniest conversation you have ever had and, to the best of your ability, transcribe it on the page.

4. From any of the previous examples, make a list of questions that puzzle you about the story or the storyteller. What *isn't* being said? What's going on beneath the surface of the narrative or conversation?

5. Go back to the exercise on page 18 in which you described an important ritual. This time, try to weave in the voices of the participants. Or start over from scratch and daydream your way back to another ritual that seems equally rich in meaning. Whose voices do you hear? What are those voices saying? Can you convey their unique texture and variety on the page?

CHAPTER 3

A Driving Question

ASKING THE QUESTIONS YOU TRULY WANT TO ASK

Here is another way that creative composition is creative: even if you are assigned a topic, you still get to select a question about that topic that you genuinely want to explore.

Why a question? Shouldn't you start with a thesis statement? Well, did you ever stop to wonder where thesis statements come from? Were you born with a prestocked supply of thesis statements in your brain? Were they implanted there by aliens? By your parents? Besides, no matter how the thesis statement got in your head, if you know what you know and believe what you believe before you sit down to write, why bother? If all you are doing is re-proving what you already know to be true, then all you need to do is list the evidence that supports your opinion and be done with the whole useless, unenlightening process. For such a piece of writing, the only form you need is the standard five-paragraph essay. *Here's what I believe. Here are three reasons I believe it. And, in conclusion, here's what I proved that I believe.* But a question implies movement. You start in ignorance and end in knowledge. Or in partial enlightenment. Or in slightly less ignorance than when you began. To quote Frank L. Cioffi, again from "Argumentation in a Culture of Discord":

> ...all academic writing starts with a problem, a hypothesis, or a question. And the idea is not to solve this problem or answer that question with previously extant notions. This kind of writing should offer something original, imaginative, something the audience would not have thought of before and might even initially reject. Yet it invites that rejection, seeks out disconfirmatory material, naysaying positions. Working against the initial rejection, it logically persuades the audience how a proposed solution betters other current solutions, covers a wider range of data, or undermines previous notions. In short, this writing looks at other answers and engages them, proving them in need of some rethinking, recontextualizing, or reimagining.

Best of all, the process by which you move from ignorance to knowledge provides the structural backbone of your essay. Writing *leads* to thinking. And what leads the writing is a driving question that propels you toward inquiry.

At first, the freedom to choose your own question might seem more frightening than exciting. Most of us are accustomed to receiving an assignment from a teacher, an editor, or a boss. Topic in hand, we visit the library, perform an Internet search, or call an expert. Then we write up what we have learned. Even if we don't experience the thrill of thinking creatively about the topic or discovering something new, at least we don't risk returning to our teacher, editor, or boss with nothing to show for a long day's work.

But even when your topic is assigned, fulfilling that assignment is more meaningful and enjoyable if you can discover something new rather than rehash what other people think. As much as libraries, Internet sites, and experts are storehouses of information that any writer is going to need and want to consult, there are other sources of enlightenment in this world, including a writer's own wisdom and experience. Part of strong academic writing is adding your own perspective, analysis, and interpretation to information that already exists (or, as Cioffi says, "rethinking, recontextualizing, or reimagining").

If you still feel nervous about coming up with a question for an essay, if you hear voices in your head insisting that the question you have come up with is stupid, naive, or obvious and assuring you that someone smarter or more qualified already has asked that question and answered it more effectively or intelligently than you could ever do, try to figure out whose voices you are hearing. Is that your father's voice telling you that you are stupid or naive? Or the voice of the sixth-grade teacher who never liked you because you weren't as polite or studious as your older brother? Talk to this person (in your mind, if not in real life). Tell him or her that you have every right to ask whatever questions you want to ask and are perfectly capable of finding answers to those questions. If all else fails, take comfort from the confession of the highly respected writer Charles Baxter, who, in his essay "Dysfunctional Narratives: or: 'Mistakes Were Made'" admits to being visited—usually late at night—by what he calls "the fraud police." We all hear members of that particular police force knocking on our door from time to time, accusing us of trying to pass ourselves off as far more competent or intelligent than we actually are. Or you can adopt William Stafford's strategy for getting past the blank page: "I don't suffer from writer's block; I just lower my standards."

Skeptical? We guarantee that by the time you were ten or twelve you had asked enough interesting questions about the world to provide you with material to last a lifetime. Another hundred questions go flitting through your mind every day. The trick is to catch these questions by the tail—or remember the questions that puzzled you as a child—and trust that most such questions would make an exciting focus for an essay. As Phillip Lopate puts it in "Writing Personal Essays: On the Necessity of Turning Oneself into a Character," what makes an essay dynamic "is the need to work out some problem, especially a problem that is not easily resolved. Fortunately, human beings are conflicted animals, so there is no shortage of tension that won't go away."

At first, your question might seem too narrow to interest anyone beyond yourself. Suppose you get up with a hangover after yet another Friday night drinking far too much alcohol at a party and wonder why you can't keep your repeated vow to confine yourself to two beers. To turn this into a question that might interest other people, all you need to do is ask yourself why so many students at your university seem to feel the same need to drink to excess. Imagine some of the lenses through which you might view this question: gender, sexuality, social class, education, communication, etc. How might these issues intersect? How might they amplify one another? What connections might you uncover? Before you know it, you will be writing toward understanding a very complex and multi-layered topic. Yet the inquiry itself grew out of a fairly ordinary and seemingly simple question.

Of course, you will want to avoid taking on a question that no one could possibly answer, at least not in a ten-page essay. "Is there a divine creator?" and "What caused the present conflict in the Middle East?" are terrific questions, but as Lopate cautions, "If you take on a problem that is too philosophically large or historically convoluted, you may choke on the details and give up." Finding a question that is the right size for the essay you are trying to write—not so small that discovering the answer is trivial, not so large that you don't have the time or resources to get the essay done in time, or done at all—is a matter of common sense and practice.

To prove that you are qualified to be an essayist, carry around a notebook and write down every question that passes through your mind, not bothering to ask if it's a good question or a silly one. Maybe winter vacation is coming up and you are curious who invented Kwanzaa and whether you might find the celebration meaningful. Or you wonder how Jews came up with the tradition of eating potato pancakes on Hanukah, or whether there is any historical truth to the legend that one small vial of oil fueled a lamp for eight days and nights. Maybe you are at a party and hate the music being played but wonder why it's suddenly so popular. Or you wonder why you can't stop thinking about the Hoover Dam, or why you keep obsessing about how you would get out of the trunk of your Camaro if someone were to lock you in.

Our bet is that if you jot down the questions flitting around your mind, by the end of the second day you will have filled an entire notebook and need to go buy a new one. Which isn't to say that writers always know what question they are trying to answer before they sit down to write. One writer might start with a question that's fairly vague, then focus the question more tightly as he conducts his initial research and writes and revises draft after draft. Another writer might begin with the question she thinks she *ought* to ask, and then realize the question she cares about is altogether different. In most cases, there's a back-and-forth interaction between the writer's initial question, which allows him or her to start the project, and the demands and revelations that present themselves at later stages. Ever since Montaigne invented the essay, with its roots in the verb *to try*, the challenge to its practitioners has been to discover what they want to say while they are trying to say it. Sometimes, you can't quite articulate your driving question until you are well into the writing process. Even then, the question might seem too eccentric or disturbing to pursue. And no matter how much you argue with those voices in your head, you might continue to worry that you lack the right credentials or expertise to answer it.

Luckily, the very process by which you acquire the courage or expertise to answer your question might be included in your essay. That's one of the beauties of creative composition. In some types of academic writing you might need to hide the obstacles in your research once you have completed it. Here, all the false starts, spilled beakers, failed experiments, and futile trips to the archives can be included; the process of discovery, with all its frustration and suspense, often provides the very backbone of your essay.

FINDING A FOCUS

As we have seen in the previous chapter, details are the building blocks of effective prose. But how do you know which details to leave out or include? The answer is: you may not. At least, not at the beginning. The first time you describe something, you might not know *why* you are describing it. But that's what rough drafts are for. If you freewrite a description of a person, place, or thing, or a memory of an experience or an event, and then you go back and reread what you have written, you will see patterns and recurring themes. Again and again, your conscious or unconscious mind will have returned to some aspect of your subject that seems troubling or important. In the next draft, you can focus your description more closely around this pattern or theme and develop its significance. As your driving question begins to take focus, the necessary details will become more apparent.

Look at the following excerpt from Barbara Ehrenreich's essay "Nickel-and-Dimed: On (Not) Getting By in America." (Ehrenreich went on to write a book with this same title; the original essay, which was published in *Harper's*, appears in its entirety in Part IV of this textbook.) Earlier in the essay, the author has told us about her job waiting tables at the Hearthside, where, if nothing else, she is able to derive some satisfaction from the companionship of her coworkers and her ability to talk to and please her customers. But her description of Jerry's, the no-frills restaurant where she takes a second job to supplement the less-than-livable wages she earns at the Hearthside, serves another goal. As you read, ask yourself why Ehrenreich might have chosen to include *these* details while omitting others—for instance, she chooses not to include descriptions of her coworkers and conversations with her customers.

What is the overall point to this description of Jerry's? What does Ehrenreich's comparison reveal about how Jerry's stacks up against the slightly classier Hearthside? What is being analyzed and scrutinized here?

> Picture a fat person's hell, and I don't mean a place with no food. Instead there
> is everything you might eat if eating had no bodily consequences—cheese fries,
> chicken-fried steaks, fudge-laden desserts—only here every bite must be paid for, one
> way or another, in human discomfort. The kitchen is a cavern, a stomach leading to
> the lower intestine that is the garbage and dishwashing area, from which issue bizarre
> smells combining the edible and the offal: creamy carrion, pizza barf, and that unique
> and enigmatic Jerry's scent—citrus fart. The floor is slick with spills, forcing us to

walk through the kitchen with tiny steps, like Susan McDougal in leg irons. Sinks everywhere are clogged with scraps of lettuce, decomposing lemon wedges, water-logged toast crusts. Put your hand down on any counter and you risk being stuck to it by the film of ancient syrup spills, and this is unfortunate, because hands are utensils here, used for scooping up lettuce onto salad plates, lifting out pie slices, and even moving hash browns from one plate to another. The regulation poster in the single unisex restroom admonishes us to wash our hands thoroughly and even offers instructions for doing so, but there is always some vital substance missing—soap, paper towels, toilet paper—and I never find all three at once. You learn to stuff your pockets with napkins before going in there, and too bad about the customers, who must eat, though they don't realize this, almost literally out of our hands.

The break room typifies the whole situation: there is none, because there are no breaks at Jerry's. For six to eight hours in a row, you never sit except to pee. Actually, there are three folding chairs at a table immediately adjacent to the bathroom, but hardly anyone ever sits here, in the very rectum of the gastro-architectural system. Rather, the function of the peri-toilet area is to house the ashtrays in which servers and dishwashers leave their cigarettes burning at all times, like votive candles, so that they don't have to waste time lighting up again when they dash back for a puff. Almost everyone smokes as if his or her pulmonary well-being depended on it—the multi-national mélange of cooks, the Czech dishwashers, the servers, who are all American natives—creating an atmosphere in which oxygen is only an occasional pollutant. My first morning at Jerry's, when the hypoglycemic shakes set in, I complain to one of my fellow servers that I don't understand how she can go so long without food. "Well, I don't understand how you can go so long without a cigarette," she responds in a tone of reproach—because work is what you do for others; smoking is what you do for yourself. I don't know why the antismoking crusaders have never grasped the element of defiant self-nurturance that makes the habit so endearing to its victims—as if, in the American workplace, the only thing people have to call their own is the tumors they are nourishing and the spare moments they devote to feeding them.

Now, the Industrial Revolution is not an easy transition, especially when you have to zip through it in just a couple of days. I have gone from craft work straight into the factory, from the air-conditioned morgue of the Hearthside directly into the flames. Customers arrive in human waves, sometimes disgorged fifty at a time from their tour buses, peckish and whiny. Instead of two "girls" on the floor at once, there can be as many as six of us running around in our brilliant pink-and-orange Hawaiian shirts. Conversations, either with customers or fellow employees, seldom last more than twenty seconds at a time. On my first day, in fact, I am hurt by my sister servers' coldness. My mentor for the day is an emotionally uninflected twenty-three-year-old, and the others, who gossip a little among themselves about the real reason someone is out sick today and the size of the bail bond someone else has had to pay, ignore me completely. On my second day, I find out why. "Well, it's good to see you again," one of them says in greeting. "Hardly anyone comes back after the first day." I feel power-fully vindicated—a survivor—but it would take a long time, probably months, before I could hope to be accepted into this sorority.

Adding Your Voice

Think of the first job you ever held (even if it was as a babysitter or newspaper carrier). Close your eyes and picture a typical day at that job. Then, without losing the memory, get down on paper what you see, hear, smell, taste, feel, say, and think. Look back at what you have written. Do you notice any common threads that connect two or more observations? Were you stunned by how spoiled some of the campers in your bunkhouse tended to be, or baffled as to how to make them behave? Were you surprised at the honesty—or dishonesty—of your fellow employees at Wal-Mart? Were you confused by the rules on the assembly line that first day at the Ford Plant? Were you proud of how your body withstood the pain as you spread gravel on a new road in the hot sun, hour after hour? Once you have figured out what larger point you were trying to make about your job, go back and write a new version of the scene, keeping the details that relate to your overall purpose, cutting the details that don't seem relevant, adding descriptions of events or dialogue that help you convey your point. Repeat the exercise, this time writing about the worst day you experienced at some job. Or the best day.

CHAPTER 4

A Natural, Organic Form

With their imposing Roman numerals and alphabetical subpoints, the logical outlines most of us learned to use in elementary school can help a writer organize a wealth of information. But logical outlines rarely correspond to anything we experience outside our heads. Nothing about such a structure draws the writer through his or her material in a natural way, and nothing pulls the reader through the finished product.

Think of the generations of reporters who learned to structure their articles in an inverted pyramid with the most important or newsworthy information across the top, leading to the least important information at the end, or the legions of science students who were taught the proper protocol for writing up their experiments, or the cadres of PhDs tutored in the only acceptable form for a dissertation, or all the law students schooled in the appropriate structure of a brief. These hand-me-down structures provide writers with a means to organize what they know but don't provide a mechanism by which they can generate or develop new ideas.

In contrast, creative nonfiction encourages its practitioners to choose—or invent— the form that seems best suited to exploring the material they wish to explore. (If you are not sure what we mean by "form," think of an essay's structure or organization.) The interplay between the driving question that guides your research and the form that helps you to organize what you learn is at the living, breathing heart of creative nonfiction. Take the genre's most common form, the reflective narrative (by which we mean a true story told in roughly chronological order). As you move forward in time, the friction between the story you are recounting and the question you are trying to answer throws up meditative sparks. That is to say, the narrative provides a chrono-logical roadmap for you to follow, and in the process of re-creating that narrative for your readers, the form inspires you to reflect more deeply on the experience than you did when it happened. When you craft a reflective narrative, you go back over what happened with the same rigor as a crime scene investigator. Your job is to make sense of the event or events you are recounting—to draw out their meaning and significance, to figure out what causes produced what effects, to come to some conclusion or reach some verdict.

Your goal is *not* to arrive at some trite lesson or moral, a folksy bromide masquerading as wisdom, or a sweeping generalization. (*Life is unfair. Family matters more than fame. I learned the greatest lesson of all: to accept myself for who I am.*) We rarely are encouraged to think about our lives in anything but clichéd terms. (*What doesn't kill you makes you stronger. Everything works out for the best. You made your bed, now lie in it.*) Yet using your experience to prove what most people already know (or think they know) tends to be tedious and dishonest. The purpose of writing an essay is to lead you, the writer, to some deeper understanding, and in so doing, to re-create for the reader the path that led you to that understanding.

If all this seems overwhelming, don't worry. No one starts out knowing exactly what question he or she wants to explore, along with the perfect way to structure the resulting essay. Like most of us, you probably will start with a tentative version of your question and do the best you can to sketch the initial draft of your narrative. Once you have written to the end, you will have a better sense of your driving question. Or you will realize that your original question was answered in the middle of page two, giving birth to a new one. During revision, you may need to rewrite the opening few paragraphs quite drastically, or perhaps cut the first page and start on page two. That's okay—it's part of the process. The advantage of using a driving question as a tool is that you are not expected to know the answer when you start. And the advantage of using forms is that they will guide you structurally as you figure all of this out.

Of course, the reflective narrative is not the only form an essay is allowed to take. A narrative is simply the most comfortable way human beings have devised to organize their experience. *First this happened, then that, then that.* But as we saw with the Facebook example in "How to Use this Book," there are numerous other structures that writers adopt to guide their inquiries.

In the sections that follow, you will encounter forms that enable you to move beyond what you already know and organize what you discover as you answer whatever questions interest or perplex you. Each set of essays will provide examples of a given form, questions to help you recognize and assimilate various techniques and tools appropriate to that form, and a series of exercises designed to allow you to add your voice to the literary and academic conversations taking place around you and provide prompts to spark your explorations of your own material. Along the way, we offer additional considerations relevant to the practice of creating and drafting essays, including how to write about one's family and friends without violating their privacy, how to carry out research, how to conduct an interview, and how to be honest about difficult topics. We hope the selection of readings in this book will give you the inspiration and confidence to see yourself as a writer, help you to understand that you can make meaning from your own experiences, and convince you that at the heart of all academic and intellectual inquiry is a simple trait to be nurtured and relied upon: curiosity.

CHAPTER 5

Habits of Mind

Nothing is more important to your progress as a writer than training yourself to think critically. Whether looking back at an incident from your childhood to analyze its significance and connecting what you know now with what you experienced back then, or objectively analyzing the importance of a person or a place, trying to uncover the essence of that individual or locale, or examining cultural trends or societal practices, you are engaged in an endeavor that demands rigorous inspection, along with the ability to make connection and draw conclusions.

This is the same set of skills that doctors use every day when analyzing their patients' symptoms: starting with a constellation of effects (a rash, a fever, a rapid heartbeat), they must connect those symptoms back to their cause. It's also the same deductive process that scientists use in laboratories to test everything from the weight-bearing properties of certain metals to the ways in which genes determine behaviors and traits in fruit flies. Whether in architecture or aeronautics, hedge-fund management or landscape design, success in any field—or any discipline in college—requires strong, sharp, critical-thinking skills.

The question is, how do you go about developing such skills? First and fundamentally, you must learn to read like a writer. As Mike Bunn says in his aptly named essay "How to Read Like a Writer" (located in Part VI of this book):

> Instead of reading for content or to better understand the ideas in the writing (which you will automatically do to some degree anyway), you are trying to understand how the piece of writing was put together by the author and what you can learn about writing by reading a particular text. As you read in this way, you think about how the choices the author made and the techniques that he/she used are influencing your own responses as a reader. ...The goal as you read like a writer is to locate what you believe are the most important writerly choices represented in the text—choices as large as the overall structure or as small as a single word used only once—to consider the effect of those choices on potential readers (including yourself). Then you can go one step further and imagine what *different* choices the author *might* have made instead, and what effect those different choices would have on readers.

This shift in the way you read, though seemingly simple, will exert a profound change on the way you think, shifting your focus from data collection (which is passive) to evaluating and synthesizing information (which is active).

It will also force you to be more attentive to language. If, as Bunn argues, you are paying attention to choices "as small as a single word used only once," then you are reading at the most granular level, a habit that will eventually come to influence your own work.

This may feel a bit foreign at first. Most of our students report that they have been trained to read for content, just as Bunn describes. One student articulated this sentiment as follows:

> To me, reading was nothing more than the painful process of discovering information, and the content of the texts was all that mattered to me. I never took the effort to analyze how the authors structured their essays or how they made their arguments compelling. So I didn't really read, all I did was extract ideas from a paragraph and store them in my brain.

By learning to pay attention to and value rhetorical devices such as word choice, sentence structure, the rhythm of language, the use of transitions, and the development of ideas, you will better understand the symbiotic relationship between thought and technique and become adept at implementing these strategies in your own work.

So where to begin? First, you need to figure out what sort of reader you already are. How do you read? Who taught you? What are you looking for? Do you highlight facts? If so, perhaps you have been trained to gather information. Do you underline favorite lines or phrases? Maybe you are reading as an apprentice, hoping to become an author someday. Do you scribble comments in the margins? Dramatize your enthusiasm for a brilliant passage with a bright pink exclamation point? Or perhaps you use red ink to note your disagreement with an author? There are many approaches to reading, depending on the context. But no matter the discipline, by learning to read like a writer, you will strengthen your ability to interrogate a text and hone your skills at creating concise, evocative language of your own.

Yet another collateral benefit of developing a writer's habits of mind will be the growing awareness that writing is a process, with steps, stages, and strategies—from drafting to research to workshop to revision to more revision—that you will develop and tailor to meet your needs. Most beginning writers think that writing is simply something that you sit down and "do." Yet writers are *not* magical creatures on whom inspiration strikes. As is true of any art or craft, developing one's skills takes patience and time.

What you will also come to find is that different projects (and disciplines) demand different writing processes. Writing a reflective narrative might require that you revisit an old photo album or journal to jog your memory about an incident from your past. Writing a portrait might involve gathering facts about the police department in your hometown and interviewing the sheriff and her deputies. Writing an essay in which you carry out an investigation might mean that you compile an annotated bibliography before you even start. If you can teach yourself to be aware of your writing process, you can use this self-reflection to adapt that process to any discipline. In other words, if you can learn to be aware of how you write English papers, you can transfer those skills to papers for the rest of your courses.

Unfortunately, some people think that "learning to write" means learning to follow a formula. As one of our students reflected in an essay:

> I learned to write as I had learned to solve problems, play sports, or play an instrument. I followed the directions. Doing exactly what I was told produced the best results. Satisfied with this consistency, I continued writing the way I was taught.

This same student noted that when he read an essay or a book, he read "only to find information. I skimmed to streamline the writing process. Reading in this way was only a means to an end. No wonder I came to hate my essay-writing routine."

No writing instructor would admit that he or she encourages formulaic thinking. Yet many of our students have been unintentionally trained to see writing as a delivery mechanism—a practical tool to demonstrate for an instructor that they have, indeed, done the reading and grasped the material they were supposed to "get." The five-paragraph essay reinforces the mistaken notion that thinking is separate from writing. Once you have your thesis, your three pieces of evidence, and your conclusion, you simply plug each element into its predetermined slot. The form requires no thought, nor does it guide the writer's process of academic inquiry.

The five-paragraph essay does teach several important lessons to young writers—that claims must be backed up by evidence, that evidence should be varied in its sources and appeals, and that a writer's position should be specific and focused. But once you begin working with more sophisticated styles of writing, you can see that the five-paragraph essay, by removing the writer from the equation, also removes the possibility that he or she will establish any individual connection to the material, let alone to the reader. In an attempt to manufacture objectivity, the writer renders the resulting essay sterile, commonplace, and dull. No wonder so many young writers approach essay writing with a sinking feeling and their instructors experience a similar dread when they receive that next batch of papers.

What better way to help student writers make the transition to college than to introduce them to an alternative that fosters intellectual curiosity. Ultimately, no one can teach you how to write—the process is individual and developmental. But a good teacher can teach you how to teach yourself to write. And if you can teach yourself to write, you can teach yourself to do just about anything.

The easiest way for this transfer to take place is through modeling. If you spend time studying how an author put together her essay—that is, if you spend time reading like a writer—then you can assess the effectiveness of her techniques and make arguments about how the form and content work together to make meaning in the text; you can then borrow these techniques and add them to your collection of writing tools. Nothing is more instructive than training yourself to notice how an essay is structured, how each argument is presented, interrogated, and supported. Writing is a thoughtful, strategic process, the very opposite of formulaic.

Some might argue that students should study more "academic" material, that few disciplines other than English will ask you to write a reflective narrative. But whether you spend a class studying how to write a scene (which is about weighing experiential evidence and the relative importance of a multiplicity of details), or how to integrate reflection into a larger narrative (which is about analysis), or how to create effective tone and voice in an essay (which is about stance), or how to position your point of view on a particular subject (which is about appeals), or how to uncover the significance of your material (which is about meaning and value), you will come to realize that writing involves selecting, adapting, and combining numerous rhetorical strategies to attack an infinite number of questions across an infinite variety of subjects and fields.

PART II

Narratives

CHAPTER 6

Literacy Narratives

Many of you are beginning writers. Some of you might enjoy writing, and others find it difficult. If it's any consolation, most of us both enjoy writing *and* find it difficult. Before we examine the varieties of forms available to you to help you explore your material, we are going to listen to writers write about writing: how they came to their craft, why writing is important, why writing matters in their lives. Such essays are called literacy narratives—that is, narratives that explore some aspect of reading or writing. Later in the book, we will read essays in which writers explore specific issues of *craft*—the technique and execution of writing—but here we are looking at essays whose driving questions revolve around the very act and impulse of writing. How does writing shape an identity? What purpose does writing serve? The essays here, as well as the ones in the craft section at the end of the book, are included to give you, as new writers, a glimpse into why more experienced writers do what they do, and how.

At its most basic level, narration is telling a story. But a meaningful, compelling narrative moves far beyond the mere description of a sequence of events. A good narrative shows how the parts of an experience are connected, how and why they cohere, why they matter, and what they mean.

The literacy narrative is a specific type of narrative that addresses an aspect of the writer's experience with writing and reading. Like the reflective narrative (discussed in Chapter 7), which is an examination of any event or series of events in the writer's past, the goal of a literacy narrative is to examine the writer's experience with books, language, writing, or reading. Here, we take you behind the scenes so you can compare your own experiences and methods to those of published writers. Sherman Alexie, in "Learning to Read and Write: Superman and Me," tells us that by reading Superman comics, he began to associate the images in the cartoon panels with the words on the page. To Alexie, reading is power and freedom. In "Me Talk Pretty One Day," David Sedaris describes his attempts to learn a foreign language—another kind of literacy—and the embarrassment, frustration, and humor that arises when we try to communicate our most basic needs without the linguistic tools we usually take for granted. These two examples suggest entirely different ways to approach the same question—an investigation of the role of literacy in your life; there are, of course, an infinite number of additional tacks and tactics you might adopt when exploring your own encounters with reading and writing.

As writers, each of us could explore the same driving question, but because of each person's unique experiences, political and religious beliefs, cultural backgrounds, and sense of aesthetics, we would produce vastly different essays. What matters is each individual writer's level of engagement with the material and commitment to analyzing his or her own experiences to illuminate some meaningful aspect of what it means to be human.

Sherman Alexie

SUPERMAN AND ME

I learned to read with a Superman comic book. Simple enough, I suppose. I cannot recall which particular Superman comic book I read, nor can I remember which villain he fought in that issue. I cannot remember the plot, nor the means by which I obtained the comic book. What I can remember is this: I was three years old, a Spokane Indian boy living with his family on the Spokane Indian Reservation in eastern Washington state. We were poor by most standards, but one of my parents usually managed to find some minimum-wage job or another, which made us middle-class by reservation standards. I had a brother and three sisters. We lived on a combination of irregular paychecks, hope, fear and government surplus food.

My father, who is one of the few Indians who went to Catholic school on purpose, was an avid reader of westerns, spy thrillers, murder mysteries, gangster epics, basket-ball player biographies and anything else he could find. He bought his books by the pound at Dutch's Pawn Shop, Goodwill, Salvation Army and Value Village. When he had extra money, he bought new novels at supermarkets, convenience stores and hos-pital gift shops. Our house was filled with books. They were stacked in crazy piles in the bathroom, bedrooms and living room. In a fit of unemployment-inspired creative energy, my father built a set of bookshelves and soon filled them with a random assort-ment of books about the Kennedy assassination, Watergate, the Vietnam War and the entire 23-book series of the Apache westerns. My father loved books, and since I loved my father with an aching devotion, I decided to love books as well.

I can remember picking up my father's books before I could read. The words themselves were mostly foreign, but I still remember the exact moment when I first understood, with a sudden clarity, the purpose of a paragraph. I didn't have the vocab-ulary to say "paragraph," but I realized that a paragraph was a fence that held words. The words inside a paragraph worked together for a common purpose. They had some specific reason for being inside the same fence. This knowledge delighted me. I began to think of everything in terms of paragraphs. Our reservation was a small paragraph within the United States. My family's house was a paragraph, distinct from the other paragraphs of the LeBrets to the north, the Fords to our south and the Tribal School to the west. Inside our house, each family member existed as a separate paragraph but still had genetics and common experiences to link us. Now, using this logic, I can see my changed family as an essay of seven paragraphs: mother, father, older brother, the deceased sister, my younger twin sisters and our adopted little brother.

At the same time I was seeing the world in paragraphs, I also picked up that Superman comic book. Each panel, complete with picture, dialogue and narrative was a three-dimensional paragraph. In one panel, Superman breaks through a door. His suit is red, blue and yellow. The brown door shatters into many pieces. I look at the narrative above the picture. I cannot read the words, but I assume it tells me that "Superman is breaking down the door." Aloud, I pretend to read the words and say, "Superman is breaking down the door." Words, dialogue, also float out of Superman's mouth. Because he is breaking down the door, I assume he says, "I am breaking down the door." Once again, I pretend to read the words and say aloud, "I am breaking down the door." In this way, I learned to read.

This might be an interesting story all by itself. A little Indian boy teaches himself to read at an early age and advances quickly. He reads "Grapes of Wrath" in kindergarten when other children are struggling through "Dick and Jane." If he'd been anything but an Indian boy living on the reservation, he might have been called a prodigy. But he is an Indian boy living on the reservation and is simply an oddity. He grows into a man who often speaks of his childhood in the third-person, as if it will somehow dull the pain and make him sound more modest about his talents.

A smart Indian is a dangerous person, widely feared and ridiculed by Indians and non-Indians alike. I fought with my classmates on a daily basis. They wanted me to stay quiet when the non-Indian teacher asked for answers, for volunteers, for help. We were Indian children who were expected to be stupid. Most lived up to those expectations inside the classroom but subverted them on the outside. They struggled with basic reading in school but could remember how to sing a few dozen powwow songs. They were monosyllabic in front of their non-Indian teachers but could tell complicated stories and jokes at the dinner table. They submissively ducked their heads when confronted by a non-Indian adult but would slug it out with the Indian bully who was 10 years older. As Indian children, we were expected to fail in the non-Indian world. Those who failed were ceremonially accepted by other Indians and appropriately pitied by non-Indians.

I refused to fail. I was smart. I was arrogant. I was lucky. I read books late into the night, until I could barely keep my eyes open. I read books at recess, then during lunch, and in the few minutes left after I had finished my classroom assignments. I read books in the car when my family traveled to powwows or basketball games. In shopping malls, I ran to the bookstores and read bits and pieces of as many books as I could. I read the books my father brought home from the pawnshops and secondhand. I read the books I borrowed from the library. I read the backs of cereal boxes. I read the newspaper. I read the bulletins posted on the walls of the school, the clinic, the tribal offices, the post office. I read junk mail. I read auto-repair manuals. I read magazines. I read anything that had words and paragraphs. I read with equal parts joy and desperation. I loved those books, but I also knew that love had only one purpose. I was trying to save my life. Despite all the books I read, I am still surprised I became a writer. I was going to be a pediatrician. These days, I write novels, short stories, and poems. I visit schools and teach creative writing to Indian kids. In all my years in the reservation school system, I was never taught how to write poetry, short stories or novels. I was certainly never taught that Indians wrote poetry, short stories and novels. Writing was something beyond Indians. I cannot recall a single time that a guest teacher visited the reservation. There must have been visiting teachers. Who were they? Where are they now? Do they exist? I visit the schools as often as possible. The Indian kids crowd the classroom. Many are writing their own poems, short stories and novels. They have read my books. They have read many other books. They look at me with bright eyes and arrogant wonder. They are trying to save their lives. Then there are the sullen and already defeated Indian kids who sit in the back rows and ignore me with theatrical precision. The pages of their notebooks are empty. They carry neither pencil nor pen. They stare out the window. They refuse and resist. "Books," I say to them. "Books," I say. I throw my weight against their locked doors. The door holds. I am smart. I am arrogant. I am lucky. I am trying to save our lives.

—1997

Learning from Other Writers (Alexie)

1. Alexie notes at the end of the second paragraph that he "decided to love books." What is the effect of his choice of the word "decided"? How is this different than saying "I loved books" or "I realized I loved books"?

2. Alexie says that as a child he realized that paragraphs are like "fences" that hold words. Why is this such a significant detail? How does he develop this idea? To what other ideas does he link the image of a paragraph as a fence?

3. Go through Alexie's essay and find words or images that have to do with the concept of choice. How do all these examples of choices contribute to your understanding of Alexie's essay?

David Sedaris

ME TALK PRETTY ONE DAY

At the age of forty-one, I am returning to school and have to think of myself as what my French textbook calls "a true debutante." After paying my tuition, I was issued a student ID, which allows me a discounted entry fee at movie theaters, puppet shows, and Festyland, a farflung amusement park that advertises with billboards picturing a cartoon stegosaurus sitting in a canoe and eating what appears to be a ham sandwich.

I've moved to Paris with hopes of learning the language. My school is an easy ten-minute walk from my apartment, and on the first day of class I arrived early, watching as the returning students greeted one another in the school lobby. Vacations were recounted, and questions were raised concerning mutual friends with names like Kang and Vlatnya. Regardless of their nationalities, everyone spoke in what sounded to me like excellent French. Some accents were better than others, but the students exhibited an ease and confidence I found intimidating. As an added discomfort, they were all young, attractive, and well dressed, causing me to feel not unlike Pa Kettle trapped backstage after a fashion show.

The first day of class was nerve-racking because I knew I'd be expected to perform. That's the way they do it here—it's everybody into the language pool, sink or swim. The teacher marched in, deeply tanned from a recent vacation, and proceeded to rattle off a series of administrative announcements. I've spent quite a few summers in Normandy, and I took a monthlong French class before leaving New York. I'm not completely in the dark, yet I understood only half of what this woman was saying.

"If you have not *meimslsxp* or *Igpdmurct* by this time, then you should not be in this room. Has everyone *apzkiubjxow*? Everyone? Good, we shall begin." She spread out her lesson plan and sighed, saying, "All right, then, who knows the alphabet?"

It was startling because (a) I hadn't been asked that question in a while and (b) I realized, while laughing, that I myself did *not* know the alphabet. They're the same letters, but in France they're pronounced differently. I know the shape of the alphabet but had no idea what it actually sounded like.

"Ahh." The teacher went to the board and sketched the letter *a*. "Do we have anyone in the room whose first name commences with an *ahh*?"

Two Polish Annas raised their hands, and the teacher instructed them to present themselves by stating their names, nationalities, occupations, and a brief list of things they liked and disliked in this world. The first Anna hailed from an industrial town outside of Warsaw and had front teeth the size of tombstones. She worked as a seamstress, enjoyed quiet times with friends, and hated the mosquito.

"Oh, really," the teacher said. "How very interesting. I thought that everyone loved the mosquito, but here, in front of all the world, you claim to detest him. How is it that we've been blessed with someone as unique and original as you? Tell us, please."

The seamstress did not understand what was being said but knew that this was an occasion for shame. Her rabbity mouth huffed for breath, and she stared down at her lap as though the appropriate comeback were stitched somewhere alongside the zipper of her slacks.

The second Anna learned from the first and claimed to love sunshine and detest lies. It sounded like a translation of one of those Playmate of the Month data sheets, the answers always written in the same loopy handwriting: "Turn-ons: Mom's famous five-alarm chili! Turnoffs: insecurity and guys who come on too strong!!!!"

The two Polish Annas surely had clear notions of what they loved and hated, but like the rest of us, they were limited in terms of vocabulary, and this made them appear less than sophisticated. The teacher forged on, and we learned that Carlos, the Argentine bandonion player, loved wine, music, and, in his words, "making sex with the womens of the world." Next came a beautiful young Yugoslav who identified herself as an optimist, saying that she loved everything that life had to offer.

The teacher licked her lips, revealing a hint of the saucebox we would later come to know. She crouched low for her attack, placed her hands on the young woman's desk, and leaned close, saying, "Oh yeah? And do you love your little war?"

While the optimist struggled to defend herself, I scrambled to think of an answer to what had obviously become a trick question. How often is one asked what he loves in this world? More to the point, how often is one asked and then publicly ridiculed for his answer? I recalled my mother, flushed with wine, pounding the tabletop late one night, saying, "Love? I love a good steak cooked rare. I love my cat, and I love..." My sisters and I leaned forward, waiting to hear our names. "Tums," our mother said. "I love Tums."

The teacher killed some time accusing the Yugoslavian girl of masterminding a program of genocide, and I jotted frantic notes in the margins of my pad. While I can honestly say that I love leafing through medical textbooks devoted to severe dermatological conditions, the hobby is beyond the reach of my French vocabulary, and acting it out would only have invited controversy.

When called upon, I delivered an effortless list of things that I detest: blood sausage, intestinal pates, brain pudding. I'd learned these words the hard way. Having given it some thought, I then declared my love for IBM typewriters, the French word for *bruise*, and my electric floor waxer. It was a short list, but still I managed to mispronounce IBM and assign the wrong gender to both the floor waxer and the typewriter. The teacher's reaction led me to believe that these mistakes were capital crimes in the country of France.

"Were you always this *palicmkrexis*?" she asked. "Even a *fiuscrzsa ticiwelmun* knows that a typewriter is feminine."

I absorbed as much of her abuse as I could understand, thinking—but not saying—that I find it ridiculous to assign a gender to an inanimate object incapable of disrobing and making an occasional fool of itself. Why refer to crack pipe or Good Sir Dishrag when these things could never live up to all that their sex implied?

The teacher proceeded to belittle everyone from German Eva, who hated laziness, to Japanese Yukari, who loved paintbrushes and soap. Italian, Thai, Dutch, Korean, and Chinese—we all left class foolishly believing that the worst was over. She'd shaken us up a little, but surely that was just an act designed to weed out the deadweight. We didn't know it then, but the coming months would teach us what it was like to spend time in the presence of a wild animal, something completely unpredictable.

Her temperament was not based on a series of good and bad days but, rather, good and bad moments. We soon learned to dodge chalk and protect our heads and stomachs whenever she approached us with a question. She hadn't yet punched anyone, but it seemed wise to protect ourselves against the inevitable.

Though we were forbidden to speak anything but French, the teacher would occasionally use us to practice any of her five fluent languages.

"I hate you," she said to me one afternoon. Her English was flawless. "I really, really hate you." Call me sensitive, but I couldn't help but take it personally.

After being singled out as a lazy *kfdtinvfm*, I took to spending four hours a night on my homework, putting in even more time whenever we were assigned an essay. I suppose I could have gotten by with less, but I was determined to create some sort of identity for myself: David the hard worker, David the cut-up. We'd have one of those "complete this sentence" exercises, and I'd fool with the thing for hours, invariably settling on something like "A quick run around the lake? I'd love to! Just give me a moment while I strap on my wooden leg." The teacher, through word and action, conveyed the message that if this was my idea of an identity, she wanted nothing to do with it.

My fear and discomfort crept beyond the borders of the classroom and accompanied me out onto the wide boulevards. Stopping for a coffee, asking directions, depositing money in my bank account: these things were out of the question, as they involved having to speak. Before beginning school, there'd been no shutting me up, but now I was convinced that everything I said was wrong. When the phone rang, I ignored it. If someone asked me a question, I pretended to be deaf. I knew my fear was getting the best of me when I started wondering why they don't sell cuts of meat in vending machines.

My only comfort was the knowledge that I was not alone. Huddled in the hallways and making the most of our pathetic French, my fellow students and I engaged in the sort of conversation commonly overheard in refugee camps.

"Sometime me cry alone at night."

"That be common for I, also, but be more strong, you. Much work and someday you talk pretty. People start love you soon. Maybe tomorrow, okay."

Unlike the French class I had taken in New York, here there was no sense of competition. When the teacher poked a shy Korean in the eyelid with a freshly sharpened pencil, we took no comfort in the fact that, unlike Hyeyoon Cho, we all knew the irregular past tense of the verb *to defeat*. In all fairness, the teacher hadn't meant to stab the girl, but neither did she spend much time apologizing, saying only, "Well, you should have been *vkkdyo* more *kdeynfulh*."

Over time it became impossible to believe that any of us would ever improve. Fall arrived and it rained every day, meaning we would now be scolded for the water dripping from our coats and umbrellas. It was mid-October when the teacher singled me out, saying, "Every day spent with you is like having a cesarean section." And it struck me that, for the first time since arriving in France, I could understand every word that someone was saying.

Understanding doesn't mean that you can suddenly speak the language. Far from it. It's a small step, nothing more, yet its rewards are intoxicating and deceptive. The teacher continued her diatribe and I settled back, bathing in the subtle beauty of each new curse and insult.

"You exhaust me with your foolishness and reward my efforts with nothing but pain, do you understand me?"

The world opened up, and it was with great joy that I responded, "I know the thing that you speak exact now. Talk me more, you, *plus*, please, *plus*."

—2000

Learning from Other Writers (Sedaris)

1. Whereas Alexie's tone is serious and uncompromising, Sedaris's tone—his trademark—is sarcastic and self-deprecating. Discuss the ways in which each author's choices as regard tone are appropriate for the subject of each essay.

2. Sedaris's struggles in his French class are funny, but in recounting them for us, he also gets at a larger, more universal concern. What is that concern? What is the essay's driving question?

3. Sedaris uses nonsense words to indicate words whose meanings he couldn't even guess at. What are some of the effects of his decision to use these nonsense words? How do they mirror his overall attitude toward learning French? His feelings in the classroom?

4. What does Sedaris mean when he says that he learned the words for blood sausage, intestinal paté, and brain pudding "the hard way"? How does this encapsulate the experience of being in a new place whose language you don't understand?

5. Sedaris states at the end of his essay: "Understanding doesn't necessarily mean that you can suddenly speak the language." How does this statement work on multiple levels? How can it be applied not only to learning a language but also to being an outsider in a country or a community of any type?

Adding Your Voice

1. Think of your earliest, most vivid memory that has to do with reading or writing. Was the experience positive or negative? What value did your parents and friends place on reading and writing? How have those early experiences or expectations about reading and writing influenced the way you approach each activity?

2. Is there a book you particularly loved as a child? A book that changed the way you think? A book that moved you or upset you? A book you found exceptionally difficult to read or understand? Reflect on your experience reading that book and why you reacted as you did.

3. Is there some activity other than reading or writing in which you have gained an above-average degree of competence or proficiency? In what ways are the two activities different, or even antithetical to each other? In what ways are they linked?

4. Why do you write? In your journal, try to address the topic now, and then revisit this same question at the end of the semester. At that later point, ask yourself: *How has my view of writing changed? How has my writing itself changed?* Then write an essay in which you trace the path you have traveled as a writer from the beginning of the semester to the end.

CHAPTER 7

Reflective Narratives

The *reflective narrative* is the most common form of creative nonfiction and the easiest to define: a writer's first-person account of something he or she has experienced, told in roughly chronological order, as a story. But as is true of most definitions, this one is clear only until you consider it more closely. A writer's experiences, observations, and use of the pronoun "I" may play a significant role in an essay that isn't primarily about the writer. And an essay based on the writer's life might assume a shape other than chronological.

Nonetheless, our basic definition of a reflective narrative will allow us to study its ingredients. Narrative is a tool for reflection. By recalling the experience precisely and analytically, you will be more able to trace the chain of events that led up to it and the parts that contribute to the whole and to see the importance of something you had overlooked in the past. The narrative form also provides readers with a naturally coherent way of encountering your reflections and ideas about the events you are narrating (after all, we are all well versed in the structure of storytelling—first this happened, then that).

As you have seen in Part I, once you have gained your audience's attention, you will need to maintain it by providing details that bring alive the people and events that figure in your narrative. In the same way that expert storytellers becomes adept at keeping their listeners interested in or even enthralled by their stories, you will learn to use the literary devices of fiction, poetry, and drama—that is, suspense, humor, evocative images and descriptions, and startling turns of phrase—to keep your readers invested in your essays.

Most of us understand these elements well enough that we can tell an amusing anecdote. And often that's enough. If you tell your friends about the day you got lost in Yellowstone Park, then tumbled off a cliff and looked up to see a bear, no doubt they will stick around to find out what happened next. And anyone with a sense of humor will enjoy an account of the time you stumbled into a classroom, barely awake after an all-nighter, and sat through an entire lecture about James Joyce's *Ulysses* before you realized that you were not in your Introduction to Anthropology class.

But the most memorable stories do more than entertain. Like the best movies, the best reflective narratives keep us thinking about the questions they raise long after the lights have gone up or we have put down the book. In fact, we have chosen to use the term "reflective narrative" rather than the more common "personal narrative" to enforce the idea that every good essay is grounded in critical thinking. Reflection is analysis. Writing a reflective narrative involves more than just describing something funny or upsetting. If your audience doesn't know you, they won't care that your father humiliated you when you were a kid because you couldn't hit a baseball. There's no context. When a stranger on a plane starts to tell you about her husband's infidelities or her own inability to stay out of bars, you want to move to another seat. *Why do I need to know this? Why would you think I care?*

What distinguishes the very best essayists is their ability to construct a compelling narrative and make meaning from a brush with death or something as seemingly trivial as getting cheated at a card game or being pressured by a friend into smoking a cigarette. Which generally means that the storyteller is using the card game or cigarette to explore some larger question about what it means to be human. Which *doesn't* mean that the storyteller is trying to teach us a lesson about honesty being the best policy or peer pressure being an evil force that causes young people to smoke and use drugs and fornicate indiscriminately. (An essay *testing* one of these clichés might be worth writing. *Is honesty the best policy? Always? Can't peer pressure be a helpful part of growing up?*)

Another way of saying this is that you need to contextualize your experience so that it's meaningful to your readers. As you write and revise, you need to ask yourself why your readers might care about what you are telling them; you need to stave off their propensity to mutter: *"So what?"* Think back to the essays by Steve Amick ("Cold Comfort") and Judith Ortiz Cofer ("*Casa:* A Partial Remembrance of a Puerto Rican Childhood") in Part I. Both Amick and Cofer are looking back on something from their past from the perspective of the present. We call this "retrospective analysis." Consider the etymology of this first word: "retro" (back) and "spective" (the same root as "spectacles"). So, "back-looking." Beyond the rituals that Amick and Cofer describe, beyond the descriptions of the settings in which these rituals take place, lies something more significant: what each ritual means to the writer. Amick uses swimming in the cold lake as a metaphor for "hurling forward" in life, and Ortiz Cofer uses the ritual of hairbrushing to illuminate the interactions among the women in her family and show how the conversations during the hour of *café con leche* gave her insight into the world of adults.

Amick is not recalling any one particular incident but rather using his memories and impressions of a place to center his essay, moving from a description of his family's house on the lake to the family's ritual of jumping in the cold water as a way to characterize what he means by the "hurling forward kind." He structures his piece around a particular, significant place in northern Michigan and zooms in to the swimming ritual, which has to do not only with the importance of the place to him but also the way diving into the cold water without hesitation becomes a symbol for his decision to propose to his girlfriend.

Note that Ortiz Cofer subtitles her piece "A Partial Remembrance." By focusing on the women in her family and Mama's tradition of telling stories, the author is able to eliminate many other events from her childhood and adolescence. We don't hear about her first love or her fights with her mother or her successes and failures at school. The focus remains on the women in her family, that very particular coffee-hour, and the story told therein.

Narrative forces us to pay attention to the ways in which relationships among people and events shift, change, and influence one another over time. A good narrative measures the distance between two points: where we were then and where we are now. Think of the reflective aspects of a narrative as a way to measure the emotional distance traveled by the writer, not in the sense of a "lesson learned" but a more complex and less predictable change in attitude, perspective, or understanding. When you begin to write, you will generally know the facts of your history but not their meaning. Most likely, you will discover the significance of what happened only as you move from draft to draft of your essay. That's what makes this form both exciting and complex.

A strong reflective narrative not only will use concrete sensory details, lively dialogue, and fresh, evocative language to convey the writer's experience, it also will place that experience within a larger societal (or historical, literary, psychological, or scientific) context. Whether you are writing about your love for deer hunting or the hardships your family suffered during and after Hurricane Katrina, you will need to formulate an interesting, driving question about your topic, develop at least a partial answer to that question, and present your findings and discoveries in a comprehensible and compelling way.

EXPOSITION AND SCENE

Two main modes of writing are used in any narrative: expository and scenic writing. In the roughest terms, you can think of exposition as "telling" and scenic writing as "showing." That is, an expository sentence conveys an opinion or a fact or sums up habitual action, while a scene re-creates a particular experience on the page. A successful narrative will contain an appropriate balance of both. When you write creative nonfiction, you don't merely tell your readers about the animals you saw at the zoo: you take your readers to the zoo with you to watch the monkeys swinging around in their cages, to smell the fetid stink in the hippos' stagnant pond, to hear the jokey comments the schoolchildren make about the colors of the baboons' butts. (A third mode of writing, reflection or meditation, can be found within either an expository passage or a scene. In this third mode, which we will cover in a moment, the writer expresses his or thoughts or feelings about what is happening in the narrative or analyzes the significance of the information or facts being conveyed.)

You probably have heard the oft-repeated advice: *Show, don't tell.* As we discussed earlier, the more you can engage your readers' senses, the better, and the best way to engage your readers' senses is by showing them what your subject looks like and using other types of sensory details to appeal to your readers' sense of taste, smell, touch, and sound. But sometimes you need to come right out and tell your readers the safety statistics of various car models, as Malcolm Gladwell does in "Big and Bad," or inform us that "Evanston was still a segregated city in 1958 when Martin Luther King, Jr., spoke there about the Greek concept of agape, or love for all humanity" as Eula Biss does in "No Man's Land."

Both expository and scenic writing allow you to re-create your subject for your reader. With exposition, you might convey the history of your hometown, the height of the mountains that surround it, the types of products sold in the shops that line the main street, the ways in which the residents of the town differ from the tourists who come there to ski. You might also use exposition to move your readers from this general evocation of your hometown to a specific event that changed and complicated your attitude toward your neighbors and/or the outsiders upon whom the town's livelihood depends. Using scenic writing, you might then re-create for your readers the day that two elderly tourists got lost on the mountain and you, as a member of the junior ski patrol, were enlisted to help find them. Scenic writing doesn't just tell the reader what happened; it places the reader right in the moment and allows him or her to experience the event, usually from the writer's perspective.

Choosing what to convey via exposition and what to convey with a scene is an important skill. If you want to tell your readers something straight out—if you want to convey a fact, summarize an event, or compress a long period of time into a short amount of space—you should use expository writing. On the other hand, scenic writing is effective when you want to bring your subject alive so your readers can experience the actual moment for themselves.

Say you are writing about a violin competition. You might tell your readers when you first started playing the violin, your feelings toward music, and the way you tended to panic before competitions. You might then show us what it was like at the breakfast table the morning before a particular competition and let us hear the way your parents spoke in low voices in the other room. (Dialogue is one of the key elements in scenic writing.) You might tell us what you were thinking when you saw your father eyeing your violin case and your mother looking at the clock, silently willing you to practice your pieces one more time. You might show us the concert hall and the other nervous musicians waiting to be judged, after which you might re-create for us the moment you walked in for your audition, the way the judges looked you up and down before you began playing, and what they said as they critiqued your performance afterward.

In shifting between exposition and scene, most writers rely on intuition. You might employ exposition at the opening of an essay to establish the context, then move quickly into scene to grab your readers' interest, and then weave in some background information on a need-to-know basis. If you feel that a passage of exposition has gone on too long, you might break it up with another scene. Pacing, in particular, is affected by these proportions. When you need to speed things up, exposition will do the trick—it's great for compressing information and delivering facts efficiently. If *how* an event happened is as important as *what* happened, you can slow down and expand your narrative with scenic prose, letting your reader experience the event just as you once did. Moving back and forth between the two types of writing will add texture and variety to your work, which will keep both you and your reader engaged. Of course, it's always good to share your draft with a trusted reader or group of readers to see if your intuition is correct.

Remember that you can use reflection within either an expository passage or a scene: reflection allows you to convey to the reader how you interpreted what was happening at the time, as well the way you see those same events now, retrospectively, at the moment of writing. Reflection is what gives the events, people, and places you describe their meaning.

For instance, you might start by telling us about your struggle with your weight when you were in high school, explaining that all your friends were as thin as ballet dancers while you were the stocky star of your rugby team, reflecting at length on the way you felt whenever you went to the mall with your classmates or changed into your gym clothes in the locker room. You might then move on to a scene at a party where you realize that your best friend ate two slices of birthday cake, then went into the bathroom and vomited. In the middle of the scene, while you are waiting outside the bathroom door, you can also employ reflection and analysis: "While I listened to my best friend throwing up, I wondered how long she had been doing this. She had always been thin, but maybe the pressure to *stay* that way was worse than I had imagined. When the door opened, she stormed out as if I weren't there. Maybe she didn't want to see my horrified expression."

Keep in mind that you shouldn't use exposition to explain what you already have shown. In the previous scene, you wouldn't need to say: "I was very upset to catch my best friend throwing up her dessert." Instead, you might use exposition to move us quickly ahead through whatever happened next:

"For the next few weeks, my best friend avoided me. She ignored my calls and claimed she had too much homework to meet me at the mall. She didn't show up to our usual lunch table at school, and I realized she probably had stopped eating altogether."

Then, you might move into another scene:

One day, two weeks after Homecoming, I found her waiting for me in my driveway. Her face was swollen from crying, but I noticed the way her jeans were folded over at the top to keep from sliding down her bony hips.

"Hi," I said.

She didn't say anything, but when I hugged her, she started to cry again. "Come inside," I said. "No one's home. You can tell me what's been going on."

Adding Your Voice

To gain a bit of practice juggling exposition and scene, go back and try the exercise in which you write one specific sentence about someone who raised you. Be sure to avoid generalizations and clichés; instead, choose one significant, revelatory detail about your parent or guardian. Now add another five or six detailed expository sentences about that same person. Finally, close your eyes and bring to mind a memory in which your subject is acting in such a way that he or she reveals something essential about his or her character. Let the memory play itself out inside your head. Where is this person? What is he or she doing or saying? How does he look? Is she interacting with other people? What do you see? Hear? Smell? Without losing your mental movie of that scene, try to get everything down on paper.

Now compare this scene with the expository sentences you wrote earlier. Which tactic is more effective? Are there aspects of the scene that couldn't be conveyed by exposition? Which expository sentences convey information that couldn't be conveyed through scene?

RATE OF REVELATION AND DRAMATIC PACING

Once you understand the basic characteristics of expository and scenic writing and the relative advantages of each, you will need to consider how to regulate the flow of information that you dispense to your readers via exposition and the length and pacing of each scene. In reality, much of a writer's skill in both arenas—rate of revelation and dramatic pacing—is acquired naturally through reading other people's prose and workshopping and revising early drafts of a manuscript. As you will see when you read the essays in this anthology, few writers begin with pages and pages of exposition whose purpose is to provide readers with the background necessary to provide the main action; instead, we get a gripping scene, followed by a paragraph or two of crucial information, then another scene, then we learn more as we go on reading, a paragraph here, a sentence there.

On the other hand, you rarely encounter a successful writer who withholds crucial facts in a misguided effort to create suspense. Real suspense comes from what readers know rather than what they don't know; to follow a mystery or a thriller, you need to have a clear idea as to what the mystery or conspiracy *is*. Instead of withholding information, mystery writers dole out clues as the narrative progresses. The resolution of a mystery shouldn't come as a complete shock; rather, the surprise of the final revelation gives way to a satisfying sense that the writer has been preparing us for that ending all along.

As to pacing, no one wants to read pages and pages of exposition about the months a soldier spends hanging around the barracks, only to rush through a scene in which he comes under attack in his first gun battle in Iraq. Most of us have watched enough movies that we have acquired an intuitive feel for pacing. We know that subjecting an audience to twenty minutes of expository voice-over is a clumsy way to start a film and that asking viewers to read chapter after chapter of historical background scrolling across a screen begs them to draw unfavorable parallels to the opening moments of *Star Wars*. Most of us are familiar with the way directors use quickly cut scenes or montages to convey the passing of empty time, only to watch the pacing slow dramatically as the two main characters are finally reunited and find themselves alone in a motel room.

All these references to movies might make you consider taking up filmmaking instead of writing. Certainly, an essayist can find it frustrating to spend twenty pages describing the visual and aural details a camera can reveal in an instant. But writers enjoy enviable advantages over filmmakers: we can convey the way something smells, tastes, or feels; we can provide important background information without resorting to stilted dialogue whose only purpose is to clue in the audience rather than the other members of the conversation; we can create the impression of habitual (rather than one-time) action simply by changing our verb tenses; we can reveal what's going on inside our characters' heads; and we can work on our own, with equipment that is easy to obtain and operate, on an extremely modest budget.

Writing is both a creative and an analytical process. In the hands of a good writer, the two are nearly inseparable. As you make your way through this book and begin generating essays of your own, you will find that in describing a moment from your life, you will see—and understand—that moment better. Partly this will occur because re-creating an event forces us to witness it more objectively, seeing what we failed to notice the first time, connecting incidents or images we didn't think to connect when we were younger or less informed or more harried or frightened. But you will also gain that new understanding because a writer's job is to interpret and contextualize. Our duty is to make meaning through analysis and examination. And by being aware of an audience—that is, re-creating the past not only for ourselves but also for some-one else—we are able to imbue our writing with significance. As you gather the vari-ous threads of analysis that have been exposed during the writing process and weave them together, whether by drawing a connection to some larger theme, by linking one circumstance to another in a causal way, or by identifying the ways in which your experience illuminates a larger aspect of society or culture, you will begin to make the specific—the particular, the personal—into the universal.

REFLECTION AND ANALYSIS

Although most of us feel comfortable telling stories about our experiences, analyzing those same experiences in a complex and original way requires confidence. Often, the writer simply gives up and says, "I don't know why I stole that bracelet," or "I will never understand why my boss refused to adopt my method for restocking the shelves more efficiently." But that's usually the whole essay right there. Don't let yourself get off so easily. Go deeper. *Think* about why you did what you did, or why your boss did what she did. Then put that meditation on the page.

A willingness to write about what you don't know rather than what you do know is the difference between a raconteur's breezy and oft-recited anecdote and an essay in which a memoirist revisits an important incident from her childhood or early adult-hood armed with a question that troubles her about that incident. In George Orwell's essay "Shooting an Elephant," which we discussed briefly in Chapter 1, the synergy between content and form is preserved in the finished product. The essay matters as it does because Orwell feels compelled to figure out why he shot an elephant that didn't need to be shot. He doesn't tell the story as a predigested anecdote, a bloody good yarn to entertain the officers at the club. Rather, he reconsiders an experience that he didn't fully understand when it happened, an experience that still disturbs him. The news that a rampaging elephant has killed a poor coolie propels the younger Orwell out the door. And yet, once he finds the elephant, he knows with "perfect certainty" that he ought not to shoot.

> It is a serious matter to shoot a working elephant—it is comparable to destroying a huge and costly piece of machinery—and obviously one not to do if it can possibly be avoided. ... I thought then and I think now that his attack of "must" was already passing off; in which case he would merely wander harmlessly about until the mahout came back and caught him. ... I decided that I would watch him for a while to make sure that he did not turn savage again, and then go home.

There Orwell stands, surrounded by a mob silently willing him to shoot the elephant for the spectacle of the thing, and there, at that moment, he grasps "the futility of the white man's dominion in the East."

> Here was I, the white man with his gun, standing in front of the unarmed native crowd—seemingly the leading actor of the piece; but in reality I was only an absurd puppet pushed to and fro by the will of those yellow faces behind. I perceived in this moment that when the white man turns tyrant it is his own freedoms that he destroys. ... For it is the condition of his rule that he shall spend his life in trying to impress the "natives," and so in every crisis he has got to do what the "natives" expect of him. ... I had got to shoot the elephant. ... To come all that way, rifle in hand, with two thousand people marching at my heels, and then to trail feebly away, having done nothing—no, that was impossible. The crowd would laugh at me. And my whole life, every white man's life in the East, was one long struggle not to be laughed at.

As Orwell answers the question of why he shot the elephant, he also partially answers the more universal question in which his conundrum nests: Why do imperialists act in ways that are not in their own best interests or the interests of the people they rule? "Shooting an Elephant" is a marvelous example of the manner in which a compelling narrative and a sincere question about that narrative work to produce an essay imbued not only with the suspense of "what will happen next" but the deeper suspense of what the experience will end up meaning. The thesis isn't presented at the start, with the rest of the essay proving it to be true. Rather, the reader watches the narrator struggling to reach his conclusion at every point along the way.

Orwell shows us the trick to making his specific experience of interest to a larger audience. When writing your own reflective narratives, ask yourself what you *don't* understand about a given experience and see if you can phrase that question in a slightly more general way so at least a few people (other than your family and friends) will be interested in the answer. That doesn't mean your question needs to interest everyone in the world. An essay in which you try to figure out why your immigrant Chinese parents never seem satisfied with your accomplishments will interest other sons of Chinese parents, not to mention the sons of Korean and Japanese parents. It also might interest the daughters of such parents, along with the sons and daughters of Russian and Kenyan immigrants. It might even interest readers who don't seem able to satisfy their American-born parents, or who teach in schools with a substantial population of immigrant students, or who are married to the offspring of immigrants, or who simply want to learn more about the trials faced by immigrants and their kids.

That's how most narratives work. The writer replays the events of a story while comparing those events at every point to the question that troubles him or her. If the writer thinks that his or her task is merely to describe an unusually dramatic or comic incident, he or she will be tempted to put in every detail, provoking the reader to ask—even for a story about a near-death experience or a horrifying instance of abuse—*why are you telling me all this?* On the other hand, if a writer sits down to ponder an abstract question (Why do imperialists act in ways that run counter to their own best interests?), the meditation will likely stall (nothing makes a mind wander more quickly to what's for lunch than an abstract question).

George Orwell

SHOOTING AN ELEPHANT

In Moulmein, in lower Burma, I was hated by large numbers of people—the only time in my life that I have been important enough for this to happen to me. I was sub-divisional police officer of the town, and in an aimless, petty kind of way anti-European feeling was very bitter. No one had the guts to raise a riot, but if a European woman went through the bazaars alone somebody would probably spit betel juice over her dress. As a police officer I was an obvious target and was baited whenever it seemed safe to do so. When a nimble Burman tripped me up on the football field and the referee (another Burman) looked the other way, the crowd yelled with hideous laughter. This happened more than once. In the end the sneering yellow faces of young men that met me everywhere, the insults hooted after me when I was at a safe distance, got badly on my nerves. The young Buddhist priests were the worst of all. There were several thousands of them in the town and none of them seemed to have anything to do except stand on street corners and jeer at Europeans.

All this was perplexing and upsetting. For at that time I had already made up my mind that imperialism was an evil thing and the sooner I chucked up my job and got out of it the better. Theoretically—and secretly, of course—I was all for the Burmese and all against their oppressors, the British. As for the job I was doing, I hated it more bitterly than I can perhaps make clear. In a job like that you see the dirty work of Empire at close quarters. The wretched prisoners huddling in the stinking cages of the lock-ups, the gray, cowed faces of the long-term convicts, the scarred buttocks of the men who had been flogged with bamboos—all these oppressed me with an intolerable sense of guilt. But I could get nothing into perspective. I was young and ill educated and I had had to think out my problems in the utter silence that is imposed on every Englishman in the East. I did not even know that the British Empire is dying, still less did I know that it is a great deal better than the younger empires that are going to supplant it. All I knew was that I was stuck between my hatred of the empire I served and my rage against the evil-spirited little beasts who tried to make my job impossible. With one part of my mind I thought of the British Raj as an unbreakable tyranny, as something clamped down, in *saecula saeculorum*, upon the will of prostrate peoples; with another part I thought that the greatest joy in the world would be to drive a bayonet into a Buddhist priest's guts. Feelings like these are the normal by-products of imperialism; ask any Anglo-Indian official, if you can catch him off duty.

One day something happened which in a roundabout way was enlightening. It was a tiny incident in itself; but it gave me a better glimpse than I had had before of the real nature of imperialism—the real motives for which despotic governments act. Early one morning the sub-inspector at a police station the other end of the town rang me up on the 'phone and said that an elephant was ravaging the bazaar. Would I please come and do something about it? I did not know what I could do, but I wanted to see what was happening and I got on to a pony and started out. I took my rifle, an old .44 Winchester and much too small to kill an elephant, but I thought the noise might be useful *in terrorem*. Various Burmans stopped me on the way and told me about the elephant's doings. It was not, of course, a wild elephant, but a tame one which had gone "must." It had been chained up, as tame elephants always are when their attack of "must" is due, but on the previous night it had broken its chain and escaped. Its mahout, the only person who could manage it when it was in that state, had set out in pursuit, but had taken the wrong direction and was now twelve hours' journey away, and in the morning the elephant had suddenly reappeared in the town. The Burmese population had no weapons and were quite helpless against it. It had already destroyed somebody's bamboo hut, killed a cow and raided some fruit-stalls and devoured the stock; also it had met the municipal rubbish van and, when the driver jumped out and took to his heels, had turned the van over and inflicted violences upon it.

The Burmese sub-inspector and some Indian constables were waiting for me in the quarter where the elephant had been seen. It was a very poor quarter, a labyrinth of squalid bamboo huts, thatched with palm-leaf, winding all over a steep hillside. I remember that it was a cloudy, stuffy morning at the beginning of the rains. We began questioning the people as to where the elephant had gone and, as usual, failed to get any definite information. That is invariably the case in the East; a story always sounds clear enough at a distance, but the nearer you get to the scene of events the vaguer it becomes. Some of the people said that the elephant had gone in one direction, some said that he had gone in another, some professed not even to have heard of any elephant. I had almost made up my mind that the whole story was a pack of lies, when we heard yells a little distance away. There was a loud, scandalized cry of "Go away, child! Go away this instant!" and an old woman with a switch in her hand came round the corner of a hut, violently shooing away a crowd of naked children. Some more women followed, clicking their tongues and exclaiming; evidently there was something that the children ought not to have seen. I rounded the hut and saw a man's dead body sprawling in the mud. He was an Indian, a black Dravidian coolie, almost naked, and he could not have been dead many minutes. The people said that the elephant had come suddenly upon him round the corner of the hut, caught him with its trunk, put its foot on his back and ground him into the earth. This was the rainy season and the ground was soft, and his face had scored a trench a foot deep and a couple of yards long. He was lying on his belly with arms crucified and head sharply twisted to one side. His face was coated with mud, the eyes wide open, the teeth bared and grinning with an expression of unendurable agony. (Never tell me, by the way, that the dead look peaceful. Most of the corpses I have seen looked devilish.) The friction of the great beast's foot had stripped the skin from his back as neatly as one skins a rabbit. As soon as I saw the dead man I sent an orderly to a friend's house nearby to borrow an elephant rifle. I had already sent back the pony, not wanting it to go mad with fright and throw me if it smelt the elephant.

The orderly came back in a few minutes with a rifle and five cartridges, and meanwhile some Burmans had arrived and told us that the elephant was in the paddy fields below, only a few hundred yards away. As I started forward practically the whole population of the quarter flocked out of the houses and followed me. They had seen the rifle and were all shouting excitedly that I was going to shoot the elephant. They had not shown much interest in the elephant when he was merely ravaging their homes, but it was different now that he was going to be shot. It was a bit of fun to them, as it would be to an English crowd; besides they wanted the meat. It made me vaguely uneasy. I had no intention of shooting the elephant—I had merely sent for the rifle to defend myself if necessary—and it is always unnerving to have a crowd following you. I marched down the hill, looking and feeling a fool, with the rifle over my shoulder and an ever-growing army of people jostling at my heels. At the bottom, when you got away from the huts, there was a metalled road and beyond that a miry waste of paddy fields a thousand yards across, not yet ploughed but soggy from the first rains and dotted with coarse grass. The elephant was standing eight yards from the road, his left side toward us. He took not the slightest notice of the crowd's approach. He was tearing up bunches of grass, beating them against his knees to clean them, and stuffing them into his mouth.

I had halted on the road. As soon as I saw the elephant I knew with perfect certainty that I ought not to shoot him. It is a serious matter to shoot a working elephant—it is comparable to destroying a huge and costly piece of machinery—and obviously one ought not to do it if it can possibly be avoided. And at that distance, peacefully eating, the elephant looked no more dangerous than a cow. I thought then and I think now that his attack of "must" was already passing off; in which case he would merely wander harmlessly about until the mahout came back and caught him. Moreover, I did not in the least want to shoot him. I decided that I would watch him for a little while to make sure that he did not turn savage again, and then go home.

But at that moment I glanced round at the crowd that had followed me. It was an immense crowd, two thousand at the least and growing every minute. It blocked the road for a long distance on either side. I looked at the sea of yellow faces above the garish clothes—faces all happy and excited over this bit of fun, all certain that the elephant was going to be shot. They were watching me as they would watch a conjurer about to perform a trick. They did not like me, but with the magical rifle in my hands I was momentarily worth watching. And suddenly I realized that I should have to shoot the elephant after all. The people expected it of me and I had got to do it; I could feel their two thousand wills pressing me forward, irresistibly. And it was at this moment, as I stood there with the rifle in my hands, that I first grasped the hollowness, the futility of the white man's dominion in the East. Here was I, the white man with his gun, standing in front of the unarmed native crowd—seemingly the leading actor of the piece; but in reality I was only an absurd puppet pushed to and fro by the will of those yellow faces behind. I perceived in this moment that when the white man turns tyrant it is his own freedom that he destroys. He becomes a sort of hollow, posing dummy, the conventionalized figure of a sahib. For it is the condition of his rule that he shall spend his life in trying to impress the "natives," and so in every crisis he has got to do what the "natives" expect of him. He wears a mask, and his face grows to fit it. I had got to shoot the elephant. I had committed myself to doing it when I sent for the rifle. A sahib has got to act like a sahib; he has got to appear resolute, to know his own mind and do definite things. To come all that way, rifle in hand, with two thousand people marching at my heels, and then to trail feebly away, having done nothing—no, that was impossible. The crowd would laugh at me. And my whole life, every white man's life in the East, was one long struggle not to be laughed at.

But I did not want to shoot the elephant. I watched him beating his bunch of grass against his knees with that preoccupied grandmotherly air that elephants have. It seemed to me that it would be murder to shoot him. At that age I was not squeamish about killing animals, but I had never shot an elephant and never wanted to. (Somehow it always seems worse to kill a *large* animal.) Besides, there was the beast's owner to be considered. Alive, the elephant was worth at least a hundred pounds; dead, he would only be worth the value of his tusks, five pounds, possibly. But I had got to act quickly. I turned to some experienced-looking Burmans who had been there when we arrived, and asked them how the elephant had been behaving. They all said the same thing: he took no notice of you if you left him alone, but he might charge if you went too close to him.

It was perfectly clear to me what I ought to do. I ought to walk up to within, say, twenty-five yards of the elephant and test his behavior. If he charged, I could shoot; if he took no notice of me, it would be safe to leave him until the mahout came back. But also I knew that I was going to do no such thing. I was a poor shot with a rifle and the ground was soft mud into which one would sink at every step. If the elephant charged and I missed him, I should have about as much chance as a toad under a steam-roller. But even then I was not thinking particularly of my own skin, only of the watchful yellow faces behind. For at that moment, with the crowd watching me, I was not afraid in the ordinary sense, as I would have been if I had been alone. A white man mustn't be frightened in front of "natives"; and so, in general, he isn't frightened. The sole thought in my mind was that if anything went wrong those two thousand Burmans would see me pursued, caught, trampled on, and reduced to a grinning corpse like that Indian up the hill. And if that happened it was quite probable that some of them would laugh. That would never do. There was only one alternative. I shoved the cartridges into the magazine and lay down on the road to get a better aim.

The crowd grew very still, and a deep, low, happy sigh, as of people who see the theater curtain go up at last, breathed from innumerable throats. They were going to have their bit of fun after all. The rifle was a beautiful German thing with cross-hair sights. I did not then know that in shooting an elephant one would shoot to cut an imaginary bar running from ear-hole to ear-hole. I ought, therefore, as the elephant was sideways on, to have aimed straight at his ear-hole; actually I aimed several inches of front of this, thinking the brain would be further forward.

When I pulled the trigger I did not hear the bang or feel the kick—one never does when a shot goes home—but I heard the devillish roar of glee that went up from the crowd. In that instant, in too short a time, one would have thought, even for the bullet to get there, a mysterious, terrible change had come over the elephant. He neither stirred, nor fell, but every line of his body had altered. He looked suddenly stricken, shrunken, immensely old, as though the frightful impact of the bullet had paralyzed him without knocking him down. At last, after what seemed a long time—it might

have been five seconds, I dare say—he sagged flabbily to his knees. His mouth slob-
bered. An enormous senility seemed to have settled upon him. One could have imagined him thousands of years old. I fired again into the same spot. At the second shot
he did not collapse but climbed with desperate slowness to his feet and stood weakly
upright, with legs sagging and head drooping. I fired a third time. That was the shot
that did for him. You could see the agony of it jolt his whole body and knock the last
remnant of strength from his legs. But in falling he seemed for a moment to rise, for
as his hind legs collapsed beneath him he seemed to tower upward like a huge rock
toppling, his trunk reaching skyward like a tree. He trumpeted, for the first and only
time. And then down he came, his belly toward me, with a crash that seemed to shake
the ground even where I lay.

I got up. The Burmans were already racing past me across the mud. It was obvious
that the elephant would never rise again, but he was not dead. He was breathing very
rhythmically with long rattling gasps, his great mound of a side painfully rising and
falling. His mouth was wide open—I could see far down into caverns of pale pink
throat. I waited a long time for him to die, but his breathing did not weaken. Finally
I fired my two remaining shots into the spot where I thought his heart must be. The
thick blood welled out of him like red velvet, but still he did not die. His body did not
even jerk when the shots hit him, the tortured breathing continued without a pause.
He was dying, very slowly and in great agony, but in some world remote from me
where not even a bullet could damage him further. I felt that I had got to put an end
to that dreadful noise. It seemed dreadful to see the great beast lying there, powerless
to move and yet powerless to die, and not even to be able to finish him. I sent back
for my small rifle and poured shot after shot into his heart and down his throat. They
seemed to make no impression. The tortured gasps continued as steadily as the ticking of a clock.

In the end I could not stand it any longer and went away. I heard later that it took
him half an hour to die. Burmans were bringing dahs and baskets even before I left,
and I was told they had stripped his body almost to the bones by the afternoon.

Afterward, of course, there were endless discussions about the shooting of the
elephant. The owner was furious, but he was only an Indian and could do nothing.
Besides, legally I had done the right thing, for a mad elephant has to be killed, like a
mad dog, if its owner fails to control it. Among the Europeans opinion was divided.
The older men said I was right, the younger men said it was a damn shame to shoot
an elephant for killing a coolie, because an elephant was worth more than any damn
Coringhee coolie. And afterward I was very glad that the coolie had been killed; it put
me legally in the right and it gave me a sufficient pretext for shooting the elephant. I
often wondered whether any of the others grasped that I had done it solely to avoid
looking a fool.

—1936

Learning from Other Writers (Orwell)

1. What is the effect of Orwell's decision to open his essay with two paragraphs of background information rather than the appearance of the elephant? Given that these opening paragraphs are written in expository rather than scenic prose, how does Orwell keep them interesting?

2. Much of Orwell's essay illustrates the racism at the heart of the British imperialism. Why doesn't Orwell make racism the point of his essay?

3. Where and how does Orwell employ the perspective of the young, ignorant policeman he was at the time he shot the elephant? Where does he speak from the perspective of the older, wiser man he is at the time he writes the essay?

4. Orwell asserts that his ambivalence about the Raj and the people it oppresses "are the normal by-products of imperialism." He also claims that it is "invariably the case in the East" that "a story always sounds clear enough at a distance, but the nearer you get to the scene of events the vaguer it becomes." What—if anything—gives him the right to make such sweeping generalizations?

5. What are the most memorable details that Orwell uses to bring alive his narrative?

6. Can you find the passages in which Orwell tries to develop an answer to his driving question? How does he use repetition to signpost these meditations?

7. Some readers think the dying elephant symbolizes British rule in India. Do you agree or disagree?

8. What is the effect of concluding the essay not with the elephant's death but with the general debate as to whether the author was right to kill it?

EPISODIC NARRATION

Elwood Reid, in his essay "My Body, My Weapon, My Shame," gives us an insider's view of the world of Big Ten football. "I did bad things for football," he begins. The essay's driving question becomes an inquiry into *why* he did those things. Like Orwell, who writes that the white man who rules a country he has colonized "wears a mask, and his face grows to fit it," Reid explores the flaws of the system in which he is caught while refusing to blame anyone else for his decisions. Like Orwell, he takes responsibility for his actions.

Because they both explore such similar questions, it's instructive to look at the different structures that Orwell and Reid employ and the way each author handles time. Orwell's essay uses *continuous narration*. He sets up his essay with two paragraphs of exposition: where he was, what he was doing in Burma, and how he felt about serving the Raj. Then, in the third paragraph, he launches into the narrative: "One day something happened. ..." The rest of the essay is a narration of this one incident. We don't jump ahead in time, nor are we provided with much backstory.

Reid, on the other hand, uses *episodic narration*. Instead of describing one specific game or practice session or party to explore his driving question, he presents a series of linked episodes, all of which are told in chronological order and are centered around his driving question about his football career: what it felt like to be both a part of the team and an outsider within its exclusive boundaries.

As we mentioned earlier, scenic writing takes us into a specific moment, using description, dialogue, reflection, and analysis. Reid's essay demonstrates the use of a fourth element, action and gesture. In the following scene from Reid's essay, his team has just won its Big Ten opener. Reporters are interviewing the game's important players, and word "percolates" through the locker room that there will be a party that night at "a fella's house." Then Reid takes us to the party. Note the way he describes the scene that we are entering. The room isn't frozen in time: it's full of people, and the people are in motion.

> When I enter the party, the room seems to be in some sort of drunken-action overload. Near the keg there is a makeshift wrestling pit, circled by grubby couches full of squealing teased-hair women who look at me briefly, decide that I am not a starter and look away. I am handed a beer and told to drink. My beertender is a huge, smiling defensive tackle named the Wall, who watches as I raise the cup to my lips and sip.

Then Reid inserts dialogue:

> "What a matter with you?" he says, pointing at the beer. "We've got beer and a roomful of chicks who want to fuck us 'cause we won the game. What more do you want?"
> "I'm just a frosh," I tell him.
> "Skip the *Leave it to Beaver* bullshit and drink," Wall says.

Notice the way Reid assigns gestures to his characters. The Wall doesn't just speak: he watches Reid take a drink; he points at the beer. These little gestures make the character come alive. They also provide a nice pacing to the dialogue so the reader can more clearly visualize the scene.

In the paragraph that follows, Reid includes more gesture, action, and description, as well as a bit of *reflection*—that is, what he thinks about what's going on in the scene:

> I nod, drain the cup and follow him to the kitchen, past heavily made-up groupies who stare at me now that I am with Wall. There are others, big guys mostly, and we keep pace with Wall, who tosses back beer as if it's water. After every round, somebody slops an arm around me or smacks me on the shoulder, and for a moment I feel the tug of the fella fraternity.

The scene ends here, and the Reid moves back into expository mode to condense what must have been hours of drunken carousing and to convey the typical behavior at such parties:

> What happens next is what happens in varying degrees at every subsequent party. Fights erupt over women, favorite teams, etc. There is a girl in an upstairs bedroom handing out blow jobs or an underclassman who is too drunk and vomits before he is stripped naked and thrown out a window or tossed down the stairs.

As you read the essay, pay attention to the way Reid alternates between exposition and scene. Notice the way he uses exposition to move through time and the way he uses scene to slow the pacing. Then highlight the passages in which he either lets us know what he was thinking or feeling at the time or reflects back on the bad things he did for football from the vantage of "a guy who used to play."

MY BODY, MY WEAPON, MY SHAME

I did bad things for football. Because I could. Because I was 19 years old, weighed 270 pounds, had 5 percent body fat and had muscle to burn. Forget touchdowns, I played football for the chance to hit another man as hard as I could—to fuck him up, move through him like wind through a door. Anybody who tells you different is a liar.

There is the fear that any hit may be your last. That some bigger, stronger, better player will come along—take you down to the turf and end your career with the snap of bone or the pop of an anterior cruciate ligament.

The moment of impact goes like this: You slam helmet-first into another person's back until you can hear the air whoosh out of his lungs. Or better yet—you ram a forearm so hard into his throat that the crunch of cartilage and the fear in his eyes give you pause. Time stops. No pain, only a sucking sound as the physics of the impact sort themselves out—who hit who first, angle, shoulder, mass, helmet, speed, forearm. Silence follows the cruel twist of limbs as the pain rushes in the way oxygen blows through the streets of a firebombed city, leaving flame in its wake. The pain is good. Both of you know it, and for a few precious seconds the world has order. Hitter and hittee. Motherfucker and motherfucked.

I came by football through my father. I played because if you were big, it was what you did in Cleveland. To do anything else was to be soft or queer. As long as I could hit and tackle, nobody made fun of my size. I played football, and that was all you needed to know about me. Then there were the men—the coaches who demanded a single-minded intensity from me each time I strapped on the pads. Even then I knew these were men who kept basements full of plaques and trophies from their glory days, collected beer steins and fell into deep depressions when the Cleveland Browns lost or their wives bore them daughters instead of sons. Their solution to everything was to hit harder. The word was forever on their lips. They scrawled it on chalkboards and spat it in my face: *Hit. Hit. Hit.* They knew how to infect eager minds with the desire to someday play in the pros. And when one of these potbellied men screamed at me to kick ass, act like a man or gut it out, I did, because I wanted to believe that a sport or even life could be boiled down to a few simple maxims. I was big, and I could hit; therefore I had purpose.

In high school, my scrawny body filled out as I moved from junior varsity to varsity and then to captain of a mediocre football team. College scouts came to time me in the forty-yard dash, watch me lift weights and eye me coming out of the shower as if I were a horse they might someday bid for at auction. I can't say I didn't enjoy the attention, but I began to realize that as a potential college-football recruit, I was expected to behave like one. I had to shake hands and look scouts in the eye and thank them for coming to see me. I had to talk sports, tell them who my favorite players were, what team I liked in the Super Bowl. I had to be smart but not too smart. Grades mattered only because colleges like "no risk" players, guys who can be recruited without the worry that they'll flunk out. I couldn't tell them that I didn't care who won the Super Bowl, that what really mattered to me was books. That when I finished *One Flew Over the Cuckoo's Nest* or *Heart of Darkness*, my heart beat faster than it ever had on the football field. I knew that I had to keep this part of me hidden and let the scouts and coaches see the bright-eyed athlete they wanted to see.

Pursuing a football scholarship became a full-time job. Everything I did was for my body. I ate well, went running at night, swallowed handfuls of vitamins, swilled gallons of protein shakes and fell asleep rubbing sore muscles. Everything fell away as I focused on using this body I'd nurtured and cared for, asking it to come back day after day, stronger, better. And it did. Even after the most torturous practices, my body responded by snapping back, fresh and ready to go. If there were limits, I had yet to find them.

On the field, I plugged my heart in, throwing my body at tailbacks with reckless abandon. I went both ways and loved every minute of it—reveling in the sheer exhaustion that came every fourth quarter, when it was all I could do to hunker down into a three-point stance and fire out. To be better than the man lined up across from you was to summon your body to do what it didn't want to do—what it would normally resist doing off the gridiron. Great ballplayers are full of hate and a kind of love for what they are capable of inflicting on another man. And in between whistles, I hated.

When the first recruiting letter arrived, I had this feeling that I was standing on the cusp of what I imagined to be greatness. I saw television, cheerleaders and, I suppose even then, the endgame—the NFL.

"This is a great opportunity," my father said, holding the letter in his hands as if it were alive.

I nodded, knowing that the ante had been raised. I was no longer playing because I liked to hit but for the chance to get out of Cleveland and escape the factory-gray fate that awaited me.

I escaped by signing a letter of intent to play ball for one of those Big Ten colleges, where football is king, the coach is feared and anybody wearing a letterman's jacket is instantly revered. I felt important, my head swirling with the possibilities that seemed to shimmer before me. I had worked hard; my friends had gone out drinking or had sat around watching television, but I'd been running and lifting. Now I felt as if I had been rewarded and everything would be OK.

That was ten years ago, and what I did both on and off the field for football is preserved forever in the aches, pains and injuries that haunt my body, lurking no matter how many aspirins I chew or how early I go to bed.

When I report to freshman summer camp, there are thirty or so other new recruits sitting around a huge indoor practice facility. Some of them are bigger and stronger than me, guys with no necks and triceps that hang off their arms like stapled-on hams. The speedsters and skill guys, mostly thick-legged black dudes with gold chains and shaved heads, pool over into their own corner, staring down at their feet as if the secret of their speed lay somewhere underground. The oddball white guys—quarterbacks, tight ends and a few gangly-looking receivers—find one another and talk like bankers, in slow, measured tones.

I make my way over to the group of big guys who stand, shifting foot to foot, in a loose semicircle, until the coaches walk in and everybody snaps to attention. I am relieved to find that they look like all the other coaches who have ever yelled at me or offered arm-swinging praise. They are the very same gray/white-haired men, swaddled head to toe in loud polyester, I've been trying to impress my whole life.

Nobody says a word. Instead, the coaches stand there looking at us the way a mechanic eyes his socket wrenches, as tools to be picked up, used and thrown aside. There is only this simple equation: As a ballplayer, I am expected to do as I'm told, lay my body on the line or else get out of the way for somebody who will. Everybody in the room knows and understands this and, when asked, will put himself in harm's way with the dim, deluded hope that he will come out the other end a star.

The speech begins, and it's like every other coach's speech, only this time the coach spouting the platitudes owns our bodies and our minds for the next four years, five if we redshirt. He lays down the rules—the same rules I've heard all my life about what I can and can't do—about how we're here to win and anything less is simply unacceptable.

Then his theory of football: "Domination through hard work, men," he says, his short body quivering with anger. "More hard work until we come together as a team of men focused on one thing: *winning.* Am I understood?"

"Yes, sir," we answer.

"Good then," he says. "I'll accept nothing less than smash-mouth, cream-them-in-the-ear-hole football. That is why you are here, and I will not tolerate softness or excuses. You are here because we think each of you will someday become a ballplayer. You are not yet ballplayers, but if you do what we ask, you will become ballplayers, and for that you are lucky."

All thirty of us grunt, "Yes, sir."

Then this no-neck guy, his face swollen with fear and desire, leans into me and says, "I wish we could skip the bullshit, strap on the pads and sort out who's who."

My first inclination is to laugh, to tell him to relax. Instead, I lid my eyes and clench my jaw and tell him that yes, that would be good, that I too like to hit.

Coach finishes his rah-rah speech, and the air is heavy with anticipation as the realization washes over everyone in the room that all of the lifting and running has come down to this—the chance to prove ourselves by putting our bodies on the line with guys who are every bit as strong and as fast.

Then we're marched off to the training room, where a team of doctors pokes and prods us as if we were cattle heading to market. By the time we're through, everybody has a nickname: Fuckhead, Slope, Rope, Sith, Crawdaddy, Pin Dick, Yo Joe, Hernia, Bible Boy, Vic, Napalm, Six-Four, Too Tall, Dead Fuck, Flat-Ass Phil, the Creeper, Revlon. Somebody tags me with Sweet Lou Reid because before every practice I listen to "Coney Island Baby."

On our first day of padded practice, the line coach, a man with steel blue-and-gray hair, cold eyes and a hatchet nose, marches us over to a row of low metal cages. "Get into a three-point," Coach says as he lines us across from one another on opposite sides of the cages.

I hunker down, straddling one of the boards, and look out at the man in front of me. "*Hit!*" Coach screams.

And with a blast of his whistle, my college football career begins. We hit and fall to the ground, fighting and spitting until he whistles us back to attention. We line up and do it over and over. After ten minutes, I am bleeding from three different places, my arms are numb, and my right thumb hangs from my hand at an angle I know is wrong. But to stop and go to the sideline is to pussy out. So I play through the pain, and after a few more hits I don't care what happens to my thumb.

The rest of practice takes place in five-second bursts, until our pads, wet with blood and sweat, hang on us like second skins. Everything is done harder and faster. Fights break out without warning. Two long-armed D-backs start swinging at each other, and the coaches let it go until the taller one splits his hand on a face mask. Blood flies from his smashed paw as he spins around like some shoulder-padded Tasmanian devil. One of the coaches finally grabs him by the face mask and drags him to the sideline, leaving his opponent alone and bewildered, with nothing to do except join the huddle. Guys suffer knee injuries, pop hamstrings, tear Achilles tendons, while others just go down with silent, allover injuries that are the same as quitting—telling the team you can no longer take it. During the first week, nine walk-ons clear out their lockers and quit.

We learn to live with injuries and spend what little free time we have complaining and scheming about our positions on the depth chart. Hernia has a bruise he can move up and down his forearm. Bible Boy's knee is fucked, and my shoulder slides in and out of place so much that I no longer notice it. All of us have scabbed-over noses and turf burns on our shins that crack and fill our shoes with warm blood the minute practice starts.

After practice and a shower, I stand in front of the mirror and stare at the road map of bruises, cuts and mysterious pink swellings. I touch each bruise, scrape and swelling until I feel something, and I know that my body is still there, capable of doing what I ask of it.

When the upperclassmen report to camp, we become their tackling dummies. Even the coaches forget about us and concentrate on the home opener four weeks off. I'm moved from defense to offense because my feet are too slow and my "opportunities," Coach says, are better on the other side of the ball. He tells me that offense is the thinking man's side of the ball, that it is about forward motion and scoring.

I adjust, and within a week I become an offensive lineman. Every day is the same grind—the same flesh-filled five yards on either side of the ball, where we grunt, shove, kick and gouge at one another. In the trenches, success is measured in feet and inches, not long touchdown runs or head-over-ass catches that bring crowds to their feet.

After three weeks, I begin to root for injuries. Not only do I want the man in front of me on the depth chart to go down but I begin to look for ways to hasten his downfall. I am not the only one. More than once I see guys twisting knees in pileups, lowering helmets into exposed spines, gouging throats and faces with the hope that a few well-placed injuries will move them up the depth chart. The coaches seem to encourage this ballplayer-eat-ballplayer mentality, pitting starter against backup and watching as the two players wrestle and pump padded fists at each other long after the play has been blown dead.

But it is off the field that the real training happens, where I learn about how the team is not really a team. Offensive players hate defensive players. Linemen hate ball handlers because they get all the glory and half the aches and pains. It goes without saying that everybody hates the kickers because of their soft bodies and clean uniforms and the way they run warm-up laps out in front, making the rest of us look bad.

There is also a silent division between blacks and whites. Any white guy who hangs with the brothers and listens to their music is called a "whigger." Black guys who hang with the white guys are called "Oreo-cookie motherfuckers" or sellouts. In the locker room, when there are only white faces around, some guy will call a black guy who fumbles the ball or hits too hard in warm-ups a stupid nigger, and I know that I am supposed to nod in agreement or high-five the racist bastard. And when I don't, there is another line drawn.

But somehow it all comes together, and there are times when black and white, offense and defense and even the kickers seem to be part of the same team, especially when practice is over and we're all glad to be walking off the field, happy to have seen our bodies through another day, united by our aches, pains and fatigue.

I learn that among the linemen there are those who belong and those who don't. To belong means to go about the game of football grim faced, cocksure of your ability to take any hit and keep moving. The guys who zone out on God, refuse the pack or are refused by it end up falling by the wayside, unnoticed by the coaching staff and their fellow players.

Then there are the guys who have already made it—broken out of the pack to start or platoon with another player in a starting position. Among the linemen, they are called "the fellas." Coaches love the fellas because they have proven themselves. But what really distinguishes a fella is not his success on the field but rather his ability to wallow in the easy gratification afforded any athlete at any university that is nuts for football. Everything is permitted—drinking, scoring chicks, fighting off the field—because he has survived the mayhem and the mindless drudgery of practices. I hear the stories over lunch or in the locker room after a workout: how to score with a woman nicknamed "the Dishwasher." How to persuade one of the brains or geeks to cheat for you. How to cop free meals at restaurants or free drinks at a bar. How to wrangle free T-shirts from the equipment manager. How to pass the drug test. And, most important, how to act like you don't give a shit, because you've got it coming to you.

We win our Big Ten opener, and for a few minutes in the locker room the air seems to vibrate with goodwill and camaraderie. Even I who have stood on the sideline getting rained on feel like a player as I listen to reporters question today's heroes. After the coaches leave, word that there will be a party at a fella's house percolates through the sweaty room.

When I enter the party, the room seems to be in some sort of drunken-action overload. Near the keg there is a makeshift wrestling pit, circled by grubby couches full of squealing teased-haired women who look at me briefly, decide that I am not a starter and look away. I am handed a beer and told to drink. My beertender is a huge, smiling defensive tackle named the Wall, who watches as I raise the cup to my lips and sip.

"What's a matter with you?" he says, pointing at the beer. "We've got beer and a roomful of chicks who want to fuck us 'cause we won the game. What more do you want?"

"I'm just a frosh," I tell him.

"Skip the *Leave It to Beaver* bullshit and drink," Wall says.

I nod, drain the cup and follow him to the kitchen, past heavily made-up groupies who stare at me now that I am with Wall. There are others, big guys mostly, and we keep pace with Wall, who tosses back beer as if it's water. After every round, somebody slops an arm around me or smacks me on the shoulder, and for a moment I feel the tug of the fella fraternity.

What happens next is what happens in varying degrees at every subsequent party. Fights erupt over women, favorite teams, etc. There is a girl in an upstairs bedroom handing out blow jobs or an underclassman who is too drunk and vomits before he is stripped naked and thrown out a window or tossed down the stairs.

I down half a bottle of Everclear grain alcohol when it is handed to me and let a sadeyed chubby girl in tight jeans sit on my lap. As the liquor hits my brain, I realize that there are no victims here, even as I watch this girl get talked into going upstairs with three guys. Later I see her in the front yard, leaning against a lamppost crying, as several players throw empty beer cans at her and call her a whore. Everybody, including the skinny-shouldered engineering student and the jock-sniffing schlub with stars in his eyes whom we occasionally torture and torment, knows the deal and comes back for more. We have something they want, and they'll take anything we have—even the laughter and the cruel pranks—just to be near us, to wear one of our sweatshirts or to talk to us about the game. And it all seems so normal. When our starting defensive tackle rams a frat boy's head into a steel grate, not once but several times, there are no repercussions because he is a star and the team needs him. There are rules on the field and in the locker room when we are around the coaches, but off the field, anything goes.

And I do bad things because I want to belong. I hide the part of me that enjoys classes and reading in my room after practice. I know better, yet I find myself doing the same stupid shit I see others do, and nobody tells me that it's wrong. Nobody blinks when I walk into a party, pick up the first girl I see and pin her to the ceiling until her laughter turns to screams and then finally to tears. I put lit cigarettes out on the back of my hand to prove to the fellas that I don't give a fuck—that I am above pain, above caring what happens to my body, because I am young and I am a ballplayer and my body seems to have no limits.

At another party, I split a frat boy's nose for no particular reason other than that I am drunk and it feels like the right thing to do. He goes down, holding his nose, and I hop up on a thick oak banister, close my eyes and walk, not caring if I fall or if someone pushes me. When I do fall down two flights of stairs, I pop right back up, though my knee doesn't seem to be working, and there are several fraternity brothers closing in on me. Instead of running, I go outside and proceed to kick in the basement windows until I hear police sirens and escape into the snowy backyards. The next day, I am sober and ready to practice, and only at that point do I feel remorse. But then there is the first hit, and my body hurts, my joints crack, and I am absolved.

One night at a party during my sophomore year, I am asked by a fella if I want to help him videotape some girl giving head to a couple of guys in an upstairs room. I nod drunkenly and follow him through the forest of oversize flesh and dull-eyed groupies to the stairs, where he turns around and winks at me. For a moment, I'm not sure if he's joking or not. The music is loud—too loud. There are women playing quarters at a table to my right and guys staring at *Hustler* magazine on a couch in the corner, while several sophomores write their names with a permanent Magic Marker on the body of a passed-out frosh and discuss shaving his balls.

"You ready?" my guide asks. I can tell he's waiting for me to say no so he can call me a pussy or a Boy Scout. I look around at the monster bodies of ballplayers acting like children grabbing at toys, and I realize that I've finally become what the coaches and my fellow players have always expected me to become—a fella, a person living in a world of no consequence. I am not a star or even a starter; still, everything I do is acceptable, allowed and in the end … empty.

I look at the hulking player as he awaits my response. Part of me wants to go upstairs and rescue the girl, take her away. But I know she'd only be back next week, drunker and more willing, and I would be there, too, and maybe then, a few beers to the better, I'd say yes when asked if I wanted to help with the videotaping, because I could, because it is expected of me and because it is what a fella does.

I turn to go, but before I can get to the door, Fuckhead jumps on my back and screams, "Isn't this great?" I shake him off and toss him to the floor, tell him no and walk outside, feeling cold and hollow. But most of all, I feel simple and stupid, because I can't see a way out. If I quit, I lose my scholarship and go back home to Cleveland having failed. If I choose not to partake in the fun, there will be a line drawn and I will be exiled into the lonely world of those who practice but who will never play or belong. That is my problem, that I want to belong at any cost. I still have the dream that someday I will become a starter, and the pro scouts will come to time me in the forty-yard dash and I will have a chance to go to the next level.

It starts with a tingling in my arm, one of a thousand jolts of pain that have run through my body that I no longer seem to notice. Only this time it doesn't go away.

I hear one of the coaches screaming, "Get up, Reid. Get the fuck up and get your ass back to the huddle."

Without thinking, I roll to my feet and try to shake it off. When I rejoin the huddle, the coach glares at me and another play is called, and I line up, hit and do it again, the pain lingering in my spine. Then one morning I awake unable to raise my arms above my head. After swallowing a handful of Tylenol Threes and a few anti-inflammatories, I go to practice and hit. My arms dangle from my shoulders, bloodless and weak, forcing me to deliver the blows with my head and helmet. The coaches scream when I am slow to rise after the whistle. And when the pills wear off, the numbness is replaced by a hot poker of pain and a dull, crunching sound in my neck. After I miss a block, Coach sends me to the sideline and motions for the trainers to have a look. I explain and point to my neck as they walk me to the training room. It is the longest walk of my life, and no one even turns a helmet in my direction. In the training room, I am told to lie still while the trainers pull my pads off and wrap ice bags around my neck.

I sit the sideline for a full week. No one except the trainers and the team doctor says a word to me, and it's all right, because for once I am outside looking in at the football machine as it whirs and clicks along without me. But by the end of the week, I want more than anything else to peel the ice bags off my neck and shoulders, strap on pads and prove that I'm still one of them. I think that this time it will be different, that I can hit and go about the game I've played and nursed my body for without acting like one of the fellas off the field.

So when the team doctor works his way up my arm with a safety pin, poking my flesh and asking, "Do you feel this?" I say, "Yes."

"And this?"

Yes, yes and yes. Although I have no idea where or if he is poking me. He plays along with the charade. There are no X rays, only ice and pills that make my head feel like it's stuffed with cotton. After the pain has subsided, I am put on a cycle of cervical steroids and must report to the training room twice a day to have my blood pressure monitored.

In a week, I am back on the field, and everything falls into place. My legs move and my body goes where it's directed, but the pain won't go away. I imagine a rotten spot in my spine, a cancer I want to cut out. My body learns to hit all over again, making small adjustments in some vain hope that the injury will go away and with it the nerve pain that seems to lurk after every collision.

Instead the pain gets worse, and most nights I'm back in the training room with the other gimps, begging for ice and more pills that I hope will somehow allow me to hit again. Nobody questions the toughness of the guys who are hauled off the field with their knees turned inside out or the players who are knocked cold and can't so much as wiggle a toe. But I look healthy. There is no blood, no bone poking through skin, no body cast, no evidence that I am injured. I can walk and talk and smile, and in the eyes of the team the real problem is that I can't stand the pain.

I go another month, practicing when my neck will allow, sitting the sideline when it won't. Finally, I'm referred to a neurologist. This time there are tests: X rays, CAT scans, an MRI and an EMG. When a nurse pumps two needles into each of my arms, telling me my mouth will taste like I have a spoon in it and that I'll feel nauseous, I smile, happy to have the pain and the sickness so controlled.

As I stare into the fluorescent lights with the taste of metal in my mouth, I know that something in my body has given out, that I somehow deserve this for not wanting to be a fella.

When the tests are over, I am not allowed to see the results. "We'll have them sent to the team doctor," the technician tells me.

"Am I OK?" I ask, wanting this guy in a white smock with his needles and nurses to tell me that I'm all right—that I'll have my body back. But I know that I'd only throw it away again, out on the field, to prove that I am one of them.

Instead, there are other tests, more pills and a neck brace. I start going to the parties, watching the fellas go about their fun, envious of what their play and performance has earned them. To prove to the fellas and myself that I still matter, I get drunk, head-butt walls and stick needles into my numb hands, despite rational thoughts that tell me what I am doing is stupid. I am careful to inflict this abuse only on myself, to show them that the injury they can't see is real and I can stand even more pain than they can imagine. So I let someone push a stapler into my biceps over and over until my shirt turns red, and for a few precious minutes the fellas pay attention to me—one even shakes his head and calls me a "sick dog motherfucker." And I'm proud. The pain leaves, and my body feels like it used to—large, powerful and capable of great things.

Then there is the morning, the staples still scabbed into my arms, the cigarette burns on the backs of my hands. But worst of all, there is the silent crunching in my neck and the dead feeling in my fingers. I stand in front of the mirror, staring at the smooth outline of my neck muscles, the slope of my shoulders. I know one thing: I no longer want to play football the way the best of them do—dying between whistles as if you are born to it and there is no other option. Still, when I'm called into the head coach's office and told that I can no longer play, I walk out of the room despising my neck, my body and the fact that it will no longer have the opportunity to hit another man.

Some guys go through life feeding the athlete inside with weekend-warrior games of touch football, season tickets, tailgate parties and war stories about what it was like to play. Athletes don't, as they say, die twice; instead, part of them remains 19 years old forever, with the body ready and willing to prove itself all over again. I had to kill that 19-year-old, the one who enjoyed being able to prove himself to the world with sheer brute force: hitting, taking and not thinking.

After college I headed for Alaska to get away from football. I became a frame carpenter and spent my days pounding nails and lifting twenty-foot sections of wall until my back and neck shivered with pain and my arms went numb. Every time I went home sore, bruised and full of splinters, it felt good—punishment for failing at football and at being a fella. Work helped to kill the jock in me. Falling off buildings and being crushed by two-by-fours dropped by stoned Hi-Lo operators finished what football had started. There were days and even weeks when I couldn't pull myself out of bed. And I liked it, because for once I could see the end—somewhere, sometime I would no longer be able to use my body, and what would be left would be the guy who loved reading and talking about books.

Later I would work as a bouncer, a bartender, a grunt laborer, a truck dispatcher and a handyman. When I needed money, I rented out my body to schizophrenia-drug-testing programs at a VA hospital. The drugs left me with waking aural and visual hallucinations for days. I thought I was Miles Davis and that I could hear ants crawling in the grass. There were other tests with needles and electric current and more drugs. I didn't care. I got paid for all of it and never once questioned why I wanted to do this to myself. But somewhere along the line, the jock in me died.

Now I'm a guy who used to play. I rise out of bed each morning to a symphony of cracks and crunches. I have pain from football injuries I don't remember. My shoulders still slop around in their sockets if I don't sleep in exactly the same position every night. Sometimes my neck and back lock up without warning, and I fall, and I'm reminded that I did bad things for football and it did bad things to me. It left me with this clear-cut of a body, a burned-out village that I sacked for a sport.

—1997

Learning from Other Writers (Reid)

1. Why, exactly, did Elwood Reid "do bad things for football"?

2. If you have never played college football, does the essay reveal anything about the sport that surprises you? If you *have* played college football, does anything in the essay surprise you? Either way, what is the effect of Reid's in-your-face approach?

3. What larger question is Elwood Reid trying to answer by evaluating his own experiences as a member of a Big Ten football team?

4. Who is the audience for this essay? How do you know?

5. What is Reid's current attitude toward the bad things he did for football? The bad things other players, coaches, or fans did for football?

6. Reid is narrating retrospectively: that is, he is recounting his experiences years after he stopped playing. What is the effect of this older perspective? What effect do the final four paragraphs have on your reaction to the essay as a whole?

7. Go through the essay and note the instances where Reid uses animal imagery. What is the effect of this language? How does it enhance the theme of the essay?

8. What if Elwood Reid had started his essay: "Football made me do bad things"? How would this change the tone of the essay? How would it change the essay's meaning and significance?

Adding Your Voice

1. Orwell writes: "He wears a mask, and his face grows to fit it." Think about a time when you had to wear a certain mask. How did you react to the mask initially? Was it self-imposed or was it placed upon you by others? Were you relieved to be able to hide behind the mask? Did you fight against wearing it? Did your face grow to fit the mask? Why or why not?

2. Write about a time when you were caught up in a system whose rules you didn't agree with or made you uncomfortable. How did you react? Looking back, do you wish you had reacted differently? Or write about a time when, like Orwell, you were important enough to be hated, or loved, or admired, or feared, by more than the usual number of people.

3. Elwood Reid, for better or worse, found his identity through his body and the pain it could endure. From what aspect of your life do you derive your identity? Do you wish you could find it elsewhere? Do you anticipate that you will always define yourself in this manner? Why or why not?

4. Think of the most interesting, upsetting, funny, or odd event that every happened to you. What don't you understand about the event? In one sentence, try to articulate your question. Then, using a balance of exposition and scenic writing, re-create your experience for your readers. Don't forget to use reflective or meditative prose to try to answer the question you have posed.

QUESTIONS AND INSIGHTS

A writer need not have served the Raj or played Big Ten football to come up with an experience worth describing or a question worth exploring. In "A Clack of Tiny Sparks," Bernard Cooper revisits the fall and winter of his ninth-grade boyhood to figure out why, when the girl who sat beside him in algebra class asked, "Are you a fag?," he lied and said no. From the safety of adulthood, happily coupled with his male partner of seven years, Cooper recounts a series of highly charged events from his adolescence in an attempt to understand how his life might have turned out differently if he hadn't been so intent on hiding from his parents and classmates his knowledge that he was gay. Although Cooper's essay doesn't tell us anything earthshakingly new about what it means to grow up gay, the author allows his audience to experience from the inside the struggle to figure out whether people choose their sexual preference or whether their sexual preference chooses them. The accuracy and honesty of Cooper's observations, his eye and ear for the perfect detail, remind us not only how ninth grade smelled but also what ninth grade felt like. Cooper's scenic depiction of his sexual turmoil, combined with his meditations on the causes of that turmoil, give "A Clack of Tiny Sparks" its emotional power and thematic significance.

Similarly, in "A Few Words About Breasts," Nora Ephron explores what it means to be a flat-chested woman. Just as Cooper uses his friend Grady as the perfect embodiment of heterosexual boyhood, Ephron uses her friend Diana Raskob to indicate her perception of the feminine ideal:

> Her hair is curled and she has a waist and hips and a bust and she is wearing a straight skirt, an article of clothing I have been repeatedly told I will be unable to wear until I have the hips to hold it up. My jaw drops, and suddenly I am crying, crying hysterically, can't catch my breath sobbing. My best friend has betrayed me. She has gone ahead without me and done it. She has shaped up.

Growing up in an era in which tight sweaters and a curvy, hourglass figure were the epitome of attractiveness, Ephron felt anything but feminine. Her tone starts out humorous and light, as does Cooper's, but the "sobbing" here signals the upcoming shift in tone. Whereas the first half of the essay uses self-deprecating humor, the second half hits notes of desperation and anger. The essay is not only about Ephron's feelings of inadequacy as a woman but also the way other women help to perpetuate and magnify such feelings. When her boyfriend's mother gives her a book on frigidity, suddenly the essay turns even darker, and Ephron's childhood feeling of betrayal regarding her best friend's "development" becomes magnified by this older woman's comment. Diana Raskob, after all, didn't intentionally try to belittle Ephron, but her boyfriend's mother did.

Yet as we read, we can't help but wonder if Ephron's harshest critic isn't Ephron herself. Note that she never comes to the conclusion that her reasoning as a girl or a younger woman was flawed, naive, or silly. Though she tells the story from a distance, we see that her present self ("I think they are full of shit") has not quite come to terms with her breast size. She resists what might be the instinct to add some words of wisdom or a change in attitude. This is not to say that your essay can't express a change in attitude or something you have learned by reflecting on your experience, but make sure your conclusion is sincere and arises naturally from the material.

Self-perception and self-realization are prominent themes in Lucy Grealy's "Mirrorings"; even the title suggests self-reflection. Grealy doesn't tack on a lesson at the end, but she does express a genuine insight that she has gained from her experience: "I know now ... that most truths are inherently unretainable, that we have to work hard all our lives to remember the most basic things." This insight is complex: each new cruelty, each new surgery, each disappointment becomes a new truth that she has to learn to face all over again. Because Grealy is struggling to see herself (or, by avoiding mirrors, has been attempting *not* to see herself), the understanding she reaches at the end is a result of both the experience and the writing.

Bernard Cooper

A CLACK OF TINY SPARKS: REMEMBRANCES OF A GAY BOYHOOD

Theresa Sanchez sat behind me in ninth-grade algebra. When Mr. Hubbley faced the blackboard, I'd turn around to see what she was reading; each week a new book was wedged inside her copy of *Today's Equations*. The deception worked; from Mr. Hubbley's point of view, Theresa was engrossed in the value of *X*, but I knew otherwise. One week she perused *The Wisdom of the Orient*, and I could tell from Theresa's contemplative expression that the book contained exotic thoughts, guidelines handed down from high. Another week it was a paperback novel whose title, *Let Me Live My Life,* appeared in bold print atop every page, and whose cover, a gauzy photograph of a woman biting a strand of pearls, head thrown back in an attitude of ecstasy, confirmed my suspicion that Theresa Sanchez was mature beyond her years. She was the tallest girl in school. Her bouffant hairdo, streaked with blond, was higher than the flaccid bouffants of other girls. Her smooth skin, plucked eyebrows, and painted fingernails suggested hours of pampering, a worldly and sensual vanity that placed her within the domain of adults. Smiling dimly, steeped in daydreams, Theresa moved through the crowded halls with a languid, self-satisfied indifference to those around her. "You are merely children," her posture seemed to say. "I can't be bothered." The week Theresa hid *101 Ways to Cook Hamburger* behind her algebra book, I could stand it no longer and, after the bell rang, ventured a question.

"Because I'm having a dinner party," said Theresa. "Just a couple of intimate friends." No fourteen-year-old I knew had ever given a dinner party, let alone used the word "intimate" in conversation. "Don't you have a mother?" I asked.

Theresa sighed a weary sigh, suffered my strange inquiry. "Don't be so naive," she said. "Everyone has a mother." She waved her hand to indicate the brick school buildings outside the window. "A higher education should have taught you that." Theresa draped an angora sweater over her shoulders, scooped her books from the graffiti-covered desk, and just as she was about to walk away, she turned and asked me, "Are you a fag?"

There wasn't the slightest hint of rancor or condescension in her voice. The tone was direct, casual. Still I was stunned, giving a sidelong glance to make sure no one had heard. "No," I said. Blurted really, with too much defensiveness, too much transparent fear in my response. Octaves lower than usual, I tried a "Why?"

Theresa shrugged. "Oh, I don't know. I have lots of friends who are fags. You remind me of them." Seeing me bristle, Theresa added, "It was just a guess." I watched her erect, angora back as she sauntered out the classroom door.

She had made an incisive and timely guess. Only days before, I'd invited Grady Rogers to my house after school to go swimming. The instant Grady shot from the pool, shaking water from his orange hair, freckled shoulders shining, my attraction to members of my own sex became a matter I could no longer suppress or rationalize.

Sturdy and boisterous and gap-toothed, Grady was an inveterate backslapper, a formidable arm wrestler, a wizard at basketball. Grady was a boy at home in his body.

My body was a marvel I hadn't gotten used to; my arms and legs would sometimes act of their own accord, knocking over a glass at dinner or flinching at an oncoming pitch. I was never singled out as a sissy, but I could have been just as easily as Bobby Keagan, a gentle, intelligent, and introverted boy reviled by my classmates. And although I had always been aware of a tacit rapport with Bobby, a suspicion that I might find with him a rich friendship, I stayed away. Instead, I emulated Grady in the belief that being seen with him, being like him, would somehow vanquish my self-doubt, would make me normal by association.

Apart from his athletic prowess, Grady had been gifted with all the trappings of what I imagined to be a charmed life: a fastidious, aproned mother who radiated calm, maternal concern; a ruddy, stoic father with a knack for home repairs. Even the Rogerses' small suburban house in Hollywood, with its spindly Colonial furniture and chintz curtains, was a testament to normalcy.

Grady and his family bore little resemblance to my clan of Eastern European Jews, a dark and vociferous people who ate with abandon—matzo and halvah and gefilte fish; foods the goyim couldn't pronounce—who cajoled one another during endless games of canasta, making the simplest remark about the weather into a lengthy philosophical discourse on the sun and the seasons and the passage of time. My mother was a chain-smoker, a dervish in a frowsy housedress. She showed her love in the most peculiar and obsessive ways, like spending hours extracting every seed from a watermelon before she served it in perfectly bite-sized, geometric pieces. Preoccupied and perpetually frantic, my mother succumbed to bouts of absentmindedness so profound she'd forget what she was saying midsentence, smile and blush and walk away. A divorce attorney, my father wore roomy, iridescent suits, and the intricacies, the deceits inherent in his profession, had the effect of making him forever tense and vigilant. He was "all wound up," as my mother put it. But when he relaxed, his laughter was explosive, his disposition prankish: "Walk this way," a waitress would say, leading us to our table, and my father would mimic the way she walked, arms akimbo, hips liquid, while my mother and I were wracked with laughter. Buoyant or brooding, my parents' moods were unpredictable, and in a household fraught with extravagant emotion it was odd and awful to keep my longing secret.

One day I made the mistake of asking my mother what a "fag" was. I knew exactly what Theresa had meant but hoped against hope it was not what I thought; maybe "fag" was some French word, a harmless term like "naive." My mother turned from the stove, flew at me, and grabbed me by the shoulders. "Did someone call you that?" she cried.

"Not me," I said. "Bobby Keagan."

"Oh," she said, loosening her grip. She was visibly relieved. And didn't answer. The answer was unthinkable.

For weeks after, I shook with the reverberations from that afternoon in the kitchen with my mother, pained by the memory of her shocked expression and, most of all, her silence. My longing was wrong in the eyes of my mother, whose hazel eyes were the eyes of the world, and if that longing continued unchecked, the unwieldy shape of my fate would be cast, and I'd be subjected to a lifetime of scorn.

During the remainder of the semester, I became the scientist of my own desire, plotting ways to change my yearning for boys into a yearning for girls. I had enough evidence to believe that any habit, regardless of how compulsive, how deeply ingrained, could be broken once and for all: The plastic cigarette my mother purchased at the Thrifty pharmacy—one end was red to approximate an ember, the other tan like a filtered tip—was designed to wean her from the real thing. To change a behavior required self-analysis, cold resolve, and the substitution of one thing for another: plastic, say, for tobacco. Could I also find a substitute for Grady? What I needed to do, I figured, was kiss a girl and learn to like it.

This conclusion was affirmed one Sunday morning when my father, seeing me wrinkle my nose at the pink slabs of lox he layered on a bagel, tried to convince me of its salty appeal. "You should try some," he said. "You don't know what you're missing."

"It's loaded with protein," added my mother, slapping a platter of sliced onions onto the dinette table. She hovered above us, cinching her housedress, eyes wet from onion fumes, the mock cigarette dangling from her lips.

My father sat there chomping with gusto, emitting a couple of hearty grunts to dramatize his satisfaction. And still I was not convinced. After a loud and labored swallow, he told me I may not be fond of lox today, but sooner or later I'd learn to like it. One's tastes, he assured me, are destined to change.

"Live," shouted my mother over the rumble of the Mixmaster. "Expand your horizons. Try new things." And the room grew fragrant with the batter of a spice cake.

The opportunity to put their advice into practice, and try out my plan to adapt to girls, came the following week when Debbie Coburn, a member of Mr. Hubbley's algebra class, invited me to a party. She cornered me in the hall, furtive as a spy, telling me her parents would be gone for the evening and slipping into my palm a wrinkled sheet of notebook paper. On it were her address and telephone number, the lavender ink in a tidy cursive. "Wear cologne," she advised, wary eyes darting back and forth. "It's a make-out party. Anything can happen."

The Santa Ana wind blew relentlessly the night of Debbie's party, careening down the slopes of the Hollywood hills, shaking the road signs and stoplights in its path. As I walked down Beachwood Avenue, trees thrashed, surrendered their leaves, and carob pods bombarded the pavement. The sky was a deep but luminous blue, the air hot, abrasive, electric. I had to squint in order to check the number of the Coburns' apartment, a three-story building with glitter embedded in its stucco walls. Above the honeycombed balconies was a sign that read BEACHWOOD TERRACE in lavender script resembling Debbie's.

From down the hall, I could hear the plaintive strains of Little Anthony's "I Think I'm Going Out of My Head." Debbie answered the door bedecked in an Empire dress, the bodice blue and orange polka dots, the rest a sheath of black and white stripes. "Op art," proclaimed Debbie. She turned in a circle, then proudly announced that she'd rolled her hair in orange juice cans. She patted the huge unmoving curls and dragged me inside. Reflections from the swimming pool in the courtyard, its surface ruffled by wind, shuddered over the ceiling and walls. A dozen of my classmates were seated on the sofa or huddled together in corners, their whispers full of excited imminence, their bodies barely discernible in the dim light. Drapes flanking the sliding glass doors bowed out with every gust of wind, and it seemed that the room might lurch from its foundations and sail with its cargo of silhouettes into the hot October night.

Grady was the last to arrive. He tossed a six-pack of beer into Debbie's arms, barreled toward me, and slapped my back. His hair was slicked back with Vitalis, lacquered furrows left by the comb. The wind hadn't shifted a single hair. "Ya ready?" he asked, flashing the gap between his front teeth and leering into the darkened room. "You bet," I lied.

Once the beers had been passed around, Debbie provoked everyone's attention by flicking on the overhead light. "Okay," she called. "Find a partner." This was the blunt command of a hostess determined to have her guests aroused in an orderly fashion. Everyone blinked, shuffled about, and grabbed a member of the opposite sex. Sheila Garabedian landed beside me—entirely at random, though I wanted to believe she was driven by passion—her timid smile giving way to plain fear as the light went out. Nothing for a moment but the heave of the wind and the distant banter of dogs. I caught a whiff of Sheila's perfume, tangy and sweet as Hawaiian Punch. I probed her face with my own, grazing the small scallop of an ear, a velvety temple, and though Sheila's trembling made me want to stop, I persisted with my mission until I found her lips, tightly sealed as a private letter. I held my mouth over hers and gathered her shoulders closer, resigned to the possibility that, no matter how long we stood there, Sheila would be too scared to kiss me back. Still, she exhaled through her nose, and I listened to the squeak of every breath as though it were a sigh of inordinate pleasure. Diving within myself, I monitored my heartbeat and respiration, trying to will stimulation into being, and all the while an image intruded, an image of Grady erupting from our pool, rivulets of water sliding down his chest. "Change," shouted Debbie, switching on the light. Sheila thanked me, pulled away, and continued her routine of gracious terror with every boy throughout the evening. It didn't matter whom I held—Margaret Sims, Betty Vernon, Elizabeth Lee—my experiment was a failure; I continued to picture Grady's wet chest, and Debbie would bellow "change" with such fervor, it could have been my own voice, my own incessant reprimand.

Our hostess commandeered the light switch for nearly half an hour. Whenever the light came on, I watched Grady pivot his head toward the newest prospect, his eyebrows arched in expectation, his neck blooming with hickeys, his hair, at last, in disarray. All that shuffling across the carpet charged everyone's arms and lips with static, and eventually, between low moans and soft osculations, I could hear the clack of tiny sparks and see them flare here and there in the dark like meager, short-lived stars.

I saw Theresa, sultry and aloof as ever, read three more books—*North American Reptiles*, *Bonjour Tristesse*, and *MGM: A Pictorial History*—before she vanished early in

December. Rumors of her fate abounded. Debbie Coburn swore that Theresa had been "knocked up" by an older man, a traffic cop, she thought, or a grocer. Nearly quivering with relish, Debbie told me and Grady about the home for unwed mothers in the San Fernando Valley, a compound teeming with pregnant girls who had nothing to do but touch their stomachs and contemplate their mistake. Even Bobby Keagan, who took Theresa's place behind me in algebra, had a theory regarding her disappearance colored by his own wish for escape; he imagined that Theresa, disillusioned with society, booked passage to a tropical island, there to live out the rest of her days without restrictions or ridicule. "No wonder she flunked out of school," I overheard Mr. Hubbley tell a fellow teacher one afternoon. "Her head was always in a book."

Along with Theresa went my secret, or at least the dread that she might divulge it, and I felt, for a while, exempt from suspicion. I was, however, to run across Theresa one last time. It happened during a period of torrential rain that, according to reports on the six o'clock news, washed houses from the hillsides and flooded the downtown streets. The halls of Joseph Le Conte Junior High were festooned with Christmas decorations: crepe-paper garlands, wreaths studded with plastic berries, and one requisite Star of David twirling above the attendance desk. In Arts and Crafts, our teacher, Gerald (he was the only teacher who allowed us—*required* us—to call him by his first name), handed out blocks of balsa wood and instructed us to carve them into bugs. We would paint eyes and antennae with tempera and hang them on a Christmas tree he'd made the previous night. "Voilà," he crooned, unveiling his creation from a burlap sack. Before us sat a tortured scrub, a wardrobe-worth of wire hangers that were bent like branches and soldered together. Gerald credited his inspiration to a Charles Addams cartoon he's seen in which Morticia, grimly preparing for the holidays, hangs vampire bats on a withered pine. "All that red and green," said Gerald. "So predictable. So *boring*."

As I chiseled a beetle and listened to rain pummel the earth, Gerald handed me an envelope and asked me to take it to Mr. Kendrick, the drama teacher. I would have thought nothing of his request if I hadn't seen Theresa on my way down the hall. She was cleaning out her locker, blithely dropping the sum of its contents—pens and textbooks and mimeographs—into a trash can. "Have a nice life," she sang as I passed. I mustered the courage to ask her what had happened. We stood alone in the silent hall, the reflections of wreaths and garlands submerged in brown linoleum.

"I transferred to another school. They don't have grades or bells, and you get to study whatever you want." Theresa was quick to sense my incredulity. "Honest," she said. "The school is progressive." She gazed into a glass cabinet that held the trophies of track meets and intramural spelling bees. "God," she sighed, "this place is so ... barbaric." I was still trying to decide whether or not to believe her story when she asked me where I was headed. "Dear," she said, her exclamation pooling in the silence, "that's no ordinary note, if you catch my drift." The envelope was blank and white; I looked up at Theresa, baffled. "Don't be so naive," she muttered, tossing an empty bottle of nail polish into the trash can. It struck bottom with a resolute thud. "Well," she said, closing her locker and breathing deeply, "bon voyage." Theresa swept through the double doors and in seconds her figure was obscured by rain.

As I walked toward Mr. Kendrick's room, I could feel Theresa's insinuation burrow in. I stood for a moment and watched Mr. Kendrick through the pane in the door. He paced intently in front of the class, handsome in his shirt and tie, reading from a thick book. Chalked on the blackboard behind him was THE ODYSSEY BY HOMER. I have no recollection of how Mr. Kendrick reacted to the note, whether he accepted it with pleasure or embarrassment, slipped it into his desk drawer or the pocket of his shirt. I have scavenged that day in retrospect, trying to see Mr. Kendrick's expression, wondering if he acknowledged me in any way as his liaison. All I recall is the sight of his mime through a pane of glass, a lone man mouthing an epic, his gestures ardent in empty air.

Had I delivered a declaration of love? I was haunted by the need to know. In fantasy, a kettle shot steam, the glue released its grip, and I read the letter with impunity. But how would such a letter begin? Did the common endearments apply? This was a message between two men, a message for which I had no precedent, and when I tried to envision the contents, apart from a hasty, impassioned scrawl, my imagination faltered.

Once or twice I witnessed Gerald and Mr. Kendrick walk together into the faculty lounge or say hello at the water fountain, but there was nothing especially clandestine or flirtatious in their manner. Besides, no matter how acute my scrutiny, I wasn't sure, short of a kiss, exactly what to look for—what semaphore of gesture, what encoded word. I suspected there were signs, covert signs that would give them away, just as I'd unwittingly given myself away to Theresa.

In the school library, a *Webster's* unabridged dictionary lay on a wooden podium, and I padded toward it with apprehension; along with clues to the bond between my teachers, I risked discovering information that might incriminate me as well. I had decided to consult the dictionary during lunch period, when most of the students would be on the playground. I clutched my notebook, moving in such a way as to appear both studious and nonchalant, actually believing that, unless I took precautions, someone would see me and guess what I was up to. The closer I came to the podium, the more obvious, I thought, was my endeavor; I felt like the model of The Visible Man in our science class, my heart's undulations, my overwrought nerves legible through transparent skin. A couple of kids riffled through the card catalogue. The librarian, a skinny woman whose perpetual whisper and rubber-soled shoes caused her to drift through the room like a phantom, didn't seem to register my presence. Though I'd looked up dozens of words before, the pages felt strange beneath my fingers. *Homer* was the first word I saw. *Hominid. Homogenize.* I feigned interest and skirted other words before I found the word I was after. Under the heading HO·MO·SEX·U·AL was the terse definition: *adj. Pertaining to, characteristic of, or exhibiting homosexuality.—n. A homosexual person.* I read the definition again and again, hoping the words would yield more than they could. I shut the dictionary, swallowed hard, and, none the wiser, hurried away.

As for Gerald and Mr. Kendrick, I never discovered evidence to prove or dispute Theresa's claim. By the following summer, however, I had overheard from my peers a confounding amount about homosexuals: They wore green on Thursday, couldn't whistle, hypnotized boys with a piercing glance. To this lore, Grady added a surefire test to ferret them out.

"A test?" I said.

"You ask a guy to look at his fingernails, and if he looks at them like this"—Grady closed his fingers into a fist and examined his nails with manly detachment—"then he's okay. But if he does this"—he held out his hands at arm's length, splayed his fingers, and coyly cocked his head—"you'd better watch out." Once he'd completed his demonstration, Grady peeled off his shirt and plunged into our pool. I dove in after. It was early June, the sky immense, glassy, placid. My father was cooking spareribs on the barbecue, an artist with a basting brush. His apron bore the caricature of a frazzled French chef. Mother curled on a chaise lounge, plumes of smoke wafting from her nostrils. In a stupor of contentment she took another drag, closed her eyes, and arched her face toward the sun.

Grady dog-paddled through the deep end, spouting a fountain of chlorinated water. Despite shame and confusion, my longing for him hadn't diminished; it continued to thrive without air and light, like a luminous fish in the dregs of the sea. In the name of play, I swam up behind him, encircled his shoulders, astonished by his taut flesh. The two of us flailed, pretended to drown. Beneath the heavy press of water, Grady's orange hair wavered, a flame that couldn't be doused.

I've lived with a man for seven years. Some nights, when I'm half-asleep and the room is suffused with blue light, I reach out to touch the expanse of his back, and it seems as if my fingers sink into his skin, and I feel the pleasure a diver feels the instant he enters a body of water.

I have few regrets. But one is that I hadn't said to Theresa, "Of course I'm a fag." Maybe I'd have met her friends. Or become friends with her. Imagine the meals we might have concocted: hamburger Stroganoff, Swedish meatballs in a sweet translucent sauce, steaming slabs of Salisbury steak.

—1991

Learning from Other Writers (Cooper)

1. Cooper opens his essay with a scene involving Theresa Sanchez. Can you find the *end* of that scene? What is it about that ending that prompts the combination of exposition and reflection that follows? How does Cooper manage to make that second section, his meditation on whether he is a "fag," so vivid and revealing? Why does the author include *this* information about his parents and not some other set of facts?

2. How does Cooper use the exposition in the first three paragraphs after the space break to move us through time? What is the function of the scenic passage after that, in which his parents urge him to try the lox?

3. After a brief bit of exposition ("The opportunity to put their advice into practice, and try out my plan to adapt to girls ..."), Cooper launches into the main section of his narrative. How would you describe the experiment the teenage Cooper carries out at Debbie Coburn's party? What are you favorite details? Bits of dialogue?

4. What is ironic about Cooper's parents trying to get him to taste lox? Or about the teacher's comment that Theresa flunked out of school because her nose was always in a book? What larger irony is Cooper trying to expose here?

5. What is the role of the final section, in which Cooper narrates his farewell encounter with Theresa? Can you highlight the passage of exposition that bridges that scene with the next, where the adolescent Cooper looks up "homosexual" in the dictionary? And the expository bridge from there to the final scene, in which the narrator and Grady are swimming in the Cooper's pool?

6. What is the function of the final two paragraphs, in which Cooper jumps forward in time to the present day? Is he playfully addressing any stereotypes here?

Nora Ephron

A FEW WORDS ABOUT BREASTS

I have to begin with a few words about androgyny. In grammar school, in the fifth and sixth grades, we were all tyrannized by a rigid set of rules that supposedly determined whether we were boys or girls. The episode in *Huckleberry Finn* where Huck is disguised as a girl and gives himself away by the way he threads a needle and catches a ball—that kind of thing. We learned that the way you sat, crossed your legs, held a cigarette, and looked at your nails—the way you did these things instinctively was absolute proof of your sex. Now obviously most children did not take this literally, but I did. I thought that just one slip, just one incorrect cross of my legs or flick of an imaginary cigarette ash would turn me from whatever I was into the other thing; that would be all it took, really. Even though I was outwardly a girl and had many of the trappings generally associated with girldom—a girl's name, for example, and dresses, my own telephone, an autograph book—I spent the early years of my adolescence absolutely certain that I might at any point gum it up. I did not feel at all like a girl. I was boyish. I was athletic, ambitious, outspoken, competitive, noisy, rambunctious. I had scabs on my knees and my socks slid into my loafers and I could throw a football. I wanted desperately not to be that way, not to be a mixture of both things, but instead just one, a girl, a definite indisputable girl. As soft and as pink as a nursery. And nothing would do that for me, I felt, but breasts.

I was about six months younger than everyone else in my class, and so for about six months after it began, for six months after my friends had begun to develop (that was the word we used, develop), I was not particularly worried. I would sit in the bathtub and look down at my breasts and know that any day now, any second now, they would start growing like everyone else's. They didn't. "I want to buy a bra," I said to my mother one night. "What for?" she said. My mother was really hateful about bras, and by the time my third sister had gotten to the point where she was ready to want one, my mother had worked the whole business into a comedy routine. "Why not use a Band-Aid instead?" she would say. It was a source of great pride to my mother that she had never even had to wear a brassiere until she had her fourth child, and then only because her gynecologist made her. It was incomprehensible to me that anyone could ever be proud of something like that. It was the 1950s, for God's sake. Jane Russell. Cashmere sweaters. Couldn't my mother see that? *I am too old to wear an undershirt.* Screaming. Weeping. Shouting. "Then don't wear an undershirt," said my mother. "But I want to buy a bra." "What for?"

I suppose for most girls, breasts, brassieres, that entire thing, has more trauma, more to do with the coming of adolescence, with becoming a woman, than anything else. Certainly more than getting your period, although that, too, was traumatic, symbolic. But you could see breasts; they were there; they were visible. Whereas a girl could claim to have her period for months before she actually got it and nobody would ever know the difference. Which is exactly what I did. All you had to do was make a great fuss over having enough nickels for the Kotex machine and walk around clutching your stomach and moaning for three to five days a month about The Curse and you could convince anybody. There is a school of thought somewhere in the women's lib / women's mag / gynecology establishment that claims that menstrual cramps are purely psychological, and I lean toward it. Not that I didn't have them finally. Agonizing cramps, heating-pad cramps, go-down-to-the-school-nurse-and-lie-on-the-cot cramps. But, unlike any pain I had ever suffered, I adored the pain of cramps, welcomed it, wallowed in it, bragged about it. "I can't go. I have cramps." "I can't do that. I have cramps." And most of all, gigglingly, blushingly: "I can't swim. I have cramps." Nobody ever used the hard-core word. Menstruation. God, what an awful word. Never that. "I have cramps."

The morning I first got my period, I went into my mother's bedroom to tell her. And my mother, my utterly-hateful-about-bras mother, burst into tears. It was really a lovely moment, and I remember it so clearly not just because it was one of the two times I ever saw my mother cry on my account (the other was when I was caught being a six-year-old kleptomaniac), but also because the incident did not mean to me what it meant to her. Her little girl, her firstborn, had finally become a woman. That was what she was crying about. My reaction to the event, however, was that I might well be a woman in some scientific, textbook sense (and could at least stop faking every month and stop wasting all those nickels). But in another sense—in a visible sense—I was as androgynous and as liable to tip over into boyhood as ever.

I started with a 28 AA bra. I don't think they made them any smaller in those days, although I gather that now you can buy bras for five-year-olds that don't have any cups whatsoever in them; trainer bras they are called. My first brassiere came from Robinson's Department Store in Beverly Hills. I went there alone, shaking, positive they would look me over and smile and tell me to come back next year. An actual fitter took me into the dressing room and stood over me while I took off my blouse and tried the first one on. The little puffs stood out on my chest. "Lean over," said the fitter. (To this day I am not sure what fitters in bra departments do except to tell you to lean over.) I leaned over, with the fleeting hope that my breasts would miraculously fall out of my body and into the puffs. Nothing.

"Don't worry about it," said my friend Libby some months later, when things had not improved. "You'll get them after you're married."

"What are you talking about?" I said.

"When you get married," Libby explained, "your husband will touch your breasts and rub them and kiss them and they'll grow."

That was the killer. Necking I could deal with. Intercourse I could deal with. But it had never crossed my mind that a man was going to touch my breasts, that breasts had something to do with all that, petting, my God, they never mentioned petting in my little sex manual about the fertilization of the ovum. I became dizzy. For I knew instantly—as naive as I had been only a moment before—that only part of what she was saying was true: the touching, rubbing, kissing part, not the growing part. And I knew that no one would ever want to marry me. I had no breasts. I would never have breasts.

My best friend in school was Diana Raskob. She lived a block from me in a house full of wonders. English muffins, for instance. The Raskobs were the first people in Beverly Hills to have English muffins for breakfast. They also had an apricot tree in the back, and a badminton court, and a subscription to *Seventeen* magazine, and hundreds of games, like Sorry and Parcheesi and Treasure Hunt and Anagrams. Diana and I spent three or four afternoons a week in their den reading and playing and eating. Diana's mother's kitchen was full of the most colossal assortment of junk food I have ever been exposed to. My house was full of apples and peaches and milk and homemade chocolate-chip cookies—which were nice, and good for you, but-not-right-before-dinner-or-you'll-spoil-your-appetite. Diana's house had nothing in it that was good for you, and what's more, you could stuff it in right up until dinner and nobody cared. Bar-B-Q potato chips (they were the first in them, too), giant bottles of ginger ale, fresh popcorn with melted butter, hot fudge sauce on Baskin-Robbins jamoca ice cream, powdered-sugar doughnuts from Van de Kamp's. Diana and I had been best friends since we were seven; we were about equally popular in school (which is to say, not particularly), we had about the same success with boys (extremely intermittent), and we looked much the same. Dark. Tall. Gangly.

It is September, just before school begins. I am eleven years old, about to enter the seventh grade, and Diana and I have not seen each other all summer. I have been to camp and she has been somewhere like Banff with her parents. We are meeting, as we often do, on the street midway between our two houses, and we will walk back to Diana's and eat junk and talk about what has happened to each of us that summer. I am walking down Walden Drive in my jeans and my father's shirt hanging out and my old red loafers with the socks falling into them and coming toward me is... I take a deep breath... a young woman. Diana. Her hair is curled and she has a waist and hips and a bust and she is wearing a straight skirt, an article of clothing that I have been repeatedly told I will be unable to wear until I have the hips to hold it up. My jaw drops, and suddenly I am crying, crying hysterically, can't catch my breath sobbing. My best friend has betrayed me. She has gone ahead without me and done it. She has shaped up.

Here are some things I did to help:
Bought a Mark Eden Bust Developer.
Slept on my back for four years.
Splashed cold water on them every night because some French actress said in *Life* magazine that that was what *she* did for her perfect bustline.
Ultimately, I resigned myself to a bad toss and began to wear padded bras. I think about them now, think about all those years in high school I went around in them, my three padded bras, every single one of them with different-sized breasts. Each time I changed bras I changed sizes: one week nice perky but not too obtrusive breasts, the next medium-sized slightly pointy ones, the next week knockers, true knockers; all the time, whatever size I was, carrying around this rubberized appendage on my chest that occasionally crashed into a wall and was poked inward and had to be poked outward—I think about all that and wonder how anyone kept a straight face through it. My parents, who normally had no restraints about needling me— why did they say nothing as they watched my chest go up and down? My friends, who

would periodically inspect my breasts for signs of growth and reassure me—why didn't they at least counsel consistency?

And the bathing suits. I die when I think about the bathing suits. That was the era when you could lay an uninhabited bathing suit on the beach and someone would make a pass at it. I would put one on, an absurd swimsuit with its enormous bust built into it, the bones from the suit stabbing me in the rib cage and leaving little red welts on my body, and there I would be, my chest plunging straight downward absolutely vertically from my collarbone to the top of my suit and then suddenly, wham, out came all that padding and material and wiring absolutely horizontally.

Buster Klepper was the first boy who ever touched them. He was my boyfriend my senior year of high school. There is a picture of him in my high-school yearbook that makes him look quite attractive in a Jewish, horn-rimmed-glasses sort of way, but the picture does not show the pimples, which were air-brushed out, or the dumbness. Well, that isn't really fair. He wasn't dumb. He just wasn't terribly bright. His mother refused to accept it, refused to accept the relentlessly average report cards, refused to deal with her son's inevitable destiny in some junior college or other. "He was tested," she would say to me, apropos of nothing, "and it came out a hundred and forty-five. That's near-genius." Had the word "underachiever" been coined, she probably would have lobbed that one at me, too. Anyway, Buster was really very sweet—which is, I know, damning with faint praise, but there it is. I was the editor of the front page of the high-school newspaper and he was editor of the back page; we had to work together, side by side, in the print shop, and that was how it started. On our first date, we went to see *April Love*, starring Pat Boone. Then we started going together. Buster had a green coupe, a 1950 Ford with an engine he had hand-chromed until it shone, dazzled, reflected the image of anyone who looked into it, anyone usually being Buster polishing it or the gas-station attendants he constantly asked to check the oil in order for them to be overwhelmed by the sparkle on the valves. The car also had a boot stretched over the back seat for reasons I never understood; hanging from the rearview mirror was a pair of angora dice. A previous girlfriend named Solange, who was famous throughout Beverly Hills High School for having no pigment in her right eyebrow, had knitted them for him. Buster and I would ride around town, the two of us seated to the left of the steering wheel. I would shift gears. It was nice.

There was necking. Terrific necking. First in the car, overlooking Los Angeles from what is now the Trousdale Estates. Then on the bed of his parents' cabana at Ocean House. Incredibly wonderful, frustrating necking, I loved it, really, but no further than necking, please don't, please, because there I was absolutely terrified of the general implications of going-a-step-further with a near-dummy and also terrified of his finding out there was next to nothing there (which he knew, of course; he wasn't that dumb).

I broke up with him at one point. I think we were apart for about two weeks. At the end of that time, I drove down to see a friend at a boarding school in Palos Verdes Estates and a disc jockey played "April Love" on the radio four times during the trip. I took it as a sign. I drove straight back to Griffith Park to a golf tournament Buster was playing in (he was the sixth-seeded teen-age golf player in southern California) and presented myself back to him on the green of the 18th hole. It was all very dramatic.

That night we went to a drive-in and I let him get his hand under my protuberances and onto my breasts. He really didn't seem to mind at all.

"Do you want to marry my son?" the woman asked me.

"Yes," I said.

I was nineteen years old, a virgin, going with this woman's son, this big strange woman who was married to a Lutheran minister in New Hampshire and pretended she was gentile and had this son, by her first husband, this total fool of a son who ran the hero-sandwich concession at Harvard Business School and whom for one moment one December in New Hampshire I said—as much out of politeness as anything else—that I wanted to marry.

"Fine," she said. "Now, here's what you do. Always make sure you're on top of him so you won't seem so small. My bust is very large, you see, so I always lie on my back to make it look smaller, but you'll have to be on top most of the time."

I nodded. "Thank you," I said.

"I have a book for you to read," she went on. "Take it with you when you leave. Keep it." She went to the bookshelf, found it, and gave it to me. It was a book on frigidity.

"Thank you," I said.

That is a true story. Everything in this article is a true story, but I feel I have to point out that that story in particular is true. It happened on December 30, 1960. I think about it often. When it first happened, I naturally assumed that the woman's son, my boyfriend, was responsible. I invented a scenario where he had had a little heart-to-heart with his mother and had confessed that his only objection to me was that my breasts were small; his mother then took it upon herself to help out. Now I think I was wrong about the incident. The mother was acting on her own, I think: that was her way of being cruel and competitive under the guise of being helpful and maternal. You have small breasts, she was saying; therefore you will never make him as happy as I have. Or you have small breasts; therefore you will doubtless have sexual problems. Or you have small breasts; therefore you are less woman than I am. She was, as it happens, only the first of what seems to me to be a never-ending string of women who have made competitive remarks to me about breast size. "I would love to wear a dress like that," my friend Emily says to me, "but my bust is too big." Like that. Why do women say these things to me? Do I attract these remarks the way other women attract married men or alcoholics or homosexuals? This summer, for example, I am at a party in East Hampton and I am introduced to a woman from Washington. She is a minor celebrity, very pretty and Southern and blond and outspoken, and I am flattered because she has read something I have written. We are talking animatedly, we have been talking no more than five minutes, when a man comes up to join us. "Look at the two of us," the woman says to the man, indicating me and her. "The two of us together couldn't fill an A cup." Why does she say that? It isn't even true, dammit, so why? Is she even more addled than I am on this subject? Does she honestly believe there is something wrong with her size breasts, which, it seems to me, now that I look hard at them, are just right? Do I unconsciously bring out competitiveness in women? In that form? What did I do to deserve it?

As for men.

There were men who minded and let me know that they minded. There were men who did not mind. In any case, I always minded.

And even now, now that I have been countlessly reassured that my figure is a good one, now that I am grown-up enough to understand that most of my feelings have very little to do with the reality of my shape, I am nonetheless obsessed by breasts. I cannot help it. I grew up in the terrible fifties—with rigid stereotypical sex roles, the insistence that men be men and dress like men and women be women and dress like women, the intolerance of androgyny—and I cannot shake it, cannot shake my feelings of inadequacy. Well, that time is gone, right? All those exaggerated examples of breast worship are gone, right? Those women were freaks, right? I know all that. And yet here I am, stuck with the psychological remains of it all, stuck with my own peculiar version of breast worship. You probably think I am crazy to go on like this: here I have set out to write a confession that is meant to hit you with the shock of recognition, and instead you are sitting there thinking I am thoroughly warped. Well, what can I tell you? If I had had them, I would have been a completely different person. I honestly believe that.

After I went into therapy, a process that made it possible for me to tell total strangers at cocktail parties that breasts were the hang-up of my life, I was often told that I was insane to have been bothered by my condition. I was also frequently told, by close friends, that I was extremely boring on the subject. And my girl friends, the ones with nice big breasts, would go on endlessly about how their lives had been far more miserable than mine. Their bra straps were snapped in class. They couldn't sleep on their stomachs. They were stared at whenever the word "mountain" cropped up in geography. And *Evangeline*, good God what they went through every time someone had to stand up and recite the Prologue to Longfellow's *Evangeline*: "… stand like druids of eld… / With beards that rest on their bosoms." It was much worse for them, they tell me. They had a terrible time of it, they assure me. I don't know how lucky I was, they say.

I have thought about their remarks, tried to put myself in their place, considered their point of view. I think they are full of shit.

—1972

Learning from Other Writers (Ephron)

1. What are some of the significant details that Ephron uses in her piece? Why are they significant? How do they help to develop the theme?

2. What is Ephron's driving question? How does each section, each anecdote, help to develop or answer that question?

3. One of the major themes of this piece is betrayal. Go through the essay and highlight language, images, or passages that illustrate this theme. How do these instances of betrayal contribute to Ephron's feelings of inadequacy?

4. What is the effect of the list of things that Ephron does to develop her bust? What is the effect of the list's placement in the essay?

MIRRORINGS

There was a long period of time, almost a year, during which I never looked in a mirror. It wasn't easy, for I'd never suspected just how omnipresent are our own images. I began by merely avoiding mirrors, but by the end of the year I found myself with an acute knowledge of the reflected image, its numerous tricks and wiles, how it can spring up at any moment: a glass tabletop, a well-polished door handle, a darkened window, a pair of sunglasses, a restaurant's otherwise magnificent brass-plated coffee machine sitting innocently by the cash register.

At the time, I had just moved, alone, to Scotland and was surviving on the dole, as Britain's social security benefits are called. I didn't know anyone and had no idea how I was going to live, yet I went anyway because by happenstance I'd met a plastic surgeon there who said he could help me. I had been living in London, working temp jobs. While in London, I'd received more nasty comments about my face than I had in the previous three years, living in Iowa, New York, and Germany. These comments, all from men and all odiously sexual, hurt and disoriented me. I also had journeyed to Scotland because after more than a dozen operations in the States my insurance had run out, along with my hope that further operations could make any *real* difference. Here, however, was a surgeon who had some new techniques, and here, amazingly enough, was a government willing to foot the bill: I didn't feel I could pass up yet another chance to "fix" my face, which I confusedly thought concurrent with "fixing" my self, my soul, my life.

Twenty years ago, when I was nine and living in America, I came home from school one day with a toothache. Several weeks and misdiagnoses later, surgeons removed most of the right side of my jaw in an attempt to prevent the cancer they found there from spreading. No one properly explained the operation to me, and I awoke in a cocoon of pain that prevented me from moving or speaking. Tubes ran in and out of my body, and because I was temporarily unable to speak after the surgery and could not ask questions, I made up my own explanations for the tubes' existence. I remember the mysterious manner the adults displayed toward me. They asked me to do things: lie still for x-rays, not cry for needles, and so on, tasks that, although not easy, never seemed equal to the praise I received in return. Reinforced to me again and again was how I was "a brave girl" for not crying, "a good girl" for not complaining, and soon I began defining myself this way, equating strength with silence.

Then the chemotherapy began. In the seventies chemo was even cruder than it is now, the basic premise being to poison patients right up to the very brink of their own death. Until this point I almost never cried and almost always received praise in return. Thus I got what I considered the better part of the deal. But now it was like a practical joke that had gotten out of hand. Chemotherapy was a nightmare and I wanted it to stop; I didn't want to be brave anymore. Yet I had grown so used to defining myself as "brave"—i.e., *silent*—that the thought of losing this sense of myself was even more terrifying. I was certain that if I broke down I would be despicable in the eyes of both my parents and the doctors.

The task of taking me into the city for the chemo injections fell mostly on my mother, though sometimes my father made the trip. Overwhelmed by the sight of the vomiting and weeping, my father developed the routine of "going to get the car," meaning that he left the doctor's office before the injection was administered, on the premise that then he could have the car ready and waiting when it was all over. Ashamed of my suffering, I felt relief when he was finally out of the room. When my mother took me, she stayed in the room, yet this only made the distance between us even more tangible. She explained that it was wrong to cry *before* the needle went in; afterward was one thing, but before, that was mere fear, and hadn't I demonstrated my bravery earlier? Every Friday for two and a half years I climbed up onto that big doctor's table and told myself not to cry, and every week I failed. The two large syringes were filled with chemicals so caustic to the vein that each had to be administered very slowly. The whole process took about four minutes; I had to remain utterly still. Dry retching began in the first fifteen seconds, then the throb behind my eyes gave everything a yellow-green aura, and the bone-deep pain of alternating extreme hot and cold flashes made me tremble, yet still I had to sit motionless and not move my arm. No one spoke to me—not the doctor, who was a paradigm of the cold-fish physician; not the nurse, who told my mother I reacted much more violently than many of "the other children"; and not my mother, who, surely overwhelmed by the sight of her child's suffering, thought the best thing to do was remind me to be brave, to try not to cry. All the while I hated myself for having wept before the needle went in, convinced that the nurse and my mother were right, that I was "overdoing it," that the throwing up was psychosomatic, that my mother was angry with me for not being good or brave enough.

Yet each week, two or three days after the injection, there came the first flicker of feeling better, the always forgotten and gratefully rediscovered understanding that to simply be well in my body was the greatest thing I could ask for. I thought other people felt this appreciation and physical joy all the time, and I felt cheated because I was able to feel it only once a week.

Because I'd lost my hair, I wore a hat constantly, but this fooled no one, least of all myself. During this time, my mother worked in a nursing home in a Hasidic community. Hasidic law dictates that married women cover their hair, and most commonly this is done with a wig. My mother's friends were now all willing to donate their discarded wigs, and soon the house seemed filled with them. I never wore one, for they frightened me even when my mother insisted I looked better in one of the few that actually fit. Yet we didn't know how to say no to the women who kept graciously offering their wigs. The cats enjoyed sleeping on them and the dogs playing with them, and we grew used to having to pick a wig up off a chair we wanted to sit in. It never struck us as odd until one day a visitor commented wryly as he cleared a chair for himself, and suddenly a great wave of shame overcame me. I had nightmares about wigs and flushed if I even heard the word, and one night I put myself out of my misery by getting up after everyone was asleep and gathering all the wigs except for one the dogs were fond of and that they had chewed up anyway. I hid all the rest in an old chest.

When you are only ten, which is when the chemotherapy began, two and a half years seem like your whole life, yet it finally did end, for the cancer was gone. I remember the last day of treatment clearly because it was the only day on which I succeeded in not crying, and because later, in private, I cried harder than I had in years; I thought now I would no longer be "special," that without the arena of chemotherapy in which to prove myself no one would ever love me, that I would fade unnoticed into the background. But this idea about *not being different* didn't last very long. Before, I foolishly believed that people stared at me because I was bald. After my hair eventually grew in, it didn't take long before I understood that I looked different for another reason. My face. People stared at me in stores, and other children made fun of me to the point that I came to expect such reactions constantly, wherever I went. School became a battleground.

Halloween, that night of frights, became my favorite holiday because I could put on a mask and walk among the blessed for a few brief, sweet hours. Such freedom I felt, walking down the street, my face hidden! Through the imperfect oval holes I could peer out at other faces, masked or painted or not, and see on those faces nothing but the normal faces of childhood looking back at me, faces I mistakenly thought were the faces everyone else but me saw all the time, faces that were simply curious and ready for fun, not the faces I usually braced myself for, the cruel, lonely, vicious ones I spent every day other than Halloween waiting to see around each corner. As I breathed in the condensed, plastic-scented air under the mask, I somehow thought that I was breathing in normality, that this joy and weightlessness were what the world was composed of, and that it was only my face that kept me from it, my face that was my own mask that kept me from knowing the joy I was sure everyone but me lived with intimately. How could the other children not know it? Not know that to be free of the fear of taunts and the burden of knowing no one would ever love you was all that anyone could ever ask for? I was a pauper walking for a short while in the clothes of the prince, and when the day ended I gave up my disguise with dismay.

I was living in an extreme situation, and because I did not particularly care for the world I was in, I lived in others, and because the world I did live in was dangerous now, I incorporated this danger into my secret life. I imagined myself to be an Indian. Walking down the streets, I stepped through the forest, my body ready for any opportunity to fight or flee one of the big cats that I knew stalked me. Vietnam and Cambodia, in the news then as scenes of catastrophic horror, were other places I walked through daily. I made my way down the school hall, knowing a land mine or a sniper might give themselves away at any moment with the subtle metal click I'd read about. Compared with a land mine, a mere insult about my face seemed a frivolous thing.

In those years, not yet a teenager, I secretly read—knowing it was somehow inappropriate—works by Primo Levi and Elie Wiesel, and every book by a survivor I could find by myself without asking the librarian. Auschwitz, Birkenau: I felt the blows of the capos and somehow knew that because any moment we might be called upon to live for a week on one loaf of bread and some water called soup, the peanut-butter sandwich I found on my plate was nothing less than a miracle, an utter and sheer miracle capable of making me literally weep with joy.

I decided to become a "deep" person. I wasn't exactly sure what this would entail, but I believed that if I could just find the right philosophy, think the right thoughts, my suffering would end. To try to understand the world I was in, I undertook to find out what was "real," and I quickly began seeing reality as existing in the lowest common denominator, that suffering was the one and only dependable thing. But rather than spend all of my time despairing, though certainly I did plenty of that, I developed a form of defensive egomania: I felt I was the only one walking about in the world who understood what was really important. I looked upon people complaining about the most mundane things—nothing on TV, traffic jams, the price of new clothes—and felt joy because I knew how unimportant those things really were and felt unenlightened superiority because other people didn't. Because in my fantasy life I had learned to be thankful for each cold, blanketless night that I survived on the cramped wooden bunks, my pain and despair were a stroll through the country in comparison. I was often miserable, but I knew that to feel warm instead of cold was its own kind of joy, that to eat was a reenactment of the grace of some god whom I could only dimly define, and that to simply be alive was a rare, ephemeral gift.

As I became a teenager, my isolation began. My nonidentical twin sister started going out with boys, and I started—my most tragic mistake of all—to listen to and believe the taunts thrown at me daily by the very boys she and the other girls were interested in. I was a dog, a monster, the ugliest girl they had ever seen. Of all the remarks, the most damaging wasn't even directed at me but was really an insult to "Jerry," a boy I never saw because every day between fourth and fifth periods, when I was cornered by a particular group of kids, I was too ashamed to lift my eyes off the floor. "Hey, look, it's Jerry's girlfriend!" they shrieked when they saw me, and I felt such shame, knowing that this was the deepest insult to Jerry that they could imagine.

When pressed to it, one makes compensations. I came to love winter, when I could wrap up the disfigured lower half of my face in a scarf: I could speak to people and they would have no idea to whom and to what they were really speaking. I developed the bad habit of letting my long hair hang in my face and of always covering my chin and mouth with my hand, hoping it might be mistaken as a thoughtful, accidental gesture. I also became interested in horses and got a job at a rundown local stable. Having those horses to go to each day after school saved my life; I spent all of my time either with them or thinking about them. Completely and utterly repressed by the time I was sixteen, I was convinced that I would never want a boyfriend, not ever, and wasn't it convenient for me, even a blessing, that none would ever want me. I told myself I was free to concentrate on the "true reality" of life, whatever that was. My sister and her friends put on blue eye shadow, blow-dried their hair, and spent interminable hours in the local mall, and I looked down on them for this, knew they were misleading themselves and being overly occupied with the "mere surface" of living. I'd had thoughts like this when I was younger, ten or twelve, but now my philosophy was haunted by desires so frightening I was unable even to admit they existed.

Throughout all of this, I was undergoing reconstructive surgery in an attempt to rebuild my jaw. It started when I was fifteen, two years after chemo ended. I had known for years I would have operations to fix my face, and at night I fantasized about how good my life would finally be then. One day I got a clue that maybe it wouldn't be so easy. An older plastic surgeon explained the process of "pedestals" to me, and told me it would take *ten years* to fix my face. Ten years? Why even bother, I thought; I'll be ancient by then. I went to a medical library and looked up the "pedestals" he talked about. There were gruesome pictures of people with grotesque tubes of their own skin growing out of their bodies, tubes of skin that were harvested like some kind of crop and then rearranged, with results that did not look at all normal or acceptable to my eye. But then I met a younger surgeon, who was working on a new way of grafting that did not involve pedestals, and I became more hopeful and once again began to await the fixing of my face, the day when I would be whole, content, loved.

Long-term plastic surgery is not like in the movies. There is no one single operation that will change everything, and there is certainly no slow unwrapping of the gauze in order to view the final, remarkable result. There is always swelling, sometimes to a grotesque degree, there are often bruises, and always there are scars. After each operation, too frightened to simply go look in the mirror, I developed an oblique method, with several stages. First, I tried to catch my reflection in an overhead lamp: the roundness of the metal distorted my image just enough to obscure details and give no true sense of size or proportion. Then I slowly worked my way up to looking at the reflection in someone's eyeglasses, and from there I went to walking as briskly as possible by a mirror, glancing only quickly. I repeated this as many times as it would take me, passing the mirror slightly more slowly each time until finally I was able to stand still and confront myself.

The theory behind most reconstructive surgery is to take large chunks of muscle, skin, and bone and slap them into the roughly appropriate place, then slowly begin to carve this mess into some sort of shape. It involves long, major operations, countless lesser ones, a lot of pain, and many, many years. And also, it does not always work. With my young surgeon in New York, who with each passing year was becoming not so young, I had two or three soft-tissue graft, two skin grafts, a bone graft, and some dozen other operations to "revise" my face, yet when I left graduate school at the age of twenty-five I was still more or less in the same position I had started in: a deep hole in the right side of my face and a rapidly shrinking left side and chin, a result of the radiation I'd had as a child and the stress placed upon the bone by the other operations. I was caught in a cycle of having a big operation, one that would force me to look monstrous from the swelling for many months, then having the subsequent revision operations that improved my looks tremendously, and then slowly, over the period of a few months or a year, watching the graft reabsorb back into my body, slowly shrinking down and leaving me with nothing but the scarred donor site the graft had originally come from.

It wasn't until was in college that I finally allowed that maybe, just maybe, it might be nice to have a boyfriend. I went to a small, liberal, predominantly female school and suddenly, after years of alienation in high school, discovered that there were other people I could enjoy talking to who thought me intelligent and talented. I was, however, still operating on the assumption that no one, not ever, would be physically attracted to me, and in a curious way this shaped my personality I became forthright and honest in the way that only the truly self-confident are, who do not expect to be rejected, and in the way of those like me, who do not even dare to ask acceptance from others and therefore expect no rejection. I had come to know myself as a person, but I would be in graduate school before I was literally, physically able to use my name and the word "woman" in the same sentence.

Now my friends repeated for me endlessly that most of it was in my mind, that, granted, I did not look like everyone else, but that didn't mean I looked bad. I am sure now that they were right some of the time. But with the constant surgery I was in a perpetual state of transfiguration. I rarely looked the same for more than six months at a time. So ashamed of my face, I was unable even to admit that this constant change affected me; I let everyone who wanted to know that it was only what was inside that mattered, that I had "grown used to" the surgery, that none of it bothered me at all. Just as I had done in childhood, I pretended nothing was wrong, and this was constantly mistaken by others for bravery I spent a great deal of time looking in the mirror in private, positioning my head to show off my eyes and nose, which were not only normal but quite pretty, as my friends told me often. But I could not bring myself to see them for more than a moment: I looked in the mirror and saw not the normal upper half of my face but only the disfigured lower half.

People still teased me. Not daily, as when was younger, but in ways that caused me more pain than ever before. Children stared at me, and I learned to cross the street to avoid them; this bothered me, but not as much as the insults I got from men. Their taunts came at me not because I was disfigured but because I was a disfigured *woman*. They came from boys, sometimes men, and almost always from a group of them. I had long, blond hair, and I also had a thin figure. Sometimes, from a distance, men would see a thin blonde and whistle, something I dreaded more than anything else because I knew that as they got closer, their tune, so to speak, would inevitably change; they would stare openly or, worse, turn away quickly in shame or repulsion. I decided to cut my hair to avoid any misconception that anyone, however briefly, might have about my being attractive. Only two or three times have I ever been teased by a single person, and I can think of only one time when I was ever teased by a woman. Had I been a man, would I have had to walk down the street while a group of young women followed and denigrated my sexual worth?

Not surprisingly, then, I viewed sex as my salvation. I was sure that if only I could get someone to sleep with me, it would mean I wasn't ugly, that I was attractive, even lovable. This line of reasoning led me into the beds of several manipulative men who liked themselves even less than they liked me, and I in turn left each short-term affair hating myself, obscenely sure that if only I had been prettier it would have worked— he would have loved me and it would have been like those other love affairs that I was certain "normal" women had all the time. Gradually, I became unable to say "I'm depressed" but could say only "I'm ugly," because the two had become inextricably linked in my mind. Into that universal lie, that sad equation of "if only..." that we are all prey to, I was sure that if only I had a normal face, then I would be happy.

The new surgeon in Scotland, Oliver Fenton, recommended that I undergo a procedure involving something called a tissue expander, followed by a bone graft. A tissue expander is a small balloon placed under the skin and then slowly blown up over the course of several months, the object being to stretch out the skin and create room and cover for the new bone. It's a bizarre, nightmarish thing to do to your face, yet I was hopeful about the end results and I was also able to spend the three months that the expansion took in the hospital. I've always felt safe in hospitals: they're the one place I feel free from the need to explain the way I look. For this reason the first tissue expander was bearable—just—and the bone graft that followed it was a success; it did not melt away like the previous ones.

The surgical stress this put upon what remained of my original jaw instigated the deterioration of that bone, however, and it became unhappily apparent that I was going to need the same operation I'd just had on the right side done to the left. I remember my surgeon telling me this at an outpatient clinic. I planned to be traveling down to London that same night on an overnight train, and I barely made it to the station on time, such a fumbling state of despair I was in.

I could not imagine going through it *again,* and just as I had done all my life, I searched and searched through my intellect for a way to make it okay, make it bearable, for a way to *do* it. I lay awake all night on that train, feeling the tracks slip beneath me with an odd eroticism, when I remembered an afternoon from my three months in the hospital. Boredom was a big problem those long afternoons, the days marked by meals and television programs. Waiting for the afternoon tea to come, wondering desperately how I could make time pass, it had suddenly occurred to me that I didn't have to make time pass, that it would do it of its own accord, that I simply had to relax and take no action. Lying on the train, remembering that, I realized I had no obligation to improve my situation, that I didn't have to explain or understand it, that I could just simply let it happen. By the time the train pulled into King's Cross station, I felt able to bear it yet again, not entirely sure what other choice I had.

But there was an element I didn't yet know about. When I returned to Scotland to set up a date to have the tissue expander inserted, I was told quite casually that I'd be in the hospital only three or four days. Wasn't I going to spend the whole expansion time in the hospital? I asked in a whisper. What's the point of that? came the answer. You can just come in every day to the outpatient ward to have it expanded. Horrified by this, I was speechless. I would have to live and move about in the outside world with a giant balloon inside the tissue of my face? I can't remember what I did for the next few days before I went into the hospital, but I vaguely recall that these days involved a great deal of drinking alone in bars and at home.

I had the operation and went home at the end of the week. The only things that gave me any comfort during the months I lived with my tissue expander were my writing and Franz Kafka. I started a novel and completely absorbed myself in it, writing for hours each day. The only way I could walk down the street, could stand the stares I received, was to think to myself, "I'll bet none of them are writing a novel." It was that strange, old, familiar form of egomania, directly related to my dismissive, conceited thoughts of adolescence. As for Kafka, who had always been one of my favorite writers, he helped me in that I felt permission to feel alienated, and to have that alienation be okay, bearable, noble even. In the same way that imagining I lived in Cambodia helped me as a child, I walked the streets of my dark little Scottish city by the sea and knew without doubt that I was living in a story Kafka would have been proud to write.

The one good thing about a tissue expander is that you look so bad with it in that no matter what you look like once it's finally removed, your face has to look better. I had my bone graft and my fifth soft-tissue graft and, yes, even I had to admit I looked better. But I didn't look like me. Something was wrong: was *this* the face I had waited through eighteen years and almost thirty operations for? I somehow just couldn't make what I saw in the mirror correspond to the person I thought I was. It wasn't only that I continued to feel ugly; I simply could not conceive of the image as belonging to me. My own image was the image of a stranger, and rather than try to understand this, I simply stopped looking in the mirror. I perfected the technique of brushing my teeth without a mirror, grew my hair in such a way that it would require only a quick, simple brush, and wore clothes that were simply and easily put on, no complex layers or lines that might require even the most minor of visual adjustments.

On one level I understood that the image of my face was merely that, an image, a surface that was not directly related to any true, deep definition of the self. But I also knew that it is only through appearances that we experience and make decisions about the everyday world, and I was not always able to gather the strength to prefer the deeper world to the shallower one. I looked for ways to find a bridge that would allow me access to both, rather than riding out the constant swings between peace and anguish. The only direction I had to go in to achieve this was to strive for a state of awareness and self-honesty that sometimes, to this day, occasionally rewards me. I have found, I believe, that our whole lives are dominated, though it is not always so clearly translatable, by the question "How do I look?" Take all the many nouns in our lives—car, house, job, family, love, friends—and substitute the personal pronoun "I." It is not that we are all so self-obsessed; it is that all things eventually relate back to ourselves, and it is our own sense of how we appear to the world by which we chart our lives, how we navigate our personalities, which would otherwise be adrift in the ocean of *other* people's obsessions.

One evening toward the end of my year-long separation from the mirror, I was sitting in a café talking to someone—an attractive man, as it happened—and we were having a lovely, engaging conversation. For some reason I suddenly wondered what I looked like to him. What was he *actually* seeing when he saw me? So many times I've asked this of myself, and always the answer is this: a warm, smart woman, yes, but an unattractive one. I sat there in the café and asked myself this old question, and startlingly, for the first time in my life, I had no answer readily prepared. I had not looked in a mirror for so long that I quite simply had no clue as to what I looked like. I studied the man as he spoke; my entire life I had seen my ugliness reflected back to me. But now, as reluctant as I was to admit it, the only indication in my companion's behavior was positive.

And then, that evening in that café, I experienced a moment of the freedom I'd been practicing for behind my Halloween mask all those years ago. But whereas as a child I expected my liberation to come as a result of gaining something, a new face, it came to me now as the result of shedding something, of shedding my image. I once thought that truth was eternal, that when you understood something it was with you forever. I know now that this isn't so, that most truths are inherently unretainable, that we have to work hard all our lives to remember the most basic things. Society is no help; it tells us again and again that we can most be ourselves by looking like someone else, leaving our own faces behind to turn into ghosts that will inevitably resent and haunt us. It is no mistake that in movies and literature the dead sometimes know they are dead only after they can no longer see themselves in the mirror; and as I sat there feeling the warmth of the cup against my palm, this small observation seemed like a great revelation to me. I wanted to tell the man I was with about it, but he was involved in his own topic and I did not want to interrupt him, so instead I looked with curiosity toward the window behind him, its night-darkened glass reflecting the whole café, to see if I could, now, recognize myself.

—1993

Learning from Other Writers (Grealy)

1. Lucy Grealy tells her story chronologically, except for her opening. What is the effect of framing the essay this way, starting in Scotland and then moving back twenty years? At what point do we return to Scotland?

2. Grealy's narrative structure is complex, so she sometimes has to cover the same period of time in two different sections. Where does this occur? Why do you think Grealy chose to tell her story this way?

3. How would you describe the tone of the essay? Why do you think she chose this tone to describe what to her was such a traumatic experience? Where do you find emotion in the writing?

4. Grealy asserts that she decided to become a "deep" person, and she is constantly trying to convince herself of certain realities. How does this tie in with the title? The theme of the essay?

5. Grealy writes about allowing herself to become very blunt as a sort of defense mechanism against being hurt. Is this true honesty, or another of her disguises?

6. Where do you see contradictions in the way Grealy thinks? How do such complexities enhance, rather than detract from, the essay?

Adding Your Voice

1. In what ways does your appearance define who you are? How do you think your appearance might mislead others? Was there a specific time in your life when your appearance played a significant role in defining how you saw yourself or how other people reacted to you?

2. Who are today's beauty icons? Who is the embodiment of femininity? Masculinity? Androgyny? How does the idea of beauty embodied in that person affect you and other people you know? Can you think of a narrative, whether continuous or episodic, that would allow you to reflect on this question?

3. For Grealy and Ephron, and to an extent for Cooper, the progression into adolescence marks a new stage of grappling with conflicts that began in childhood. What is the most significant change you noticed, or feared, or welcomed, in your adolescence? Was it physical? Emotional? Philosophical?

ARGUING FROM EXPERIENCE

As we discussed in Part I, a good academic argument is about joining a conversation, not having the last word, and what better way to join a conversation than by starting with your own experience? The subjects that interest, perplex, and enrage you are great places to begin. In his essay "Final Cut," Atul Gawande details his close encounters with the autopsy, an unpleasant but necessary part of the practice of medicine. As a doctor, Gawande has noticed that the autopsy no longer is performed as frequently as once was the case. He writes:

> The autopsy is in a precarious state these days. A generation ago, it was routine; now it has become a rarity. Human beings have never quite become comfortable with the idea of having their bodies cut open after they die. Even for a surgeon, the sense of violation is inescapable.

Beginning with a clear driving question—why is the autopsy in decline?—Gawande uses a narrative of his own experiences to introduce and interrogate his subject. But from there, he moves into a more complex exploration of a practice the medical community has used for millennia to ascertain the cause of death. Gawande notes that one of the earliest autopsies was performed in 44 B.C. on Julius Caesar, and that in 1410, "the Catholic Church itself ordered an autopsy— on Pope Alexander V, to determine whether this successor had poisoned him." He weaves this historical research into his narrative not simply to entertain the reader, but also to contextualize the material and to illustrate how powerful this mysterious new agent of change must be to disrupt such a longstanding and respected practice.

Likewise, the author conducts scholarly research, discovering that about 40 percent of autopsies "turn up major misdiagnosis in the cause of death" and that "in about a third of the misdiagnoses the patients would have been expected to live if proper treatment had been administered." From here he turns to theories on the nature of fallibility to further illuminate medicine's inability to provide exact diagnoses for every patient.

In short: Gawande uses his own experiences, historical research, and scholarly sources in multiple disciplines to arrive at and support his position that an increased reliance on sophisticated medical technology has given doctors a false sense of confidence in their diagnoses, leading them to discard the autopsy out of discomfort, despite its continued importance as a learning tool. This conclusion is significant because if doctors don't realize that their misdiagnoses are incorrect, then they won't learn from their mistakes and become better healers.

This is not material for the faint-hearted. Gawande opens his essay in the second person, telling us to imagine that we are doctors ourselves, that our patient is dead, and that we must now ask the grieving family members for permission to conduct an autopsy. Similarly, the descriptions of the autopsies are graphic (though never gratuitously so).

This stark, almost detached attention to physical detail doesn't mean that the essay is cold. Rather, the use of precise, unflinching description allows the author to evoke emotion. In essays about death and trauma—common concerns for reflective narratives, although certainly not the only possible topics—the driving question plays an additional role in that it gives the writer a purpose greater than merely evoking our pity or grief. Think of sentiment as an honest emotional response to an event, and sentimentality as the expression of an unearned, generic, wildly excessive, or insincere emotion. When Nora Ephron describes "crying hysterically" the moment she sees her friend Diane, she is sincerely recollecting the event and her response. But if you were to tell the story of your first romantic breakup and say that a single tear rolled down your cheek as you placed your hand over your broken heart, your readers might accuse you of being sentimental or melodramatic (that is, trying too hard to be dramatic).

To repeat: Details matter. If you revisit an experience while trying to answer a question that intrigues you about that experience, certain aspects of the story—objects, images, gestures, and bits of dialogue—will gradually assume a greater thematic weight than they might otherwise have attained. To think like a writer, pay attention to such details, allow yourself to identify and reflect on the links among them, and then work to illuminate those connections. As you read Atul Gawande's essay, notice his description of the autopsy procedures. What tools are used? What actions are described? More importantly, *how* are they described? What sort of language does the author employ? What types of words does he choose?

Autul Gawande

FINAL CUT

Your patient is dead; the family is gathered. And there is one last thing that you have to ask about: the autopsy. How should you go about it? You could do it offhandedly, as if it were the most ordinary thing in the world: "Shall we do an autopsy, then?" Or you could be firm, use your Sergeant Joe Friday voice: "Unless you have strong objections, we will need to do an autopsy, ma'am." Or you could take yourself out of it: "I am sorry, but they require me to ask, Do you want an autopsy done?"

What you can't be nowadays is mealymouthed about it. I once took care of a woman in her eighties who had given up her driver's license only to get hit by a car—driven by someone even older—while she was walking to a bus stop. She sustained a depressed skull fracture and cerebral bleeding, and, despite surgery, she died a few days later. So, on the spring afternoon after the patient took her last breath, I stood beside her and bowed my head with the tearful family. Then, as delicately as I could—not even using the awful word—I said, "If it's alright, we'd like to do an examination to confirm the cause of death."

"An *autopsy*?" a nephew said, horrified. He looked at me as if I were a buzzard circling his aunt's body. "Hasn't she been through enough?"

The autopsy is in a precarious state these days. A generation ago, it was routine; now it has become a rarity. Human beings have never quite become comfortable with the idea of having their bodies cut open after they die. Even for surgeon, the sense of violation is inescapable.

Not long ago, I went to observe the dissection of a thirty-eight-year-old woman I had taken care of who had died after a long struggle with heart disease. The dissecting room was in the sub-basement, past the laundry and a loading dock, behind an unmarked metal door. It had high ceilings, peeling paint, and brown tiled floor that sloped down to a central drain. There was a Bunsen burner on a countertop, and an old-style grocer's hanging scale, with a big clock-face red-arrow gauge and a pan underneath, for weighing organs. On shelves all around the room there were gray portions of brain, bowel and other organs soaking in formalin in Tupperware-like containers. The facility seemed rundown, chintzy, low-tech. On a rickety gurney in the corner was my patient, sprawled out, completely naked. The autopsy team was just beginning its work.

Surgical procedures can be grisly, but dissections are somehow worse. In even the most gruesome operations—skin grafting, amputations—surgeons maintain some tenderness and aestheticism toward their work. We know that the bodies we cut still pulse with life, and that these are people who will wake again. But in the dissecting room, where the person is gone and only the shell remains, you naturally find little delicacy, and the difference is visible in the smallest details. There is, for example, the simple matter of how a body is moved from gurney to table. In the operating room, we follow a careful, elaborate procedure for the unconscious patient, involving a canvas-sleeved rolling board and several gentle movements. We don't want so much as a bruise. Down here, by contrast, someone grabbed my patient's arm, another person a leg, and they just yanked. When her skin stuck to the stainless-steel dissecting table, they had to wet her and the table down with a hose before they could pull her the rest of the way.

The young pathologist for the case stood on the sidelines and let a pathology assistant take the knife. Like many of her colleagues, the pathologist had not been drawn to her field by autopsies but by the high-tech detective work that she got to do on tissue from living patients. She was happy to leave the dissection to the assistant, who had more experience at it anyway.

The assistant was a tall, slender woman of around thirty with straight sandy-brown hair. She was wearing the full protective garb of mask, face shield, gloves, and blue plastic gown. Once the body was on the table, she placed a six-inch metal block under the back, between the shoulder blades, so that the head fell back and the chest arched up. Then she took a scalpel in her hand, a big No. 6 blade, and made a huge Y-shaped incision that came down diagonally from each shoulder, curving slightly around each breast before reaching the midline, and then continued down the abdomen to the pubis.

Surgeons get used to the opening of bodies. It is easy to detach yourself from the person on the table and become absorbed by the details of method and anatomy. Nevertheless, I couldn't help wincing as she did her work: she was holding the scalpel like a pen, which forced her to cut slowly and jaggedly with the tip of the blade. Surgeons are taught to stand straight and parallel to their incision, hold the knife between the thumb and four fingers, like a violin bow, and draw the belly of the blade through the skin in a single, smooth slice to the exact depth desired. The assistant was practically sawing her way through my patient.

From there, the evisceration was swift. The assistant flayed back the skin flaps. With an electric saw, she cut through the exposed ribs along both sides. Then she lifted the rib cage as if it were the hood of a car, opened the abdomen, and removed all the major organs—including the heart, the lungs, the liver, the bowels, and the kidneys. Then the skull was sawed open, and the brain, too, was removed. Meanwhile, the pathologist was at a back table, weighing and examining everything, and preparing samples for microscopy and thorough testing.

For all this, however, I had to admit: the patient came out looking remarkable undisturbed. The assistant had followed the usual procedure and kept the skull incision behind the woman's ears, where it was completely hidden by her hair. She had also taken care to close the chest and abdomen really neatly, sewing the incision tight with weaved seven-cord thread. My patient seemed much the same as before, except now a little collapsed in the middle. (The standard consent allows the hospital to keep organs for testing and research. This common and long-established practice has caused huge controversy in Britain—the media have branded it "organ stripping"—but in America it remains generally accepted.) Most families, in fact, still have open-casket funerals after autopsies. Morticians employ fillers to restore a corpse's shape, and when they're done you cannot tell that an autopsy has been performed.

Still, when it is time to ask for a family's permission to do such a thing, the images weigh on everyone's mind—not least the doctor's. You strive to achieve a cool, dispassionate attitude toward these matters. But doubts nevertheless creep in.

One of the first patients for whom I was expected to request an autopsy was a seventy-five-year-old retired New England doctor who died one winter night while I was with him. Herodotus Sykes (not his real name, but not unlike it, either) had been rushed to the hospital with an infected, rupturing abdominal aortic aneurysm and taken to emergency surgery. He survived it, and recovered steadily until, eighteen days later, his blood pressure dropped alarmingly and blood began to poor from the drainage tube in his abdomen. "The aortic stump must have blown out," his surgeon said. Residual infection must have weakened the suture line where the infected aorta had been removed. We could have operated again, but the patient's chances were poor, and his surgeon didn't think he would be willing to take any more.

He was right. No more surgery, Sykes told me. He'd been through enough. We called Mrs. Sykes, who was staying with a friend about two hours away, and she set out for the hospital.

I was about midnight. I sat with him as he lay silent bleeding, his arms slack at his sides, his eyes without fear. I imagined his wife out on the Mass Pike, frantic, helpless, with six lanes, virtually empty at that hour, stretching far ahead.

Sykes held on, and at 2:15 A.M. his wife arrived. She turned ashen at the sight of him, but she steadied herself. She gently took his hand in hers. She squeezed, and he squeezed back. I left them to themselves.

At 2:45, the nurse called me in. I listened with my stethoscope, then turned to Mrs. Sykes and told her that he was gone. She had her husband's Yankee reserve, but she broke into quiet tears, weeping into her hands, and seemed suddenly frail and small. A friend who had come with her soon appeared, took her by the arm, and led her out of the room.

We are instructed to request an autopsy on everyone as a means of confirming the cause of death and catching our mistakes. And this was the moment I was supposed to ask—with the wife despondent and reeling with shock. But surely, I began to think, here was a case in which an autopsy would be pointless. We knew what had happened—a persistent infection, a rupture. We were sure of it. What would cutting the man apart accomplish?

And so I let Mrs. Sykes go. I could have caught her as she walked through the ICU's double doors. Or even called her on the phone later. But I never did.

Such reasoning, it appears, has become commonplace in medicine. Doctors are seeking so few autopsies that in recent years the *Journal of the American Medical Association* has twice felt the need to declare "war on the nonautopsy." According to the most recent statistics available, autopsies have been done in fewer than 10 percent of deaths; many hospitals do none. This is a dramatic turnabout. Through much of the twentieth century, doctors diligently obtained autopsies in the majority of all deaths—and it had taken centuries to reach this point. As Kenneth Iserson recounts in his fascinating almanac, *Death to Dust*, physicians have performed autopsies for more than two thousand years. But for most of history they were rarely performed. If religions permitted them at all—Islam, Shinto, orthodox Judaism, and the Greek Orthodox Church still frown on them—it was generally only for legal purposes. The Roman physician Antistius performed one of the earliest forensic examinations on record, in 44 B.C., on Julius Caesar, a documenting twenty-three wounds, including a final, fatal stab to the chest. In 1410, the Catholic Church itself ordered an autopsy—on Pope Alexander V, to determine whether his successor had poisoned him. No evidence of this was apparently found.

The first documented postmortem examination in the New World was actually done for religious reasons, though. It was performed on July 19, 1533, on the island of Española (now the Dominican Republic), upon conjoined females twins connected at the lower chest, to determine if they had one soul or two. The twins had been born alive, and a priest baptized them as two separate souls. A disagreement subsequently ensued about whether he was right to have done so, and when the "double monster" died at eight days of age an autopsy was ordered to settle the issue. A surgeon, one Johan Camacho, found two virtually complete sets of internal organs, and it was declared that two souls had lived and died.

Even in the nineteenth century, however, long after church strictures had loosened, people in the West seldom allowed doctors to autopsy their family members for medical purposes. As a result, the practice was largely clandestine. Some doctors went ahead and autopsied hospital patients immediately after death, before relatives could turn up to object. Others waited until burial and then robbed the graves, either personally or through accomplices, and activity that continued into the twentieth century. To deter such autopsies, some families would post nighttime guards at the grave site—hence the term "graveyard shift." Others placed heavy stones on the coffins. In 1878, one company in Columbus, Ohio, even sold "torpedo coffins," equipped with pipe bombs rigged to blow up if they were tampered with. Yet doctors remained undeterred. Ambrose Bierce's The Devil's Dictionary, published in 1906, defined "grave" as "a place in which the dead are laid to await the coming of the medical student."

By the turn of the twentieth century, however, prominent physicians such as Rudolf Virchow in Berlin, Karl Rokitansky in Vienna, and William Osler in Baltimore began to win popular support for the practice of autopsy. They defended it as a tool of discovery, one that had already been used to identify the cause of tuberculosis, reveal how to treat appendicitis, and establish the existence of Alzheimer's disease. They also showed that autopsies prevented errors—that without them doctors could not know when their diagnoses were incorrect. Moreover, most deaths were a mystery then, and perhaps what clinched the argument was the notion that autopsies could provide families with answers—give the story of a loved one's life a comprehensible ending. Once doctors had insured a dignified and respectful dissection at the hospital, public opinion turned. With time, doctors who did not obtain autopsies were viewed with suspicion. By the end of the Second World War, the autopsy was firmly established as a routine part of death in Europe and North America.

So what accounts for its decline? In truth, it's not because families refuse—to judge from recent studies, they still grant that permission up to 80 percent of the time. Instead, doctors, once so eager to perform autopsies that they stole bodies, have simply stopped asking. Some people ascribe this to shady motives. It has been said that hospitals are trying to save money by avoiding autopsies, since insurers don't pay for them, or that doctors avoid them in order to cover up evidence of malpractice. And yet autopsies lost money and uncovered malpractice when they were popular, too.

Instead, I suspect, what discourages autopsies is medicine's twenty-first-century, tall-in-the-saddle confidence. When I failed to ask Mrs. Sykes where we could autopsy her husband, it was not because of the expense, or because I feared that the autopsy would uncover an error. It was the opposite: I didn't see much likelihood that an error would be found. Today, we have MRI scans, ultrasound, nuclear medicine, molecular testing, and much more. When somebody dies, we already know why. We don't need an autopsy to find out.

Or so I thought. Then I had a patient who changed my mind.

He was in his sixties, whiskered and cheerful, a former engineer who had found success in retirement as an artist. I will call him Mr. Jolly, because that's what he was. He was also what we call a vasculopath—he did not seem to have an undiseased artery in him. Whether because of his diet or his genes or the fact that he used to smoke, he had had, the previous decade, one heart attack, two abdominal aortic aneurysm repairs, four bypass operations to keep blood flowing past blockages in his leg arteries, and several balloon procedures to keep hardened arteries open. Still, I never knew him to take a dark view of his lot. "Well, you can't get miserable about it," he'd say. He had wonderful children. He had beautiful grandchildren. "But, aargh, the wife," he'd go on. She would be sitting right there at the bedside and would roll her eyes, and he'd break into a grin.

Mr. Jolly had come into the hospital for treatment of a wound infection in his legs. But he soon developed congestive heart failure, causing fluid to back up into his lungs. Breathing became steadily harder for him, until we had to put him in the ICU, intubate him, and place him on a ventilator. A two-day admission turned into two weeks. With a regimen of diuretics and a change in heart medications, however, his heart failure reversed, and his lungs recovered. And one bright Sunday morning he was reclining in bed, breathing on his own, watching the morning shows on the TV set that hung from the ceiling. "You're doing marvelously," I said. I told him we would transfer him out of intensive care by the afternoon. He would probably be home in a couple of days.

Two hours later, a code-blue emergency call went out on the overhead speakers. When I got to the ICU and saw the nurse hunched over Mr. Jolly, doing chest compressions, I blurted out an angry curse. He'd been fine, the nurse explained, just watching TV, when suddenly he sat upright with a look of shock and then fell back, unresponsive. At first, he was asystolic—no heart rhythm on the monitor—and then the rhythm came back, but he had no pulse. A crowd of staffers set to work. I had him intubated, gave him fluids and epinephrine, had someone call the attending surgeon at home, someone else check the morning lab test results. An X-ray technician shot a portable chest film.

I mentally ran through possible causes. There were not many. A collapsed lung, but I heard good breath sounds with my stethoscope, and when his X-ray came back the lungs looked fine. A massive blood loss, but his abdomen wasn't swelling, and his decline happened so quickly that bleeding just didn't make sense. Extreme acidity of the blood could do it, but his lab tests were fine. Then there was cardiac tamponade—bleeding into the sac that contains the heart. I took a six-inch spinal needle on a syringe, pushed it through the skin below the breastbone, and advanced it to the heart sac. I found no bleeding. That left only one possibility: a pulmonary embolism—a blood clot that flips into the lung and instantly wedges off all blood flow. And nothing could be done about that.

I went out and spoke to the attending surgeon by phone and then to the chief resident, who had just arrived. An embolism was the only logical explanation, they agreed. I went back into the room and stopped the code. "Time of death: 10:23 A.M.," I announced. I phoned the wife at home, told her that things had taken a turn for the worse, and asked her to come in.

This shouldn't have happened; I was sure of it. I scanned the records for clues. Then I found one. In a lab test done the day before, the patients clotting had seemed to slow, which wasn't serious, but an ICU physician had decided to correct it with vitamin K. A frequent side effect of vitamin K is blood clots. I was furious. Giving the vitamin was completely unnecessary—just fixing a number on a lab test. Both the chief resident and I lit into the physician. We all but accused him of killing the patient.

When Mrs. Jolly arrived, we took her to a family room where it was quiet and calm. I could see from her face that she'd already surmised the worst. His heart had stopped suddenly, we told her, because of a pulmonary embolism. We said the medicines we gave him may have contributed to it. I took her in to see him and left her with him. After a while, she came out, her hands trembling and her face stained with tears. Then, remarkably, she thanked us. We had kept him for her all these years, she said. Maybe so, but neither of us felt any pride about what had just happened.

I asked her the required question. I told her that we wanted to perform an autopsy and needed her permission. We thought we already knew what had happened, but an autopsy would confirm it, I said. She considered my request for a moment. If an autopsy would help us, she finally said, then we could do it. I said, as I was supposed to, that it would. I wasn't sure I believed it.

I wasn't assigned to the operating room the following morning, so I went down to observe the autopsy. When I arrived, Mr. Jolly was already laid out on the dissecting table, his arms splayed, skin flayed back, chest exposed, abdomen open. I put on a gown, gloves, and a mask, and went up close. The assistant began buzzing through the ribs on the left side with the electric saw, and immediately blood started seeping out, as dark and viscous as crankcase oil. Puzzled, I helped him lift open the rib cage. The left side of the chest was full of blood. I felt along the pulmonary arteries for a hardened, embolized clot, but there was none. He hadn't had an embolism after all. We suctioned out three liters of blood, lifted the left lung, and the answer appeared before our eyes. The thoracic aorta was almost three times larger than it should have been, and there was a half-inch hole in it. The man had ruptured an aortic aneurysm and had bled to death almost instantly.

In the days afterward, I apologized to the physician I'd reamed out over the vitamin, and pondered how we had managed to miss the diagnosis. I looked through the patient's old X-rays and now saw a shadowy outline of what must have been his aneurysm. But none of us, not even the radiologists, had caught it. Even if we had caught it, we wouldn't have dared to do anything about it until weeks after treating his infection and heart failure, and that would have been too late. It disturbed me, however, to have felt so confident about what had happened that day and to have been so wrong.

The most perplexing thing was his final chest X-ray, the one we had taken during the code blue. With all that blood filling the chest, I should have seen at least a haze over the left side. But when I pulled the film out to look again, there was nothing.

How often do autopsies turn up a major misdiagnosis in the cause of death? I would have guessed this happened rarely, 1 or 2 percent of cases at most. According to three studies done in 1998 and 1999, however, the figure is about 40 percent. A large review of autopsy studies concluded that in about a third of the misdiagnoses the patients would have been expected to live if proper treatment had been administered. George Lundberg, a pathologist and former editor of the *Journal of the American Medical Association*, has done more than anyone to call attention to these figures. He points out the most surprising fact of all: the rates at which misdiagnosis is detected in autopsy studies have not improved since at least 1938.

With all the recent advances in imaging and diagnostics, it's hard to accept that we not only get the diagnosis wrong in two out of five of our patients who die but that we have also failed to improve over time. To see if this could really be true, doctors at Harvard put together a simple study. They went back into their hospital records to see how often autopsies picked up missed diagnoses in 1960 and 1970, before the advent of CT, ultra-sound, and nuclear scanning, and other technologies, and then in 1980, after those technologies became widely used. The researchers found no improvement. Regardless of the decade, physicians missed a quarter of fatal infections, a third of heart attacks, and almost two-thirds of pulmonary emboli in their patients who died.

In most cases, it wasn't technology that failed. Rather, the physicians did not consider the correct diagnosis in the first place. The perfect test or scan may have been available, but the physicians never ordered it.

In a 1976 essay, the philosophers Samuel Gorovitz and Alasdair MacIntyre explored the nature of fallibility. Why would a meteorologist, say, fail to correctly predict where a hurricane was going to make landfall? They saw three possible reasons. One was ignorance: perhaps science affords only a limited understanding of how hurricanes behave. A second reason was ineptitude: the knowledge is available, but the weatherman fails to apply it correctly. Both of these are surmountable sources of error. We believe that science will overcome ignorance, and that training and technology will overcome ineptitude. The third possible cause of error the philosophers posited, however, was an insurmountable kind, one they termed "necessary fallibility."

There may be some kinds of knowledge that science and technology will never deliver, Gorovitz and MacIntyre argued. When we ask science to move beyond explaining how things (say, hurricanes) generally behave to predicting exactly how a particular thing (say, Thursday's storm off the South Carolina coast) will behave, we may be asking it to do more than it can. No hurricane is quite like any other hurricane. Although all hurricanes follow predictable laws of behavior, each one is continuously shaped by myriad uncontrollable, accidental factors in the environment. To say precisely how one specific hurricane will behave would require a complete understanding of the world in all its particulars—in other words, omniscience.

It's not that it's impossible to predict anything; plenty of things are completely predictable. Gorovitz and MacIntyre give the example of a random ice cube in a fire. Ice cubes are so simple and so alike that you can predict with complete assurance that an ice cube will melt. But when it comes to inferring exactly what is going on in a particular person, are people more like ice cubes or like hurricanes?

Right now, at about midnight, I am seeing a patient in the emergency room, and I want to say that she is an ice cube. That is, I believe I can understand what's going on with her, that I can discern all her relevant properties. I believe I can help her.

Charlotte Duveen, as we will call her, is forty-nine years old, and for two days she has had abdominal pain. I begin observing her from the moment I walk through the curtains into her room. She is sitting cross-legged in the chair next to her stretcher and greets me with a cheerful, tobacco-beaten voice. She does not look sick. No clutching the belly. No gasping for words. Her color is good—neither flushed nor pale. Her shoulder-length brown hair has been brushed, her red lipstick neatly applied.

She tells me the pain started out crampy, like a gas pain. But then, during the course of the day, it became sharp and focused, and as she says this she points to a spot in the lower right part of her abdomen. She has developed diarrhea. She constantly feels as if she has to urinate. She doesn't have a fever. She is not nauseated. Actually, she is hungry. She tells me that she ate a hot dog at Fenway Park two days ago and visited the exotic birds at the zoo a few days before that, and she asks if either might have anything to do with this. She has two grown children. Her last period was three months ago. She smokes half a pack a day. She used to use heroin but says she's clean now. She once had hepatitis. She has never had surgery.

I feel her abdomen. It could be anything, I think: food poisoning, a virus, appendicitis, a urinary-tract infection, an ovarian cyst, a pregnancy. Her abdomen is soft, without distention, and there is an area of particular tenderness in the lower right quadrant. When I press there, I feel her muscles harden reflexively beneath my fingers. On the pelvic exam, her ovaries feel normal. I order some lab tests. Her white blood cell count comes back elevated. Her urinalysis is normal. A pregnancy test is negative. I order an abdominal CT scan.

I am sure I can figure out what's wrong with her, but, if you think about it, that's a curious faith. I have never seen this woman before in my life, and yet I presume that she is like the others I've examined. Is it true? None of my other patients, admittedly, were forty-nine-year-old women who had had hepatitis and a drug habit, had recently been to the zoo and eaten a Fenway frank, and had come in with two days of mild lower-right-quadrant pain. Yet I still believe. Every day, we take people to surgery and open their abdomens, and, broadly speaking, we know what we will find: not eels or tiny chattering machines or a pool of blue liquid but coils of bowel, a liver to one side, a stomach to the other, a bladder down below. There are, of course, differences—an adhesion in one patient, an infection in another—but we have catalogued and sorted them by the thousands, making a statistical profile of mankind.

I am leaning toward appendicitis. The pain is in the right place. The timing of her symptoms, her exam, and her white blood cell count all fit with what I've seen before. She's hungry, however; she's walking around, not looking sick, and this seems unusual. I go to the radiology reading room and stand in the dark, looking over the radiologist's shoulder at the images of Duveen's abdomen flashing up on the monitor. He points to the appendix, wormlike, thick, surrounded by gray, streaky fat. It's appendicitis, he says confidently. I call the attending surgeon on duty and tell him what we've found. "Book the OR," he says. We're going to do an appendectomy.

This one is as sure as we get. Yet I've worked on similar cases in which we opened the patient up and found a normal appendix. Surgery itself is a kind of autopsy. "Autopsy" literally means "to see for oneself," and despite our knowledge and technology, when we look we're often unprepared for what we find. Sometimes we turn out wrong despite doing everything right.

Whether with living patients or dead, however, we cannot know until we look. Even in the case of Mr. Sykes, I now wonder whether we put our stitches in correctly, or whether the bleeding had come from somewhere else entirely. Doctors are no longer asking such questions. Equally troubling, people seem happy to let us off the hook. In 1995, the United States National Center for Health Statistics stopped collecting autopsy statistics altogether. We can no longer even say how rare autopsies have become.

From what I've learned looking inside people, I've decided human beings are somewhere between a hurricane and an ice cube: in some respects, permanently mysterious, but in others—with enough science and careful probing—entirely scrutable. It would be as foolish to think we have reached the limits of human knowledge as it is to think we could ever know everything. There is still room enough to get better, to ask questions of even the dead, to learn from knowing when or simple certainties are wrong.

—2002

Learning from Other Writers (Gawande)

1. Though his essay is told predominately in the first person, in the opening paragraph Gawande employs the second-person point of view: "Your patient is dead; the family is gathered." Why do you think he chooses to begin in this manner?

2. How does Gawande position himself as someone with the authority to argue from personal experience? How does he build himself into a character?

3. Assuming that you are not a surgeon or medical professional, how might you investigate the status of the autopsy in the medical community today? What sources might you consult? What types of research might you carry out?

4. Why does Gawande provide such careful, vivid, crude details about the dissecting room and the procedure he watches there? What is the purpose of this passage?

6. How does Gawande transition from his personal experiences to background information? How does he move back into recounting more personal experience? What is the effect of this balance?

7. Why do you think Gawande provides the etymology of the word "autopsy" ("to see for oneself") at the end of the essay and not the beginning?

Adding Your Voice

Think of an experience that strongly affected you and whose story you could tell before branching into a larger argument. For instance, you might have experienced the pitfalls of fraternity hazing and would now like to examine the hazards of the practice beyond your own experience. Perhaps you were cyber-bullied in high school and want to tell your story yet also go beyond it, making an argument about the power and danger of this specific type of harassment.

BEGINNINGS AND ENDINGS

Now that you have read the reflective narratives in this chapter and attempted at least a few of the suggested exercises, you are ready to write your own. How to begin? As paradoxical as this seems, you may not find your beginning until after you start writing; often, you will need to engage in some warm-up writing, perhaps in a notebook or journal, to discover where the story should start. Or you might begin writing and realize that your fifth paragraph is actually where the essay heats up; the first four paragraphs were necessary to get you there but no longer belong in the narrative.

Nevertheless, the way you begin your essay is crucial. A good hook establishes your tone and intrigues your readers. Let's review the ways each essay in this section starts:

- "In Moulmein, in lower Burma, I was hated by large numbers of people—the only time in my life that I have been important enough for this to happen to me."

- "I did bad things for football."

- "Theresa Sanchez sat behind me in ninth-grade algebra."
- "I have to begin with a few words about androgyny."
- "There was a long period of time, almost a year, during which I never looked in a mirror."
- "Your patient is dead; the family is gathered."

Look at the questions that arise from these beginnings: Why were you hated? What bad things did you do for football? Who is Theresa Sanchez and why is she so important? Why begin with "androgyny" when your essay seems to be about breasts? Why didn't you look in the mirror? Why did your patient die? Was the death your fault? What is his or her family waiting for you to say? As these examples demonstrate, an essay's opening lines should be intriguing enough to keep the reader reading while remaining concrete enough that she doesn't feel lost.

Even so, most of you will find writing the introduction to your essay easier than writing the ending. If you begin at a place of puzzlement or intrigue, how do you know when to stop? Rest assured that you don't have to provide a complete answer to your driving question. If there are aspects of your question left open at the end, that's okay; sometimes the best writing acknowledges the contradictions and ambiguity of an experience or a set of emotions. But you should have spent enough time developing and exploring your driving question so the reader feels satisfied that the essay has gone somewhere.

If you have ever written a five-paragraph essay, you might be struggling to break the habit of tacking on a "conclusion" that says the same thing as your introduction. With a reflective narrative, you most likely won't introduce your main points in your introduction, and you don't need to sum them up at the end. But a good narrative will, to paraphrase Frank L. Cioffi, carry the reader over the distance the writer has traveled to get where he or she ended up. By the essay's final paragraphs, the writer not only has told us about a certain experience but also has traced his or her emotional and intellectual response to that experience.

It can be helpful to think of your essay as having both a conclusion and a resolution. For our purposes, let's think of the conclusion as *philosophical* and the resolution as *dramatic*: the conclusion is the (partial) answer to the driving question, whatever you have come to understand in researching and writing your essay; the resolution is the wrap-up of the actual events you are narrating.

Which comes first? You might end your narrative the way Cooper does, with a conclusion: he regrets never having told Theresa Sanchez that he was gay. But the resolution of the story comes with Grady swimming in his pool, a "flame that couldn't be doused." On the other hand, George Orwell realizes before he shoots the elephant that imperialism is wrong and that he was only a puppet to the regime (note that his conclusion arrives when we are only halfway through the essay!), while the resolution of the story is his actual shooting of the elephant.

Looking at the places in which the authors of the essays in this chapter conclude their meditations and resolve their plots will help you to write your own endings.

By realizing that an essay is a movement, a progression, each part building toward the conclusion and resolution, you will liberate yourself from feeling as though you must put all your thinking and analysis into that final paragraph. You will realize that the entire essay is building toward its conclusion and resolution and that an ending isn't just something you tack on at the end.

An additional exercise is to look at the first few paragraphs of an essay and the last few. How are the beginning and ending in each essay linked? How has the introduction become cast in a new light once you have read the ending?

ADDITIONAL CONSIDERATIONS: HOW PERSONAL IS TOO PERSONAL?

Most of us are comfortable with the narrative form. What could be more natural than coming home after a long day at work or school and telling a friend or relative what happened? And some of us have no trouble writing about ourselves: the more personal, the better.

But some writers squirm at the idea of any sort of personal revelation; they dislike even those first few moments of a new class in which the teacher asks students to introduce themselves and say a few words about what they are studying and where they are from. Anything but that! To those writers, we say: Relax. In writing a reflective narrative, you only need to write from your own perspective, in your own voice, about something that happened to you or someone you know. You don't necessarily have to bare your soul about a traumatic or embarrassing event.

In his essay "Writing Personal Essays: On the Necessity of Turning Oneself into a Character," Phillip Lopate notes that most young essayists are "torn between two contrasting extremes," the first being the idea that "I am so weird that I could never tell on the page what is really, secretly going on in my mind" and the second that "I am so boring, nothing ever happens to me out of the ordinary, so who would want to read about me?" Lopate speculates that both extremes "are rooted in shame, and both reflect a lack of worldliness," the first exaggerating "how isolated one is in one's 'wicked' thoughts, instead of recognizing that everyone has strange, surreal, immoral notions," and the second requiring a "reeducation" so the essayist can acknowledge "the charm of the ordinary" in his or her loves and friendships, brushes with history, and interactions with the natural world and thereby "recognize that life remains a mystery—even one's own so-called boring life."

Which isn't to say that you won't be troubled by the repercussions of telling the truth about your life and the lives of others. Although a reflective narrative need not be confessional, the very difficulty of writing about certain events or topics is often a sign that the topic or event demands to be written about. Deciding what to say about yourself and others and taking responsibility for any repercussions is as much a part of writing a good essay as developing a natural, clear, original voice, selecting an interesting topic and driving question, and finding a useful, effective form.

KEY FEATURES OF THE FORM

As you draft your reflective narrative, perhaps using the writing you have done in response to *Adding Your Voice* activities throughout this chapter, consider the common features of the reflective narrative:

- Examine a driving question by using chronological time as a structuring device;
- Move the reader clearly through time and space;
- Explore some sort of conflict—the struggle is the story;
- Effectively balance expository and scenic writing;
- Reveal information to create tension and suspense;
- Develop a clear sense of the narrator's character for the reader;
- Use careful, thoughtful analysis and reflection to answer the writer's driving question and deepen the reader's understanding of the significance of the narrative;
- Focus on significant, concrete details relevant to the driving question;
- Employ an engaging voice and appropriate tone;
- End with a dramatic resolution and a philosophical conclusion that show the emotional and/or intellectual distance traveled;
- Use the writer's experience to tap into something universal, to illuminate the subject in a unique way.

PART III

Portraits

CHAPTER 8

People

I f we use narratives to make sense of events, we use portraits to discover the essence of a person, place, or community. In creating a portrait, your goal is to define your subject for your readers, then probe beneath the surface to give your subject meaning by analyzing what it represents—why it has significance, and for whom. In the portraits in this chapter, the writers seek to define their relationships to their subjects, each writer using a particular lens (e.g., social class, motherhood, work) through which to view that relationship and thereby make claims about those subjects.

In Part II, we discussed the difference between a narrative's plot and the analysis or reflection that gives it meaning. You can think about a portrait in comparable terms. Analogous to the reflective narrative's plot are the *facts* about your subject: who, what, when, where, why, and how. While the research you might find on the Internet or in books or magazines might help you with the basics, a portrait is not just a report. A good portrait examines its subject from a particular standpoint. Just as an optical lens focuses rays of light to create an image, the lens of a portrait focuses—and filters out—information and experience to create a clear, vivid representation of a subject. This is what we mean by capturing the "essence" of a person or a place.

But it's impossible for a subject to have only one essence. As is true of any good argument, a writer's position is based on interpretation and point of view. A son writing a portrait of his father might approach the material from the viewpoint of masculinity or labor. Filtered through these particular lenses, the essence of the father that emerges would be slightly different than the portrait of the father that the writer's sister might create. How you understand and interpret the world is an individual experience. This is why analysis and critical thinking are such an integral part of the work we do as writers—our job is to give our readers a new way of seeing our subjects.

Although the focus of a portrait is different from that of a narrative, the two forms share certain rhetorical techniques. As you practice writing portraits, you will continue to hone the skills you developed in earlier chapters: paying attention to audience, learning to balance scene and exposition, selecting significant details, creating rich characterizations, developing a unique point of view, and weaving analysis and reflection into your work. Likewise, an awareness of chronology and the way in which events relate to and affect one another is important to most essays written in the portrait form. The difference is that while a reflective narrative tends to re-create a story in order to illuminate something about a writer's own identity or experience, a portrait that employs narrative uses it to give meaning to a subject other than the writer.

Think of the difference between two forms this way: in a reflective narrative, you can consider yourself to be the lead actor or actress in the events you are relating; in a portrait, you play the supporting role—necessary to the material but not its central focus. You are still looking at something from your perspective, but you are no longer the primary player on the stage.

In "Tracks and Ties," Andre Dubus III uses the technique of the reflective narrative—structuring a story in chronological order—but here he turns his focus on his childhood best friend rather than on himself. In fact, the essay is written in the second-person point of view ("you"), as if the author were writing a letter to that friend. Scene by scene, as Dubus re-creates a series of events from their shared childhood and adolescence in the gritty, working-class town of Haverhill, Massachusetts, he focuses on his friend rather than on himself in order to figure out the significance of his friend's life—and death—in comparison to the path his own life has taken.

In particular, Dubus is haunted by questions about the ties that once bound him to his friend and the forces that eventually led their tracks to diverge so radically. Why was this friend shunted off to trade school, while Dubus, who hated gym and was failing algebra, managed to go to college? How did the author evade the lure of drugs that even his sister sold? How and why did that "hawny" fourteen-year-old grow up to be a wife beater, while Dubus grew up to be a man who pulls on his boots and jacket and goes for a walk rather than risk an argument with his girlfriend? The answer, as you might guess, is that he can never be entirely sure. Yet by exploring these questions through the form of a portrait and trying to capture the essence of his friend's life—and by contrast, his own—Dubus is able to say something meaningful about what it is like to grow up in this sort of place under these sorts of conditions, and how the struggles of our childhoods have the potential to shape our futures.

PROFILES IN ACTION

Sitting down to capture the essence of a person might seem a daunting task. Where do you start? How can you be sure you are capturing your subject's essence, even if "essence" is subject to interpretation? And how do you know if you haven't missed something or left out the most important part? Luckily, the combination of a natural, organic structure and a specific driving question once again come to the writer's rescue.

You needn't approach your subject in an abstract way, trying to pull essential facts and characteristics out of the air and setting them down on the page in a random manner. Instead, you can allow the subject to inspire you and provide the structure of your essay. Writing about a person sitting behind a desk isn't very dramatic, but you might use the person's physical presence behind that desk to order your reflections.

For example, imagine that your mother is the senior vice-president of a major insurance company. What objects decorate her office, and what messages do those objects—whether intentionally or not—transmit to her colleagues and clients? You might also wonder why she chooses to wear her hair short and carefully coiffed now, in contrast to the waist-length flowing locks she sported in her hippie college years. And what's with those pearls? Didn't she once tell you that pearls remind her of her prissy, snobbish grandmother? Then there's the intercom she uses to endlessly page her administrative assistant. How does your mother treat that young woman, especially in light of the horror stories your mom has told you about her early days trying to advance in a company where no female employee had ever progressed higher than the level of secretary? Analyzing these seemingly contradictory sides of your mother might yield interesting insights into the personas we adopt at work, or how work changes us, or the changing role of women in business. The key is to remember that the form helps to drive and shape the inquiry.

Of course, a profile written about a subject who does nothing but sit behind her desk all day isn't likely to be as dynamic as a profile of a person in action, doing whatever characterizes his or her essential nature. If you can persuade your subject to get up from behind his or her desk, the activity you are recounting will provide your essay with a pleasing forward movement and development. Obviously, you can create an engrossing profile-in-action of a Navy Seal performing some heroic act. But even the everyday experiences of ordinary people can yield fascinating material for an essay. Structuring a profile around a day in the life of a zookeeper, dentist, air traffic controller, or trash collector, or the process by which a computer, hammer, or surfboard is designed and manufactured can afford your readers access to lives they might otherwise never witness, understand, or appreciate.

More important, the activity or process you are recounting will provide you, the writer, with a clear, engaging structure for your meditations. What ultimately matters is that you arrive at a deeper insight about your material. Regardless of whether your argument is implied or explicit (as we discussed in Part I), you are making claims about your subject through the process of inquiry and analysis. This is at the core of uncovering a subject's essence and giving it meaning.

To do so, you will need to formulate a driving question so your readers know why that subject merits their attention. It's often easiest to start with a specific, personal angle. For example, when your mother goes to work, does she become a completely different person? Is that efficient, pearl-and-suit-wearing corporate executive behind the desk as much your real mother as the woman who cooks vegetarian chili in her sweatpants on the weekends and who once attended Grateful Dead shows? Does your mother change when she goes to work, or has work changed *her* in certain important ways over the years? By allowing your question to narrow your focus, you won't feel compelled to put in every detail about your mother's job at that insurance company. Instead, you will be able to pay specific attention to those details or scenes related to issues of gender, power dynamics, and the changing demographics of the work force.

As you explore your driving question in the specific context of your mother and her relationship to work, however, you will begin to see the way in which her experience is a *microcosm* of a larger phenomenon: how men and women act differently (or not) in corporate America than they do in their private lives; how the business world of the twenty-first century has different expectations (or not) for women and men; or how our personal identities are shaped (or not) by our professional lives. The point here is that we illuminate—and make claims about—the world at large through specific, individual experience. This is what gives our work depth and meaning.

Andre Dubus III

TRACKS AND TIES

Years later, when I was twenty-six, she said in the *New York Times* you would tie her naked and spread-eagled on the bed, that you would take a bat to her. She said you'd hit her for any reason. But in Haverhill, Massachusetts, you were my best friend, my brother's too. I was fifteen and you two were fourteen and in 1974 we walked the avenues on cold gray days picking through dumpsters for something to beat off to. We'd beat off to anything, though I was shy about it and couldn't do it just anywhere.

One February morning we skipped school and went downtown. It was ten or eleven degrees and the dirty snow piled along both sides of River Street had become ice; the air made my lungs hurt and our noses, ears, and fingers felt burned, but you wore your faded blue jean jacket with the green magic marker peace signs drawn all over it. You wore sneakers and thin fake denim pants that looked more purple than blue. It was so cold I pulled the rubber band from my ponytail and let my hair down around my neck and leather-jacketed shoulders. Your hair was long too, brown and stringy. My brother, barely fourteen, needed a shave.

We had a dollar between us so we sat in a booth at Vahally's Diner and drank coffee with so much milk and sugar in it you couldn't call it coffee anymore. The Greek man behind the counter hated us; he folded his black hairy forearms across his chest and watched us take our free refills until we were giddy with caffeine. You went for your seventh cup and he yelled something at you in Greek. On the way out you stole two dollars someone had left on their check under a sugar shaker.

You paid our way on the city bus that was heated and made a loop all the way through town, along the river, up to the Westgate shopping center, then back again. We stayed on it for two hours, taking the loop six times. In the far rear, away from the driver, you took out your black-handled Buck knife and carved a peace sign into the aluminum-backed seat in front of you. For a while I looked out the window at all the red brick factory buildings, the store-fronts with their dusty windows, bright neon price deals taped to the bottom and top. Barrooms on every block. I probably thought of the high school algebra I was flunking, the gym class I hated, the brown mescaline and crystal meth and THC my sister was selling. The bus was warm, too warm, and more crowded than before. A woman our mothers' age sat in her overcoat and scarf in the seat in front of you both. Her back was to you and I'm sure she heard you laughing but she didn't see my brother hunched forward in his seat, jerking back and forth on his penis and coming in no time, catching it all in his hand. I think I looked away and I don't remember what he did with it.

After the bus, we made our way through the narrow factory streets, most of the buildings' windows covered with gray plywood, though your mother still worked at Schwartz's Shoe, on the fifth floor, when she wasn't drinking. We walked along the railroad tracks, its silver rails flush with the packed snow, the wooden ties gone under. And we laughed about the summer before when we three built a barricade for the train, a wall of broken creosote ties, an upside-down shopping cart, cinder blocks, and a rusted oil drum. We covered it with brush, then you siphoned gas from a Duster behind Schwartz's and poured it on. My brother and I lit it, air sucked by us in a whoosh, and we ran down the bank across the parking lot into the abandoned brewery to the second floor to watch our fire, to wait for the Boston & Maine, to hear the screaming brakes as it rounded the blind curve just off the trestle over the river. But a fat man in a good shirt and tie showed up at the tracks, then a cop, and we ran laughing to the first floor where we turned on the keg conveyor belt, lay on it belly-first, and rode it up through its trap door over and over.

As we made our way through town it began to snow. My brother and I were hungry, but you were never hungry; you were hawny, you said. One morning, as we sat in the basement of your house and passed a homemade pipe between us, your mother upstairs drunk on Kappy's vodka and Pepsi, singing to herself, you said: "I'm always hawny in the mawnin'."

My brother and I laughed and you didn't know why, then you inhaled resin on your next hit and said, "Shit man, the screem's broken."

"The *what?*"

"The screem. You know, the screem. Like a *screem* door?"

By the time we reached the avenues the snow had blanketed the streets. There were two sisters on Seventh who lived in the projects that always had motorcycles in front of them, and trash, and bright-colored babies' toys. Trish and Terry were older, sixteen and seventeen and so skinny their breasts looked like prunes beneath their shirts, but they had dark skin and long hair and sometimes, if they were high, they'd suck you. But there was a day party on the first floor of their building, and it had only been two weeks since Harry Wright and Kevin McConigle, rent collectors for Fat Billy, both twenty-three or -four, beat us up, you and me, just walked us out of a pot party we were both quiet at, walked us off the front porch into the mud then kicked and punched us until they were through. So we kept walking, heading for a street close to the highway where we knew three girls who would fuck if you had wine and rubbers, though after the wine they didn't mention the rubbers.

On Cedar Street, cars spun out snow as they drove from the curb or the corner store. You let out a yelp and a holler and went running after a Chevy that had just pulled away, skidding slightly as it went. You ran low, bent over so the driver wouldn't see you, and when you reached the back bumper you grabbed it and squatted on your sneakers, your butt an inch or two from the road. And you skied away, just like that, the snow shooting out from under the wheels of the car, out from under your Zayre Department Store sneakers, blue exhaust coughing out its pipe beside you.

In the spring and summer we hopped trucks. A mile from the highway was a cross-walk on Main with a push-button traffic signal pole that we three leaned against until a truck came along and one of us pressed the button to turn red. I was the decoy that day, for a white refrigerator truck from Shoe City Beef. It stopped at the line, and I crossed the street jerking my head like a chicken to keep his attention from the mirrors while you two ran around to the back and climbed up on the foot-wide iron ledge at the bottom of its rear doors. As soon as I got to the sidewalk I heard the driver shift from neutral to first, heard him give it the gas. I waited for a car to drive by from the opposite direction, then I ran out into the street behind the truck, which was only shifting up to second. You and my brother stood on the ledge waiting, smiling, nodding your heads for me to hurry. I reached the ledge just as the truck moved into higher gear and I grabbed the bolt lock on its back doors and pulled myself up, the truck going faster now, shifting again, dipping and rattling through a low spot in the road. You both held an iron handle on opposite sides of the door so I stayed down, gripping the bolt lock with both hands, sitting on the ledge.

A car horn behind us honked and the driver, some man who combed his hair to the side like a teacher, shook his head and honked his horn again. You gave him the finger and we laughed but it was a scared laugh because the truck wasn't slowing down as it got to the gas stations and Kappy's Liquor near the highway, it was speeding up. Before, we'd jumped off into the grass of the highway ramp, but now we couldn't; he took the turn without leaving third gear and you yelled: "He *knows!* He friggin' *knows!*" My brother wasn't smiling anymore, and he stuck his head around the corner and let the growing wind hit him in the face, run through the hair on his cheeks as he squeezed the handle with both hands and I wanted to stand, to get my feet on something solid, but there was no room and now the driver was in fourth gear, heading north on 495, going fifty, then sixty, then sixty-five. He moved to the middle lane and I tried not to look down at the zip of the asphalt a foot beneath my dangling boots, but it was worse looking out at the cars, at the drivers looking at us like we might be a circus act they should catch sometime. Some honked as they passed so I looked up at you, at the side of your face as you looked around the corner, the June wind snapping your hair back past your forehead and ears, your mouth open in a scream I could barely hear. You smiled and shook your head at my brother then down at me, your brown eyes wet from the wind, your cheeks flushed in a satisfaction so deep I had to look back at the cars behind us, at the six or seven I was convinced would run me over one after the other, after my fingers failed. Miles later, at the tollbooths of the New Hampshire line, the truck slowed to a stop and we jumped off exhausted, our fingers stiff, and thumbed home.

That fall you went to the trade school, my brother joined me at the high school, and I saw you six years later in an all-night store in Monument Square. I was buying cigarettes for my college girl-friend. She waited in the car. It was winter. The floor was dirty with people's slush and mud tracks, the overhead light was fluorescent and too bright, and I was waiting my turn at the register when I saw you, watching me, smiling as you walked up. You carried a carton of ice cream and a quart of Coke. I had on a sweater and a jacket but you wore only a T-shirt, green Dickie work pants, and sneakers. You were taller than me, lean, and your young black mustache and goatee made you look sinister until you started talking in that high voice that hadn't changed since you'd told us you were hawny in the mawnin'. You said you were living down on the avenues, that you were getting married soon. I said congratulations, then I was at the counter asking for a pack of Parliaments and you touched me on the shoulder, said to say hi to my brother. I said I would. At the door I glanced back at you and watched you dig into your front pocket for crumpled bills. You nodded and smiled at me, winked even, and as I left the store, the cold tightening the skin on my face, I remembered the time your mother went to visit her sister in Nebraska for a whole month. I could never understand why she went alone, why she'd leave her family like that to go off for a visit. Then my mother told me it was detox she went to, some twenty-eight-day program in Boston. When I told you I knew, you laughed and said, "Nah," but you swallowed twice and walked away to do nothing in particular.

Six months after I saw you in the store my brother and I got invitations to your wedding. We didn't go.

Four more years and you were dead.

I heard about it after you were buried. They said your wife stabbed you in the back. That was it; she stabbed you. But a year later I was behind the bar at McMino's Lounge and Fat Billy's son, Bill Jr., told me what really happened, that you were cooked, always thinking your wife was cheating on you, always beating her up. That night you ran outside off the porch to go kill the guy you thought she was fucking. This was down on one of the avenues, behind the projects, and you took the trail in back of your house. But your wife opened your black-handled Buck knife and chased after you, screaming. She was short and small, barely five feet, and just as you reached the weeds she got to you and drove it in low, sinking the blade into your liver, snipping something called the portal artery. You went down without a sound. You curled up in a heap. But your wife spent four hours at a neighbor's house crying before they called anyone, and then it was the cops, and you were gone.

I served Bill Jr. another White Russian and for a second I felt sure it was him she went to that night, and I thought about hitting him for not making a faster call, but I felt no heat in my hands, no pull inside me. And I've always hated woman beaters. Part of me thought you got what you deserved. I left Bill Jr. to finish his too-sweet drink.

The following winter I was living in New York City, in a one-room studio with my girlfriend. It was late on a Sunday morning and we both sat with our feet up on the couch reading the *New York Times*. Outside our barred window snow fell on parked cars, on the sidewalk and street. I got tired of the movie section and picked up a story about three women in prison, all there for the same reason, for killing the husbands who beat them. And your wife was one of them; they gave her full name, *your* name. They wrote how she chased you outside and stabbed you. They described the town you both lived in as economically depressed, once a thriving textile town but no more. I lowered the paper and started to tell my girlfriend all about you, but she and I weren't doing so well, both past wanting to hear anything extra about each other, so I pulled on my boots and jacket and went walking. I crossed Third Avenue and Second and First. A car alarm went off in front of some Chinese laundry. I stuck my hands in my pockets and wished I'd worn a hat. I passed an empty basketball court, then I waited for the traffic on FDR Drive and walked the last block to the East River. To my right and left were bridges over to Queens. Though from where I stood I could see only the backs of warehouses, dry weeds five feet tall, then the gray river, swirling by fast.

The snow had stopped and I started walking along the cobblestone walk. One morning I skipped school and cut through back yards to your house. I didn't know your mother was home from Nebraska and I almost stepped back when she answered the door. She'd dyed her brown hair black, she wore sweatpants and a sweater, she had a cold sore on her bottom lip, and she'd gained weight, but she smiled and kissed me on the cheek and invited me in. The small kitchen was clean and warm. It smelled like coffee and cinnamon rolls. She put one on a napkin and handed it to me. I thanked her, and while I chewed the sweet buttery bread, she lit up a cigarette and asked about my mother. Then you came downstairs in just your jeans, no shirt, your chest pale and thin, your nipples pink, and your mother rushed over and kissed and hugged you like you'd been gone and just gotten home. And you didn't pull away, you hugged her back, and when your eyes caught mine, you lowered your face into the hair at her shoulder, and kept hugging.

—1993

Learning from other Writers (Dubus)

1. Dubus uses the second-person point of view ("you") to narrate his essay. What is the effect of this unusual form of address?

2. The main narrative describes the three boys' journey around Haverhill on a single winter's day in February 1974. How does chronology function in this essay?

3. What details does the author select, and how do those details serve to characterize both his friend and their hometown? Why do these details matter to us as readers, even though we didn't grow up in Dubus's hometown and will never meet his friend?

4. What is the function of the scene at McMino's Lounge? In particular, why does Dubus report Bill Jr.'s dialogue rather than presenting it in an actual scene?

5. What is the purpose of the scene in New York City that comes near the end? How does it connect back to the beginning? How does this juxtaposition of past and present enhance the way you read the essay and indicate the essay's driving question?

Adding Your Voice

Think of a time where you ran into a friend you hadn't seen in many years or with whom you had deliberately reconnected after a long separation. Try to remember the encounter. Was it awkward? Nostalgic? Did the place where it happened affect your interaction? Evoke that moment in a scene, including description, dialogue, action, and interiority (what you were thinking or feeling). Next, think of your most vivid memory of an earlier experience you shared with this friend. Capture that memory in a second scene, again trying to engage all the senses. As you re-create this previous experience, pay attention to how you and your friend once interacted. What roles did you each play? What do you remember that surprises you? What is different about the earlier experience as compared to the more recent encounter? What remains the same? Are the two scenes linked? How and why? Finally, try to analyze what that person represented to you in the past and what role he or she plays in your current life. In short: you are trying to *measure the distance* between your relationship then versus where it is now. What conclusions can you draw about how each of you has changed, or not?

BALANCING INTIMACY AND DISTANCE

In her short, concise essay "Sibling Rivalry at the Stove," Tamar Adler writes about her brother, John, and their shared—yet very different—relationships to cooking. For as long as Adler can remember, food has played a central role in her family:

> My brother and I grew up in a household rich with meals: our mother's hands reeked of garlic in an inside-the-veins way. Our lunches weren't like our friends'. Every day we watched quizzically while they bit into soft bread filled with floppy disks of pink meat, garish mustard, waxy squares of cheese, then unpacked our own heavily seeded sesame semolina rolls dripping with oily roasted eggplant and smoked mozzarella.

As they grow older, both siblings become chefs. Yet their culinary paths are characterized not only by fierce competition but also by entirely different philosophies regarding what constitutes the art of cooking. Adler's brother ends up at the famed New York restaurant Per Se, where order rules, while Adler moves to the West Coast, taking a position at Chez Panisse, where "[m]easuring was contemptuous, uniformity prosaic." Each believes that only he or she understands the soul of "true cooking," and this, in turn, becomes the driving question of the essay: "What is cooking, why do we do it, and what purpose does it serve in our lives beyond simply eating?"

Not until the end of the essay, however, do we learn the *narrative occasion* of the essay: a recent Thanksgiving when the siblings' mother got sick and they were forced to cook together. "Worried more about my mother than who cooked the beets," Adler writes, "we haltingly began negotiations." This compromise and eventual collaboration is made possible by the mother's illness. Yet Adler recognizes that the passage of time and the successes that she and her brother have achieved in their respective careers—Adler writing a book, her brother now an esteemed *sous* chef in New York—have also played a role, because neither sibling has anything left to prove to the other. Just as Dubus uses the newspaper article about his friend's death as the catalyst for his own reflection, Adler conceives her essay from the vantage point of her family's Thanksgiving meal. You might think of your essay's narrative occasion as when and where you are standing when you are writing—how you have positioned yourself in relation to your material and from what point of view you are considering your subject. This is particularly important to establish when you are analyzing subjects with whom you have an intimate relationship; as you might expect, writing about your family or friends makes it that much harder to develop the distance necessary to objectively create or analyze meaning.

Another challenge that arises when writing about a person you know intimately is the sheer volume of information at your disposal. Most of us could write books about our friends, our siblings, and our parents. So what do we include? What do we leave out? This is why identifying a particular lens of examination is so important.

In "Sibling Rivalry at the Stove," Adler chooses to get at her brother's essence—and the essence of their relationship—through the lens of cooking. She and her brother may have played sports, they may have taken family vacations, and they may have watched a lot of television growing up, but by focusing her essay on food, she can eliminate anything that doesn't fit into this category. Finding a lens allows us to discard extraneous information and to focus exclusively on what matters.

Like Adler, Dan Rivas has a complicated relationship with an intimate subject, in his case his father. By structuring his essay "Master of Machines" around images and scenes of his father at work making tortillas, or *trying* to make tortillas, Rivas is able to focus his analysis on a concrete element of his father's personality, omitting anything not related to his job. As Rivas grapples with his father's preoccupation with his tortilla-making machine, his subsequent failures as a businessman, and his struggles with his deteriorating marriage and health, the author continually returns to the essay's driving question: Why were the rest of Rivas's family members able to better themselves, while his father—despite a tremendous work ethic—seemed unable to do so? Had Rivas not structured his essay around those images of his father at work, he wouldn't have hit upon the central analogy between his father's talent for fixing machines and his helplessness when it came to fixing his marriage, his body, or his life. This reflection, in large part, is what gives the essay depth and complexity.

For a profile—or any essay—to truly succeed, it must go beyond a mere description of the subject to say something meaningful about the world, to give readers a new way of seeing. Though "Master of Machines" is principally about Rivas's father's failures as a businessman, the essay is also about social class. In particular, it exposes the myth of the American Dream—that all you have to do to succeed is work hard. More important, the essay explores the ways in which work *defines us* as human beings, how integral work is to our sense of self. This is why the essay has significance and matters.

The intersecting themes of work and identity are also at the center of Caitlin Flanagan's "To Hell With All That." By looking at the way her mother's decision to go back to work affected her as a girl, Flanagan is prompted to examine her feelings about mothers who work outside the home, stay-at-home mothers, and modern-day parenting. By comparing the way her mother approached her job as a medical-claims adjustor and then a nurse with her own attitudes toward work and childrearing, the author is able to articulate some of her own anxieties about motherhood and to consider how her generation negotiates the tension between family and career.

Adding Your Voice

Find a photo that shows you interacting with someone with whom you have a complicated relationship. Examine the photo closely. Do you notice anything you hadn't noticed before? Where was the photo taken? On what occasion? What does the photo remind you of? What *isn't* in the photo? Freewrite about the ways in which this photo is emblematic of (or deceptive about) your relationship with this person. Imagine that a stranger had found this photo on the sidewalk. What could the stranger never know about this individual and how he or she has affected your life? Narrate for us what is not visible in the photo. Let us in behind the scenes.

Tamar Adler

SIBLING RIVALRY AT THE STOVE

My brother and I grew up in a household rich with meals: our mother's hands reeked of garlic in an inside-the-veins way. Our lunches weren't like our friends'. Every day we watched quizzically while they bit into soft bread filled with floppy disks of pink meat, garish mustard, waxy squares of cheese, then unpacked our own heavily seeded sesame semolina rolls dripping with oily roasted eggplant and smoked mozzarella. We sheepishly offered around crunchy fried chickpeas and hard olives, whose pits we'd suck on through class.

We became cooks without realizing it. My brother says it happened for him one night when my mother baked him brownies to mollify an especially heartbreaking moment in adolescence. He wrote me about them recently. They were "rich, dense with a double dose of chocolate in chips and batter; a single bite causing the following series of reactions: eyes widening, slight, blush-inducing moans beginning, a smile developing, finishing with the inevitable, 'Oh my god.'" He is that dramatic about all food.

I have been a cook since I received a birthday present of glass beakers painted lightly with the names of spices: turmeric, African bird pepper, cardamom, each filled with a mysterious powder.

When I was twenty-five, an editor at a magazine, a *cri de coeur* rose from somewhere inside me: the spice filled beakers, the deep pleasure I felt at the evening energy humming from my favorite restaurant, which I walked by each day: they were what I longed for. I got an unpaid part-time job cooking there, hiding it from my fellow editors.

As soon as my brother heard the news, he snapped: after years trailing behind me through elementary, middle, and high school, always chilled by what he by cooking professionally, I had trespassed onto the sovereign territory to which he had secretly laid claim. Tightly called my "intellectual shadow," he decided that by cooking professionally I had trespassed onto the sovereign territory to which he had secretly laid claim.

And we were off.

He got a job as a line cook at the only good restaurant in our hometown of Pleasantville, NY. Enraged at my intrusion, he'd walked into the restaurant, resumé full of accomplishments like "student body president," "fraternity treasurer," "stage-manager, numerous student productions," and made an argument like the one I'd made to the chef who let me into her kitchen. Because small town kitchens are different from big city ones, he wasn't offered a tentative weekend job, but an oily chef's coat, a pair of ugly hounds-tooth pants, and a grueling work schedule.

The early battles were pure sibling predictability. I didn't *know* anything, but I had lived longer and cooked at a better-known restaurant. I am stubborn and utterly sure I'm right. Our contests pitted my mistrust of him against whatever he did, no matter how legitimate his experience. I watched him like a hawk. I embarrassedly recall the holiday meal we grandly offered to cook for my mother and her husband in the little apartment where they were living while repairs were done on our childhood home. I had chosen it from a magazine: fillets of sea bass with *cippollini* onions *agrodolce*.

My brother and I each took our places and heated our pans. He let his get smoking hot. I observed his machismo and felt superior about my more moderate approach. I added a thin stream of oil to my delicately warm pan. He told me to wait. I imperiously told him I knew what I was doing. I added a fillet of fish, which settled in calmly. He turned red and waited and heated and waited for an eternal minute before oiling his pan and adding his fish, whose middle threatened to buckle in an ugly way the instant it felt heat and had to be subdued with a spatula.

When it was the time to flip our fishes, I nudged my pan, expecting a whisper of an arc as my fillet gracefully turned itself over. When it didn't budge, I nudged harder. Then I tried nudging with a spatula. When that didn't work I began to press and scrape frantically. It still stuck, and I eventually gave up and turned broken pieces of sad, white fillet over, even more pathetically using my fingers.

Out of the corner of my eye I watched John tap his pan and his crisp-skinned fish obediently upend itself. I stalked around while he cooked the rest of the fish. We all sat down to eat. I hid my homely, broken fillets under dark onions. Everyone marveled at the gloriously browned bass skin. My brother and I eyed each other coolly over our plates. Point, John.

We got older. Our cooking plodded ahead. I followed my college roommate to Georgia where friends of ours wanted a restaurant attached to their farm, and we were to be chefs. My brother stayed in New York and moved slowly up the ladder at Blue Hill at Stone Barns. I tenuously ruled a kitchen of tattooed Southern teenagers who called me "ma'am," grabbed heavy pots out of my hands against my protests, and ignored everything I said.

Each day I cooked with the sole purpose of maintaining my authority. Each day my brother relinquished more of his.

Our divide created strange, if occasionally delicious, meals. I flew home every few months and in a flurry cooked great, salty, buttery pots of grits, ignoring any objections my family dared make. I made quarts of sugary jam, mouth-puckering pickled okra and chilies, remanded any ingredient in my sightlines to a smoker. I made mayonnaise in a blender, drank soda out of plastic quart containers, strutted around the kitchen, displaying my burns.

My brother insisted on staying clean and straight in a white chef's coat and apron on the hot Saturdays we managed to both be in our home kitchen. For an easy family dinner, he'd first steep garlic cloves in a shallow pot of olive oil and cook them at a bare murmur until they were soft; he'd maintain that it was absolutely imperative to cook onions in duck fat until they were a single teaspoon of sweet, sticky, rich onion confit; then he'd make a fennel stock with a sachet of herbs, straining it and cooking it again. Two hours into his preparations, aromatic confits and fortified fennel stock in hand, he would retie his apron, wipe down his cutting board, and feel ready to cook.

We were considerate and civil. He admired my power; I was impressed by his skill. When I was in a terrible mess over having to butcher and prepare 70 ducks for a fancy dinner in Georgia, he flew to teach me. Each week, I sat on the phone with him late into the night reassuring him that if I could do one soul-crushing, back-breaking service after another, he could, too. We regarded each other across our mother's kitchen island: he wondering at my authoritative pickles, I intrigued by the submissive decorum of his fennel tian. It was an era of amicable draws. We'd not think too hard about it, and go wash our knives.

Then, our détente broke. John spent three months cooking at Arzac in Spain, St. John in London, *Le Manoir aux Quat' Saisons* in Oxford. I moved from Georgia to California to cook at Chez Panisse. John returned and quickly got a job cooking at Per Se.

At Per Se, the universe's contents were uniform; survival meant being able to measure existence in precise, replicable shapes. Berated for having trouble creating Balsamic dots that decreased proportionally in size and distance, he spent days off alone in his home kitchen, reducing two gallons of Balsamic vinegar to a syrup then solemnly dotting his roommate's mismatched plates. Daily, as though gravity itself hinged on it, he wrestled ingredients into tiny perfect cubes.

On the West Coast, cooking was a spinning top; the universe a tilted gyroscope. I cut vegetables and meat directly on huge wooden cutting blocks. Measuring was contemptuous, uniformity prosaic. Our ladles were mismatched, and too small or too big. Unpredictability was the soul of true cooking, so we forgot our towels' places, decided we didn't like aprons, cooked directly in deep fireplaces and ended up smudged with coal.

My brother came to visit me in Berkeley. We planned to cook a dinner party for a group of my friends, chefs he respected from the area. I assured him it was just a few people. I assured him we had enough food. I mocked him for wanting to stop drinking beer and make lists. When we took inventory a few hours before the dinner was scheduled to start, our booty looked perfectly reasonable to me and catastrophic to him.

We had two pounds of grits, three packages of ground pork, one of spare ribs, a few frozen sausages and the fat from a cured pig shoulder. We had ten pounds of green tomatoes, good garlic, and a garden full of kale and Swiss chard. I was cheerful and triumphant. We could make grits and pork ragu of all the different cuts, and griddled green tomatoes, and sautéed greens. There wasn't exactly enough of anything, but I was sanguine. I knew I could muddle my way toward dinner and end up with something delicious, certainly. My brother saw things differently.

He refused to participate. This wasn't cooking. He fumed. He stomped. He huffed. Then he stopped talking to me altogether and began to punctiliously brunoise green tomatoes. He salted them. Then he drained them. Then he drizzled them with white wine vinegar. Then he sifted and drained them. Then he let them sit. I realized, suddenly, that he was going to make me cook the rest of the meal alone, and I scrambled to brown meat, cook grits, stem greens. He ignored me, daintily stirring his pickles occasionally.

Eighteen of us: chefs and their children, housemates that wandered in, sat down late to a Sunday supper of grits and pork and pickles. Everyone loved the grits and the long table. Everyone loved the pickles. The joy of dinner was muzzled, though, marred by something we'd learned and now couldn't shake. Neither of us thought the other could cook. My brother thought I was careless. I thought he was a prig.

I flew back east for a holiday. We cooked in unpalatable doubt. Dinners were stilted and cold. John did preposterous things to beets: he picked them for identical size, then scrubbed them, peeled them, blanched them, braised them, seasoning the oil he used with garlic and herbs, then straining both out, cooking everything covered in parchment paper. I made a big fuss of imagining I was acting on vegetables' behalf. I never washed anything well: what wasn't overwrought was gritty. John went in for gilded architectural masterpieces. I served anything I could raw.

But maybe I'm not telling the story correctly.

Our cooking is probably a story of two people withdrawing from rage. When we were fifteen and eleven, after six terrible months of illness, our father died, and our house and table emptied. I am sure our meals were still good, but there were fewer guests. My mother's oily eggplant sandwiches tasted sodden. I stopped eating lunch altogether. My brother became insatiable. Our appetites warped by empty, searing rage.

Maybe the rage of loss drove us each to cook as we did, as if we had no choice and each of us like ourselves and not at all like the other.

For the two years I was at Chez Panisse and John at Per Se, the food we cooked, which seemed to work fine for each of us alone, was terrible when we came together. Mutual doubt bred mistakes. Mistakes bred doubt. We botched and bungled. The kitchen could clearly only hold one of us; the other would sit outside and gloat. I would innocently lament to my mother how unfortunate it was that John had been cooking so long and still not become truly excellent. She would sigh, turn a page of her magazine, and assure me that he was excellent. I don't know what John said about me. The gist was evident. If he convened the menu and prep meetings that in our house stand in for deciding what to eat for dinner, I would be coldly assigned washing lettuce, then table-setting.

Then, one Thanksgiving, our mother got sick and requested that John and I cook a small dinner at home.

He had left the tense pantomime of Per Se a few months earlier. When that subdued Thanksgiving rolled around, John was already sous chef of a rustic Brooklyn restaurant called Franny's where he cooked in a big deep oven with a live fire. I'd come back to New York to write a book about home cooking. I had spent weeks of research flipping through recipes from an earlier time, among which were quaint, lovely ones, like "Crème Vichyssoise with sizzled baby leeks and buckwheat blini" that had, along with African bird pepper, pulled me toward the living, perishable world of the kitchen.

Worried more about my mother than about who cooked the beets, we haltingly began negotiations.

We spoke gingerly, all discussion hypothetical. One of us: "I might do halved eggs with anchovies to start. I don't know, just cook them until the whites are set and halve them, and sprinkle them with a little crunchy salt, olive oil, then an anchovy filet. But what do you think?" The other, timidly: "Parsley?" "Yes." "With a few pickled onions?" Then a brave question: "Pickled in brine, or just soaked in vinegar?" And then—because even the tiniest confidence breeds as much and as fertilely as doubt—the respondent would reply and mean: "Either way."

That first meal was good. We complimented each other unceasingly. We took photographs of each of us clowning in front of the stove. My blowing kisses to his herby fingerling potatoes, his salivating over my buttery roast chicken. The relief made us giddy.

But maybe I'm telling it incorrectly again.

Our mother's illness was discomforting but not terrible. It's probably simple. John's thinking about food now involved mandatory disorder. Mine included a recognition of the necessity, in certain circumstances—like making blini—of precision. In his new, esteemed position as sous chef, he had nothing to prove; contented to be writing the book I'd always dreamed of, neither did I. We had done what children who share mourning do as over time their rage breathes life into their passions. We'd grown together. And grown up.

—2011

Learning from Other Writers (Adler)

1. Adler documents the exact moments when she and her brother became chefs: for him, the night their mother baked him brownies "to mollify an especially heartbreaking moment in adolescence"; for her, the birthday present she received of "glass beakers painted lightly with the names of spices." How does this initial comparison help to characterize the different approaches to cooking the author and her brother eventually take? Where else in the text do you see examples of this dichotomy?

2. What is the "essence" of Adler's brother as she portrays him in this essay?

3. When the author's brother visits her in Berkeley, they are supposed to cook together for a dinner party. Yet once he arrives and sees what she has planned (or, more accurately, has *not* planned), he refuses to participate. To her brother, what she is doing isn't "cooking." Why not? How does this example deepen the analysis of this essay? What is illuminated?

4. In several places, Adler speaks directly to the reader (or perhaps to herself), saying, "But maybe I'm not telling the story correctly," and: "But maybe I'm telling it incorrectly again." How do these statements affect your reading of the essay? What would the essay lose without them?

5. What is the effect of Adler's revelation that her father is dead? Why might she have chosen to wait to reveal this fact until she is more than three-quarters of the way through the essay, even though her father actually died when she and her brother were children? And how does this revelation change the way you view the author's rivalry with her brother?

Daniel Rivas

THE MASTER OF MACHINES

This was my father: he turns on the gas, lights his paper-sack torch, and carries it to the six-foot-long tub where he cooks corn. Leaves of glowing ash abscise behind him as he extends the torch toward the rows of burners, a rush of air preceding the blue flames. I warm myself there—the mornings were cold, even in summer—careful not to get too close, while he stirs with a lime-crusted two-by-four.

He dips a metal basket deep into the tub with his bare hand. Most of the small squares of the once-porous sieve are filled with petrified kernels (to extract them would require a good hammer, chisel, and at least an hour). He has to shake it a few times to get most of the water out, but even then, corn juice runs down his arm and onto the floor as he carries the basket to the stainless-steel grinder that conceals a stone wheel at its centre. From the ceiling hangs a thin black hose that drops a dribbling stream of water into the grinder to give the ground corn the right consistency. Almost instantly, golden flecks begin clinging to the sides of a rectangular steel bin, and within moments, those flecks become sticky lumps, then one mass—*masa*. The cavernous *tortilleta* begins to fill with a bodily smell I sometimes encounter in alleys after rain or on towels left wet on the bathroom floor.

While masa collects in viscid lumps, he prepares the machines. He lights the oven first, again taking up his paper torch; a thousand tiny flames pop into being, glow blue in neat rows. The conveyor squeaks into motion.

Masa goes into the wide-open top of the machine that slowly metes it out in the shape of a fan, my father reaching up and into the mouth to help push masa through to the two rolling presses that flatten it before it reaches the die that cuts either oblong tortillas or chips.

Through the oven, over and through again, the tortillas cook three times before they emerge the colour and texture of baked sand. They travel again on another conveyor—fifty feet long and canted up and at a right angle to the oven—cooling as they bounce left to right, right to left, back again; the purpose is to take them a long way but not far, like the lines at Disneyland. And when they become cool enough to touch, I wait with the women who count tortillas with practised speed, then bag the stack to start again.

It has been more than eleven years since this ritual ended, since my father's factory closed. It feels like the end of a particular history, one both uniquely American and outside of America's vision.

With seven hundred dollars and a house full of working children, my grandparents left the ghettos of Denver, the fields of Greeley, Toppenish, and the Skagit Valley behind and opened the Mexico Cafe in 1965. It was the first Mexican restaurant in northwestern Washington State. Within a few years, my grandfather decided they needed to make their own tortillas because those from El Ranchito in Toppenish often arrived mouldy after a long journey across the Cascades in the warm belly of a Greyhound bus. In the late sixties, my father and grandfather went down to California where they bought a tub to cook corn, a grinder, an oven, and a conveyor belt and brought them back to the long, cinder-block building beside my grandmother's house.

For more than twenty years, my father made tortillas, at first with his father, who could never cook the corn right, then alone, as a business after his father died of a heart attack in 1970. My parents met in the restaurant. My mother was a cook. In April of 1978, they eloped to Hawaii—the only way my mother's Pentecostal Christian parents would allow her to marry this Mexican man who was twelve years her senior and who did not even go to church. In 1981, my father built a large yellow house on a mound of fill dirt in the middle of a field used to grow hay and test motorcycles. My grandmother died in 1988 and made my uncle Adolph, who still runs the restaurant, the sole owner.

In 1992, when I was in eighth grade, health inspectors closed the tortilleta. My father blamed the dinginess of the building and the ignorance of the inspectors, and for the next month or two, drove my mother, sister, and me past a number of buildings for lease, none of which he could afford and none of which had the proper drainage. Soon after, he suffered a cerebral hemorrhage—a stroke—the first in a litany of illness and loss I cannot help but confuse in number and sequence: heart attack (maybe two), broken left foot, house sold due to bankruptcy, amputated right foot, diabetes.

My mother took care of him as best she could, but once he began to ease into the convalescent life, and she could think of herself again, she wanted out. By my own estimate, it took her five years and another man before she found the courage to leave him.

My sister and I were made to work in our father's factory. We were poor workers and hated the place. In fog or darkness, we pulled on clothes we could dirty and followed slowly behind our mother who was always late to work but who usually would drop us off at the tortilleta on her way.

We did not earn money, but we did earn school clothes and maybe a week-long sports camp—baseball for me, tennis for my sister—though clothes and camps were not why we were there. My father and his machines were our babysitters when school was not in session because real babysitters were often too expensive. We viewed the place as a kind of prison complex with a work element. My sister would sit obstinate, refusing to count or stack, playing instead with whatever she could find, which was not much: a pen, her hair, the flaps on a cardboard box. Though I worked harder, I would sometimes escape for long stretches, walking around the imposing concrete box that also housed a cheese factory and Skagit Valley Hospital's laundry services.

This was my father: he can leave the machines only for a few moments; too often they break down when he is on a delivery or errand, and there is no one to fix them until he returns. He comes out looking for me, and when he finds me, says, "*Get* in there," a broad, forceful sweep of his arm gesturing toward the "in," the "there." He hurries back, and I follow, the noise of the creaking machines echoing so loudly between those concrete walls that a stranger might think some kind of doomsday device were housed within. It is nearly impossible to speak to him, even if he is near. By the time I enter the factory, he is already feeding the masa into the die, his whole arm deep within the mouth of the machine.

He learned early in life that machines could be a living. His father used to take him and his brother Frankie out in their Ford pickup to collect newspapers, bottles, and scrap metal. But the real treasures, for they were rare and infinitely valuable, were the machines they would find or be given by white people who enjoyed charity. They once salvaged an 8 mm projector and reels of cartoons. They found or received Victrolas, toasters, radios, and cameras, which they spent their afternoons fixing. My grandfather taught his son, my father, to see the worth in old, broken, or disused objects.

My father still collected machines when I was a kid, though he had little time or need for them by then. We had a pachinko machine my father had picked up at some swap meet or flea market; the launching device never worked right, so my sister and I used to roll the metal balls across the basement floor or stick them up our noses. He had a Rototiller, automatic garage door, chainsaw, cars no one drove because they were broken—a Mazda RX-7 and at least one van in addition to the two or three my mother and father did drive—four-wheel motorcycle, hydraulic jack, rock polisher, electric sander. In the house my father built, he installed the infrastructure for a central vacuuming system and windows that cranked open.

My father's machines were always a source of conflict between him and my mother. She found the machines unsightly and useless, especially when they were in the yard or at the side of the house. Even in the years when I was young and they seemed happy, his machines were driving them apart.

Now that he is alone, the lessons he learned from his junk-man father keep him going still. He makes furniture from salvaged wood. Garage sales and handiwork helped him fill his house with appliances after my mother left. He recently received a broken-down Dodge van for free and fixed it, drives it now nearly every day.

Once, my father brought home a gigantic piece of blue canvas and laid it out along the wide stretch of sloping lawn at the side of the house. I remember puzzling over this stretch of fabric, walking on it and finding frogs in the pools that gathered in its thick folds after the rain. I had no concept of it until my father attached a fan and I watched it grow, shedding the water and frogs slowly, like a resurfacing submarine. When it was full of air, my sister and I unzipped the doorway and ran around in the breezy half-light feeling a sense of space and freedom we had never felt when this patch of grass had been surrounded by open air. It was for a swimming pool, he told us. We knew he did not mean *our* swimming pool, but a hypothetical pool, the purpose for this invention. Where it went I'm not certain, probably to the soggy field behind my uncle Steve's tool repair shop, but what remained for months afterwards was a long rectangle of mud and yellow grass.

In the time between the closing of my father's tortilla factory and the beginning of his litany of illness, he and I alone moved iron and steel. Though he had nowhere to take them, no factory where he could begin anew, his machines had to go. We used jacks, dollies, and hand trucks to get each one, piece by piece, onto the box truck he used for deliveries. Conveyor belts; ovens; grinder with stone wheel; the vacuum sealer I used to run just to hear the release of air, just to see the bags seize instantly; mixer with hooked arm to knead flour tortilla dough; machine to roll the dough into balls to be flattened and stretched; fryer for chips—we wheeled them out, a procession of now useless parts.

My father tested my strength and my trust in him. He rigged a series of cranks and pulleys, suspended these tons of metal, then swung them into the truck, easing them down. We drove them over to the site of the first tortilleta, a decaying, rat-infested building. The machines that had been there before, returned. The newer machines, the ones that my father had made payments on for years and that had forced him to declare bankruptcy, joined them. It became a machine cemetery. And like gravestones in remote cemeteries of former mill or gold-rush towns, my father's machines were forgotten and left to nature. Grasses grew tall around the building, obscuring entrances and glassless windows. Weeds sprouted on the mossy roof and inside, between the cracks. Pigeon or crow shit encrusted every surface. Owl pellets mixed among the dust. Rats nested in the belly of the oven and finches lodged in the exhaust pipe. Spiders saw infinite points of connection and wove long filaments.

During my junior or senior year of high school, he took me again to that weather-beaten shed, cleared the grass and weeds, and began scrubbing the machines clean. He said someone wanted to buy them and he had to get them ready. It took him weeks before he could get the masa right, keep the tortillas from falling apart. He made a batch and I ate one. It had a hollow, dirty aftertaste, but I told him it was good. I do not know what happened to that buyer. The machines were not sold.

"Jack of all trades, master of none," my father says about the handiwork he does to get by. Yet, he did know tortillas and the machines that made them. Of these alone, he was a master. His father sloughed off the responsibility soon after they started the factory, left it for my father, who came home from Weyerhaeuser after an eight-hour shift to nap until Adolph and Natalie—his youngest brother and niece—came home from school to stack and bag tortillas. Sometimes, when the machines were not running well, the kids would go inside to sleep or do homework, and my father would be left alone to make sure the corn had been cooked, ground, pressed flat, cut, and baked. He'd stay alone all night if he had to. In a short time, he built a business that delivered tortillas as far south as Tacoma and as far north as Vancouver, British Columbia.

I'm sure my father felt gratitude that the tortilleta was his own, but now he tells me he feels "left out." He explains it as begrudging glances he gets from Adolph's wife when he pours himself a cup of coffee or a soda in their restaurant, but I know he means to say he feels excluded from all his family's class climbing, feels left out of their collective success. While his brothers and sisters buy nice cars and pay off their homes, my father pays the mortgage on his small, poorly built tract house with his social security cheque. To pay bills and buy food, he rents out the rooms vacated by my sister and me to a young Mexican girl, who works at the restaurant, and her boyfriend, who is still in high school. My father spends his mornings and afternoons at the restaurant, putting chips into baskets for the bus kids, unpacking groceries from Food Service, or fixing the cooler or the plumbing, not only for the few dollars my uncle gives him, but also because he has no other way to fill his day, no job to go to. When I am back home, and we arrange to meet for lunch, I usually find him sitting at one of the tables off to the side where he can watch the customers come and go.

This is my father:

- *Hey Daaaan-el. How are things? Okay? How's school?*

- *I'm thinking about opening up a Mexican deli. All prepared stuff. For lunch, you know. And then we'll sell tortillas, fresh. There are a lot of Mexican people. I think it would be real good.*

- *Hey, I think I got someone to buy those machines. We're going to be partners.*

- *You know those machines, well this guy who lives across the street has a brother who's interested.*

- *I'm going to open up a little carneceria like in Mexico and then we'll sell corn tortillas too.*

- *Hey, I'm going to take those chip bins over to El Cazador. The owner maybe wants to buy one.*

Over the years, I have heard too many of his plans to distinguish one from another. He waffles between going into business again for himself and selling the machines with the stipulation that he be hired to run them, at least for a while. His plans always include the machines, which is practical in its way. In a very real sense, these machines are all the capital he has. He cannot lend his body—two bad feet, a bad heart, too much weight—to Weyerhaeuser or Norm Nelson Potatoes the way he did when he was young, the way the men of his generation were taught to do. Nor can he conjure money out of the capital of his mind in offices the way men who have been to college seem able to do. Yet, I cannot help but think the machines are about something more.

Even when machines are mysterious, when they won't run, if you continue to turn bolts, disassemble parts, grease or oil what ought to move, tighten what ought to remain firm, if you replace what is broken with a part, new or refurbished, then you can continue as before; and if the machine runs well, you will soon forget it was ever broken.

Much that has happened to my father must seem to him to be out of his control. Of course, he did have some control, and in fact, his doctors, family, my mother, and even I have placed most of the blame on him, on his inattention to sanitation, his wilful ignorance of his own health, his stubbornly bad business sense, and his worka-holism. But my father sees different causes. To him, a bureaucracy closed his business; a stroke kept him from working and caused him to lose his tortilleta and the home he had built; diabetes, a disease, took his foot; all this and more caused my mother to leave, caused his loneliness. Infirmity and poverty have excluded him from climbing in class as his brothers and sisters have done. He feels helpless.

Life is not a machine. It cannot be fixed. He knows this better than I do, yet he still believes in machines. He believes in the power of machines to save him—*deus ex machina* descending to put his life improbably back in order.

Until recently, my father has relied most heavily on his prosthetic foot. It is a simple machine—hard plastic shin, Velcro straps to keep it tight around the bulbous nub where his leg ends, a joint where two plastics meet to form an ankle. The doctors at the VA hospital in Seattle have put him in a purple cast because his foot does not fit well. After a long day of walking or standing, he always has a bloody sore where flesh and plastic meet. The cast embarrasses him because now it is plain to everyone that he is missing this part. The doctors have advised him that if the sores do not heal, they will have to amputate a few more inches. They tell him that after the procedure, he would have a newer, more flexible limb. He is not convinced.

"Those doctors," he says to me as I drive him out of the parking lot. "They cut off a little, then a little more, pretty soon they want the whole leg. They don't know when to stop."

After I return to school, I call him and ask about his foot. "It's just about healed," he tells me. "I've only got a little bit left. And when it heals I can get that business started."

He says no more about the business or his machines, and I don't ask. A few minutes later, he asks if I have heard from my mother. I tell him no.

"I sometimes think about her. ... It's a sad thing being alone," he says.

I sit in silence. I want so badly to find the words, but nothing comes to me. Instead I retreat into imagination. I know he will likely never run another business, will likely end his days as he began them—with nothing to his name but family. And for this reason, I decide to believe with him in the power of machines to save him. I forget his infirmities, his trouble managing a business, the rusty volatility of his machines, and think only of him examining the tortillas on two good feet, running things again, the master of machines.

—2004

Learning from Other Writers (Rivas)

1. What is the effect of Rivas's decision to begin his portrait with a description of his father making tortillas? How does the use of the present tense affect the scene?

2. How do you interpret the author's statement that the tortilla-making ritual feels to him "like the end of a particular history, one both uniquely American and outside of America's vision"?

3. What details from his family's history does Rivas choose to include in the second main movement of the essay? Why these details and not others?

4. At what point does the author seem to understand the driving question at the heart of this portrait? Highlight his closing meditations on this question. If the author seems to discover his true question only toward the end of his portrait, how do you think he managed to produce such a coherent and well-organized essay?

5. Just as Andre Dubus III chooses to end "Tracks and Ties" with an image of his dead friend from an earlier and happier time, Rivas ends his essay with an image of his father at work: "... I decide to believe with him in the power of machines to save him. I forget his infirmities, his trouble managing a business, the rusty volatility of his machines, and think only of him examining the tortillas on two good feet, running things again, the master of machines." Compare the endings of these two essays.

By Caitlin Flanagan

TO HELL WITH ALL THAT

Throughout my childhood, the thirty-five-cent Cardinal edition of Dr. Spock sat on a kitchen counter beside another font of domestic good counsel, "The Settlement Cookbook." The books have fallen into my hands now, their spines mended with tape, their pages buckling with age. The two homely volumes (decommissioned and reclassified as mementos) are capable of a profound act of evocation: of my mother, certainly, but more powerfully of the qualities she embodied for me—competence, benevolence, calm authority. To be a child with a mother who possessed those two books and the cheerful willingness to follow their practical and time-honored suggestions was to live in a world that seems to me now a bygone age, as remote and unrecoverable as Camelot: a world of good meals turned out in orderly fashion, of fevers cooled without a single frantic call to the pediatrician, of clothes mended and pressed back into useful service rather than discarded to the rag heap as soon as a button pops or a sleeve unravels. If a household is a tiny state, as of course it is, then my mother was the potentate of ours—her command unchallenged—although our fealty was rarely vociferous. (If, while wandering through the kitchen, I caught sight of her cooking dinner, I would not have taken any more note of her than I did of the humming refrigerator or the shining toaster; it was her absences I noticed, but she was not often absent.) Her subjects were assured of safety, continuity, comfort of the highest order. God was in his heaven, and a rump roast was in the oven, seasoned with salt, pepper, and ginger, and basted with fat from the pan.

This was before housewifery was understood to be an inherently oppressive state, before a marriage soured was a marriage abandoned; this was in the time when thrift and economy were still the cornerstones of middle-class American life. It was a rare night that the family ate dinner at a restaurant; "convenience" foods consisted of Swanson frozen dinners, their aluminum trays saved for all eternity (for mixing up four colors of poster paint for a bored child; for catching a drip from a leaking roof). They were called TV dinners then, but in my experience they were not eaten in front of the television. They were eaten—convivially and with gusto—in the dining room of our California home, with placemats, folded napkins, glasses to the right of knives. In my childish apprehension of things, my father was happiest when he was sitting in his armchair reading a big, fat book, and my mother when she was standing at her ironing board transforming a chaotic basket of wash into a set of sleek and polished garments.

Which is why it came as such a shock when my mother suddenly pulled the plug on the whole operation. It was 1973; I was twelve. The story, as she always told it: One morning, she cooked breakfast for my father and me and sent us on our way (a scramble for lunchbox and briefcase, the daily struggle to get my hair brushed and braided, two sets of feet stumping down the front steps, and then—quiet). The morning was hers, and she had big plans for it. She filled a basin with warm, soapy water, set it on the utility ledge of the kitchen stepladder, and climbed up. Her intention was to wash down the wallpaper, of which she was rather fond (it had a cheerful blue-and-white pattern with a Dutch motif; she had hung it herself). But as she stood on the ladder, dripping sponge in hand, something happened. In one clear moment, staring at a little windmill or a tiny Dutch girl, she realized that it was no longer possible for her to go on living that particular life. I would have been just arriving at school; my father would have been getting off the bus at the bottom of Euclid Avenue, headed for the English department and his morning class. The fogs and mists that settle on the Berkeley Hills every night would have been just lifting when my mother threw the sponge back in the basin and said—out loud, to no one but herself, and apparently with finality—"To hell with it." And then she climbed off the ladder.

It must have been a bleak moment. She would have sat down at the kitchen table and lit a cigarette with trembling hands. Whiskey, the wirehaired terrier, would have been hovering solicitously close by, confused by the outburst. And all the while she would have been looking around the homey little kitchen—my favorite room of the house! location of bacon sandwiches and homemade root beer and apple betties, warm from the oven—and suddenly seeing it for what it was: the center of her working life. The place where she turned out meal after meal and washed the same dishes and pots over and over again, and waited around, with her books and her cigarettes, for everyone to come home.

She was a person on whom history tended to operate in broad strokes and with enduring effect. The impulses of her Depression-era childhood never left her, even later in life when there was no longer any reason to cut corners. She possessed the sense of civic responsibility and personal fortitude of many people who were young during the Second World War. And on that day in the kitchen a third historical force was at work on her. If an inchoate cultural movement can sweep down into one woman's kitchen and put words to feelings, the words of this one were "To hell with it!"

But—to hell with *what*, exactly? This was the question that plagued me for many unhappy months after the step-ladder resolution. Suffice it to say, to hell with the demoralizing nature of make-work cleaning projects—hadn't Betty Friedan aptly entitled a chapter of "The Feminine Mystique" "Housewifery Expands to Fill the Time Available"? And to hell with wasting her education: Hadn't she sailed through nursing school on a sea of A's? Wasn't she still consulted about ailments and remedies by half the people she knew? She was not willing to say to hell with her marriage, which was of the volatile but imperishable variety. But as for cheerily bustling around the kitchen while the union endured one of the dreary interludes that often attend the halfway mark—to hell with that, too. If she had lived in another time or place, certain solutions to these familiar and perhaps inevitable discontents might have presented themselves. She might have hosted faculty-wife teas or read *Middlemarch* or taken up watercolor. But my mother climbed off that stepladder during a moment when there was a single panacea for what ailed her: work. "A no-nonsense nine-to-five job" was what Betty Friedan recommended, and that was what my mother got.

It had been nearly twenty years since she'd worked in a doctor's office, and she was nervous about going back to nursing after such a long time. But a health-insurance company in San Francisco hired her as a medical-claims adjuster. She bought some drip-dry pants suits and half a dozen Ship 'n Shore blouses in pretty colors; she bought a BART commuter ticket and studied the route map. The Sunday afternoon before she started, she went into the kitchen and made five casseroles and stacked them in the freezer. She left defrosting instructions under a magnet on the refrigerator door, and when I got up on Monday morning she was gone.

Almost as soon as my mother began working, she cheered up. The sulks that had so often descended upon her lifted miraculously. (Wretched little egomaniac that I was, I hadn't taken any note of them until they vanished.) The other members of the family were more or less untroubled by her transformation from housewife to working woman. My sister was away at college and had no opinion about it, and my father was the last person to squelch a money-making scheme (not that he saw any of the cash; the pin money went toward trips to Disneyland and carpet tiles for the sun porch and new clothes and shoes all around). I was miserable. To my thinking, my mother's change of heart constituted child abandonment, plain and simple. "Being home alone is a stressful experience for children," David Elkind, the author of the 1981 book *The Hurried Child*, has observed, and he's dead right. Just walking through the front door each afternoon to be met by the quiet gloom of the empty living room was depressing. Not that it was easily accomplished. On my first day as a latchkey child, I lost the key. Another key was hidden under a stone for me, but I used it once and forgot to return it, and it vanished. Frustrated, my mother tied a third key on a thick white string and hung it around my neck, a weighty reminder that I'd been dumped by Mom.

Afternoons alone in the house were often frightening. It did not help that I am a hysteric by nature. When Patty Hearst was kidnapped across town, I became convinced that I was next. We had so much in common—pale skin and brown hair, terry-cloth bathrobes, Catholic girlhoods. That her father was one of the richest men in California and mine was a college professor with a mortgage and a car loan did not factor into my threat assessment. Still, in the early nineteen-seventies in Berkeley, there were plenty of bad things happening on a more random basis. One day, there was a knock at our front door, the top half of which was a big, swing-out window. I opened the window to two young men whose question to me (I can't now recall it) was so obviously trumped up, whose interest was so clearly in the living room beyond me, that I swung the window shut in mid-sentence and locked it. I stood watching from behind a curtain as they made their way up the street, knocking on doors and peering through windows. I reported the incident to my parents, who advised me not to let my imagination run wild.

My terror of kidnappers and burglars eventually reached such a pitch that my mother—who by then had left the insurance company and returned to nursing, taking a job at a convalescent hospital—arrived at a novel solution to the problem, a kind of one-woman Take Our Daughters to Work Day. She bought a couple of yards of blue-and-white ticking, ran up a candy-striper uniform on the sewing machine, and introduced me, at age thirteen, to a career in the health-care industry. In lieu of a lunch hour, she would leave the hospital at three o'clock, pick me up from school, and take us both back to work to finish the shift. I would change out of my school uniform into my work clothes and spend the rest of the afternoon officiously copying chart headings, wheeling patients around the facility (a courtesy they tended to endure rather than appreciate), and making an endless series of tongue-depressor houses and cotton-ball bunnies in the dayroom, where I was encouraged in my work by the young, friendly occupational therapist.

I did not last in my new post. I would grow bored long before quitting time, and it was hard for my mother to do her job and also put up with my pestering suggestions that we knock off early and swing by McDonald's for shakes. And eventually she took a better job, at a hospital in Oakland, which was too far away for her to pick me up each afternoon. Once again, I was on my own, fretting about unseen dangers while the defrosting casserole sat unappetizingly on the counter, in a puddle of melt.

No mother today who could afford to do otherwise would go to work without making any provision for her young child except to tie a key around her neck and hope for the best. My mother was by no means indifferent about me; I was her pet, the baby of the family. But children then were not under constant adult supervision, even if their mothers were housewives. By the time I was five, I was allowed to wander away from the house so long as I didn't cross any big streets; I had the run of the neighborhood at six. So the idea that I would be home alone in the afternoons at the age of twelve was not a radical or an overly worrisome one for my mother. A good friend of mine was only nine when her mother took a volunteer job and left the child on her own in the afternoons. Such an arrangement was not then seen as a shocking dereliction of duty: a nine-year-old could be trusted with a key; a nine-year-old knew how to work a telephone if anything went wrong.

Moreover, anxiety as a precondition of the maternal experience had not yet been invented. We kids were topped up with Salk vaccine, our fathers had saved the world, and our neighborhoods were chock-full of busybody housewives who delighted in scolding other people's errant children. Terrible things happened then, just as they do today. But they tended not to have the titanic significance of the contemporary event. Once, when I was in third grade, we were all given purple-and-white mimeographed letters to bring home to our mothers. The letters reported that a child molester had been preying on children walking home from the next elementary school over. "What's a child molester?" I kept asking my mother, who stood in the kitchen reading the letter in a concerned way. That was not for me to know—but neither was it sufficient cause for my mother to forbid me to roam the neighborhood after school. I should just "be careful." ("Careful of what?" Just careful.) My mother and her friends probably would not have made a best-seller of "The Lovely Bones."

At age twelve, I wasn't doing much that required my mother's presence. The notion that after-school hours might constitute prime time for improvement—athletic, academic, social, psychiatric—was still years away. When I think of what it was like to be a girl then, I remember an endless series of afternoons, each an ungraspable piece of time. I watched television, and hurtled perilously down our steep block on my Schwinn, and dressed the cats in baby clothes. Children didn't have "passions" and "talents"; we had hobbies and collections—glass animals and plastic horses for girls, baseball cards for boys, and stamps for geeks of both genders. These were activities that required no parental involvement and produced just as little quantifiable enrichment. Why should my mother have to sulk around the kitchen, weepy with frustration, her only job to provide me with a beacon of reassurance—and to muscle off the S.L.A. if it came for me—while I wrestled the cats into pinafores and watched reruns of "Lost in Space"?

The rhetoric of liberation exhorted women to go to work not in spite of their children but—at least partly—because of them. The notion was that housewives made poor mothers. Betty Friedan reported "strange new problems" with those children "whose mothers were always there, driving them around, helping them with their homework—an inability to endure pain or discipline or pursue any self-sustained goal of any sort, a devastating boredom with life." Being on my own recognizance was supposed to toughen me up, to deliver me from my mother's crippling cosseting and vault me to new levels of independence—not an unreasonable theory. If I had had a different temperament, it might have worked. (As it is, however, I remain an inveterate loser of keys—and sunglasses and credit cards—and my anxiety about being alone in a house borders on the pathological.) In a 1970 discussion of day care, the feminists Louise Gross and Phyllis Taube Greenleaf wrote that the institution could be a means of liberating not only women but also children. For what were the tots learning at home except that it was a place of female enslavement?

My mother's tenure as a working woman was short-lived. We spent a year overseas while my father was on sabbatical—requiring my mother to give up the best job of the lot—and by the time we returned he had reinvented himself as a successful novelist, a surprising turn of events that energized and occupied them both. She was happy to accompany him on book tours and at publishing events, a combination of glamorous literary wife and girl Friday. But I always guiltily assumed that it was at least in part my whining and balking that was responsible for her giving up. She and I were exceedingly close—"enmeshed" is the term now in vogue—and although I was the only one in the household who hated my mother's job, I was also the only one who really understood what it meant to her. Like most marriages, hers traded interludes of excitement with long stretches of tedious overfamiliarity. As an adult, I have often thought of how much better off my mother would have been if she'd had a job—money of her own, power of her own—as she faced the hard times.

Thirty years later, the notion of a woman's being blindsided by the stultification of housekeeping is positively quaint—upper-middle-class women have been so thoroughly indoctrinated about the politics of housework that we can hardly scrape a dish without fuming about the inequitable distribution of domestic labor within a marriage. What surprises successive waves of women is how difficult it is to conduct family life along recognizably bourgeois lines and also maintain a career. It's even harder today than it was in my mother's era, because the modern professional-class mother is not pursuing the kind of women's work for which my mother and her friends had been trained, and to which they eventually returned: nursing and elementary-school teaching and secretarial work and the like. Those were posts that could be abandoned and returned to without a significant loss of stature, and were usually predictable in terms of hours and workload.

Today's career moms are often trying to make partner or become regional sales manager or executive editor, jobs that require a tremendous number of hours and a willingness to allow urgent appeals, via Blackberry or cell phone, to interrupt even the best-laid plans for family time. And all the while, not giving an inch, there are the women who have chosen to stay home. They've forfeited the power and autonomy of work for one reason: to insure that their children get the very best of them. And, in a hundred different ways, at-home mothers are eager to remind working mothers that they're not quite measuring up.

To call these tensions a preoccupation among the mothers I know would be to commit a grave act of understatement. Last year, I went to a fund-raiser for the Los Angeles nursery school that my twin sons attended. It was a dinner dance with an auction, and the signal items up for bid were chairs hand-painted by the members of each class, a project that had been laboriously created and supervised by an exceedingly earnest and energetic at-home mother. She was at the podium, a little flustered and flush with pride about the furniture, the decorating of which she was describing in effusive terms. Leaning against a far column watching her, with drinks in their hands and sardonic half smiles on their faces, were two of my friends: a lawyer and a movie producer. I was propelled toward them the way I was once propelled toward the cool girls in high school. And I suddenly had the bona fides to join them: my writing had recently begun to be published. We looked at the woman—think of all she'd sacrificed to stay home with her children, think of the time she'd spent dipping our own children's hands in paint so that they could press their little prints on the miniature Adirondack chairs. "Get a life," one of us said, and we all laughed and drank some more. And then we turned our backs on the auction and talked about work.

But I'm craven enough to change colors if the occasion calls for it. "Is that poor child's mother *ever* at school?" someone hissed when a (perfectly happy) little girl marched off with her nanny one recent afternoon. "I've never seen her," I clucked back, feeling guilty about knifing the absent mother and glad as hell that I hadn't sent my own nanny to pick up the boys that day.

When my children were born, six years ago, there was no question where I stood on all of this: I was certain that it was better for children—much better—if their mothers stayed home with them, and that is exactly what I did. It was a mixed experience. The emotion I felt gazing down into their bassinets was akin to romantic fervor, but I'm a woman who likes ideas and good jokes, and the poor little babies didn't seem to know any. The three of us were invited to plenty of places—to a twins-only playgroup, to a regular meeting of mothers in the park—but at the crucial moment of departure one of the boys would nod off into a sound sleep, or they would both become transfixed by the branches scraping against the living-room windows, a turn of events that only a fool would fail to recognize as a sign from God that it was time to make a nice cup of tea and have a chat on the telephone. (It was my friends from work whom I wanted to talk to, not the mothers in the park.) Slowly, the invitations dried up, and I became one of those lonely, out-of-synch mothers patrolling the streets with my enormous stroller at odd hours, ransacking my library of baby-care books for signs of lagging development or rare medical syndromes. People began to worry about me. My mother called and gently suggested that I go back to work, a remark that (needless to say) infuriated me on several levels. I wasn't going anywhere: if the last gasp of my youth was to be spent sitting on a lawn chair in a tiny back yard watching the little boys poke at things with sticks, so be it. There was only one thing about motherhood of which I was certain: these early years of my sons' lives would one day constitute my happiest memories. I was also certain that there would be a big payoff for the kids. The starting bell of the academic decathlon was about to ring: nursery school (carefully chosen, highly regarded) was around the corner. There, I naïvely assumed, the children would fall into two easily recognizable camps: the wan and neurotic kids of working mothers and the emotionally hardy, confident kids of stay-at-home moms. What a bust. There was no difference at all that I could divine—if anything, the kids of the working mothers seemed a little more on the ball. My boys (who had been slavishly catered to by besotted late-life parents) would drop their sweaters and toys on the playground and forget they existed, while their friends whose mothers worked took care of their own things, putting sweaters in cubbies, keeping track of toys and shoes. Many of the children of the working mothers marched into the classroom without a backward glance; they were used to not having their mothers beside them. They looked ready to take over the world.

In the end, what did my boys gain from those thousand days they spent with me before school took them out into the larger world? Nothing, it seems to me, of any quantifiable value—no head start in life assuring them some prize that forever eludes the children of working mothers. All they gained was an immersion in the most powerful force on earth: mother love. And perhaps there is something of worth in that alone.

Support for this opinion was readily at hand in my mother's kitchen, in the Cardinal edition of Dr. Spock. He addresses the issue of the working mother in a dire final section called "Special Problems," for in those unreconstructed days having a working mother landed you in the same luckless category as the premature baby and the handicapped child. Spock, though, was an exceptionally decent man, quick to soothe the wounds his early opinions caused. Indeed, the sixth edition of "Baby and Child Care" (which I was given when I had my children) puts the topic of combining work and family right up front, in Chapter 1, and aims it as much at Dad as at Mom. (The chapter also addresses such with-it concepts as "Men need liberating, too" and "The subordination of women is brought about by countless small acts.") But I'm not so quick to dismiss his earlier thoughts on the subject. As I read them now, in the crumbling pages of my mother's book, I find them politically radical, morally compelling, and honest.

"Some mothers *have* to work to make a living," he begins, reasonably. "It doesn't make sense to let mothers go to work making dresses in factories or tapping typewriters in offices, and have them pay other people to do a poorer job of raising their children." His solution? The government should "pay a comfortable allowance to all mothers (of young children) who would otherwise be compelled to work."

Of mothers who work for more complicated reasons, at more exalted jobs, he says this: "A few mothers, particularly those with professional training, feel they have to work because they wouldn't be happy otherwise. I wouldn't disagree if a mother felt strongly about it, provided she had an ideal arrangement for her children's care. After all, an unhappy mother can't bring up very happy children."

And then he identifies a third type: "What about the mothers who don't absolutely have to work but would prefer to, either to supplement the family income, or because they think they will be more satisfied themselves and therefore get along better at home?" His answer to this question has angered many women, but it proceeds from nothing more malevolent than absolute respect for the maternal bond: "The important thing for a mother to realize is that the younger the child the more necessary it is for him to have a steady, loving person taking care of him. In most cases, the mother is the best one to give him this feeling of 'belonging,' safely and surely. She doesn't quit on the job, she doesn't turn against him, she isn't indifferent to him.... If a mother realizes clearly how vital this kind of care is to a small child, it may make it easier for her to decide that the extra money she might earn, or the satisfaction she might receive from an outside job, is not so important after all."

What Spock could not have predicted was how many women would fall into his second category. Mothers with professional training are thick on the ground these days, and their desire to work is at once more complex and more profound than Spock imagined. A woman with an education and a desire to take part in the business of the world—someone who wants a public life even a thousandth as vital and exciting as Spock's—may not be uniquely suited to the simple routines of child care. In fact, the life of the nursery can handily diminish what is most hard-fought-for in a person. It isn't simply a matter of "extra money" or "satisfaction." For many women, the choice amounts to the terrible prospect of either relinquishing a measure of influence over their children or abandoning—to some extent—the work they love. For them, this will always be the stuff of grinding anxiety and regret.

My mother died the way Mike lost his money in *The Sun Also Rises*: very slowly and then all at once. I had been with her two weeks before, and any fool could have seen that she was near the end. But she was my mother; I thought she was going to live forever.

In the modern way, my family had a memorial service instead of a funeral. There had been heavy rain on the terrible day in the hospital, but the day of the memorial was glorious. An overflow crowd sat on wooden folding chairs in my parents' garden and ate lunch. Then everyone pressed into the living room for the speeches. People remembered the countless dinner parties my mother had thrown over the years, and also the encouragement she had given with her famous pep talks and cheery phone calls, the excursions she would plan if anybody was feeling low. Sitting on her writing desk in a corner, unnoticed and unremarked upon, was her old nursing-school portrait, which had been taken in a photographer's studio more than half a century earlier, and which she had paid for with her very first wages.

—2004

Learning from Other Writers (Flanagan)

1. In the opening paragraph of the essay, Flanagan likens her mother to a kitchen appliance. How is this comparison important to the development of the essay's theme and Flanagan's subsequent analysis of her driving question?

2. Writers often use smaller "micro questions" to propel their inquiry. What are some of the micro questions the author implicitly poses that allow her to move further into her material?

3. Unlike the other authors in this section, Flanagan brings outside sources into her portrait. What are these sources, where does the author employ them, and when are they most effective?

4. How does Flanagan handle the progression of time in her essay? Locate at least three transitions that move the reader from one stage of the essay to the next.

5. What is the significance of the final image? Why do you think Flanagan chose to focus on her mother's picture as the conclusion for her portrait?

Adding Your Voice

Think of a parent, older relative, or neighbor whose work defined him or her for you when you were younger. This work doesn't have to be a job. Maybe your grandfather enjoyed restoring furniture, and every time you visited, he smelled of paint thinner, his white t-shirts were stained with varnish, and the first thing he did when you arrived was to take you out to his workshop in the garage. Or maybe your father was a fly-fisherman and each evening he spent his spare hours tying intricate flies in the den, surrounded by thread and pliers and bright colored feathers, with maps of rivers and lakes on the walls. Whomever you choose, find an activity and its accompanying details that will help you to capture that person's essence. Then, as Rivas does in the opening of his essay, craft a scene that allows us to see that individual in action. You may even wish to borrow Rivas's opening line to get you started: "This was my father/mother/grand-father/uncle." From there, allow the work and the details of your subject's activities to reveal something about his or her character. Does your subject's job still define him or her for you? What, if anything, has changed about this definition? What hasn't? Why?

OUTSIDE YOUR CIRCLE

So far, the authors in this section have written portraits about people they know, but a portrait doesn't have to be about someone who already is in your life. After all, through writing the portrait, you will become part of your subject's life, and he or she will become part of yours. As long as you include your viewpoint in the essay—why the person intrigues you, how you became interested in his or her story, how you went about discovering something about him or her, or the ways in which your subject's life might parallel, provide a contrast to, or illuminate something about your own life—you can write about anyone you want. Your distance from and intimacy with your subjects will vary from essay to essay, but you will usually place yourself in the essay in some relation to the person you are profiling. Remember, a portrait is not just a *report*; it is a documentation of your engagement with and analysis of the subject.

In "XXXXL," Michael Paterniti travels to Ukraine to meet the world's largest man, eight-foot-tall, 480-pound Leonid Stadnik, whose existence Paterniti first became aware of through a newswire story he could not forget. Though his decision to travel to Ukraine, his arrival in Kiev, his drive to Leonid's small village, and his account of his visits with Leonid at the family farm are all part of the essay—and serve as a narrative backbone for his work—what Paterniti does so beautifully in this portrait is to capture Leonid's personality: the huge but soft-spoken and unassuming man who knows that his life will not give him all the freedoms and pleasures that more conventionally packaged human beings might enjoy, a man who is happiest in his garden, where what grows does not judge him by his size.

In addition to capturing Leonid's essence as an individual and ideas of what it means to be "normal" or "other," the author uses this portrait as an opportunity to meditate on ideas of family. In his hotel room in Kiev, Paterniti reflects on Leonid's life and offers thoughts about the family he himself has left behind. Throughout his time with the giant he also pays close attention to the role Leonid plays in his community and among the members of his family, creating a natural comparison to the author's own life, one that Paterniti describes as having been "subsumed by fatherhood." Again, you need not have an intimate relationship with your subject to make important and personal connections. In fact, much of the meaning of this essay emerges *because* of the separation between author and subject, and what that comparison reveals.

Finally, as noted above, Paterniti's essay is structured around the basic form of the narrative—it moves chronologically from the seed of the essay to his trip to Ukraine to his return home. And because the writer has left home specifically to investigate a certain subject (versus looking back on something that took place in the past), we could classify this essay as a journey, a form we will study more carefully in the next section. Because his primary subject is a person, however, we are including "XXXXL" as a portrait. As we have said, the lines between the forms are fluid; what matters is that you become adept at using various forms to structure and frame your research and writing.

XXXXL

ONE DAY while loitering at my desk, I happened upon a newswire story about a giant. The story was of the variety that appears from time to time, offering a brief snapshot of the oldest/smallest/fattest person on earth, a genre in which I take a keen interest. But there was something else about this one. The giant was reported to be thirty-three years old, residing in a small village with no plumbing in a very poor region of the Ukraine. He lived with his mother and sister, who happened to be tiny. How he'd gotten so huge wasn't entirely known, because the giant wasn't interested in seeing doctors anymore. Something inside of him had been broken or left open, like a faucet, pulsing out hormones as if his body presumed that it still belonged to that of a pro-liferating pubescent boy. This apparently was the result of an operation he'd had as a child. Under the knife that saved him from a blood clot in his brain, his pituitary gland had been nicked. Now he was over eight feet tall—and still growing.

In the article, the giant was pictured sitting at his small dining-room table, reach-ing up to change a light bulb at a height that a normal-sized person couldn't have reached standing. Another picture captured the giant in an unguarded moment, star-ing in astonishment at his hand, as if he'd just picked an exotic, oversized starfish from a coral reef. Near the end of the article, he said something that killed me. He said that his happiest hours were spent in his garden because only the apples and beets don't care what size you are.

Beyond my admittedly voyeuristic interest in the facts of the giant's life—his huge hands, his constant search for clothes that fit, the way he traveled by horse and cart—that one comment brought with it the intimation of something heartbreaking and holy. It began a story: *Once upon a time, there was a giant who kept growing...* And yet this was a real life. And what kind of life was it when you had to find solace among fruits and vegetables? Maybe he was an angel. Turned out of heaven, or thrown down to save the world. What other explanation could there be?

In the days and weeks after I'd read the article, the giant came back to me as I stood in the kitchen making dinner (did he use an oversized spatula?) and while bathing my kids (how did he bathe if he couldn't fit in a shower or tub?). He returned to me in the lulls, while I was brushing my teeth or driving among a trance of red taillights. Maybe I cracked an egg when he did, and maybe I didn't and just believed I had.

Fall arrived. The leaves changed. I didn't forget about the giant; no, he'd only become more insistent. He was out there, and stuck inside of me, too. Why? It made no sense, really. It was almost irresponsible. I had two great kids and a pregnant wife whom I loved, but a part of me—my old self or soul or me-ness—had been subsumed by fatherhood. I'd let it happen, of course, but then there were still moments when I found myself going a bit haywire. Having children was its own kind of prolifera-tion. You suddenly found yourself at the center of something that was growing wildly around you. Extra hands and feet and voices getting louder, a world of sippy cups, dirty diapers, and sleepless nights stretching from here to 2020. I felt as if I were lost in a kid world, unable to form an adult sentence. Except this one:

It was time to see the giant.

I broke the idea gently to my wife, Sara, expecting the worst.

"OK," she said calmly. In her mind, maybe she was already imagining the days she was going to cash out in return, the eighty-miles-per-hour drive with a friend to the nearest hotel that offered room service and in-house salt glows, what the Romans called quid pro quo and others call "me-time." I know that most guys spend theirs on rounds of golf or buddy weekends at a casino, but that's never quite worked for me.

So I packed a bag, said my goodbyes to the children—it never hurts any less—and made a beeline for the airport. There, I strode straight up to the Northwest Airlines counter like a black-market-arms dealer and bought a ticket to Kiev. It may rank as one of the most pleasing, impulsive things I've ever done. Maybe I was already imagining a fable in which some essential truth is revealed. Or maybe I was just hoping to escape, for a moment, what I was growing into and return to who I'd been. Either way, hadn't I earned a little me-time with a Ukrainian giant?

There was only one road leading to the giant—a ribbon of battered, unlined pavement wide enough for exactly two and a half cars. Landing in Kiev, I was able to pick up a translator and a driver, whose beat-up black Audi smelled like the inside of a gas tank. Before leaving the city, we stopped and bought a cake. Somehow cake seemed like the right sort of gift for a giant, lest he confuse his hunger, as giants sometimes did in fairy tales, for a normal person like me.

We drove west toward Poland and Slovakia, through all the small villages inhabited by all the small and average-sized human beings of the country. The people here—the babushkas and the hunched old men—looked as if they might have been out meandering on this same road three hundred years ago. Ancient and ruddy-faced, they wore old wool hats and sat on the hard benches of their carts, driving their horses, hauling their beets to market, payloads of what looked to be purple hearts.

We followed the Teterev River, winding westward through flat-lands, and knew we were close when we came upon a town called Chudnive, or "Miracle." The giant allegedly lived nearby, in Podoliantsi, a tiny backwater of four hundred people, which sat on a vein of blue granite. We drifted off the highway near a rail yard, came over the tracks, which were lit by a string of indigo lights that seemed to stretch all the way to Minsk, then skirted the edge of an endless field, finally turning right on a dirt road.

There was no WELCOME TO PODOLIANTSI sign, just a bunch of hens running loose and the smell of wood smoke. It was dusk, without much light left in the sky, though the sun had come down under the gloom and momentarily lit the land crosswise, throwing long, spindly shadows, catching a nearby cloud, making it glow orange over the village until the last beams of light tipped higher into space as the sun fell beneath the horizon line, like a spotlight suddenly diverted. That's when panic rose in my throat, a stifled up-chuck.

What in the name of bullcrap was I doing here?

We asked directions to the giant's house from a woman at a well, drawing water, and without a word she blushed and pointed ahead to another little dirt lane. We turned and stopped before a stone one-story with a blue-painted gate. Apple trees loomed everywhere over the house. When we got out of the car, my eyes were slow to adjust to the shadows. There was mostly silence, some wind blowing quietly out across the fields rustling some faraway trees, until a hinge squeaked loudly, which caused the air to exhale from my lungs and my heart to skim seven or eight beats. I could feel a thuding reverberation emanating up into my body from the earth. Suddenly, a voice passed through the dark: it had its own special reverberation, too.

"*Dobryi den*," the giant said from behind the gate, among the trees. He didn't boom it out in some Fee-fi-fo-fum, he said it almost delicately, politely, so as not to startle anyone. He was behind the trees, and among them. Slowly, I could make out the low, interleaving branches and then some higher branches, with silver apples trembling there, on a level with the gutter of his stone house. And just above them, breaching, came the giant's head. It was enormous, and he ducked down to come to our level.

"*Dobryi den*," he said again. Good day. As if he'd been waiting. He was smiling as he undid the gate, teeth like mahjong tiles. He was tall. The top of my head reached only to his elbows. And he was wide. On his own, he was a walking family of four, maybe five. My hand instinctively shot out, and he hesitated, then took it. Hand in hand, mine vanished in his like a small goldfish. He seemed to measure its weight a moment, considered its smallness, then squeezed. Yes, ouch — without realizing it, trying to be gentle — very hard! His palm was too wide to clasp fingers around. Meanwhile, he was crushing certain fine bones I didn't realize I had. But I was doing what you do when you meet a real giant in a strange, faraway land: I was smiling like hell, nervously gesturing toward the cake in my other hand.

"*Dobryi den*," I said. And these two small words were a spell cast over everything. Holding my hand, he ceased to be a giant at all. Rather, in his world now, I became the dwarf.

His name was Leonid Stadnik. He had a thicket of chestnut-colored hair cut neatly over the ears and hazel eyes that squinted ever so slightly. His feet were shod in black leather shoes, size twenty-six, so large that later, when I tried to lift one, I needed two hands. When he walked, he did so heavily, with knocked knees and a precipitous forward lean, his legs trying to keep pace with the momentum of his upper body. He led me into the house, ducking and squeezing through doorways as he went, doorways through which I passed with an easy foot of clearance. His head brushed the ceiling that I couldn't reach without leaping.

We entered a cluttered foyer into the kitchen, where there was a small refrigerator, a wood stove, and various religious icons on the wall, including Saint Mary and, as he put it, "Saint Jesus." Leonid took me into a little living room off the kitchen. Spanning almost its entire length stood a bed—not a normal bed but one that was at least ten feet long, extra wide, covered with a green blanket of synthetic fur and, up near the pillows, three stuffed bunnies. There were heavy rugs hung from the wall, cheaply made Orientals, and several Soviet-era wardrobes along the near wall, spilling over with unruly swatches of fabric: exceptionally long shirtsleeves or stray pant legs, the world's largest gray suit, a bright sweater with enough wool to make a half-dozen sweaters. It brought to mind parachutes and gift-wrapping the Reichstag.

He offered me a chair and sat on the bed, reclining with his back against the wall. In the light, he was good-looking and boyish. He was perfectly proportional to himself, if no one else. If his growth surge had been the result of a surgeon's errant knife, he didn't technically suffer from gigantism, which is almost always caused by tumors on the pituitary gland. And he didn't *look* like other giants, with their heavy foreheads, prognathic jaws, abundant body hair, joints and limbs gnarled and misshapen. Also, unlike other giants about whom I'd read, his skin wasn't coarse or oily, and he was not odoriferous in the least. I don't know that he smelled at all, because the only detectable scent was that of the house, the land, the air here — of the Ukraine — a strong, earthy, manure-laced, rotting-apple odor that suffused everything. It was the smell of agriculture, of human beings living partially submerged in the earth, in the mud and muck from which they originally came, and it wasn't at all unpleasant.

In the days leading up to my visit, I'd done some research. Being big — the kind of big that happened in the one foot of stratosphere above the seven-foot-six Yao Mings of the world and was the province of only an elite group of giants — was both physically and psychologically traumatic. Problems ranged from crippling arthritis to lost vision, severe headaches to sleep apnea, tumors to impotence. Many giants simply could not be supported by their enlarged hearts. To find one alive past fifty was a rarity; forty was an accomplishment. And many ended up living alone, on the margins of society, their only claim to fame being their height. There were Web sites devoted to tracking these people the way stocks are tracked: Hussain Bisad, a man from Somalia, was reported to be seven feet nine inches tall. Ring Kuot, a fifteen-year-old Sudanese boy, was rumored to be eight feet three. And until Leonid's emergence at eight feet four inches last spring, people generally assumed that Radhouane Charbib of Tunisia, at seven feet nine, was the tallest documented man in the world. Which was fine with Leonid, because he didn't want the title. To have it meant that it was only a matter of time before his body betrayed him. It meant an early death. It might be next year, it might be ten years from now, but the clocks in the house were echoing.

We began with the easy stuff. Leonid talked about his favorite foods, which included a dish of rice and ground meat wrapped in cabbage leaves called *holubtsi*. "I like sweet things, too — cakes and candies," he said. "I adore ice cream, like a child. Pancakes with jam. But I'm not demanding. We grow all that we use: potatoes, cucumbers, carrots, tomatoes, pumpkins, apples, pears, grapes, plums, cherries ..."

The list continued, and he cut himself short, saying it would take another fifteen minutes to name everything they cultivated in their fields and garden and then differentiate between the categories of apples and cherries, the ten kinds of grapes and squashes. "You know, when I was in Germany, I could not understand why they live so well," he said. He'd traveled to Germany last spring, and not only was it the epic event of his life, but it remained a constant point of reference. "They have very bad land," he continued, "and we have great land. We have natural resources and the Germans don't, but they have a better life."

That first night, he talked while I marveled, as one marvels in the presence of seemingly impossible creations, whether they be exalted paintings or unusual horses.

He sat hugging himself, in a red-plaid shirt and heavy brown slacks. When he raised a finger to make a point, it was dramatic, huge, as if he were waving a nightstick. He had a twitch in his left eye and a way of dreamily staring into space as he spoke that suggested he saw something there or was merely trying to see something through the opacity of his life.

Every once in a while, Leonid's sister, Larisa, appeared. She was elfin, under five feet tall, and looked more like a boy than a woman in her early forties. Her only nod to femininity was a *hustina*, the traditional Ukrainian scarf that she wore over her head. At one point, she ferried plates of brown bread, fish, tomatoes, teacups, vodka glasses, cheese, and cold uncooked pig fat called *salo* to the table, as well as an unlabeled bottle of vodka. She didn't try to communicate with us, just nodded once and disappeared again. By this time it was very dark — and cold — and Leonid said she was going out to bring in the cows, who'd been grazing somewhere at the edge of the village.

From another room came the sound of a television and the intermittent voice of Leonid's mama, Halyna. She was even shorter than Larisa, wrapped in crocheted blankets in the classic rounded, robust shape of a sixtysomething babushka, her leg heavily bandaged. The family had suffered a shock in July when, while lugging a large milk jug up the front step, she had stumbled and fallen, the jug crushing one of her legs. "Mama tried to save the milk," said Leonid.

Not owning a car — not having the money to buy one and not being able to fit in anything smaller than a microbus — Leonid and his sister had driven their horse and cart miles to visit their mother in the hospital. This is how he'd been traveling for over a decade, and how people had been traveling here since before the birth of Christ. It was an investment the family made after Leonid couldn't bear the traumas of riding the bus — where he became a target of derision — and after his weight had destroyed several bikes. "My sister stayed near the horse, and I went to see Mama in the hospital," he said. "Then we shifted, and I stayed with the horse and my sister visited Mama. That's the problem with a horse and cart: someone always has to stay with the horse."

After her release, Leonid's mama had returned home to her bed where she'd been for months ever since. But if there was any doubt, she was still very much in charge, barking orders, overhearing snippets of conversation, and shouting spirited rejoinders.

"Yes, Mama," Leonid called back.

"I know, Mama," he said.

"OK, Mama."

We drank, all of us except Leonid, who claimed never to have had a drop of alcohol in his life. The vodka was very good, homemade from potatoes. I asked him how he could avoid drinking when their family made vodka this good. "It's a matter of principle. It's not that I don't drink. I do drink. Water, juice—cherry juice especially—but I don't drink alcohol. I have a motto: 'Try to do without the things that you can.' Look at me. I've been broken by my height. Probably I would become a drunk if I started drinking."

He wasn't looking at anyone when he said it but gazed out the dark window again—at something, or nothing. If people throw off vibrations, if certain people move molecules because of their words or actions or presence, Leonid sat in the room like a herd of buffaloes about to thunder. "In my life, I've done my best to become a normal person," he said, "to reach something. But because of my unusual body. I will never have a family or wealth or a future. I'm telling you, I've done my best. Everything that depended on me. I've done."

He was silent again, but his whole disposition had suddenly changed, as if he'd been thrown down on dungeon stones. "There's a saying here in the Ukraine," he said. "God punishes the ones he loves most.'"

I returned early the next morning. Leonid didn't seem to mind my presence or my questions, he just took me on as his little-man apprentice. He had risen sometime after five, as he always did, and started by milking the cows. It was as dark outside as when I'd left him the night before—the air wrapped close around the morning bodies in cloaks of purple and black—and it was just as cold.

He put on his shoes at the door and walked across the flat granite patio of the inner yard, past two chained dogs rolling in their own feces, through the muddy passage between the small barn and the granary and the outhouse, past towering piles of stacked wood, and entered a room where LaSonya and Bunny, the cows, stood munching hay. Following him and imagining him simply as a form moving through the predawn, one could say he was, physically speaking, a true behemoth. His back was several tectonic plates; his head was more rectangular than round—his nose was a straight, emphatic line; his chin, a mesa—but he didn't give the impression of being sharp-edged, willful, or stressed by these geometries. He was just 150 percent as big as the world in which he lived and had figured long ago that the only way to live in it at all was to remain absolutely calm—and to make himself as small and invisible as possible. Here, at home, was the only place where he was still Leonid, the boy.

He towered over those cows as they chewed cud, and though be professed that they could be unmanageable, they grew still in his presence. The evening before, he'd said that one of his loves, one of his gifts, was the way he communed with animals, the way they fell under his sway. This was evident with the cat, called Striped One, who constantly sought him out, like a persistent lover, to have his ears scratched. But when it came to the cows and horses, the animals seemed to sense that, in this one case, they were in the company of a much larger being. So they became followers.

When milking, he used only his forefinger and thumb, because that's all that fit down there, squeezing out the teats, streams of white liquid clinking in a metal bucket. He sat on a stool, which left him lowly placed, and because of his size, he had to reach down so far to the udder that he rested his head on top of the cows' haunches. I kept having an image of him, after he'd finished, hoisting the cow up over his shoulder just because he could.

Having once worked at the local collective as a vet, Leonid knew his way around a farm. He loved digging, the feel of the earth in his hands. But unlike others in the village, he was fairly well-educated, having attended a local institute, graduating with honors. And yet his height defined everything. At fifteen, he was closing in on seven feet, growing several inches a year. By the time he went to college, he was a full-fledged giant. He needed new clothes every four to six months, and finding them was nearly impossible. After he'd outgrown store-bought clothes, he turned to a local dressmaker. "Sometimes she was successful, and sometimes she was not," he said. His eyesight became poor, and his legs began to fail. He slipped on the ice and broke his leg. He got frostbite commuting the seven kilometers to work and finally quit his job. By then, he'd long ago let go of his friends; he'd become afraid of crowds, afraid of anyone who might point a finger and laugh.

"I don't like to look at myself from the outside," he said. "I don't like the way I walk. I don't like the way I move. When I became tall, I felt shy and separated from my friends. A friend is a person with whom you can share your happiness and unhappiness. My best and most loyal friend is my mother."

When he spoke in his deep baritone, the trivial things he said felt metaphoric: "Lilies that don't work are more beautiful than any other flower in the world. But this is controversial." Or: "I wouldn't say I like to fish, but I like to look at people who like to fish." Or: "Everything depends on pigs and how fast they grow."

After milking, he took the buckets and emptied them into large jugs and then went out to meet the milkman. It was nearly ten before he made himself some rice and ground beef and rested for a while, reading the Bible.

"Here you're so busy," said Leonid, seated on his bed again. "You work until you see the moon in the sky, and that means it's evening. When I was in Germany, there were days when we didn't have to do anything; we had no special plans. So we could not wait for the end of the day, because there was nothing we had to do and nothing to do. Here every day seems very short."

Ah, Germany. He explained how a Ukrainian expat named Volodymyr, now living in Germany, had read an article and contacted him. It turned out that the two were distant relatives, and Volodymyr invited Leonid to visit Germany, all expenses paid. He had a special bus to pick him up and then drove him all the way through the western Ukraine and Poland to southern Germany, a two-day trip. At each stop along the way, the giant of Podoliantsi emerged from the bus as a great spectacle, to the awe of people who wanted his picture, his autograph, a few words. "You're a movie star," said Volodymyr. This was somehow different from the reaction he sometimes faced at home in the Ukraine. In this case, the awe wasn't mean or intrusive; it was "cultured," as Leonid said. In one town where there was a festival that included carnival performers, he walked into a restaurant and sat down, drinking apple juice with Volodymyr. People assumed he was part of the carnival, too, and couldn't help staring.

If they were looking at him, Leonid was looking back. He shared their sense of awe, even if the source of his were the amazing little things he saw around him. "There were so many bikes in the street," he said. "And the roads! Compared to ours, there is no comparison. I had a small table in my bus where I could put my glass with tea, and in the Ukraine there was great movement and in Poland a slight movement, and when we were driving in Germany there was no movement at all!"

He wanted me to know, however, that German roads and prosperity did not make Germany a better place. "When we went to Germany, we crossed the border, and even looking around, we could see that it's another country," he said in professorial tones. "Germany is a specific country. It is a strict country. Even the color of their buildings is usually gray, brown, some pale colors." He paused seriously, marshaling the full force of his memory. Surely few from Podoliantsi had ever been to Germany, and it was clear that some relatives, and maybe some of his mother's friends, had sat rapt through these recollections before, wondering what secrets he had brought back from abroad.

"The ornaments on the wall were different," he said.

At the end of each day with Leonid, I went back to Kiev, where, for me, the ornaments on the wall were different—as were my strange, empty hotel on Vozdvyzhenska Street and the late-night drunks lurching through the shadows. I thought about Leonid and how he seemed trapped inside of something growing out of control. Not just his body but the effect his body had on the world around him. Shy and sensitive, his only defense had been to withdraw. In so many ways, he was still a child who'd missed so much of life: first love, friends, marriage, children of his own. He no longer had a profession, just a business card with a picture, one made up for him by Japanese businessmen who had come to visit, of Leonid towering over a seven-story building.

He was a full-time giant now, waiting. But for what?

I called home and spoke to my wife. I could hear the kids in the background. By being here, I hadn't escaped them at all; in that hotel room, they seemed everywhere. And yet, by not being able to touch them—wrestling around with my son, Leo, or getting power hugs from my daughter, May—I felt more lost. They were growing, changing, proliferating, and I wasn't there. I was here, halfway around the world, trying to find some glimmer of what I thought I'd lost.

Over the days, the routine with Leonid was similar: I usually brought food and gifts. I gave Leonid's mother a scented candle and she responded happily, tickled, saying, "I've smelled one of these before and will look forward to smelling it again!" Then she barked to Larisa. "Matches!"

We spent many hours in the room with the big bed off the kitchen, chatting with Leonid, who sometimes brought a plate of walnuts to the table, crushing three or four at a time in his hand, then picking bits of meat from the serving tray of his palm. It was hard to say enough about his hands, to describe their power and enormousness. He was proud of them, the one thing he was unafraid to show the world. He also knew that if he ever hit someone with them, "that person would be dead," as he succinctly put it.

Larisa came and went, harried, rosy cheeked. She regarded us openly, without expression, like an animal. A squirrel, to be exact. Sometimes she became impatient with Leonid's loafing and stood for an extra moment glaring at him — even muttering single words like "carrots" or "cows" to signify the task at hand — while he spoke on, oblivious, staring out the window into space. "I don't always have the will to pursue my goals," he said. "I force myself to finish very dull work. But my sister, she is persistent. She never gives up. I can give up, but she can't."

So that was her role, the sister of the giant of Podoliantsi. To work twice as hard while caring for her mother and brother. And that would be the role for the rest of her life, as both of them became more and more infirm. And Leonid's role, for us at least, was to reflect on his life, to offer it like some gilded manuscript, one with missing pages, of the things he'd actually missed in life and the things that were too painful to recall. He wouldn't discuss his operation at all, for instance, even when I pressed for details. "All you ask about is trifles and some negative moments in my life," he said, almost angrily. "Ask me about something gay and something happy, though I have few moments like that."

About his height, he said it was something he couldn't comprehend when he was young. He said everything seemed normal after the operation until one day, in ninth grade, the class was measured and the two-meter tape was too short for him. After that, he became acutely aware of people laughing out loud when there wasn't a block of empty seats on the bus and, unable to stand on his legs, Leonid would squat, as if over a hole in the ground. "One in a million would have survived what I survived on that bus," he said.

But somehow he did. He kept surviving.

And if God was punishing him. God had also kept him alive.

Leonid had nearly died five times. In the first year of his life, he slipped into a coma and couldn't breathe. His parents bid their last goodbyes and made preparations for his burial — and he came back. When he was twelve, the Lord was more emphatic, letting loose the blood clot in his brain. Leonid couldn't move his hands or legs. To alleviate the paralysis, a risky procedure was performed inside the brain. Before he was put under, he remembered being wheeled through a ward of paralyzed children and then his parents saying goodbye once more. But whatever saved him that day doomed him to be a giant forever.

Realizing his fate over time, suffering the unbearable loneliness of giants, he twice tried suicide by hanging. ("My angels were awake," he said of those two attempts. "They did not want me to die. And my skeleton would not be broken.") And then, in his cart a few years ago, being pulled by his horse Tulip, he hit a rut. The cart toppled, and all 480 pounds of him were suddenly in the air, then beneath the heavy cart. What would have killed anyone else, what would have cleanly snapped a spine or neck, did not kill him. He came up from under the cart and went chasing his horse.

God had kept him alive. That's what he believed, so that's what the truth was. And he believed he'd been kept alive for a purpose.

"Do you talk to God and ask him?" I said.

"I ask him, but He doesn't hear me," Leonid said. "The Bible says that those who cry in this world will then be happy in heaven. I'm not sure it will be like this, but I want to believe it. But secretly, I think those that suffer here will suffer in heaven, too."

"But why did God choose you for this?" I asked.

"I'm too tired to think about it," he said, finding the last bit of meat from the walnuts. "I used to think about it all the time, and now I don't want to think about it anymore. My future is only black."

Almost on cue, Larisa appeared again, muttering the word "apples." Her appearance was perfectly timed. This time Leonid smiled broadly and said, "Come," waving his hand for me to follow. "We'll go pick some." He forced himself to his feet and ducked through the first doorway, listing through the cramped house without so much as disturbing a spoon. He grabbed his coat and cap, squeezed through two more doorways, then went out into the day, which was still full of light.

Leonid was a prankster — and a giggler. He had a sweet giggle, very boyish and innocent. At one point, seated on his bed, he reached into his pocket, as if suddenly remembering something important, and produced a mobile phone, which he seemed to check for missed messages. With his pointer finger, he somehow plinked out a number. To give him his privacy, the translator and I began chatting, until her phone engaged, too, and she formally excused herself to take the call. She answered, "*Dobryi den*" and then Leonid answered back from three feet away, in his booming baritone, "*DOBRYI DEN!*"

Watching the translator's surprise, his eyes became slits, his cheeks rose, and there was an enormous uplift at the corners of his mouth. His face, which was wind-chapped from so many hours in the garden, became its own planet. His ears, the shape and size of a hefty split Idaho potato, wiggled; his prodigious chin raised to reveal a patch of whiskers he'd missed while shaving; his two eyes were ponds of hazel water, suddenly lit by a downpour of sun. All the features of his face were complementary and, taken together, offered no clue that he was a giant. It's only when they were set against the rest of humanity that he became, in every way, more exaggerated . . . and, well, gigantic.

And yet his happiness was such a feathery, redemptive force. He had the same smile in one of the only pictures that still existed from when he was a boy — a picture that hung in a frame over his mama's bed, of a towheaded three-year-old with almond-shaped eyes. It had been taken on a special outing at the Kiev Zoo, one of the few times the family had been out of their village together, on a proper trip. It was sepia-toned, as if taken a century ago.

Looking up at that little-boy face in the picture and then looking at Leonid's now was like watching the arc of an entire life being drawn between two points. More than anything, the primary experience of Leonid's life had been his growing, though his primary desire had been to go back to that moment when he was simply a child again.

"I was a little guy, and now I'm a big one," Leonid said when he showed me the photograph, his mama sitting nearby, still bundled in blankets.

"He was so nice when he was small," she said, with a touch of longing. "At least he has a suit for his funeral."

So it came down to this: on the day his life was saved by doctors operating on his brain, Leonid lost the ability to determine his own fate. On that day, he became chosen, as he pointed out — but he also became powerless. No wonder he was so dedicated to the Bible, reciting certain parables to whoever would listen. Long ago, he had thrown his life over to God, with his Old Testament temper, because nothing could explain what was happening to him. God was his hands and his feet and his mahjong teeth.

Maybe because of my size, mere mortal that I was, I had choices. And my god wasn't his god. In fact, I wasn't sure about who my god was. Maybe he was a feeling I got sometimes, a feeling that there *could* be a god. Or a glimmer I occasionally saw in the trees.

God was in the apple trees and red oaks or a bend in the river that we'd come upon yesterday where leaves fell into the current and were borne to the Black Sea in gold trails. God was the cows chewing cud and Tulip the horse pulling the cart and the dogs rolling in their own shit. God was the vein of blue granite running beneath the ground here and the milk in the jugs that pinned Leonid's mama, crushing her leg.

God was that moment when Leonid went out to pick apples and I followed. He used a little stool, and I took a crude metal ladder and leaned it against the house. We levitated way up in the top boughs of the trees, and the apples thudded as they were dropped in the buckets. We were up in the trees, Leonid and I, and he began singing, in his own tongue, gently twisting fruit from each branch. His voice, that sweet song, sounded as if it came from some deep underground river.

The town of Miracle lay beyond him. Across the fields, a train sounded. God was the trees and the apples and the glowing clouds overhead. We were part of the same body, the earth as it was, as it had been created by some cosmic force. When I think of this, I still get that feeling, up there in that tree, that feeling of belonging to something sizeless.

I get that feeling of being up in the trees with Leonid, and everything that really matters, everything worth it, is up there with us, too: my children, his mama. All of our giants and dwarves. The apples are sources of warmth on that cold day, as if heated from within. To touch them was divine.

My time with Leonid was coming to an end. I'd gotten fleas — or something — from my hotel bed and was itching like a possessed maniac. When I'd filled the tub to wash, cold, smelly green water had eagerly obliged. Anyway, Halloween was approaching, and I would be returning to my kids, returning to watch them grow. And I was returning to one day set them free of this giant body, our family: to eventually put them on a bus somewhere so that they might come back and tell us of the ornaments they saw out there. I realized that once I left Leonid, I was really returning for good, that my next probable meeting with the giant would come some random afternoon at my desk, when I'd stumble across a newspaper item about his death, the tallest man in the world finally subsumed by his size.

Here were the basic facts: he would die having grown to eight and a half, nine, nine and a half feet, perhaps as the tallest man that ever lived, a title he'd never wanted. He would die a virgin, without ever having had a lover. Without having close friends, for that matter. He would die without children, having made it to Germany once, but no farther. It would have been many years since he'd been able to run or swim. He might or might not have a suit to fit him when he was put in his casket and lowered by the village men, at least a dozen of them, into the earth of Podoliantsi.

Until then, he clung to his otherworld, half made of dream and half made of manure. "I have no bad thoughts about the end," he said. He ate ice cream, sucked down a dozen raw eggs at a time, chewed cold pig fat, sang, and slept with three stuffed bunnies. He fell into bitter moods, cursed his God, then contritely read his Bible. He received his pilgrims and told them the tale of his life, hugging himself, gazing out the window, while Larisa came and went, muttering words like "beets" and "melon." He wasn't an angel or a beast after all, just a man, forming his beliefs from the body he'd been given. He said goodbye among the apple trees, where he'd first said hello, crushing my hand again, turning the colors of the leaves as we drove away.

But I remember him most vividly in a moment just before leaving. I went for a little walk to see the cows. When I returned, I came upon him standing in the shadow of the apple trees, leaning against his gate, looking out from his stone house at the landscape, the red oaks on fire now, villagers using their wooden plows to turn the fields, the sun coming down just opposite him in the melancholic end of day. He had no idea I was there. He just breathed it all in. There was a presence behind his eyes — not just his enormous brain and eardrums, but *him*, his himness or soul or whatever. It was a moment where he just *was*. Contented.

He stood against the fence, and a neighbor child drifted by. The neighbors had cherubic boys and girls, blond and fresh and smiling, like he once was. Maybe, in another life, one of them would have been his own, light enough to hold up in one hand. But now, hidden in the shadows beneath the apple tree, invisible, Leonid gently said, "*Dobryi den,*" which sent the boy skyward. He hadn't seen the giant there at all, and that was before factoring in that the voice belonged to an actual *giant* who happened to be his neighbor.

"*Dobryi den,*" the boy said in a startled whisper. He looked up into the branches, gazed upon Leonid's face there, and stumbled. Then he put his head down and hurried on.

It took two days to get home. In the lounge at the airport in Munich, still itching madly, I realized that something smelled. Did anyone bathe in Germany? Yes, they did. It was me: I smelled like Podoliantsi, and I could tell people were thinking twice about sitting near me. I got up and found a terminal shower that I could use and stood in warm, clear water for nearly a half hour, washing it all away.

On the flight to Boston, I looked down on the world for all signs of life on land and sea, but from that height many of the fine details of the earth, including large houses and tankers, were simply erased. After landing at Logan, I waited in line, passed through customs, and again waited for my luggage to appear from behind rubber ribbons, trusting it would. The minute it did, I ran like a madman for the bus. I was so shot through with adrenaline, I was floating.

Soon the bus cloverleafed onto the highway. Two hours north now, to home, fitting neatly in my seat. When I saw this familiar land outside the window — fall here, too, flat land with its own forest flaring — and when I saw my wife, her stomach rounded against her sweater, and my daughter in funny pigtails there at the station, waiting, and I could finally touch them again, and when I lifted and held my little boy, Leo, in my arms again and felt my heart beating hard enough to know that I wanted to live a very long time. I took his hand up against mine, just to check, just to see what had occurred in my absence.

His hand lay in mine, and I felt its weight: the little bones and the smooth, scarless skin so soft it didn't seem real. Mine dwarfed his, but still I held his hand up and inspected his fingers for a moment. He thought I was being funny, and he laughed, a little-boy giggle. His breath smelled like cookies. Yes, his fingers were bigger, and I was not frightened. Maybe the betrayals lay out before us somewhere in our murky future. Maybe we were all growing until someday nothing would work for us anymore. But I was not frightened. I was filled with joy.

It read 4:00 on the wall — on the east coast of the United States of America — and at that very moment, somewhere, the giant was sleeping on his oversized bed. His huge shoes lay empty near the doorway, his pants thrown over the chair. His enormous suit hung in the closet, waiting.

Soon he would rise to milk the cows, feed the pigs, pick the rest of the apples. In the dirt lane before his house, carts would come and go, bearing payloads of huge purple hearts. And there he would be, the giant, alone up in the apple tree, gently picking fruit, humming the notes again.

At the bus station, my children began singing.

—2005

Learning from Other Writers (Paterniti)

1. What is the effect of the author spending the first nine paragraphs describing how he learned of the giant's existence and the way in which he couldn't get him out of his thoughts?

2. How would you classify or categorize the sorts of details used to physically describe Leonid? Do they change over the course of the essay? If so, why? If not, why not?

3. Leonid tells the author about his trip to Germany and says that he didn't much care for that country. Why and how is the trip to Germany significant in capturing Leonid's essence? The way he views his home? His village? His life?

4. How does Paterniti's role as an outsider shape both the structure of the essay and his analysis? How would this essay have been different if *you* had written it? What might you have focused on that Paterniti omits, downplays, or neglects?

5. The author ends by describing the moment he returns home and holds his young son's—*Leo's*—hand in his. What is the effect of this scene? Why end here?

ADDITIONAL CONSIDERATIONS: THE ART OF THE INTERVIEW

As any reporter will tell you, the more you prepare for an interview, the more likely you will use that time wisely. Although you might not be sure of your driving question before you get a chance to spend time with your subject, you will need to develop a preliminary focus so that you can draw up a list of questions to ask and suggest an activity or location that might provide the narrative backbone or physical backdrop for your interview and resulting portrait. (If you feel anxious about your ability to interview your subject while he or she is carrying out whatever activity you are using to structure your portrait, you might want to conduct the stationary part of the interview before or after you accompany your subject on that activity.)

Nor do you want to waste time by asking your subject obvious questions. If your subject is a public figure, you can figure out from published sources when he was born or where she went to college. Even if you are interviewing a taxidermist who lives in a secluded shack ten miles out of town, you can read up on the basics of taxidermy before you get there. And in many cases, you can save your factual questions for a preliminary or follow-up email.

Not only will your initial research guide you to a possible focus for your interview, but you can use this information to set your subject at ease. "So," you might begin, "your aunt says that when you were a little girl you were terrified of the water. But here you are, swimming across Lake Michigan. What were you so afraid of when you were a kid? How did you overcome that fear?" Once your subject begins talking, sit back and listen to what he or she says. Don't jump ahead to the next question on your list if your subject has just told you something that begs to be pursued. We interview subjects not only to get answers, but with the hope that we will stumble upon the unexpected. So feel free to charge course when the opportunity presents itself. We call this "following the conversation."

Rather than asking yes-or-no questions, you should also try to provide your subject with more open-ended prompts. Asking a plastic surgeon if he likes his job might elicit little more than "yes." Asking him *why* he likes his job, what aspect of the job he dislikes, what his favorite (or least favorite) type of surgical procedure might be is likely to produce lengthier and more revealing answers. The same is true for questions your subject doesn't usually get asked. Does the physicist you are interviewing ever read her horoscope? What frightens the otherwise fearless member of the SWAT team you want to profile? And no matter what question you ask, give your subject a chance to answer it. A nice *long* chance. Silence makes most people so ill at ease that they eventually will begin to speak.

As you can see from the essays in this chapter, dialogue plays an important role in most portraits. Even if an author doesn't give us very many lines of actual dialogue, what lines she does provide usually are startling (i.e., Flanagan's mother's "To hell with that," or the snippets of Rivas's father talking about starting a new business). How do you capture the way your subjects speak? The decision will vary from writer to writer and subject to subject. If the person with whom you are spending time is an important political figure or his or her statements might be controversial—or the basis for a lawsuit—you will want to get that subject's words on tape. (A reporter's dated notes constitute a legal record of a conversation, but a tape recording is better evidence if a lawsuit goes to court.) But in most instances, your decision as to whether to record an interview or rely on your ability to take notes depends on which method increases your chances of coming away with good material.

Early in Eileen's career she found that she didn't like to spend time fussing with a tape recorder or worried that a set of batteries might die in the middle of an interview or that the recording might come out garbled. Her mind wandered if she knew that whatever her subject said would be recorded by a machine. And she hated to spend days, if not weeks, transcribing an interview from a recording, then try to knit together everything her subject said into a coherent essay. If she didn't rely on a recorder, she listened more closely to what her subject said and only wrote down his or her most interesting quotes, along with surreptitious observations about the person's mannerisms, appearance, dress, and taste in home decor. (Most reporters develop their own incomprehensible shorthand, or tiny indecipherable writing a subject can't read, especially upside down.)

Jeremiah, on the other hand, swears that relying on a recorder frees him to focus on what the subject is saying and to follow the conversation in a more organic way. Also, because the recorder catches everything, people are less likely to feel intimidated than when the reporter suddenly begins jotting down what is clearly a "good" quote. This can leave the subject feeling as if the writer is cherry picking what he or she is saying, rather than listening for the whole story, even though both styles of reporting rely on this subjective selectivity. The recording device simply makes that selectivity less apparent. Just be sure to always bring a backup recorder—recorders run out of batteries and digital hard-drives fill up.

Although every writer or reporter can tell you stories about the time he blew an interview because his tape recorder didn't work or she wasn't adept at taking notes, most people eventually master the mechanics of the interview. What doesn't get easier is navigating your relationship to your subject. You might think that you are the only writer who feels queasy at the prospect of calling a stranger to set up an interview or ask for information. But even Joan Didion, one of the boldest and most successful writers in the country, makes the following admission:

> I am bad at interviewing people. I avoid situations in which I have to talk to anyone's press agent. (This precludes doing pieces on most actors, a bonus in itself.) I do not like to make telephone calls, and would not like to count the mornings I have sat on some Best Western motel bed somewhere and tried to force myself to put through the call to the assistant district attorney.

For most of us, the dread of calling strangers stems from the fear that we will need to ask that person difficult questions, the fear that, in the end, the person who was kind enough to let us tag along and interrupt and pry will feel upset or embarrassed by what we write about him or her. You can warn people not to say or do anything they wouldn't want to see in print. You can remind them that unless they specify that something they are about to say or do must be kept off the record, you are legally allowed to publish it, and that specifying that something is off the record *after* they have said or done it does not legally oblige you to leave it out. But no matter how careful you are, there is always the possibility that something you write might strike your subject as a betrayal, if for no other reason than your purpose in writing about someone's life is going to be different from his purpose in living his life or allowing you to watch.

Which doesn't mean that you shouldn't write about other people. Most ordinary human beings are deeply honored to find themselves worthy of your attention. Most are happy to share their stories for the simple reason that you find their experiences interesting or valuable. So long as you don't set out with an axe to grind or a score to settle, rest assured that you are probably being generous with your portrayal. Most of us make our peace with the proposition that what we write will bring about more good than harm. If not for Joan Didion's willingness to pick up that phone and dial that assistant district attorney, we wouldn't now be able to pull down from our shelves *Slouching toward Bethlehem* and *The White Album,* her valuable chronicles of the 1960s and 1970s, two very important and tumultuous decades in American history.

Adding Your Voice

1. Think of a friend or relative who has lived through an event of larger social or historical significance. Spend time with that person, getting down his or her description of that event and what he or she was thinking and feeling as the event unfolded. If necessary, supplement your interview(s) with other forms of research. Re-create your subject's experiences for your readers. Be sure that you convey the flavor of your subject's language and a sense of his or her interior world, as well as the larger social or historical significance of the events he or she lived through.

2. Choose someone whose work or hobby interests you. Prepare to spend time with that person as he or she engages in that activity. Write a portrait in which you describe your subject performing the activity you observed while you try to answer a larger thematic question about the person and his or her activity. This could be an ideal opportunity to talk with someone who works in the field you hope to pursue, either in the professional world or on your campus.

GROUP PORTRAITS

When your subject concerns the behavior or characteristics of a group of people rather than an individual or a place, you will want to consider the form known as the group portrait. *Hiroshima,* John Hersey's groundbreaking portrayal of six survivors of the atomic blast that ended World War II, not only tells the stories of these six victims of the bomb but also quietly poses the question of who does or doesn't survive a nuclear catastrophe, and why.

Before Hersey received his assignment (from William Shawn, the editor of *The New Yorker*) to visit Hiroshima, accounts of the bombing had focused almost exclusively on the physical devastation the bomb had wreaked. Hersey could have taken the same approach. Instead, he chose to focus on the bomb's effects on six inhabitants of the city, five of them Japanese civilians and one a German priest who had been living and working in Japan, a radical decision given that the Japanese and German people (civilians as well as soldiers) had been demonized and dehumanized by Allied propaganda.

If Hersey's approach seems familiar to us now, that's because nearly every disaster movie—and every spoof of every disaster movie—takes the shape of a group portrait of the lucky or unlucky victims who do or do not survive a malfunctioning airline engine, an earthquake, a political uprising, a shipwreck, an avalanche, an alien invasion, or an outbreak of an epidemic. In fact, as the form's popularity has increased, it also has become the dominant structure for documentaries. Journalists and academics often use the form to structure their analyses of social or public policies, illustrating or supporting their arguments with case histories or mini-profiles of people whom the policies help or hurt (Jonathan Cohn's recent book *Sick: The Untold Story of America's Health Care Crisis* documents the effects of the lack of universal health care on various Americans). So versatile is the group portrait that it can be used to structure an ethnographic or sociological study; all you have to do is add a few members to the group, some rules for initiation, and a definition as to who belongs and who doesn't, and you have an essay that explores the nature of a culture or a community (for an example of an ethnological group portrait, look back at Elwood Reid's "My Body, My Weapon, My Shame" in Chapter 7).

Finally, unlike the portrait of a person, which focuses on a single subject, most group portraits require a second level of organization to allow the writer to move smoothly from one member of the group to the next. In *Hiroshima*, Hersey cuts from character to character as he moves along a timeline from the moments immediately before the atomic blast to the hours and weeks that follow. But other organizational plans are possible. If you wanted to write about life on a naval destroyer, you might arrange your subjects according to their functions, from the lowest swabbie to the captain. The only thing that matters is that you're consistent in whatever organizational model you adopt. This will give your work a feeling of unity.

FROM: *HIROSHIMA*

A Noiseless Flash

At exactly fifteen minutes past eight in the morning, on August 6, 1945, Japanese time, at the moment when the atomic bomb flashed above Hiroshima, Miss Toshiko Sasaki, a clerk in the personnel department of the East Asia Tin Works, had just sat down at her place in the plant office and was turning her head to speak to the girl at the next desk. At that same moment, Dr. Masakazu Fujii was settling down cross-legged to read the Osaka *Asahi* on the porch of his private hospital, overhanging one of the seven deltaic rivers which divide Hiroshima; Mrs. Hatsuyo Nakamura, a tailor's widow, stood by the window of her kitchen, watching a neighbor tearing down his house because it lay in the path of an air-raid-defense fire lane; Father Wilhelm Kleinsorge, a German priest of the Society of Jesus, reclined in his underwear on a cot on the top floor of his order's three-story mission house, reading a Jesuit magazine, *Stimmen der Zeit*; Dr. Terufumi Sasaki, a young member of the surgical staff of the city's large, modern Red Cross Hospital, walked along one of the hospital corridors with a blood specimen for a Wassermann test in his hand; and the Reverend Mr. Kiyoshi Tanimoto, pastor of the Hiroshima Methodist Church, paused at the door of a rich man's house in Koi, the city's western suburb, and prepared to unload a handcart full of things he had evacuated from town in fear of the massive B-29 raid which everyone expected Hiroshima to suffer. A hundred thousand people were killed by the atomic bomb, and these six were among the survivors. They still wonder why they lived when so many others died. Each of them counts many small items of chance or volition—a step taken in time, a decision to go indoors, catching one streetcar instead of the next—that spared him. And now each knows that in the act of survival he lived a dozen lives and saw more death than he ever thought he would see. At the time, none of them knew anything.

The Reverend Mr. Tanimoto got up at five o'clock that morning. He was alone in the parsonage, because for some time his wife had been commuting with their year-old baby to spend nights with a friend in Ushida, a suburb to the north. Of all the important cities of Japan, only two, Kyoto and Hiroshima, had not been visited in strength by *B-san*, or Mr. B, as the Japanese, with a mixture of respect and unhappy familiarity, called the B-29; and Mr. Tanimoto, like all his neighbors and friends, was almost sick with anxiety. He had heard uncomfortably detailed accounts of mass raids on Kure, Iwakuni, Tokuyama, and other nearby towns; he was sure Hiroshima's turn would come soon. He had slept badly the night before, because there had been several air-raid warnings. Hiroshima had been getting such warnings almost every night for weeks, for at that time the B-29s were using Lake Biwa, northeast of Hiroshima, as a rendezvous point, and no matter what city the Americans planned to hit, the Superfortresses streamed in over the coast near Hiroshima. The frequency of the warnings and the continued abstinence of Mr. B with respect to Hiroshima had made its citizens jittery; a rumor was going around that the Americans were saving something special for the city.

Mr. Tanimoto was a small man, quick to talk, laugh, and cry. He wore his black hair parted in the middle and rather long; the prominence of the frontal bones just above his eyebrows and the smallness of his mustache, mouth, and chin gave him a strange, old-young look, boyish and yet wise, weak and yet fiery. He moved nervously and fast, but with a restraint which suggested that he was a cautious, thoughtful man. He showed, indeed, just those qualities in the uneasy days before the bomb fell. Besides having his wife spend the nights in Ushida, Mr. Tanimoto had been carrying all the portable things from his church, in the close-packed residential district called Nagaragawa, to a house that belonged to a rayon manufacturer in Koi, two miles from the center of town. The rayon man, a Mr. Matsui, had opened his then unoccupied estate to a large number of his friends and acquaintances, so that they might evacuate whatever they wished to a safe distance from the probable target area. Mr. Tanimoto had had no difficulty in moving chairs, hymnals, Bibles, altar gear, and church records by pushcart himself, but the organ console and an upright piano required some aid. A friend of his named Matsuo had, the day before, helped him get the piano out to Koi; in return, he had promised this day to assist Mr. Matsuo in hauling out a daughter's belongings. That is why he had risen so early.

Mr. Tanimoto cooked his own breakfast. He felt awfully tired. The effort of moving the piano the day before, a sleepless night, weeks of worry and unbalanced diet, the cares of his parish—all combined to make him feel hardly adequate to the new day's work. There was another thing, too: Mr. Tanimoto had studied theology at Emory College, in Atlanta, Georgia; he had graduated in 1940; he spoke excellent English; he dressed in American clothes; he had corresponded with many American friends right up to the time the war began; and among a people obsessed with a fear of being spied upon—perhaps almost obsessed himself—he found himself growing increasingly uneasy. The police had questioned him several times, and just a few days before, he had heard that an influential acquaintance, a Mr. Tanaka, a retired officer of the Toyo Kisen Kaisha steamship line, an anti-Christian, a man famous in Hiroshima for his showy philanthropies and notorious for his personal tyrannies, had been telling people that Tanimoto should not be trusted. In compensation, to show himself publicly a good Japanese, Mr. Tanimoto had taken on the chairmanship of his local *tonarigumi*, or Neighborhood Association, and to his other duties and concerns this position had added the business of organizing air-raid defense for about twenty families.

Before six o'clock that morning, Mr. Tanimoto started for Mr. Matsuo's house. There he found that their burden was to be a *tansu*, a large Japanese cabinet, full of clothing and household goods. The two men set out. The morning was perfectly clear and so warm that the day promised to be uncomfortable. A few minutes after they started, the air-raid siren went off—a minute-long blast that warned of approaching planes but indicated to the people of Hiroshima only a slight degree of danger, since it sounded every morning at this time, when an American weather plane came over. The two men pulled and pushed the handcart through the city streets. Hiroshima was a fan-shaped city, lying mostly on the six islands formed by the seven estuarial rivers that branch out from the Ota River; its main commercial and residential districts, covering about four square miles in the center of the city, contained three-quarters of its population, which had been reduced by several evacuation programs from a wartime peak of 380,000 to about 245,000. Factories and other residential districts, or suburbs, lay compactly around the edges of the city. To the south were the docks, an airport, and the island-studded Inland Sea. A rim of mountains runs around the other three sides of the delta. Mr. Tanimoto and Mr. Matsuo took their way through the shopping center, already full of people, and across two of the rivers to the sloping streets of Koi, and up them to the outskirts and foothills. As they started up a valley away from the tight-ranked houses, the all-clear sounded. (The Japanese radar operators, detecting only three planes, supposed that they comprised a reconnaissance.) Pushing the handcart up to the rayon man's house was tiring, and the men, after they had maneuvered their load into the driveway and to the front steps, paused to rest awhile. They stood with a wing of the house between them and the city. Like most homes in this part of Japan, the house consisted of a wooden frame and wooden walls supporting a heavy tile roof. Its front hall, packed with rolls of bedding and clothing, looked like a cool cave full of fat cushions. Opposite the house, to the right of the front door, there was a large, finicky rock garden. There was no sound of planes. The morning was still; the place was cool and pleasant.

Then a tremendous flash of light cut across the sky. Mr. Tanimoto has a distinct recollection that it travelled from east to west, from the city toward the hills. It seemed a sheet of sun. Both he and Mr. Matsuo reacted in terror—and both had time to react (for they were 3,500 yards, or two miles, from the center of the explosion). Mr. Matsuo dashed up the front steps into the house and dived among the bedrolls and buried himself there. Mr. Tanimoto took four or five steps and threw himself between two big rocks in the garden. He bellied up very hard against one of them. As his face was against the stone, he did not see what happened. He felt a sudden pressure, and then splinters and pieces of board and fragments of tile fell on him. He heard no roar. (Almost no one in Hiroshima recalls hearing any noise of the bomb. But a fisherman in his sampan on the Inland Sea near Tsuzu, the man with whom Mr. Tanimoto's mother-in-law and sister-in-law were living, saw the flash and heard a tremendous explosion; he was nearly twenty miles from Hiroshima, but the thunder was greater than when the B-29s hit Iwakuni, only five miles away.)

When he dared, Mr. Tanimoto raised his head and saw that the rayon man's house had collapsed. He thought a bomb had fallen directly on it. Such clouds of dust had risen that there was a sort of twilight around. In panic, not thinking for the moment of Mr. Matsuo under the ruins, he dashed out into the street. He noticed as he ran that the concrete wall of the estate had fallen over—toward the house rather than away from it. In the street, the first thing he saw was a squad of soldiers who had been burrowing into the hillside opposite, making one of the thousands of dugouts in which the Japanese apparently intended to resist invasion, hill by hill, life for life; the soldiers were coming out of the hole, where they should have been safe, and blood was running from their heads, chests, and backs. They were silent and dazed.

Under what seemed to be a local dust cloud, the day grew darker and darker.

At nearly midnight, the night before the bomb was dropped, an announcer on the city's radio station said that about two hundred B-29s were approaching southern Honshu and advised the population of Hiroshima to evacuate to their designated "safe areas." Mrs. Hatsuyo Nakamura, the tailor's widow, who lived in the section called Nobori-cho and who had long had a habit of doing as she was told, got her three children—a ten-year-old boy, Toshio, an eight-year-old girl, Yaeko, and a five-year-old girl, Myeko—out of bed and dressed them and walked with them to the military area known as the East Parade Ground, on the northeast edge of the city. There she unrolled some mats and the children lay down on them. They slept until about two, when they were awakened by the roar of the planes going over Hiroshima.

As soon as the planes had passed, Mrs. Nakamura started back with her children. They reached home a little after two-thirty and she immediately turned on the radio, which, to her distress, was just then broadcasting a fresh warning. When she looked at the children and saw how tired they were, and when she thought of the number of trips they had made in past weeks, all to no purpose, to the East Parade Ground, she decided that in spite of the instructions on the radio, she simply could not face starting out all over again. She put the children in their bedrolls on the floor, lay down herself at three o'clock, and fell asleep at once, so soundly that when planes passed over later, she did not waken to their sound.

The siren jarred her awake at about seven. She arose, dressed quickly, and hurried to the house of Mr. Nakamoto, the head of her Neighborhood Association, and asked him what she should do. He said that she should remain at home unless an urgent warning—a series of intermittent blasts of the siren—was sounded. She returned home, lit the stove in the kitchen, set some rice to cook, and sat down to read that morning's Hiroshima Chugoku. To her relief, the all-clear sounded at eight o'clock. She heard the children stirring, so she went and gave each of them a handful of peanuts and told them to stay on their bedrolls, because they were tired from the night's walk. She had hoped that they would go back to sleep, but the man in the house directly to the south began to make a terrible hullabaloo of hammering, wedging, ripping, and splitting. The prefectural government, convinced, as everyone in Hiroshima was, that the city would be attacked soon, had begun to press with threats and warnings for the completion of wide fire lanes, which, it was hoped, might act in conjunction with the rivers to localize any fires started by an incendiary raid; and the neighbor was reluctantly sacrificing his home to the city's safety. Just the day before, the prefecture had ordered all able-bodied girls from the secondary schools to spend a few days helping to clear these lanes, and they started work soon after the all-clear sounded.

Mrs. Nakamura went back to the kitchen, looked at the rice, and began watching the man next door. At first, she was annoyed with him for making so much noise, but then she was moved almost to tears by pity. Her emotion was specifically directed toward her neighbor, tearing down his home, board by board, at a time when there was so much unavoidable destruction, but undoubtedly she also felt a generalized, community pity, to say nothing of self-pity. She had not had an easy time. Her husband, Isawa, had gone into the Army just after Myeko was born, and she had heard nothing from or of him for a long time, until, on March 5, 1942, she received a seven-word telegram: "Isawa died an honorable death at Singapore." She learned later that he had died on February 15th, the day Singapore fell, and that he had been a corporal. Isawa had been a not particularly prosperous tailor, and his only capital was a Sankoku sewing machine. After his death, when his allotments stopped coming, Mrs. Nakamura got out the machine and began to take in piecework herself, and since then had supported the children, but poorly, by sewing.

As Mrs. Nakamura stood watching her neighbor, everything flashed whiter than any white she had ever seen. She did not notice what happened to the man next door; the reflex of a mother set her in motion toward her children. She had taken a single step (the house was 1,350 yards, or three-quarters of a mile, from the center of the explosion) when something picked her up and she seemed to fly into the next room over the raised sleeping platform, pursued by parts of her house.

Timbers fell around her as she landed, and a shower of tiles pommelled her; everything became dark, for she was buried. The debris did not cover her deeply. She rose up and freed herself. She heard a child cry, "Mother, help me!," and saw her youngest—Myeko, the five-year-old—buried up to her breast and unable to move. As Mrs. Nakamura started frantically to claw her way toward the baby, she could see or hear nothing of her other children.

In the days right before the bombing, Dr. Masakazu Fujii, being prosperous, hedonistic, and at the time not too busy, had been allowing himself the luxury of sleeping until nine or nine-thirty, but fortunately he had to get up early the morning the bomb was dropped to see a house guest off on a train. He rose at six, and half an hour later walked with his friend to the station, not far away, across two of the rivers. He was back home by seven, just as the siren sounded its sustained warning. He ate breakfast and then, because the morning was already hot, undressed down to his underwear and went out on the porch to read the paper. This porch—in fact, the whole building—was curiously constructed. Dr. Fujii was the proprietor of a peculiarly Japanese institution: a private, single-doctor hospital. This building, perched beside and over the water of the Kyo River, and next to the bridge of the same name, contained thirty rooms for thirty patients and their kinfolk—for, according to Japanese custom, when a person falls sick and goes to a hospital, one or more members of his family go and live there with him, to cook for him, bathe, massage, and read to him, and to offer incessant familial sympathy, without which a Japanese patient would be miserable indeed. Dr. Fujii had no beds—only straw mats—for his patients. He did, however, have all sorts of modern equipment: an X-ray machine, diathermy apparatus, and a fine tiled laboratory. The structure rested two-thirds on the land, one-third on piles over the tidal waters of the Kyo. This overhang, the part of the building where Dr. Fujii lived, was queer-looking, but it was cool in summer and from the porch, which faced away from the center of the city, the prospect of the river, with pleasure boats drifting up and down it, was always refreshing. Dr. Fujii had occasionally had anxious moments when the Ota and its mouth branches rose to flood, but the piling was apparently firm enough and the house had always held.

Dr. Fujii had been relatively idle for about a month because in July, as the number of untouched cities in Japan dwindled and as Hiroshima seemed more and more inevitably a target, he began turning patients away, on the ground that in case of a fire raid he would not be able to evacuate them. Now he had only two patients left—a woman from Yano, injured in the shoulder, and a young man of twenty-five recovering from burns he had suffered when the steel factory near Hiroshima in which he worked had been hit. Dr. Fujii had six nurses to tend his patients. His wife and children were safe; his wife and one son were living outside Osaka, and another son and two daughters were in the country on Kyushu. A niece was living with him, and a maid and a manservant. He had little to do and did not mind, for he had saved some money. At fifty, he was healthy, convivial, and calm, and he was pleased to pass the evenings drinking whiskey with friends, always sensibly and for the sake of conversation. Before the war, he had affected brands imported from Scotland and America; now he was perfectly satisfied with the best Japanese brand, Suntory.

Dr. Fujii sat down cross-legged in his underwear on the spotless matting of the porch, put on his glasses, and started reading the Osaka *Asahi*. He liked to read the Osaka news because his wife was there. He saw the flash. To him—faced away from the center and looking at his paper—it seemed a brilliant yellow. Startled, he began to rise to his feet. In that moment (he was 1,550 yards from the center), the hospital leaned behind his rising and, with a terrible ripping noise, toppled into the river. The Doctor, still in the act of getting to his feet, was thrown forward and around and over; he was buffeted and gripped; he lost track of everything, because things were so speeded up; he felt the water.

Dr. Fujii hardly had time to think that he was dying before he realized that he was alive, squeezed tightly by two long timbers in a V across his chest, like a morsel suspended between two huge chopsticks—held upright, so that he could not move, with his head miraculously above water and his torso and legs in it. The remains of his hospital were all around him in a mad assortment of splintered lumber and materials for the relief of pain. His left shoulder hurt terribly. His glasses were gone.

Father Wilhelm Kleinsorge, of the Society of Jesus, was, on the morning of the explosion, in rather frail condition. The Japanese wartime diet had not sustained him, and he felt the strain of being a foreigner in an increasingly xenophobic Japan; even a German, since the defeat of the Fatherland, was unpopular. Father Kleinsorge had, at thirty-eight, the look of a boy growing too fast—thin in the face, with a prominent Adam's apple, a hollow chest, dangling hands, big feet. He walked clumsily, leaning forward a little. He was tired all the time. To make matters worse, he had suffered for two days, along with Father Cieslik, a fellowpriest, from a rather painful and urgent diarrhea, which they blamed on the beans and black ration bread they were obliged to eat. Two other priests then living in the mission compound, which was in the Nobori-cho section—Father Superior LaSalle and Father Schiffer—had happily escaped this affliction.

Father Kleinsorge woke up about six the morning the bomb was dropped, and half an hour later—he was a bit tardy because of his sickness—he began to read Mass in the mission chapel, a small Japanese-style wooden building which was without pews, since its worshippers knelt on the usual Japanese matted floor, facing an altar graced with splendid silks, brass, silver, and heavy embroideries. This morning, a Monday, the only worshippers were Mr. Takemoto, a theological student living in the mission house; Mr. Fukai, the secretary of the diocese; Mrs. Murata, the mission's devoutly Christian housekeeper; and his fellow-priests. After Mass, while Father Kleinsorge was reading the Prayers of Thanksgiving, the siren sounded. He stopped the service and the missionaries retired across the compound to the bigger building. There, in his room on the ground floor, to the right of the front door, Father Kleinsorge changed into a military uniform which he had acquired when he was teaching at the Rokko Middle School in Kobe and which he wore during air-raid alerts.

After an alarm, Father Kleinsorge always went out and scanned the sky, and in this instance, when he stepped outside, he was glad to see only the single weather plane that flew over Hiroshima each day about this time. Satisfied that nothing would happen, he went in and breakfasted with the other Fathers on substitute coffee and ration bread, which, under the circumstances, was especially repugnant to him. The Fathers sat and talked awhile, until, at eight, they heard the all-clear. They went then to various parts of the building. Father Schiffer retired to his room to do some writing. Father Cieslik sat in his room in a straight chair with a pillow over his stomach to ease his pain, and read. Father Superior LaSalle stood at the window of his room, thinking. Father Kleinsorge went up to a room on the third floor, took off all his clothes except his underwear, and stretched out on his right side on a cot and began reading his *Stimmen der Zeit*.

After the terrible flash—which, Father Kleinsorge later realized, reminded him of something he had read as a boy about a large meteor colliding with the earth—he had time (since he was 1,400 yards from the center) for one thought: A bomb has fallen directly on us. Then, for a few seconds or minutes, he went out of his mind.

Father Kleinsorge never knew how he got out of the house. The next things he was conscious of were that he was wandering around in the mission's vegetable garden in his underwear, bleeding slightly from small cuts along his left flank; that all the buildings round about had fallen down except the Jesuits' mission house, which had long before been braced and double-braced by a priest named Gropper, who was terrified of earthquakes; that the day had turned dark; and that Murata-*san*, the housekeeper, was nearby, crying over and over, "*Shu Jesusu, awaremi tamai!* Our Lord Jesus, have pity on us!"

On the train on the way into Hiroshima from the country, where he lived with his mother, Dr. Terufumi Sasaki, the Red Cross Hospital surgeon, thought over an unpleasant nightmare he had had the night before. His mother's home was in Mukaihara, thirty miles from the city, and it took him two hours by train and tram to reach the hospital. He had slept uneasily all night and had wakened an hour earlier than usual, and, feeling sluggish and slightly feverish, had debated whether to go to the hospital at all; his sense of duty finally forced him to go, and he had started out on an earlier train than he took most mornings. The dream had particularly frightened him because it was so closely associated, on the surface at least, with a disturbing actuality. He was only twenty-five years old and had just completed his training at the Eastern Medical University, in Tsingtao, China. He was something of an idealist and was much distressed by the inadequacy of medical facilities in the country town where his mother lived. Quite on his own, and without a permit, he had begun visiting a few sick people out there in the evenings, after his eight hours at the hospital and four hours' commuting. He had recently learned that the penalty for practicing without a permit was severe; a fellow-doctor whom he had asked about it had given him a serious scolding. Nevertheless, he had continued to practice. In his dream, he had been at the bedside of a country patient when the police and the doctor he had consulted burst into the room, seized him, dragged him outside, and beat him up cruelly. On the train, he just about decided to give up the work in Mukaihara, since he felt it would be impossible to get a permit, because the authorities would hold that it would conflict with his duties at the Red Cross Hospital.

At the terminus, he caught a streetcar at once. (He later calculated that if he had taken his customary train that morning, and if he had had to wait a few minutes for the streetcar, as often happened, he would have been close to the center at the time of the explosion and would surely have perished.) He arrived at the hospital at seven-forty and reported to the chief surgeon. A few minutes later, he went to a room on the first floor and drew blood from the arm of a man in order to perform a Wassermann test. The laboratory containing the incubators for the test was on the third floor. With the blood specimen in his left hand, walking in a kind of distraction he had felt all morning, probably because of the dream and his restless night, he started along the main corridor on his way toward the stairs. He was one step beyond an open window when the light of the bomb was reflected, like a gigantic photographic flash, in the corridor. He ducked down on one knee and said to himself, as only a Japanese would, "Sasaki, *gambare!* Be brave!" Just then (the building was 1,650 yards from the center), the blast ripped through the hospital. The glasses he was wearing flew off his face; the bottle of blood crashed against one wall; his Japanese slippers zipped out from under his feet—but otherwise, thanks to where he stood, he was untouched.

Dr. Sasaki shouted the name of the chief surgeon and rushed around to the man's office and found him terribly cut by glass. The hospital was in horrible confusion: heavy partitions and ceilings had fallen on patients, beds had overturned, windows had blown in and cut people, blood was spattered on the walls and floors, instruments were everywhere, many of the patients were running about screaming, many more lay dead. (A colleague working in the laboratory to which Dr. Sasaki had been walking was dead; Dr. Sasaki's patient, whom he had just left and who a few moments before had been dreadfully afraid of syphilis, was also dead.) Dr. Sasaki found himself the only doctor in the hospital who was unhurt.

Dr. Sasaki, who believed that the enemy had hit only the building he was in, got bandages and began to bind the wounds of those inside the hospital; while outside, all over Hiroshima, maimed and dying citizens turned their unsteady steps toward the Red Cross Hospital to begin an invasion that was to make Dr. Sasaki forget his private nightmare for a long, long time.

Miss Toshiko Sasaki, the East Asia Tin Works clerk, who was not related to Dr. Sasaki, got up at three o'clock in the morning on the day the bomb fell. There was extra housework to do. Her eleven-month-old brother, Akio, had come down the day before with a serious stomach upset; her mother had taken him to the Tamura Pediatric Hospital and was staying there with him. Miss Sasaki, who was about twenty, had to cook breakfast for her father, a brother, a sister, and herself, and—since the hospital, because of the war, was unable to provide food—to prepare a whole day's meals for her mother and the baby, in time for her father, who worked in a factory making rubber earplugs for artillery crews, to take the food by on his way to the plant. When she had finished and had cleaned and put away the cooking things, it was nearly seven. The family lived in Koi, and she had a forty-five-minute trip to the tin works, in the section of town called Kannonmachi. She was in charge of the personnel records in the factory. She left Koi at seven, and as soon as she reached the plant, she went with some of the other girls from the personnel department to the factory auditorium. A prominent local Navy man, a former employee, had committed suicide the day before by throwing himself under a train—a death considered honorable enough to warrant a memorial service, which was to be held at the tin works at ten o'clock that morning. In the large hall, Miss Sasaki and the others made suitable preparations for the meeting. This work took about twenty minutes.

Miss Sasaki went back to her office and sat down at her desk. She was quite far from the windows, which were off to her left, and behind her were a couple of tall bookcases containing all the books of the factory library, which the personnel department had organized. She settled herself at her desk, put some things in a drawer, and shifted papers. She thought that before she began to make entries in her lists of new employees, discharges, and departures for the Army, she would chat for a moment with the girl at her right. Just as she turned her head away from the windows, the room was filled with a blinding light. She was paralyzed by fear, fixed still in her chair for a long moment (the plant was 1,600 yards from the center).

Everything fell, and Miss Sasaki lost consciousness. The ceiling dropped suddenly and the wooden floor above collapsed in splinters and the people up there came down and the roof above them gave way; but principally and first of all, the bookcases right behind her swooped forward and the contents threw her down, with her left leg horribly twisted and breaking underneath her. There, in the tin factory, in the first moment of the atomic age, a human being was crushed by books.

—1945

Learning from Other Writers (Hersey)

1. What is the purpose of the opening paragraph of *Hiroshima?* What is the effect of beginning with Miss Sasaki as opposed to any of the other five characters?

2. Where and how does Hersey weave in background about the war, the bombing, and the city of Hiroshima?

3. What is the effect of including the information about the Japanese soldiers who had been burrowing into the hills above the city?

4. How and when does Hersey cut from person to person?

5. How does Hersey make his subjects seem familiar to American readers? Unfamiliar?

6. What is the implied argument of Hersey's text?

SUBCULTURES

Although many group portraits concern troubling themes of war, racism, and death, essays that adhere to this form also can inspire levity, as is true of Megan Daum's "Music Is My Bag." Instead of focusing on a handful of specific individuals within the subculture of amateur musicians, Daum attempts to portray the group as a whole, using archetypal behavior as opposed to the quirks of a few carefully selected subjects. The light, sarcastic tone of her essay allows for this sort of treatment. By spending the first five paragraphs carefully defining the Music Is My Bag subculture, she paints a funny yet endearing portrait of the group of musicians to which she once belonged but from which she slowly grew apart. Even if we are unfamiliar with the subculture Daum is describing, we immediately begin to think of what our "bag" might be (golf? soccer? fishing? horseback riding? dance?) and what trappings, signs, and codes signal our membership in that community.

After Daum defines this subculture, she describes her experiences playing the oboe and expresses her regret that she eventually gave up the instrument. At the end, she notes that what caused her to stop playing was her aversion to this subculture, the almost desperate attempts of the people around her to self-identify as musicians, rather than any distaste for the instrument itself. Although her essay is bitterly funny, the concluding three paragraphs end on a far more poignant, wistful note.

MUSIC IS MY BAG

The image I want to get across is that of the fifteen-year-old boy with the beginning traces of a mustache who hangs out in the band room after school playing the opening bars of a Billy Joel song on the piano. This is the kid who, in the interests of adopting some semblance of personal style, wears a fedora hat and a scarf with a black-and-white design of a piano keyboard. This is the kid who, in addition to having taught himself some tunes from the *Songs from the Attic* sheet music he bought at the local Sam Ash, probably also plays the trombone in the marching band, and experienced a seminal moment one afternoon as he vaguely flirted with a not-yet-kissed, clarinet-playing girl, a girl who is none too popular but whose propensity for leaning on the piano as the boy plays the opening chords of "Captain Jack" give him a clue as to the social possibilities that might be afforded him via the marching band.

If the clarinet-playing girl is an average student musician, she carries her plastic Selmer in the standard-issue black plastic case. If she has demonstrated any kind of proficiency, she carries her Selmer in a tote bag that reads "Music Is My Bag." The boy in the piano-key scarf definitely has music as his bag. He may not yet have the tote bag, but the hat, the Billy Joel, the tacit euphoria brought on by a sexual awakening that, for him, centers entirely around band, is all he needs to be delivered into the unmistakable realm that is Music Is My Bagdom.

I grew up in Music Is My Bag culture. The walls of my parents' house were covered with framed art posters from musical events: The San Francisco Symphony's 1982 production of St. Matthew's Passion, The Metropolitan Opera's 1976 production of Aida, the original Broadway production of Sweeney Todd. Ninety percent of the books on the shelves were about music, if not actual musical scores. Childhood ceramics projects made by my brother and me were painted with eighth notes and treble clef signs. We owned a deck of cards with portraits of the great composers on the back. A baby grand piano overtook the room that would have been the dining room if my parents hadn't forgone a table and renamed it "the music room." This room also contained an imposing hi-fisystem and a $300 wooden music stand. Music played at all times: Brahms, Mendelssohn, cast recordings of Sondheim musicals, a cappella Christmas albums. When my father sat down with a book, he read musical scores, humming quietly and tapping his foot. When I was ten, my mother decided we needed to implement a before-dinner ritual akin to saying grace, so she composed a short song, asking us all to contribute a lyric, and we held hands and sang it before eating. My lyric was, "There's a smile on our face and it seems to say all the wonderful things we've all done today." My mother insisted on harmonizing at the end. She also did this when singing "Happy Birthday."

Harmonizing on songs like "Happy Birthday" is a clear indication of the Music Is My Bag personality. If one does not have an actual bag that reads "Music Is My Bag"—as did the violist in the chamber music trio my mother set up with some women from the Unitarian Church—a $300 music stand and musical-note coasters will more than suffice. To avoid confusion, let me also say that there are many different Bags in life. Some friends of my parents have a $300 dictionary stand, a collection of silver bookmarks, and once threw a dinner party wherein the guests had to dress up as members of the Bloomsbury Group. These people are Literature Is My Bag. I know people who are Movies Are My Bag (detectable by key chains shaped like projectors, outdated copies of *Halliwell's Film Guide*, and one too many T-shirts from things like the San Jose Film Festival), people who are Cats Are My Bag (self-explanatory), and, perhaps most annoyingly, Where I Went To College Is My Bag (Yale running shorts, plastic Yale tumblers, Yale Platinum Plus MasterCard, and, yes, even Yale screensavers—all this in someone aged forty or more, the perennial contributor to the class notes).

Having a Bag connotes the state of being overly interested in something, and yet, in a certain way, not interested enough. It has a hobbyish quality to it, a sense that the enthusiasm developed at a time when the enthusiast was lacking in some significant area of social or intellectual life. Music Is My Bag is the mother of all Bags, not just because in the early 1980s some consumer force of the public radio fund-drive variety distributed a line of tote bags that displayed that slogan, but because its adherents, or, as they tend to call themselves, "music lovers," give off an aura that distinguishes them from the rest of the population. It's an aura that has to do with a sort of benign cluelessness, a condition that, even in middle age, smacks of that phase between prepubescence and real adolescence. Music Is My Bag people have a sexlessness to them. There is a pastiness to them. They can never seem to find a good pair of jeans. You can spot them on the street, the female French horn player in concert dress hailing a cab to Lincoln Center around seven o'clock in the evening, her earrings too big, her hairstyle unchanged since 1986. The fifty-something recording engineer with the running shoes and the shoulder bag. The Indiana marching band kids in town for the Macy's Thanksgiving Day Parade, snapping photos of each other in front of the Hard Rock Cafe, having sung their parts from the band arrangement of *Hello, Dolly!* the whole way on the bus, thinking, knowing, that it won't get better than this. Like all Music Is My Bag people, they are a little too in love with the trappings. They know what their boundaries are and load up their allotted space with memorabilia, saving the certificates of participation from regional festivals, the composer-a-month calendars, the Mostly Mozart posters. Their sincerity trumps attempts at snideness. The boys' sarcasm only goes a fraction of the way there, the girls will never be great seducers. They grow up to look like high school band directors even if they're not. They give their pets names like Wolfgang and Gershwin. Their hemlines are never quite right.

I played the oboe. This is not an instrument to be taken lightly. The oboist runs a high risk of veering into Music Is My Bag culture, mostly because to get beyond the entry level is to give oneself over to an absorption with technique that can make a person vulnerable to certain vagaries of a subcategory, the oboe phylum. This inevitably leads to the genus of wind ensemble culture, which concerns itself with the socio-political infrastructure of the woodwind section, the disproportionate number of solo passages, a narcissistic pride in sounding the A that tunes the orchestra. Not many people play the oboe. It's a difficult instrument, beautiful when played well, horrifying when played poorly. I was self-conscious about playing the oboe, mostly because so many people confuse it with the bassoon, its much larger, ganglier cousin in the double-reed family. The act of playing the oboe, unlike the graceful arm positions of the flute or the violin, is not a photogenic one. The embouchure puckers the face into a grimace; my childhood and adolescence is documented by photos that make me look slightly deformed—the lipless girl. It's not an instrument for the vain. Oboe playing revolves almost entirely around saliva. Spit gets caught in the keys and the joints and must be blown out using cigarette rolling paper as a blotter (a scandalous drugstore purchase for a twelve-year-old). Spit can accumulate on the floor if you play for too long. Spit must constantly be sucked out from both sides of the reed. The fragile, temperamental reed is the player's chronic medical condition. It must be tended to constantly. It must be wet but never too wet, hard enough to emit a decent sound, but soft enough to blow air through. The oboist must never stray far from moisture; the reed is forever in her mouth, in a paper cup of water that teeters on the music stand, being doused at a drinking fountain in Parsippany High School at the North Jersey Regional Band and Orchestra Audition. After a certain age, the student oboist must learn to make her own reeds, build them from bamboo using knives and shavers. Most people don't realize this. Reed-making is an eighteenth-century exercise, something that would seem to require an apprenticeship before undertaking solo. But oboists, occupying a firm, albeit wet, patch of ground under the tattered umbrella of Music Is My Bag, never quite live in the same era as everyone else.

Though I did, at one point, hold the title of second-best high school player in the state of New Jersey, I was a mediocre oboist. My discipline was lacking, my enthusiasm virtually nil, and my comprehension of rhythm (in keeping with a lifelong math phobia) held me back considerably. But being without an aptitude for music was, in my family, tantamount to being a Kennedy who knows nothing of politics. Aptitude was something, perhaps even the only thing, I possessed. As indifferent to the oboe as I was—and I once began an orchestra rehearsal without noticing that I had neglected to screw the bell, which is the entire bottom portion, onto the rest of my instrument—I managed to be good enough to play in the New Jersey All-State High School Orchestra as well as a local adult symphony. I even gained acceptance into a music conservatory. These aren't staggering accomplishments unless you consider the fact that I rarely practiced. If I had practiced with any amount of regularity, I could have been, as my parents would have liked me to be, one of those kids who was schlepped to Juilliard on Saturdays. If I had practiced slightly more than that, I could have gone to Juilliard for college. If I had practiced a lot I could have ended up in the New York Philharmonic. This is not an exaggeration, merely a moot point. I didn't practice. I haven't picked up the oboe since my junior year in college, where, incidentally, I sat first chair in the orchestra even though I did not practice once the entire time.

I never practiced and yet I always practiced. My memory is always of being unprepared, yet I was forced to sit in the chair for so many hours that I suspect something else must have been at work, a lack of consciousness about it, an inability to practice on my own. "Practice" was probably among the top five words spoken in our family, the other four probably being the names of our family members. Today, almost ten years since I've practiced, the word has lost the resonance of our usage. I now think of practice in terms of law or medicine. There is a television show called *The Practice*, and it seems odd to me that I never associate the word sprawled across the screen with the word that wove relentlessly throughout our family discourse. For my entire child-hood and adolescence, practicing was an ongoing condition. It was both a given and a punishment. When we were bad, we practiced. When we were idle, we practiced. Before dinner and TV and friends coming over and bedtime and a thousand other things that beckoned with the possibility of taking place without all that harrowing noise, we practiced. "You have practicing and homework," my mother said every day. In that order. My father said the same thing without the homework part.

Much of the reason I could never quite get with the oboe-playing program was that I developed, at a very young age, a deep contempt for the Music Is My Bag world. Instead of religion, my family had music, and it was the church against which I rebelled. I had clergy for parents. My father: professional composer and arranger, keyboard player and trombonist, brother of a high school band director in Illinois. My mother: pianist and music educator of the high school production of *Carousel* genre. My own brother was a reluctant Christ figure. A typically restless second child in youth (he quit piano les-sons but later discovered he could play entirely by ear), my brother recently completed the final mix of a demo CD of songs he wrote and performed—mid-eighties pop, late Doobie Brothers groove. His house is littered with Billy Joel and Bruce Hornsby sheet music, back issues of Stereo Review, the liner notes to the digital remastering of John Williams's score for *Star Wars*. Music is the Bag.

I compose songs in my sleep. I can't do it awake. I'll dream of songwriters singing onstage. I'll hear them perform new songs, songs I've never heard, songs I therefore must have written. In childhood I never put one thought toward composing a song. It would have been like composing air, creating more of something of which there was already quite enough. Wind players like flutists and saxophonists need as much air as they can get. Oboists are always trying to get rid of air. They calibrate what they need to get the reed to vibrate, end up using even less, and dispense with the rest out the corners of their mouths. It's all about exhaling. On an eighth rest, they're as likely to blow air out as they are to steal a breath. There's always too much air for oboists, too much of everything, too many bars when they're not playing and too many bars where there's hardly anyone playing but them, too many percussion players dropping triangles on the floor, too many violinists playing "Eleanor Rigby" before the rehearsal starts. Orchestras have only two oboists, first chair and second chair, pilot and copilot, though the "co" in this case is, like all "co's," a misnomer. The second oboist is the perpetual backup system, the one on call, the one who jumps in and saves the other when his reed dries up in the middle of a solo, when he misses his cue, when he freezes in panic before trying to hit a high D. I've been first oboist and I've been second oboist and, let me tell you, first is better, but not by much. It's still the oboe. Unlike the gregarious violinist or the congenial cellist, the oboist is a lone wolf. To play the oboe in an orchestra is to complete an obstacle course of solos and duets with the first flutist who, if she is hard-core Music Is My Bag, will refer to herself as a "flautist."

Oboe solos dot the great symphonies like land mines, the pizzicati that precede them are drumrolls, the conductor's pointing finger an arrow for the whole audience to see: Here comes the oboe, two bars until the oboe, now, *now*. It's got to be nailed, one flubbed arpeggio, one flat half note, one misplaced pinky in the middle of a run of sixteenth notes, and *everyone* will hear, everyone.

My parents' presence at a high school orchestra concert turned what should have been a routine event into something akin to the finals of the Olympic women's figure skating long program. Even from the blinding, floodlit stage I could practically see them in the audience, clucking at every error, grimacing at anything even slightly out of tune. Afterwards, when the other parents—musically illiterate chumps—were patting their kids on the head and loading the tuba into the station wagon, I would receive my critique. "You were hesitating in the second movement of the Haydn Variations." "You over-anticipated in the berceuse section of the Stravinsky." "Your tone was excellent in the first movement but then your chops ran out." My brother, who was forced for a number of years to play the French horn, was reduced to a screaming fight with our father in the school parking lot, the kind of fight only possible between fathers and sons. He'd bumbled too many notes, played out of tune, committed some treasonous infraction against the family reputation. My father gave him the business on the way out to the car, eliciting the alto curses of a fourteen-year-old, pages of music everywhere, an instrument case slammed on the pavement.

This sort of rebellion was not my style. I cried instead. I cried in the seventh grade when the letter telling me I'd been accepted to the North Jersey regional orchestra arrived three days late. I cried in the tenth grade, when I ended up in the All-State Band instead of the orchestra. I cried when I thought I'd given a poor recital (never mind that the audience thought I was brilliant—all morons), cried before lessons (under-prepared), cried after lessons (sentenced to a week of reviewing the loathsome F-sharp étude). Mostly I cried during practice drills supervised by my father. These were torture sessions wherein some innocent tooting would send my father racing downstairs from his attic study, screaming, "Count, count, you're not counting! Jesus Christ!" Out would come a pencil—if not an actual conductor's baton—hitting the music stand, forcing me to repeat the tricky fingerings again and again, speeding up the tempo so I'd be sure to hit each note when we took it back down to real time. These sessions would last for hours, my mouth muscles shaking from atrophy, tears welling up from fatigue and exasperation. If we had a copy of the piano part, my mother would play the accompaniment, and together my parents would bark commands. "Articulate the eighth notes more. More staccato on the tonguing. Don't tap your foot, tap your toe inside your shoe." The postman heard a lot of this. The neighbors heard all of it. After practicing we'd eat dinner, but not before that song—"There's a smile on our face, and it seems to say all the wonderful things ..." "Good practice session today," my mother would say, dishing out the casserole, WQXR's *Symphony Hall* playing over the kitchen speakers. "Yup, sounding pretty good," my father would say. "How about one more go at it before bed?"

My mother called my oboe a "horn." This infuriated me. "Do you have your horn?" she'd ask every single morning. "Do you need your horn for school today?" She maintained that this terminology was technically correct, that among musicians, a "horn" was anything into which air was blown. My oboe was a $4,000 instrument, high-grade black grenadilla with sterling silver keys. It was no horn. But such semantics are a staple of Music Is My Bag, the overfamiliar stance that reveals a desperate need for subcultural affiliation, the musical equivalent of people in the magazine business who refer to publications like *Glamour* and *Forbes* as "books." As is indicated by the use of "horn," there's a subtly macho quality to Music Is My Bag. The persistent insecurity of musicians, especially classical musicians, fosters a kind of jargon that would be better confined to the military or major league baseball. Cellists talk about rock stops and rosin as though they were comparing canteen belts or brands of glove grease. They have their in-jokes and aphorisms, "The rock stops here," "Eliminate Violins In Our Schools."

I grew up surrounded by phrases like "rattle off that solo," "nail that lick," and "build up your chops." Like acid-washed jeans, "chops" is a word that should only be invoked by rock-and-roll guitarists but is more often uttered with the flailing, badly timed anti-authority of the high school clarinet player. Like the violinist who plays "Eleanor Rigby" before rehearsal, the clarinet player's relationship to rock and roll maintains its distance. Rock and roll is about sex. It is something unloved by parents and therefore unloved by Music Is My Bag people, who make a vocation of pleasing their parents, of studying trig and volunteering at the hospital and making a run for the student government even though they're well aware they have no chance of winning. Rock and roll is careless and unstudied. It might possibly involve drinking. It most certainly involves dancing. It flies in the face of the central identity of Music Is My Baggers, who chose as their role models those painfully introverted characters from young adult novels—"the klutz," "the bookworm," "the late bloomer." When given a classroom assignment to write about someone who inspires her, Music Is My Bag will write about her grandfather or perhaps Jean-Pierre Rampal. If the bad-attitude kid in the back row writes about AC/DC's Angus Young, Music Is My Bag will believe in her heart that this student should receive a failing grade. Rock and roll is not, as her parents would say when the junior high drama club puts on a production of *Grease,* "appropriate for this age group." Even in the throes of adolescence, Music Is My Bag will deny adolescence. Even at age sixteen, she will hold her ears when the rock and roll gets loud, saying it ruins her sense of overtones, saying she has sensitive ears. Like a retiree, she will classify the whole genre as nothing but a bunch of noise, though it is likely she is a fan of Yes.

During the years that I was a member of the New Jersey All-State Orchestra I would carpool to rehearsals with the four or so other kids from my town who made All State every year. This involved spending as much as two hours each way in station wagons driven by people's parents and, inevitably, the issue would arise of what music would be played in the car. Among the most talented musicians in school was a freshman who, in addition to being hired by the Boston Symphony Orchestra at age twenty-two, possessed, as a fifteen-year-old, a ripe enthusiasm for the singer Amy Grant. This was back in the mid-1980s when Amy Grant's hits were still relegated to the Christian charts. Our flute-playing carpool-mate loved Amy Grant. Next to Prokofiev and the

Hindemith Flute Sonata, Amy Grant occupied the number one spot in this girl's studious, late-blooming heart. Since her mother, like many parents of Baggers, was devoted solely to her daughter's musical and academic career, she did most of the driving to these boony spots—Upper Chatham High School, Monmouth Regional, Long Branch Middle School. Mile after New Jersey Turnpike mile, we were serenaded by the wholesome synthesizers of songs like "Saved By Love" and "Wait for the Healing," only to spill out of the car and take no small relief in the sound of twenty-five of New Jersey's best student violinists playing "Eleanor Rigby" before the six-hour rehearsal.

To participate in a six-hour rehearsal of the New Jersey All-State Band or Orchestra is to enter a world so permeated by Music Is My Bagdom that it becomes possible to confuse the subculture with an entire species, as if Baggers, like lobsters or ferns, require special conditions in order to thrive. Their ecosystem is the auditorium and the adjacent band room, any space that makes use of risers. To eat lunch and dinner in these venues is to see the accessories of Badgom tumble from purses, knapsacks, and totes; here more than anyplace are the real McCoys, actual Music Is My Bag bags, canvas satchels filled with stereo Walkmen and A.P. math homework and Trapper Keeper notebooks featuring the piano-playing Schroeder from the *Peanuts* comic strip. The dinner break is when I would embark on oboe maintenance, putting the reed in water, swabbing the instrument dry, removing the wads of wax that, during my orthodontic years, I placed over my front teeth to keep the inside of my mouth from bleeding. Just as I had hated the entropy of recess back in my grade-school years, I loathed the dinner breaks at All-State rehearsals. To maximize rehearsal time, the wind section often ate separately from the strings, which left me alone with the band types. They'd wolf down their sandwiches and commence with their jam session, a cacophonous white noise of scales, finger exercises, and memorized excerpts from their hometown marching band numbers. During these dinner breaks I'd generally hang with the other oboist. For some reason, this was almost always a tall girl who wore sneakers with corduroy pants and a turtleneck with nothing over it. This is fairly typical Music Is My Bag garb, though oboists have a particular spin on it, a spin characterized more than anything by lack of spin. Given the absence in most classical musicians of a style gene, this is probably a good thing. Oboists don't accessorize. They don't wear buttons on their jackets that say "Oboe Power" or "Who Are You Going to Tune To?"

There's high-end Bagdom and low-end Bagdom, with a lot of room in between. Despite my parents' paramilitary practice regimes, I have to give them credit for being fairly high-end Baggers. There were no piano-key scarves in our house, no "World's Greatest Trombonist" figurines, no plastic tumblers left over from my father's days as director of the Stanford University Marching Band. Such accessories are the mandate of the lowest tier of Music Is My Bag, a stratum whose mascot is P.D.Q. Bach, whose theme song is "Piano Man," and whose regional representative is the kid in high school who plays not only the trumpet but the piano, saxophone, flute, string bass, accordion, and wood block. This kid, considered a wunderkind by his parents and the rest of the band community, plays none of these instruments well, but the fact that he knows so many different sets of fingerings, the fact that he has the potential to earn some college money by performing as a one-man band at the annual state teacher's conference, makes him a hometown hero. He may not be a football player. He may not even gain access to the Ivy League. But in the realm of Music Is My Bag, the kid who plays every instrument, particularly when he can play Billy Joel songs on every instrument, is the Alpha Male.

The flip side of the one-man-band kid are those Music Is My Baggers who are not musicians at all. These are the kids who twirl flags or rifles in the marching band, kids who blast music in their rooms and play not air guitar but air keyboards, their hands fluttering out in front of them, the hand positions not nearly as important as the attendant head motions. This is the essence of Bagdom. It is to take greater pleasure in the reverb than the melody, to love the lunch break more than the rehearsal, the rehearsal more than the performance, the clarinet case more than the clarinet. It is to think nothing of sending away for the deluxe packet of limited-edition memorabilia that is being sold for the low, low price of one's entire personality. It is to let the trinkets do the talking.

I was twenty-one when I stopped playing the oboe. I wish I could come up with a big, dramatic reason why. I wish I could say that I sustained some kind of injury that prevented me from playing (it's hard to imagine what kind of injury could sideline an oboist—a lip strain? carpal tunnel?) or that I was forced to sell my oboe in order to help a family member in crisis or, better yet, that I suffered a violent attack in which my oboe was used as a weapon against me before being stolen and melted down for artillery. But the truth, I'm ashamed to say, has more to do with what in college I considered to be an exceptionally long walk from my dormitory to the music building, and the fact that I was wrapped up in a lot of stuff that, from my perspective at the time, precluded the nailing of Rachmaninoff licks. Without the prodding of my parents or the structure of a state-run music education program, my oboe career had to run on self-motivation alone—not an abundant resource—and when my senior year started I neither registered for private lessons nor signed up for the orchestra, dodging countless calls from the director imploring me to reassume my chair.

Since then, I haven't set foot in a rehearsal room, put together a folding music stand, fussed with a reed, marked up music, practiced scales, tuned an orchestra or performed any of the countless activities that had dominated my existence up until that point. There are moments every now and then when I'll hear the oboe-dominated tenth movement of the Bach Mass in B Minor or the berceuse section of Stravinsky's *Firebird* and long to find a workable reed and pick up the instrument again. But then I imagine how terrible I'll sound after eight dormant years and put the whole idea out of my mind before I start to feel sad about it. I can still smell the musty odor of the inside of my oboe case, the old-ladyish whiff of the velvet lining and the tubes of cork grease and the damp fabric of the key pads. Unlike the computer on which I now work, my oboe had the sense of being an ancient thing. Brittle and creaky, it was vulnerable when handled by strangers. It needed to be packed up tight, dried out in just the right places, kept away from the heat and the cold and from anyone stupid enough to confuse it with a clarinet.

What I really miss about the oboe is having my hands on it. I could come at that instrument from any direction or any angle and know every indentation on every key, every spot that leaked air, every nick on every square inch of wood. When enough years go by, the corporeal qualities of an instrument become as familiar to its player as, I imagine, those of a longstanding lover. Knowing precisely how the weight of the oboe was distributed between my right thumb and left wrist, knowing, above all, that the weight would feel the same way every time, every day, for every year that I played, was a feeling akin to having ten years of knowledge about the curve of someone's back. But I put my oboe down, and I never picked it back up. I could have been a pretty good oboist if I had practiced, if I had ignored the set design and just played the instrument. But I didn't and I wasn't. When I look back I hardly recognize myself, that person who could play a Mozart sonata by memory, whose fingers could move three times faster than I now type—a person who was given a gift, but who walked away from it because of piano-key scarves and fedora hats and all those secondary melodies that eventually became the only thing I could hear.

—2000

Learning from Other Writers (Daum)

1. Megan Daum begins her essay with a humorous portrait of "the unmistakable world of Music Is My Bag." How does she leverage parody as a kind of analysis in the first section?

2. By the third paragraph the author has revealed that she herself grew up in this world. Does this give Daum permission to make fun? What is the fine line between humor and generalization, between satire and stereotype?

3. What elements of the narrative form does Daum utilize for her portrait? How does she organize her portrait in terms of chronology?

4. How might Daum's essay appeal to readers who aren't musicians? How does she present her work to appeal to a wider audience, particularly with regards to her central analysis?

5. What if Daum had decided to profile five specific musicians rather than the subculture as a whole? How would that structure change the goal of the essay? Her driving question? Her use of humor?

Adding Your Voice

1. Think of a group of people who have something in common (for example, theater students, rugby players, patients in a pediatric cancer ward, deer hunters, or stand-up comics). Think of a question that applies to this group. Write a group portrait, bearing in mind the larger question about the group you are trying to answer. Remember, you might need a secondary structure to help you find an order for the portraits. Is there some action or event in which your group participated (e.g., a tryout for a musical, or the opening day of deer season)? If so, you might want to use the chronology of that event to help you figure out when

to describe each person in the group. You could structure your essay around the parts being auditioned for in the musical, or you might profile those deer hunters according to age, from youngest to most experienced. The trick here is to get at the essence of the group without creating a caricature of the members, or devolving into stereotype.

2. Choose a community to which you belong (whether as an insider or an insider/outsider). Freewrite about the ways in which that community is defined. How are insiders distinguished from outsiders? Do members display special ways of speaking? Dressing? Eating? Telling jokes? Are they characterized by particular desires or goals? Are there any rituals or superstitions that insiders follow or believe in? Based on this freewriting, come up with a definition of your community and/or the process by which certain people can become members. Freewrite about the significance of this community and the community's effect on members, outsiders, or society at large. What does the existence of the community say about some larger aspect of American culture? Should we celebrate or condemn the existence of this community? Work to change it, abolish it, or preserve its existence? Based on personal experience, research, interviews, or a combination of all three, write an essay in which you define your community and explore one of the questions you came up with in your freewriting. Make sure you know whether your audience consists of members of the community, outsiders, or both.

3. Select a set of signs or behaviors that interests you (e.g., a style of dress, a group of objects that people buy and/or display, the rituals that people in your group follow when dating or mating, the protocols that you and your friends follow when communicating via text messaging). Define and decipher the "code" you have selected, helping an audience of outsiders to understand the significance of the code and what is going on at a deeper level. To defamiliarize the code and help your audience see it in a new light, you might pretend that you are explaining it to an alien from another planet or a time-traveler from the future or the past. Structure your essay according to the order in which you or someone else might encounter these signs or behaviors in everyday life. If that seems too complicated, you can structure your essay according to a list of the signs or behaviors you are decoding.

CHAPTER 9

Place

When you write a profile of a person, you have available to you many methods of gaining information about your subject—your memories of the person, interviews with him or her, letters, journals, historical documents, books, and scholarly articles. When you write about a place, many of these same sources might be relevant. Whether you are describing a French city on the Mediterranean or a small mining town in Montana, you might want to interview people who live there. You might obtain access to historical societies and libraries. And, most fruitful of all, you might travel to that place and spend time wandering the beaches, climbing the mountains, descending to the old silver mines, or sifting through the trash at the local dump.

But the power of memory as it relates to writing about a place should not be underestimated. E. B. White's "Once More to the Lake" uses the tension between the author's memories and present-day experiences to help evoke a place. The way you once viewed a place versus the way you view that same place now, or the way a place once was as contrasted with the way it is now, can provide a nice juxtaposition in an essay. Often, writers attempt to answer their driving question about the essence of a place through this type of temporal comparison.

E. B. White's essay revolves around the time that he returned with his son to the lake that he used to visit every summer as a child. So many aspects of life on the lake, from the dragonflies to the waitresses, strike the author as unchanging; other aspects—the loud outboard motors, the two tracks on the dirt roads instead of three (showing the switch from horse-drawn transportation to wheeled automobiles)—are different. What White realizes is that the lake hasn't changed so much as he has aged. The lake to which he brings his son becomes emblematic of his own grappling with mortality. White finds it difficult not to imagine himself as both his son and his father, and the sensation, which he describes as "creepy," persists the entire visit. With careful, almost reverent attention to the sensory details of the place, White captures the essence of what this lake meant to him as a boy and what it now means to him as a father, although the aforementioned meditations on mortality, change, and progress are what give the essay its significance.

E. B. White

ONCE MORE TO THE LAKE

August 1941

One summer, along about 1904, my father rented a camp on a lake in Maine and took us all there for the month of August. We all got ringworm from some kittens and had to rub Pond's Extract on our arms and legs night and morning, and my father rolled over in a canoe with all his clothes on; but outside of that the vacation was a success and from then on none of us ever thought there was any place in the world like that lake in Maine. We returned summer after summer—always on August 1 for one month. I have since become a salt-water man, but sometimes in summer there are days when the restlessness of the tides and the fearful cold of the sea water and the incessant wind that blows across the afternoon and into the evening make me wish for the placidity of a lake in the woods. A few weeks ago this feeling got so strong I bought myself a couple of bass hooks and a spinner and returned to the lake where we used to go, for a week's fishing and to revisit old haunts.

I took along my son, who had never had any fresh water up his nose and who had seen lily pads only from train windows. On the journey over to the lake I began to wonder what it would be like. I wondered how time would have marred this unique, this holy spot—the coves and streams, the hills that the sun set behind, the camps and the paths behind the camps. I was sure that the tarred road would have found it out, and I wondered in what other ways it would be desolated. It is strange how much you can remember about places like that once you allow your mind to return into the grooves that lead back. You remember one thing, and that suddenly reminds you of another thing. I guess I remembered clearest of all the early mornings, when the lake was cool and motionless, remembered how the bedroom smelled of the lumber it was made of and of the wet woods whose scent entered through the screen. The partitions in the camp were thin and did not extend clear to the top of the rooms, and as I was always the first up I would dress softly so as not to wake the others, and sneak out into the sweet outdoors and start out in the canoe, keeping close along the shore in the long shadows of the pines. I remembered being very careful never to rub my paddle against the gunwale for fear of disturbing the stillness of the cathedral.

The lake had never been what you would call a wild lake. There were cottages sprinkled around the shores, and it was in farming country although the shores of the lake were quite heavily wooded. Some of the cottages were owned by nearby farmers, and you would live at the shore and eat your meals at the farmhouse. That's what our family did. But although it wasn't wild, it was a fairly large and undisturbed lake and there were places in it that, to a child at least, seemed infinitely remote and primeval.

I was right about the tar: it led to within half a mile of the shore. But when I got back there, with my boy, and we settled into a camp near a farmhouse and into the kind of summertime I had known, I could tell that it was going to be pretty much the same as it had been before—I knew it, lying in bed the first morning, smelling the bedroom and hearing the boy sneak quietly out and go off along the shore in a boat. I began to sustain the illusion that he was I, and therefore, by simple transposition, that I was my father. This sensation persisted, kept cropping up all the time we were there. It was not an entirely new feeling, but in this setting it grew much stronger. I seemed to be living a dual existence. I would be in the middle of some simple act, I would be picking up a bait box or laying down a table fork, or I would be saying something, and suddenly it would be not I but my father who was saying the words or making the gesture. It gave me a creepy sensation.

We went fishing the first morning. I felt the same damp moss covering the worms in the bait can, and saw the dragonfly alight on the tip of my rod as it hovered a few inches from the surface of the water. It was the arrival of this fly that convinced me beyond any doubt that everything was as it always had been, that the years were a mirage and that there had been no years. The small waves were the same, chucking the rowboat under the chin as we fished at anchor, and the boat was the same boat, the same color green and the ribs broken in the same places, and under the floorboards the same fresh-water leavings and debris—the dead hellgrammite, the wisps of moss, the rusty discarded fishhook, the dried blood from yesterday's catch. We stared silently at the tips of our rods, at the dragonflies that came and went. I lowered the tip of mine into the water, tentatively, pensively dislodging the fly, which darted two feet away, poised, darted two feet back, and came to rest again a little farther up the rod. There had been no years between the ducking of this dragonfly and the other one—the one that was part of memory. I looked at the boy, who was silently watching his fly, and it was my hands that held his rod, my eyes watching. I felt dizzy and didn't know which rod I was at the end of.

We caught two bass, hauling them in briskly as though they were mackerel, pulling them over the side of the boat in a businesslike manner without any landing net, and stunning them with a blow on the back of the head. When we got back for a swim before lunch, the lake was exactly where we had left it, the same number of inches from the dock, and there was only the merest suggestion of a breeze. This seemed an utterly enchanted sea, this lake you could leave to its own devices for a few hours and come back to, and find it had not stirred, this constant and trustworthy body of water. In the shallows, the dark, water-soaked sticks and twigs, smooth and old, were undulating in clusters on the bottom against the clean ribbed sand, and the track of the mussel was plain. A school of minnows swam by, each minnow with its small individual shadow, doubling the attendance, so clear and sharp in the sunlight. Some of the other campers were in swimming, along the shore, one of them with a cake of soap, and the water felt thin and clear and unsubstantial. Over the years there had been this person with the cake of soap, this cultist, and here he was. There had been no years.

Up to the farmhouse to dinner through the teeming, dusty field, the road under our sneakers was only a two-track road. The middle track was missing, the one with the marks of the hooves and the splotches of dried, flaky manure. There had always been three tracks to choose from in choosing which track to walk in; now the choice was narrowed down to two. For a moment I missed terribly the middle alternative. But the way led past the tennis court, and something about the way it lay there in the sun reassured me; the tape had loosened along the backline, the alleys were green with plantains and other weeds, and the net (installed in June and removed in September) sagged in the dry noon, and the whole place steamed with midday heat and hunger and emptiness. There was a choice of pie for dessert, and one was blueberry and one was apple, and the waitresses were the same country girls, there having been no passage of time, only the illusion of it as in a dropped curtain—the waitresses were still fifteen; their hair had been washed, that was the only difference—they had been to the movies and seen the pretty girls with the clean hair.

Summertime, oh summertime, pattern of life indelible, the fade-proof lake, the woods unshatterable, the pasture with the sweetfern and the juniper forever and ever, summer without end; this was the background, and the life along the shore was the design, their tiny docks with the flagpole and the American flag floating against the white clouds in the blue sky, the little paths over the roots of the trees leading from camp to camp and the paths leading back to the outhouses and the can of lime for sprinkling, and at the souvenir counters at the store the miniature birch-bark canoes and the postcards that showed things looking a little better than they looked. This was the American family at play, escaping the city heat, wondering whether the newcomers in the camp at the head of the cove were "common" or "nice," wondering whether it was true that the people who drove up for Sunday dinner at the farmhouse were turned away because there wasn't enough chicken.

It seemed to me, as I kept remembering all this, that those times and those summers had been infinitely precious and worth saving. There had been jollity and peace and goodness. The arriving (at the beginning of August) had been so big a business in itself, at the railway station the farm wagon drawn up, the first smell of the pine-laden air, the first glimpse of the smiling farmer, and the great importance of the trunks and your father's enormous authority in such matters, and the feel of the wagon under you for the long ten-mile haul, and at the top of the last long hill catching the first view of the lake after eleven months of not seeing this cherished body of water. The shouts and cries of the other campers when they saw you, and the trunks to be unpacked, to give up their rich burden. (Arriving was less exciting nowadays, when you sneaked up in your car and parked it under a tree near the camp and took out the bags and in five minutes it was all over, no fuss, no loud wonderful fuss about trunks.)

Peace and goodness and jollity. The only thing that was wrong now, really, was the sound of the place, an unfamiliar nervous sound of the outboard motors. This was the note that jarred, the one thing that would sometimes break the illusion and set the years moving. In those other summertimes all the motors were inboard; and when they were at a little distance, the noise they made was a sedative, an ingredient of summer sleep. They were one-cylinder and two-cylinder engines, and some were make-and-break and some were jump-spark, but they all made a sleepy sound across the lake. The one-lungers throbbed and fluttered, and the twin-cylinder ones purred and purred, and that was a quiet sound, too. But now the campers all had outboards. In the daytime, in the hot mornings, these motors made a petulant, irritable sound;

at night, in the still evening when the afterglow lit the water, they whined about one's ears like mosquitoes. My boy loved our rented outboard, and his great desire was to achieve single-handed mastery over it, and authority, and he soon learned the trick of choking it a little (but not too much), and the adjustment of the needle valve. Watching him I would remember the things you could do with the old one-cylinder engine with the heavy flywheel, how you could have it eating out of your hand if you got really close to it spiritually. Motorboats in those days didn't have clutches, and you would make a landing by shutting off the motor at the proper time and coasting in with a dead rudder. But there was a way of reversing them, if you learned the trick, by cutting the switch and putting it on again exactly on the final dying revolution of the flywheel, so that it would kick back against the compression and begin reversing. Approaching a dock in a strong following breeze, it was difficult to slow up sufficiently by the ordinary coasting method, and if a boy felt he had complete mastery over his motor, he was tempted to keep it running beyond its time and then reverse it a few feet from the dock. It took a cool nerve, because if you threw the switch a twentieth of a second too soon you would catch the flywheel when it still had speed enough to go up past center, and the boat would leap ahead, charging bull-fashion at the dock.

We had a good week at camp. The bass were biting well and the sun shone endlessly, day after day. We would be tired at night and lie down in the accumulated heat of the little bedrooms after the long hot day and the breeze would stir almost imperceptibly outside and the smell of the swamp drift in through the rusty screens. Sleep would come easily and in the morning the red squirrel would be on the roof, tapping out his gay routine. I kept remembering everything, lying in bed in the mornings—the small steamboat that had a long rounded stem like the lip of a Ubangi, and how quietly she ran on the moonlight sails, when the older boys played their mandolins and the girls sang and we ate doughnuts dipped in sugar, and how sweet the music was on the water in the shining night, and what it had felt like to think about girls then. After breakfast we would go up to the store and the things were in the same place—the minnows in a bottle, the plugs and spinners disarranged and pawed over by the youngsters from the boys' camp, the Fig Newtons and the Beeman's gum. Outside, the road was tarred and cars stood in front of the store. Inside, all was just as it had always been, except there was more Coca-Cola and not so much Moxie and root beer and birch beer and sarsaparilla. We would walk out with the bottle of pop apiece and sometimes the pop would backfire up our noses and hurt. We explored the streams, quietly, where the turtles slid off the sunny logs and dug their way into the soft bottom; and we lay on the town wharf and fed worms to the tame bass. Everywhere we went I had trouble making out which I was, the one walking at my side, the one walking in my pants.

One afternoon while we were there at that lake a thunderstorm came up. It was like the revival of an old melodrama that I had seen long ago with childish awe. The second-act climax of the drama of the electrical disturbance over a lake in America had not changed in any important respect. This was the big scene, still the big scene. The whole thing was so familiar, the first feeling of oppression and heat and a general air around camp of not wanting to go very far away. In mid-afternoon (it was all the same) a curious darkening of the sky, and a lull in everything that had made life tick; and then the way the boats suddenly swung the other way at their moorings with the coming of a breeze out of the new quarter, and the premonitory rumble. Then the kettle drum, then the snare, then the bass drum and cymbals, then the crackling light against the dark, and the gods grinning and licking their chops in the hills. Afterward the calm, the rain steadily rustling in the calm lake, the return of light and hope and spirits, and the campers running out in joy and relief to go swimming in the rain, their bright cries perpetuating the deathless joke about how they were getting simply drenched, and the children screaming with delight at the new sensation of bathing in the rain, and the joke about getting drenched linking the generations in a strong indestructible chain. And the comedian who waded in carrying an umbrella.

When the others went swimming, my son said he was going in, too. He pulled his dripping trunks from the line where they had hung all through the shower and wrung them out. Languidly, and with no thought of going in, I watched him, his hard little body, skinny and bare, saw him wince slightly as he pulled up around his vitals the small, soggy, icy garment. As he buckled the swollen belt, suddenly my groin felt the chill of death.

—1941

Learning from Other Writers (White)

1. Every essay teaches the reader how to read it. How does White lead the reader through his first paragraph? How does he set up our experience of the text?

2. White is an expert at crafting significant details. In the second paragraph, he describes his son as someone "who had never had any fresh water up his nose and who had seen lily pads only from train windows." What do we know from this sentence about where White and his family live? What do we know about their vacation habits? What else can you deduce from this description?

3. What are some of White's other telling details in this essay? In particular, how do these details reinforce the author's reflections on "time"?

4. How does White characterize his son? How do the boy's actions and his personality as evoked by White provide opportunities of analysis by the author?

5. White doesn't simply list the similarities and differences between the lake as it once was and how he finds the lake to be during his recent visit with his son. Rather, he makes meaning by comparing and contrasting those similarities and differences. How so?

Adding Your Voice

Think about a time you returned to a place you hadn't visited in a while. It could be a place where you vacationed as a child, your grandparents' house, or even your hometown as it appears to you after your first semester away at college. Try to describe the way you saw the place when you were younger, using retrospective narration to provide a contrast between the way you see the place now and the way you saw it then. For example: What do you notice now that you didn't notice before? What were you more aware of as a child? Is the place less magical now than you used to think it was? Pick specific details that coalesce to give us a new understanding of your experience of returning to this place after such a long absence.

In addition to developing your skills in using details and description, this is also an exercise in perspective—analyzing a place in a new light to see how it truly is, or maybe how it was all along. Pay attention to details that engage the senses, allowing your readers both to experience the place vividly and to understand its essence in a complex way. Doing so will help give the essay significance by tackling bigger issues. For example: White uses details to show us the scenery *and* to reflect on aging, mortality, and father-son relationships.

USING NARRATIVE TO CAPTURE THE ESSENCE OF A PLACE

As mentioned earlier, narrative is a common way to structure an essay because story-telling is such a natural form. The next two essayists use straight narrative to structure their portraits of places about which they care deeply. In "We Don't Swim in Our Cemeteries," Jesmyn Ward recounts the trauma of surviving Hurricane Katrina and its aftermath, and in so doing creates a revealing portrait of the African-American community in the Mississippi gulfside town in which she was raised, all while exposing the racial tensions inherent in the place as well as the tensions exacerbated by the disaster.

Notice how she begins her essay the day before the hurricane and moves directly into describing the way her family prepared for the coming destruction. The situation of the essay is the hurricane, but the story is far more complicated; Ward's essay becomes an exploration of what *home* means, as well as the story of a place abandoned, a community overlooked.

Pay attention to the way Ward releases information about her hometown, her race, and her family, what she chooses to tell and when she tells it. For instance, you may be startled that Ward brings up the death of her brother then moves on so quickly. And yet, when she later ties her brother's death to the idea of grieving for a place and a way of life, we understand why her brother's death is part of the essay. "Grief is learning to live with that love." Moreover, Ward uses this detail to illustrate her attachment to the place: no matter where she travels, her brother's memory remains in her Mississippi gulf town.

Similarly, in Naomi Shihab Nye's "Thank You in Arabic," the author recounts the year that her family left St. Louis—where she and her brother had been born—to settle briefly in her father's homeland of Palestine. Like Ward, who grapples with the way in which her ideas of "home" have changed following the hurricane, Nye seeks to understand how she belongs to a place to which she's rooted culturally, even though she has never been there before, and how fundamentally her sense of "home" will change once she returns to the United States.

Jesmyn Ward

WE DON'T SWIM IN OUR CEMETERIES

The summer of 2005 was like any other summer in DeLisle, Mississippi: by August, the heat was bearing down on the land and wringing it like a wet towel. I was home on vacation from the University of Michigan, and my days were bright with riding along Highway 90 while the water of the Gulf stretched out across the horizon like a metallic, dirty green fish. My nights were bright with dancing and drinking at a club along the beach where the lights of the night fishers searched lonely in the inky water. My favorite memory of that summer, though, is of a long day spent with my family swimming in Wolf River, a small swimming hole, amber and brown. The water was unusually cold on that day, the sand muddy and slimy with leaves at the bottom. We swam, ate baloney sandwiches, and played music loudly. Near the end of the day, I sat and shared a bag of potato chips with my three-year-old nephew and stared at the bristling pines, at the green shimmering in the distance. Every summer, I came back to the Mississippi Gulf Coast as to a lover.

And then, of course, came news of the storm.

My family prepared for Katrina like any other hurricane. We never evacuated so we didn't evacuate this time. For one thing, we couldn't afford to leave. My mother made seven dollars per hour as a teaching assistant, my middle sister made ten dollars per hour as a dental assistant, and my youngest, pregnant sister made two dollars and fifty cents per hour as a waitress. My father made eight dollars per hour as a gas-station attendant. I was unemployed for the summer.

On the Gulf Coast, we were used to facing at least one hurricane every year, sometimes more. We filled bottles with water for drinking, filled the bathtub with water so we'd have some to flush the toilets and bathe in, stocked up on canned goods and gas lanterns and batteries and flashlights. We tried securing everything in the yard that could be blown away by a storm. We nailed plywood boards and tin over the windows. We packed overnight bags and, with her most important documents, my mother put all the pictures of my deceased brother in the trunk of her car.

"I was eleven when Camille hit," she said, "and I promised myself that if another one like that ever came along again, I was going to leave." In heavy-duty garbage bags she wrapped childhood pictures of me and my sisters and put them in dresser drawers. Because my mother's house is a doublewide trailer, which we knew couldn't survive a hurricane, we and another group of relatives left for my grandmother's brick house at nine P.M. on Sunday, August 28, to ride out the storm.

At six in the morning, I awoke on my grandmother's floor. My two sisters said the wind had awoken them; it sounded, they said, like a freight train.

The lights had gone out. We wandered around the house in the dark, peering out of the doors and cracks in the windows at the gray whirlwind whipping up the pines and bending them in two. The wind whistled as it rushed around. Outside, a dog barked madly and circled houses looking for shelter.

There was nothing for us to do except wait. I went back to sleep on the pallets we'd made on the living-room floor. When I woke up again a few hours later, it was to my aunt saying, "Come see the den." There was an inch of water on the floor, brown and cold, and my mother and my relatives were trying to move photo albums, bibles, and other keepsakes to even higher spots.

My grandmother downplayed the water in the den: it was only coming up because the den was a walk-down: it was at least a foot lower than the rest of the rooms in the house. We would be okay. But on the living-room floor, water began to spread beneath our feet, darkening the carpet. I tried to find my shoes but couldn't. We began throwing bags on top of the sofas. The water came up through the floor of the house. The carpet, soaked through and buoyed by the water, began to rise from the floor. Water was everywhere: in the kitchen, in my grandmother's bedroom, here in the living room. My grandmother stood in the hallway with her mouth open, but saying nothing.

When the water was up to our thighs, my grandfather said it was time to leave. I slung a bag over my shoulder and grabbed my two-year-old nephew, who was screaming hysterically, and followed my mother out of the house. The water was now at my waist. A tree fell on the roof. I put my head down against the wind, trying to ignore the snap and fall of trees, and the tumultuous water, and waded to higher ground where my uncle and stepfather had moved their trucks. A brown sweep of water overwhelmed my sisters' cars, which hadn't been moved, and shoved them across the road where they spun lazily. Caught between the roar of the wind and the force of the water, we split up: my uncle, his wife, my sister, and my nephews got into my uncle's truck and disappeared around a curve.

My grandmother stood on a small hill by my stepfather's truck, gesturing at us to come up there. The trees in the forest around us crackled like electricity as the wind snapped them and tossed them along the road. I waded with Charine, my pregnant little sister, toward my grandmother. I kept my hands on Charine's arm and back, pushing her forward; her pregnant stomach cut the water like a prow.

We made it up and into my stepfather's truck, which rocked from side to side. As we clung to the doors, cowering between gusts, I allowed myself to think how my father might have felt the same during Camille when he was in his house as it swayed and swayed. We just prayed we wouldn't flip.

The water flowed in channels from the forest to the street to the ditches and created rapids, which blocked us from heading to the west to the interstate, or to the east to the local Catholic church, which my grandmother insisted would be a safe place. The small hill we were on belonged to some white neighbors. The neighbors emerged from the house to check out their pickup trucks and cars and an old Mardi Gras float in the field. We shouted at them over the wind.

"Our house flooded! We couldn't stay!" my grandfather said.

They eyed my pregnant sister, my gray-haired grandparents and, I thought, *our black skin.*

"We got a houseful!" one of them called back between gusts. "You can sit in this field till the storm ends!"

They left us to a Category 5 storm in an open field.

Over and over again, as I huddled with my freezing sister in the swaying truck, I thought, *They didn't even have any room for us to stand.*

The water began to recede.

"Go to the church," my grandmother said. The street was a river but one that we could now ford. We drove east, dodging felled pines and power lines. My stepfather drove as far as the local elementary school, where we saw water charging out of the doors. Here we were a mile inward from the Gulf and still the water rushed through. Most of the houses were flooded or ripped away. A family who'd fled their house was in one of the school buses. My stepfather drove a little farther, as far as he could with the trees and power lines on the road, and found my uncle and sister and nephews. I saw them waving frantically from the porch of an antebellum house. We joined them and sat on the floor of the owner's living room. They'd had to abandon the truck when the water washed into the cab. They had been rescued by some neighbors in a boat. Along-side us were two white families, poor as we were, who'd also been rescued by boat, whose houses were also completely submerged.

The wind outside, more dramatic now, sounded like jet fighter planes. My mother, resigned to the fact that our trailer was gone, lay down on the floor with her head in Nerissa's lap. Charine could not stop crying. I sat on the wet floor and wrapped my arms around my legs and looked at my bare feet. I was cold. The hurricane was ripping the landscape away.

When my daddy talked about Hurricane Camille of '69, he talked about water, not the wind. He was thirteen at the time, and he and his mother, five sisters, and one brother were living next to the tracks in Pass Christian in a three-bedroom house with twelve-foot ceilings. He said the water from the storm surged into the house, salty and cold. It rose steadily. While the winds roared outside, the sea climbed up their walls. He and his mother and his sisters and his uncle climbed the furniture: a sofa, a dresser, iron bunk beds, until they could ascend no higher, until the furniture began to topple and float, and they were paddling. The water was relentless. They scrambled into the attic. The water pushed through the floor, and still they climbed boxes. They held to the rafters and clung to the house and one another in the dark attic. My father said that as the surge grew stronger, the house lifted from the foundations. It began to rock with the current, swaying from side to side like a boat tied uneasily in a slip: left, right, left, right. He said his Uncle Butch counted it for them, made them ready themselves as if they were playing jump rope, eyeing the circling rope, trying to get into the game: "Here we go again, y'all." The house lifted and settled. "Here we go again."

My grandmother's children were at her sister Eunice's house. Aunt Eunice put two of my uncles and her own boys in her sons' room. As Camille bore down on them, something nagged at her to move the boys to another room. After wrestling with the impulse, Aunt Eunice woke them up and put them back to bed in another room in the house. Minutes later, all the windows in her sons' bedroom shattered, and the glass flew and pierced the beds where the boys had lain. (Hours later, part of the roof ripped from the house.)

My grandmother had been in the hospital for a hysterectomy during Camille: she'd been on the third floor, and the water had come up to the bottom of her bed. She'd hitched a ride home afterward to DeLisle to find trees tossed and bent, roofs ripped from houses, and her house undamaged and the only one with freshwater: there was an artesian well in the backyard. For months, my grandmother supplied water for the entire neighborhood.

When I was younger, my father told me that, after Camille, bodies were everywhere: these included those of the recently buried. They littered the beach along with uprooted trees, cars, furniture, and the remains of houses. They turned blue and soft. My mother said the smell of things decomposing in the sun permeated the air. Everything stank. My neighbor's entire family had been killed when they'd taken shelter in a church; down at DeLisle cemetery, his family's tombstone has eleven names etched into it, all of them victims of the storm.

When the wind abated its lashing, the landscape was flat. My two sisters and I climbed fallen trees and waded through ditches to find our trailer, much to our surprise, intact: the trees had fallen in a circle around it as if the trailer had been a centrifugal force, bading them to spin outwards and away.

When water left my grandmother's house, she and my grandfather cleaned off the screened-in porch to live in and began trying to salvage the rest of the house. In the neighborhood, I saw that most roofs had peeled away during the storm and showed the skeleton of the houses: the ribs of the ceiling beams, the hollow innards of the rooms. Other houses had collapsed or trees had destroyed entire rooms. The storm had uprooted, or broken in two, every tree over fifteen feet: pines, oak, birch, and magnolia, all equally affected. The power lines lay like slinky Mardi Gras beads along the streets. A trampoline had flown through the air, across the street, and molded itself to the severed trunks of several trees. It perched there in the foliage like a blue and silver bird with long black wings. My sisters and I walked the streets in a parade of people who eyed one another somberly, but stopped to hug or wave, and talk. *We had to jump out the windows of the car and swim. We had to leave the house in the middle of the storm and the water came up to the ceiling; these the only clothes the kids got now. The wall caved in, the ceiling came off the house, and the windows shattered. The water came up so fast and we had to leave; when we looked back, it was all gone and we couldn't even see the roof.* We were barefoot and muddy and tired, but, we confirmed, alive, alive, alive, alive.

We walked home as the sun set. The rumble of generators sounded like the cicadas and frogs had before the storm.

We woke, the day after the storm, to an awful, bright hot morning. We were coated with grime. We used one cup of water from the bathtub to rinse ourselves and our rags, soaped and scrubbed, and then used another cup of water to rinse the dry soap scum from our bodies. We had six gallons of drinkable water, two bathtubs filled for washing and flushing the toilets, and one generator that was only powerful enough to run one appliance at once: my mother alternated plugging in the refrigerator and deep freezer, hoping to save the meat. We began chopping at the trees that blanketed the yard and the streets. We dragged the foliage, still green, and stacked it to burn. We are canned tuna and SpaghettiO's, cold. My mother began taking the meat out of the deep freezer and cooking all of it on a small propane grill she had. She said it was better to cook it and eat it than lose it. The entire neighborhood smelled like barbecue; everyone was cooking meat.

We rationed cups of water, but our supply still got very low. There were nine of us: my mother, her brother, Charine, her boyfriend, my other sister, her boyfriend, my two little cousins, and me, and we could not help but to run through our meager stores.

Even though I was constantly hungry, all I could think about was drinking water. I tipped my cups and waited for the last drop to roll down the plastic, and worried about the fast-depleting jugs. And yet, there were those who had less. My sister Charine's boyfriend and his brothers and cousins had lost everything in Pass Christian. His family was living down at the park under a cement gazebo, and out of their cars: a nomadic tribe of a dozen or so. They sat at the park all day in the heat with their T-shirts draped over their heads because there was no shade anymore, anywhere. As if in the center of a Northern winter, the trees that could still stand were denuded of leaves.

We spent our days chopping and dragging and hauling, and collecting rainwater in plastic buckets. No one came to help us.

Sometimes my mother hooked the television up to the generator and we caught the local news: where to go for water and ice, which shelters were open, when curfews started, etc. People drove to gas stations at five A.M. and waited all day in line, only for no one to turn up. There was one station opened on the Gulf Coast, and it was all the way in D'Iberville, some thirty miles away. Who could get there? There were some who couldn't even make it to the drop spots. We were trying to siphon gas out of cars that had been damaged by water to put in our generators to keep the food for a bit longer. Crackheads rode up and down the street and tried to sell gas for ten dollars a gallon.

My two nephews developed heat rashes: the tiny bumps spread along their bodies and made their faces look like those of old men, textured and lined. Charine developed heatstroke on the first day after the sun, and had to spend the rest of her time in the bed in the hot, hot house. Bugs ate at us constantly. I broke out in a rash from the standing water, a rash that spread along the front of my thighs and itched and burned constantly. My middle sister, Nerissa, developed the same kind of rash that spread along her torso and back and made her skin swell.

When it rained. Charine and I took showers in the downpour and experienced true happiness.

Two friends and I used the last of our gas to ride to Pass Christian, which is across the bayou from DeLisle: it's a small, beautiful city that lies directly on the Gulf of Mexico. The water from the bayou had seeped across the road; we drove through the water and it splattered the sides of the Cutlass. In Pass Christian, we crept down roads gummy with mud. Most of the houses had been washed from their foundations and deposited in the middle of the streets, their windows blown out, their curtains fluttering like eyelashes. Houses sat squarely on the railroad tracks. Every other house was a pile of debris. Cars squatted on houses that squatted on houses. Most roads were blocked by homes or debris so we had to get out of the car and walk. We walked down to the beach. All the old mansions on the beach had been smashed flat. Gas stations and restaurants had simply disappeared. The only things left of the Peoples Bank and the Winn-Dixie on the beach were the concrete bases and a few twisted metal beams which reached out and up like bonsai trees. The old oaks that had lined Highway 90 were ripped from the earth by the root and lay on their sides. Pieces of the road had caved in and been ripped away, leaving gaping holes many feet wide and deep, so we could see the red earth underneath. A river ran down Highway 90. Sofas and mattresses and cars lay on the beach like sunbathers. It was so quiet we only heard the whispering of the breeze and the lapping of the Gulf.

People gathered along North Street. Recent Mexican immigrants to the city waited at corners, with their possessions in small plastic bags, for someone to pick them up and take them away from their waterlogged apartment homes. Older black men draped plywood over the low branches of small trees and sat under them, hiding and living. On the iron harnesses of decimated trailers, entire Vietnamese families lived in small tents made of siding and sheets. Old poor white men sat in rickety chairs on the porches of smashed houses. Black teenagers and older women shifted through the merchandise of an open Dollar Store, scavenging for usable goods.

In Gulfport, giant reams of paper, eighteen-wheeler trailer beds, and sacks of raw, decomposing chicken littered downtown. In DeLisle, we heard that Gulfport and Biloxi had help, but we saw no one.

At least three days passed before I saw the first truck, an eighteen-wheeler. It was parked next to the decimated firehouse and from the back of the truck, a man, the trucker, gave away free boxes of water.

He was a private driver, not attached to any federal or state campaign. Truckers like him swarmed the area after the storm, and drove places where no one else cared to go. We were starving, but at least we had water to drink and ice to shove into the refrigerators to try to keep the meat from turning bad. We were grateful. But we still wondered where FEMA was, where the Red Cross was.

The trucker told us that police were guarding the Wal-Mart in Pass Christian, guarding the empty shell of the building that the hurricane had gutted, guarding the goods strewn across the neighborhoods behind the store that were of no use to anyone. In Gulfport, they were guarding the outlet malls and the malls and the strip malls. All along the Coast, they were guarding large chain stores. Meanwhile, all along the Coast, we were starving in our homes.

When my friend Mariha and her family—two of whom were elderly and infirm—ran out of water in Gulfport, she and her friend got what gas they could and drove the family to Gulf Shores in Florida, where they sat in hotel rooms and watched CNN and Fox and MSNBC. She watched people cower on rooftops in New Orleans. She watched them swim through floodwaters. She watched them beg the cameramen for food, for help, because they were dying. She watched an older white woman give an interview, and in response to what they heard about the situation in New Orleans, that woman whispered the word *genocide*.

Plenty of us, though, couldn't leave.

President Bush visited the Gulf Coast. I saw photo-ops with him and young minority women, and I heard that he had thanked the man in charge of the nonexistent relief effort and said he was really looking forward to sitting on Trent Lott's porch. One visit, two visits. He talked about rebuilding. But I wondered where the food was. I heard inklings about what was going on in New Orleans. My Uncle Bookie had evacuated from New Orleans on the day before the storm. He and his family had gotten as far as a hotel in the middle of central Mississippi where they'd run out of gas and money, so they slept in the lobby. My aunt drove from North Carolina to fetch them, and took them back to the Carolinas with her. The small, dilapidated neighborhood in New Orleans where I'd spent the previous weekend with my Uncle Bookie and his wife and another couple, drinking in several hole-in-the-wall clubs with jukeboxes, and tiny curved bars shaped like red beans, was flooded. A commentator from a New Orleans radio station said his crew saw a shark swimming in the floodwaters of downtown New Orleans.

One of the truckers told us that when he was driving through Gulfport, he saw two men with hammers beating at something on the beach. He paused his truck and peered at them through his window. The men were pummeling a casket that had washed up on the beach. They were trying to knock the hinges off. They were eager to get at what was inside.

A week after the storm, the federal government showed up with supplies.

Months later, after back-and-forth accusations and finger-pointing between Mayor Ray Nagin and George W. Bush and Governor Kathleen Blanco and the firing of FEMA chieftain Mike Brown, little had improved. In Gulfport, the mammoth barges that had supported the casinos in water still blocked the highway. In Pass Christian, the government bulldozed the houses to the sides of the streets. They cleared the roads, but they were slow to clear away the piles of siding and wood and concrete and crushed automobiles and collapsed houses. They emptied the streets of debris, but there was nowhere for anyone to go because everything: the schools, the library, the fire station, the city hall, the restaurants, and the homes had been hollowed out and left sagging. In DeLisle, and everywhere along the Coast, relatives were squeezing in with other relatives, the ones who still had homes. My mother's four-bedroom double-wide trailer housed six people: my immediate family and other relatives. My mother made food stretch.

FEMA, advocating relocation, offered out-of-state apartments and free rent for three months. People I knew who had lived in Pass Christian and Bay St. Louis and New Orleans migrated to Atlanta, Oklahoma City, Jacksonville, Houston, and Dallas. Some of those who left are happy where they are, and some are not. After a few months, my Uncle Bookie returned to New Orleans, to the city of his birth, only to find the wood of his house wet-warped and uninhabitable. My cousin moved from one ghetto to another: he lived in Atlanta in another poor community in an apartment FEMA allocated to him and his girlfriend and her child for a time before he too returned home. Those who remained and never left now live in a fundamental disconnect between the landscape they knew and the reality they encounter.

More months passed. Watching the progress was like watching the foliage grow back, the oaks sprout tufts of green at the joints where their limbs joined the trunk, stubbornly pushing back to life, but slowly. My half sister and her mother, after having narrowly escaped the storm in New Orleans, were still living in a shelter in Shreveport. Her mother followed her to the restroom in fear that she would be raped. My sixty-year-old grandmother was still living in one damp room of her house and on her porch. She was surviving on her meager social-security checks and waiting for some sort of insurance money so she could begin salvaging the foundation of the flooded house and begin rebuilding. My pregnant sister had her baby but lost her job because the restaurant where she worked was destroyed.

Small FEMA trailers dotted the landscape between the savaged trees and punctured houses.

There was some comfort for me when I looked at the photographs of my mother and her brothers that were taken immediately after Camille. There was something reassuring in recognizing the stunted landscape and the grim black and brown and yellow and white faces, of knowing that we recovered once, that my family rebuilt once. Still: I wondered if my Uncle Bookie would ever be able to return to Sousberry in New Orleans, or would he be developed out of the city he had known since he was born, a city where that branch of my family has lived for as far as they can remember? I wondered if the casinos on the Coast would move inland, if crude development would spread across the piney landscape like an infection, leaving red earth, bare plots, and new, cheap, overly expensive houses and apartment complexes, if the Coast I loved would become something else, a plastic girl like all the other plastic girls of the world: developed to suburb highlights, track mall outfits, a tourist tan. Would she become denuded to anonymity, interchangeable with Panama City, Orlando, or Jacksonville?

My brother died on October 2, 2000. Losing him taught me one great lesson: Even after that which you love dies, the love you have for it does not die. Grief is learning to live with that love. My small town dies and becomes something else. People are building their houses up on stilts, and have multiple stairway entrances. The country loses its luster, its horse pastures, its wild stretches, and is marked by houses, pricey subdivision developments or commercial developments where restaurants pop up selling food too expensive for the people who live in the neighborhood. The casinos remain on the ground on which they landed. Yanked from the barges they rested on to the shore, they now glitter and spread over the landscape. Our lawmakers in Jackson have given them the right to build on land (previously, casinos had to float, by law, on water); they rooted themselves deeper into the Gulf Coastal economy and grow even fatter on the senior pensions and bi-weekly paychecks of the poor. It took me three years to learn that I could never return home, because the home I knew was gone. Yet I still love her.

I haven't been swimming at Wolf River in a year. We resort to tin or inflatable yard pools, and we avoid swimming in the Gulf of Mexico, which is now dotted with twenty-story condos. I have heard that these condos sell well with investors, but not with actual clients. The water on the Gulf Coast of Mississippi, at least, refuses to turn tourist; it will not turn blue green. Maybe some day they will dye it, but for now, it remains just as dirty, coppery, dull green, and silt-ridden as it was before the storm. We would not swim there even if it were green, because we heard stories from people on clean-up crews right after the storm that they discovered dead bodies out in the water every day. (Right after the storm, the newspapers published the numbers of dead and we gossiped that they were not revealing the true numbers because our clean-up crews could not stop finding bodies. We thought it was a publicity trick.) The water cloaks the shoreline, and we are scared of what it holds. We do not swim in our cemeteries. We imagine sunken houses like whales, bodies turning to seaweed, cars rusted to coral. Sometimes I imagine home is there, sunk under the waters, wild and silent as it used to be.

Today, my grandmother is back in her house. She's taken out the carpet, and installed all tile floors. Her furniture sits higher. My two sisters have found better jobs, and they are trying to finish up college. I've worked at home for the past two years, and I am leaving at the end of the summer, driven by opportunity and the need to get away from the Coast where wages have risen only a fraction while rent, gas, food, housing, and property prices have doubled. My mother resumed working as a teaching assistant and is making her same pre-Katrina wage. With the recent spike in gas prices, she worries over being able to fill her gas tank because she must drive miles for groceries. Even though hundreds died along the Coast in Hurricane Camille, my mother says that Camille was a weakling compared to Katrina. She says, "It was nothing like this." When the next big one hits, in another thirty years, she promises she'll leave. Then she changes her mind. By then, she says, she hopes she'll be dead.

—2008

Learning from Other Writers (Ward)

1. Examine the structure of Ward's narrative. How much time in the essay is spent on the build-up to the hurricane, and how much on the aftermath? Why?

2. Ward begins her essay with a scene in which she is swimming in the Wolf River, on a summer day like any other. How does this moment take on a greater significance by the end of the essay?

3. The essay is full of figurative language: find five instances of a metaphor or simile. What is the effect of such language? How does this use of metaphor and simile enhance our understanding of Ward's ideas of home?

4. Ward also pays great attention to the natural world. Why, in this essay about place, is this aspect of the essay particularly resonant?

5. Ward's tone grows angrier and her frustration becomes more apparent as the essay progresses. How does this tonal shift match the content of the essay?

6. What is the argument of this essay?

Naomi Shihab Nye

THANK YOU IN ARABIC

Shortly after my mother discovered my brother had been pitching his Vitamin C tablets behind the stove for years, we left the country. Her sharp alert, "Now the truth be known!" startled us at the breakfast table as she poked into the dim crevice with the nozzle of her vacuum. We could hear the pills go click, click, up the long tube.

My brother, an obedient child, a bright-eyed, dark-skinned charmer who scored high on all his tests and trilled a boy's sweet soprano, stared down at his oatmeal. Four years younger than I, he was also the youngest and smallest in his class. Somehow he maintained an intelligence and dignity more notable than that of his older, larger companions, and the pills episode, really, was a pleasant surprise to me.

Companions in mischief are not to be underestimated, especially when everything else in your life is about to change.

We sold everything we had and left the country. The move had been brewing for months. We took a few suitcases each. My mother cried when the piano went. I wished we could have saved it. My brother and I had sung so many classics over its keyboard—"Look for the Silver Lining" and "Angels We Have Heard on High"—that it would have been nice to return to a year later, when we came straggling back. I sold my life-size doll and my toy sewing machine. I begged my mother to save her red stove for me, so I could have it when I grew up—no one else we knew had a red stove. So my mother asked some friends to save it for me in their barn.

Our parents had closed their imported-gifts stores, and our father had dropped out of ministerial school. He had attended the Unity School of Christianity for a few years, but decided not to become a minister after all. We were relieved, having felt like impostors the whole time he was enrolled. He wasn't even a Christian, to begin with, but a gently non-practicing Muslim. He didn't do anything like fasting or getting down on his knees five times a day. Our mother had given up the stern glare of her Lutheran ancestors, raising my brother and me in the Vedanta Society of St. Louis. When anyone asked what we were, I said, "Hindu." We had a Swami, and sandalwood incense. It was over our heads, but we liked it and didn't feel very attracted to the idea of churches and collection baskets and chatty parish good-will.

Now and then, just to keep things balanced, we attended the Unity Sunday School. My teacher said I was lucky my father came from the same place Jesus came from. It was a passport to notoriety. She invited me to bring artifacts for Show and Tell. I wrapped a red and white *keffiyah* around my friend Jimmy's curly blond head while the girls in lacy socks giggled behind their hands. I told about my father coming to America from Palestine on the boat and throwing his old country clothes overboard before docking at Ellis Island. I felt relieved he'd kept a few things, like the *keffiyah* and its black braided band. Secretly it made me mad to have lost the blue pants from Jericho with the wide cuffs he told us about.

I enjoyed standing in front of the group talking about my father's homeland. Stories felt like elastic bands that could stretch and stretch. Big fans purred inside their metal shells. I held up a string of olive wood camels. I didn't tell our teacher about the Vedanta Society. We were growing up ecumenical, though I wouldn't know that word till a long time later in college. One night I heard my father say to my mother in the next room, "Do you think they'll be confused when they grow up?" and knew he was talking about us. My mother, bless her, knew we wouldn't be. She said, "At least we're giving them a choice." I didn't know then that more clearly than all the stories of Jesus, I'd remember the way our Hindu swami said a single word three times, "Shanti, shanti, shanti"—peace, peace, peace.

Our father was an excellent speaker—he stood behind pulpits and podiums easily, delivering gracious lectures on "The Holy Land" and "The Palestinian Question." He was much in demand during the Christmas season. I think that's how he had fallen into the ministerial swoon. While he spoke, my brother and I hovered toward the backs of the auditoriums, eyeing the tables of canapés and tiny tarts, slipping a few into our mouths or pockets.

What next? Our lives were entering a new chapter, but I didn't know its title yet.

We had never met our Palestinian grandmother, Sitti Khadra, or seen Jerusalem, where our father had grown up, or followed the rocky, narrow alleyways of the Via Dolorosa, or eaten an olive in its own neighborhood. Our mother hadn't either. The Arabic customs we knew had been filtered through the fine net of folktales. We did not speak Arabic, though the lilt of the language was familiar to us—our father's endearments, his musical blessings before meals—but that language had never lived in our mouths.

And that's where we were going, to Jerusalem. We shipped our car, a wide golden Impala the exact color of a cigarette filter, over on a boat. We would meet up with it later.

The first plane flight of my whole life was the night flight out of New York City across the ocean. I was fourteen years old. Every glittering light in every skyscraper looked like a period at the end of the sentence. Good-bye, our lives.

We stopped in Portugal for a few weeks. We were making a gradual transition. We stopped in Spain and Italy and Egypt, where the pyramids shocked me by sitting right on the edge of the giant city of Cairo, not way out in the desert as I had imagined them. While we waited for our baggage to clear customs, I stared at six tall African men in brilliantly patterned dashikis negotiating with an Egyptian customs agent and realized I did not even know how to say "Thank you" in Arabic. How was this possible? The most elemental and important of human phrases in my father's own tongue had evaded me till now. I tugged on his sleeve, but he was busy with visas and passports. "Daddy," I said. "Daddy, I have to know. Daddy, tell me. Daddy, why didn't we ever *learn*?" An African man adjusted his turban. Always thereafter, the word *shookrun*, so simple, with a little roll in the middle, would conjure up the vast African baggage, the brown boxes looped and looped in African twine.

We stayed one or two nights at the old Shepherd's Hotel downtown, but couldn't sleep because of the heat and honking traffic beneath our windows. So our father moved us to the famous Mena House Hotel next to the pyramids. We rode camels for the first time, and our mother received a dozen blood-red roses at her hotel room from a rug vendor who apparently liked her pale brown ponytail. The belly dancer at the hotel restaurant twined a gauzy pink scarf around my brother's astonished ten-year-old head as he tapped his knee in time to her music. She bobbled her giant cleavage under his nose, huge bosoms prickled by sequins and sweat.

Back in our rooms, we laughed until we fell asleep. Later that night, my brother and I both awakened burning with fever and deeply nauseated, though nobody ever threw up. We were so sick that a doctor hung a Quarantine sign in Arabic and English on our hotel room door the next day. Did he know something we didn't know? I kept waiting to hear that we had malaria or typhoid, but no dramatic disease was ever mentioned. We lay in bed for a week. The aged doctor tripped over my suitcase every time he entered to take our temperatures. We smothered our laughter. "Shookrun," I would say. But as soon as he left, to my brother, "I feel bad. How do you feel?"

"I feel really, really bad."

"I think I'm dying."

"I think I'm already dead."

At night we heard the sound and lights show from the pyramids drifting across the desert air to our windows. We felt our lives stretching out across thousands of miles. The Pharaohs stomped noisily through my head and churning belly. We had eaten spaghetti in the restaurant. I would not be able to eat spaghetti again for years.

Finally, finally, we appeared in the restaurant again, thin and weakly smiling, and ordered the famous Mena House *shorraba*, lentil soup, as my brother nervously scanned the room for the belly dancer. Maybe she wouldn't recognize him now.

In those days Jerusalem, which was then a divided city, had an operating airport on the Jordanian side. My brother and I remember flying in upside down, or in a plane dramatically tipped, but it may have been the effect of our medicine. The land reminded us of a dropped canvas, graceful brown hillocks and green patches. Small and provincial, the airport had just two runways, and the first thing I observed as we climbed down slowly from the stuffy plane was all my underwear strewn across one of them. There were my flowered cotton briefs and my pink panties and my slightly embarrassing raggedy ones and my extra training bra, alive and visible in the breeze. Somehow my suitcase had popped open in the hold and dropped its contents the minute the men pried open the cargo door. So the first thing I did on the home soil of my father was recollect my underwear, down on my knees, the posture of prayer over that ancient holy land.

Our relatives came to see us at a hotel. Our grandmother was very short. She wore a long, thickly embroidered Palestinian dress, had a musical, high-pitched voice and a low, guttural laugh. She kept touching our heads and faces as if she couldn't believe we were there. I had not yet fallen in love with her. Sometimes you don't fall in love with people immediately, even if they're your own grandmother. Everyone seemed to think we were all too thin.

We moved into a second-story flat in a stone house eight miles north of the city, among fields and white stones and wandering sheep. My brother was enrolled in the

Friends Girls School and I was enrolled in the Friends Boys School in the town of Ramallah a few miles farther north—it seemed a little confused. But the Girls School offered grades one through eight in English and high school continued at the Boys School. Most local girls went to Arabic-speaking schools after eighth grade.

I was a freshman, one of seven girl students among two hundred boys, which would cause me problems later. I was called in from the schoolyard at lunchtime, to the office of our counselor who wore shoes so pointed and tight her feet bulged out pinkly on top.

"You will not be talking to them anymore," she said. She rapped on the desk with a pencil for emphasis.

"To whom?"

"All the boy students at this institution. It is inappropriate behavior. From now on, you will only speak with the girls."

"But there are only six other girls! And I only like one of them!" My friend was Anna, from Italy, whose father ran a small factory that made matches. I'd visited it once with her. It felt risky to walk the aisles among a million filled matchboxes. Later we visited the factory that made olive oil soaps and stacked them in giant pyramids to dry.

"No, thank you," I said. "It's ridiculous to say that girls should only talk to girls. Did I say anything bad to a boy? Did anyone say anything bad to me? They're my friends. They're like my brothers. I won't do it, that's all."

The counselor conferred with the headmaster and they called a taxi. I was sent home with a note requesting that I transfer to a different school. The charge: insolence. My mother, startled to see me home early and on my own, stared out the window when I told her.

My brother came home from his school as usual, full of whistling and notebooks. "Did anyone tell you not to talk to girls?" I asked him. He looked at me as if I'd gone goofy. He was too young to know the troubles of the world. He couldn't even imagine them.

"You know what I've been thinking about?" he said. "A piece of cake. That puffy white layered cake with icing like they have at birthday parties in the United States. Wouldn't that taste good right now?" Our mother said she was thinking about mayonnaise. You couldn't get it in Jerusalem. She'd tried to make it and it didn't work. I felt too gloomy to talk about food.

My brother said, "Let's go let Abu Miriam's chickens out." That's what we always did when we felt sad. We let our fussy landlord's red and white chickens loose to flap around the yard happily, puffing their wings. Even when Abu Miriam shouted and waggled his cane and his wife waved a dishtowel, we knew the chickens were thanking us.

My father went with me to the St. Tarkmanchatz Armenian School, a solemnly ancient stone school tucked deep into the Armenian Quarter of the Old City of Jerusalem. It was another world in there. He had already called them on the telephone and tried to enroll me, though they didn't want to. Their school was for Armenian students only, kindergarten through twelfth grade. Classes were taught in three languages,

Armenian, Arabic and English, which was why I needed to go there. Although most Arab students at other schools were learning English, I needed a school where classes were actually taught in English—otherwise I would have been staring out the windows triple the usual amount.

The head priest wore a long robe and a tall cone-shaped hat. He said, "Excuse me, please, but your daughter, she is not an Armenian, even a small amount?"

"Not at all," said my father. "But in case you didn't know, there is a stipulation in the educational code books of this city that says no student may be rejected solely on the basis of ethnic background, and if you don't accept her, we will alert the proper authorities."

They took me. But the principal wasn't happy about it. The students, however, seemed glad to have a new face to look at. Everyone's name ended in -ian, the beautiful, musical Armenian ending—Boghossian, Minassian, Kevorkian, Rostomian. My new classmates started calling me Shihabian. We wore uniforms, navy blue pleated skirts for the girls, white shirts, and navy sweaters. I waited during the lessons for the English to come around, as if it were a channel on television. While my friends were on the other channels, I scribbled poems in the margins of my pages, read library books, and wrote a lot of letters filled with exclamation points. All the other students knew three languages with three entirely different alphabets. How could they carry so much in their heads? I felt humbled by my ignorance. Again and again and again. One day I felt so frustrated in our physics class—still another language—that I pitched my book out the open window. The professor made me go collect it. All the pages had let loose at the seams and were flapping into the gutters along with the white wrappers of sandwiches.

Every week the girls had a hands-and-fingernails check. We had to keep our nails clean and trim, and couldn't wear any rings. Some of my new friends would invite me home for lunch with them, since we had an hour-and-a-half break and I lived too far to go to my own house.

Their houses were a thousand years old, clustered beehive fashion behind ancient walls, stacked and curled and tilting and dark, filled with pictures of unsmiling relatives and small white cloths dangling crocheted edges. We ate spinach pies and white cheese. We dipped our bread in olive oil, as the Arabs did. We ate small sesame cakes, our mouths full of crumbles. They taught me to say, "I love you" in Armenian, which sounded like yes-kay-see-goo-see-rem. I felt I had left my old life entirely.

Every afternoon I went down to the basement of the school where the kindergarten class was having an Arabic lesson. Their desks were pint-sized, their full white smocks tied around their necks. I stuffed my fourteen-year-old self in beside them. They had rosy cheeks and shy smiles. They must have thought I was a very slow learner.

More than any of the lessons, I remember the way the teacher rapped the backs of their hands with his ruler when they made a mistake. Their little faces puffed up with quiet tears. This pained me so terribly I forgot all my words. When it was my turn to go to the blackboard and write in Arabic, my hand shook. The kindergarten students whispered hints to me from the front row, but I couldn't understand them. We learned horribly useless phrases: "Please hand me the bellows for my fire." I wanted words simple as tools, simple as *food* and *yesterday* and *dreams*. The teacher never rapped my hand, especially after I wrote a letter to the city newspaper, which my father edited, protesting such harsh treatment of young learners. I wished I had known how to talk to those little ones, but they were just beginning their English studies and didn't speak much yet. They were at the same place in their English that I was in my Arabic.

From the high windows of St. Tarkmanchatz, we could look out over the Old City, the roofs and flapping laundry and television antennas, the pilgrims and churches and mosques, the olive-wood prayer beads and fragrant *falafel* lunch stands, the intricate interweaving of cultures and prayers and songs and holidays. We saw the barbed wire separating Jordan from Israel then, the bleak, uninhabited strip of no-man's land reminding me how little education saved us after all. People who had differing ideas still came to blows, imagining fighting could solve things. Staring out over the quiet roofs of afternoon, it seemed so foolish to me. I asked my friends what they thought about it and they shrugged.

"It doesn't matter what we think about it. It just keeps happening. It happened in Armenia too, you know. Really, really bad in Armenia. And who talks about it in the world news now? It happens everywhere. It happens in *your* country one by one, yes? Murders and guns. What can we do?"

Sometimes after school, my brother and I walked up the road that led past the crowded refugee camp of Palestinians who owned even less than our modest relatives did in the village. The kids were stacking stones in empty tin cans and shaking them. We waved our hands and they covered their mouths and laughed. We wore our beat-up American tennis shoes and our old sweatshirts and talked about everything we wanted to do and everywhere else we wished we could go.

"I want to go back to Egypt," my brother said. "I sort of feel like I missed it. Spending all that time in bed instead of exploring—what a waste."

"I want to go to Greece," I said. "I want to play a violin in a symphony orchestra in Austria." We made up things. I wanted to go back to the United States most of all. Suddenly I felt like a patriotic citizen. One of my friends, Sylvie Markarian, had just been shipped off to Damascus, Syria, to marry a man who was fifty years old, a widower. Sylvie was exactly my age—we had turned fifteen two days apart. She had never met her future husband before. "Tell your parents no thank you," I urged her. I thought this was the most revolting thing I had ever heard of. "Tell them you *refuse*."

Sylvie's eyes were liquid, swirling brown. I could not see clear to the bottom of them.

"You don't understand," she told me. "In United States you say no. We don't say no. We have to follow someone's wishes. This is the wish of my father. Me, I am scared. I never slept away from my mother before. But I have no choice. I am going because they tell me to go." She was sobbing, sobbing on my shoulder. And I was stroking her long, soft hair. After that, I carried two fists inside, one for Sylvie and one for me.

Most weekends my family went to the village to sit with the relatives. We sat and sat and sat. We sat in big rooms and little rooms, in circles, on chairs or on woven mats or brightly-covered mattresses piled on the floor. People came in and out to greet my family. Sometimes even donkeys and chickens came in and out. We were like movie stars or dignitaries. They never seemed to get tired of us.

My father translated the more interesting tidbits of conversation, the funny stories my grandmother told. She talked about angels and food and money and people and politics and gossip and old memories from my father's childhood, before he emigrated away from her. She wanted to make sure we were going to stick around forever, which made me feel very nervous. We ate from mountains of rice and eggplant on large silver trays—they gave us plates of our own since it was not our custom to eat from the same plate as other people. We ripped the giant wheels of bread into triangles. Shepherds passed through town with their flocks of sheep and goats, their long canes and cloaks, straight out of the Bible. My brother and I trailed them to the edge of the village, past the lentil fields to the green meadows studded with stones, while the shepherds pretended we weren't there. I think they liked to be alone, unnoticed. The sheep had differently colored dyed bottoms, so shepherds could tell their flocks apart.

During these long, slow, smoke-stained weekends—the men still smoked cigarettes a lot in those days, and the old *taboon*, my family's mounded bread-oven, puffed billowy clouds outside the door—my crying jags began. I cried without any warning, even in the middle of a meal. My crying was usually noiseless but dramatically wet— streams of tears pouring down my cheeks, onto my collar or the back of my hand.

Everything grew quiet.

Someone always asked in Arabic, "What is wrong? Are you sick? Do you wish to lie down?"

My father made valiant excuses in the beginning. "She's overtired," he said. "She has a headache. She is missing her friend who moved to Syria. She is feeling homesick."

My brother stared at me as if I had just landed from Planet X.

Worst was our drive to school every morning, when our car came over the rise in the highway and all Jerusalem lay sprawled before us in its golden, stony splendor pock-marked with olive trees and automobiles. Even the air above the city had a thick, religious texture, as if it were a shining brocade filled with broody incense. I cried hardest then. All those hours tied up in school lay just ahead. My father pulled over and talked to me. He sighed. He kept his hands on the steering wheel even when the car was stopped and said, "Someday, I promise you, you will look back on this period in your life and have no idea what made you so unhappy here."

"I want to go home." It became my anthem. "This place depresses me. It weighs too much. I hate all these old stones that everybody keeps kissing. I'm sick of pilgrims. They act so pious and pure. And I hate the way people stare at me here." Already I'd been involved in two street skirmishes with boys who stared too hard and long, clucking with their tongues. I'd socked one in the jaw and he socked me back. I hit the other one straight in the face with my purse.

"You could be happy here if you tried harder," my father said. "Don't compare it to the United States all the time. Don't pretend the United States is perfect. And look at your brother—he's not having any problems!"

"My brother is eleven years old."

I had crossed the boundary from uncomplicated childhood where happiness was a good ball and a horde of candy-coated Jordan almonds.

One problem was that I had fallen in love with four different boys who all played in the same band. Two of them were even twins. I never quite described it to my parents, but I wrote reams and reams of notes about it on loose-leaf paper that I kept under my sweaters in my closet.

Such new energy made me feel reckless. I gave things away. I gave away my necklace and a whole box of shortbread cookies that my mother had been saving. I gave my extra shoes away to the gypsies. One night when the gypsies camped in a field down the road from our house, I thought about their mounds of white goat cheese lined up on skins in front of their tents, and the wild *oud* music they played deep into the black belly of the night, and I wanted to go sit around their fire. Maybe they could use some shoes.

I packed a sack of old loafers that I rarely wore and walked with my family down the road. The gypsy mothers stared into my shoes curiously. They took them into their tents. Maybe they would use them as vases or drawers. We sat with small glasses of hot, sweet tea until a girl bellowed from deep in her throat, threw back her head, and began dancing. A long bow thrummed across the strings. The girl circled the fire, tapping and clicking, trilling a long musical wail from deep in her throat. My brother looked nervous. He was remembering the belly dancer in Egypt, and her scarf. I felt invisible. I was pretending to be a gypsy. My father stared at me. Didn't I recognize the exquisite oddity of my own life when I sat right in the middle of it? Didn't I feel lucky to be here? Well, yes I did. But sometimes it was hard to be lucky.

When we left Jerusalem, we left quickly. Left our beds in our rooms and our car in the driveway. Left in a plane, not sure where we were going. The rumbles of fighting with Israel had been growing louder and louder. In the barbed-wire no-man's land visible from the windows of our house, guns cracked loudly in the middle of the night. We lived right near the edge. My father heard disturbing rumors at the newspaper that would soon grow into the infamous Six-Day War of 1967. We were in England by then, drinking tea from thin china cups and scanning the newspapers. Bombs were blowing up in Jerusalem. We worried about the village. We worried about my grandmother's dreams, which had been getting worse and worse, she'd told us. We worried about the house we'd left, and the chickens, and the children at the refugee camp. But there was nothing we could do except keep talking about it all.

My parents didn't want to go back to Missouri because they'd already said goodbye to everyone there. They thought we might try a different part of the country. They weighed the virtues of various states. Texas was big and warm. After a chilly year crowded around the small gas heaters we used in Jerusalem, a warm place sounded appealing. In roomy Texas, my parents bought the first house they looked at. My father walked into the city newspaper and said, "Any jobs open around here?"

I burst out crying when I entered a grocery store—so many different kinds of bread.

A letter on thin blue airmail paper reached me months later, written by my class-mate, the bass player in my favorite Jerusalem band. "Since you left," he said, "your empty desk reminds me of a snake ready to strike. I am afraid to look at it. I hope you are having a better time than we are."

Of course I was, and I wasn't. *Home* had grown different forever. *Home* had dou-bled. Back *home* again in my own country, it seemed impossible to forget the place we had just left: the piercing call of the *muezzin* from the mosque at prayer time, the dusky green tint of the olive groves, the sharp, cold air that smelled as deep and old as my grandmother's white sheets flapping from the line on her roof. What story hadn't she finished?

Our father used to tell us that when he was little, the sky over Jerusalem crackled with meteors and shooting stars almost every night. They streaked and flashed, ignit-ing the dark. Some had long golden tails. For a few seconds, you could see their whole swooping trails lit up. Our father and his brothers slept on the roof to watch the sky. "There were so many of them, we didn't even call out every time we saw one."

During our year in Jerusalem, my brother and I kept our eyes cast upwards when-ever we were outside at night, but the stars were different since our father was a boy. Now the sky seemed too orderly, stuck in place. The stars had learned where they belonged. Only people on the ground kept changing.

—1996

Learning from other Writers (Nye)

1. What is the goal of beginning this essay with the anecdote about the mother finding Nye's brother's Vitamin C tablets behind the stove?

2. What is the role of objects in this essay? What objects represent "America" and what objects represent "Palestine"? How do these artifacts accumulate or trans-mit meaning?

3. Upon meeting her paternal grandmother for the first time, Nye recounts: "I had not yet fallen in love with her. Sometimes you don't fall in love with people immediately, even if they're your own grandmother." Why is this reflection significant to the text?

4. How is the theme of "difference" analyzed in this essay, not just culturally or politically, but in terms of age, gender, and language? What meaning does Nye draw from such differences?

6. Compare the ways in which time is used as a structural device in both Ward's and Nye's essays. How do the authors manipulate chronology differently? What are the effects of those differences?

HOME AND AWAY

In "No-Man's-Land," Eula Biss parallels her experiences as a new resident in a gentrifying Chicago neighborhood with those of the author of the classic pioneer novel *Little House on the Prairie*. In doing so, Biss interrogates what it means to be a "pioneer" and why she finds it troubling when people refer to her and her husband in this manner. She paints a picture of her diverse neighborhood, where on the beach she sits with an African-American girl and a Polish immigrant, where in the park Spanish families enjoy picnics and Indian families play cricket. She does not feel unsafe in her neighborhood, but by including other people's reactions to where she lives, she allows her essay to develop into a meditation on the nature of fear and the unknown.

Because Biss uses headings in her essay, the structure may at first glance appear to be nontraditional. But on closer examination, we can see that the essay's form is fairly straightforward. First, Biss describes her childhood reaction to reading *Little House on the Prairie*, using this interesting introduction to hook her readers and to set up one of the essay's themes. Then, as we will see in many essays, Biss provides us with some context and personal history, relating the way she and her husband moved to this neighborhood, what the neighborhood was like back then, how her family and friends reacted to her choice of dwelling. Using this as a natural springboard to analyze the nature of fear and the difference between fears that are true versus fears that are imagined, she brings in outside research, from crime statistics to psychology. Then Biss braids together all her ideas: the history of her neighborhood, the concept of being a pioneer, Laura Ingalls Wilder and her novel, and real and imagined fears. She writes: "To imagine oneself as a pioneer in a place as densely populated as Chicago is either to deny the existence of your neighbors or to cast them as natives who must be displaced. Either way, it is a hostile fantasy." As Biss's essay so vividly illustrates, the question of who belongs to a place—and who doesn't—is rarely simple.

NO-MAN'S-LAND

ON THE PRAIRIE

"What is it about water that always affects a person?" Laura Ingalls Wilder wrote in her 1894 diary. "I never see a great river or lake but I think how I would like to see a world made and watch it through all its changes."

Forty years later, she would reflect that she had "seen the whole frontier, the woods, the Indian country of the great plains, the frontier towns, the building of the railroads in wild unsettled country, homesteading and farmers coming in to take possession." She realized, she said, that she "had seen and lived it all...."

It was a world made and unmade. And it was not without some ambivalence, not without some sense of loss, that the writer watched the Indians, as many as she could see in either direction, ride out of the Kansas of her imagination. Her fictional self, the Laura of *Little House on the Prairie*, sobbed as they left.

Like my sister, like my cousin, like so many other girls, I was captivated, in my childhood, by that Laura. I was given a bonnet, and I wore it earnestly for quite some time. But when I return to *Little House on the Prairie* now as an adult, I find that it is not the book I thought it was. It is not the gauzy frontier fantasy I made of it as a child. It is not a naïve celebration of the American pioneer. It is the document of a woman interrogating her legacy. It is, as the scholar Ann Romines has called it, "one of our most disturbing and ambitious narratives about failures and experiments of acculturation in the American West."

In that place and time where one world was ending and another was beginning, in that borderland between conflicting claims, the fictional Laura, the child of the frontier, struggles through her story. She hides, she cowers, she rages, she cries. She asks, "Will the government make these Indians go west?" and she asks, "Won't it make the Indians mad to have to—" but then she is cut off and told to go to sleep. She falls ill and wakes from a fever to find a black doctor attending her. She picks up beads at an abandoned Indian camp and strings them for her sister. The real Laura grows up riding back and forth in covered wagons across the Middle West, passing through immigrant towns and towns where she notes in her diary seeing "a great many colored people." She marries a farmer named Almanzo and settles, finally, in the Ozarks.

Laura Ingalls Wilder loved the land enough to know exactly what had been stolen to make her world. "If I had been the Indians," she wrote in her 1894 diary, as she looked out over a river and some bluffs in South Dakota, "I would have scalped more white folks before I ever would have left it."

ON THE BORDER

Shortly after we married, my husband and I moved to a part of Chicago that was once known as "No-Man's-Land." At the turn of the century, when Chicago had already burned and been rebuilt again, this was still a sandy forest of birch and oak trees. It was the barely populated place between the city of Chicago and the city of Evanston, the place just north of the boundary that once designated Indian Territory, a place where the streets were unpaved and unlit.

Now this neighborhood is called Rogers Park, and the city blocks of Chicago, all paved and lit, run directly into the city blocks of Evanston, with only a cemetery to mark the boundary between the two municipalities. The Chicago trains end here, and the tracks turn back in a giant loop around the gravel yard where idle trains are docked. Seven blocks to the east of the train station is the shore of Lake Michigan, which rolls and crashes past the horizon, reminding us, with its winds and spray, that we are on the edge of something vast.

There are a dozen empty store-fronts on Howard Street between the lake and the train station—a closed Chinese restaurant, a closed dry cleaner, a closed thrift shop, a closed hot dog place. There is an open Jamaican restaurant, a Caribbean American bakery, a liquor store, a shoe store, and several little grocery markets. Women push baby carriages here, little boys eat bags of chips in front of the markets, and men smoke outside the train station while the trains rattle the air.

We moved to Chicago because I was hired to teach at the university in Evanston, which is within walking distance of Rogers Park. Walking to campus along the lakeshore for the first time, I passed the cemetery, and then a block of brick apartment buildings much like the ones on my block, and then I began to pass houses with gables and turrets and stone walls and copper gutters and huge bay windows and manicured lawns and circular drives. I passed beaches where sailboats were pulled up on the sand, where canoes and kayaks were stacked; I passed fountains, I passed parks with willow trees, I passed through one block that was gated at both ends. I passed signs that read PRIVATE ROAD, NO ACCESS, POLICE ENFORCED.

Evanston was still an officially segregated city in 1958 when Martin Luther King Jr. spoke there about the Greek concept of agapē, love for all humanity. On my first visit to Evanston, after my job interview, I experienced a moment of panic during which I stood with the big cool stone buildings of the university and its lawns and trees behind me while I called my sister to tell her that I was afraid this might not be the life for me. I was afraid, I told her, that if I became a professor I would be forever cloistered here, forever insulated from the rest of the world. My sister, who is herself training to be a professor, was not moved. There are, she reminded me, worse fates.

Of the seventy-seven official "community areas" of Chicago, twenty-four are populated by more than 90 percent of one race, and only twelve have no racial majority. Rogers Park is one of those few. It is celebrated as the most diverse neighborhood in a hypersegregated city. By the time I moved to Rogers Park, quite a few people had already warned me about the place. Two of them were my colleagues at the university, who both made mention of gangs. Others were near strangers, like my sister's roommate's mother, who asked her daughter to call me on the day I was packing my moving truck to share her suspicion that I might be moving somewhere dangerous. And then there was my mother, who grew up in a western suburb of Chicago but has, for almost twenty years now, lived in an old farmhouse in rural New York. She told me that she had heard from someone that the neighborhood I was moving to might not be safe, that there were gangs there. "Ma," I said to her, "what do you know about gangs?" And she said, "I know enough—I know that they're out there." Which is about as much as I know, and about as much as most white folks who talk about gangs seem to know, which is to say, nothing.

IN THE IMAGINATION

Gangs are real, but they are also conceptual. The word *gang* is frequently used to avoid using the word *black* in a way that might be offensive. For instance, by pairing it with a suggestion of fear.

My cousin recently traveled to South Africa, where someone with her background would typically be considered neither white nor black, but colored, a distinct racial group in South Africa. Her skin is light enough so that she was most often taken to be white, which was something she was prepared for, having traveled in other parts of Africa. But she was not prepared for what it meant to be white in South Africa, which was to be reminded, at every possible opportunity, that she was not safe, and that she must be afraid. And she was not prepared for how seductive that fear would become, how omnipresent it would be, so that she spent most of her time there in taxis, and in hotels, and in "safe" places where she was surrounded by white people. When she returned home she told me, "I realized this is what white people do to each other— they cultivate each other's fear. It's very violent."

We are afraid, my husband suggests, because we have guilty consciences. We secretly suspect that we might have more than we deserve. We know that white folks have reaped some ill-gotten gains in this country. And so, privately, quietly, as a result of our own complicated guilt, we believe that we deserve to be hated, to be hurt, and to be killed.

But, for the most part, we are not. Most victims of violent crimes are not white. This is particularly true for "hate" crimes. We are far more likely to be hurt by the food we eat, the cars we drive, or the bicycles we ride than by the people we live among. This may be lost on us in part because we are surrounded by a lot of noise that suggests otherwise. Within the past month, for example, the *Chicago Tribune* reported an "unprovoked stabbing spree," a "one-man crime wave," a boy who was beaten in a park, and a bartender who was beaten behind her bar, the story being, again and again, that none of us are safe in this city.

IN THE CITY

In the spring of 2006, the *New York Times* published an analysis of all the murders that had been committed in New York City during the previous three years—a total of 1,662 murders. The article revealed one trend: people who were murdered tended to be murdered by other people like them. Most of the killers were men and boys (a disturbing 93 percent—a number that, if we weren't so accustomed to thinking of men as "naturally" violent, might strike us as the symptom of an alarming mass pathology), and most killed other men and boys. The majority of children were killed by a parent, and in more than half of all the cases, the victim and the killer knew each other. In over three fourths of the killings, the killer and the victim were of the same race, and less than 13 percent of the victims were white or Asian.

Even as it made this point, the article undid its own message by detailing a series of stranger-murders. There was the serial murderer who shot shopkeepers, the KFC customer who stabbed a cashier, the man who offered a ride to a group of strangers and was then murdered for his car. These are the murders we find most compelling, of course, because these are the murders that allow us to be afraid of the people we want to be afraid of.

In a similar layering of popular fantasy with true information, the article went on to mention specific precincts in Brooklyn, the Bronx, and Harlem where murders were concentrated, and then quoted Andrew Karmen, an expert in victimology, who explained, "The problem of crime and violence is rooted in neighborhood conditions—high rates of poverty, family disruption, failing schools, lack of recreational opportunities, active recruitment by street gangs, drug markets. People forced to reside under those conditions are at a greater risk of getting caught up in violence, as victims or as perpetrators." In other words, particular neighborhoods are not as dangerous as the conditions within those neighborhoods. It's a fine line, but an important one, because if you don't live in those conditions, you aren't very likely to get killed. Not driving through, not walking through, not even renting an apartment.

I worked, during my first year in New York, in some of the city's most notorious neighborhoods: in Bed-Stuy, in East New York, in East Harlem, in Washington Heights. That was before I knew the language of the city, and the codes, so I had no sense that these places were considered dangerous. I was hired by the Parks Department to inspect community gardens, and I traveled all over the city, on train and on bus and on foot, wearing khaki shorts and hiking boots, carrying a clipboard and a Polaroid camera.

I did not understand then that those city blocks on which most of the lots were empty or full of the rubble of collapsed buildings would be read, by many New Yorkers, as an indication of danger. I understood that these places were poverty stricken, and ripe with ambient desperation, but I did not suspect that they were any more dangerous than anywhere else in the city. I was accustomed to the semirural poverty and postindustrial decay of upstate New York. There, by the highways, yards were piled with broken plastic and rusting metal, tarps were tacked on in place of walls, roof beams were slowly rotting through. And in the small cities, in Troy and Watervliet, in Schenectady and Niskayuna, in Amsterdam and in parts of Albany, old brick buildings crumbled, brown-stones stood vacant, and factories with huge windows waited to be gutted and razed.

Beyond the rumor that the old hot-dog factory was haunted, I don't remember any mythology of danger clinging to the urban landscape of upstate New York. And the only true horror story I had ever heard about New York City before I moved there was the story of my grandmother's brother, a farm boy who had gone to the city and died of gangrene after cutting his bare foot on some dirty glass. "Please," my grandmother begged me with tears in her eyes before I moved to New York, "always wear your shoes."

And I did. But by the time I learned what I was really supposed to be afraid of in New York, I knew better—which isn't to say that there was nothing to be afraid of, because, as all of us know, there are always dangers, everywhere.

But even now, at a much more wary and guarded age, what I feel when I am told that my neighborhood is dangerous is not fear but anger at the extent to which so many of us have agreed to live within a delusion—namely that we will be spared the dangers that others suffer only if we move within certain very restricted spheres, and that insularity is a fair price to pay for safety.

Fear is isolating for those that fear. And I have come to believe that fear is a cruelty to those who are feared. I once met a man of pro-football-size proportions who saw something in my body language when I shook his hand that inspired him to tell me he was pained by the way small women looked at him when he passed them on the street—pained by the fear in their eyes, pained by the way they drew away—and as he told me this he actually began to cry.

One evening not long after we moved to Rogers Park, my husband and I met a group of black boys riding their bikes on the sidewalk across the street from our apartment building. The boys were weaving down the sidewalk, yelling for the sake of hearing their own voices, and drinking from forty-ounce bottles of beer. As we stepped off the sidewalk and began crossing the street toward our apartment, one boy yelled, "Don't be afraid of us!" I looked back over my shoulder as I stepped into the street and the boy passed on his bike so that I saw him looking back at me also, and then he yelled again, directly at me, "Don't be afraid of us!"

I wanted to yell back, "Don't worry, we aren't!" but I was, in fact, afraid to engage the boys, afraid to draw attention to my husband and myself, afraid of how my claim not to be afraid might be misunderstood as bravado begging a challenge, so I simply let my eyes meet the boy's eyes before I turned, disturbed, toward the tall iron gate in front of my apartment building, a gate that gives the appearance of being locked but is in fact always open.

IN THE WATER

My love of swimming in open water, in lakes and oceans, is tempered only by my fear of what I cannot see beneath those waters. My mind imagines into the depths a nightmare landscape of grabbing hands and spinning metal blades and dark sucking voids into which I will be pulled and not return. As a charm against my terror of the unseen I have, for many years now, always entered the water silently repeating to myself this command: *Trust the water.* And for some time after an incident in which one of my feet brushed the other and I swam for shore frantically in a gasping panic, breathing water in the process and choking painfully, I added: *Don't be afraid of your own feet.*

I am accustomed to being warned away from the water, to being told that it is too cold, too deep, too rocky, that the current is too strong and the waves are too powerful. Until recently, what I learned from these warnings was only that I could safely defy them all. But then I was humbled by a rough beach in Northern California where I was slammed to the bottom by the surf and dragged to shore so forcefully that sand was embedded in the skin of my palms and my knees. That beach happened to have had a sign that read HOW TO SURVIVE THIS BEACH, which made me laugh when I first arrived, the first item in the numbered list being DO NOT GO WITHIN 500 FEET OF THE WATER.

It is only since I have discovered that some warnings are legitimate that my fears of open water have become powerful enough to fight my confidence in my own strength. I tend to stay closer to shore now, and I am always vigilant, although for what, exactly, I do not know. It is difficult to know what to be afraid of and how cautious to be when there are so many imagined dangers in the world, so many killer sharks, and so many creatures from the Black Lagoon.

Now that we share a bookshelf, I am in possession of my husband's dog-eared, underlined copy of Barry Glassner's *The Culture of Fear*. Every society is threatened by a nearly infinite number of dangers, Glassner writes, but societies differ in what they choose to fear. Americans, interestingly, tend to be most preoccupied with those dangers that are among the least likely to cause us harm, while we ignore the problems that are hurting the greatest number of people. We suffer from a national confusion between true threats and imagined threats.

And our imagined threats, Glassner argues, very often serve to mask true threats. Quite a bit of noise, for example, is made about the minuscule risk that our children might be molested by strange pedophiles, while in reality most children who are sexually molested are molested by close relatives in their own homes. The greatest risk factor for these children is not the proximity of a pedophile or a pervert but the poverty in which they tend to live. And the sensationalism around our "war" on illegal drugs has obscured the fact that legal drugs, the kind of drugs that are advertised on television, are more widely abused and cause more deaths than illegal drugs. Worse than this, we allow our misplaced, illogical fears to stigmatize our own people. "Fear Mongers," Glassner writes, "project onto black men precisely what slavery, poverty, educational deprivation, and discrimination have ensured that they do not have—great power and influence."

Although I do not pretend to understand the full complexity of local economies, I suspect that fear is one of the reasons that I can afford to live where I live, in an apartment across the street from a beach, with a view of the lake and space enough for both my husband and me to have rooms in which to write. "Our lake home," we sometimes call it, with a wink to the fact that this apartment is far better than we ever believed two writers with student loan debt and one income could hope for. As one Chicago real estate magazine puts it: "For decades, a low rate of owner occupancy, a lack of commercial development… and problems with crime have kept prices lower in East Rogers Park than in many North Side neighborhoods." And so my feelings about fear are somewhat ambivalent, because fear is why I can afford to swim every day now.

One of the paradoxes of our time is that the War on Terror has served mainly to reinforce a collective belief that maintaining the right amount of fear and suspicion will earn one safety. Fear is promoted by the government as a kind of policy. Fear is accepted, even among the best-educated people in this country, even among the professors with whom I work, as a kind of intelligence. And inspiring fear in others is often seen as neighborly and kindly, instead of being regarded as what my cousin recognized it for—a violence.

On my first day in Rogers Park, my downstairs neighbors, a family of European immigrants whom I met on my way out to swim, warned me that a boy had drowned by the breakwater not too long ago. I was in my bathing suit when they told me this, holding a towel. And, they told me, another neighbor walking his dog on the beach had recently found a human arm. It was part of the body of a boy who had been killed in gang warfare, and then cut up with a tree saw. The torso was found later, they told me, farther up the shore, but the head was never found.

I went for my swim, avoiding the breakwater and pressing back a new terror of heads with open mouths at the bottom of the lake. When I retold the neighbors' story to my husband later, he laughed. "A tree saw?" he asked, still laughing.

ON THE FRONTIER

When the Irish immigrant Phillip Rogers built a log cabin nine miles north of the Chicago courthouse in 1834, there were still some small Indian villages there. He built his home on the wooded ridges along the north shore after noticing that this is where the Native Americans wintered.

Rogers built just south of the Northern Indian Boundary Line, which was the result of an 1816 treaty designating safe passage for whites within a twenty-mile-wide tract of land that ran from Lake Michigan to the Mississippi River, a treaty that was rendered meaningless by the Indian Removal Act of 1830, which dictated that all of the land east of the Mississippi would be open to white settlement. The Northern Indian Boundary Line, which was originally an Indian trail, would eventually become Rogers Avenue. And my apartment building would be built on the north corner of Rogers Avenue, just within the former Indian Territory.

During my first weeks in Rogers Park, I was surprised by how often I heard the word *pioneer*. I heard it first from the white owner of an antiques shop with signs in the windows that read WARNING, YOU ARE BEING WATCHED AND RECORDED. When I stopped off in his shop, he welcomed me to the neighborhood warmly and delivered an introductory speech dense with code. This was a "pioneering neighborhood" he told me, and it needed "more people like you." He and other "people like us" were gradually "lifting it up."

And then there was the neighbor across the street, a white man whom my husband met while I was swimming. He told my husband that he had lived here for twenty years, and asked how we liked it. "Oh, we love it," my husband said. "We've been enjoying Clark Street." The tone of the conversation shifted with the mention of Clark Street, our closest shopping street, which is lined with taquerias and Mexican groceries. "Well," the man said, in obvious disapproval, "we're pioneers here."

The word *pioneer* betrays a disturbing willingness to repeat the worst mistake of the pioneers of the American West—the mistake of considering an inhabited place uninhabited. To imagine oneself as a pioneer in a place as densely populated as Chicago is either to deny the existence of your neighbors or to cast them as natives who must be displaced. Either way, it is a hostile fantasy.

My landlord, who grew up in this apartment building, the building his grandfather built, is a tattooed Harley-riding man who fought in Vietnam and has a string of plastic skulls decorating the entrance to his apartment. When I ask him about the history of this neighborhood he speaks so evasively that I don't learn anything except that he once felt much safer here than he does now. "We never used to have any of this," he says, gesturing toward the back gate and the newly bricked wall that now protects the courtyard of this building from the alley. "We never even used to lock our doors even—I used to come home from school and let myself in without a key."

For some time, the front door of the little house that Laura's pa built on the prairie was covered with only a quilt, but when Pa built a door, he designed it so that the latch-string could be pulled in at night and no one could enter the house from outside. Pa padlocked the stable as soon as it was built, and then, after some Indians stopped by and asked Ma to give them her cornmeal, Pa padlocked the cupboards in the kitchen. These padlocks now strike me as quite remarkable, considering that Pa did not even have nails with which to construct the little house, but used wooden pegs instead.

In one scene of *Little House*, the house is ringed by howling wolves; in another, a roaring prairie fire sweeps around the house; in another a panther screams an eerie scream and the girls are kept inside. And then there are the Indians. The Indians who ride by silently, the Indian who occasionally come to the door of the house and demand food or tobacco, the Indians who are rumored—falsely, as Pa reveals—to have started the prairie fire to drive out the settlers. Toward the end the book, the Indians hold a "jamboree," singing and chanting all night so that the family cannot sleep. Pa stays up late making bullets and Laura wakes to see Pa sitting on a chair by the door with his gun across his knees.

This is our inheritance, those us who imagine ourselves as pioneers. We don't seem to have retained the frugality of the original pioneers, or their resourcefulnes but we have inherited a ring wolves around a door covered on by a quilt. And we have inherited padlocks on our pantries. That we carry with us a residue of the pioneer experience is my best explantion for the fact that my which neighbors seem to feel besieged this neighborhood. Because the feeling cannot be explained by anything else that I know to be true about our lives here.

The adult characters in *Little House*, all of them except for Pa, a fond of saying, "The only good Indian is a dead Indian." And for this reason some people don't want their children reading the book. It may be true that *Little House* is no after all, a children's book, but it is book that does not fail to interregate racism. And although Laura guilty of fearing the Indians, she among the chief interrogators:

"Why don't you like Indians, Ma?" Laura asked, and she caught a drip of molasses with her tongue.

"I just don't like them; and don't lick your fingers, Laura," said Ma.

"This is Indian country, isn't it?" Laura said. "What did we come to their country for, if you don't like them?"

With the benefit of sixty years of hindsight, Laura Ingalls Wilder knew, by the time she wrote *Little House*, that the pioneers who had so feared Native Americans had been afraid of a people whom they were in the process of nearly exterminating. And so as a writer she took care, for instance, to point out that the ribs of the Indians were showing, a reminder that they came, frighteningly, into the house for food not because they were thieves but because they were starving. They were starving because the pioneers were killing all their game. If anyone had a claim on fear, on terror, in the American frontier, it was obviously the Indians, who could not legally own or buy the land they lived on, and so were gradually being driven out of their lives.

Near the very end of *Little House*, after the nights of whooping and chanting that had been terrifying the Ingalls family, and after marry repetitions of the phrase "the only good Indian is a dead Indian," Pa meets an Indian in the woods, the first Indian he has met who speaks English, and he learns from him that the tall Indian who recently came into the house and ate some food and smoked silently with Pa has saved their lives. Several tribes came together for a conference and decided to kill the settlers, but this tall Indian refused, thus destroying a federation of tribes and saving the settlers. One reporting the news to his family, Pa declares, "That's one good Indian."

This turn of events has the advantage of offering a lesson and also of being a fairly accurate account of what took place in Kansas in 1869. Because Laura Ingalls Wilder was actually only a toddler during the time her family lived in Kansas, she did quite a bit of research for *Little House*, traveling back to Kansas with her daughter and writing to historians, in the process discovering the story of the tall Indian, Soldat du Chene.

And so Wilder, the writer and the researcher, knows that the land the Ingalls have made their home on in *Little House* is part of the Osage Diminished Reserve. It is unclear whether Pa knows this, but it is clear that he knows he is in Indian Territory. He goes into Indian Territory on speculation, because he has heard that the government is about to open it up to settlers. At the end of the book, he gets word from his neighbors that the government has decided to uphold its treaty with the Indians, and soldiers will be coming to move the settlers off the land.

"If some blasted politicians in Washington hadn't sent out word it would be all right to settle here, I'd never have been three miles over the line into Indian Territory," Pa admits, in a rare moment of anger and frustration. "But I'll not wait for the soldiers to take us out. We're going now!"

The Ingalls family did indeed leave their home in Kansas under these circumstances. But the possibility the book suggests, by ending where it does, is that the settlers left Indian Territory to the Indians. "It's a great country, Caroline," Pa says, as they ride off in their covered wagon. "But there will be wild Indians and wolves here for many a long day."

This is how it could have been, Laura Ingalls Wilder seems to be proposing. The government could have enforced a fair policy. The settlers could have left and stayed away. But, as it happened, the government revoked its treaty with the Plains tribes within what one historian estimates was a few weeks after the Ingalls family abandoned their house in Kansas.

Laura Ingalls Wilder does not tell us this. She tells us, instead, that Pa digs up the potatoes he just planted and they eat them for dinner. The next day they get back into their covered wagon, leaving the plow in the field and leaving their new glass windows, leaving their house and their stable, and leaving the crop they have just planted. This is the end of the book, and this, I believe, is the moral of the story.

ON THE LAKE

Leaving my apartment one morning, I found a piece of paper on the sidewalk that read, "Help! We have no hot water." This message was printed in pink ink above an address that I recognized as nearby, but farther inland from the lake. The paper was carried by the wind to the water's edge. I imagined, as a reminder of the everyday inconveniences, the absent landlords and the delayed buses and the check-cashing fees, of the world beyond.

"Everyone who lives in a neighborhood belongs to it, is part of it," Geoff Dyer writes in *Out of Sheer Rage*. "The only way to opt out of a neighborhood is to move out...." But this does not seem to hold true of the thin sliver of Rogers Park bordering the lake, which many of our white neighbors drive in and out of without ever touching the rest of the neighborhood. They do not walk down Howard to the train station, do not visit the corner store for milk or beer, do not buy vegetables in the little markets, do not, as one neighbor admitted to me, even park farther inland than one block from the lake, no matter how long it takes to find a spot.

Between my apartment building and the lake there is a small park with a stony beach and some cracked tennis courts where people like to let their dogs run loose. In the winter, the only people in the park are people with dogs, people who stand in the tennis courts holding bags of shit while their dogs run around in circles and sniff each other. In the summer, the park fills with people. Spanish-speaking families make picnics on the grass and Indian families have games of cricket and fathers dip their babies in the lake and groups of black teenagers sit on the benches and young men play volleyball in great clouds of dust until dusk. "The warm weather," my landlord observed to me not long after I moved in, "brings out the riffraff."

When my landlord said this, I was standing on the sidewalk in front of our building in my bathing suit, still dripping from the lake, and a boy leaving the park asked if I had a quarter. I laughed and told the boy that I don't typically carry change in my bathing suit, but he remained blank-faced, as uninterested as a toll collector. His request, I suspect, had very little to do with any money I may have had, or any money he may have needed. The exchange was intended to be, like so many of my exchanges with my neighbors, a ritual offering. When I walk from my apartment to the train I am asked for money by all variety of people—old men and young boys and women with babies. Their manner of request is always different, but they are always black and I am always white. Sometimes I give money and sometimes I do not, but I do not feel good about it either way, and the transaction never fails to be complicated. I do not know whether my neighbors believe, like I do, that I am paying paltry reparations, but I understand that the quarters and dollars I am asked for are a kind of tax on my presence here. A tax that, although I resent it, is more than fair.

One day in the late summer after we moved to Rogers Park, my husband came home from the fruit market with a bag of tomatoes and a large watermelon he had carried the half mile from the market to our house, stopping once to let some children feel how heavy it was. He was flushed from the sun and as he split the melon, still warm, my husband mused. "I hope more white people don't move here." My husband isn't prone to sentimentality of any kind, or to worrying about white people, so I asked him why and he said, "Because kids were playing basketball by the school, and they had cheerleaders cheering them on, and black men say hello to me on the street, and I love our little fruit market, and I don't want this place to change."

But this place probably will change, if only because this is not a city where integrated neighborhoods last very long. And we are the people for whom the new coffee shop has opened. And the pet grooming store. "You know your neighborhood is gentrifying," my sister observes, "when the pet grooming store arrives." *Gentrification* is a word that agitates my husband. It bothers him because he thinks that the people who tend to use the word negatively, white artists and academics, people like me, are exactly the people who benefit from the process of gentrification. "I think you should define the word *gentrification*," my husband tells me now. I ask him what he would say it means and he pauses for a long moment. "It means that an area is generally improved," he says finally, "but in such a way that everything worthwhile about it is destroyed."

My dictionary defines *gentrification* as meaning "to renovate or improve (esp. a house or district) so that it conforms to middle-class taste." There is definitely the sense among the middle-class people in this neighborhood that they are improving the place. New condos fly banners that read LUXURY! The coffee shop and pet grooming store have been billed as a "revitalization." And if some people lose their neighborhood in the process, there is bound to be someone like Mrs. Scott of *Little House* who will say, "Land knows, they'd never do anything with this country themselves. All they do is roam around over it like wild animals. Treaties or no treaties, the land belongs to folk that'll farm it. That's only common sense and justice."

Meanwhile, when I walk home from the train station at night, I watch unmarked cars pull up in front of black teenagers who are patted down quickly and wordlessly. Some of the teenagers, my husband observes, carry their IDs in clear cases hanging from their belts for easy access. One evening, I watch the police interrogate two boys who have set a large bottle of Tide down on the sidewalk next to them, and I cannot forget this detail, the bottle of Tide, and the mundane tasks of living that it evokes. I consider going to one of the monthly beat meetings the police hold for each neighborhood and making some kind of complaint, but month after month I do not go.

Walking down Clark Street, I pass a poster on an empty storefront inviting entrepreneurs to start businesses in Rogers Park, "Chicago's most diverse neighborhood."

It takes me some time, standing in front of this poster, to understand why the word *diverse* strikes me as so false in this context, so disingenuous. It is not because this neighborhood is not full of many different kinds of people, but because that word implies some easy version of this difficult reality, some version that is not full of sparks and averted eyes and police cars. But still, I'd like to believe in the promise of that word. Not the sun-shininess of it, or the quota-making politics of it, but the real complexity of it.

ON THE COAST

There are three of us here on the beach, with Lake Michigan stretching out in front of us. We are strangers, but we have the kind of intimacy that can exist between people who are lying on the same deserted beach. Aisha, a young black woman, sits on one side of me, and Andre, a middle-aged Polish immigrant, sits on the other.

We bury our feet in the sand and talk of the places we have lived Aisha is from Chicago, and she has never, in her twenty-one years, lived anywhere else. Andre left Poland when he was seventeen, looking for more opportunities. Now, he says he isn't entirely sure that he didn't make a mistake. We all fall silent after this confession.

This beach is a kind of no-man's-land. To the south are the last city blocks of Chicago, where the beaches are free but rocky and plagued with chunks of concrete. To the north are the first city blocks of Evanston, where the beaches are expansive and sandy but require a fee of seven dollars. To the west, beyond the wall of rocks directly behind us, is the cemetery that separates Chicago from Evanston, and a sign that forbids entry to this stretch of beach. To the east is an endless prairie of water.

When I mention that yesterday a lifeguard from Evanston came down in a boat while I was swimming and informed me that it was illegal to be here and that I had to leave because this land belongs to Evanston, Aisha rolls her eyes and says, gesturing back toward the cemetery, "This land belongs to the dead people." Andre, the immigrant, the pioneer, looks out across the water and says, "This land belongs to God."

—2008

Learning from Other Writers (Biss)

1. Biss begins by discussing Laura Ingalls Wilder. Trace where and how the theme of "pioneers" is woven throughout this essay. How does the author re-define our concept of the word "pioneer" throughout "No-Man's-Land"? What is the implied argument of this essay?

2. Biss's essay is divided into eight sections. Each section begins with either "on" or "in" (for example, "On the Prairie" or "In the City"). What is the effect of ordering the essay in this way? How does this strategy focus your attention as a reader?

3. On the surface, this essay is a profile of Rogers Park, Illinois. More generally, it is a profile of a neighborhood "in transition." But at its most fundamental level, the essay examines the nature of fear. How does Biss's fear compare to her mother's fear? Why does this contrast matter?

4. In addition to referencing and analyzing *Little House on the Prairie*, Biss incorporates other outside sources. Where does she employ them in her text? What purpose do they serve?

5. In the third paragraph of the second-to-last section ("On the Lake"), Biss paints a bucolic scene of the park near her house. She gives readers a lengthy, beautiful description of who is playing outdoors—families, fathers, children, teenagers—and then punctures that image with a hurtful comment from her landlord. How does this moment serve as evidence for the argument she's making? How is it related to the scene where the boys ride by on their bicycles and tell her not to be afraid of them?

6. The final scene of Biss's essay is written in present tense. What is the effect of this decision? What risks does Biss take by shifting tense? What benefits might she gain?

Adding Your Voice

Both Naomi Shihab Nye and Eula Biss move to places where they are outsiders—Nye doesn't speak Arabic and Biss is a white woman living in "the most diverse neighborhood in a hypersegregated city." Recount a time when you felt like an outsider in a place. Whether you moved to a new state or a foreign country, whether you visited a city where you had relatives but had never been before, or whether you finally ventured to the part of town where your parents had forbidden you to go, your goal here is to capture the feeling of not belonging.

Using a narrative structure, describe your arrival in the place where you felt like an outsider and the subsequent days, weeks, or months that followed—however long it took you to feel the first twinges of belonging. Or perhaps you never did come to belong. If not, why not? If so, how? Also, be sure to analyze your expectations. What did you expect to find? Why? Were those expectations met or foiled? What details about this place—objects, artifacts, clothing, temperature, architecture, etc.—surprised you? Focus on creating and analyzing the difference between "home" and this place.

KEY FEATURES OF THE FORM

As you draft your portraits, perhaps using the writing you have done in response to *Adding Your Voice* activities throughout this chapter, consider the common features of the portrait and note the similarities with the reflective narrative:

- Examine a driving question by using a particular lens to focus on the crucial information and eliminate what's insignificant;

- Reveal information to capture and convey your subject's particular essence and to go beyond basic reporting on the subject;

- Develop a clear sense of your relationship to the subject;

- Explore some sort of conflict or complicated relationship with the subject;

- Effectively balance expository and scenic writing;

- Use careful, thoughtful analysis and reflection to answer your driving question and deepen your readers' understanding of your subject;

- Use carefully consulted resources to provide new information on the subject by means of library research, interviews, journals, letters, photographs, memories, and so forth;

- Employ significant, concrete details relevant to your driving question and chosen lens;

- Employ an engaging voice and appropriate tone;

- End with a conclusion that shows an emotional and/or intellectual distance traveled;

- Use the subject you are portraying to tap into something universal and/or try to illuminate your subject in a new or unique way.

PART IV
Investigations

As we have discussed, form is a tool that writers use to uncover meaning. We employ narratives to analyze events that happened in the past; we craft portraits to define and illuminate the essence of our subject so we can better understand what it represents; and we undertake investigations in which we employ rigorous research, analysis, and meditation to discover connections between our subject and ourselves, as well as to make claims about that subject and the larger culture, society, or environment to which it belongs. Regardless of what form we choose, our goal is to expose what is hidden, to illuminate what is unseen, to give the reader a more complex understanding of the world.

As you will notice, investigations often incorporate the characteristics of both the narrative (a chronological, storytelling structure) and the portrait (an attempt to define the essence of a subject). The primary difference between investigations and these other two forms has less to do with content and more to do with stance. In an investigation—whether a research analysis, an experiment, a journey, or a meditation—the writer approaches his or her material with a forensic state of mind. With narratives, we look *inward* at incidents from our past and re-create them to discover their true meaning; with portraits, we look *head on* at our subjects as we try to capture their essence; and with investigations, we look *forward* as we attempt to uncover new information and insights about our material.

In all three forms, the writer's exploration of the essay's driving question allows him or her to arrive at a position in relation to the material. Some authors explicitly delineate this position, as Atul Gawande does in "Final Cut" (Chapter 7), clearly stating his claim that an increased reliance on sophisticated technology has given doctors a false sense of confidence in their diagnoses, leading them to discard the autopsy out of discomfort, despite the fact that it still remains an important learning tool for medicine. Other writers develop their arguments more implicitly, as Dan Rivas does in "Master of Machines (Chapter 8), when he uses his portrait of his father's failures to reveal that the American Dream might be a myth and that working hard doesn't necessarily guarantee success. Either way, the writer's search for a position in relation to his or her material is what gives the work meaning and significance.

CHAPTER 10

Research and Examination

Many of the essays in this chapter are centered on causes and effects: the driving question seeks first to uncover the reasons for a phenomenon and then to delineate its benefits and harms. Recognizing such cause-and-effect patterns, or looking at behaviors we take for granted from a different perspective, can change the way we think about the world. Although the sections in this book move further and further from the strictly personal, your experiences will still be useful in carrying out an investigation. James McBride, in his essay "Hip-Hop Planet," uses his initial distaste for hip-hop to launch an investigation into its roots and relevance. Nicholas Carr follows his hunch that the Internet has changed the way he thinks and lessened his ability to concentrate as he investigates the question posed in the essay's title: "Is Google Making Us Stupid?"

As we will see, many writers place themselves directly in their essays as the primary means to investigate their subjects, whether by traveling, interviewing experts, or conducting experiments. But we can't overlook the importance of traditional research using books, journal articles, statistical data, museum exhibits, historical archives, and so forth. Libraries, as old-fashioned as they might seem, hold treasures that haven't yet been digitized—not only books, but also newspapers, diaries, letters, and magazines (you would be amazed at the sorts of interesting and important details that get lost when hard copies of periodicals are turned into digital images), as well as collections of musical instruments, campaign buttons, pin cushions, and bat skulls. Most useful of all: libraries come equipped with people called librarians, who delight in helping writers find answers to their questions.

ON THE DAY YOU WERE BORN

Ken Macrorie, in his old but wise standby for composition courses, *The I-Search Paper*, suggests an exercise to combat the sorts of boring assignments that used to lead students to go to the encyclopedia (we told you his book was old), look up information (being careful to change the wording), and turn in the resulting hash of quotes (thereby proving they could re-search and re-find what superior beings known as experts already had searched and found). Instead, Macrorie advised instructors to nudge their students toward coming up with questions that genuinely intrigued them, then going out in the world and discovering their own answers to those questions.

In one assignment, Macrorie prompted students to visit the library and peruse newspapers and periodicals from the day or week they were born, with instructions that they find an interesting invention, cultural artifact, or event that had exerted a significant effect on their lives (and/or the lives of other members of their generation). Over the years, our students have responded to Macrorie's assignment by incorporating into their essays the excitement of the search, how one item jumped out from the mass of print, how this article or that advertisement prompted them to consider the effect of the invention of the digital watch on their perception of time, the effect of the Kent State riots on their family members' lives, or the effect of *Star Wars* on the fantasies and moral values of millions of young men their age. Eileen once had a biracial student who, while reading magazines from the week of his birth, discovered that his parents' marriage had been an act of miscegenation (his mother was black and his father white), making the union illegal in the state they lived in, a discovery that shocked him into a lengthy reconsideration of how much braver and more rebellious his parents must have been than he previously had understood.

The mere fact that you were born into an age in which technological innovations keep changing the way we experience reality qualifies you to write a cause-and-effect essay. After all, who is more of an expert than you on the psychological and sociological changes wrought by email and instant-messaging systems, cell phones, iPods, online gambling and online porn, cable TV, antidepressants, safe and effective birth control, treatments for AIDS and other medical conditions, global warming, genetic testing ... well, you get the point. Just as the reflective narrative addresses the tension between past and present—where you were then versus where you are now—a cause-and-effect essay examines the tension between before and after. What was the effect of the Ford Company's decision to build the Explorer? What does America's love affair with the S.U.V. say about us as consumers? (We will consider the answer when we read Malcolm Gladwell's essay "Big and Bad.")

Not only did Macrorie's assignment provide students with a motive to go to the library and conduct research that seemed exciting rather than dreary, but something about his exercise inspired our students to think. The structure of the essay pushes its writer right up to the brink of a cliff and says: Okay, now you must consider the effects of the microwave oven on the way your family ate its meals, or the effects of the first Gulf War on your aunt Jane and uncle Mark, or the effects of video games on the lives of girls your age. And most of our students took that leap ... only to discover that they were indeed able to think original thoughts, and that thinking such thoughts could be exhilarating.

When most people are *told* to think, their brains freeze up and they become too nervous or self-conscious to remember what they ate for breakfast, let alone to generate great thesis statements or arguments. (Anyone who tells you to think great thoughts or to generate a thesis statement or argument out of nothing has the process backwards:

we start with questions, not answers; we arrive at positions and claims, we don't begin there.) Many of the finest essays achieve their thematic coherence and depth of insight indirectly, if for no other reason than that telling a story with a question simmering in the back of your mind will lead you to notice or select the details that relate to that question. Your analysis comes from the material. If you know what question you are supposed to be thinking about, if you care about that question, and if you come up with a structure that pulls you naturally along the path toward answering that question, your mind will begin making connections and unraveling puzzles you previously overlooked, which you can then supplement by talking to other people or performing various types of explicit research. Again, analysis entails exposing what is hidden, noticing and developing connections that previously have remained unseen, mapping out the relationships among phenomenon so that we understand the effects on the world and the culture that surround our daily lives.

This isn't to say that the more meditation you put in an essay the better it will be, only that the basic elements are the same whether you are writing a narrative to examine your years as a high school quarterback or undertaking an experiment that involves eating dog food in order to analyze the powerful effects of marketing and branding on the purchases we make for our pets.

Similarly, your language needn't sound more "academic" when you write about cultural phenomenon or a research-driven project than when you write about the time you got sent home from school for standing up to a bully and knocking him unconscious. You should strive to write all of your essays in natural, concise, cliché-free prose. (Macrorie uses the word "Engfish" for the sort of fake, fishy prose that many people, including professors, slip into when they write academic or analytical papers.) If you read Malcolm Gladwell's "Big and Bad" or Margot Talbot's "Little Hotties," you won't find much difference between the language these authors use and the language used by authors in the reflective narrative section of this book. And while Nicholas Carr and Michael Rudin are writing about digital technology, they never use jargon-heavy or overly specialized language; their essays are accessible to a general audience. Let your ideas be complicated, not your sentences. This will not only allow you to produce more complex thinking, but also imbue your work with clarity and depth.

Adding Your Voice

Make a trip to the periodicals room of your library (or visit via an electronic database) and search through newspapers or magazines from the day or week of your birth until you find an event or an invention, a book, a movie, an article of clothing, or another product that affected your life and the lives of some segment of the population. Write an essay in which you make a case for the existence of this cause-and-effect relationship and explain its larger significance. Be careful to distinguish between a *causal* relationship, in which one event can be proved to have caused another event, and a *noncausal* relationship, in which two events happen at the same time or in sequence but don't necessarily affect one another (unless you are writing a humor piece, you won't want to blame your propensity to fall in love with the wrong people on the fact that a satellite landed on Venus the day you were born). If the effects of the phenomenon you have chosen seem too small to warrant an essay, or if you are finding it difficult to prove the existence of a link between an invention or historical event and the fairly major effect on society you are claiming it produced, try structuring your essay as a series of smaller cause-and-effect relationships. Think of dominoes: one domino falls and hits another, which hits another, which hits another.

INTEGRATING RESEARCH AND RESISTANCE

Before we move into the readings for this section, we would like to talk about integrating research and resistance into your work. Though some of the essays we introduced in earlier chapters do employ research, the authors have done so principally to contextualize elements of their own experience. For example, Caitlin Flanagan engages with theories of feminism and child psychology to distinguish her own child-rearing practices from her mother's, and Eula Biss employs facts about how, where, to whom, and *by* whom violence happens to better understand why we fear what we fear. In short, research is a secondary component of these authors' writing.

Yet many of the authors in Part IV of this book—and particularly in this chapter on research and examination—use research in a more primary way. In these essays, the lives of the writers and their personal experiences serve more as framing devices or entry points for their research rather than the other way around. Coupled with a driving question, the research process itself becomes the primary engine for investigation.

However, it is still the case that a question rather than an argument or a claim sparks the initial inquiry. To uncover their arguments or claims, the authors need to conduct a variety of investigations in a variety of disciplines—history, sociology, psychology, and so on. Visits to libraries and archives, encounters with focus groups, interviews with experts, and trips to interesting and exciting places will all play a part here.

But once you have conducted such research, what do you do with your findings?

First, remember that you are not writing a traditional "research paper" when you write an investigative essay. The goal of a research paper is often to collect as many articles on a topic as you can and then distill that vast amount of information into a more manageable format. That's certainly a useful skill. After all, gathering, categorizing, and distilling research is foundational work in many fields, particularly in the sciences and the humanities. Likewise, creating an annotated bibliography (which requires you to summarize the salient points of a series of texts in a concise and cohesive manner) can be an important starting point for any critical project. Creating such a bibliography forces you to uncover a range of materials and demands that you approach the material in a fair and unbiased way rather than simply looking for evidence that will back up your position.

But writing an investigative essay is different from writing a research paper or an annotated bibliography in that your presence as a writer—your point of view, your background, your way of seeing the world—is integral to the process. After all, without "you" there can be no position, no real meaning. Even an essay that has stripped the "I" out of the text still has an author who makes decisions, weighs evidence, and comes to conclusions based on interpretation, regardless of how objective he or she is attempting to be. By recognizing our own subjectivity—and being honest about where we stand—we actually become more objective in our readers' eyes in that they can trust us and more accurately assess our point of view and weigh our conclusions for themselves.

Analysis is about interpretation. Research doesn't inherently "prove" anything. Rather, you analyze facts and data to *extract* meaning, which you will then use to propel your work further, allowing you to ask more questions. After all, what one person sees as supporting evidence, another person might see as a counter argument.

That said, we should note that the term "counter argument" is overly simplistic and doesn't accurately reflect the way sophisticated writers engage with other points of view. Further, the term can foster the divisiveness that Frank L. Cioffi warns against in his essay "Argumentation in a Culture of Discord" (Chapter 16), in which he notes that his students have come to view the practice of argumentation not as an honest exploration of different ideas, but as a war of opposing sides. He blames this shift in attitude on the lack of a genuine forum for debate on television, where shows like *Crossfire* dominate. "In terms of discussing issues, they offer two sides, pick one: Either you are for gay marriage or against it, either for abortion or for life, either for pulling the feeding tube or for 'life.'"

Instead of using the term "counter argument," we encourage our students to think about where a reader might resist their ideas. By anticipating resistance, and then either addressing that resistance—by offering an alternative interpretation, by re-contextualizing a position, by narrowing a claim, by conceding a point, by incorporating the resistance into the work—investigation becomes a less combative and more exploratory position.

Frankly, we find it easier to understand where a reader might "resist" our ideas than where someone might "counter argue" them. Counter argument implies the exact *opposite* of your ideas, when it's actually rare that someone diametrically opposes someone else. Talking about disagreements in terms of "counter arguments" feels combative and disingenuous. When we *resist* an idea, we often find ourselves saying, "Yes, but. ..." In fact, our own position usually emerges in the very important space between those two words—"yes" and "but." Even when we agree with another writer's basic argument, there's usually something in there that we don't agree with entirely. Explore that territory—a good essay idea is often hiding in that partial disagreement.

To help train yourself to anticipate resistance, you might imagine reading your work aloud to a crowd of people made up of different backgrounds and opinions. Where do you think someone in the crowd might raise a hand to say, "Excuse me, but have you considered 'X'?" Where might someone say, "That's a bit of an over-simplification, isn't it?" Or, "Aren't you ignoring this?" Once you can anticipate what a reader might resist in your work, you will have an easier time fine-tuning your essay to make sure that those reservations are addressed.

You can also use your imaginary audience and that audience's imagined questions in your text as a way of propelling your investigation forward. In Cioffi's essay about argumentation, he begins a paragraph this way: "Now this might be very well for philosophical or literary-critical discourse, but what of scientific discourse? I suggest that all these fields require an argumentative stance, if not in the papers that students write at the freshman or even undergraduate level, then in professional journals and monographs, and that stance should be the model for student writing." See how he anticipates the resistance a scientist might put up and, instead of rejecting or ignoring it and hoping no one will bring it up, re-contextualizes what scientific writing requires and how an argumentative stance will benefit a young scientist? Cioffi takes the criticism he envisions his imaginary readers leveling at him and incorporates that resistance into his argument.

Rather than ignoring your potential critics or treating them as the enemy, you will want those critics to help you shape your work and give it nuance. This is part of joining the larger intellectual conversation that is going on around you. To honestly engage with a driving question so that you *arrive* at a position rather than begin with one, you will have a much easier time if you consider all the evidence related to your material rather than only that evidence you think will support your argument. So embrace resistance. Let research be the tool that guides your inquiry.

BRANCHING OUT FROM PERSONAL EXPERIENCE

In the next section, two authors use their experiences with digital technology to inspire and inform their investigations. Nicholas Carr, in "Is Google Making Us Stupid?," points out that his ability to concentrate has surely changed in the ten years that he has been using the Internet. Michael Rudin calls upon his experience working for the video-game designer Activision to demonstrate that today's video games exhibit the complexity and nuance of art. In "Writing the Great American Novel Video Game," he argues that the games are as sophisticated and emotionally resonant as the best novels, then goes on to show the ways in which the writers of video games use many of the same creative impulses and skills as our best novelists. He cleverly points out that video games as a genre are reviewed in *The New York Times* alongside books, films, plays, and museum exhibits, and goes on to compare the narrative devices of novels with those of video games. All along, he weaves in his experience and uses it to launch into more research and analysis.

What matters here is that these authors balance their personal points of view with objective evidence and analysis, using their knowledge of the world to contextualize their claims and add a layer of investment to the subject.

By Nicholas Carr

IS GOOGLE MAKING US STUPID?

"Dave, stop. Stop, will you? Stop, Dave. Will you stop, Dave?" So the supercomputer HAL pleads with the implacable astronaut Dave Bowman in a famous and weirdly poignant scene toward the end of Stanley Kubrick's 2001: *A Space Odyssey*. Bowman, having nearly been sent to a deep-space death by the malfunctioning machine, is calmly, coldly disconnecting the memory circuits that control its artificial " brain. "Dave, my mind is going," HAL says, forlornly. "I can feel it. I can feel it."

I can feel it, too. Over the past few years I've had an uncomfortable sense that someone, or something, has been tinkering with my brain, remapping the neural circuitry, reprogramming the memory. My mind isn't going—so far as I can tell—but it's changing. I'm not thinking the way I used to think. I can feel it most strongly when I'm reading. Immersing myself in a book or a lengthy article used to be easy. My mind would get caught up in the narrative or the turns of the argument, and I'd spend hours strolling through long stretches of prose. That's rarely the case anymore. Now my concentration often starts to drift after two or three pages. I get fidgety, lose the thread, begin looking for something else to do. I feel as if I'm always dragging my wayward brain back to the text. The deep reading that used to come naturally has become a struggle.

I think I know what's going on. For more than a decade now, I've been spending a lot of time online, searching and surfing and sometimes adding to the great databases of the Internet. The Web has been a godsend to me as a writer. Research that once required days in the stacks or periodical rooms of libraries can now be done in minutes. A few Google searches, some quick clicks on hyperlinks, and I've got the telltale fact or pithy quote I was after. Even when I'm not working, I'm as likely as not to be foraging in the Web's info-thickets reading and writing e-mails, scanning headlines and blog posts, watching videos and listening to podcasts, or just tripping from link to link to link. (Unlike footnotes, to which they're sometimes likened, hyperlinks don't merely point to related works; they propel you toward them.)

For me, as for others, the Net is becoming a universal medium, the conduit for most of the information that flows through my eyes and ears and into my mind. The advantages of having immediate access to such an incredibly rich store of information are many, and they've been widely described and duly applauded. "The perfect recall of silicon memory," *Wired*'s Clive Thompson has written, "can be an enormous boon to thinking." But that boon comes at a price. As the media theorist Marshall McLuhan pointed out in the 1960s, media are not just passive channels of information. They supply the stuff of thought, but they also shape the process of thought. And what the Net seems to be doing is chipping away my capacity for concentration and contemplation. My mind now expects to take in information the way the Net distributes it: in a swiftly moving stream of particles. Once I was a scuba diver in the sea of words. Now I zip along the surface like a guy on a Jet Ski.

I'm not the only one. When I mention my troubles with reading to friends and acquaintances—literary types, most of them—many say they're having similar experiences. The more they use the Web, the more they have to fight to stay focused on long pieces of writing. Some of the bloggers I follow have also begun mentioning the phenomenon. Scott Karp, who writes a blog about online media, recently confessed that he has stopped reading books altogether. "I was a lit major in college, and used to be [a] voracious book reader," he wrote. "What happened?" He speculates on the answer: "What if I do all my reading on the web not so much because the way I read has changed, i.e. I'm just seeking convenience, but because the way I THINK has changed?"

Bruce Friedman, who blogs regularly about the use of computers in medicine, also has described how the Internet has altered his mental habits. "I now have almost totally lost the ability to read and absorb a longish article on the web or in print," he wrote earlier this year. A pathologist who has long been on the faculty of the University of Michigan Medical School, Friedman elaborated on his comment in a telephone conversation with me. His thinking, he said, has taken on a "staccato" quality, reflecting the way he quickly scans short passages of text from many sources online. "I can't read *War and Peace* anymore," he admitted. "I've lost the ability to do that. Even a blog post of more than three or four paragraphs is too much to absorb. I skim it."

Anecdotes alone don't prove much. And we still await the long-term neurological and psychological experiments that will provide a definitive picture of how Internet use affects cognition. But a recently published study of online research habits , conducted by scholars from University College London, suggests that we may well be in the midst of a sea change in the way we read and think. As part of the five-year research program, the scholars examined computer logs documenting the behavior of visitors to two popular research sites, one operated by the British Library and one by a U.K. educational consortium, that provide access to journal articles, e-books, and other sources of written information. They found that people using the sites exhibited "a form of skimming activity," hopping from one source to another and rarely returning to any source they'd already visited. They typically read no more than one or two pages of an article or book before they would "bounce" out to another site. Sometimes they'd save a long article, but there's no evidence that they ever went back and actually read it. The authors of the study report:

It is clear that users are not reading online in the traditional sense; indeed there are signs that new forms of "reading" are emerging as users "power browse" horizontally through titles, contents pages and abstracts going for quick wins. It almost seems that they go online to avoid reading in the traditional sense.

Thanks to the ubiquity of text on the Internet, not to mention the popularity of text-messaging on cell phones, we may well be reading more today than we did in the 1970s or 1980s, when television was our medium of choice. But it's a different kind of reading, and behind it lies a different kind of thinking—perhaps even a new sense of the self. "We are not only *what* we read," says Maryanne Wolf, a developmental psychologist at Tufts University and the author of *Proust and the Squid: The Story and Science of the Reading Brain*. "We are *how* we read." Wolf worries that the style of reading promoted by the Net, a style that puts "efficiency" and "immediacy" above all else, may be weakening our capacity for the kind of deep reading that emerged when an earlier technology, the printing press, made long and complex works of prose commonplace. When we read online, she says, we tend to become "mere decoders of information." Our ability to interpret text, to make the rich mental connections that form when we read deeply and without distraction, remains largely disengaged.

Reading, explains Wolf, is not an instinctive skill for human beings. It's not etched into our genes the way speech is. We have to teach our minds how to translate the symbolic characters we see into the language we understand. And the media or other technologies we use in learning and practicing the craft of reading play an important part in shaping the neural circuits inside our brains. Experiments demonstrate that readers of ideograms, such as the Chinese, develop a mental circuitry for reading that is very different from the circuitry found in those of us whose written language employs an alphabet. The variations extend across many regions of the brain, including those that govern such essential cognitive functions as memory and the interpretation of visual and auditory stimuli. We can expect as well that the circuits woven by our use of the Net will be different from those woven by our reading of books and other printed works.

Sometime in 1882, Friedrich Nietzsche bought a typewriter—a Malling-Hansen Writing Ball, to be precise. His vision was failing, and keeping his eyes focused on a page had become exhausting and painful, often bringing on crushing headaches. He had been forced to curtail his writing, and he feared that he would soon have to give it up. The typewriter rescued him, at least for a time. Once he had mastered touch-typing, he was able to write with his eyes closed, using only the tips of his fingers. Words could once again flow from his mind to the page.

But the machine had a subtler effect on his work. One of Nietzsche's friends, a composer, noticed a change in the style of his writing. His already terse prose had become even tighter, more telegraphic. "Perhaps you will through this instrument even take to a new idiom," the friend wrote in a letter, noting that, in his own work, his "'thoughts' in music and language often depend on the quality of pen and paper."

"You are right," Nietzsche replied, "our writing equipment takes part in the forming of our thoughts." Under the sway of the machine, writes the German media scholar Friedrich A. Kittler , Nietzsche's prose "changed from arguments to aphorisms, from thoughts to puns, from rhetoric to telegram style."

The human brain is almost infinitely malleable. People used to think that our mental meshwork, the dense connections formed among the 100 billion or so neurons inside our skulls, was largely fixed by the time we reached adulthood. But brain researchers have discovered that that's not the case. James Olds, a professor of neuroscience who directs the Krasnow Institute for Advanced Study at George Mason University, says that even the adult mind "is very plastic." Nerve cells routinely break old connections and form new ones. "The brain," according to Olds, "has the ability to reprogram itself on the fly, altering the way it functions."

As we use what the sociologist Daniel Bell has called our "intellectual technologies"—the tools that extend our mental rather than our physical capacities—we inevitably begin to take on the qualities of those technologies. The mechanical clock, which came into common use in the 14th century, provides a compelling example. In *Technics and Civilization*, the historian and cultural critic Lewis Mumford described how the clock "disassociated time from human events and helped create the belief in an independent world of mathematically measurable sequences." The "abstract framework of divided time" became "the point of reference for both action and thought."

The clock's methodical ticking helped bring into being the scientific mind and the scientific man. But it also took something away. As the late MIT computer scientist Joseph Weizenbaum observed in his 1976 book, *Computer Power and Human Reason: From Judgment to Calculation*, the conception of the world that emerged from the widespread use of timekeeping instruments "remains an impoverished version of the older one, for it rests on a rejection of those direct experiences that formed the basis for, and indeed constituted, the old reality." In deciding when to eat, to work, to sleep, to rise, we stopped listening to our senses and started obeying the clock.

The process of adapting to new intellectual technologies is reflected in the changing metaphors we use to explain ourselves to ourselves. When the mechanical clock arrived, people began thinking of their brains as operating "like clockwork." Today, in the age of software, we have come to think of them as operating "like computers." But the changes, neuroscience tells us, go much deeper than metaphor. Thanks to our brain's plasticity, the adaptation occurs also at a biological level.

The Internet promises to have particularly far-reaching effects on cognition. In a paper published in 1936, the British mathematician Alan Turing proved that a digital computer, which at the time existed only as a theoretical machine, could be programmed to perform the function of any other information-processing device. And that's what we're seeing today. The Internet, an immeasurably powerful computing system, is subsuming most of our other intellectual technologies. It's becoming our map and our clock, our printing press and our typewriter, our calculator and our telephone, and our radio and TV.

When the Net absorbs a medium, that medium is re-created in the Net's image. It injects the medium's content with hyperlinks, blinking ads, and other digital gewgaws, and it surrounds the content with the content of all the other media it has absorbed. A new e-mail message, for instance, may announce its arrival as we're glancing over the latest headlines at a newspaper's site. The result is to scatter our attention and diffuse our concentration.

The Net's influence doesn't end at the edges of a computer screen, either. As people's minds become attuned to the crazy quilt of Internet media, traditional media have to adapt to the audience's new expectations. Television programs add text crawls and pop-up ads, and magazines and newspapers shorten their articles, introduce capsule summaries, and crowd their pages with easy-to-browse info-snippets. When, in March of this year, the *New York Times* decided to devote the second and third pages of every edition to article abstracts , its design director, Tom Bodkin, explained that the "shortcuts" would give harried readers a quick "taste" of the day's news, sparing them the "less efficient" method of actually turning the pages and reading the articles. Old media have little choice but to play by the new-media rules.

Never has a communications system played so many roles in our lives—or exerted such broad influence over our thoughts—as the Internet does today. Yet, for all that's been written about the Net, there's been little consideration of how, exactly, it's reprogramming us. The Net's intellectual ethic remains obscure.

About the same time that Nietzsche started using his typewriter, an earnest young man named Frederick Winslow Taylor carried a stopwatch into the Midvale Steel plant in Philadelphia and began a historic series of experiments aimed at improving the efficiency of the plant's machinists. With the approval of Midvale's owners, he recruited a group of factory hands, set them to work on various metalworking machines, and recorded and timed their every movement as well as the operations of the machines. By breaking down every job into a sequence of small, discrete steps and then testing different ways of performing each one, Taylor created a set of precise instructions—an "algorithm," we might say today—for how each worker should work. Midvale's employees grumbled about the strict new regime, claiming that it turned them into little more than automatons, but the factory's productivity soared.

More than a hundred years after the invention of the steam engine, the Industrial Revolution had at last found its philosophy and its philosopher. Taylor's tight industrial choreography—his "system," as he liked to call it—was embraced by manufacturers throughout the country and, in time, around the world. Seeking maximum speed, maximum efficiency, and maximum output, factory owners used time-and-motion studies to organize their work and configure the jobs of their workers. The goal, as Taylor defined it in his celebrated 1911 treatise, *The Principles of Scientific Management*, was to identify and adopt, for every job, the "one best method" of work and thereby to effect "the gradual substitution of science for rule of thumb throughout the mechanic arts." Once his system was applied to all acts of manual labor, Taylor assured his followers, it would bring about a restructuring not only of industry but of society, creating a utopia of perfect efficiency. "In the past the man has been first," he declared; "in the future the system must be first."

Taylor's system is still very much with us; it remains the ethic of industrial manufacturing. And now, thanks to the growing power that computer engineers and software coders wield over our intellectual lives, Taylor's ethic is beginning to govern the realm of the mind as well. The Internet is a machine designed for the efficient and automated collection, transmission, and manipulation of information, and its legions of programmers are intent on finding the "one best method"—the perfect algorithm—to carry out every mental movement of what we've come to describe as "knowledge work."

Google's headquarters, in Mountain View, California—the Googleplex—is the Internet's high church, and the religion practiced inside its walls is Taylorism. Google, says its chief executive, Eric Schmidt, is "a company that's founded around the science of measurement," and it is striving to "systematize everything" it does. Drawing on the terabytes of behavioral data it collects through its search engine and other sites, it carries out thousands of experiments a day, according to the *Harvard Business Review*, and it uses the results to refine the algorithms that increasingly control how people find information and extract meaning from it. What Taylor did for the work of the hand, Google is doing for the work of the mind.

The company has declared that its mission is "to organize the world's information and make it universally accessible and useful." It seeks to develop "the perfect search engine," which it defines as something that "understands exactly what you mean and gives you back exactly what you want." In Google's view, information is a kind of commodity, a utilitarian resource that can be mined and processed with industrial efficiency. The more pieces of information we can "access" and the faster we can extract their gist, the more productive we become as thinkers.

Where does it end? Sergey Brin and Larry Page, the gifted young men who founded Google while pursuing doctoral degrees in computer science at Stanford, speak frequently of their desire to turn their search engine into an artificial intelligence, a HAL-like machine that might be connected directly to our brains. "The ultimate search engine is something as smart as people—or smarter," Page said in a speech a few years back. "For us, working on search is a way to work on artificial intelligence." In a 2004 interview with *Newsweek*, Brin said, "Certainly if you had all the world's information directly attached to your brain, or an artificial brain that was smarter than your brain, you'd be better off." Last year, Page told a convention of scientists that Google is "really trying to build artificial intelligence and to do it on a large scale."

Such an ambition is a natural one, even an admirable one, for a pair of math whizzes with vast quantities of cash at their disposal and a small army of computer scientists in their employ. A fundamentally scientific enterprise, Google is motivated by a desire to use technology, in Eric Schmidt's words, "to solve problems that have never been solved before," and artificial intelligence is the hardest problem out there. Why wouldn't Brin and Page want to be the ones to crack it?

Still, their easy assumption that we'd all "be better off" if our brains were supplemented, or even replaced, by an artificial intelligence is unsettling. It suggests a belief that intelligence is the output of a mechanical process, a series of discrete steps that can be isolated, measured, and optimized. In Google's world, the world we enter when we go online, there's little place for the fuzziness of contemplation. Ambiguity is not an opening for insight but a bug to be fixed. The human brain is just an outdated computer that needs a faster processor and a bigger hard drive.

The idea that our minds should operate as high-speed data-processing machines is not only built into the workings of the Internet, it is the network's reigning business model as well. The faster we surf across the Web—the more links we click and pages we view—the more opportunities Google and other companies gain to collect information about us and to feed us advertisements. Most of the proprietors of the commercial Internet have a financial stake in collecting the crumbs of data we leave behind as we flit from link to link—the more crumbs, the better. The last thing these companies want is to encourage leisurely reading or slow, concentrated thought. It's in their economic interest to drive us to distraction.

Maybe I'm just a worrywart. Just as there's a tendency to glorify technological progress, there's a countertendency to expect the worst of every new tool or machine. In Plato's *Phaedrus*, Socrates bemoaned the development of writing. He feared that, as people came to rely on the written word as a substitute for the knowledge they used to carry inside their heads, they would, in the words of one of the dialogue's characters, "cease to exercise their memory and become forgetful." And because they would be able to "receive a quantity of information without proper instruction," they would "be thought very knowledgeable when they are for the most part quite ignorant." They would be "filled with the conceit of wisdom instead of real wisdom." Socrates wasn't wrong—the new technology did often have the effects he feared—but he was short-sighted. He couldn't foresee the many ways that writing and reading would serve to spread information, spur fresh ideas, and expand human knowledge (if not wisdom).

The arrival of Gutenberg's printing press, in the 15th century, set off another round of teeth gnashing. The Italian humanist Hieronimo Squarciafico worried that the easy availability of books would lead to intellectual laziness, making men "less studious" and weakening their minds. Others argued that cheaply printed books and broadsheets would undermine religious authority, demean the work of scholars and scribes, and spread sedition and debauchery. As New York University professor Clay Shirky notes, "Most of the arguments made against the printing press were correct, even prescient." But, again, the doomsayers were unable to imagine the myriad blessings that the printed word would deliver.

So, yes, you should be skeptical of my skepticism. Perhaps those who dismiss critics of the Internet as Luddites or nostalgists will be proved correct, and from our hyperactive, data-stoked minds will spring a golden age of intellectual discovery and universal wisdom. Then again, the Net isn't the alphabet, and although it may replace the printing press, it produces something altogether different. The kind of deep reading that a sequence of printed pages promotes is valuable not just for the knowledge we acquire from the author's words but for the intellectual vibrations those words set off within our own minds. In the quiet spaces opened up by the sustained, undistracted reading of a book, or by any other act of contemplation, for that matter, we make our own associations, draw our own inferences and analogies, foster our own ideas. Deep reading, as Maryanne Wolf argues, is indistinguishable from deep thinking.

If we lose those quiet spaces, or fill them up with "content," we will sacrifice something important not only in our selves but in our culture. In a recent essay, the playwright Richard Foreman eloquently described what's at stake:

I come from a tradition of Western culture, in which the ideal (my ideal) was the complex, dense and "cathedral-like" structure of the highly educated and articulate personality—a man or woman who carried inside themselves a personally constructed and unique version of the entire heritage of the West. [But now] I see within us all (myself included) the replacement of complex inner density with a new kind of self—evolving under the pressure of information overload and the technology of the "instantly available."

As we are drained of our "inner repertory of dense cultural inheritance," Foreman concluded, we risk turning into "'pancake people'—spread wide and thin as we connect with that vast network of information accessed by the mere touch of a button."

I'm haunted by that scene in 2001. What makes it so poignant, and so weird, is the computer's emotional response to the disassembly of its mind: its despair as one circuit after another goes dark, its childlike pleading with the astronaut—"I can feel it. I can feel it. I'm afraid"—and its final reversion to what can only be called a state of innocence. HAL's outpouring of feeling contrasts with the emotionlessness that characterizes the human figures in the film, who go about their business with an almost robotic efficiency. Their thoughts and actions feel scripted, as if they're following the steps of an algorithm. In the world of 2001, people have become so machinelike that the most human character turns out to be a machine. That's the essence of Kubrick's dark prophecy: as we come to rely on computers to mediate our understanding of the world, it is our own intelligence that flattens into artificial intelligence.

—2008

Learning from Other Writers (Carr)

1. What is the effect of Carr's decision to open and close his essay with Stanley Kubrick's 2001: A Space Odyssey? How does the reference at the end demonstrate distance traveled?

2. How would your reading of this essay have changed if Carr hadn't first examined the way the Internet has affected his *own* ability to concentrate?

3. Trace the way Carr builds his argument. (For instance, he begins with his own experience, then moves to other people's experiences.) How and where does he anticipate his readers' potential resistance to his argument?

4. What type of research has Carr done to provide evidence for his argument? How does he use his evidence, and analysis of this evidence, to launch into the next stage of his argument?

5. Carr writes: "As people's minds become attuned to the crazy quilt of Internet media, traditional media have to adapt to the audience's new expectations." Besides the examples that Carr provides, how do you see this phenomenon operating in your daily life? In your opinion, does the Internet enhance the quality of your daily life, or detract from it?

By Michael Rudin

WRITING THE GREAT AMERICAN ~~NOVEL~~ VIDEO GAME

Last summer, I found myself at a typical family barbecue. I was bored, bloated, and a look at my watch confirmed it: there was another hour until dessert. A disc jockey friend of mine had accompanied me that day, and we agreed a cultural crash-course might be more satisfying than a fourth round of ribs. I sent my DJ pal toward my parents' record player. A few moments later, the opera playing out of their living room evolved into a new kind of Hip Hop—"Hip-Hopera," if you will—and my parents' assumption that record players simply played records changed forever. The piece of equipment had been theirs for decades—its secret life was troubling, but also exhilarating. If a record player could do this, what was the microwave capable of? The toaster?

I share this story because the keyboard we writers know so intimately is no less different or shocking. Like my parents' record player, it lives a double life, spellbound in passionate affairs with a video game community that dotes on it as affectionately as we authors ever have. For every keystroke a writer uses to describe character or establish scene, somewhere in cyberspace a gamer uses these same keys to navigate gunships and commandeer submarines. Hone your fast-twitch muscles, and that slender spacebar can control more than just space—a boxer's jab, a racer's gear-shift, a sniper's scope.

My parents learned that day that record players exist in a parallel universe; what they thought was simply a musical utility—a tool—audiophiles and DJs have turned into a device by which musical art can be both created and consumed. Similarly, there are some 34 million PC gamers who might say we writers haven't a clue what the keyboard is capable of delivering. For them, the keyboard grants far more than access to entertainment. In this brave new virtual world, gamers have discovered—and are creating with each keystroke—an entirely new art form.

LEVEL ONE

INSTALLATION

The history of video games is told in *generations*. A big, weighty word for a thirty-year old industry, but fitting nonetheless—this is, after all, a marketplace that refreshes cyclically by purging its own technologies. Wholly and wholeheartedly, manufacturers abandon their video game console "families" for newer, shinier ones. Today, after three decades of hitting the *Reboot* button, the industry finds itself amidst a seventh generation that is doing just so. This seventh go is the period fanboys and journalists refer to as the *Next Generation*, the forward-looking term first coined in 2005 when Microsoft's Xbox 360 console released. "Next-Gen" encapsulated the industry's optimism for innovation—we were gunning it, leaving "Current-Generation" tech behind, a dusty box for little brother.

I joined Activision Blizzard on the heels of this hype, and spent the next three years as a Brand Manager as the company grew to become the largest and most profitable third-party publisher in the world. Like my former employer, the industry has refused to break stride. Since it began, Next-Gen has netted out prodigious advancements in graphical fidelity (the stuff that looks cool) and playability (the cool stuff you can control), but what makes Next-Gen worth writing about, and what makes Next-Next Gen worth dreaming about, is the recent leap forward in artistic achievement and experimentation.

For some time I felt alone in this view, one of few standing firmly in both camps—writer *and* gamer, fiction-fiend *and* pixel-popper—but Next-Gen has, with its leaps in technology and massive install-base, brought the water to the masses. You no longer need three years in Activision's trenches to spot the trend: games have developed depth, and the future of gaming will look a lot more like literature than flight simulators. This is, in many ways, the rise of a new novel. Like its lexicographic predecessor, the pixilated form revels in moral ambiguity, character motivations, conflicts between free will and fate. Take, for example, Activision's recent record-breaking release of the game *Call of Duty: Modern Warfare 2*. In Seth Schier's review for the *New York Times*— yep, a *game* review in the *Times*—he called the title "unflinching yet empathetic." Describing the series, Schiesel writes:

> With its shift to the Modern Warfare line two years ago Infinity Ward clearly wanted to deliver a present-day shooter experience that not only trotted out the latest, greatest technologies for killing efficiently, but that also prompted the player to consider the emotional and psychological consequences. In the first Modern Warfare that was demonstrated most clearly in a now-famous sequence in which the player, acting as the gunner on an airship high above a battleground, obliterated the ghostly infrared images of people displayed on a screen with detachment and precision. It was a subtly powerful moment, with a game imitating life imitating games.

Reviews like Schiesel's hint at what is evolving under the hood—a new generation of games as mature and complex as any art form available to audiences today. And such games capture the depth and scope of the human condition through the power of collaboration, rather than singular artistic vision. Even the term for the gaming audience—"install base"—reinforces the integration of participant and medium. For these individuals are not merely "connected to" or "invested in" their form: they are *installed*.

LEVEL TWO

THE NEW BAKERY

The renaissance and risk-taking that Next-Gen represents could just as easily describe gaming's evolving audience as it does its technologies and stories. This is a worldwide install-base tiptoeing toward a future of "game imitating life imitating games." And as this tip-toe toward sophistication swells into a march millions-of-gamers deep, devotees to the book and letter can appreciate what directs its path: games and the players who love them aren't locusts devouring time and attention from other art forms; rather, they are honeybees finding the nectar in narrative and then pollinating the desire for more of it, no matter the medium.

The only thing more exciting than the purity in this relentless hunt is the sheer number of hunters involved—the gaming audience is massive and still growing. Those spellbound keyboard-wielding PC gamers mentioned earlier compose the smallest slice of the gaming pie. Add console and handheld gamers and the medium comes to entertain 100 million people in America alone. The video game industry already beats Hollywood in revenue annually. Gaming hasn't carved a piece out of the entertainment pie—it's built a whole new bakery.

As a writer, I was excited to learn the empire wasn't built on a secret recipe so much as some very familiar ingredients. There are protagonists and antagonists, epilogues and prologues, first-person and third-person. But it's the sum of these parts—the finished good—that gamers hold dear above all else, and which fans of literature can identify with most. Gamers, like readers, covet immersion. It is the Holy Grail. Gamers want something they can sit down and lose time in, consuming level after level until their eyes can take no more and the urge to know what happens next gives reluctant way to body clocks that have timed out.

But this is no longer an issue of curfew, of child's play. According to the Electronic Software Association, the average gamer is thirty-five years old and has on average played games for twelve years. These men and women (females compose forty percent of all gamers) outspend every other form of entertainment, not because they are drawn to great games but because they stay drawn by their complexity and artistry.

So, yes, at their core, games are stories, consumed with great fanfare but also built with the same tools and materials we authors stash in our own toolboxes. That said, a game's construction is highly specialized. Though expenses vary, your average novel costs time and energy, a laptop, and equal parts espresso and sanity. A video game needs these things too, but to the tune of around twenty-five million dollars in technical support. Nevertheless, here is the most important distinction: a game, though at one point written, is not created by a *writer*. Games are brought to life by *developers*. In my three years in the industry, the term never ceased to give me pause, given the extended family *developers* share in the wide world of storytellers. Whereas authors, journalists, screenwriters and playwrights can hypothetically create a finished product on their own, at their own pace, developers must "develop" their games gradually, usually over a two-year cycle of incremental gains. Games evolve from ideas into prototypes into weekly game "builds," each week's build increasingly fleshed out from an art, sound, and design standpoint. In linear games, each game "level" contains an environment, plot points, and like the chapters of a novel, these levels come together to form a larger narrative.

In most cases, the team that creates all this ranges from twenty to 200 dedicated individuals. The art department conceptualizes the game's style, characters, and environments. Designers take those building blocks and create a set of features that will govern the game's mechanics—what will the action look like and how will it stay interesting for ten to twenty hours? Sound engineers construct effects and music scores to complete the experience. Producers are the glue, making sure everything happens in-sync, on-budget and on-time. Amongst all of this: one writer.

He is a lot of things, our cousin. He is on his own, for one. Few writers have entered this space. He is both an explorer, stewarding the march of Next-Gen down a worthy path, and a pilgrim, setting up camp for the rest of us. He is also a prospector, a new-millennium 49er. As viewed against the full scope of the storytelling pantheon, gaming is an infant—the industry is new money, less than a half-a-century old. It boasts an unscarred landscape, veins of rich ore lying undiscovered just below the surface. The opportunity may be best put by Guillermo Del Toro, director of Oscar-winner *Pan's Labrynth*, who told *Wired* magazine:

"We are used to thinking of stories in a linear way—act one, act two, act three. We're still on the Aristotelian model. What the digital approach allows you to do is take a tangential and nonlinear model and use it to expand the world. For example: If you're following Leo Bloom from Ulysses on a certain day and he crosses a street, you can abandon him and follow someone else...We could be doing so much more...In the next 10 years, there will be an earthshaking *Citizen Kane* of games."

Forget the riches of revenue for a moment; right now, as you read this, gaming is rich in something far more valuable to us writers: gaming is rich with *storytelling possibility*. For all my insider knowledge of what the medium has done, and Del Toro's optimism at what it might do, the idea that games might not have done it yet means that we, as storytellers, have reason to be a smidge jealous of our "developer" brethren and their install base. Their art is still maturing. Someone will soon make history. Gaming will evolve.

Independent game developers—stewards of the new and different, and usually on the cheap—are more aware of this than anyone. One of these developers, Jason Rohrer, creator of *Passage*, is credited by some as creating the first tear-jerker video game. In a recent *New York Times Magazine* article by Joshuah Bearman, he discusses the way in which video games will inevitably have to escape the influence of film to distinguish themselves, just as film had to do the same with its predecessor, the stage. "Eventually film figured out editing, camera movement—the tools that made movies movies," he says. "Video games need to discover what's special and different about their own medium to break out of their cultural ghetto."

Given the process and team dynamic described above, the question, then, is how does writing fit into the game industry's creative process, and how will that relationship evolve as game development and the medium itself matures? Why should we care about the gaming recipe or, for that matter, whether or not it breaks out of its "cultural ghetto"? After all, if it does, what kind of art form will have escaped?

LEVEL THREE

SWEAT AND TREMBLE

Fair questions, for if members of the development team are drawing the game up, making it work, giving it sound, and constructing it from scratch, then what in the world does the writer really do? A game concept must be nurtured from something fun into something immersive, but how this is achieved through narrative is the writer's responsibility. Though you may not pick up and play a game and immediately see the writer's contribution, if you keep playing it, if you experience it beginning to end, those realizations become paramount. There is a script. A plot. Characters have dialogue. For gamers, winning the game is a formality, an expectation; beyond stepping into the boots of their favorite characters and watching these protagonists grow and evolve, they want to become experts on each character's biography and relationships, each distant planet's geography, the effects and counter effects of countless spells, weapons and artifacts. They game to experience. To understand. To learn.

The writer is busiest before the project has a team, conceptualizing all these details and developments so that when the artists and designers sit down to create, they are working not off ideas but a cohesive game, a narrative. Depth, rather than polish. Gaming is the ultimate show-over-tell medium. But for it to matter, for a gamer to remember it years later, and want to play it again, what's shown must be rooted in a story worth telling.

But that's just it, isn't it? How can show-over-tell, a literary term, apply to a medium that shows-and-tells-everything? The act of reading and gaming are so fundamentally different that whereas they both require writers, any developer who hopes to raise gaming out of its "cultural ghetto" must first be tapped not into what the gaming audience experiences, but *how*—they need to get how games affect gamers emotionally. Literature has evolved; though today we read for different reasons than ever before, certain truths hold eternal: we read to understand characters different than ourselves, to experience other lives, to grow and learn through stepping into others' shoes. Gamers play for these same reasons, but they also want to *control* characters different from themselves—to not only experience and see other lives, but *guide* them. Perhaps this is why winning is a formality, a diploma to hang in the garage. Winning comes after gamers have sweated and trembled, paused the game to compose themselves. Screamed and thrashed. As an audience, they are immersed on another level altogether. This level increasingly requires two things: new kinds of storytelling and new storytellers to bring it forth.

At Activision, I worked on award-winning titles and the opposite—games meant solely to entertain and fill rainy afternoons. The latter is what Rohrer referred to as the "cultural ghetto"; as in any other form, money still drives decision making and more often than not, game publishers will pick simpler premises to develop. This is not merely because they have proven audiences; they're also more affordable to build out. Think Tom Clancy, Danielle Steele, Clive Cussler, or any other writer whose work has become a franchise of predictability.

But the kind of game Rohrer dreams of exists. I've played and worked on both types of games, and as a writer, toiling in each tier taught me as much about what makes art as what makes entertainment. For an outsider trying to understand the difference, the problem is that games, no matter their purpose or depth, can often look equally breathtaking. Even for hardcore gamers, graphics can be the most effective common denominator in judging a title's ability to immerse; and to that end, games, and the characters and environments therein, have become uncommonly pretty. Female characters like Lara Croft are so beautifully rendered that they've become bona fide sex symbols—transcending off the small screen and onto the big. We've gone from 16-bit graphics to environments where blades of grass sway against the breeze. On the surface, these graphical advances might mean that to a non-scrutinizing gamer, most titles are looking good, or looking "cool." What the graphical advances really mean is that under the hood, the processing power has gone up—developers can do more, experiment more, risk more. It means that a game writer's narrative can be enhanced by craft—details, objects, expressions and atmospherics can all augment storytelling. Mood is now a factor.

Distill this further and the opportunity for artistic achievement in the games space becomes that much more exciting. True, like its brother-in-law the beach-ready paperback, there will always be mindless video games; scoring touchdowns and zapping aliens provide the same cracker-barrel escapism as pulp detective novels and bodice-rippers. But if we observe the last few years' most popular games, they illustrate a clear shift in consumer palate toward more complex narrative. And it's this small batch of sophisticated stories that have evolved what used to be called a good game into Great Gaming, a difference in quality akin to the disparity between good reads and Great Literature. Today they might compose a narrow bandwidth amidst the hundreds available to consumers, but these are the games tasked with evolving, growing big and strong into *Citizen Kanes* that might one day provide gaming with a permanent path out from its casual and iterative "ghetto." And as game consoles become more technically powerful and developers more savvy, impressive graphics and gameplay will continue to shed their role as competitive advantages, and instead storytelling will emerge as the critical instrument teams will use to differentiate their art. Narrative and art are becoming less a bright possibility for gaming's future and more likely the only path to the top of its mountain.

Of course, the ascent never really seemed necessary until recently. Game stories have historically been raw, a means to an end, form-fitted to help players understand and uncover game features and content. Players didn't care if Pac-Man had daddy issues—they wanted to gobble ghosts. Things have changed. Video game writing is now recognized and awarded by the Writers Guild of America. 2009's five nominees come from five different genres, ranging from casual to action to role-playing. The establishment of the award and its broad view is in ways a reflection of the depth game-writing now encompasses. The 'gobbling ghost' has become a ghost itself. Though every game writer contributes to the game's design document, dialogue and story, the exceptional ones are working hand in hand to see what else they can do to build unprecedented immersion. These are the artists, creating games that are art. They suspend disbelief with their storytelling. Juxtapose vivid new worlds against meticulously researched historical fact. They are increasingly intimate, driven by characters that compel. They probe morality relentlessly. Like any great work of art, they challenge their audience, destabilize it, and demand collaboration.

LEVEL FOUR
AVOID THE RAILS

In Pac-Man, our hero's quest is simple: clear the screen while avoiding certain ghosts and gobbling others. By today's development standards, it's an archaic design. Whereas an author might give her character a fork in the road and pick one for the reader, game writers now work in concert with designers to challenge gamers by giving characters countless forks. In short, complete rein over a character's destiny. So that in this new future, Pac-Man can jump off your screen, gobble any ghost he wants, maybe even stop for a beer and some Thai before outsourcing his contract to another Pac-Assassin. Today's gamers demand depth through choice, and today's great games challenge their audience not only through the minutiae of mini-quests but with mini-bouts of moral plight. Clint Hocking, a Creative Director at Ubisoft, the world's fourth largest game company, refers to the successful experimentation in the "indie" development circuit as games that "have used what is innate to games—their interactivity—to make a statement about the human condition."

Though in no way a perfect example, I personally worked on one title that attempted to extract this effect through a popular proxy: your friendly neighborhood Spider-Man. *Spider-Man: Web of Shadows* was built so that the player would not only have the tools to defeat enemies, but to mold temperament. Righteous or antihero, staying a "friendly" neighborhood Spider-Man was solely the player's choice. We did this because the novelty of simply swinging around town as Spider-Man had worn off. Immersion had to evolve beyond wearing the costume. So with every intention of challenging our audience, we redefined Spider-Man as ambiguous, left it up to the gamer to return verdict on Spidey—in turn, returning verdict on the gamer himself. A variety of reasons kept us from only scratching the surface, as in true "open world" games, choices have consequences beyond whether a city cheers or fears a Red or Black-Suited Spider-Man, or who in turn becomes Spidey's ally or villain.

Character creation and development arguably hits its apex in the franchise *Fable*, where the entire game is based on the decisions a player makes, as the character will evolve into whatever he or she desires. The appeal lies in the immersion this provides—this is self-invention fused with complex consequences. Imagine a Choose Your Own Adventure book where in addition to affecting the character's path, your choices affect the book's page color, the book's fonts, the book-jacket's imagery. Complete control comes when every decision matters, when destiny is rewritten with each one. For games like these, an ambitious writer can spend weeks and months brainstorming "quests" and paths for his audience. The payoff? A gamer can spend years replaying them, experimenting with different causal relationships, observing change, learning. The idea that game stories may be less profound than short stories because they boast more outcomes is beside the point—this is a new art form, and just as film and television learned to inspire their audiences, video game writers are learning their medium is one that can embrace its replayability to reinvent how gaming narrative can challenge its audience.

But what about games that challenge more than their audience? A great work of art can destabilize far more than its following—it can infect the periphery. Whether destabilizing our senses of right and wrong or simply what's proper, the capability of games to shake things up by literally providing the audience with the shaker makes it one of the most powerful art forms in history. When an art form is banned over violated codes of "...excess vulgar language, sexual scenes, things concerning moral issues, excessive violence, and anything dealing with the occult," we need to ask ourselves if this censorship is truly protecting our citizens, or whether we simply haven't recognized the artistry in the work. Yes, many games cash in on the liquid gold of blood, the silver of silicon'ed heroines, but can we honestly say that today's morally challenging video games do little more than erode our morals? What if, instead, some are breaking down boundaries of thought and expression? Just by sitting on the receiving end of politicians' ire and parental fear, video games are joining a fraternity, walking a well-worn path: after all, the violated codes listed above refer not to a particular game, but were cited by a Canadian library in 1982 as grounds for banning *The Catcher in the Rye*.

I've seen the value of destabilization first-hand, watching as the developers of *Call of Duty* invested in it devotedly, dividends returning the favor promptly, elevating their property from risk-taker to headline-stealer to chart-topper. *Call of Duty* is by classification a first-person shooter, a typically linear experience that creates immersion through action intensity and tactical combat decisions. Publishers can differentiate their shooters with different weapons, time periods and villains, but some of the best games in recent history have leaned on writing to differentiate with risky and unique narrative devices. While at Activision I had the great fortune of working on *Call of Duty 4: Modern Warfare*, a title that inspired contempt for its fictional villains by placing the player into the shoes of a kidnapped politician in the very first scene of the game. Though the player can control the camera, he can control little else, forced to watch as he is driven through a war-ravaged Middle Eastern city to the center of a town hall where camcorder and wooden post await. The player watches as he is stood up, strung in, and executed—out of commission before he can affect a single thing. Later in the game, players crash-land after a nuclear bomb goes off. Although able to walk, there is no escaping the radiation that blankets a devastated playground the player finds himself in. There is nothing he can do—he falls to the ground and dies in what was one of the most overpowering moments in any game to date. *Call of Duty* was the first commercially successful shooter to kill off the protagonist, and though the game is unprecedented on all levels—gameplay, polish, sound design—it was this kind of risk that endeared the title to its audience. They were neither coddled nor shoved from level to level. Rather, they were immersed, invested, and thus affected. It was this level of artistic ambition that took *Call of Duty* from wildly popular with gamers to wildly popular period, the best selling shooter of all time.

Then came the sequel, and *Call of Duty* grew from a best-selling shooter to the best-selling form of *entertainment* of all time, earning $310 million on its first-day in stores in North America and the United Kingdom alone. It has gone on to shatter every record. The success can be attributed to a perfect storm of sorts, but one undeniable component was the storm of controversy *Modern Warfare* 2 brewed by extending the moral boundaries it drew in the first game to an entirely new order of magnitude for the sequel. Now came the slaughter of civilians. Though the gamer is allowed to skip a scene prefaced as potentially offensive, if he continues, it is wholly up to him to follow orders that demand he murders an airport full of innocent civilians. The narrative warns the gamer that accepting the mission will "cost a piece of yourself," and the explosion of news and headlines following *Modern Warfare* 2's release clearly indicate that it broke not just sales records, but social and societal boundaries. Whether one finds the game's airport mission reprehensible or not, the ethical dilemmas it embraced represent a massive step-forward for gaming. Through narratives that "cost" gamers pieces of themselves, titles like *Modern Warfare* 2 have begun destabilizing not only their audience but every audience, using moral complexities in ways this new art form will only echo and grow upon.

In the aforementioned level, gamers were given a variety of options: they could cry foul and return the game in a huff; they could skip the level in question altogether; they could continue conservatively, allowing computer-controlled members of the team to shoot civilians instead; or they could lock and load, mow down every digital innocent. No matter their selection, the five million individuals who bought *Modern Warfare* 2 on its opening day were engaged in a way that makes video games so uniquely powerful as an art form: they were given a choice in the first place.

The collaboration between game and gamer is intrinsic to what a game is, who a gamer can be—without a gamer's input, the game's narrative will stall and fail. Some might say that the entire *point* of literature is for a reader to experience an individual point of view, a unique and singular vision of the world. But certainly the best novels and stories make demands on its readership. In fact, readers have plenty to do. They must piece language with pieces of themselves; they must imagine and make connections; they must think forward and back. In his ode to craft, *On Writing*, Stephen King whittled down an author's main job to three categories: narration, description, and dialogue. From there, it is dependent upon the reader to weave our words with their imagination, to work, build, and create life. The greatest novels I've read are the ones that demanded the most from me—as the stories became more fully mine, they became richer, more meaningful. Similarly, the worst novels I've read have demanded the least—these were the slideshows, pages of prose sliding past my eyes but never penetrating their glassy gaze.

The collaboration that games demand follows suit. The worst-reviewed games are often "on rails," a game-critic's term for linearity which is a nice way of saying the title was too simple, demanded too little, and was therefore a bore. On the other hand, the best-reviewed games *demand* investment from their audience; unlike collaboration between reader and author, gamers are not *imagining* settings and time periods so much as *exploring* them. Yet both these actions require deciding what details matter and what don't, acting on those decisions and then living with those consequences.

And herein lies collaboration's pay-off: gamers and readers feel their stories more profoundly, the art resonates, rings true. Of course, the roads to emotional pay-off in reading and gaming are one-way streets heading in different directions, something developers are aware of and increasingly experimenting with. Whereas in words we feel with protagonists as the action unfolds, in games we feel by unfolding the action ourselves, unfurling the carpet and then walking it.

BioShock, 2007's Video Game Awards' Game of the Year, placed the gamer in an underworld utopia ravaged by its own citizens, individuals who in their attempts to perfect life with genetic enhancement poisoned themselves and their world. In the game, players come upon a choice: heal a possessed little girl or harvest her. Though she may assist you later, you need her power to survive now. Throughout the adventure, gamers picked life or death for countless individuals in a narrative device that stretched the moral fibers of what most players had come to expect from their games. Taking it further, the developers programmed "Achievements" for gamers who stayed true to their code of ethics—rewards lay in wait for those who remained consistent to their heal versus harvest policies. BioShock was revered because it gave gamers free will. Bioshock will be remembered because that free will came with a price. To keep the story moving along, gamers had to collaborate, make decisions and live with them; but while decision-making was nothing new, the accompanying emotional ramifications certainly were. The pride, the shame. The realization that one felt neither. As games continue to challenge, it is their inherent ability to collaborate that will make them increasingly complex. A gamer's "work" is a cornerstone to what makes his game art—it is the promise of enrichment in return for engagement, a way to break "off the rails" and take himself to places he has never been.

LEVEL FIVE

INDEBTEDNESS, CONNECTEDNESS

If you still can't see the artistry inherent in video games; if you don't see the magic in a record player the way my parents did, all I ask is this: hang on. The game industry will adapt. In order to satisfy the fractured and particular tastes of its audience, publishers are creating new genres, game types, and brand extensions with dizzying disregard for how many games players can actually afford to buy. Your local GameStop retailer may still organize its shelves by platform—Xbox 360, PlayStation 3, Wii—but one day soon it may be forced to drill down not just by audience—All Ages, Teen, Mature—or game type—Action, Shooter, Strategy—but also story type: Sci-Fi, Horror, Mystery, History, Sport. With a compartmentalized marketplace, fans will flock to the stories they love most. They already seek out their favorite developers; who is to say they won't begin looking within them, for their favorite writers?

It could also be the other way around. Just as Steven Spielberg has begun producing games, maybe an established novelist will adopt this new creative domain as well, helping migrate a readership by offering his or her next narrative in the form of a game. Guillermo can't do it alone; the Citizen Kane of games may well come from one of you, or your students. But it is coming. After all, until quite recently, many people thought the only place graphic novels belonged were in the basements and bedrooms of teenage boys—the same environment most critics have relegated video games, coincidentally. Yet with the emergence of work like Art Spiegelman's *Maus* and Marjane Satrapi's *Persepolis*, to name just two, graphic novels have found a place on the shelf with literature. And even a Pulitzer nod, in the case of Spiegelman.

The narrative devices in *Fable, Call of Duty*, and *BioShock* introduce far more than perspective and pace into a story—they inject emotion. And whereas the game designers and art department and sound engineers take away a writer's need to describe and establish scene, they cannot create the most important differentiating factor outside of fresh content and innovative gameplay: storytelling with consequences. Immersion that resonates and moves a player the way great literature resonates and moves a reader. As a form, writers interested in video games can be empowered in ways their peers have never known. If they can operate within timelines and technical limitations, if they can share the process with a large cross-functional team of equally dedicated individuals, they will be at the forefront of an entirely new storytelling medium—the first art form to empower its audience through direct action and consequence.

In her 2007 *Harper's* essay "Literary Entrails," Cynthia Ozick distilled a letter of James Wood's to get to the core of why Gustave Flaubert might have fathered the modern novel. For Ozick and Wood, Flaubert's rank at the top has less to do with his personally evolving literature than how generation to generation of the written word reflects the evolution he set forth. For Ozick, "The key is indebtedness. The key is connectedness."

Video games are as indebted and connected to literature as television and film once were. The pixel and the page are linked, now and forever, and as gaming continues to build a stage to one day stand tall upon, we, as fiction writers, would be wise to stand in solidarity with our fellow artists. If the key is indebtedness, connectedness, we may soon see literature tap into the video game install-base, as indebted and connected to gaming as games are today. Because video game popularity is transitive. It is popularity in story and narrative, something challenging, destabilizing and collaborative. Because it is popularity in art. This new frontier in creativity may come to mean new audiences for every form, hordes of fiction-fiends and pixel-poppers seeking what one camp provides and the other cannot, what both provide without fail. Games aren't toys, but we would be wise to play them. The hope for Great American Art can be sourced to the hunger of a Great American Audience.

—2010

Learning from Other Writers (Rudin)

1. Rudin opens with an anecdote about his parents and a record player. What is the purpose of this humorous introduction?

2. Like many of the authors whose work we have read, Michael Rudin uses questions at the ends of paragraphs and sections to propel his essay forward. What are some of the micro questions that Rudin uses as transitions and building blocks? How does he answer these smaller questions? How does he use those answers to complicate and develop his larger driving question?

3. Given that Rudin's essay was originally published on the Website of *Fiction Writers Review*, whom would you judge to be the audience? Do you imagine that Rudin's audience would be sympathetic to his argument? Skeptical? How does Rudin address possible resistance from his readers?

4. What is the effect of the essay's sub-headings? How do the sub-heads and sub-titles ("Installation," "The New Bakery," etc.) help to shape the movement of the essay?

5. Rudin's essay is a comparative analysis: he is looking at video games through the lens of art and literature. List the ways in which he finds video games to be similar to novels. How does he incorporate each new similarity into his essay?

TRENDS AND MISCONCEPTIONS

Often a writer sets out to investigate a trend or to correct a common misconception. James McBride, in "Hip-Hop Planet," examines his aversion to hip-hop music. Beginning with his early disdain for the genre, he challenges his reaction by investigating the history and significance of hip hop, examining the musical genre through the lens of its political relevance, even going so far as to travel to Senegal to investigate the music's roots. You may not have the time or money to leave the country, but plenty of library sources exist that could help you to investigate such a question.

As McBride's essay shows, investigating the true causes of a cultural or economic trend can provide the driving question for an essay. In "Big and Bad," Malcolm Gladwell sets out to understand the sudden, surprising popularity of S.U.V.s. Notice the way he builds his essay, letting each new discovery lead to another question that propels the essay forward. He talks to engineers and marketing executives; he studies statistics correlating driver deaths to various makes of sedans and S.U.V.s; he test-drives cars and S.U.V.s on obstacle courses designed to compare the maneuverability of various types of vehicles. All this research culminates in the author's analysis of the psychology of what we buy and how our consumer choices might reflect our feelings of safety or vulnerability. In fact, Gladwell discovers that the shift in American attitudes toward safety has been largely responsible for the rise in popularity of S.U.V.s, that in the late 1900s and early 2000s, "feeling safe" became more important than actually "being safe." The effect of Americans' changed attitudes toward safety—our belief that accidents are inevitable rather than avoidable—is reflected in the kinds of vehicles we buy and the way they are marketed to us.

In her essay "Little Hotties," Margot Talbot asks: What does the change from the elegant, albeit proportionally incorrect, Barbie to the pouty-lipped, bedroom-eyed, large-headed but sexy-bodied Bratz doll reflect about our culture? What sort of message is the Bratz doll sending to young girls—look like a pole dancer? Are these toys *reflecting* attitudes already at play in our culture, or are they *advancing* new attitudes?

Marketing and sexuality also play a role in "Orthodox Chic" by Meaghan Winter, although not in ways you might expect. The essay examines the paradox of wig wearing by Orthodox Jewish women, specifically the practice of wearing wigs that are meant to make a woman look sexually desirable, when the point of covering one's hair is religious modesty, an attempt to *subvert* sexiness. Like Gladwell's essay, "Orthodox Chic" follows the structure of a traditional investigative essay: the author begins with something she noticed (high-end wig shops), provides a bit of context, and then presents her driving question: "How does spending two grand on a shiny wig called Rebel Yell, which Shevy's website promises 'brings out the independent spirit,' fulfill a young woman's covenant with her husband, community, and God?"

Winter then turns to the blogosphere, where she finds Orthodox women responding in various ways to the idea of head coverings. Next, she provides some history of Jewish women covering their hair and includes comments from Orthodox women on relevant aspects of religious observance and obligation. She also incorporates the voices of rabbis, theology professors, and sociologists. The essay provides an examination of age-old traditions as they are juxtaposed with our modern world and the way an observant Jewish woman might negotiate both. The essay's significance goes beyond the Orthodox community: Winter raises questions about why we believe what we believe, the importance of tradition, and the ways in which contradictions are inherently part of contemporary religious life.

One practical note: As you will notice as you read the selections in this chapter, the answer to the writer's driving question is usually developed throughout the essay, with a more complete conclusion at the end. While we consider this a perfectly acceptable (and often preferable) approach to locating your essay's major argument, finding, or claim, we also recognize that professors in other classes might not always agree. In a traditional research paper, the writer may be expected to state his or her argument, claim or finding—i.e., the answer to the driving question—at or near the beginning of the paper. To satisfy such a requirement, all you need to do is to write your essay following the methods detailed in this book, and then, once you have arrived at your final draft, insert a statement of your argument, claim, or finding near the start of the paper, directly after your statement of the essay's driving question. This foreshadowing might spoil the suspense for your readers, but it will satisfy a professor who wants to see your paper's thesis somewhere in the introduction.

By James McBride

HIP HOP PLANET

This is my nightmare: *My daughter comes home with a guy and says, "Dad, we're getting married." And he's a rapper, with a mouthful of gold teeth, a do-rag on his head, muscles popping out his arms, and a thug attitude. And then the nightmare gets deeper, because before you know it, I'm hearing the pitter-patter of little feet, their offspring, cascading through my living room, cascading through my life, drowning me with the sound of my own hypocrisy, because when I was young, I was a knucklehead, too, hearing my own music, my own sounds. And so I curse the day I saw his face, which is a reflection of my own, and I rue the day I heard his name, because I realize to my horror that rap—music seemingly without melody, sensibility, instruments, verse, or harmony, music with no beginning, end, or middle, music that doesn't even seem to be music—rules the world. It is no longer my world. It is his world. And I live in it. I live on a hip-hop planet.*

High-stepping

I remember when I first heard rap. I was standing in the kitchen at a party in Harlem. It was 1980. A friend of mine named Bill had just gone on the blink. He slapped a guy, a total stranger, in the face right in front of me. I can't remember why. Bill was a fellow student. He was short-circuiting. Problem was, the guy he slapped was a big guy, a dude wearing a do-rag who'd crashed the party with three friends, and, judging by the fury on their faces, there would be no Martin Luther King moments in our immediate future.

There were no white people in the room, though I confess I wished there had been, if only to hide the paleness of my own frightened face. We were black and Latino students about to graduate from Columbia University's journalism school, having learned the whos, whats, wheres, whens, and whys of American reporting. But the real storytellers of the American experience came from the world of the guy that Bill had just slapped. They lived less than a mile (1.6 kilometers) from us in the South Bronx. They had no journalism degrees. No money. No credibility. What they did have, however, was talent.

Earlier that night, somebody tossed a record on the turntable, which sent my fellow students stumbling onto the dance floor, howling with delight, and made me, a jazz lover, cringe. It sounded like a broken record. It was a version of an old hit record called "Good Times," the same four bars looped over and over. And on top of this loop, a kid spouted a rhyme about how he was the best disc jockey in the world. It was called "Rapper's Delight." I thought it was the most ridiculous thing I'd ever heard. More ridiculous than Bill slapping that stranger.

Bill survived that evening, but in many ways, I did not. For the next 26 years, I high-stepped past that music the way you step over a crack in the sidewalk. I heard it pounding out of cars and alleyways from Paris to Abidjan, yet I never listened. It came rumbling out of boomboxes from Johannesburg to Osaka, yet I pretended not to hear. I must have strolled past the corner of St. James Place and Fulton Street in my native

Brooklyn where a fat kid named Christopher Wallace, aka Biggie Smalls, stood amusing his friends with rhyme, a hundred times, yet I barely noticed. I high-stepped away from that music for 26 years because it was everything I thought it was, and more than I ever dreamed it would be, but mostly, because it held everything I wanted to leave behind.

In doing so, I missed the most important cultural event in my lifetime.

Not since the advent of swing jazz in the 1930s has an American music exploded across the world with such overwhelming force. Not since the Beatles invaded America and Elvis packed up his blue suede shoes has a music crashed against the world with such outrage. This defiant culture of song, graffiti, and dance, collectively known as hip-hop, has ripped popular music from its moorings in every society it has permeated. In Brazil, rap rivals samba in popularity. In China, teens spray-paint graffiti on the Great Wall. In France it has been blamed, unfairly, for the worst civil unrest that country has seen in decades.

Its structure is unique, complex, and at times bewildering. Whatever music it eats becomes part of its vocabulary, and as the commercial world falls into place behind it to gobble up the powerful slop in its wake, it metamorphoses into the Next Big Thing. It is a music that defies definition, yet defines our collective societies in immeasurable ways. To many of my generation, despite all attempts to exploit it, belittle it, numb it, classify it, and analyze it, hip-hop remains an enigma, a clarion call, a cry of "I am" from the youth of the world. We'd be wise, I suppose, to start paying attention.

Burning Man

Imagine a burning man. He is on fire. He runs into the room. You put out the flames. Then another burning man arrives. You put him out and go about your business. Then two, three, four, five, ten appear. You extinguish them all, send them to the hospital. Then imagine no one bothers to examine why the men caught fire in the first place. That is the story of hip-hop.

It is a music dipped in the boiling cauldron of race and class, and for that reason it is clouded with mystics, snake oil salesmen, two-bit scholars, race-baiters, and sneaker salesmen, all professing to know the facts, to be "real," when the reality of race is like shifting sand, dependent on time, place, circumstance, and who's telling the history. Here's the real story: In the mid-1970s, New York City was nearly broke. The public school system cut funding for the arts drastically. Gone were the days when you could wander into the band room, rent a clarinet for a minimal fee, and march it home to squeal on it and drive your parents nuts.

The kids of the South Bronx and Harlem came up with something else. In the summer of 1973, at 1595 East 174th Street in the Bronx River Houses, a black teenager named Afrika Bambaataa stuck a speaker in his mother's first-floor living room window, ran a wire to the turntable in his bedroom, and set the housing project of 3,000 people alight with party music. At the same time, a Jamaican teenager named Kool DJ Herc was starting up the scene in the East Bronx, while a technical whiz named Grandmaster Flash was rising to prominence a couple of miles south. The Bronx became a music magnet for Puerto Ricans, Jamaicans, Dominicans, and black Americans from the surrounding areas. Fab 5 Freddy, Kurtis Blow, and Melle Mel were only a few of the pioneers. Grand Wizard Theodore, Kool DJ AJ, the Cold Crush Brothers, Spoony Gee, and the Rock Steady Crew of B-boys showed up to "battle"—dance, trade quips and rhymes, check out each other's records and equipment—not knowing as they strolled through the doors of the community center near Bambaataa's mother's apartment that they were writing musical history. Among them was an MC named Lovebug Starski, who was said to utter the phrase "hip-hop" between breaks to keep time.

This is how it worked: One guy, the DJ, played records on two turntables. One guy—or girl—served as master of ceremonies, or MC. The DJs learned to move the record back and forth under the needle to create a "scratch," or to drop the needle on the record where the beat was the hottest, playing "the break" over and over to keep the folks dancing. The MCs "rapped" over the music to keep the party going. One MC sought to outchat the other. Dance styles were created — "locking" and "popping" and "breaking." Graffiti artists spread the word of the "I" because the music was all about identity: I am the best. I spread the most love in the Bronx, in Harlem, in Queens. The focus initially was not on the MCs, but on the dancers, or B-boys. Commercial radio ignored it. DJs sold mix tapes out of the back of station wagons. "Rapper's Delight" by the Sugarhill Gang—the song I first heard at that face-slapping party in Harlem—broke the music onto radio in 1979.

That is the short history.

The long history is that spoken-word music made its way here on slave ships from West Africa centuries ago: Ethnomusicologists trace hip-hop's roots to the dance, drum, and song of West African griots, or storytellers, its pairing of word and music the manifestation of the painful journey of slaves who survived the middle passage. The ring shouts, field hollers, and spirituals of early slaves drew on common elements of African music, such as call and response and improvisation. "Speech-song has been part of black culture for a long, long time," says Samuel A. Floyd, director of the Center for Black Music Research at Columbia College in Chicago. The "dozens," "toasts," and "signifying" of black Americans—verbal dueling, rhyming, self-deprecating tales, and stories of blacks outsmarting whites—were defensive, empowering strategies.

You can point to jazz musicians such as Oscar Brown, Jr., Edgar "Eddie" Jefferson, and Louis Armstrong, and blues greats such as John Lee Hooker, and easily find the foreshadowing of rap music in the verbal play of their work. Black performers such as poet Nikki Giovanni and Gil Scott-Heron, a pianist and vocalist who put spoken political lyrics to music (most famously in "The Revolution Will Not Be Televised"), elevated spoken word to a new level.

But the artist whose work arguably laid the groundwork for rap as we know it was Amiri Baraka, a beat poet out of Allen Ginsberg's Greenwich Village scene. In the late 1950s and '60s, Baraka performed with shrieks, howls, cries, stomps, verse floating ahead of or behind the rhythm, sometimes in staccato syncopation. It was performance art, delivered in a dashiki and Afro, in step with the anger of a bold and sometimes frightening nationalistic black movement, and it inspired what might be considered the first rap group, the Last Poets.

I was 13 when I first heard the Last Poets in 1970. They scared me. To black America, they were like the relatives you hoped wouldn't show up at your barbecue because the boss was there—the old Aunt Clementine who would arrive, get drunk, and pull out her dentures. My parents refused to allow us to play their music in our house—so my siblings waited until my parents went to work and played it anyway. They were the first musical group I heard to use the N-word on a record, with songs like "N——Are Scared of Revolution." In a world where blacks were evolving from "Negroes" to "blacks," and the assassinations of civil rights leaders Malcolm X and Martin Luther King, Jr., still reverberated in the air like a shotgun blast, the Last Poets embodied black power. Their records consisted of percussion and spoken-word rhyme. They were wildly popular in my neighborhood. Their debut recording sold 400,000 records in three months, says Last Poet member Umar Bin Hassan. "No videos, no radio play, strictly word of mouth." The group's demise coincided with hip-hop's birth in the 1970s.

It's unlikely that the Last Poets ever dreamed the revolution they sang of would take the form it has. "We were about the movement," Abiodun Oyewole, a founder of the group, says. "A lot of today's rappers have talent. But a lot of them are driving the car in the wrong direction."

The Crossover

Highways wrap around the city of Dayton, Ohio, like a ribbon bow-tied on a box of chocolates from the local Esther Price candy factory. They have six ladies at the plant who do just that: Tie ribbons around boxes all day. Henry Rosenkranz can tell you about it. "I love candy," says Henry, a slim white teenager in glasses and a hairnet, as he strolls the factory, bucket in hand. His full-time after-school job is mopping the floors.

Henry is a model American teenager—and the prototypical consumer at which the hip-hop industry is squarely aimed, which has his parents sitting up in their seats. The music that was once the purview of black America has gone white and gone commercial all at once. A sea of white faces now rises up to greet rap groups as they perform, many of them teenagers like Henry, a NASCAR fanatic and self-described redneck. "I live in Old North Dayton," he says. "It's a white, redneck area. But hip-hop is so prominent with country people … if you put them behind a curtain and hear them talk, you won't know if they're black or white. There's a guy I work with, when Kanye West sings about a gold digger, he can relate because he's paying alimony and child support."

Obviously, it's not just working-class whites, but also affluent, suburban kids who identify with this music with African-American roots. A white 16-year-old hollering rap lyrics at the top of his lungs from the driver's seat of his dad's late-model Lexus may not have the same rationale to howl at the moon as a working-class kid whose parents can't pay for college, yet his own anguish is as real to him as it gets. What attracts white kids to this music is the same thing that prompted outraged congressmen to decry jazz during the 1920s and Tipper Gore to campaign decades later against violent and sexually explicit lyrics: life on the other side of the tracks; its "cool" or illicit factor, which black Americans, like it or not, are always perceived to possess.

Hip-hop has continually changed form, evolving from party music to social commentary with the 1982 release of Grandmaster Flash and the Furious Five's "The Message." Today, alternative hip-hop artists continue to produce socially conscious songs, but most commercial rappers spout violent lyrics that debase women and gays. Beginning with the so-called gangsta rap of the '90s, popularized by the still unsolved murders of rappers Biggie Smalls and Tupac Shakur, the genre has become dominated by rappers who brag about their lives of crime. 50 Cent, the hip-hop star of the moment, trumpets his sexual exploits and boasts that he has been shot nine times.

"People call hip-hop the MTV music now," scoffs Chuck D, of Public Enemy, known for its overtly political rap. "It's Big Brother controlling you. To slip something in there that's indigenous to the roots, that pays homage to the music that came before us, it's the Mount Everest of battles."

Most rap songs unabashedly function as walking advertisements for luxury cars, designer clothes, and liquor. Agenda Inc., a "pop culture brand strategy agency," listed Mercedes-Benz as the number one brand mentioned in Billboard's top 20 singles in 2005. Hip-hop sells so much Hennessy cognac, listed at number six, that the French makers, deader than yesterday's beer a decade ago, are now rolling in suds. The company even sponsored a contest to win a visit to its plant in France with a famous rapper.

In many ways, the music represents an old dream. It's the pot of gold to millions of kids like Henry, who quietly agonizes over how his father slaves 14 hours a day at two tool-and-die machine jobs to make ends meet. Like teenagers across the world, he fantasizes about working in the hip-hop business and making millions himself.

"My parents hate hip-hop," Henry says, motoring his 1994 Dodge Shadow through traffic on the way home from work on a hot October afternoon. "But I can listen to Snoop Dogg and hear him call women whores, and I know he has a wife and children at home. It's just a fantasy. Everyone has the urge deep down to be a bad guy or a bad girl. Everyone likes to talk the talk, but not everyone will walk the walk."

Full Circle

You breathe in and breathe out a few times and you are there. Eight hours and a wake-up shake on the flight from New York, and you are on the tarmac in Dakar, Senegal. Welcome to Africa. The assignment: Find the roots of hip-hop. The music goes full circle. The music comes home to Africa. That whole bit. Instead it was the old reporter's joke: You go out to cover a story and the story covers you. The stench of poverty in my nostrils was so strong it pulled me to earth like a hundred-pound ring in my nose. Dakar's Sandaga market is full of "local color"—unless you live there. It was packed and filthy, stalls full of new merchandise surrounded by shattered pieces of life everywhere, broken pipes, bicycle handlebars, fruit flies, soda bottles, beggars, dogs, cell phones. A teenage beggar, his body malformed by polio, crawled by on hands and feet, like a spider. He said, "Hey brother, help me." When I looked into his eyes, they were a bottomless ocean.

The Hotel Teranga is a fortress, packed behind a concrete wall where beggars gather at the front gate. The French tourists march past them, the women in high heels and stonewashed jeans. They sidle through downtown Dakar like royalty, haggling in the market, swimming in the hotel pool with their children, a scene that resembles Birmingham, Alabama, in the 1950s—the blacks serving, the whites partying. Five hundred yards (460 meters) away, Africans eat off the sidewalk and sell peanuts for a pittance. There is a restlessness, a deep sense of something gone wrong in the air.

The French can't smell it, even though they've had a mouthful back home. A good amount of the torching of Paris suburbs in October 2005 was courtesy of the children of immigrants from former French African colonies, exhausted from being bottled up in housing projects for generations with no job prospects. They telegraphed the punch in their music—France is the second largest hip-hop market in the world—but the message was ignored. Around the globe, rap music has become a universal expression of outrage, its macho pose borrowed from commercial hip-hop in the U.S.

In Dakar, where every kid is a microphone and turntable away from squalor, and American rapper Tupac Shakur's picture hangs in market stalls of folks who don't understand English, rap is king. There are hundreds of rap groups in Senegal today. French television crews troop in and out of Dakar's nightclubs filming the kora harp lute and tama talking drum with regularity. But beneath the drumming and the dance lessons and the jingling sound of tourist change, there is a quiet rage, a desperate fury among the Senegalese, some of whom seem to bear an intense dislike of their former colonial rulers.

"We know all about French history," says Abdou Ba, a Senegalese producer and musician. "We know about their kings, their castles, their art, their music. We know everything about them. But they don't know much about us."

Assane N'Diaye, 19, loves hip-hop music. Before he left his Senegalese village to work as a DJ in Dakar, he was a fisherman, just like his father, like his father's father before him. Tall, lean, with a muscular build and a handsome chocolate face, Assane became a popular DJ, but the equipment he used was borrowed, and when his friend took it back, success eluded him. He has returned home to Toubab Dialaw, about 25 miles (40 kilometers) south of Dakar, a village marked by a huge boulder, perhaps 40 feet (12 meters) high, facing the Atlantic Ocean.

About a century and a half ago, a local ruler led a group of people fleeing slave traders to this place. He was told by a white trader to come here, to Toubab Dialaw. When he arrived, the slavers followed. A battle ensued. The ruler fought bravely but was killed. The villagers buried him by the sea and marked his grave with a small stone, and over the years it is said to have sprouted like a tree planted by God. It became a huge, arching boulder that stares out to sea, protecting the village behind it. When the fishermen went deep out to sea, the boulder was like a lighthouse that marked the way home. The Great Rock of Toubab Dialaw is said to hold a magic spirit, a spirit that Assane N'Diaye believes in.

In the shadow of the Great Rock, Assane has built a small restaurant, Chez Las, decorated with hundreds of seashells. It is where he lives his hip-hop dream. At night, he and his brother and cousin stand by the Great Rock and face the sea. They meditate. They pray. Then they write rap lyrics that are worlds away from the bling-bling culture of today's commercial hip-hoppers. They write about their lives as village fishermen, the scarcity of catch forcing them to fish in deeper and deeper waters, the hardship of fishing for 8, 10, 14 days at a time in an open pirogue in rainy season, the high fee they pay to rent the boat, and the paltry price their catches fetch on the market. They write about the humiliation of poverty, watching their town sprout up around them with rich Dakarians and richer French. And they write about the relatives who leave in the morning and never return, surrendered to the sea, sharks, and God.

The dream, of course, is to make a record. They have their own demo, their own logo, and their own name, Salam T. D. (for Toubab Dialaw). But rap music represents a deeper dream: a better life. "We want money to help our parents," Assane says over dinner. "We watch our mothers boil water to cook and have nothing to put in the pot."

He fingers his food lightly. "Rap doesn't belong to American culture," he says. "It belongs here. It has always existed here, because of our pain and our hardships and our suffering."

On this cool evening in a restaurant above their village, these young men, clad in baseball caps and T-shirts, appear no different from their African-American counterparts, with one exception. After a dinner of chicken and rice, Assane says something in Wolof to the others. Silently and without ceremony, they take every bit of the leftover dinner—the half-eaten bread, rice, pieces of chicken, the chicken bones—and dump them into a plastic bag to give to the children in the village. They silently rise from the table and proceed outside. The last I see of them, their regal figures are outlined in the dim light of the doorway, heading out to the darkened village, holding on to that bag as though it held money.

The City of Gods

Some call the Bronx River Houses the City of Gods, though if God has been by lately, he must've slipped out for a chicken sandwich. The 10 drab, red-brick buildings spread out across 14 acres (5.7 hectares), coming into view as you drive east across the East 174th Street Bridge. The Bronx is the hallowed holy ground of hip-hop, the place where it all began. Visitors take tours through this neighborhood now, care of a handful of fortyish "old-timers," who point out the high and low spots of hip-hop's birthplace.

It is a telling metaphor for the state of America's racial landscape that you need a permit to hold a party in the same parks and playgrounds that produced the music that changed the world. The rap artists come and go, but the conditions that produced them linger. Forty percent of New York City's black males are jobless. One in three black males born in 2001 will end up in prison. The life expectancy of black men in the U.S. ranks below that of men in Sri Lanka and Colombia. It took a massive hurricane in New Orleans for the United States to wake up to its racial realities.

That is why, after 26 years, I have come to embrace this music I tried so hard to ignore. Hip-hop culture is not mine. Yet I own it. Much of it I hate. Yet I love it, the good of it. To confess a love for a music that, at least in part, embraces violence is no easy matter, but then again our national anthem talks about bombs bursting in air, and I love that song, too. At its best, hip-hop lays bare the empty moral cupboard that is our generation's legacy. This music that once made visible the inner culture of America's greatest social problem, its legacy of slavery, has taken the dream deferred to a global scale. Today, 2 percent of the Earth's adult population owns more than 50 percent of its household wealth, and indigenous cultures are swallowed with the rapidity of a teenager gobbling a bag of potato chips. The music is calling. Over the years, the instruments change, but the message is the same. The drums are pounding out a warning. They are telling us something. Our children can hear it.

The question is: Can we?

—2007

Learning from Other Writers (McBride)

1. Why does McBride begin by telling us about his so-called nightmare? Does the author's race change the way you react to or interpret the nightmare? If so, how?

2. The author begins with a personal anecdote and then slowly weaves in his research. What is the effect of this authorial presence?

3. McBride gives two histories of hip hop: the short and the long. Why do you think he starts with the most recent (South Bronx and Harlem in the 1970s) instead of starting with the slave ships from West Africa? How does he connect the two histories?

4. What types of research does McBride incorporate here? Why?

5. McBride equates the image of a burning man whose flames are extinguished again and again, without anyone bothering to figure out the source of the fire, to the history of hip hop. How is this analogy reflected in the way he structures his essay?

6. How would you describe the tone of the essay's introduction versus the tone of the ending? What sort of emotional journey has the author taken?

By Malcolm Gladwell

BIG AND BAD

In the summer of 1996, the Ford Motor Company began building the Expedition, its new, full-sized S.U.V., at the Michigan Truck Plant, in the Detroit suburb of Wayne. The Expedition was essentially the F-150 pickup truck with an extra set of doors and two more rows of seats—and the fact that it was a truck was critical. Cars have to meet stringent fuel-efficiency regulations. Trucks don't. The handling and suspension and braking of cars have to be built to the demanding standards of drivers and passengers. Trucks only have to handle like, well, trucks. Cars are built with what is called unit-body construction. To be light enough to meet fuel standards and safe enough to meet safety standards, they have expensive and elaborately engineered steel skeletons, with built-in crumple zones to absorb the impact of a crash. Making a truck is a lot more rudimentary. You build a rectangular steel frame. The engine gets bolted to the front. The seats get bolted to the middle. The body gets lowered over the top. The result is heavy and rigid and not particularly safe. But it's an awfully inexpensive way to build an automobile. Ford had planned to sell the Expedition for thirty-six thousand dollars, and its best estimate was that it could build one for twenty-four thousand—which, in the automotive industry, is a terrifically high profit margin. Sales, the company predicted, weren't going to be huge. After all, how many Americans could reasonably be expected to pay a twelve-thousand-dollar premium for what was essentially a dressed-up truck? But Ford executives decided that the Expedition would be a highly profitable niche product. They were half right. The "highly profitable" part turned out to be true. Yet, almost from the moment Ford's big new S.U.V.s rolled off the assembly line in Wayne, there was nothing "niche" about the Expedition.

Ford had intended to split the assembly line at the Michigan Truck Plant between the Expedition and the Ford F-150 pickup. But, when the first flood of orders started coming in for the Expedition, the factory was entirely given over to S.U.V.s. The orders kept mounting. Assembly-line workers were put on sixty- and seventy-hour weeks. Another night shift was added. The plant was now running twenty-four hours a day, six days a week. Ford executives decided to build a luxury version of the Expedition, the Lincoln Navigator. They bolted a new grille on the Expedition, changed a few body panels, added some sound insulation, took a deep breath, and charged forty-five thousand dollars—and soon Navigators were flying out the door nearly as fast as Expeditions. Before long, the Michigan Truck Plant was the most profitable of Ford's fifty-three assembly plants. By the late nineteen-nineties, it had become the most profitable factory of any industry in the world. In 1998, the Michigan Truck Plant grossed eleven billion dollars, almost as much as McDonald's made that year. Profits were $3.7 billion. Some factory workers, with overtime, were making two hundred thousand dollars a year. The demand for Expeditions and Navigators was so insatiable that even when a blizzard hit the Detroit region in January of 1999—burying the city in snow, paralyzing the airport, and stranding hundreds of cars on the freeway—Ford officials got on their radios and commandeered parts bound for other factories so that the Michigan Truck

Plant assembly line wouldn't slow for a moment. The factory that had begun as just another assembly plant had become the company's crown jewel.

In the history of the automotive industry, few things have been quite as unexpected as the rise of the S.U.V. Detroit is a town of engineers, and engineers like to believe that there is some connection between the success of a vehicle and its technical merits. But the S.U.V. boom was like Apple's bringing back the Macintosh, dressing it up in color-ful plastic, and suddenly creating a new market. It made no sense to them. Consumers said they liked four-wheel drive. But the overwhelming majority of consumers don't need four-wheel drive. S.U.V. buyers said they liked the elevated driving position. But when, in focus groups, industry marketers probed further, they heard things that left them rolling their eyes. As Keith Bradsher writes in "High and Mighty"—perhaps the most important book about Detroit since Ralph Nader's "Unsafe at Any Speed"—what consumers said was "If the vehicle is up high, it's easier to see if something is hiding underneath or lurking behind it." Bradsher brilliantly captures the mixture of baffle-ment and contempt that many auto executives feel toward the customers who buy their S.U.V.s. Fred J. Schaafsma, a top engineer for General Motors, says, "Sport-utility owners tend to be more like 'I wonder how people view me,' and are more willing to trade off flexibility or functionality to get that." According to Bradsher, internal industry market research concluded that S.U.V.s tend to be bought by people who are insecure, vain, self-centered, and self-absorbed, who are frequently nervous about their marriages, and who lack confidence in their driving skills. Ford's S.U.V. designers took their cues from seeing "fashionably dressed women wearing hiking boots or even work boots while walking through expensive malls." Toyota's top marketing executive in the United States, Bradsher writes, loves to tell the story of how at a focus group in Los Angeles "an elegant woman in the group said that she needed her full-sized Lexus LX 470 to drive up over the curb and onto lawns to park at large parties in Beverly Hills." One of Ford's senior marketing executives was even blunter. "The only time those S.U.V.s are going to be off-road is when they miss the driveway at 3 A.M."

The truth, underneath all the rationalizations, seemed to be that S.U.V. buyers thought of big, heavy vehicles as safe: they found comfort in being surrounded by so much rubber and steel. To the engineers, of course, that didn't make any sense, either: if consumers really wanted something that was big and heavy and comforting, they ought to buy minivans, since minivans, with their unit-body construction, do much better in accidents than S.U.V.s. (In a thirty-five-m.p.h. crash test, for instance, the driver of a Cadillac Escalade—the G.M. counterpart to the Lincoln Navigator—has a sixteen-per-cent chance of a life-threatening head injury, a twenty-per-cent chance of a life-threat-ening chest injury, and a thirty-five-per-cent chance of a leg injury. The same numbers in a Ford Windstar minivan—a vehicle engineered from the ground up, as opposed to simply being bolted onto a pickup-truck frame—are, respectively, two per cent, four per cent, and one percent.) But this desire for safety wasn't a rational calculation. It was a *feel-ing.* Over the past decade, a number of major automakers in America have relied on the services of a French-born cultural anthropologist, G. Clotaire Rapaille, whose special-ity is getting beyond the rational—what he calls "cortex"—impressions of consumers and tapping into their deeper, "reptilian" responses. And what Rapaille concluded from countless, intensive sessions with car buyers was that when S.U.V. buyers thought about safety they were thinking about something that reached into their deepest unconscious. "The No. 1 feeling is that everything surrounding you should be round and soft, and should give," Rapaille told me. "There should be air bags everywhere. Then there's this notion that you need to be up high. That's a contradiction, because the people who buy these S.U.V.s know at the cortex level that if you are high there is more chance of a roll-over. But at the reptilian level they think that if I am bigger and taller I'm safer. You feel secure because you are higher and dominate and look down. That you can look down is psychologically a very powerful notion. And what was the key element of safety when you were a child? It was that your mother fed you, and there was warm liquid. That's why cupholders are absolutely crucial for safety. If there is a car that has no cupholder, it is not safe. If I can put my coffee there, if I can have my food, if everything is round, if it's soft, and if I'm high, then I feel safe. It's amazing that intelligent, educated women will look at a car and the first thing they will look at is how many cupholders it has." During the design of Chrysler's PT Cruiser, one of the things Rapaille learned was that car buyers felt unsafe when they thought that an outsider could easily see inside their vehicles. So Chrysler made the back window of the PT Cruiser smaller. Of course, making windows smaller—and thereby reducing visibility—makes driving *more* dangerous, not less so. But that's the puzzle of what has happened to the automobile world: feeling safe has become more important than actually being safe.

One day this fall, I visited the automobile-testing center of Consumers Union, the organization that publishes *Consumer Reports*. It is tucked away in the woods, in south-central Connecticut, on the site of the old Connecticut Speedway. The facility has two skid pads to measure cornering, a long straightaway for braking tests, a meandering "handling" course that winds around the back side of the track, and an accident-avoidance obstacle course made out of a row of orange cones. It is headed by a trim, white-haired Englishman named David Champion, who previously worked as an engineer with Land Rover and with Nissan. On the day of my visit, Champion set aside two vehicles: a silver 2003 Chevrolet TrailBlazer—an enormous five-thousand-pound S.U.V.—and a shiny blue two-seater Porsche Boxster convertible.

We started with the TrailBlazer. Champion warmed up the Chevrolet with a few quick circuits of the track, and then drove it hard through the twists and turns of the handling course. He sat in the bucket seat with his back straight and his arms almost fully extended, and drove with practiced grace: every movement smooth and relaxed and unhurried. Champion, as an engineer, did not much like the TrailBlazer. "Cheap interior, cheap plastic," he said, batting the dashboard with his hand. "It's a little bit heavy, cumbersome. Quiet. Bit wallowy, side to side. Doesn't feel that secure. Accelerates heavily. Once it gets going, it's got decent power. Brakes feel a bit spongy." He turned onto the straightaway and stopped a few hundred yards from the obstacle course.

Measuring accident avoidance is a key part of the Consumers Union evaluation. It's a simple setup. The driver has to navigate his vehicle through two rows of cones eight feet wide and sixty feet long. Then he has to steer hard to the left, guiding the vehicle through a gate set off to the side, and immediately swerve hard back to the right, and enter a second sixty-foot corridor of cones that are parallel to the first set. The idea is to see how fast you can drive through the course without knocking over any cones. "It's like you're driving down a road in suburbia," Champion said. "Suddenly, a kid on a bicycle veers out in front of you. You have to do whatever it takes to avoid the kid. But there's a tractor-trailer coming toward you in the other lane, so you've got to swing back into your own lane as quickly as possible. That's the scenario."

Champion and I put on helmets. He accelerated toward the entrance to the obstacle course. "We do the test without brakes or throttle, so we can just look at handling," Champion said. "I actually take my foot right off the pedals." The car was now moving at forty m.p.h. At that speed, on the smooth tarmac of the raceway, the TrailBlazer was very quiet, and we were seated so high that the road seemed somehow remote. Champion entered the first row of cones. His arms tensed. He jerked the car to the left. The TrailBlazer's tires squealed. I was thrown toward the passenger-side door as the truck's body rolled, then thrown toward Champion as he jerked the TrailBlazer back to the right. My tape recorder went skittering across the cabin. The whole maneuver had taken no more than a few seconds, but it felt as if we had been sailing into a squall. Champion brought the car to a stop. We both looked back: the TrailBlazer had hit the cone at the gate. The kid on the bicycle was probably dead. Champion shook his head. "It's very rubbery. It slides a lot. I'm not getting much communication back from the steering wheel. It feels really ponderous, clumsy. I felt a little bit of tail swing."

I drove the obstacle course next. I started at the conservative speed of thirty-five m.p.h. I got through cleanly. I tried again, this time at thirty-eight m.p.h., and that small increment of speed made a dramatic difference. I made the first left, avoiding the kid on the bicycle. But, when it came time to swerve back to avoid the hypothetical oncoming eighteen wheeler, I found that I was wrestling with the car. The protests of the tires were jarring. I stopped, shaken. "It wasn't going where you wanted it to go, was it?" Champion said. "Did you feel the weight pulling you sideways? That's what the extra weight that S.U.V.s have tends to do. It pulls you in the wrong direction." Behind us was a string of toppled cones. Getting the TrailBlazer to travel in a straight line, after that sudden diversion, hadn't been easy. "I think you took out a few pedestrians," Champion said with a faint smile.

Next up was the Boxster. The top was down. The sun was warm on my forehead. The car was low to the ground; I had the sense that if I dangled my arm out the window my knuckles would scrape on the tarmac. Standing still, the Boxster didn't feel safe: I could have been sitting in a go-cart. But when I ran it through the handling course I felt that I was in perfect control. On the straightaway, I steadied the Boxster at forty-five m.p.h., and ran it through the obstacle course. I could have balanced a teacup on my knee. At fifty m.p.h., I navigated the left and right turns with what seemed like a twitch of the steering wheel. The tires didn't squeal. The car stayed level. I pushed the Porsche up into the mid-fifties. Every cone was untouched. "Walk in the park!" Champion exclaimed as we pulled to a stop.

Most of us think that S.U.V.s are much safer than sports cars. If you asked the young parents of America whether they would rather strap their infant child in the back seat of the TrailBlazer or the passenger seat of the Boxster, they would choose the TrailBlazer. We feel that way because in the TrailBlazer our chances of surviving a collision with a hypothetical tractor-trailer in the other lane are greater than they are in the Porsche. What we forget, though, is that in the TrailBlazer you're also much more likely to hit the tractor-trailer because you can't get out of the way in time. In the parlance of the automobile world, the TrailBlazer is better at "passive safety." The Boxster is better when it comes to "active safety," which is every bit as important.

Consider the set of safety statistics compiled by Tom Wenzel, a scientist at Lawrence Berkeley National Laboratory, in California, and Marc Ross, a physicist at the University of Michigan. The numbers are expressed in fatalities per million cars, both for drivers of particular models and for the drivers of the cars they hit. (For example, in the first case, for every million Toyota Avalons on the road, forty Avalon drivers die in

Make/Model	Type	Driver Deaths	Other Deaths	Total
Toyota Avalon	large	40	20	60
Chrysler Town & Country	minivan	31	36	67
Toyota Camry	mid-size	41	29	70
Volkswagen Jetta	subcompact	47	23	70
Ford Windstar	minivan	37	35	72
Nissan Maxima	mid-size	53	26	79
Honda Accord	mid-size	54	27	82
Chevrolet Venture	minivan	51	34	85
Buick Century	mid-size	70	23	93
Subaru Legacy/Outback	compact	74	24	98
Mazda 626	compact	70	29	99
Chevrolet Malibu	mid-size	71	34	105
Chevrolet Suburban	S.U.V.	46	59	105
Jeep Grand Cherokee	S.U.V.	61	44	106
Honda Civic	subcompact	84	25	109
Toyota Corolla	subcompact	81	29	110
Ford Expedition	S.U.V.	55	57	112
GMC Jimmy	S.U.V.	76	39	114
Ford Taurus	mid-size	78	39	117
Nissan Altima	compact	72	49	121
Mercury Marquis	large	80	43	123
Nissan Sentra	subcompact	95	34	129
Toyota 4Runner	S.U.V.	94	43	137
Chevrolet Tahoe	S.U.V.	68	74	141
Dodge Stratus	mid-size	103	40	143
Lincoln Town Car	large	100	47	147
Ford Explorer	S.U.V.	88	60	148
Pontiac Grand Am	compact	118	39	157
Toyota Tacoma	pickup	111	59	171
Chevrolet Cavalier	subcompact	146	41	186
Dodge Neon	subcompact	161	39	199
Pontiac Sunfire	subcompact	158	44	202
Ford F-Series	pickup	110	128	238

car accidents every year, and twenty people die in accidents involving Toyota Avalons.) The numbers below have been rounded:

Are the best performers the biggest and heaviest vehicles on the road? Not at all. Among the safest cars are the midsize imports, like the Toyota Camry and the Honda Accord. Or consider the extraordinary performance of some subcompacts, like the Volkswagen Jetta. Drivers of the tiny Jetta die at a rate of just forty-seven per million, which is in the same range as drivers of the five-thousand-pound Chevrolet Suburban and almost half that of popular S.U.V. models like the Ford Explorer or the GMC Jimmy. In a head-on crash, an Explorer or a Suburban would crush a Jetta or a Camry. But, clearly, the drivers of Camrys and Jettas are finding a way to avoid head-on crashes with Explorers and Suburbans. The benefits of being nimble—of being in an automobile that's capable of staying out of trouble—are in many cases greater than the benefits of being big.

I had another lesson in active safety at the test track when I got in the TrailBlazer with another Consumers Union engineer, and we did three emergency-stopping tests, taking the Chevrolet up to sixty m.p.h. and then slamming on the brakes. It was not a pleasant exercise. Bringing five thousand pounds of rubber and steel to a sudden stop involves lots of lurching, screeching, and protesting. The first time, the TrailBlazer took 146.2 feet to come to a halt, the second time 151.6 feet, and the third time 153.4 feet. The Boxster can come to a complete stop from sixty m.p.h. in about 124 feet. That's a difference of about two car lengths, and it isn't hard to imagine any number of scenarios where two car lengths could mean the difference between life and death.

The S.U.V. boom represents, then, a shift in how we conceive of safety—from active to passive. It's what happens when a larger number of drivers conclude, consciously or otherwise, that the extra thirty feet that the TrailBlazer takes to come to a stop don't really matter, that the tractor-trailer will hit them anyway, and that they are better off treating accidents as inevitable rather than avoidable. "The metric that people use is size," says Stephen Popiel, a vice-president of Millward Brown Goldfarb, in Toronto, one of the leading automotive market-research firms. "The bigger something is, the safer it is. In the consumer's mind, the basic equation is, If I were to take this vehicle and drive it into this brick wall, the more metal there is in front of me the better off I'll be."

This is a new idea, and one largely confined to North America. In Europe and Japan, people think of a safe car as a nimble car. That's why they build cars like the Jetta and the Camry, which are designed to carry out the driver's wishes as directly and efficiently as possible. In the Jetta, the engine is clearly audible. The steering is light and precise. The brakes are crisp. The wheelbase is short enough that the car picks up the undulations of the road. The car is so small and close to the ground, and so dwarfed by other cars on the road, that an intelligent driver is constantly reminded of the necessity of driving safely and defensively. An S.U.V. embodies the opposite logic. The driver is seated as high and far from the road as possible. The vehicle is designed to overcome its environment, not to respond to it. Even four-wheel drive, seemingly the most beneficial feature of the S.U.V., serves to reinforce this isolation. Having the engine provide power to all four wheels, safety experts point out, does nothing to improve braking, although many S.U.V. owners erroneously believe this to be the case. Nor does the feature necessarily make it safer to turn across a slippery surface: that is largely a function of how much friction is generated by the vehicle's tires. All it really does is improve what engineers call tracking—that is, the ability to accelerate without slipping in perilous conditions or in deep snow or mud. Champion says that one of the occasions when he came closest to death was a snowy day, many years ago, just after he had bought a new Range Rover. "Everyone around me was slipping, and I was thinking, *Yeahhh.* And I came to a stop sign on a major road, and I was driving probably twice as fast as I should have been, because I could. I had traction. But I also weighed probably twice as much as most cars. And I still had only four brakes and four tires on the road. I slid right across a four-lane road." Four-wheel drive robs the driver of feedback. "The car driver whose wheels spin once or twice while backing out of the driveway knows that the road is slippery," Bradsher writes. "The SUV driver who navigates the driveway and street without difficulty until she tries to brake may not find out that the road is slippery until it is too late." Jettas are safe because they make their drivers feel unsafe. S.U.V.s are unsafe because they make their drivers feel safe. That feeling of safety isn't the solution; it's the problem.

Perhaps the most troublesome aspect of S.U.V. culture is its attitude toward risk. "Safety, for most automotive consumers, has to do with the notion that they aren't in complete control," Popiel says. "There are unexpected events that at any moment in time can come out and impact them—an oil patch up ahead, an eighteen-wheeler turning over, something falling down. People feel that the elements of the world out of their control are the ones that are going to cause them distress."

Of course, those things really aren't outside a driver's control: an alert driver, in the right kind of vehicle, can navigate the oil patch, avoid the truck, and swerve around the thing that's falling down. Traffic-fatality rates vary strongly with driver behavior. Drunks are 7.6 times more likely to die in accidents than nondrinkers. People who wear their seat belts are almost half as likely to die as those who don't buckle up. Forty-year-olds are ten times less likely to get into accidents than sixteen-year-olds. Drivers of minivans, Wenzel and Ross's statistics tell us, die at a fraction of the rate of drivers of pickup trucks. That's clearly because minivans are family cars, and parents with children in the back seat are less likely to get into accidents. Frank McKenna, a safety expert at the University of Reading, in England, has done experiments where he shows drivers a series of videotaped scenarios—a child running out the front door of his house and onto the street, for example, or a car approaching an intersection at too great a speed to stop at the red light—and asks people to press a button the minute they become aware of the potential for an accident. Experienced drivers press the button between half a second and a second faster than new drivers, which, given that car accidents are events measured in milliseconds, is a significant difference. McKenna's work shows that, with experience, we all learn how to exert some degree of control over what might otherwise appear to be uncontrollable events. Any conception of safety that revolves entirely around the vehicle, then, is incomplete. Is the Boxster safer than the TrailBlazer? It depends on who's behind the wheel. In the hands of, say, my very respectable and prudent middle-aged mother, the Boxster is by far the safer car. In my hands, it probably isn't. On the open road, my reaction to the Porsche's extraordinary road manners and the sweet, irresistible wail of its engine would be to drive much faster than I should. (At the end of my day at Consumers Union, I parked the Boxster, and immediately got into my own car to drive home. In my mind, I was still at the wheel of the Boxster. Within twenty minutes, I had a two-hundred-and-seventy-one-dollar speeding ticket.) The trouble with the S.U.V. ascendancy is that it excludes the really critical component of safety: the driver.

In psychology, there is a concept called learned helplessness, which arose from a series of animal experiments in the nineteen-sixties at the University of Pennsylvania. Dogs were restrained by a harness, so that they couldn't move, and then repeatedly subjected to a series of electrical shocks. Then the same dogs were shocked again, only this time they could easily escape by jumping over a low hurdle. But most of them didn't; they just huddled in the corner, no longer believing that there was anything they could do to influence their own fate. Learned helplessness is now thought to play a role in such phenomena as depression and the failure of battered women to leave their husbands, but one could easily apply it more widely. We live in an age, after all, that is strangely fixated on the idea of helplessness: we're fascinated by hurricanes and terrorist acts and epidemics like SARS—situations in which we feel powerless to affect our own destiny. In fact, the risks posed to life and limb by forces outside our control are dwarfed by the factors we can control. Our fixation with helplessness distorts our perceptions of risk. "When you feel safe, you can be passive," Rapaille says of the fundamental appeal of the S.U.V. "Safe means I can sleep. I can give up control. I can relax. I can take off my shoes. I can listen to music." For years, we've all made fun of the middle-aged man who suddenly trades in his sedate family sedan for a shiny red sports car. That's called a midlife crisis. But at least it involves some degree of engagement with the act of driving. The man who gives up his sedate family sedan for an S.U.V. is saying something far more troubling—that he finds the demands of the road to be overwhelming. Is acting out really worse than giving up?

On August 9, 2000, the Bridgestone Firestone tire company announced one of the largest product recalls in American history. Because of mounting concerns about safety, the company said, it was replacing some fourteen million tires that had been used primarily on the Ford Explorer S.U.V. The cost of the recall—and of a follow-up replacement program initiated by Ford a year later—ran into billions of dollars. Millions more were spent by both companies on fighting and settling lawsuits from Explorer owners, who alleged that their tires had come apart and caused their S.U.V.s to roll over. In the fall of that year, senior executives from both companies were called to Capitol Hill, where they were publicly berated. It was the biggest scandal to hit the automobile industry in years. It was also one of the strangest. According to federal records, the number of fatalities resulting from the failure of a Firestone tire on a Ford Explorer S.U.V., as of September, 2001, was two hundred and seventy-one. That sounds like a lot, until you remember that the total number of tires supplied by Firestone to the Explorer from the moment the S.U.V. was introduced by Ford, in 1990, was four-teen million, and that the average life span of a tire is forty-five thousand miles. The allegation against Firestone amounts to the claim that its tires failed, with fatal results, two hundred and seventy-one times in the course of six hundred and thirty billion vehicle miles. Manufacturers usually win prizes for failure rates that low. It's also worth remembering that during that same ten-year span almost half a million Americans died in traffic accidents. In other words, during the nineteen-nineties hundreds of thousands of people were killed on the roads because they drove too fast or ran red lights or drank too much. And, of those, a fair proportion involved people in S.U.V.s who were lulled by their four-wheel drive into driving recklessly on slick roads, who drove aggressively because they felt invulnerable, who disproportionately killed those they hit because they chose to drive trucks with inflexible steel-frame architecture, and who crashed because they couldn't bring their five-thousand-pound vehicles to a halt in time. Yet, out of all those fatalities, regulators, the legal profession, Congress, and the media chose to highlight the .0005 per cent that could be linked to an alleged defect in the vehicle.

But should that come as a surprise? In the age of the S.U.V., this is what people worry about when they worry about safety—not risks, however commonplace, involv-ing their own behavior but risks, however rare, involving some unexpected event. The Explorer was big and imposing. It was high above the ground. You could look down on other drivers. You could see if someone was lurking behind or beneath it. You could drive it up on someone's lawn with impunity. Didn't it seem like the safest vehicle in the world?

—2004

Learning from Other Writers (Gladwell)

1. What is the role of the first section of this essay? How does Gladwell use this introduction to introduce his driving question (no pun intended)?

2. Each section ends with the answer to an earlier question, which prompts Gladwell to try to figure out why that answer might be true. For example, section one ends: "Feeling safe has become more important than being safe." Section two then sets out to discover what might have caused that mindset. The eventual answer: there are two types of safety—active and passive—and Americans have decided to rely on the latter rather than the former. This, then, prompts the author to wonder, "Why?" And so on. Examine the end of each section and the beginning of the section that follows in order to articulate how these micro ques-tions propel Gladwell to his ultimate conclusion.

3. How does Gladwell anticipate his audience's possible reactions to what he is saying? Point out instances where Gladwell anticipates his audience's resistance and discuss how well he does or doesn't forestall that resistance.

4. Gladwell introduces evidence from psychology, social science, statistics, and so on. How does this range of sources affect his argument?

5. Ultimately, Gladwell cannot prove his argument—the best he can do is to trace a possible link between the trend he has observed (the rise in S.U.V. sales) and the various factors that might have led to that trend. Where does he best make his case? Where is his claim of causality weakest or most vulnerable?

6. Why does Gladwell end with the incident about the Firestone tires?

By Margaret Talbot

LITTLE HOTTIES

Barbie is forty-seven years old, and forty-seven years is a long time to have been the alpha doll. Over the decades, many competitors have been sent out into the world to get what Mattel's doll had: hugely profitable sovereignty over the imaginations of little girls. Some of these rivals briefly grabbed a small share of the fashion-doll market. The Tammy doll, which had a wholesome teen-aged look and came encumbered with parents, stuck around from 1962 to 1966, before Barbie squashed her flat. In 1969, Ideal Toy created Crissy, whose hair grew with the push of a button; you can still find Crissy on eBay, but not in Toys R Us. Kenner's spookily big-headed Blythe, whose eye color could be changed from green to blue to pink to orange, lasted for one year: 1972. (She has since been rediscovered by hipster collectors; a photographer named Gina Garan poses her in myriad scenarios, as if she were a plastic Cindy Sherman.) In the mid-eighties, Hasbro launched Jem—corporate by day, rock and roll by night. Mattel moved swiftly to undercut her with its own Rock Star Barbie. And then there were the earnest attempts to make more "realistic" fashion dolls, an enterprise doomed to oxymoronic failure. The Happy to Be Me doll, which came out in the early nineties, when childhood anorexia was a bigger media trope than childhood obesity, had a thicker waist, wider hips, and larger feet than Barbie, and left little girls cold. As M. G. Lord, the author of "Forever Barbie" (1994), wrote, "She may have been happy to be herself, but it was obvious, even to kids, that she had extremely low standards." And the Get Real Girls—muscular, sporty dolls who were supposed to be snowboarders, soccer players, and the like—might have appealed to athletic girls, except that athletic girls preferred to play sports. "They can kick Barbie's butt like you wouldn't believe," a promotional Web site promised in 2000. On store shelves, though, Barbie kicked theirs.

In June, 2001, M.G.A. Entertainment, a small toy company in Southern California, unveiled a line of dolls called Bratz. It was not an auspicious début. M.G.A. had enjoyed some success with handheld electronic toys imported from Japan—M.G.A. stands for Micro Games of America—and with a baby doll called Singing Bouncy Baby, but never with a fashion doll. The company was privately owned, and its headquarters were in a drab stretch of the San Fernando Valley, amid a jumble of taquerias and doughnut shops near the Van Nuys airport. Its C.E.O., Isaac Larian, an Iranian immigrant with a degree in civil engineering whose first company imported brass tchotchkes from South Korea, still made sales calls himself. When a doll designer and on-and-off-again Mattel employee named Carter Bryant brought Larian a drawing of a new doll he had in mind, Larian at first saw little to admire. "To be honest, to me it looked weird—it looked ugly," Larian told me. But Larian's attitude toward the tastes of children is respectful to the point of reverence, and his daughter Jasmin, then eleven years old, happened to be hanging out in his office that day. Larian asked her what she thought of the drawing. "And, you know, I saw this sparkle that you see in kids' eyes," he recalled. "They talk with their body language more than their voice. And she says, 'Yeah, it's cute.'" For Larian, that was enough: "I said, 'O.K., we'll do it.'"

At first, M.G.A. struggled to give Bryant's drawings three-dimensional form. The design showed a face in which the lips and eyes were cartoonishly prominent and the nose was vanishingly small: it was as if the doll had undergone successive rounds of plastic surgery. Molding that micronose in vinyl wasn't easy. At the Hong Kong toy fair in January, 2001, Larian and his team had only a rough sample to show venders; the hair was Scotch-taped on. And in October of that year Toys R Us cancelled its order for Bratz because initial sales were not what Larian had predicted. He borrowed money to fund more advertising; by Christmas, Bratz dolls had taken off.

In the five years since then, M.G.A. has sold a hundred and twenty-five million Bratz worldwide, and it has become the top fashion doll in the United Kingdom and Australia. Global sales of Bratz products reached two billion dollars in 2005; sales of Barbie remained higher, at three billion dollars, but they declined by 12.8 per cent. Last December, after five years in which domestic Barbie sales had either declined or stagnated for all but three quarters, Mattel replaced Matthew Bousquette, who had headed the Barbie line, with Neil Friedman and Chuck Scothon, who together had been running its successful Fisher-Price division. (Friedman, a president at Mattel, is known to be gifted at turning around flagging toy lines.) According to Sean McGowan, a toy-industry analyst at Wedbush Morgan Securities, Bratz has now captured about forty per cent of the fashion-doll market, compared with Barbie's sixty per cent. Barbie is still an instantly recognizable brand name, like Kleenex or Coke, but even Scothon says, "The competition has changed. There's no denying that."

Bratz dolls have large heads and skinny bodies; their almond-shaped eyes are tilted upward at the edges and adorned with thick crescents of eye-shadow, and their lips are lush and pillowy, glossed to a candy-apple sheen and rimmed with dark lip liner. They look like pole dancers on their way to work at a gentlemen's club. Unlike Barbie, they can stand unassisted. I've heard mothers say that they would never buy their daughters a doll that couldn't stand on its own, but perhaps they should have been more careful what they wished for. To change a Bratz doll's shoes, you have to snap off its feet at the ankles. (It's creepy but ingenious; because the footwear is attached to the legs, all those little shoes are harder to lose.) Their out-sized feet are oddly insinuating: you can picture the Bratz dolls tottering around on their stalklike legs, like fauns waking up from a tranquillizer dart. Bratz dolls don't have Barbie's pinup-girl measurements—they're not as busty and they're shorter. But their outfits include halter tops, faux-fur armlets, and ankle-laced stiletto sandals, and they wear the sly, dozy expression of a party girl after one too many mojitos. They are the "girls with a passion for fashion," as the slogan has it, so their adventures—as presented in all those "sold separately" books and other paraphernalia—run to all-night mall parties and trips to Vegas. ("Deck out and step out for a party in the streets, as you spend the weekend with the girls in the city that never sleeps.") A Bratz Princess—one of the newer versions—wears a tiara and, instead of a ball gown, a tight camouflage T-shirt and a short skirt. You could never imagine a Bratz doll assuming any of the dozens of careers Barbie has pursued over the decades: not Business Executive or Surgeon or Summit Diplomat—not even Pan Am Flight Attendant or Pet Doctor. Bratz girls seem more like kept girls, or girls trying to convert a stint on reality TV into a future as the new Ashlee or Lindsay or Paris.

Whereas Mattel's Scothon likes to talk about Barbie's "aspirational" qualities—how she might inspire "a girl to run for President and look good while she was doing it"—Larian prefers to talk about "fashion and fantasy" and what's "cute."

The Bratz girls also tend to look ethnic, or, rather, ethnically indeterminate: blond dolls are in the minority in the Bratz world, as they increasingly are in the world of Bratz consumers. At the Toy Fair, the industry's giant annual trade show in New York, Larian told me, "When we came out with these dolls, one of the things we did not want to do was just label them. Don't call them African-American. Don't call them Hispanic. Don't call them Middle Eastern. Don't call them white. Just convey difference." Larian is fifty-two years old, and he has graying, closely cropped curls and shrewd, dark eyes; he was wearing a nicely cut gray suit and an understated tie. Nearby, a group of toy retailers from around the country, most of them middle-aged white men, milled around a magenta-and-purple showroom, solemnly handling Bratz dolls and their diminutive accessories. (No one under eighteen is allowed into the Toy Fair.) Southern California, where Larian immigrated on his own, at the age of seventeen, was an inspiration for Bratz, he said, because it is a place where racial mixing is commonplace. Larian and his team picked names for the Bratz dolls that didn't align them with any one ethnic group—made-up-sounding names (Nevra, Kiana) or names with offbeat spellings (Meygan, Roxxi) or "exotic" names with crossover appeal (Jade, Yasmin). "I was in Brazil," Larian recalled. "I asked some girls, 'Where do you think Yasmin is from?' and they said, 'Oh, she's Brazilian, she's Latin.' Then I was in Israel, and I asked, 'Where do you think Yasmin is from?' and they thought she was Middle Eastern. It's fascinating to see that, everywhere you go." When Mattel came out with the first black Barbie, in 1968, it seemed like a well-meaning afterthought. Bratz girls were born as a multiracial pack; each one is a slightly different shade. That is enough to earn them the approval of Naomi Wolf, the feminist writer. "If I were betting on culture as a form of stocks, I would get out of skinny Barbie and into multiethnic, imaginative Bratz dolls," she wrote recently.

What Bratz dolls are both contributing to and feeding on is a culture in which girls play at being "sassy"—the toy industry's favored euphemism for sexy—and discard traditional toys at a younger age. (Girls seem to be growing out of toys earlier than boys are, industry analysts say.) Toy marketers now invoke a phenomenon called K.G.O.Y.— Kids Getting Older Younger—and talk about it as though it were a fact of modern life over which they have no control, rather than one which they have largely created. Mattel's Scothon said, "Kids are certainly exposed to more things at earlier ages. Their scope of reference is wider. Their exposure to media is greater." Larian told me, "Little girls are really much more sophisticated now than they used to be."

Barbie was originally intended for nine- to twelve-year-olds; today, girls widely perceive it as a toy for three- to six-year-olds. The association of Barbie with preschool girls sometimes leads slightly older girls to repudiate the doll with sadistic élan. Agnes Nairn and Patricia Gaya Wicks, professors of business at the University of Bath, and Christine Griffin, their colleague in the psychology department, published a study earlier this year revealing that seven-to-eleven-year-old girls enjoyed destroying Barbies.

As one subject put it, "I just kept having to squish their heads off." Sometimes, the interviewers seemed taken aback by the girls' ingenuity in punishing their Barbies:

FIRST GIRL: Our friend does that with Barbies.
SECOND GIRL: Yeah, she microwaves them.
INTERVIEWER: She microwaves them? Oh, gosh.
FIRST GIRL: Did she parachute one out of the house?
SECOND GIRL: Yeah, she parachuted one out of the house and it landed in the next-door neighbour's garden.

The study concluded that girls turned on Barbie because she seemed out of fashion and disposable (children had so many of them, in so many different guises, that they were "simply being imaginative" in getting rid "of an excessive commodity in the same way as one might crush cans for recycling"), but most of all because she was "babyish," and the girls "saw her as representing their younger childhood out of which they felt they had now grown."

You used to hear the opposite theory: when girls rejected Barbie it was because she represented a sexualized womanhood they felt ambivalent about entering. But Larian, for one, thinks that Barbie now represents a "mommy figure" for many girls, and they don't particularly want to play with a doll who reminds them of their mothers. In any case, there are some toys that kids love until they hate, and some they do not. Sean McGowan, the toy-industry analyst, said, "Nobody gets to a certain age and says, 'I hate Mickey Mouse.' But Barbie is now like Barney. Three-year-olds are addicted to it like crack, but all it takes is for one kid to be embarrassed and they turn on it."

For M.G.A., holding on to the six-to-twelve-year-old market—a group that, until the eighties, wasn't yet letting go of childish things—means making dolls that look like celebrity hotties. As Larian wrote in *Brand Strategy* earlier this year, "Bratz are not merely dolls but 'fashion icons' that look to the runways and what kids wear in and out of school for inspiration." With Bratz, the company is selling the notion that divahood is something for girls to aspire to, with or without a talent to go with it. This is the attitude that fuels, for example, the success of Club Libby Lu, the chain of mall stores where six-year-olds can get makeovers for their birthdays, complete with hair extensions and lip gloss; it's also the attitude behind T-shirts for little girls bearing slogans such as "So Many Boys, So Little Time" and "My Heart Belongs to Shopping." Many parents find this aesthetic weird, even repellent, but somehow hard to dodge.

Indeed, marketers counsel companies not to feel guilty about "going around moms," as the 2004 book "The Great Tween Buying Machine" puts it, and advertising products that parents dislike. The book's co-authors, David L. Siegel, Timothy J. Coffey, and Gregory Livingston, who run the marketing agency WonderGroup, write that, thanks to the "nag factor," there are "plenty of examples of successful products that moms really don't like for themselves, but they buy anyway." They cite unusual color innovations like green Heinz ketchup and blue Hawaiian Punch: "Moms do not like any one of these products, yet each has generated millions of dollars in sales."

Calling "Mom-centricity" a "heinous disease," they remind marketers that all they have to do is "appease" parents, not please them. With Bratz, a parent might think, Sure, they're sexy-looking, but at least a ten-year-old girl playing with them is a ten-year-old still playing with dolls. Fara Warner, the author of "Power of the Purse: How Smart Businesses Are Adapting to the World's Most Important Consumers—Women," goes further, writing that Bratz represent "a future where young girls don't need their dolls to show them the career choices they have open to them. They already know they can choose any career and pursue it. It's a future where the rules about the size and shape of women's bodies, and how women express their sexuality, are far broader and more open." Whether a seven-year-old actually needs a doll that hints at how broad the rules of sexuality now are is not a question Warner addresses. This line of thinking gets even trickier when it comes to M.G.A.'s Bratz Babyz: baby dolls with makeup, lacy lingerie, and bikinis, and bottles slung on chains around their necks. ("Step back in time with the Bratz and see how it all began, as they xpress themselves with lots of style, and Baby 'Brattitude!'") Parents buy Bratz Babyz for girls as young as two. A ten-year-old might see irony—or humor—in the outrageous shoes, collagen-plump lips, and attitude-laden pout of a Bratz doll; irony is generally lost on toddlers.

A few weeks ago, a couple named Christopher and Tiffany Himes were in the doll section of a Toys R Us in Rockville, Maryland, having a half-joking argument about Bratz dolls. Tiffany, who is twenty-seven, is a stay-at-home mother of three daughters: Emma, seven; Madison, six; and Olivia, three. She said, "Unfortunately, the girls are really into them. I say 'unfortunately' because Bratz are just really trashy. My husband can't stand them."

"Oh, yeah," Chris, a thirty-two-year-old comedy writer, said. "I have some strong opinions on Bratz." He strode over to one of the Bratz shelves and peered at a box that contained something called the Wicked Twiins. Ciara was the "spunky" twin ("'cuz I'm always causing trouble"); Diona was the "sparkly" twin ("'cuz I'm in love with my own reflection"). Both Wicked Twiins were wearing black chokers, tight black T-shirts that said "Bad Girl," low-slung skirts (one chartreuse, one hot pink), and lace-up, high-heeled boots; one had bare legs, the other wore black fishnet stockings. "I mean, these are dolls that look like streetwalkers," Chris said. "Or, you know these underground 'pumping parties' you hear about, where people go for plastic surgery on the cheap? Well, they look like pumping-party victims." Tiffany and Chris had considered not letting the girls have Bratz—the first doll had come into their home as a gift—but Tiffany felt that banning toys was likely to backfire. Madison, the six-year-old, "was just really into fashion," Tiffany said, which was why she liked Bratz, and little Olivia liked them because her older sister did. Tiffany said she had noticed that the Bratz dolls did not elicit the kind of imaginative role-playing she had engaged in with Barbie as a child but, rather, focussed her girls' minds entirely on taking the dolls' clothes off and putting them back on.

Chris pushed a button on a talking Bratz doll named Jade, which was dressed in a rhinestone-studded micromini, a tank top emblazoned with a biker tattoo, and a cropped fur-trimmed black vinyl jacket. "Do you ever get fashion ideas from celebrities?" Jade asked, and then confided, "Sometimes I get ideas from celeb photos in magazines." She added, rather unconvincingly, "Being smart is cool." Chris snorted, and Tiffany said, "Bratz will fizzle out. Barbie will stay. She might have to get sexier, but she'll stay."

In 2002, Mattel introduced a new line of dolls: My Scene Barbie, which kept Barbie's basic dimensions but had bigger eyes, plumper, shinier lips, and hotter clothes. A recent incarnation of the line is the unsubtly named My Bling Bling Barbie. (The Barbie Web site says of one of these dolls, "Chelsea burns up the Bling Bling scene, in an ultra hot halter top and sassy skirt *sooo* scorchin'.") When not "getting their groove on," the Bling Bling girls are "mall maniacs." An animated video on the Barbie Web site depicts them struggling to lay off shopping for a day. They manage only a brief visit to the park—where the puppies they coo over turn into high-heeled boots, the fountain spouts jewelry, and the clouds above them spell out "SALE"—before they give in and head to the mall.

The competition between Bratz and Barbie has grown increasingly nasty. In April, 2004, Mattel sued the doll designer Carter Bryant, accusing him of developing his designs for Bratz while working at Mattel and taking them to M.G.A., thereby breaching his contract.

Bryant, who claims that he was not working for Mattel when he envisioned Bratz, countersued, alleging that Mattel required him to sign an overly broad and unlawful confidentiality agreement, which he claims kept him from divulging even the names of its employees. And in April, 2005, M.G.A. sued Mattel, accusing the company of trying to "muscle M.G.A. out of the business" while engaging in "serial copycatting" of M.G.A.'s products. The complaint makes much of the allegedly proprietary look of the Bratz eye, and the ways in which, it claims, the My Scene eye has evolved to mimic it:

The "My Scene" eye [originally had] lashes that radiate almost straight out, circumferentially, from the eyelids and, although the eye is more almond shaped than a "Barbie" eye, the eye is not so sleepy and heavy lidded as a "Bratz" eye and is only lightly shadowed. The new "My Scene" eye, in contrast, is dramatically more similar to a "Bratz" eye....The doe-eyed innocent look of the "My Scene" eye [has been] replaced with a sultrier look, characteristic of "Bratz." The new "My Scene" eye ... boasts lashes that sweep out and away from the outer corner of the eye, just like the "Bratz" eye. The new "My Scene" eye is also more heavily lidded and thickly lined, and the make-up is more markedly pronounced and dramatic.

Barbie, chided the M.G.A. lawyers, "does not 'play nice' with others (particularly her competitors), and needs to be taught to 'share' (at least in the fashion doll marketplace)." The suit also alleges that Mattel has unfairly tried to lock up the market on Saran doll hair—the long tresses that crown the vinyl heads of both Barbie and Bratz dolls and that girls love to comb—by "buying up the supply from the two main hair supply companies."

Mattel will not comment on the lawsuits, because they are still pending in California district court—and may be for years. (It has filed court papers denying M.G.A.'s accusations.) On November 20th, Mattel amended its lawsuit against Bryant to include both M.G.A. and Isaac Larian as defendants. The new complaint alleges that "M.G.A. intentionally stole not just specific Mattel property, such as Bratz designs, prototypes and related materials, but also a vast array of trade secrets and other confidential information that comprise Mattel's intellectual infrastructure." Larian said in response, "This lawsuit just proves that Mattel is desperate. They are living in a fantasyland. They wish they owned Bratz but they know that they don't. We will continue to beat them in the marketplace in the old-fashioned American way, through better product innovation, better sales, and better marketing." When I spoke with Scothon, he avoided referring to M.G.A. or Bratz by name. He said, "The competition has done an awful lot of following. Barbie will be around for another forty-seven years. The same can't be said for the competition."

When I visited Larian at the Bratz headquarters in Van Nuys, he was full of righteous scoffing about Mattel. After Mattel reintroduced the Ken doll, in February—Ken had endured a two-year exile from store shelves after the company announced that Barbie had dumped him—Larian had told reporters that it was "stupid publicity" and that "Ken is not going to save Barbie." (And indeed the whole Ken-is-back theme seemed so tongue-in-cheek—the campy Hollywood stylist Phillip Bloch effused on CNN about the new metrosexual look he'd developed for him—that it was hard to imagine his having much appeal for little girls.) During our interview, Larian dispatched an assistant to gather up a pile of My Scene dolls that he had on his desk; she dumped them on the table where we were eating lunch, so that I could study them. "My Scene was a knockoff," he declared. "They don't even look like Barbie! They look like Bratz!" Take the dolls home and show them to your six-year-old, he urged me more than once; see if she agrees that they look alike. Part of M.G.A.'s suit depends on its ability to prove that customers have been confused about which product is which. But in practice few Bratz- or Barbie-loving girls seem to have any trouble telling the difference.

Barbie occupies a unique place in the history of American toys. Before she was launched, in 1959, most of the dolls that children played with were baby dolls or sturdy-legged little-girl dolls. In 1987, the staff of the Strong Museum, a toy museum in Rochester, New York, interviewed ninety-eight women about their early-twentieth-century childhoods—specifically, how they had played. The recollections were often about climbing trees, jumping in haystacks, skating, and sledding; one woman remembered splashing in a stream and "getting bloodsuckers all over my legs." Many of the girls played with dolls into their teen-age years. They lavished baby dolls with maternal care—diapering and feeding them as they'd seen their mothers do with younger siblings. The Dy-Dee Doll, invented by a Brooklyn schoolteacher named Marie Wittam, in the early thirties, even wet herself: you pushed a button on her stomach and water came out of a tube. The popular Betsy Wetsy, which was introduced soon afterward, performed the same dubious trick. The little-girl dolls—such as Patsy, whose manufacturer, Effanbee, touted her as a "lovable imp" with tiltable head and moveable limbs—were more like cheery companions to have tea with, read to, or take on special romps. "The dolls that looked like infants I would mother," recalled one woman. "The dolls that looked like they could be miniatures of me were my friends." Another woman recalled that she had played with her baby dolls until she was nine, when she acquired a baby brother.

Barbie was different—she was meant to be a young adult, a gal about town, possessor of a glamorous wardrobe and an imposing pair of breasts. Barbie was invented by Ruth Handler, the tenth child of a Polish Jewish immigrant family in Denver, Colorado. Her father, Jacob Mosko, was an entrepreneur who started a successful business making custom truck bodies. As a young woman, Ruth Mosko moved to Southern California, where she worked as a stenographer at Paramount Pictures and married Elliot Handler, in 1945, the couple, along with Harold Mattson, founded Mattel. It became the most successful toy company in the world.

One of Handler's inspirations for the Barbie doll was a postwar cartoon character who had originally been featured in the German newspaper *Bild*. Lilli, as she was called, was a tough little blonde with an eye for the main chance; eventually, she had been turned into a lewd three-dimensional novelty item intended for purchase by men. Handler saw possibilities in Lilli, though she had to look past some of her trappings, as she recalled in her 1994 autobiography, "Dream Doll." Lilli's face was "too hard-looking," but her body was "another story":

Here were the breasts, the small waist, the long tapered legs I had enthusiastically described for the designers all those years ago.

The idea had been the result of the many times I had observed my daughter Barbara playing with paperdolls with her friends. While the toy counters in the early 1950s were heavy with paperdolls of every size, shape, and form, Barbara and her friends always insisted on buying only *adult* female paperdolls. They simply were not interested in baby paperdolls or even those representing ten-year-olds, their own age. Pretending to be doing something else, I'd listen, fascinated, to the girls as they played with these paperdolls hour after hour. And I discovered something very important: They were using these dolls to project their dreams of their own futures as adult women.... It dawned on me that this was a basic, much needed play pattern that had never before been offered by the doll industry to little girls. Oh, sure, there were so-called fashion dolls, those who came with more than one outfit. But these dolls had flat chests, big bellies, and squatty legs—they were built like overweight six- or eight-year-olds. The idea of putting a prom dress on such a doll, had such a dress even been available, was ludicrous.

Handler worried that "little girls would be intimidated by too much beauty" in a doll, but, unlike some of Barbie's future critics, she decided that the girls could handle it, and, after the first models, she made the dolls still prettier. Initially, Mattel produced brunet and red-headed Barbies, but the blondes were the runaway best-sellers.

In 1958, a year before Barbie's début, Mattel commissioned a study of toys by Ernest Dichter, one of the marketing gurus anatomized in Vance Packard's "The Hidden Persuaders" (1957). A Jewish émigré from Vienna who had trained as a psychoanalyst, Dichter reinvented himself with vulpine glee in the United States, offering his services to American brands such as Ivory soap and Chrysler. Like some sitcom parody of a Freudian, he tirelessly dug up sexual explanations for consumers' reactions to products. (Thus, the Edsel failed because its designer had "castrated" it by putting an artful hole between the front fenders; it was a challenge to market hot dogs to women, because, as one man whom Dichter interviewed said, "My wife gets mad at me when I munch or suck contentedly on my frankfurter.") Dichter's work for Mattel, which is discussed in detail in Lord's excellent "Forever Barbie," was a prescient example of conducting focus groups with a psychological edge. Dichter detected a notable and exploitable wedge between mothers and daughters when it came to Barbie. Many girls loved her, many mothers did not—and the disapproval they expressed sounded a lot like the disapproval you hear mothers expressing about Bratz today. Either the complaints that children are becoming too knowing too early are to some extent perennial, or companies keep pushing the bounds of what parents find acceptable, and parents are limited in what they can do to push back. (Both explanations probably have some truth.)

One mother told Dichter, "I know little girls want dolls with high heels but I object to that sexy costume. I wouldn't walk around the house like that. I don't like that influence on my little girl. If only they would let children remain young a little longer. . . . It's hard enough to raise a lady these days without undue moral pressure." Another admitted that her daughter would be "fascinated" by Barbie, but said she wouldn't buy the doll for her. "It has too much of a figure. . . . I'm sure she would like to have one, but I wouldn't buy it. All these kids talk about is how the teachers jiggle."

As Lord reports, Dichter believed that mothers could be bought off. One mother who initially found the doll too racy changed her mind when she heard her daughter say how "well groomed" Barbie was. Could Barbie make tidy little hair-combers out of grubby tomboys? If so, then maybe those pontoon breasts could be overlooked. Dichter concluded, "The type of arguments which can be used successfully to overcome parental objection are in the area of the doll's function in awakening in the child a concern with proper appearance." At the same time, a doll with a "sophisticated, even wicked" wardrobe would satisfy a girl's urge to rebel against her mother.

There were always mothers who refused to allow Barbie in the house. (Anna Quindlen once wrote of her desire to drive a "silver lamé stake" through Barbie's "plastic heart.") And there were always girls who didn't particularly care for dolls. In the past, they probably called themselves tomboys; now they're more likely to refer to themselves as what they are not—they aren't girly-girls. Annie, a smart, dog-loving ten-year-old I know, says she's just "not a doll person" and dismisses Barbie as "so twentieth century." Other dolls invite a different fantasy than Barbie does, and tend to unite mothers and daughters more. Groovy Girls, made by Manhattan Toy, are soft dolls that wear trendy but not revealing clothes, smile rather than pout, look to be tweens themselves, and seem to fulfill the old doll-as-pal role. But Groovy Girls don't command anywhere near the shelf space at major retailers that Barbie and Bratz do.

American Girl, the line of dolls from different historical eras, has positioned itself as a brand that helps girls hold on to little-girlhood for a bit longer. The dolls are meant to be nine-year-olds; they come with books that offer historically correct, if bland, details of life in the American past and tell slightly anachronistic tales of feminine pluck. (Felicity, from the eighteenth century, dons boys' clothes to ride a horse she isn't supposed to; Whartonian-rich-girl Samantha democratically befriends the Irish maid next door.) The American Girl Place stores in Chicago, New York, and Los Angeles offer themselves as approachably elegant, slightly retro sites for mother-daughter bonding; at in-store cafes, shiny-haired girls in party dresses and mothers with just-freshened lipstick and switched-off cell phones chat over tea sandwiches and chocolate mousse. (The restaurants even place a box full of conversation-starting questions on each table: If you were a character from a book, who would you be? Would you rather have the power of flying or becoming invisible?) Last year, American Girl launched a campaign to "Save Girlhood." Its Web site bore the message: "Save unicorns. Save dreams. Save rainbows. Save girlhood." It went on, "The way we see it, girls are growing up too fast. From every angle, today's girls are bombarded by influences pushing them towards womanhood at too early an age—at the expense of their innocence, their playfulness, their imagination." Even some girls see American Girl dolls as an antidote to the K.G.O.Y. poison. "They look like regular girls—they don't have all that makeup on like Bratz" is how Annie puts it. But the dolls are expensive—nearly a hundred dollars for a starter kit of doll and book—and sold only by catalogue, on their Web site, or at American Girl Place. American Girl, whose parent company has been owned since 1998 by Mattel, will never be a mass consumer brand, like Bratz or Barbie dolls, which cost less than thirty dollars on average. (Based on M.G.A. figures, Bratz products outsold American Girl last year by a rate of five to one.)

American Girl dolls—expensive, innocent-looking, and old-fashioned—are on one side of a class and cultural divide. Judging from the families you see shopping at American Girl Place, the dolls appeal disproportionately to well-off white parents willing to spend whatever it takes to help prolong their daughters' childhood. Bratz and My Scene Barbies, by contrast, are peddling the toy world's version of gangsta chic. Fara Warner notes that Bratz dolls mimic the fashions that their very young owners regularly see "on cable channels such as MTV and BET." And Sean McGowan, even more candidly, says that Bratz have the same allure that "makes rap popular with white kids in the suburbs."

Isaac Larian may hate Mattel, but he admires Ruth Handler, whom he calls a "true entrepreneur." Larian grew up in Tehran, where his father owned a textile shop, and he helped out from the time he was eleven. When he was seventeen, he told his parents he wanted to go to the United States. They sent him to Los Angeles "with seven hundred and fifty dollars—a lot of money for them." In his first job, he washed dishes from eleven at night to seven in the morning at a coffee shop in the predominantly Hispanic city of Lawndale. Later, he waited tables and put himself through school at California State University, Los Angeles, where he got a degree in civil engineering. Entre-preneurship is what appealed to him, though. After graduating, he began importing cheap brass doodads from South Korea, starting a company called Surprise Gift Wagon. In the late eighties, he persuaded Nintendo to give him the American rights to their handheld games. "The first year, we sold twenty-two million dollars in games, and we had a thirty-five-per-cent profit," he recalled. "But the next year we had ten million dollars' worth of Nintendo games that nobody wanted anymore. The kids wanted something new." He concluded from that experience that a company marketing to kids has to keep an avid eye on trends. "With Bratz, we need to change them every three, four months," he explained. "What you see in the stores today was not in the stores last year. And when we come out with our fall line, what's in the stores in the spring is not going to be there. And the key is to be fresh, to listen to the kids carefully, because they change literally every week. And you have to think, What are they into *now*, and come up with products that let them be ahead of the curve. If we stop doing that, the same thing that happened to Barbie is going to happen to us. They're gonna throw us in the trash can."

Larian likes to tell a story about the first Bratz doll, which wore pants with fashionable embroidery trim at the cuffs. When M.G.A. released the doll for the international market, Larian decided that the trim was too expensive and it was left off the pants. He thought nobody would notice. But, he recalled, "You wouldn't *believe* how many letters we got from kids in the U.K. saying, 'I was in New York, and the Cloe doll or the Yasmin doll that I saw in America had this little embroidery on the pants and the one I bought in London didn't have that.'" Kids, he learned from that experience, notice visual details at a level of precision that surprises adults. And kids' opinions about toys, Larian believes, are always right. "I have insomnia—people in my company think I never sleep," Larian said, smiling but not joking. "I take home all these fan letters, and I read them at night. Our designers—it's mandatory for them to read those letters carefully, too. We pay attention—we make toys kids want. The secret formula is to listen carefully to kids. They tell you. If they don't like something, they say, 'This sucks.' If they like it, they tell you. And if they want you to make it better they tell you."

One recent afternoon, I sat in a darkened room behind a one-way mirror with Larian and Rachel Griffin, of the M.G.A. publicity team, as they watched a focus group for a new product line: the Bratz Genie Magic dolls. The four little girls gathered inside—Ember, Emily, Kristine, and Morgan—were between the ages of eight and ten. They all had sneakers on, and their sweatpants and windbreakers bore the marks of the back yard or the classroom: grass-stained knees, a dusting of chalk. They sat on bright-colored bean-bag chairs, looking alert and easily amused, happy to have got out of school a little early. The interviewer was a beautiful young woman with spike-heeled boots, extravagant black curls, and a humorless mien. She started by asking why the girls liked Bratz. Kristine, who was ten, cited the difficulty of losing their shoes. Ember, who was nine, called out, "They're just so fashionable!" And Morgan, who was eight and had long straight dark hair, remarked that Barbies "all look the same. They're all blond." Larian, who sat next to me, murmured contentedly, "Good girl. Kids are so smart." In fact, Barbies now come in a number of hair and skin colors, but for Morgan an annoying aura of blondness still clung to the Mattel doll.

Kristine was the expert, the one who had seen "Bratz," the tie-in television show, and who appreciated specific qualities about the dolls' hair and shoes. Emily and Ember were more reticent. Morgan had a goofy, anarchic way about her. Maybe it was because she was younger—"Dang, why am I so young?" she asked cheerily, of no one in particular—but she seemed to see something faintly ridiculous in the self-serious world of fashionistas. Still, she, like the other girls, had a disconcerting tendency to spout ad-style triads of adjectives when asked what she'd tell others about Bratz products. "How would you describe these to your mom?" the interviewer asked, gesturing to the Genie Magic dolls and accessories. "Cool. Fun. Playful," Morgan recited. "Awesome. New, Fantastic," Kristine added.

After a while, the interviewer left the room, having invited the girls to play with the Genie Magic dolls and some of their accessories, including a flying carpet and a bottle from which the genie was supposed to emerge. The girls didn't know one another, but they slipped into companionability easily enough. A couple of them made the magic carpet fly around the room. There was some desultory talk about which of the Bratz Genies had a boyfriend, and there were invitations to tea—amazingly, tea remains a central trope of doll play, no matter how incongruous. (It's hard to imagine Jade, say, being excited by her grandmother's quilted tea cozies.)

Kristine, who wore her dark curly hair in a ponytail, spent a lot of time combing the long straight hair of the big-headed Bratz Genie doll. "I've combed her hair, and it's finally pretty," she said after a while. "I love combing hair."

To which Morgan replied, "I know, but it's so boring."

"It's actually fun," Kristine insisted.

The girls seemed to regard the word "sassy" as code for something more exciting and scandalous. By the time the interviewer came back into the room, Morgan was bouncing around, knocking over packages and singing, "I'm sassy! I'm *sassy!* Yeah!" and the girls were cracking up.

"O.K., guys," the interviewer said primly. "I need you to focus for a couple more minutes."

Meanwhile, on the other side of the one-way mirror, there were signs of distress. Larian was hanging on these little girls' every word. Again and again, he fired off messages on his BlackBerry based on their more or less idle chatter. The girls were the unwitting lords of this realm, although their power was of a limited sort—the answers children's marketers listen to so keenly are only to questions they have designed in pursuit of parents' money. Nevertheless, in the moment, the keenness of the listening and the watching made Ember and Morgan and Kristine and Emily seem influential indeed. For instance, the girls had been blithely referring to a Bratz Genie's bottle as her "house" or her "castle," causing Larian to groan and type agitatedly into his BlackBerry. "Jesus Christ, we've got to fix that," he said. The packaging and advertising campaign clearly called it a bottle.

The interviewer asked the girls, "What are you calling this over here?"

"The royal castle!" the girls cried out at once.

"If we call it a bottle, is that wrong?"

Yes, they said. They liked the "genie's castle" or the "genie's royal house." Later, the interviewer asked about their preferences between genies and princesses. Bratz was putting a lot of resources behind the Genies this season. "Princesses!" the girls chorused.

"Most girls really want to be princesses," Kristine explained. "Like Queen Elizabeth—girls at my school, they want to be like Queen Elizabeth's daughter." (Somehow, I don't think she meant Princess Anne.) "When we were smaller, we used to play princess in the castle. A princess—you *really* want to be one. You're really rich and stuff."

Morgan chimed in: "Genies are really unexpected, but princesses are something you really like." And she added, with daffy precision, "Girls will choose princesses because they'd rather be one—technically, of all the girls in the world, let's say five to one."

"Oh, my God," Larian moaned.

Other problems were discovered. The girls didn't realize that a design on the Bratz Princess box was supposed to be a picture frame; one of the girls thought it was coiled hair. Larian tried to take comfort in the fact that the girls recognized the handle on the box as a tiara that they could wear themselves. Still, he grumbled, "That frame costs a dollar-fifteen more a unit." Larian typed into his BlackBerry. "People from product development should be here," he said crossly.

Within a few weeks, M.G.A. had changed the labelling on the Genie Bottle—it was now a Genie Magic Royal Castle. By the end of the summer, the Genie Magic line had taken off, selling more than a million dolls. M.G.A. soon expanded, by acquiring the Little Tikes toy company, and began planning a move to bigger headquarters in the San Fernando Valley. Morgan, Kristine, Ember, and Emily had spoken.

—2006

Learning from Other Writers (Talbot)

1. In the opening lines of Talbot's essay, she writes that what's at stake in the toy industry's battle over who is the "alpha doll" is "the hugely profitable sovereignty over the imaginations of little girls." How is this sovereignty important beyond sales figures? What is the effect of "owning" imagination?

2. What is the implied claim of this essay? Why doesn't Talbot state that claim explicitly?

3. How does Talbot weigh her sources? Though she presents her case in a fairly objective way, can you tell when she puts more weight on one side of her argument rather than another? How so? Where?

4. How does the author structure her essay in terms of chronology? What role does the history of dolls and toy manufacturing play in her investigation?

5. The dolls that boys play with are called "action figures." The toy industry's euphemism for "sexy" is "sassy." How is "naming" an important component of this essay? How does what we call something affect that thing?

Meaghan Winter

ORTHODOX CHIC

I. THE SEXINESS OF MINIMIZED SEXINESS

In Brooklyn's Orthodox Jewish neighborhoods, where religious married women are expected to cover their hair in public, dozens of high-end shops sell glossy human-hair wigs for upward of five thousand dollars. One such retailer, Shevy, offers among the most expensive on the market, in New York or anywhere. Its wares run from nineteen hundred for a standard pixie cut to forty-eight hundred for The Knockout, advertised as a "curtain of luxurious locks, ever-so-slightly layered for maximum movement and show-stopping glamour." These wigs have been sewn by hand overseas, by a seamstress who used a tiny hooked needle to loop each strand of hair through minuscule netting the color of a white woman's scalp. The hair is stitched so tightly and evenly that it can be laid along any part, unlike machine-sewn or synthetic-hair wigs, which give themselves away with artificial parts and hairlines.

Until recently, when an Orthodox Jewish woman in Brooklyn needed a hair covering she visited a neighbor who sewed wigs in her living room. The traditional wig was basically a synthetic helmet. When a woman wore an obvious wig she showed her neighbors that she was religious and married, and she unapologetically signaled her faith to gentiles. These living-room businesses are quickly disappearing, however, as the wigs worn by some Orthodox women become less brazenly wig-like. In Orthodox neighborhoods, hair doesn't hang or stick or pucker. Each woman wears a dome of dark gloss, and if these hairpieces' names—Roman Holiday, Sassy Swoon, Downtown Edge, Hamptons Chic—are any indication, Orthodox customers now aspire to signify more than just faithfulness. It's not uncommon for a wig distributor to play up the sex appeal of products hypothetically intended to minimize sexiness. Shevy's website plays low-toned mood music and flashes pictures of full-lipped models performing sultriness. They're all cheekbones and narrowed side-glances. In defense of their marketing tactics, it should be said that Brooklyn's up-scale wig retailers don't cater just to Orthodox customers: celebrities and cancer patients buy, too. Snoop Dogg's ex-wife has shopped at Shevy. Yet soon-to-be-married Orthodox women still make up a large portion of these retailers first-time wig buyers. How *does* spending two grand on a shiny wig called Rebel Yell, which Shevy's website promises "brings out the independent spirit," fulfill a young woman's covenant with her husband, community, and God?

II. TAMING THE INHERENTLY LECHEROUS

On July 2, 2009, Hadassah Sabo Milner, mother of seven and resident of a small town in Rockland County, New York, described on a friend's blog the grief she'd felt after her divorce. By most contemporary measures, Milner's decision to write publicly about her private "pain and suffering" seems unremarkable. Yet Milner's post so departed from her community's expectations that it inspired nearly two hundred comments, many of them angry. Like many Orthodox Jewish women, Milner wore a wig to cover her natural hair during her marriage. In her post, she wrote that after her divorce she stopped wearing wigs because they'd always "felt like… shackles," and once she was single she'd told herself: "I am doing what I want."

Milner's words subvert two thousand years of religious discourse. For hundreds of years, women of many faiths wore headscarves, but among Jews today, only Orthodox women routinely cover their hair with hats or scarves, snoods (bell-shaped knit hats like those favored by Rasta-farians) or wigs. In the first written records of Jewish law, penned around 200 CE, rabbis assert that women's hair is erotic. Men are inherently lecherous, the rabbis write, and women must not tempt them.

In the past several years, though, on blogs and online forums, Orthodox women have begun publishing for the first time their unfettered thoughts about hair covering. Some online commentators argue with such lawyerly precision that their exchanges mimic Talmudic discourse; others write the confessionals and beauty secrets typical of mainstream women's magazines. On dozens of sites, women describe covering their hair as a "daily struggle." Protected by anonymity, they leave comments that they're understandably reluctant to voice in public: "I still hate covering my hair, and it does not help that I originally did so at my husband's insistence, without having any say (i.e. guts to argue)"; when wearing scarves to work, women claim they "developed poor self-esteem and felt incredibly self-conscious."

Unlike most of the internet's angry dribblers, Orthodox bloggers and their readers parcel out each "operative word" in a Bible passage as often as they spew emotional reactions. And precision is needed, because the hair-covering tradition hinges on a single word. In Numbers 5:18 a man suspects his wife of adultery. He is overcome with jealousy and brings her before a priest, who performs a ritual to prove her guilty or innocent. This ritual involves a clay bowl and the priest doing *something* to the woman's hair, an action encapsulated by the verb *parah*, the meaning of which has been understood as either "uncovered" or "disheveled." If *parah* is understood to mean "uncovered," as a majority of early rabbis decided it meant, the passage suggests that in ancient Israel, women covered their hair, and covered hair was central to wifely virtue. Because the woman's chastity was called into question, the priest uncovered her hair. But if the word *parah* means "disheveled," as others have argued, the passage contains little information about how biblical women kept their hair, and how God thus ordered them to dress and behave. Disheveling the alleged adulteress's hair reads as a generic form of humiliation.

No matter how *parah* is translated, the story is not ambiguous. The passage submits a woman to her husband and to the priest's authority, and those men use her hair to judge her. The priest says that if the woman is found guilty of adultery, she bears responsibility for her transgression, but if she is innocent and the jealous husband has falsely accused her, the wife is still responsible, for she has provoked his jealousy.

When an Orthodox blogger posted his tongue-in-cheek riff "Judging Women Based on How They Cover Their Hair," commentators cited the adulteress story and offered opinions so diverse and contradictory that a reader wouldn't be able to retrieve solid answers to basic questions. But no one who responded to "Judging Women Based on How They Cover Their Hair" doubted that Orthodox women *are* judged by the way they cover their hair. Because women may opt for various head coverings, Orthodox men and women can size up a passerby's religiosity in a glance.

Each kind of covering occupies a rung on a perceived ladder of sacrifice. Generally, it's thought that the more obvious (and uglier) the covering, the more pious and admirable the woman. Different coverings are also associated with various communities. For example, a woman I'll call Deborah (women referred to by first name only are protected by a pseudonym) belongs to an ultra-Orthodox community, and she's worn a scarf over her head every day since her wedding. She shaves her head at the end of each menstrual cycle to be sure not a single hair will ever peek out.

Deborah explains that a woman almost always covers her hair the way her mother or mother-in-law does. Matchmakers keep mothers' hair in mind when pairing couples, for similar coverings indicate shared lifestyles. Modern Orthodox women may consider hair covering a choice, as their rabbis are less likely to interpret the Numbers story as a biblical mandate, but Hasidic and ultra-Orthodox women take it for granted. Deborah says that in her community, "not even the rebels would consider not doing it."

III. DON'T TRUST YOURSELF UNTIL THE DAY YOU DIE

As recently as fifty years ago, few Orthodox women in the United States covered their hair. At the turn of the century, when established immigrants collected their newly arrived relatives at the docks, they brought them American-style outfits. The quick-to-assimilate left their wigs on Ellis Island. Over the years, however, a greater number of American Orthodox women have begun covering their hair. The Haredi refugees who hunkered down in Brooklyn after World War II covered their hair, and postwar revivalism rekindled an interest in traditional Jewish life. Later, multiculturalism made advertising one's heritage acceptable, if not faddish, so hair coverings came back into style. Ironically, however, wig retailers owe a bulk of their sales to the 1970s feminist movement and its focus on liberating women from traditional gender roles.

Joan, who turned to Orthodox Judaism in her twenties, says her community "believes gender roles are holy and good—to deny your role is to deny who you are." Joan is one of many Orthodox women who desired to publicly reaffirm their commitment to the traditional role of religious wife and mother.

Historically, that role involved facilitating her husband's Bible study by keeping house. Today, in most Orthodox synagogues, men and women sit separately, and women are prohibited from singing in the company of men: beautiful bodies and voices may distract men from their prayers. Many of Orthodox Judaism's rules, like mandatory hair covering, rest on the premise that even a glimpse of a woman may overcome a man with temptation and lead him from righteousness. Suppressing any suggestion of pre- or extramarital lust is considered community preservation. At weddings and other parties, a curtain or screen divides the room into male and female sides so men don't see women dance.

I hesitantly suggested to Barbara, an ultra-Orthodox woman who writes for a Jewish website, that maybe all the emphasis on not touching or looking or thinking might actually make people *more* aware of erotic undertones. Don't all these rules assume the worst of people, and of men in particular? Barbara said that we *should of course* expect the worst of people. Human nature is weak, and even with religious rules for a guide, "you shouldn't trust yourself until the day you die," she warned.

If a community relies on a collective adherence to such rules, no wonder Orthodox readers respond so passionately to what they read online; Orthodoxy's reliance on social policing and its tradition of argumentation seem to necessitate online debate. Hadassah Sabo Milner's readers discuss to what extent modesty rules pull women into "social coercion," and whether a husband "owns his wife's sexuality." When Milner insists that "my sexuality belongs to ME," she provokes a few readers. But nothing fills her or anyone's comment board quite like the mention of wigs. In Israel, right-wing groups routinely picket outside wig retailers because they believe women should wear only scarves. "Sexy momma wigs," many write, are "pure hypocrisy." The popularity of these human-hair wigs, not unlike Muslim headscarves, is thought to measure the extent to which secular influences, like feminism, have co-opted traditional religious values.

Orthodox women say they cover their hair (and knees, thighs, shoulders, collarbones, elbows, and of course, breasts) to be modest. More than a dress code, modesty is considered a way of being in the world. "I tell my children, modesty is class," says Edith, Deborah's mother. "It's about being soft-spoken, carrying yourself with dignity, and not elbowing your way through life." Edith says there's no official mandate, but ultra-Orthodox women don't drink or smoke, and few exercise in public. Joan doesn't scream, curse, or even "use coarse words," and generally behaves in keeping with David's oft-quoted line in the Psalms. "The glory of the king's daughter is in her inwardness."

Never mind the tacit expectation that brides will be virgins; in some communities women and girls aren't even told about sex until they're engaged. Preserving girls "innocence," or ignorance, however you look at it, is one of the primary reasons television, the internet, secular books, and other outside influences are so frowned upon. As with hair covering, opinions concerning the internet vary depending on a community's stringency, but most Hasidic rabbis ban it and many Modern Orthodox rabbis discourage it. Edith eagerly showed me a new iPhone app that locates nearby synagogues; she said that many Orthodox Jews go online anyway, in part because it's necessary for holding a job.

Despite her appreciation for GPS. Edith agrees that the internet is dangerous and that girls should be kept sheltered. Her daughter Alona effused that she'd been "naive, totally clueless, without an idea about *anything*" until Deborah pulled her aside a few months before her wedding, when she was twenty. "I had to tell her!" Deborah says, smiling. "Then I learned on the job!" Alona laughs, crossing her arms and blushing. Premarital "family purity" courses give women their first sex education. Proponents of hair covering argue that once a woman loses her virginity, she's more aware of and in control of her sexuality. Because she can work her prowess, she needs to literally keep a lid on it. Taking her nephew in her arms, Alona noted that the whole experience of moving from her parents' house and being married was "such a huge change, such a whirlwind" that starting to wear a hat felt like a minor issue, even though she cried as she stood in the shower and her mother shaved her head.

IV. DOWNSIDES AND UPSIDES

Because many ultra-Orthodox women value tradition for its own sake, they might appear to think of covering their hair as I think of wearing clothes. If someone questioned me about my tendency to wear a shirt in public, I would have a hard time explaining my thoughts on the matter. I don't like or dislike shirt-wearing, and other than when shopping or laundering, I don't give it much thought. In my world, basic decency necessitates shirts. Accordingly, Edith said in response to my incessant *whys* that "the significance is tradition. Nothing else. It's not that it's acceptable to me, or significant to me. This is me. The thought of why doesn't enter my mind."

Aside from the obvious differences in cultural meaning, however, a wig is not analogous to a shirt. The Orthodox women I met all acknowledged that covering their hair is difficult, painful, and can have permanent physical consequences. Hair coverings pinch and may cause headaches. They're hot and itchy, insufferable in the summer. And after years of routine squishing, natural hair looks flat and dull; often it falls out.

In contrast, a Modern Orthodox woman named Leah says she considers hair covering "just a commandment [she] chose to keep." Leah began covering because her husband asked her to, and at the time she "was nineteen and naive and in love, and it was 'anything for you, my darling.'" Leah's mother didn't cover her hair and was furious. She called the practice ridiculous and old-fashioned, a nuisance and a health hazard. "You'll get sores! You'll get infections! Your natural hair will thin and fall out! Once you start, you can't stop!" she shouted. And she was right: Leah is now losing her hair and concedes that wearing a wig for the past forty-five years hasn't been easy.

The most stringent women shrug these grievances off as annoyances, pittances beside the importance of fulfilling God's wishes. Others, however, point to real emotional costs. Those women sighed and told me, repeatedly, that they wanted me to know that they'd had beautiful hair. It had been their "defining feature," their "crowning glory." They missed it. Lynne Schreiber, editor of *Hide and Seek*, a 2003 collection of oral testimonies focused on Orthodox women's perspectives on hair covering, covered her hair for four years, before she went bareheaded during a camping trip with her children and female friends. Leaving the woods, head covered again, she felt "a marked difference" within herself, as though her scarf suppressed her personality. She stopped covering her hair. Then friends stopped calling. She soon felt so alienated and disillusioned that she left Orthodoxy. (She also regrets that; *Hide and Seek* is "so pro-covering." If it weren't, however, the book likely wouldn't have existed, and even if it had, no one would have bought it. Few Orthodox women are willing to openly admit their ambivalence about hair covering, and Orthodox audiences are wary of anything that doesn't toe the sanctioned line.)

After the journal *Judaism* published a debate over hair covering, Lillian Krakowski wrote a letter criticizing its male authors for failing to mention how women suffer when they cover their hair. Krakowski wrote that many women have stopped covering "for the sake of eliminating cruelty, humiliation, ostracism and pain," and that losing one's hair "is a cruel price to pay for marriage." Krakowski's sentiment is not uncommon, but her voice is rare. I've yet to find an equally impassioned anti-covering perspective from an Orthodox woman published formally anywhere else. Only beyond the confines of the establishment, on their personal blogs and anonymous online forums, have women been able to broadcast their points of view.

In those online discussions, women have lamented hair covering in such numbers that they could form a virtual mob. Yet they don't. Plenty of readers write that they won't cover, or that there's no biblical basis for a mandate. But as counterintuitive as it may seem, when a blogger says she's ambivalent about her scarf, readers overwhelmingly respond that hearing about her struggle reinforces their own commitment to covering. Why? How does acknowledging a custom's difficulty persuade someone to stick with it?

The difficulty must provide something. Rebbetzin Feige Twerski, a rabbi's wife, writes an online column with champion salesmanship—dozens of her readers have commented that she's helped them stay observant—and calls each commandment "a communication" that "forges a personal relationship with the Master of the universe." Feige says that "the objective of God's commandments is not the betterment of society as a whole... but rather how the commandments speak to us personally, and how they enhance and promote the requisite spiritual growth of the individual who observes them."

When Judaism was formed, however, no one could have possibly viewed the commandments as conduits for a personal relationship with God, because the whole concept of the personal had yet to be invented. "Modernity itself is about the individual," Dr. Shuly Schwartz, a professor at the Jewish Theological Seminary, tells me. In traditional Judaism, people submitted to God's commandments simply because they were God's commandments, Schwartz explains, which reminds me of Edith's insistence that she never asks herself *why* she covers her hair. The needs of the community came first and foremost in classical Judaism, as they do in Hasidism. Today, though, most people want something for themselves in return for their obedience, and they're more inclined to believe that God cares about them personally.

Rebbetzin Feige Twerski's readers also seem to prioritize personal rather than social reasons for covering: "I felt that I was doing this for me and God, not the rest of the world," one woman writes. Hadassah Sabo Milner wrote that after liberating herself from the "shackles" of hair covering when she divorced, she decided to cover her hair again during her second marriage, "on my own terms, because it is what I feel is right for where I am in life." Forget saving men from lechery and keeping their communities intact; these women want to strengthen their own spiritual practice and sense of self. They're taught that modesty codes turn their focus from their bodies to their internal selves to elevate their feelings of self-worth. But if individualism is a modern concept, the idea that a commandment might serve a woman's needs is straight-up avant-garde. Rabbi Judith Hauptman of the Jewish Theological Seminary says it's great that so many women have found meaning in hair covering, but Jewish regulations and customs were originally created to facilitate men's worship. Anything that a woman feels is for herself is something that she or her community has reinterpreted.

V. FEMINISM IS WHAT WE TELL OURSELVES IT IS

When rabbis chose to read *parah* as uncovered, they sentenced its runner-up meaning to obscurity. Edith probably won't start blogging about personal freedom anytime soon. But like her Modern Orthodox counterparts, she does believe modesty rules exist in part to help women, a nuance that represents a change. There's no way to know how assumptions will continue to evolve, especially if bloggers keep validating each others' choices.

Will their new interpretations empower women or just give them an illusion of control? Susan Weiss, a sociologist and lawyer, writes that feel-good associations like devotion to a beloved husband or commitment to God are passed down by authorities to deflect the "underlying power relations" that keep Orthodox women "the chattel of their husbands." Wigs and scarves themselves are not oppressive, Weiss argues, but they represent the bargain Orthodox women must make to earn acceptance within their repressive communities. Without the promise of personal gratification, a modern necessity, women may be more likely to question if not also reject such rigid gender roles.

So have Leah and Hadassah been brainwashed? Are they lying to themselves? Part of me wants to accept at face value everything Leah tells me about why she covers her hair. Allowing a woman to define her own life is what feminism is all about, right? Besides, I like Leah. We sit and joke around in her kitchen and she feeds me cookies. I would want my guest to believe my stated reasons for doing what I do. The meaning I have woven for myself is very real to me.

Another part of me, though, accepts Weiss's Stockholm syndrome—like hypothesis. Of course we can never really know the reasons we do what we do. We can only know the reasons we tell ourselves, and those explanations adapt to our environment with incredible dexterity. Or, we adapt them.

—2011

Learning from Other Writers (Winter)

1. Like Michael Rudin's essay on video games, "Orthodox Chic" is divided into sections with subheadings. How do Winter's subheads function similarly to or differently from Rudin's? How do they guide the reader? Shape the essay's analysis?

2. Winter notes that "[a]s recently as fifty years ago, few Orthodox women in the United States covered their hair." How does this detail, which suggests that the practice is a rekindling of a waning tradition, affect the way you read the essay? Might it suggest that wig wearing is as much a way of asserting a religious identity as it is a demonstration of religious piety?

3. What is the writer's position on wig wearing? Where do we see her perspective come through? Where does she acknowledge her position but try to subvert it?

4. Winter notes that it is rare to find a woman willing to speak out openly against hair covering, but the number of women speaking out anonymously is much higher. Why does she include this information? What does it illuminate about this debate?

5. Winter writes about Orthodox Jewish women. How can her portrait be applied to practices in other cultures? Why is her driving question significant beyond the community about which she writes?

Adding Your Voice

1. In "Is Google Making Us Stupid?," Nicholas Carr writes: "The process of adapting to new intellectual technologies is reflected in the changing metaphors we use to explain ourselves to ourselves. When the mechanical clock arrived, people began thinking of their brains as operating 'like clockwork.' Today, in the age of software, we have come to think of them as operating 'like computers.'" Think about the way in which the technology you use has affected your language, personality, or behavior. How might this line of thought lead you to a driving question to explore in an essay? Use your evolving relationship with a particular technology to research and write an investigation on the topic.

2. Choose a trend in music, fashion, film, speech, or sexual behavior that you have noticed among your friends, your peers, or the culture in general. Where did this trend start? Did the appearance of the trend surprise you? Did you buy into the trend? Do you understand the origins of the trend? Have there been trends like this before? Do some research on the trend and the genre to which it belongs; then, as Gladwell does in "Big and Bad," write an investigation in which you analyze the causes of the trend and its effects on the group that practices it and/or society at large.

CHAPTER 11

Experiments

S ometimes, the questions that pop up in your mind when you think about writing an essay lead you to consider performing an experiment to figure out the answer. "What would happen if ...?" "What's it really like to ...?" "Could that urban legend be based in fact?" One of the most successful recent documentaries was *Super Size Me*, in which Morgan Spurlock vows to eat at McDonald's, and only at McDonald's, three meals a day for thirty days, to investigate what such a diet does to a person's physical and mental health. Even Spurlock's doctors, who predict that eating nothing but the food served at McDonald's will probably harm his body, are shocked at the outcome. Spurlock, in perfect health when he begins his experiment, gains 24.5 pounds. His cholesterol level spikes to 230. Toward the end of his experiment, his physician fears such irreparable damage to Spurlock's organs that he urges him to stop immediately, but Spurlock continues for the entire thirty days.

Super Size Me is an eye-opening film. What might have begun as a simple question, a *what if* tossed around among friends, turns into a cultural, social, and political phenomenon. Though McDonald's claimed that Spurlock's documentary had nothing to do with its decision, six weeks after the film premiered at Sundance, the company discontinued its Supersize campaign.

The experiment form isn't new. George Orwell's first novel, *Down and Out in Paris and London*, which he published in 1933, is deeply rooted in the experiment he undertook to shake off his upper-class British childhood by washing dishes in the kitchen of a fancy French restaurant and living in British slums among paupers, tramps, and beggars. Starting in the mid 1960s, George Plimpton risked serious injury to his body and pride in a series of exercises in what he called *immersion journalism*, trying out as a rookie quarterback for the Detroit Lions, tending goal for the Boston Bruins, pitching against some of baseball's all-time greats, and playing professional golf for a month on the PGA tour (see, in order, Plimpton's nonfiction books *Paper Lion, Open Net, Out of My League*, and *Bogey Man*). But the experiment form seems to have assumed a recent upsurge in popularity, perhaps because of the popularity of reality TV shows, with writers stripping onstage in men's clubs or trying to live for a year on food that comes from within a hundred-mile radius of their houses, all in an attempt to learn from doing—regardless of how farcical some of the experiments might seem to be.

REALITY CHECKS: TESTING THEORIES AND MYTHS

Carrying out an experiment doesn't necessarily require a team of doctors monitoring your vitals, and you don't need an advanced degree in physics or biology to pull it off. Often, the form requires little more than possessing a strong stomach, as you will see in Ann Hodgman's essay "No Wonder They Call Me a Bitch," for which she samples various kinds of dog food to determine if the advertising claims surrounding them are true, or owning a car, as you will see in Philip Weiss's "How to Get out of a Locked Trunk," in which he figures out how to perform the mechanical act indicated by his title. On the surface, such experiments are designed to answer factual questions. But the answers also need to matter for deeper analytical reasons. Hodgman makes us wonder why we so often treat our pets like humans and why we allow ourselves to be duped by advertising claims we know to be unfounded, while Weiss seeks to understand why the threat of a living burial haunts him, especially on the eve of his marriage to a woman he thinks he loves.

The philosophical or ideological position you stake out as you undertake an experiment can vary from project to project, but most writers try to be neither too antagonistic toward nor too fanatically enamored of their subjects. This isn't to say that you need to be completely objective. Had Morgan Spurlock not been deeply interested in the outcome of eating McDonald's food for thirty days he would have quit after the first week, when he gained nine pounds and felt awful. You obviously will have biases, preconceived notions, fears, and hopes for your experiment, and letting your reader know what these are—and why you are the right person to undertake the experiment anyway—is important.

In the essay version of Barbara Ehrenreich's nonfiction book *Nickel-and-Dimed: On (Not) Getting By in America*, which we include in this chapter, the author describes her attempt to survive on the pittance she earns working several jobs that pay the minimum wage. In the first two sections, Ehrenreich outlines her experiment, sets up her parameters, and addresses her misgivings ("And with my real-life assets ... I am, of course, thoroughly insulated from the terrors that afflict the genuinely poor"), in addition to providing information about minimum-wage jobs and the economic realities of living on such a wage. Then she shows us the lead-up to the experiment: her search for a job. In the third section, she begins her career waiting on tables at both the Hearthside and Jerry's; the rest of her essay chronicles her encounters with her coworkers, bosses, and customers and the day-in, day-out struggles endemic to this profession.

As will be true with the journey/quest form in the following chapter, you will need to decide how much time to spend telling your readers how and why you came to formulate your experiment and what was entailed in your preparations. (In Ehrenreich's book, she devotes an entire introductory chapter to explaining her methodology and addressing her readers' possible objections to her project.) You might choose to meditate on your findings along the way, or save such meditations for the end, in which you sit back and analyze your discoveries in the sort of "results" section you are required to include in the write-up for a lab in physics. Just be careful to perform the literary equivalent of wearing gloves and goggles, by which we mean that you will need to take precautions so your experiment doesn't land you in the hospital or in jail.

Ann Hodgman

NO WONDER THEY CALL ME A BITCH

I've always wondered about dog food. Is a Gaines-burger really like a hamburger? Can you fry it? Does dog food "cheese" taste like real cheese? Does Gravy Train actually make gravy in the dog's bowl, or is that brown liquid just dissolved crumbs? And exactly what *are* by-products?

Having spent the better part of a week eating dog food, I'm sorry to say that I now know the answers to these questions. While my dachshund, Shortie, watched in agonies of yearning, I gagged my way through can after can of stinky, white-flecked mush and bag after bag of stinky, fat-drenched nuggets. And now I understand exactly why Shortie's breath is so bad.

Of course, Gaines-burgers are neither mush nor nuggets. They are, rather, a miracle of beauty and packaging—or at least that's what I thought when I was little. I used to beg my mother to get them for our dogs, but she always said they were too expensive. When I finally bought a box of cheese-flavored Gaines-burgers—after 20 years of longing—I felt deliciously wicked.

"Dogs love real beef," the back of the box proclaimed proudly. "That's why Gaines-burgers is the only beef burger for dogs with real beef and no meal by-products!" The copy was accurate: meat by-products did not appear in the list of ingredients. Poultry by-products did, though—right there next to preserved animal fat.

One Purina spokesman told me that poultry by-products consist of necks, intestines, undeveloped eggs and other "carcass remnants," but not feathers, heads or feet. When I told him I'd been eating dog food, he said, "Oh, you're kidding! Oh no!" (I came to share his alarm when, weeks later, a second Purina spokesman said that Gaines-burgers *do* contain poultry heads and feet—but *not* undeveloped eggs.)

Up close my Gaines-burger didn't much resemble chopped beef. Rather, it looked—and felt—like a single long, extruded piece of redness that had been chopped into segments and formed into a patty. You could make one at home if you had a Play-Doh Fun Factory.

I turned on the skillet. While I waited for it to heat up I pulled out a shred of cheese-colored material and palpated it. Again, like Play-Doh, it was quite malleable. I made a little cheese bird out of it; then I counted to three and ate the bird.

There was a horrifying rush of cheddar taste, followed immediately by the dull tang of soybean flour—the main ingredient in Gaines-burgers. Next I tried a piece of red extrusion. The main difference between the meat-flavored and cheese-flavored extrusions is one of texture. The "cheese" chews like fresh Play-Doh, whereas the "meat" chews like Play-Doh that's been sitting out on a rug for a couple of hours.

Frying only turned the Gaines-burger black. There was no melting, no sizzling, no warm meat smells. A cherished childhood illusion was gone. I flipped the patty into the sink, where it immediately began leaking rivulets of red dye.

As alarming as the Gaines-burgers were, their soy meal began to seem like an old friend when the time came to try some *canned* dog foods. I decided to try the Cycle foods first. When I opened them, I thought about how rarely I use can openers these days, and I was suddenly visited by a long-forgotten sensation of can-opener distaste. *This* is the kind of unsavory place can openers spend their time when you're not watching! Every time you open a can of, say, Italian plum tomatoes, you infect them with invisible particles of by-product.

I had been expecting to see the usual homogeneous scrapple inside, but each can of Cycle was packed with smooth, round, oily nuggets. As if someone at Gaines had been tipped off that a human would be tasting the stuff, the four Cycles really were different from one another. Cycle-1, for puppies, is wet and soyish. Cycle-2, for adults, glistens nastily with fat, but it's passably edible—a lot like some canned Swedish meatballs I once got in a care package at college. Cycle-3, the "lite" one, for fatties, had no specific flavor; it just tasted like dog food. But at least it didn't make me fat.

Cycle-4, for senior dogs, had the smallest nuggets. Maybe old dogs can't open their mouths as wide. This kind was far sweeter than the other three Cycles—almost like baked beans. It was also the only one to contain "dried beef digest," a mysterious substance that the Purina spokesman defined as "enzymes" and my dictionary defined as "the products of digestion."

Next on the menu was a can of Kal-Kan Pedigree with Chunky Chicken. Chunky chicken? There were chunks in the can, certainly—big, purplish-brown chunks. I forked one chunk out (by now I was becoming more callous) and found that while it had no discernible chicken flavor, it wasn't bad except for its texture—like meat loaf with ground-up chicken bones.

In the world of canned dog food, a smooth consistency is a sign of low quality—lots of cereal. A lumpy, frightening, bloody, stringy horror is a sign of high quality—lots of meat. Nowhere in the world of wet dog foods was this demonstrated better than in the fanciest I tried—Kal Kan's Pedigree Select Dinners. These came not in a can but in a tiny foil packet with a picture of an imperious Yorkie. When I pulled open the container, juice spurted all over my hand, and the first chunk I speared was trailing a long gray vein. I shrieked and went instead for a plain chunk, which I was able to swallow only after taking a break to read some suddenly fascinating office equipment catalogs. Once again, though, it tasted no more alarming than, say, canned hash.

Still, how pleasant it was to turn to *dry* dog food! Gravy Train was the first I tried, and I'm happy to report that it really does make a "thick, rich, real beef gravy" when you mix it with water. Thick and rich, anyway. Except for a lingering rancid-fat flavor, the gravy wasn't beefy, but since it tasted primarily like tap water, it wasn't nauseating either.

My poor dachshund just gets plain old Purina Dog Chow, but Purina also makes a dry food called Butcher's Blend that comes in Beef, Bacon & Chicken flavor. Here we see dog food's arcane semiotics at its best: a red triangle with a *T* stamped into it is supposed to suggest beef; a tan curl, chicken; and a brown *S*, a piece of bacon. Only dogs understand these messages. But Butcher's Blend does have an endearing slogan: "Great Meaty Tastes—without bothering the Butcher!" *You know, I wanted to buy some meat, but I just couldn't bring myself to bother the butcher....*

Purina O.N.E. ("Optimum Nutritional Effectiveness") is targeted at people who are unlikely ever to worry about bothering a tradesperson. "We chose chicken as a primary ingredient in Purina O.N.E. for several reasonings," the long, long essay on the back of the bag announces. Chief among these reasonings, I'd guess, is the fact that chicken appeals to people who are—you know—*like us*. Although our dogs do nothing but spend 18-hour days alone in the apartment, we still want them to be *premium* dogs. We want them to cut down on red meat, too. We also want dog food that comes in a bag with an attractive design, a subtle type-face and no kitschy pictures of slobbering golden retrievers.

Besides that, we want a list of the Nutritional Benefits of our dog food—and we get it on O.N.E. One thing I especially like about this list is its constant references to a dog's "hair coat," as in "Beef tallow is good for the dog's skin and hair coat." (On the other hand, beef tallow merely provides palatability, while the dried beef digest in Cycle provides palatability *enhancement*.)

I hate to say it, but O.N.E. was pretty palatable. Maybe that's because it has about 100 percent more fat than, say, Butcher's Blend. Or maybe I'd been duped by the packaging; that's been known to happen before.

As with people food, dog snacks taste much better than dog meals. They're better-looking too. Take Milk-Bone Flavor Snacks. The loving-hands-at-home prose describing each flavor is colorful; the writers practically choke on their own exuberance. Of bacon they say, "It's so good, your dog will think it's hot off the frying pan." Of liver: "The only taste your dog wants more than liver—is even more liver!" Of poultry: "All those farm fresh flavors deliciously mixed in one biscuit. Your dog will bark with delight!" And of vegetable: "Gardens of taste! Specially blended to give your dog that vegetable flavor he wants—but can rarely get!"

Well, I may be a sucker, but advertising *this* emphatic just doesn't convince me. I lined up all seven flavors of Milk-Bone Flavor Snacks on the floor. Unless my dog's palate is a lot more sensitive than mine—and considering that she steals dirty diapers out of the trash and eats them, I'm loath to think it is—she doesn't detect any more difference in the seven flavors than I did when I tried them.

I much preferred Bonz, the hard-baked, bone-shaped snack stuffed with simulated marrow. I liked the bone part, that is: it tasted almost exactly like the cornmeal it was made of. The mock-marrow inside was a bit more problematic: in addition to looking like the sludge that collects in the treads of my running shoes, it was bursting with tiny hairs.

I'm sure you have a few dog food questions of your own. To save us time, I've answered them in advance.

Q. *Are those little cans of Mighty Dog actually branded with the sizzling word BEEF, the way they show in the commercials?*
A. You should know by now that that kind of thing never happens.
Q. *Does chicken-flavored dog food taste like chicken-flavored cat food?*
A. To my surprise, chicken cat food was actually a little better—more chickeny. It tasted like inferior canned pâté.

Q. Was there any dog food that you just couldn't bring yourself to try?
A. Alas, it was a can of Mighty Dog called Prime Entree with Bone Marrow. The meat was dark, dark brown, and it was surrounded by gelatin that was almost black. I knew I would die if I tasted it, so I put it outside for the raccoons.

—1989

Learning from Other Writers (Hodgman)

1. What is the role of humor in this essay? How does the humor shape the author's analysis?

2. How does Hodgman characterize herself? Why is this important to the essay's success?

3. Does Hodgman honestly expect the dog food to live up to the marketing claims? If not, why does she undertake this experiment? Could she have written the essay *without* eating dog food?

4. Describing how something tastes and smells is difficult, in part because translating sensory experiences into words is difficult, in part because finding new ways to describe familiar tastes and smells is hard. Look closely at Hodgman's description of each product in terms of its appearance, taste, smell, and texture (and sound, if any of the foods make a sound). Do her descriptions strike you as effective? If so, what does she do to achieve this result?

5. How do the ideas in Hodgman's essay relate to those in Gladwell's "Big and Bad" or Talbot's "Little Hotties"? What sort of experiment could be devised to examine the choice of cars we drive or the appeal of certain toys to parents and children?

Philip Weiss

HOW TO GET OUT OF A LOCKED TRUNK

On a hot Sunday last summer my friend Tony and I drove my rental car, a '91 Buick, from St. Paul to the small town of Waconia, Minnesota, forty miles southwest. We each had a project. Waconia is Tony's boyhood home, and his sister had recently given him a panoramic postcard of Lake Waconia as seen from a high point in the town early in the century. He wanted to duplicate the photograph's vantage point, then hang the two pictures together in his house in Frogtown. I was hoping to see Tony's father, Emmett, a retired mechanic, in order to settle a question that had been nagging me: Is it possible to get out of a locked car trunk?

We tried to call ahead to Emmett twice, but he wasn't home. Tony thought he was probably golfing but that there was a good chance he'd be back by the time we got there. So we set out.

I parked the Buick, which was a silver sedan with a red interior, by the graveyard near where Tony thought the picture had been taken. He took his picture and I wandered among the headstones, reading the epitaphs. One of them was chillingly anti-individualist. It said, "Not to do my will, but thine."

Trunk lockings had been on my mind for a few weeks. It seemed to me that the fear of being locked in a car trunk had a particular hold on the American imagination. Trunk lockings occur in many movies and books—from *Goodfellas* to *Thelma and Louise* to *Humboldt's Gift*. And while the highbrow national newspapers generally shy away from trunk lockings, the attention they receive in local papers suggests a widespread anxiety surrounding the subject. In an afternoon at the New York Public Library I found numerous stories about trunk lockings. A Los Angeles man is discovered, bloodshot, banging the trunk of his white Eldorado following a night and a day trapped inside; he says his captors went on joyrides and picked up women. A forty-eight-year-old Houston doctor is forced into her trunk at a bank ATM and then the car is abandoned, parked near the Astrodome. A New Orleans woman tells police she gave birth in a trunk while being abducted to Texas. Tests undermine her story, the police drop the investigation. But so what if it's a fantasy? That only shows the idea's hold on us.

Every culture comes up with tests of a person's ability to get out of a sticky situation. The English plant mazes. Tropical resorts market those straw finger-grabbers that tighten their grip the harder you pull on them, and Viennese intellectuals gave us the concept of childhood sexuality—figure it out, or remain neurotic for life.

At least you could puzzle your way out of those predicaments. When they slam the trunk, though, you're helpless unless someone finds you. You would think that such a common worry should have a ready fix, and that the secret of getting out of a locked trunk is something we should all know about.

I phoned experts but they were very discouraging.

"You cannot get out. If you got a pair of pliers and bat's eyes, yes. But you have to have a lot of knowledge of the lock," said James Foote at Automotive Locksmiths in New York City.

Jim Frens, whom I reached at the technical section of *Car and Driver* in Detroit, told me the magazine had not dealt with this question. But he echoed the opinion of experts elsewhere when he said that the best hope for escape would be to try and kick out the panel between the trunk and the backseat. That angle didn't seem worth pursuing. What if your enemies were in the car, crumpling beer cans and laughing at your fate? It didn't make sense to join them.

The people who deal with rules on auto design were uncomfortable with my scenarios. Debra Barclay of the Center for Auto Safety, an organization founded by Ralph Nader, had certainly heard of cases, but she was not aware of any regulations on the matter. "Now, if there was a defect involved —" she said, her voice trailing off, implying that trunk locking was all phobia. This must be one of the few issues on which she and the auto industry agree. Ann Carlson of the Motor Vehicle Manufacturing Association became alarmed at the thought that I was going to play up a nonproblem: "In reality this very rarely happens. As you say, in the movies it's a wonderful plot device," she said. "But in reality apparently this is not that frequent an occurrence. So they have not designed that feature into vehicles in a specific way."

When we got to Emmett's one-story house it was full of people. Tony's sister. Carol, was on the floor with her two small children. Her husband, Charlie, had one eye on the golf tournament on TV, and Emmett was at the kitchen counter, trimming fat from meat for lunch. I have known Emmett for fifteen years. He looked better than ever. In his retirement he had sharply changed his diet and lost a lot of weight. He had on shorts. His legs were tanned and muscular. As always, his manner was humorous, if opaque.

Tony told his family my news: I was getting married in three weeks. Charlie wanted to know where my fiancée was. Back East, getting everything ready. A big-time hatter was fitting her for a new hat.

Emmett sat on the couch, watching me. "Do you want my advice?"

"Sure."

He just grinned. A gold tooth glinted. Carol and Charlie pressed him to yield his wisdom.

Finally he said, "Once you get to be thirty, you make your own mistakes."

He got out several cans of beer, and then I brought up what was on my mind. Emmett nodded and took off his glasses, then cleaned them and put them back on.

We went out to his car, a Mercury Grand Marquis, and Emmett opened the trunk. His golf clubs were sitting on top of the spare tire in a green golf bag. Next to them was a toolbox and what he called his "burglar tools," a set of elbowed rods with red plastic handles he used to open door locks when people locked their keys inside.

Tony and Charlie stood watching. Charlie is a banker in Minneapolis. He enjoys gizmos and is extremely practical. I would describe his as unflappable. That's a word I always wanted to apply to myself, but my fiancée had recently informed me that I am high-strung. Though that surprised me, I didn't quarrel with her.

For a while we studied the latch assembly. The lock closed in much the same way that a lobster might clamp on to a pencil. The claw portion, the jaws of the lock, was mounted inside the trunk lid. When you shut the lid, the jaws locked on to the bend of a U-shaped piece of metal mounted on the body of the car. Emmett said my best bet would be to unscrew the bolts. That way the U-shaped piece would come loose and the lock's jaws would swing up with it still in their grasp.

"But you'd need a wrench," he said.

It was already getting too technical. Emmett had an air of endless patience, but I felt defeated. I could only imagine bloodied fingers, cracked teeth. I had hoped for a simple trick.

Charlie stepped forward. He reached out and squeezed the lock's jaws. They clicked shut in the air, bound together by heavy springs. Charlie now prodded the upper part of the left-hand jaw, the thicker part. With a rough flick of his thumb, he was able to force the jaws to snap open. Great.

Unfortunately, the jaws were mounted behind a steel plate the size of your palm in such a way that while they were accessible to us, standing outside the car, had we been inside the trunk the plate would be in our way, blocking the jaws.

This time Emmett saw the way out. He fingered a hole in the plate. It was no bigger than the tip of your little finger. But the hole was close enough to the latch itself that it might be possible to angle something through the hole from inside the trunk and nudge the jaws apart. We tried with one of my keys. The lock jumped open.

It was time for a full-dress test. Emmett swung the clubs out of the trunk, and I set my can of Schmidt's on the rear bumper and climbed in. Everyone gathered around, and Emmett lowered the trunk on me, then pressed it shut with his meaty hands. Total darkness. I couldn't hear the people outside. I thought I was going to panic. But the big trunk felt comfortable. I was pressed against a sort of black carpet that softened the angles against my back.

I could almost stretch out in the trunk, and it seemed to me I could make them sweat if I took my time. Even Emmett, that sphinx, would give way to curiosity. Once I was out he'd ask how it had been and I'd just grin. There were some things you could only learn by doing.

It took a while to find the hole. I slipped the key in and angled it to one side. The trunk gasped open.

Emmett motioned the others away, then levered me out with his big right forearm. Though I'd only been inside for a minute, I was disoriented—as much as anything because someone had moved my beer while I was gone, setting it down on the cement floor of the garage. It was just a little thing, but I could not be entirely sure I had gotten my own beer back.

Charlie was now raring to try other cars. We examined the latch on his Toyota, which was entirely shielded to the trunk occupant (i.e., no hole in the plate), and on the neighbor's Honda (ditto). But a 1991 Dodge Dynasty was doable. The trunk was tight, but its lock had a feature one of the mechanics I'd phoned described as a "tailpiece": a finger-like extension of the lock mechanism itself that stuck out a half inch into the trunk cavity: simply by twisting the tailpiece I could free the lock. I was even faster on a 1984 Subaru that had a little lever device on the latch.

We went out to my rental on Oak Street. The Skylark was in direct sun and the trunk was hot to the touch, but when we got it open we could see that its latch plate had a perfect hole, a square in which the edge of the lock's jaw appeared like a face in a window.

The trunk was shallow and hot. Emmett had to push my knees down before he could close the lid. This one was a little suffocating. I imagined being trapped for hours, and even before he had got it closed I regretted the decision with a slightly nauseous feeling. I thought of Edgar Allan Poe's live burials, and then about something my fiancée had said more than a year and a half before. I had been on her case to get married. She was divorced, and at every opportunity I would reissue my proposal—even during a commercial. She'd interrupted one of these chirps to tell me, in a cold, throaty voice, that she had no intention of ever going through another divorce: "This time, it's death out." I'd carried those words around like a lump of wet clay.

As it happened, the Skylark trunk was the easiest of all. The hole was right where it was supposed to be. The trunk popped open, and I felt great satisfaction that we'd been able to figure out a rule that seemed to apply about 60 percent of the time. If we publicized our success, it might get the attention it deserved. All trunks would be fitted with such a hole. Kids would learn about it in school. The grip of the fear would relax. Before long a successful trunk-locking scene would date a movie like a fedora dates one today.

When I got back East I was caught up in wedding preparations. I live in New York, and the wedding was to take place in Philadelphia. We set up camp there with five days to go. A friend had lent my fiancée her BMW, and we drove it south with all our things. I unloaded the car in my parents' driveway. The last thing I pulled out of the trunk was my fiancée's hat in its heavy cardboard shipping box. She'd warned me I was not allowed to look. The lid was free but I didn't open it. I was willing to be surprised.

When the trunk was empty it occurred to me I might hop in and give it a try. First I looked over the mechanism. The jaws of the BMW's lock were shielded, but there seemed to be some kind of cable coming off it that you might be able to manipulate so as to cause the lock to open. The same cable that allowed the driver to open the trunk remotely...

I fingered it for a moment or two but decided I didn't need to test out the theory.

—1992

Learning from Other Writers (Weiss)

1. Weiss states his driving question at the end of the first paragraph of the essay. What is the purpose of each of the eight paragraphs that follow the first? How is the remainder of the essay structured?

2. Given that most of us aren't obsessed with how to get out of a locked trunk, why should we care about Weiss's fears?

3. Why doesn't the author feel the need to test his ability to get out of the trunk of his fiancée's BMW?

4. How serious is the author's claim that the real reason for his fears about getting out of a locked trunk stem from his apprehension about his upcoming marriage? Is he in any way making fun of the popular conception of Freudian psychology, in which a phobia will be cured if only the sufferer figures out the secret reason for his fear? If the essay's tone is at least partially tongue-in-cheek, does that tone invalidate the author's discoveries about his fears? About most people's fears? About locked trunks?

Barbara Ehrenreich

NICKEL-AND-DIMED: ON (NOT) GETTING BY IN AMERICA

At the beginning of June 1998 I leave behind everything that normally soothes the ego and sustains the body—home, career, companion, reputation, ATM card—for a plunge into the low-wage workforce. There, I become another, occupationally much diminished "Barbara Ehrenreich"—depicted on job-application forms as a divorced homemaker whose sole work experience consists of housekeeping in a few private homes. I am terrified, at the beginning, of being unmasked for what I am: a middle-class journalist setting out to explore the world that welfare mothers are entering, at the rate of approximately 50,000 a month, as welfare reform kicks in. Happily, though, my fears turn out to be entirely unwarranted: during a month of poverty and toil, my name goes unnoticed and for the most part unuttered. In this parallel universe where my father never got out of the mines and I never got through college, I am "baby," "honey," "blondie," and, most commonly, "girl."

My first task is to find a place to live. I figure that if I can earn $7 an hour—which, from the want ads, seems doable—I can afford to spend $500 on rent, or maybe, with severe economies, $600. In the Key West area, where I live, this pretty much confines me to flophouses and trailer homes—like the one, a pleasing fifteen-minute drive from town, that has no air-conditioning, no screens, no fans, no television, and, by way of diversion, only the challenge of evading the landlord's Doberman pinscher. The big problem with this place, though, is the rent, which at $675 a month is well beyond my reach. All right, Key West is expensive. But so is New York City, or the Bay Area, or Jackson Hole, or Telluride, or Boston, or any other place where tourists and the wealthy compete for living space with the people who clean their toilets and fry their hash browns.[1] Still, it is a shock to realize that "trailer trash" has become, for me, a demographic category to aspire to.

So I decide to make the common trade-off between affordability and convenience, and go for a $500-a-month efficiency thirty miles up a two lane highway from the employment opportunities of Key West, meaning forty-five minutes if there's no road construction and I don't get caught behind some sun-dazed Canadian tourists. I hate the drive, along a roadside studded with white crosses commemorating the more effective head-on collisions, but it's a sweet little place—a cabin, more or less, set in the swampy back yard of the converted mobile home where my landlord, an affable TV repairman, lives with his bartender girlfriend. Anthropologically speaking, a bustling trailer park would be preferable, but here I have a gleaming white floor and a firm mattress, and the few resident bugs are easily vanquished.

---

[1] According to the Department of Housing and Urban Development, the "fair-market rent" for an efficiency is $551 here in Monroe County, Florida. A comparable rent in the five boroughs of New York City is $704; in San Francisco, $713; and in the heart of Silicon Valley, $808. The fair-market rent for an area is defined as the amount that would be needed to pay rent plus utilities for "privately owned, decent, safe, and sanitary rental housing of a modest (non-luxury) nature with suitable amenities."

Besides, I am not doing this for the anthropology. My aim is nothing so mistily subjective as to "experience poverty" or find out how it "really feels" to be a long-term low-wage worker. I've had enough unchosen encounters with poverty and the world of low-wage work to know it's not a place you want to visit for touristic purposes; it just smells too much like fear. And with all my real-life assets—bank account, IRA, health insurance, multiroom home—waiting indulgently in the background, I am, of course, thoroughly insulated from the terrors that afflict the genuinely poor.

No, this is a purely objective, scientific sort of mission. The humanitarian rationale for welfare reform—as opposed to the more punitive and stingy impulses that may actually have motivated it—is that work will lift poor women out of poverty while simultaneously inflating their self-esteem and hence their future value in the labor market. Thus, whatever the hassles involved in finding child care, transportation, etc., the transition from welfare to work will end happily, in greater prosperity for all. Now there are many problems with this comforting prediction, such as the fact that the economy will inevitably undergo a downturn, eliminating many jobs. Even without a downturn, the influx of a million former welfare recipients into the low-wage labor market could depress wages by as much as 11.9 percent, according to the Economic Policy Institute (EPI) in Washington, D.C.

But is it really possible to make a living on the kinds of jobs currently available to unskilled people? Mathematically, the answer is no, as can be shown by taking $6 to $7 an hour, perhaps subtracting a dollar or two an hour for child care, multiplying by 160 hours a month, and comparing the result to the prevailing rents. According to the National Coalition for the Homeless, for example, in 1998 it took, on average nation-wide, an hourly wage of $8.89 to afford a onebedroom apartment, and the Preamble Center for Public Policy estimates that the odds against a typical welfare recipient's landing a job at such a "living wage" are about 97 to 1. If these numbers are right, low-wage work is not a solution to poverty and possibly not even to homelessness.

It may seem excessive to put this proposition to an experimental test. As certain family members keep unhelpfully reminding me, the viability of low-wage work could be tested, after a fashion, without ever leaving my study. I could just pay myself $7 an hour for eight hours a day, charge myself for room and board, and total up the num-bers after a month. Why leave the people and work that I love? But I am an experimen-tal scientist by training. In that business, you don't just sit at a desk and theorize; you plunge into the everyday chaos of nature, where surprises lurk in the most mundane measurements. Maybe, when I got into it, I would discover some hidden economies in the world of the low-wage worker. After all, if 30 percent of the workforce toils for less than $8 an hour, according to the EPI, they may have found some tricks as yet unknown to me. Maybe—who knows?—I would even be able to detect in myself the bracing psychological effects of getting out of the house, as promised by the welfare wonks at places like the Heritage Foundation. Or, on the other hand, maybe there would be unexpected costs—physical, mental, or financial—to throw off all my calcu-lations. Ideally, I should do this with two small children in tow, that being the welfare average, but mine are grown and no one is willing to lend me theirs for a month-long vacation in penury. So this is not the perfect experiment, just a test of the best possible case: an unencumbered woman, smart and even strong, attempting to live more or less off the land.

On the morning of my first full day of job searching, I take a red pen to the want ads, which are auspiciously numerous. Everyone in Key West's booming "hospitality industry" seems to be looking for someone like me—trainable, flexible, and with suitably humble expectations as to pay. I know I possess certain traits that might be advantageous—I'm white and, I like to think, well-spoken and poised—but I decide on two rules: One, I cannot use any skills derived from my education or usual work—not that there are a lot of want ads for satirical essayists anyway. Two, I have to take the best-paid job that is offered me and of course do my best to hold it, no Marxist rants or sneaking off to read novels in the ladies' room. In addition, I rule out various occupations for one reason or another: Hotel front-desk clerk, for example, which to my surprise is regarded as unskilled and pays around $7 an hour, gets eliminated because it involves standing in one spot for eight hours a day. Waitressing is similarly something I'd like to avoid, because I remember it leaving me bone tired when I was eighteen, and I'm decades of varicosities and back pain beyond that now. Telemarketing, one of the first refuges of the suddenly indigent, can be dismissed on grounds of personality. This leaves certain supermarket jobs, such as deli clerk, or housekeeping in Key West's thousands of hotel and guest rooms. Housekeeping is especially appealing, for reasons both atavistic and practical: it's what my mother did before I came along, and it can't be too different from what I've been doing part-time, in my own home, all my life.

So I put on what I take to be a respectful-looking outfit of ironed Bermuda shorts and scooped-neck T-shirt and set out for a tour of the local hotels and supermarkets. Best Western, Econo Lodge, and Hojo's all let me fill out application forms, and these are, to my relief, interested in little more than whether I am a legal resident of the United States and have committed any felonies. My next stop is Winn-Dixie, the supermarket, which turns out to have a particularly onerous application process, featuring a fifteen-minute "interview" by computer since, apparently, no human on the premises is deemed capable of representing the corporate point of view. I am conducted to a large room decorated with posters illustrating how to look "professional" (it helps to be white and, if female, permed) and warning of the slick promises that union organizers might try to tempt me with. The interview is multiple choice: Do I have anything, such as child-care problems, that might make it hard for me to get to work on time? Do I think safety on the job is the responsibility of management? Then, popping up cunningly out of the blue: How many dollars' worth of stolen goods have I purchased in the last year? Would I turn in a fellow employee if I caught him stealing? Finally, "Are you an honest person?"

Apparently, I ace the interview, because I am told that all I have to do is show up in some doctor's office tomorrow for a urine test. This seems to be a fairly general rule: if you want to stack Cheerio boxes or vacuum hotel rooms in chemically fascist America, you have to be willing to squat down and pee in front of some health worker (who has no doubt had to do the same thing herself). The wages Winn-Dixie is offering—$6 and a couple of dimes to start with—are not enough, I decide, to compensate for this indignity.[2]

I lunch at Wendy's, where $4.99 gets you unlimited refills at the Mexican part of the Superbar, a comforting surfeit of refried beans and "cheese sauce." A teenage employee, seeing me studying the want ads, kindly offers me an application form, which I fill out, though here, too, the pay is just $6 and change an hour. Then it's off for a round of the locally owned inns and guesthouses. At "The Palms," let's call it, a bouncy manager actually takes me around to see the rooms and meet the existing housekeepers, who, I note with satisfaction, look pretty much like me—faded ex-hippie types in shorts with long hair pulled back in braids. Mostly, though, no one speaks to me or even looks at me except to proffer an application form. At my last stop, a palatial B&B, I wait twenty minutes to meet "Max," only to be told that there are no jobs now but there should be one soon, since "nobody lasts more than a couple weeks." (Because none of the people I talked to knew I was a reporter, I have changed their names to protect their privacy and, in some cases perhaps, their jobs.)

Three days go by like this, and, to my chagrin, no one out of the approximately twenty places I've applied calls me for an interview. I had been vain enough to worry about coming across as too educated for the jobs I sought, but no one even seems interested in finding out how overqualified I am. Only later will I realize that the want ads are not a reliable measure of the actual jobs available at any particular time. They are, as I should have guessed from Max's comment, the employers' insurance policy against the relentless turnover of the low-wage workforce. Most of the big hotels run ads almost continually, just to build a supply of applicants to replace the current workers as they drift away or are fired, so finding a job is just a matter of being at the right place at the right time and flexible enough to take whatever is being offered that day. This finally happens to me at a one of the big discount hotel chains, where I go, as usual, for housekeeping and am sent, instead, to try out as a waitress at the attached "family restaurant," a dismal spot with a counter and about thirty tables that looks out on a parking garage and features such tempting fare as "Pollish [sic] sausage and BBQ sauce" on 95-degree days. Phillip, the dapper young West Indian who introduces himself as the manager, interviews me with about as much enthusiasm as if he were a clerk processing me for Medicare, the principal questions being what shifts can I work and when can I start. I mutter something about being woefully out of practice as

---

[2] According to the Monthly Labor Review (November 1996), 28 percent of work sites surveyed in the service industry conduct drug tests (corporate workplaces have much higher rates), and the incidence of testing has risen markedly since the Eighties. The rate of testing is highest in the South (56 percent of work sites polled), with the Midwest in second place (50 percent). The drug most likely to be detected—marijuana, which can be detected in urine for weeks—is also the most innocuous, while heroin and cocaine are generally undetectable three days after use. Prospective employees sometimes try to cheat the tests by consuming excessive amounts of liquids and taking diuretics and even masking substances available through the Internet.

a waitress, but he's already on to the uniform: I'm to show up tomorrow wearing black slacks and black shoes; he'll provide the rust-colored polo shirt with HEARTHSIDE embroidered on it, though I might want to wear my own shirt to get to work, ha ha. At the word "tomorrow," something between fear and indignation rises in my chest. I want to say, "Thank you for your time, sir, but this is just an experiment, you know, not my actual life."

So begins my career at the Hearthside, I shall call it, one small profit center within a global discount hotel chain, where for two weeks I work from 2:00 till 10:00 P.M. for $2.43 an hour plus tips.[3] In some futile bid for gentility, the management has barred employees from using the front door, so my first day I enter through the kitchen, where a red-faced man with shoulder-length blond hair is throwing frozen steaks against the wall and yelling, "Fuck this shit!" "That's just Jack," explains Gail, the wiry middle-aged waitress who is assigned to train me. "He's on the rag again"—a condition occasioned, in this instance, by the fact that the cook on the morning shift had forgotten to thaw out the steaks. For the next eight hours, I run after the agile Gail, absorbing bits of instruction along with fragments of personal tragedy. All food must be trayed, and the reason she's so tired today is that she woke up in a cold sweat thinking of her boyfriend, who killed himself recently in an upstate prison. No refills on lemonade. And the reason he was in prison is that a few DUIs caught up with him, that's all, could have happened to anyone. Carry the creamers to the table in a monkey bowl, never in your hand. And after he was gone she spent several months living in her truck, peeing in a plastic pee bottle and reading by candlelight at night, but you can't live in a truck in the summer, since you need to have the windows down, which means anything can get in, from mosquitoes on up.

At least Gail puts to rest any fears I had of appearing overqualified. From the first day on, I find that of all the things I have left behind, such as home and identity, what I miss the most is competence. Not that I have ever felt utterly competent in the writing business, in which one day's success augurs nothing at all for the next. But in my writing life, I at least have some notion of procedure: do the research, make the outline, rough out a draft, etc. As a server, though, I am beset by requests like bees: more iced tea here, ketchup over there, a to-go box for table fourteen, and where are the high chairs, anyway? Of the twenty-seven tables, up to six are usually mine at any time, though on slow afternoons or if Gail is off, I sometimes have the whole place to myself. There is the touch-screen computer-ordering system to master, which is, I suppose, meant to minimize server-cook contact, but in practice requires constant verbal fine-tuning: "That's gravy on the mashed, okay? None on the meatloaf," and so forth—while

---

[3] According to the Fair Labor Standards Act, employers are not required to pay "tipped employees," such as restaurant servers, more than $2.13 an hour in direct wages. However, if the sum of tips plus $2.13 an hour falls below the minimum wage, or $5.15 an hour, the employer is required to make up the difference. This fact was not mentioned by managers or otherwise publicized at either of the restaurants where I worked.

the cook scowls as if I were inventing these refinements just to torment him. Plus, something I had forgotten in the years since I was eighteen: about a third of a server's job is "side work" that's invisible to customers—sweeping, scrubbing, slicing, refilling, and restocking. If it isn't all done, every little bit of it, you're going to face the 6:00 P.M. dinner rush defenseless and probably go down in flames. I screw up dozens of times at the beginning, sustained in my shame entirely by Gail's support—"It's okay, baby, everyone does that sometime"—because, to my total surprise and despite the scientific detachment I am doing my best to maintain, I care.

The whole thing would be a lot easier if I could just skate through it as Lily Tomlin in one of her waitress skits, but I was raised by the absurd Booker T. Washingtonian precept that says: If you're going to do something, do it well. In fact, "well" isn't good enough by half. Do it better than anyone has ever done it before. Or so said my father, who must have known what he was talking about because he managed to pull himself, and us with him, up from the mile-deep copper mines of Butte to the leafy suburbs of the Northeast, ascending from boilermakers to martinis before booze beat out ambition. As in most endeavors I have encountered in my life, doing it "better than anyone" is not a reasonable goal. Still, when I wake up at 4:00 A.M. in my own cold sweat, I am not thinking about the writing deadlines I'm neglecting; I'm thinking about the table whose order I screwed up so that one of the boys didn't get his kiddie meal until the rest of the family had moved on to their Key Lime pies. That's the other powerful motivation I hadn't expected—the customers, or "patients," as I can't help thinking of them on account of the mysterious vulnerability that seems to have left them temporarily unable to feed themselves. After a few days at the Hearthside, I feel the service ethic kick in like a shot of oxytocin, the nurturance hormone. The plurality of my customers are hardworking locals—truck drivers, construction workers, even housekeepers from the attached hotel—and I want them to have the closest to a "fine dining" experience that the grubby circumstances will allow. No "you guys" for me; everyone over twelve is "sir" or "ma'am." I ply them with iced tea and coffee refills; I return, mid-meal, to inquire how everything is; I doll up their salads with chopped raw mushrooms, summer squash slices, or whatever bits of produce I can find that have survived their sojourn in the cold-storage room mold-free.

There is Benny, for example, a short, tight-muscled sewer repairman, who cannot even think of eating until he has absorbed a half hour of air-conditioning and ice water. We chat about hyperthermia and electrolytes until he is ready to order some finicky combination like soup of the day, garden salad, and a side of grits. There are the German tourists who are so touched by my pidgin "Willkommen" and "Ist alles gut?" that they actually tip. (Europeans, spoiled by their trade-union-ridden, high-wage welfare states, generally do not know that they are supposed to tip. Some restaurants, the Hearthside included, allow servers to "grat" their foreign customers, or add a tip to the bill. Since this amount is added before the customers have a chance to tip or not tip, the practice amounts to an automatic penalty for imperfect English.) There are the two dirt-smudged lesbians, just off their construction shift, who are impressed enough by my suave handling of the fly in the piña colada that they take the time to praise me to

Stu, the assistant manager. There's Sam, the kindly retired cop, who has to plug up his tracheotomy hole with one finger in order to force the cigarette smoke into his lungs.

Sometimes I play with the fantasy that I am a princess who, in penance for some tiny transgression, has undertaken to feed each of her subjects by hand. But the non-princesses working with me are just as indulgent, even when this means flouting management rules—concerning, for example, the number of croutons that can go on a salad (six). "Put on all you want," Gail whispers, "as long as Stu isn't looking." She dips into her own tip money to buy biscuits and gravy for an out-of-work mechanic who's used up all his money on dental surgery, inspiring me to pick up the tab for his milk and pie. Maybe the same high levels of agape can be found throughout the "hospitality industry." I remember the poster decorating one of the apartments I looked at, which said "If you seek happiness for yourself you will never find it. Only when you seek happiness for others will it come to you," or words to that effect—an odd sentiment, it seemed to me at the time, to find in the dank one-room basement apartment of a bellhop at the Best Western. At the Hearthside, we utilize whatever bits of autonomy we have to ply our customers with the illicit calories that signal our love. It is our job as servers to assemble the salads and desserts, pouring the dressings and squirting the whipped cream. We also control the number of butter patties our customers get and the amount of sour cream on their baked potatoes. So if you wonder why Americans are so obese, consider the fact that waitresses both express their humanity and earn their tips through the covert distribution of fats.

Ten days into it, this is beginning to look like a livable lifestyle. I like Gail, who is "looking at fifty" but moves so fast she can alight in one place and then another without apparently being anywhere between them. I clown around with Lionel, the teenage Haitian busboy, and catch a few fragments of conversation with Joan, the svelte fortyish hostess and militant feminist who is the only one of us who dares to tell Jack to shut the fuck up. I even warm up to Jack when, on a slow night and to make up for a particularly unwarranted attack on my abilities, or so I imagine, he tells me about his glory days as a young man at "coronary school"—or do you say "culinary"?—in Brooklyn, where he dated a knock-out Puerto Rican chick and learned everything there is to know about food. I finish up at 10:00 or 10:30, depending on how much side work I've been able to get done during the shift, and cruise home to the tapes I snatched up at random when I left my real home—Marianne Faithfull, Tracy Chapman, Enigma, King Sunny Ade, the Violent Femmes—just drained enough for the music to set my cranium resonating but hardly dead. Midnight snack is Wheat Thins and Monterey Jack, accompanied by cheap white wine on ice and whatever AMC has to offer. To bed by 1:30 or 2:00, up at 9:00 or 10:00, read for an hour while my uniform whirls around in the landlord's washing machine, and then it's another eight hours spent following Mao's central instruction, as laid out in the Little Red Book, which was: Serve the people.

I could drift along like this, in some dreamy proletarian idyll, except for two things. One is management. If I have kept this subject on the margins thus far it is because I still flinch to think that I spent all those weeks under the surveillance of men (and later women) whose job it was to monitor my behavior for signs of sloth, theft, drug abuse, or worse. Not that managers and especially "assistant managers" in low-wage settings like this are exactly the class enemy. In the restaurant business, they are mostly former cooks or servers, still capable of pinch-hitting in the kitchen or on the floor, just as in hotels they are likely to be former clerks, and paid a salary of only about $400 a week. But everyone knows they have crossed over to the other side, which is, crudely put, corporate as opposed to human. Cooks want to prepare tasty meals; servers want to serve them graciously; but managers are there for only one reason—to make sure that money is made for some theoretical entity that exists far away in Chicago or New York, if a corporation can be said to have a physical existence at all. Reflecting on her career, Gail tells me ruefully that she had sworn, years ago, never to work for a corporation again. "They don't cut you no slack. You give and you give, and they take."

Managers can sit—for hours at a time if they want—but it's their job to see that no one else ever does, even when there's nothing to do, and this is why, for servers, slow times can be as exhausting as rushes. You start dragging out each little chore, because if the manager on duty catches you in an idle moment, he will give you something far nastier to do. So I wipe, I clean, I consolidate ketchup bottles and recheck the cheesecake supply, even tour the tables to make sure the customer evaluation forms are all standing perkily in their places—wondering all the time how many calories I burn in these strictly theatrical exercises. When, on a particularly dead afternoon, Stu finds me glancing at a *USA Today* a customer has left behind, he assigns me to vacuum the entire floor with the broken vacuum cleaner that has a handle only two feet long, and the only way to do that without incurring orthopedic damage is to proceed from spot to spot on your knees.

On my first Friday at the Hearthside there is a "mandatory meeting for all restaurant employees," which I attend, eager for insight into our overall marketing strategy and the niche (your basic Ohio cuisine with a tropical twist?) we aim to inhabit. But there is no "we" at this meeting. Phillip, our top manager except for an occasional "consultant" sent out by corporate headquarters, opens it with a sneer: "The break room—it's disgusting. Butts in the ashtrays, newspapers lying around, crumbs." This windowless little room, which also houses the time clock for the entire hotel, is where we stash our bags and civilian clothes and take our half-hour meal breaks. But a break room is not a right, he tells us. It can be taken away. We should also know that the lockers in the break room and whatever is in them can be searched at any time. Then comes gossip; there has been gossip; gossip (which seems to mean employees talking among themselves) must stop. Off-duty employees are henceforth barred from eating at the restaurant, because "other servers gather around them and gossip." When Phillip has exhausted his agenda of rebukes, Joan complains about the condition of the ladies' room and I throw in my two bits about the vacuum cleaner. But I don't see any backup coming from my fellow servers, each of whom has subsided into her own personal funk; Gail, my role model, stares sorrowfully at a point six inches from her nose. The meeting ends when Andy, one of the cooks, gets up, muttering about breaking up his day off for this almighty bullshit.

Just four days later we are suddenly summoned into the kitchen at 3:30 P.M., even though there are live tables on the floor. We all—about ten of us—stand around Phillip, who announces grimly that there has been a report of some "drug activity" on the night shift and that, as a result, we are now to be a "drug-free" workplace, meaning that all new hires will be tested, as will possibly current employees on a random basis. I am glad that this part of the kitchen is so dark, because I find myself blushing as hard as if I had been caught toking up in the ladies' room myself. I haven't been treated this way—lined up in the corridor, threatened with locker searches, peppered with carelessly aimed accusations—since junior high school. Back on the floor, Joan cracks, "Next they'll be telling us we can't have sex on the job." When I ask Stu what happened to inspire the crackdown, he just mutters about "management decisions" and takes the opportunity to upbraid Gail and me for being too generous with the rolls. From now on there's to be only one per customer, and it goes out with the dinner, not with the salad. He's also been riding the cooks, prompting Andy to come out of the kitchen and observe—with the serenity of a man whose customary implement is a butcher knife—that "Stu has a death wish today."

Later in the evening, the gossip crystallizes around the theory that Stu is himself the drug culprit, that he uses the restaurant phone to order up marijuana and sends one of the late servers out to fetch it for him. The server was caught, and she may have ratted Stu out or at least said enough to cast some suspicion on him, thus accounting for his pissy behavior. Who knows? Lionel, the busboy, entertains us for the rest of the shift by standing just behind Stu's back and sucking deliriously on an imaginary joint.

The other problem, in addition to the less-than-nurturing management style, is that this job shows no sign of being financially viable. You might imagine, from a comfortable distance, that people who live, year in and year out, on $6 to $10 an hour have discovered some survival stratagems unknown to the middle class. But no. It's not hard to get my co-workers to talk about their living situations, because housing, in almost every case, is the principal source of disruption in their lives, the first thing they fill you in on when they arrive for their shifts. After a week, I have compiled the following survey:

- Gail is sharing a room in a well-known downtown flophouse for which she and a roommate pay about $250 a week. Her roommate, a male friend, has begun hitting on her, driving her nuts, but the rent would be impossible alone.

- Claude, the Haitian cook, is desperate to get out of the two-room apartment he shares with his girlfriend and two other, unrelated, people. As far as I can determine, the other Haitian men (most of whom only speak Creole) live in similarly crowded situations.

- Annette, a twenty-year-old server who is six months pregnant and has been abandoned by her boyfriend, lives with her mother, a postal clerk.

- Marianne and her boyfriend are paying $170 a week for a one-person trailer.

- Jack, who is, at $10 an hour, the wealthiest of us, lives in the trailer he owns, paying only the $400-a-month lot fee.

- The other white cook, Andy, lives on his dry-docked boat, which, as far as I can tell from his loving descriptions, can't be more than twenty feet long. He offers to take me out on it, once it's repaired, but the offer comes with inquiries as to my marital status, so I do not follow up on it.

- Tina and her husband are paying $60 a night for a double room in a Days Inn. This is because they have no car and the Days Inn is within walking distance of the Hearthside.

- When Marianne, one of the breakfast servers, is tossed out of her trailer for subletting (which is against the trailer-park rules), she leaves her boyfriend and moves in with Tina and her husband.

- Joan, who had fooled me with her numerous and tasteful outfits (hostesses wear their own clothes), lives in a van she parks behind a shopping center at night and showers in Tina's motel room. The clothes are from thrift shops.[4]

It strikes me, in my middle-class solipsism, that there is gross improvidence in some of these arrangements. When Gail and I are wrapping silverware in napkins—the only task for which we are permitted to sit—she tells me she is thinking of escaping from her roommate by moving into the Days Inn herself. I am astounded: How can she even think of paying between $40 and $60 a day? But if I was afraid of sounding like a social worker, I come out just sounding like a fool. She squints at me in disbelief, "And where am I supposed to get a month's rent and a month's deposit for an apartment?" I'd been feeling pretty smug about my $500 efficiency, but of course it was made possible only by the $1,300 I had allotted myself for start-up costs when I began my low-wage life: $1,000 for the first month's rent and deposit, $100 for initial groceries and cash in my pocket, $200 stuffed away for emergencies. In poverty, as in certain propositions in physics, starting conditions are everything.

There are no secret economies that nourish the poor; on the contrary, there are a host of special costs. If you can't put up the two months' rent you need to secure an apartment, you end up paying through the nose for a room by the week. If you have only a room, with a hot plate at best, you can't save by cooking up huge lentil stews that can be frozen for the week ahead. You eat fast food, or the hot dogs and styrofoam cups of soup that can be microwaved in a convenience store. If you have no money for health insurance—and the Hearthside's niggardly plan kicks in only after three months—you go without routine care or prescription drugs and end up paying the price. Gail, for

---

[4] I could find no statistics on the number of employed people living in cars or vans, but according to the National Coalition for the Homeless's 1997 report "Myths and Facts About Homelessness," nearly one in five homeless people (in twenty-nine cities across the nation) is employed in a full- or part-time job.

example, was fine until she ran out of money for estrogen pills. She is supposed to be on the company plan by now, but they claim to have lost her application form and need to begin the paperwork all over again. So she spends $9 per migraine pill to control the headaches she wouldn't have, she insists, if her estrogen supplements were covered. Similarly, Marianne's boyfriend lost his job as a roofer because he missed so much time after getting a cut on his foot for which he couldn't afford the prescribed antibiotic.

My own situation, when I sit down to assess it after two weeks of work, would not be much better if this were my actual life. The seductive thing about waitressing is that you don't have to wait for payday to feel a few bills in your pocket, and my tips usually cover meals and gas, plus something left over to stuff into the kitchen drawer I use as a bank. But as the tourist business slows in the summer heat, I sometimes leave work with only $20 in tips (the gross is higher, but servers share about 15 percent of their tips with the busboys and bartenders). With wages included, this amounts to about the minimum wage of $5.15 an hour. Although the sum in the drawer is piling up, at the present rate of accumulation it will be more than a hundred dollars short of my rent when the end of the month comes around. Nor can I see any expenses to cut. True, I haven't gone the lentil-stew route yet, but that's because I don't have a large cooking pot, pot holders, or a ladle to stir with (which cost about $30 at Kmart, less at thrift stores), not to mention onions, carrots, and the indispensable bay leaf. I do make my lunch almost every day—usually some slow-burning, high-protein combo like frozen chicken patties with melted cheese on top and canned pinto beans on the side. Dinner is at the Hearthside, which offers its employees a choice of BLT, fish sandwich, or hamburger for only $2. The burger lasts longest, especially if it's heaped with gut-puckering jalapeños, but by midnight my stomach is growling again.

So unless I want to start using my car as a residence, I have to find a second, or alternative, job. I call all the hotels where I filled out housekeeping applications weeks ago—the Hyatt, Holiday Inn, Econo Lodge, HoJo's, Best Western, plus a half dozen or so locally run guesthouses. Nothing. Then I start making the rounds again, wasting whole mornings waiting for some assistant manager to show up, even dipping into places so creepy that the front-desk clerk greets you from behind bulletproof glass and sells pints of liquor over the counter. But either someone has exposed my real-life housekeeping habits—which are, shall we say, mellow—or I am at the wrong end of some infallible ethnic equation: most, but by no means all, of the working housekeepers I see on my job searches are African Americans, Spanish-speaking, or immigrants from the Central European post-Communist world, whereas servers are almost invariably white and monolingually English-speaking. When I finally get a positive response, I have been identified once again as server material. Jerry's, which is part of a well-known national family restaurant chain and physically attached here to another budget hotel chain, is ready to use me at once. The prospect is both exciting and terrifying, because, with about the same number of tables and counter seats, Jerry's attracts three or four times the volume of customers as the gloomy old Hearthside.

Picture a fat person's hell, and I don't mean a place with no food. Instead there is everything you might eat if eating had no bodily consequences—cheese fries, chicken-fried steaks, fudge-laden desserts—only here every bite must be paid for, one way or another, in human discomfort. The kitchen is a cavern, a stomach leading to the lower intestine that is the garbage and dishwashing area, from which issue bizarre smells combining the edible and the offal: creamy carrion, pizza barf, and that unique and enigmatic Jerry's scent—citrus fart. The floor is slick with spills, forcing us to walk through the kitchen with tiny steps, like Susan McDougal in leg irons. Sinks everywhere are clogged with scraps of lettuce, decomposing lemon wedges, waterlogged toast crusts. Put your hand down on any counter and you risk being stuck to it by the film of ancient syrup spills, and this is unfortunate, because hands are utensils here, used for scooping up lettuce onto salad plates, lifting out pie slices, and even moving hash browns from one plate to another. The regulation poster in the single unisex restroom admonishes us to wash our hands thoroughly and even offers instructions for doing so, but there is always some vital substance missing—soap, paper towels, toilet paper—and I never find all three at once. You learn to stuff your pockets with napkins before going in there, and too bad about the customers, who must eat, though they don't realize this, almost literally out of our hands.

The break room typifies the whole situation: there is none, because there are no breaks at Jerry's. For six to eight hours in a row, you never sit except to pee. Actually, there are three folding chairs at a table immediately adjacent to the bathroom, but hardly anyone ever sits here, in the very rectum of the gastro-architectural system. Rather, the function of the peritoilet area is to house the ashtrays in which servers and dishwashers leave their cigarettes burning at all times, like votive candles, so that they don't have to waste time lighting up again when they dash back for a puff. Almost everyone smokes as if his or her pulmonary well-being depended on it—the multinational mélange of cooks, the Czech dishwashers, the servers, who are all American natives—creating an atmosphere in which oxygen is only an occasional pollutant. My first morning at Jerry's, when the hypoglycemic shakes set in, I complain to one of my fellow servers that I don't understand how she can go so long without food. "Well, I don't understand how you can go so long without a cigarette," she responds in a tone of reproach—because work is what you do for others; smoking is what you do for yourself. I don't know why the antismoking crusaders have never grasped the element of defiant self-nurturance that makes the habit so endearing to its victims—as if, in the American workplace, the only thing people have to call their own is the tumors they are nourishing and the spare moments they devote to feeding them.

Now, the Industrial Revolution is not an easy transition, especially when you have to zip through it in just a couple of days. I have gone from craft work straight into the factory, from the air-conditioned morgue of the Hearthside directly into the flames. Customers arrive in human waves, sometimes disgorged fifty at a time from their tour buses, peckish and whiny. Instead of two "girls" on the floor at once, there can be as many as six of us running around in our brilliant pink-and-orange Hawaiian shirts. Conversations, either with customers or fellow employees, seldom last more than twenty seconds at a time. On my first day, in fact, I am hurt by my sister servers' coldness. My mentor for the day is an emotionally uninflected twenty-three-year-old, and the others, who gossip a little among themselves about the real reason someone is out sick today and the size of the bail bond someone else has had to pay, ignore me completely. On my second day, I find out why. "Well, it's good to see you again," one of them says in greeting. "Hardly anyone comes back after the first day." I feel powerfully vindicated—a survivor—but it would take a long time, probably months, before I could hope to be accepted into this sorority.

I start out with the beautiful, heroic idea of handling the two jobs at once, and for two days I almost do it: the breakfast/lunch shift at Jerry's, which goes till 2:00, arriving at the Hearthside at 2:10, and attempting to hold out until 10:00. In the ten minutes between jobs, I pick up a spicy chicken sandwich at the Wendy's drive-through window, gobble it down in the car, and change from khaki slacks to black, from Hawaiian to rust polo. There is a problem, though. When during the 3:00 to 4:00 P.M. dead time I finally sit down to wrap silver, my flesh seems to bond to the seat. I try to refuel with a purloined cup of soup, as I've seen Gail and Joan do dozens of times, but a manager catches me and hisses "No eating!" though there's not a customer around to be offended by the sight of food making contact with a server's lips. So I tell Gail I'm going to quit, and she hugs me and says she might just follow me to Jerry's herself.

But the chances of this are minuscule. She has left the flophouse and her annoying roommate and is back to living in her beat-up old truck. But guess what? she reports to me excitedly later that evening: Phillip has given her permission to park overnight in the hotel parking lot, as long as she keeps out of sight, and the parking lot should be totally safe, since it's patrolled by a hotel security guard! With the Hearthside offering benefits like that, how could anyone think of leaving?

Gail would have triumphed at Jerry's, I'm sure, but for me it's a crash course in exhaustion management. Years ago, the kindly fry cook who trained me to waitress at a Los Angeles truck stop used to say: Never make an unnecessary trip; if you don't have to walk fast, walk slow; if you don't have to walk, stand. But at Jerry's the effort of distinguishing necessary from unnecessary and urgent from whenever would itself be too much of an energy drain. The only thing to do is to treat each shift as a one-time-only emergency: you've got fifty starving people out there, lying scattered on the battlefield, so get out there and feed them! Forget that you will have to do this again tomorrow, forget that you will have to be alert enough to dodge the drunks on the drive home tonight—just burn, burn, burn! Ideally, at some point you enter what servers call "a rhythm" and psychologists term a "flow state," in which signals pass from the sense organs directly to the muscles, bypassing the cerebral cortex, and a Zen-like emptiness sets in. A male server from the Hearthside's morning shift tells me about the time he "pulled a triple"—three shifts in a row, all the way around the clock—and then got off and had a drink and met this girl, and maybe he shouldn't tell me this, but they had sex right then and there, and it was like, beautiful.

But there's another capacity of the neuromuscular system, which is pain. I start tossing back drugstore-brand ibuprofen pills as if they were vitamin C, four before each shift, because an old mouse-related repetitive-stress injury in my upper back has come back to fullspasm strength, thanks to the tray carrying. In my ordinary life, this level of disability might justify a day of ice packs and stretching. Here I comfort myself with the Aleve commercial in which the cute blue-collar guy asks: If you quit after working four hours, what would your boss say? And the not-so-cute blue-collar guy, who's lugging a metal beam on his back, answers: He'd fire me, that's what. But fortunately, the commercial tells us, we workers can exert the same kind of authority over our painkillers that our bosses exert over us. If Tylenol doesn't want to work for more than four hours, you just fire its ass and switch to Aleve.

True, I take occasional breaks from this life, going home now and then to catch up on e-mail and for conjugal visits (though I am careful to "pay" for anything I eat there), seeing *The Truman Show* with friends and letting them buy my ticket. And I still have those what-am-I-doing-here moments at work, when I get so homesick for the printed word that I obsessively reread the six-page menu. But as the days go by, my old life is beginning to look exceedingly strange. The e-mails and phone messages addressed to my former self come from a distant race of people with exotic concerns and far too much time on their hands. The neighborly market I used to cruise for produce now looks forbiddingly like a Manhattan yuppie emporium. And when I sit down one morning in my real home to pay bills from my past life, I am dazzled at the two- and three-figure sums owed to outfits like Club Body Tech and Amazon.com.

Management at Jerry's is generally calmer and more "professional" than at the Hearthside, with two exceptions. One is Joy, a plump, blowsy woman in her early thirties, who once kindly devoted several minutes to instructing me in the correct one-handed method of carrying trays but whose moods change disconcertingly from shift to shift and even within one. Then there's B.J., a.k.a. B.J.-the-bitch, whose contribution is to stand by the kitchen counter and yell, "Nita, your order's up, move it!" or, "Barbara, didn't you see you've got another table out there? Come on, girl!" Among other things, she is hated for having replaced the whipped-cream squirt cans with big plastic whipped-cream-filled baggies that have to be squeezed with both hands—because, reportedly, she saw or thought she saw employees trying to inhale the propellant gas from the squirt cans, in the hope that it might be nitrous oxide. On my third night, she pulls me aside abruptly and brings her face so close that it looks as if she's planning to butt me with her forehead. But instead of saying, "You're fired," she says, "You're doing fine." The only trouble is I'm spending time chatting with customers: "That's how they're getting you." Furthermore I am letting them "run me," which means harassment by sequential demands: you bring the ketchup and they decide they want extra Thousand Island; you bring that and they announce they now need a side of fries; and so on into distraction. Finally she tells me not to take her wrong. She tries to say things in a nice way, but you get into a mode, you know, because everything has to move so fast.[5]

---

[5] In *Workers in a Lean World: Unions in the International Economy* (Verso, 1997), Kim Moody cites studies finding an increase in stress-related workplace injuries and illness between the mid-1980s and the early 1990s. He argues that rising stress levels reflect a new system of "management by stress," in which workers in a variety of industries are being squeezed to extract maximum productivity, to the detriment of their health.

I mumble thanks for the advice, feeling like I've just been stripped naked by the crazed enforcer of some ancient sumptuary law: No chatting for you, girl. No fancy service ethic allowed for the serfs. Chatting with customers is for the beautiful young college-educated servers in the downtown carpaccio joints, the kids who can make $70 to $100 a night. What had I been thinking? My job is to move orders from tables to kitchen and then trays from kitchen to tables. Customers are, in fact, the major obstacle to the smooth transformation of information into food and food into money—they are, in short, the enemy. And the painful thing is that I'm beginning to see it this way myself. There are the traditional asshole types—frat boys who down multiple Buds and then make a fuss because the steaks are so emaciated and the fries so sparse—as well as the variously impaired—due to age, diabetes, or literacy issues—who require patient nutritional counseling. The worst, for some reason, are the Visible Christians—like the ten-person table, all jolly and sanctified after Sunday-night service, who run me mercilessly and then leave me $1 on a $92 bill. Or the guy with the crucifixion T-shirt (SOMEONE TO LOOK UP TO) who complains that his baked potato is too hard and his iced tea too icy (I cheerfully fix both) and leaves no tip. As a general rule, people wearing crosses or WWJD? (What Would Jesus Do?) buttons look at us disapprovingly no matter what we do, as if they were confusing waitressing with Mary Magdalene's original profession.

I make friends, over time, with the other "girls" who work my shift: Nita, the tattooed twenty-something who taunts us by going around saying brightly, "Have we started making money yet?" Ellen, whose teenage son cooks on the graveyard shift and who once managed a restaurant in Massachusetts but won't try out for management here because she prefers being a "common worker" and not "ordering people around." Easy-going fiftyish Lucy, with the raucous laugh, who limps toward the end of the shift because of something that has gone wrong with her leg, the exact nature of which cannot be determined without health insurance. We talk about the usual girl things—men, children, and the sinister allure of Jerry's chocolate peanut-butter cream pie—though no one, I notice, ever brings up anything potentially expensive, like shopping or movies. As at the Hearthside, the only recreation ever referred to is partying, which requires little more than some beer, a joint, and a few close friends. Still, no one here is homeless, or cops to it anyway, thanks usually to a working husband or boyfriend. All in all, we form a reliable mutual-support group: If one of us is feeling sick or overwhelmed, another one will "bev" a table or even carry trays for her. If one of us is off sneaking a cigarette or a pee,[6] the others will do their best to conceal her absence from the enforcers of corporate rationality.

---

[6] Until April 1998, there was no federally mandated right to bathroom breaks. According to Marc Linder and Ingrid Nygaard, authors of *Void Where Prohibited: Rest Breaks and the Right to Urinate on Company Time* (Cornell University Press, 1997), "The right to rest and void at work is not high on the list of social or political causes supported by professional or executive employees, who enjoy personal workplace liberties that millions of factory workers can only daydream about.... While we were dismayed to discover that workers lacked an acknowledged

But my saving human connection—my oxytocin receptor, as it were—is George, the nineteen-year-old, fresh-off-the-boat Czech dishwasher. We get to talking when he asks me, tortuously, how much cigarettes cost at Jerry's. I do my best to explain that they cost over a dollar more here than at a regular store and suggest that he just take one from the halffilled packs that are always lying around on the break table. But that would be unthinkable. Except for the one tiny earring signaling his allegiance to some vaguely alternative point of view, George is a perfect straight arrow—crew-cut, hardworking, and hungry for eye contact. "Czech Republic," I ask, "or Slovakia?" and he seems delighted that I know the difference. "Václav Havel," I try. "Velvet Revolution, Frank Zappa?" "Yes, yes, 1989," he says, and I realize we are talking about history.

My project is to teach George English. "How are you today, George?" I say at the start of each shift. "I am good, and how are you today, Barbara?" I learn that he is not paid by Jerry's but by the "agent" who shipped him over—$5 an hour, with the agent getting the dollar or so difference between that and what Jerry's pays dishwashers. I learn also that he shares an apartment with a crowd of other Czech "dishers," as he calls them, and that he cannot sleep until one of them goes off for his shift, leaving a vacant bed. We are having one of our ESL sessions late one afternoon when B.J. catches us at it and orders "Joseph" to take up the rubber mats on the floor near the dishwashing sinks and mop underneath. "I thought your name was George," I say loud enough for B.J. to hear as she strides off back to the counter. Is she embarrassed? Maybe a little, because she greets me back at the counter with "George, Joseph—there are so many of them!" I say nothing, neither nodding nor smiling, and for this I am punished later when I think I am ready to go and she announces that I need to roll fifty more sets of silverware and isn't it time I mixed up a fresh four-gallon batch of bluecheese dressing? May you grow old in this place, B.J., is the curse I beam out at her when I am finally permitted to leave. May the syrup spills glue your feet to the floor.

I make the decision to move closer to Key West. First, because of the drive. Second and third, also because of the drive: gas is eating up $4 to $5 a day, and although Jerry's is as high-volume as you can get, the tips average only 10 percent, and not just for a newbie like me. Between the base pay of $2.15 an hour and the obligation to share tips with the busboys and dishwashers, we're averaging only about $7.50 an hour. Then there is the $30 I had to spend on the regulation tan slacks worn by Jerry's servers—a setback it could take weeks to absorb. (I had combed the town's two downscale department stores hoping for something cheaper but decided in the end that these marked-down Dockers, originally $49, were more likely to survive a daily washing.) Of my fellow servers, everyone who lacks a working husband or boyfriend seems to have a second job: Nita does something at a computer eight hours a day; another welds. Without the

---

legal right to void at work, [the workers] were amazed by outsiders' naive belief that their employers would permit them to perform this basic bodily function when necessary....

A factory worker, not allowed a break for six-hour stretches, voided into pads worn inside her uniform; and a kindergarten teacher in a school without aides had to take all twenty children with her to the bathroom and line them up outside the stall door when she voided."

forty-five-minute commute, I can picture myself working two jobs and having the time to shower between them.

So I take the $500 deposit I have coming from my landlord, the $400 I have earned toward the next month's rent, plus the $200 reserved for emergencies, and use the $1,100 to pay the rent and deposit on trailer number 46 in the Overseas Trailer Park, a mile from the cluster of budget hotels that constitute Key West's version of an industrial park. Number 46 is about eight feet in width and shaped like a barbell inside, with a narrow region—because of the sink and the stove—separating the bedroom from what might optimistically be called the "living" area, with its two-person table and half-sized couch. The bathroom is so small my knees rub against the shower stall when I sit on the toilet, and you can't just leap out of the bed, you have to climb down to the foot of it in order to find a patch of floor space to stand on. Outside, I am within a few yards of a liquor store, a bar that advertises "free beer tomorrow," a convenience store, and a Burger King—but no supermarket or, alas, laundromat. By reputation, the Overseas park is a nest of crime and crack, and I am hoping at least for some vibrant, multicultural street life. But desolation rules night and day, except for a thin stream of pedestrian traffic heading for their jobs at the Sheraton or 7-Eleven. There are not exactly people here but what amounts to canned labor, being preserved from the heat between shifts.

In line with my reduced living conditions, a new form of ugliness arises at Jerry's. First we are confronted—via an announcement on the computers through which we input orders—with the new rule that the hotel bar is henceforth off-limits to restaurant employees. The culprit, I learn through the grapevine, is the ultra-efficient gal who trained me—another trailer-home dweller and a mother of three. Something had set her off one morning, so she slipped out for a nip and returned to the floor impaired. This mostly hurts Ellen, whose habit it is to free her hair from its rubber band and drop by the bar for a couple of Zins before heading home at the end of the shift, but all of us feel the chill. Then the next day, when I go for straws, for the first time I find the dry-storage room locked. Ted, the portly assistant manager who opens it for me, explains that he caught one of the dishwashers attempting to steal something, and, unfortunately, the miscreant will be with us until a replacement can be found—hence the locked door. I neglect to ask what he had been trying to steal, but Ted tells me who he is—the kid with the buzz cut and the earring. You know, he's back there right now.

I wish I could say I rushed back and confronted George to get his side of the story. I wish I could say I stood up to Ted and insisted that George be given a translator and allowed to defend himself, or announced that I'd find a lawyer who'd handle the case pro bono. The mystery to me is that there's not much worth stealing in the dry-storage room, at least not in any fenceable quantity: "Is Gyorgi here, and am having 200—maybe 250—ketchup packets. What do you say?" My guess is that he had taken—if he had taken anything at all— some Saltines or a can of cherry-pie mix, and that the motive for taking it was hunger.

So why didn't I intervene? Certainly not because I was held back by the kind of moral paralysis that can pass as journalistic objectivity. On the contrary, something new—something loathsome and servile—had infected me, along with the kitchen odors that I could still sniff on my bra when I finally undressed at night. In real life I am moderately brave, but plenty of brave people shed their courage in concentration camps, and maybe something similar goes on in the infinitely more congenial milieu of the low-wage American workplace. Maybe, in a month or two more at Jerry's, I might have regained my crusading spirit. Then again, in a month or two I might have turned into a different person altogether—say, the kind of person who would have turned George in.

But this is not something I am slated to find out. When my month-long plunge into poverty is almost over, I finally land my dream job—housekeeping. I do this by walking into the personnel office of the only place I figure I might have some credibility, the hotel attached to Jerry's, and confiding urgently that I have to have a second job if I am to pay my rent and, no, it couldn't be front-desk clerk. "All right," the personnel lady fairly spits, "So it's housekeeping," and she marches me back to meet Maria, the housekeeping manager, a tiny, frenetic Hispanic woman who greets me as "babe" and hands me a pamphlet emphasizing the need for a positive attitude. The hours are nine in the morning till whenever, the pay is $6.10 an hour, and there's one week of vacation a year. I don't have to ask about health insurance once I meet Carlotta, the middle-aged African-American woman who will be training me. Carla, as she tells me to call her, is missing all of her top front teeth.

On that first day of housekeeping and last day of my entire project—although I don't yet know it's the last—Carla is in a foul mood. We have been given nineteen rooms to clean, most of them "checkouts," as opposed to "stay-overs," that require the whole enchilada of bed-stripping, vacuuming, and bathroom-scrubbing. When one of the rooms that had been listed as a stay-over turns out to be a checkout, Carla calls Maria to complain, but of course to no avail. "So make up the motherfucker," Carla orders me, and I do the beds while she sloshes around the bathroom. For four hours without a break I strip and remake beds, taking about four and a half minutes per queen-sized bed, which I could get down to three if there were any reason to. We try to avoid vacuuming by picking up the larger specks by hand, but often there is nothing to do but drag the monstrous vacuum cleaner—it weighs about thirty pounds—off our cart and try to wrestle it around the floor. Sometimes Carla hands me the squirt bottle of "BAM" (an acronym for something that begins, ominously, with "butyric"; the rest has been worn off the label) and lets me do the bathrooms. No service ethic challenges me here to new heights of performance. I just concentrate on removing the pubic hairs from the bathtubs, or at least the dark ones that I can see.

I had looked forward to the breaking-and-entering aspect of cleaning the stay-overs, the chance to examine the secret, physical existence of strangers. But the contents of the rooms are always banal and surprisingly neat—zipped up shaving kits, shoes lined up against the wall (there are no closets), flyers for snorkeling trips, maybe an empty wine bottle or two. It is the TV that keeps us going, from *Jerry* to *Sally* to *Hawaii Five-O* and then on to the soaps. If there's something especially arresting, like

"Won't Take No for an Answer" on *Jerry*, we sit down on the edge of a bed and giggle for a moment as if this were a pajama party instead of a terminally dead-end job. The soaps are the best, and Carla turns the volume up full blast so that she won't miss anything from the bathroom or while the vacuum is on. In room 503, Marcia confronts Jeff about Lauren. In 505, Lauren taunts poor cuckolded Marcia. In 511, Helen offers Amanda $10,000 to stop seeing Eric, prompting Carla to emerge from the bathroom to study Amanda's troubled face. "You take it, girl," she advises. "I would for sure."

The tourists' rooms that we clean and, beyond them, the far more expensively appointed interiors in the soaps, begin after a while to merge. We have entered a better world—a world of comfort where every day is a day off, waiting to be filled up with sexual intrigue. We, however, are only gatecrashers in this fantasy, forced to pay for our presence with backaches and perpetual thirst. The mirrors, and there are far too many of them in hotel rooms, contain the kind of person you would normally find pushing a shopping cart down a city street—bedraggled, dressed in a damp hotel polo shirt two sizes too large, and with sweat dribbling down her chin like drool. I am enormously relieved when Carla announces a half-hour meal break, but my appetite fades when I see that the bag of hot-dog rolls she has been carrying around on our cart is not trash salvaged from a checkout but what she has brought for her lunch.

When I request permission to leave at about 3:30, another housekeeper warns me that no one has so far succeeded in combining housekeeping at the hotel with serving at Jerry's: "Some kid did it once for five days, and you're no kid." With that helpful information in mind, I rush back to number 46, down four Advils (the name brand this time), shower, stooping to fit into the stall, and attempt to compose myself for the oncoming shift. So much for what Marx termed the "reproduction of labor power," meaning the things a worker has to do just so she'll be ready to work again. The only unforeseen obstacle to the smooth transition from job to job is that my tan Jerry's slacks, which had looked reasonably clean by 40-watt bulb last night when I handwashed my Hawaiian shirt, prove by daylight to be mottled with ketchup and ranch-dressing stains. I spend most of my hour-long break between jobs attempting to remove the edible portions with a sponge and then drying the slacks over the hood of my car in the sun.

I can do this two-job thing, is my theory, if I can drink enough caffeine and avoid getting distracted by George's ever more obvious suffering.[7] The first few days after being caught he seemed not to understand the trouble he was in, and our chirpy little conversations had continued. But the last couple of shifts he's been listless and unshaven, and tonight he looks like the ghost we all know him to be, with dark half-

<hr>

[7] In 1996, the number of persons holding two or more jobs averaged 7.8 million, or 6.2 percent of the workforce. It was about the same rate for men and for women (6.1 versus 6.2), though the kinds of jobs differ by gender. About two thirds of multiple jobholders work one job full-time and the other part-time. Only a heroic minority—4 percent of men and 2 percent of women—work two full-time jobs simultaneously. (From John F. Stinson Jr., "New Data on Multiple Jobholding Available from the CPS," in the *Monthly Labor Review*, March 1997.)

moons hanging from his eyes. At one point, when I am briefly immobilized by the task of filling little paper cups with sour cream for baked potatoes, he comes over and looks as if he'd like to explore the limits of our shared vocabulary, but I am called to the floor for a table. I resolve to give him all my tips that night and to hell with the experiment in low-wage money management. At eight, Ellen and I grab a snack together standing at the mephitic end of the kitchen counter, but I can only manage two or three mozzarella sticks and lunch had been a mere handful of McNuggets. I am not tired at all, I assure myself, though it may be that there is simply no more "I" left to do the tiredness monitoring. What I would see, if I were more alert to the situation, is that the forces of destruction are already massing against me. There is only one cook on duty, a young man named Jesus ("Hay-Sue," that is) and he is new to the job. And there is Joy, who shows up to take over in the middle of the shift, wearing high heels and a long, clingy white dress and fuming as if she'd just been stood up in some cocktail bar.

Then it comes, the perfect storm. Four of my tables fill up at once. Four tables is nothing for me now, but only so long as they are obligingly staggered. As I bev table 27, tables 25, 28, and 24 are watching enviously. As I bev 25, 24 glowers because their bevs haven't even been ordered. Twenty-eight is four yuppyish types, meaning everything on the side and agonizing instructions as to the chicken Caesars. Twenty-five is a middle-aged black couple, who complain, with some justice, that the iced tea isn't fresh and the tabletop is sticky. But table 24 is the meteorological event of the century: ten British tourists who seem to have made the decision to absorb the American experience entirely by mouth. Here everyone has at least two drinks—iced tea and milk shake, Michelob and water (with lemon slice, please)—and a huge promiscuous orgy of breakfast specials, mozz sticks, chicken strips, quesadillas, burgers with cheese and without, sides of hash browns with cheddar, with onions, with gravy, seasoned fries, plain fries, banana splits. Poor Jesus! Poor me! Because when I arrive with their first tray of food—after three prior trips just to refill bevs—Princess Di refuses to eat her chicken strips with her pancake-and-sausage special, since, as she now reveals, the strips were meant to be an appetizer. Maybe the others would have accepted their meals, but Di, who is deep into her third Michelob, insists that everything else go back while they work on their "starters." Meanwhile, the yuppies are waving me down for more decaf and the black couple looks ready to summon the NAACP.

Much of what happened next is lost in the fog of war. Jesus starts going under. The little printer on the counter in front of him is spewing out orders faster than he can rip them off, much less produce the meals. Even the invincible Ellen is ashen from stress. I bring table 24 their reheated main courses, which they immediately reject as either too cold or fossilized by the microwave. When I return to the kitchen with their trays (three trays in three trips), Joy confronts me with arms akimbo: "What is this?" She means the food—the plates of rejected pancakes, hash browns in assorted flavors, toasts, burgers, sausages, eggs. "Uh, scrambled with cheddar," I try, "and that's . . . " "NO," she screams in my face. "Is it a traditional, a super-scramble, an eye-opener?" I pretend to study my check for a clue, but entropy has been up to its tricks, not only on the plates but in my head, and I have to admit that the original order is beyond reconstruction. "You don't know an eye-opener from a traditional?" she demands in outrage. All I know, in fact, is that my legs have lost interest in the current venture and have announced their intention to fold. I am saved by a yuppie (mercifully not one of mine) who chooses this moment to charge into the kitchen to bellow that his food is twenty-five minutes late. Joy screams at him to get the hell out of her kitchen, please, and then turns on Jesus in a fury, hurling an empty tray across the room for emphasis.

I leave. I don't walk out, I just leave. I don't finish my side work or pick up my credit-card tips, if any, at the cash register or, of course, ask Joy's permission to go. And the surprising thing is that you can walk out without permission, that the door opens, that the thick tropical night air parts to let me pass, that my car is still parked where I left it. There is no vindication in this exit, no fuck-you surge of relief, just an overwhelming, dank sense of failure pressing down on me and the entire parking lot. I had gone into this venture in the spirit of science, to test a mathematical proposition, but somewhere along the line, in the tunnel vision imposed by long shifts and relentless concentration, it became a test of myself, and clearly I have failed. Not only had I flamed out as a housekeeper/server, I had even forgotten to give George my tips, and, for reasons perhaps best known to hardworking, generous people like Gail and Ellen, this hurts. I don't cry, but I am in a position to realize, for the first time in many years, that the tear ducts are still there, and still capable of doing their job.

When I moved out of the trailer park, I gave the key to number 46 to Gail and arranged for my deposit to be transferred to her. She told me that Joan is still living in her van and that Stu had been fired from the Hearthside. I never found out what happened to George.

In one month, I had earned approximately $1,040 and spent $517 on food, gas, toiletries, laundry, phone, and utilities. If I had remained in my $500 efficiency, I would have been able to pay the rent and have $22 left over (which is $78 less than the cash I had in my pocket at the start of the month). During this time I bought no clothing except for the required slacks and no prescription drugs or medical care (I did finally buy some vitamin B to compensate for the lack of vegetables in my diet). Perhaps I could have saved a little on food if I had gotten to a supermarket more often, instead of convenience stores, but it should be noted that I lost almost four pounds in four weeks, on a diet weighted heavily toward burgers and fries.

How former welfare recipients and single mothers will (and do) survive in the low-wage workforce, I cannot imagine. Maybe they will figure out how to condense their lives—including child-raising, laundry, romance, and meals—into the couple of hours between full-time jobs. Maybe they will take up residence in their vehicles, if they have one. All I know is that I couldn't hold two jobs and I couldn't make enough money to live on with one. And I had advantages unthinkable to many of the long-term poor—health, stamina, a working car, and no children to care for and support. Certainly nothing in my experience contradicts the conclusion of Kathryn Edin and Laura Lein, in their recent book *Making Ends Meet: How Single Mothers Survive Welfare*

and Low-Wage Work, that low-wage work actually involves more hardship and deprivation than life at the mercy of the welfare state. In the coming months and years, economic conditions for the working poor are bound to worsen, even without the almost
inevitable recession. As mentioned earlier, the influx of former welfare recipients into
the low-skilled workforce will have a depressing effect on both wages and the number
of jobs available. A general economic downturn will only enhance these effects, and
the working poor will of course be facing it without the slight, but nonetheless often
saving, protection of welfare as a backup.

The thinking behind welfare reform was that even the humblest jobs are morally
uplifting and psychologically buoying. In reality they are likely to be fraught with
insult and stress. But I did discover one redeeming feature of the most abject low-
wage work—the camaraderie of people who are, in almost all cases, far too smart
and funny and caring for the work they do and the wages they're paid. The hope, of
course, is that someday these people will come to know what they're worth, and take
appropriate action.

—1999

Learning from Other Writers (Ehrenreich)

1. How does Ehrenreich anticipate her readers' objections to the terms of her experiment and her reasons for carrying it out? Is she successful in heading off or countering such resistance?

2. What are Ehrenreich's qualifications for writing this essay? What research does she do to supplement her experiences as a waitress and housekeeper? How does she integrate this research into her essay? Is this approach successful or intrusive?

3. Where and how does Ehrenreich use scenic (as opposed to expository) writing? How do these choices shape her analysis or lead her to new insights?

4. What are some of the discoveries that Ehrenreich makes about work? Poverty? Human behavior? Economics? What can you say about the author's intended audience? What (if anything) might this essay persuade an economist, business owner, or politician to change or do?

5. What measures does Ehrenreich take to protect the people with whom she worked? Might she have asked them to reflect on their experiences in a more direct way (rather than merely quoting what she overheard)? Why or why not?

6. What theory is Ehrenreich testing?

UNDERSTANDING OTHER CULTURES

There are many ways to study another culture. As we saw in previous chapters, you might write a portrait of a place or a person as filtered through a particular lens, or travel to a foreign city with the goal of writing about the culture you find there. Often, studying another society requires participating in the rituals of a culture not your own.

Beth Ann Fennelly, who was not born in the South but who is married to a Southerner, is fascinated by the practice of geophagy, the (predominately Southern) practice of eating dirt. In an attempt to understand her husband's roots, she decides to sample some dirt herself. Her experiment leads her to a surprising conclusion about social class and the ways in which we revere certain behaviors if practiced by the learned or the rich but malign similar tastes if they belong to the uneducated or the poor.

In "Throumbes of Thassos," Christopher Bakken, a poet/professor who lives in Pennsylvania, travels to Greece to take part in the olive harvest on the island of Thassos. By focusing on the facts—how olives are harvested, where they grow, what characterizes the local culture on the island, and how he came to visit this place—he gives us insights into the business of olive picking and an astute analysis of how our work defines us.

By Beth Ann Fennelly

THE WIDE WORLD OF EATING DIRT

I knew it was wrong, but I couldn't help myself. I was curious: too curious. Finally, late one night, I returned to a website I'd bookmarked, one which promised "discrete shipping on all orders." I placed the illicit item in my shopping cart. Confirm purchase? You betcha. And so I took one small step closer to full membership in my adopted home, my quest to be a Southerner. I would eat dirt.

Not that dirt-eating—also known as geophagy—is limited to the South, of course. The practice has been found in all continents, in various peoples, even in animals. And in all times: Apparently, people have been eating the earth since they've been walking the earth. Clays meant for consumption have been discovered at sites occupied by early humans. Historical references date as far back as Aristotle and Hippocrates of Kos (460–377 B.C.), who warned that "if a pregnant woman feels the desire to eat earth or charcoal and then eats them, the child will show signs of these things." Traditionally, Haitian women dry mud cookies on their roofs. Clay eaters in Africa purchase their chosen variety in open-air markets and keep it in cloth belts, close at hand. In India, where Mahatma Gandhi advocated geophagy to cleanse the body, people have been known to drink tea from newly formed clay cups—and then eat the cups.

In the U.S., geophagy has become associated with pregnant women—especially African-American ones—in poor, rural areas. Scholars such as Donald E. Vermeer and Dennis Frate consider geophagy a culture transfer from Africa; slaves brought the habit with them to plantations, where it became known as Cachexia Africana. Plantation owners became concerned when slaves who ate too much clay acted lethargic, and some owners went so far as to force their slaves to wear face masks. Yet while it is true that overindulging can indeed lead to anemia, intestinal blockages, and ruptured colons, Vermeer and Frate find it more likely that malnutrition, not geophagy, was responsible for the slaves' ill health. And despite the slave owners' vigilance, the practice remained, and spread to poor whites as well, as suggested by a nickname for South Carolinians, "Sandlappers." My husband tells me his relations (poor white Alabamians) ate the clay mortar grouting the stones of the hearth at the family's home, the "Old Place"—weakening the structure until it threatened to collapse.

Geophagy's a dying tradition now. Due to the stigma attached, what remains has gone underground: Vermeer tells of the nurse in Holmes County, Mississippi, who pulled him aside one day to confess, "I just wanted you to know that I am also a practitioner." How much of the population shares her guilty habit is hard to determine; according to Susan Allport, author of "Women Who Eat Dirt" in *Gastronomica*, "In the 1970s, fifty percent of Black women admitted to eating clay, about four times the frequency among white women," but notes the percentage has since dropped. Vermeer hypothesizes that between thirty and fifty percent of pregnant African-American women in the rural South consume clay.

That geophagy is a habit of indigent Southerners perhaps explains why it has such negative connotations. Geophagy is a subset of *pica*, a word that comes from the Latin for magpie, a bird known for its indiscriminate diet. The American Psychiatric Association defines pica as "persistent eating of non-nutritive substances that is inappropriate to development level" and "occurs outside culturally sanctioned practice." No wonder the habit has gone underground, then; who would ask their doctor about its effects when Alexander Woywodt, M.D., writes starchily in 2002 in the *Journal of the Royal Society of Medicine* that "concealment of the aberrant eating behavior is an important issue. The diagnosis commonly emerges when a patient is accidentally discovered during a 'binge' of geophagia. Abdominal radiography can be of great help in the occasional patient who denies the habit"?

Perhaps because there's no money to be made from advocating either for, or against, the eating of dirt, geophagy is ill-understood by the medical community. In fact, not only do doctors disagree about whether it's healthy or harmful, they disagree about why people do it. This much we do know: Cravings are site-specific, which is to say, only a certain location yields the desired flavor and texture. The nineteenth-century Otomac tribe of South America preferred a fine red clay and would hike long distances to obtain it. North Carolinians, as historian Hilda Hertz reported in her 1947 "Notes on Clay and Starch Eating Among Negroes in a Southern Urban Community," prefer smooth white clay. The residents of Holmes County, Mississippi, prefer "hill dirt" to Delta dirt, and Frate tells of the popularity of a certain hill he visited where he found cars lined up "like at a drive-in bank." Nonhuman animals also demonstrate the same highly selective connoisseurship. East African elephants and the mountain gorillas of Rwanda return every year to particular sites. The Peruvian Amazon scarlet macaws eat only a certain band of exposed clay in a bend of the Manu River—so loyal are the birds that these sites "attract 4,000 bird watching tourists each year," according to UCLA evolutionary biologist Jared M. Diamond.

What's the dirt? We know that practitioners aren't running out into the garden to lap up any old surface mulch. It's pretty much the opposite of what Gabriel García Márquez describes in *One Hundred Years of Solitude*, where a woman in love

> got up in the middle of the night and ate handfuls of earth in the garden with a
> suicidal drive, weeping with pain and fury, chewing tender earthworms and chipping
> her teeth on snail shells.

Preferred clay is usually located in a band beneath ground level, and as such uncontaminated with manure, parasites, or pesticides. Sometimes such a subsoil band will be exposed along a river bed or, in contemporary times, through construction. Digging for clay in roadbanks has caused enough damage in some cases, according to Vermeer, to prompt the highway department to post signs requesting locals to stop digging.

While sometimes such clay is eaten right at the "dirt-hole," often it is stockpiled and baked into hard nuggets for gnawing, sometimes seasoned. Packages—with the clay's origin clearly marked—are sold even today across the South, in convenience stores. Southern women who migrate north find themselves dirt-poor in a new way—and then send letters to relatives pleading for shipments. Luther Brown, director of the Delta Center for Culture and Learning, says it may be apocryphal but he's heard "the post office in Anguilla was shipping huge volumes of clay up north." John B. Strait, geographer at Sam Houston State University, told me that he's tasted clay from Midnight, Mississippi, and The Plains, Georgia, in Otha's Soul Food on Chicago's South Side. "It wasn't bad," he e-mailed. "I had it with some vinegar and pepper, like one would eat with cucumbers."

Is geophagy an illness or an affirming cultural practice? Experts disagree. Even the *New York Times* can only conclude, "Why hundreds of millions of people and dozens of animal species consume earth remains a mystery, and information about the health effects is contradictory and incomplete." Every expert I spoke to disagreed with the others, but there are, to my count, five main theories.

The first theory is that pica satisfies hunger. Here we might look to the heroine of Pearl Buck's 1931 novel, *The Good Earth*, set during the reign of the last emperor of China, who serves her starving children "the good earth." There are similar historical cases—after a seventeenth-century famine in England, a Saxony official reported that "people finally started baking this earth and...the hill containing this white earth was undermined and collapsed killing five." But it's also true that geophagy exists in times of plenty.

Another hypothesis suggests that people ingest earth to gain minerals lacking in their diets. This theory helps account for earth-eating among pregnant women, whose nutritional needs are greater. Jared M. Diamond found that "soils sold in Ghanaian markets to pregnant African women are richer in iron and copper than the dietary supplement pills made by pharmaceutical companies specifically for prenatal use." Susan Allport notes that pregnant women in Africa often visit termite mounds, which "are rich in both calcium and iron and supply a woman who eats at least twenty grams a day with more than one hundred percent of her RDA for iron." Animals, too, such as monkeys, take iron supplements in the form of clay. The only problem with this tidy theory is that subsoils differ so much in mineral quality and composition. In fact, for every pregnant woman who staves off anemia through clay, there might be a woman who induces anemia from clay, as it can bind with iron molecules and prevent their absorption.

A third theory argues that clay can neutralize poisons, especially in plants that have evolved toxins to prevent being eaten. This explains, perhaps, how the wild Andes potato became domesticated. The wild potato is toxic, but ethnobotanists have seen Andes Indians dipping the potatoes in a slurry of wet clay (essentially mud) while eating them. As Allport writes, clays make effective antitoxins because:

> their very fine particles give them a large surface area and make it likely that those particles will come into contact with the toxins in foods. And their crystalline structure is layered with positively charged ions, primarily of silicon and aluminum. Since many organic toxins are also positively charged particles, they essentially trade places with the ions in the clays, then pass harmlessly through the digestive system.

Animals, also, can use clay to detoxify plants. Biologist Cindy Engel suggests that the scarlet macaws who eat clay from the Manu riverbed do so because their diet is high in toxic tree seeds, which the macaws detoxify by ingesting clay.

Yet a fourth hypothesis, and another that can account for pregnant women's cravings, is that it reduces nausea and indigestion. For years, the main ingredient in stomach-soothing Kaopectate was a white Georgia clay called kaolin. Formed millions of years ago of feldspar eroded from the Appalachians and carried by ancient rivers to the sea, these bands of kaolin are now covered by surface dirt. Kaolin has been found to reduce upset stomach and diarrhea, but it's valued more as an ingredient for high-quality glossy paper—it's what makes slick magazines slick. The story of how mining companies tricked poor Georgia Piedmont farmers into leasing away their mineral rights for a song is told in *Red Clay, Pink Cadillacs, and White Gold: The Kaolin Chalk Wars*, an unexpectedly gripping read. In it, authors Charles Seabrook and Marcy Louza describe how

> women in chalk country, like their mothers and grandmothers before them, still
> stroll occasionally down the back country roads, spoons in hand, to scoop chalk right
> out the ground.

But they also quote from a Macon physician who feels so strongly that eating clay can aggravate anemia that he goes on the radio to issue warnings.

Finally, scientists suggest that perhaps we eat dirt because dirt is good for us. Jane E. Brody, in a 2009 *New York Times* piece, ponders why children learn to explore the world by putting it in their mouths. Such reflection leads her to consider "the hygiene hypothesis," which argues that we've become too clean; because children no longer play in dirt, they no longer ingest "the millions of bacteria, viruses and especially worms that enter the body along with 'dirt'" that help develop immune systems. *Why Dirt is Good* by Mary Ruebush suggests that sheathing our children in mucus-y layers of Purell is not only misguided but accounts for the rise in childhood asthma and allergies. Ruebush argues that when children eat dirt, they are allowing their immune systems to practice responding; in addition, dirt "plays a critical role in teaching the immature immune response what is best ignored."

Could it be, then, that we are merely grown-up babies eating dirt out of an atavistic impulse that has survived because it gave us an evolutionary advantage? Diamond wonders, "Do curious dirt-licking babies deserve our encouragement for their experiments with self-medication?" A provocative question, but it is only that—a question—as even so-called experts do little more than conclude that more research is necessary.

Perhaps these experts will get their wish, for there is a renewed interest in dirt, and this time it's coming from fashionable folk. In recent years, oenophiles have enjoyed discussing terroir, meaning "sense of place"—the climate, soil type, and topography of a region that lend unique properties to a wine. (Interestingly, these are the same qualities Southern geophagists have long noted and compared.) Extreme oenophiles have moved from merely discussing terroir of a certain vineyard to actually tasting terroir. These wine lovers sometimes mate with locavores, who eat only locally grown food, and subsequently there's a lot of consideration of the qualities local dirt imparts. Throw in the foodies' wish to know more about the earth that grows the grain that fattens the hog that fattens the folks. (One cheese artisan I know claims to be able to determine, from the taste of a bite of cheese, the grass the cow ate and the season in which it was milked.) Put them all together, and voilà: You have a fad, the latest manifestation of which is a soil tasting.

People living in San Francisco can find a soil tasting in a nearby art gallery; the rest of us can e-participate through a website (tasteofplace.info) run by performance artist and "agricultural activist" Laura Parker. Parker strives to answer the question "how does soil touch our lives and affect our food; and why does it matter?" To stimulate public dialogue, Parker fills wine goblets with various soils and adds a few teaspoons of water to release the aromas and flavors. The soils aren't ingested, but participants place their noses deep into the wine bowls, inhaling the newly released molecules to the backs of their tongues, where taste receptors lie. The website even provides "Tasting Notes," such as the soil of "Apple Farm-Indian Camp Ground, 'Arrowhead Reserve,'" which has a "texture like ground espresso between your fingertips with a rich, chocolate color. The nose is both flinty and grassy with finesse and subtlety." After the soil tasting, participants dine on food grown in the various soils and identify the qualities of the dirt in the food to strengthen the connection between what we eat and where it's grown.

One factor that Parker addresses that few scientists address is taste. Which brings me to a sixth reason tht people might eat dirt: They like it. Certainly, that's what dirt eaters themselves, who praise its pleasant sourness, indicate. One online message board informed me that Scott from Scottsdale, Arizona, finds that "kaolite tastes like rain with a hint of peanuts and it melts in your mouth like chocolate." Sharlita from Batesville, Mississippi, reminisces wistfully that her family would "fry it and eat it warm."

While I might not have access to the fireplace where my husband's Alabama ancestors dug their clay, I want to experience their South, at least as much of it as remains. So I found the next best thing to Alabama dirt: Georgia dirt. "Home Grown Georgia White Dirt," kaolin from Toomsboro, was shipped UPS, discretely, as promised, in a brown wrapper. The label on the ziplock containing the large, white chalky chunks reads NOVELTY ITEM: NOT INTENDED FOR HUMAN CONSUMPTION. Humbug. My teeth sank satisfactorily into a chunk. Like an iceberg calving, a small slab fell onto my tongue and I chewed it just a few times until it dissolved into a smooth paste. This two-stage texture was probably the best part—mouthfeel is what food scientists call it—like gnawing on a solid chocolate Easter Bunny come August. Or, as my husband said, eating very stale Parmesan cheese. But the taste? Well, rather tasteless; chalky, with a strong finish of...chalk. I'd prefer the stale chocolate bunny. Or the stale Parmesan. Wondering if the hankering skips a generation, I handed a hunk to my four-year-old, who, um, didn't care for it. His tasting note: "Big fat butt dirt."

New research shows that, while in the uterus, fetuses and their mothers exchange stem cells. So, of course, we feel close to our offspring; we have become—at the cellular level—each other. And in many religions, we allow the body of another to become our own; the eating of bread, the symbol of a body, brings about rebirth. As for me, I took the body of the South into my body, and truth be told, I do not feel redeemed. What is this white powder on my fingers? Million-year-old feldspar washed from the eroding Appalachians by roiling rivers and carried down to the seething sea. Dirty girl, Sister Mary Agnes once labeled me in St. Mary's Catholic school, and proceeded to wash my mouth out with soap. Oh, she should see my dirty mouth now.

—2010

Learning from Other Writers (Fennelly)

1. Beth Ann Fennelly's opening suggests that she is buying something other than dirt online. Why does she deceive us this way? Why does she evoke the emotions of shame, embarrassment, or secrecy associated with pornography in describing her curiosity about geophagy?

2. Fennelly's actual experiment doesn't involve more than buying the dirt online and tasting it, but these simple acts provide the structural spine for her larger investigations. If her concrete question is: "Why do people eat dirt and what does dirt taste like?," then what is her larger, more abstract question?

3. Why does Fennelly note in the beginning that this would be one more step in her quest to become a Southerner? Why does she mention her outsider status here?

4. Fennelly immediately gives her readers some background about dirt eating. Why is this important? If you had never heard of the practice and knew nothing of the cultural history of geophagy, how would you react when you read that she had purchased dirt online?

5. How does Fennelly's driving question develop as the essay progresses? That is, even though she sets out to understand why people eat dirt, her question gradually morphs to something else. How does she resolve these new concerns?

6. Map the structure of this essay. What are its parts? How do they intersect and relate to one another?

Christopher Bakken

THE THROUMBES OF THASSOS

Tassos of Thassos, whose olives we shall pick, has been drinking *tsipouro* at a wedding until daylight, until just an hour ago in other words, so when he greets us at the port we can see that he's a cheerful disaster.

"It hurts me to drive slowly," he tells us, "so put on your seatbelts." And yes, in spite of his hangover, he attacks each switchback with bombastic acceleration. Abruptly, as we round the southern shoulder of the island, the dense shag of pines and oak disappears and we are speeding through a barren forest of boulders, which drop jaggedly down to the sea. Today, the wind is blowing hard from the southeast, so it is perfectly clear. The island of Samothraki, perpetually terrifying, still the most haunted and pagan of all the Greek islands, agitates the horizon like a purple gash directly to the east. Beyond that we can see the faintly pulsating outline of Asia Minor, the low molars of Limnos, and around two more bends in the road we see Mt. Athos in the distance.

It was just a few degrees above freezing on the mainland at Keramoti, where I waited with my brother and my good friend George Kaltsas two hours earlier. Even the seagulls seemed unwilling to move from their perches along the sea wall. We waited for the ferry in a closet-sized kafenion on the fishing dock. The proprietor, still evidently asleep, was busy trying to light a little wood stove in the middle of the room when we entered. He boiled sweet mountain tea and Greek coffee for us on little propane burners, grumbled now and then toward the first gestures of conversation. My brother, Aaron, who had just arrived in Greece from California, sat in an attentive stupor, his hood pulled over his head.

Just a year ago, at only thirty-seven years old, in the space of about a month, Aaron suffered a heart attack and a divorce. After years in which he had worked himself nearly to death in the competitive world of San Francisco advertising, all of a sudden both his marriage and his health abandoned him (or he abandoned them), and he agreed to join me for a week of olive picking in Greece, no cell phone or Blackberry within reach. I've promised him no place on earth will feel as far away from San Francisco as the stunning double bays of Aliki and the Pension Archontissa, which will be our home for the next week. Since we are the children of dairy farmers in Wisconsin, we have built into our genes the theory that physical work is the antidote to every ailment, a theory we are willing to test in such exquisite surroundings.

Tassos left his parents behind in the olive grove so he could fetch us at the port, so we drop our bags at the pension and join them immediately. "Don't worry, we came here to work," I remind him. When we arrive at the nearest of the Kouzis family olive groves, his parents are just pouring out the first coffees of the day and are unloading a crate full of breakfast things: bread, boiled eggs, canned meat, *tiropita*, oranges just plucked from the tree, and cold spring water in plastic Coke bottles. Tassos's father, Stamatis, rises to greet me with a leathery handshake and two kisses. His mother, Evantheia, gives me an enthusiastic hug. They seem a little stunned that I have actually come;

surely my oath to join their olive harvest, uttered after a long night of drinking *tsipouro* the previous summer, was not meant to be taken seriously. Yet here I am—with my brother in tow—stocking-capped, combat-booted, and armored in canvas and fleece– a little overdressed for the work we're about to do. As it turns out, Tassos is picking olives in his Armani jeans.

Truly, the labor isn't much to master. Tassos hands us *tsougrana*, the only neces-sary implement: benign little plastic rakes mounted upon foot-long wooden broom handles. With these, he demonstrates, you rake—or comb—the olive trees with choppy downward strokes. There is no particular pattern to our combing, no rule about mov-ing clockwise, say, or keeping a certain distance from the next person; where you see olives, you bring them down, shuffling your feet along the nets so as not to trample the booty you've already liberated from the tree. It is effective, I find, to gather three or four branches together at a time, arranging them into a kind of impromptu braid before combing out its thousand knots.

In the space of my first hour standing inside an olive tree, I cover a lot of useless mental territory: reciting to myself every Robert Frost poem I can recall from memory, inventing the lines I don't remember; contemplating a distant cousin I haven't thought of for years; worrying about my children back at home; counting the strokes of my *tsougrana*, then losing count; pondering how to fix the last stanza of a poem I drafted the week before; wishing for cold beer, then revising that wish for a glass of *tsipouro*. In fact, I cover so much useless territory that I begin to realize how little time I usually give myself over to daydreaming; on task, on topic, on subject, on location, most of my waking hours at home are a spent in a regulated blur of focused activity.

Here, a day's work is measured in *telara*, the ubiquitous and sturdy red plastic crates distributed by the local olive oil cooperative. Today, five of us work an hour to fill two or three of these crates, which cannot translate to a very substantial hourly wage. But, in fact, there is no wage; we work for the oil, which has always been more valuable than money in countries like Greece. With the oil comes nutrition and fuel and light. This is why property is often apportioned according not to acreage but to the number of olive trees growing on it. In Greece one is lucky to inherit trees.

2.

"What do you call that mountain?" I ask during one of our coffee breaks on the sec-ond morning of our work. We have moved our equipment to the abstractly terraced, boulder-strewn grove where the Kouzis family grazes its twenty sheep. The crag above us is nearly barren, too steep to support any plant life except for the most determined brambles.

From that Cyclopean forehead, the shoulders of the valley drop east and west, vested in a thick hide of pine and scrub oak that runs down to the sea below.

"*Einai vouno*," Stamatis says without hesitation—"it's a mountain"—with a dismis-sive wave of his hand.

"Well, but the old timers, if they want to be specific, call this hill Kleftoyianni Brachos," Eva interjects, the Hill of Yiannis the Thief.

"Who is Kleftoyiannis," I ask, "what did he steal?" But no one seems interested enough to remember.

This morning we can see our breath, and a light drizzle has left us damp and decidedly cold now that we have stopped our work to rest. No one is much in the mood for conversation. We pull our coffee cups up close to our faces, peel boiled eggs and oranges, and bash open walnuts with stones, staring down bleakly at the forty or so olive trees we'll need to conquer here. "But as for me," Horace says in one of his satires, "my simple meal consists of chicory and mallow from the garden ... [and] olives from the little olive tree." In spite of the cold, it's impossible not to take pleasure in this laborer's meal, in knowing that all of it was grown within a square mile of this grove, this mountain, and we are working today so others can eat olives tomorrow.

The sheep gather around us and bleat plaintively for offerings of food. The most persistent ewe has only one good eye (the other was put out by a stalk of bristle grass and is now gray as the yolk of an over-boiled egg); she actually nudges her way into our midst and must be shooed away with curses and a threatening stomping of boots upon the ground. "Oh, my darling, my pretty," my brother says to her each time she approaches, and we are punchy enough to find his flirtations hilarious every time.

Each year most of the ewes will escort one or two lambs into this hardscrabble palace of red rock, where they will feed off their mother's milk from December until just before Easter. That is, just until they are weaned; then their throats are cut for the sake of the Kouzis family restaurant. One would think that such a profound annual betrayal would make the sheep wary, if not hateful of their human captors. On the contrary, they are tame and cheerful as dogs, though they lack any of the human manners dogs learn to manipulate in favor of themselves. The moment the sheep hear, deep in the invisible depths of the canyon, the idiosyncratic grind of the transmission on Stamatis' pick-up, they begin bleating desperately, trotting off in the direction of the gate where their beloved man will soon arrive, his truck clattering and coughing from the climb, with plastic buckets of shell corn for them to gobble from filthy troughs.

By contrast, yesterday's work was play. The trees were young and virile, evenly spaced on relatively flat ground, since the poultry farm was spread out across three wide terraces that had been dug with a bulldozer. We simply stretched the nets across level earth and attacked the branches with vigor. Most important, those branches were visibly heavy with swollen black fruit the size of obese almonds; each robust stroke of the *tsougrana* unleashed a joyful pattering of olives down upon the nets. Each tree yielded at least a full *telaro* of fruit, and some trees left us with even more to gather than that. Still, regarding such remarkable trees, Tassos and Stamatis had nothing but disdain. "Some years the larger trees will give ten full *telara* each," Tassos tells me, "this is nothing." Today, beneath Kleftoyiannis Brachos, Stamatis surveys the trees in his domain with the suspicious, painfully resigned wince farmers everywhere from Attica to Alabama employ when faced with the catastrophic sight of a lame harvest.

The trees here have drilled themselves impossibly into bare rock. It seems only every third tree has enough olives to bother harvesting, and those that do all seem to be cruelly hovering into spaces that will beguile our attempts to bring down their fruit. Sometimes our nets have to be stretched over tall shrubs and tangles of evil berry-vines that rake our forearms. After combing the easiest branches—those we can reach with both feet planted on the ground—we begin an absurd, slow-motion dance: balancing on one foot, or on just the outer edge of one boot sole, leaning out over a pile of jagged stone while hanging on to a branch with one hand, just to rake down twelve or thirteen olives with the other.

In the end, most trees yield little more than a single, sorry layer in the bottom of an empty *telaro*. We are all cold and discouraged. Thankfully, the drizzle becomes a downpour. Stamatis starts the engine on his truck and shouts, "We're not slaves, let's behave like free men and quit before we drown."

A few nights later at the bar, we get a few titillating details about the hill of the elusive Klephtoyianni. We have just eaten a feast of *ortikia*, tiny local quail which Tassos's cousin, also named Tassos, has grilled with astonishing dexterity over the roaring flames of a fireplace in the corner of his restaurant. Even the men at our table know they are being treated to a delicacy, and they nod with gratitude toward the man who shot the quail, a resident of Kavala famous even here, on an island across the water, for his ability to bring down these tiny wildfowl with his gun.

Tassos's uncle, Triandafillos, cuts an imposing figure: his enormous shoulders seem even broader since he cradles one arm in a sling at the middle of his chest. A black windbreaker has been slung across his shoulders like a cape. He's just muttered a *kalinichta*, his good hand raised in farewell, when Tassos begs him to tell us what he knows about Yiannis the Thief.

"During the Turkish years, this man Yiannis lived alone," Triandafillos explains, "who knows why, and would keep himself alive by pinching a tomato or a watermelon here and there from the gardens of the shepherd's wives. Or he'd make off with a handful of their eggs. Never too much. Everyone understood that the man needed to eat, so out of charity no one reported him. These were human crimes. Anyway, they couldn't have caught him if they wanted to, since he followed paths up into the mountain that only the goats knew and he kept his loot in a cave there that no one has ever found. The mountain was named for him."

In few landscapes is history as legible as in the local earth of Greece, where all the place names bear the weight of too much classical association: Sparta, Corinth, Thebes. I find it refreshing, and somewhat touching, to learn that far more recent history—or mythology—has been inscribed here, on an obscure bluff in an obscure corner of a once famous little island. When Triandafillos leaves, I ask Tassos if all the hills have names, if all the old people have such history in their veins.

"No, people like my uncle are hard to find now. These details are being forgotten," Tassos says.

The famous bird killer of Kavala, depositing one last bit of quail carcass in the ashtray before him, concurs, and then raises his glass while proclaiming a village proverb everyone else around the table seems to know:

"If you don't have an old man in your family, then you should buy one."

3.

A few days later, the weather suddenly turns beautiful. We take the day off from olive picking to explore Thassos. It turns out that the entire island is busy with the olives. The coastal road vibrates with the noise of pick-up trucks, all of them heavy with ten or twenty crates of gleaming olives on the way to the local oil-press. Little groups of people are in every fields, hillside, and grove, spreading their nets, combing trees, sometimes barely visible underneath the endless seas of olive trees.

When we arrive in Thassos Town, we find only one restaurant open. We are the only guests and for us to dine they have to turn on the lights. Our friendly waiter at Taverna Simi shows no interest in speaking Greek; he's lived in London for years while finishing his MBA and only spends his winters here, "bored out of his skull," he says. To our delight, since we are somehow famished yet again, the food is perfectly fresh: a plate of wilted *horta*, a smear of *chtipiti*, a plump tentacle of grilled octopus, and a rectangular plate of crispy eggplant and zucchini slices accompanied with *tzatziki*.

And at last, I eat an olive—a *throumbes* olive from Thassos. It is as wrinkled as anything ancient should be—a black eye made blind by salt. The taste of an island is in this fruit. Let all the others give oil; this one has enough meat to stall every other need. The smooth-skinned Kalamata olives, typically pitted and then exported every-where on earth, offer only two pleasures to the palate: brine and a spongy uniformity of texture. Forgive me Peloponnesians, but I've come to think of Kalamata olives as little more than a delivery system for salt. Throumbes, on the other hand, attack the palate with contrasting motives: they are at shriveled and reduced in size by almost half, and yet the flesh has an expansive, almost meaty texture; the opening flavors are nutty, but then the tongue gets involved with dusky tannins, as it does with wine, moving on toward notes of bay leaf and bitter thyme. The olive's farewell gesture, which has been there all along of course, is its salty finish: throumbes *are* salty, like most olives, but since they never touch a drop of liquid brine the salt comes at the last moment, with about as much grace as salt can be proffered.

Finally, just last night, Tassos revealed his method for making throumbes, the recipe I've come to Thassos to discover. While sorting the olives from our day's work, we reserve only the very biggest olives, those entirely free of blemish, perfectly black and nearly obese with oil. The recipe, which I'm sure must involve actual bay leaves, and perhaps even some citrus or curing agent, turns out to be moronically simple. Tassos leads me to a pile of what look like white plastic bricks.

"What's this?" I ask him.

"All you'll need to make your throumbes," he replies.

Clearly marked on each brick is "Salt for Olives." Nothing more, nothing less. There is no curing agent, no seasoning, no sulfites anywhere to be found. Tassos fills a large plastic garbage bag with the largest of the olives, dumps in a handful of the coarse salt now and then, and punctures the bottom of the bag with his pocket knife a few times so it can drain. He ties the bag shut with some twine, places a brick on top of the bag and walks away.

"That's it?" I ask.

"Yes. They'll be ready in about two weeks. You can taste them next summer when you come."

When our waiter at Taverna Simi comes around to refill our tin carafe of white wine and clear away some of our empty plates, his curiosity gets the best of him. "So you live in Greece ... or are you just visiting? You know, we don't see many foreigners on Thassos this time of year."

When I tell him we have paid to fly across the Atlantic Ocean, and paid again to fly from Athens to Kavala, and again to churn across the water on the ferry from Keramoti, all to work someone's olives, he is frozen in disbelief.

"But why?" he asks. "This is boring work. Drudgery. And don't they have olives in America?"

"That is a good question," my brother replies, clicking his wine glass to mine, "and in fact we do have olive trees where I live in California."

How can we explain to him what this labor represents? For my brother: a reprieve from a life tethered to his three or four computerized devices, from the still simmering psychodramas of his recent divorce, freedom from the wasted hours of rage he endures each day while sitting in traffic, from the opulent poverty known to those who pay through the teeth to live in exquisite San Francisco.

For me: a perfect antidote to the life of the mind, that redundant rhythm of reading and lecturing and talking that makes up the life of a professor; a pause in my duties as a father, with its mixture of anxiety and joy; relief from my own poetry, which always waits to be written, which is (I suddenly realize, while eating an olive on this island) the source of the weight I always feel in my chest when I really stop to pay attention to my body for a moment, something lodged there like the weight of any true need—buried close to the heart, fed by oxygen, hope and despair. I've let that pressure go these past few days, it occurs to me now, unleashed it just enough so it might toss about in the branches of the olive trees I'm combing, the joyful spirit of my poetry liberated from its intellectual jail.

When he returns later with our bill, the waiter glances at us devilishly and says, "You know, when you are done paying Tassos to harvest *his* olives at Aliki, I'd be willing to let you pay me to harvest *mine*. I've got about two hundred trees down by Limenaria that are waiting to be picked."

—2009

Learning from Other Writers (Bakken)

1. How is Bakken an insider to the world in which he carries out his experiment? How is he an outsider?

2. What are the roles of Tassos, George Kaltsas, and Aaron in the journey? What are their roles in relation to the essay's driving question?

3. In the first hour of olive picking, Bakken finds himself daydreaming. Why is his list of the topics he thinks about important? Why is the recognition of this daydreaming so important in the context of his driving question?

4. The line "... property is often apportioned according not to acreage but to the number of olive trees growing on it" is a statement of fact. But the fact so stated also becomes thematically important in the essay. How so?

5. Bakken notes that many of the place names in Greece "bear the weight of too much classical association: Sparta, Corinth, Thebes." What does he mean here? Why might this be a problem?

6. Bakken is surprised to find that all that is needed to cure the olives is salt. Why is this discovery also thematically relevant?

Adding Your Voice

Think of a statement whose truth you have always doubted (urban legends, Internet myths, family stories, proverbs, and other bits of conventional wisdom are a good place to start). Is there any way for you to test the validity of this claim? Alternatively, think of a theory of human behavior you have often heard bandied about (perhaps this theory has to do with education, economics, psychology, government, or law). Is there any way you might conduct some sort of research or experiment that would allow you to check this theory against reality? Write a narrative proposal of how you would undertake your experiment if money and time weren't an option.

CHAPTER 12

Journeys and Quests

One of the joys of a journey or a quest is the potential for learning by experience—leaving your house and discovering something you never could have imagined before you set out. You might not have the time or means to journey to the North Pole by dog sled or to the rainforest by canoe, but you can still plan and carry out an essay-worthy trip. A bicycle ride through the farmland behind your campus, a pilgrimage to the grave of the first female graduate of your college, or a quest to the Salvation Army to find the perfect sofa might provide you with more than enough material to create an impressive example of this form. What matters is not the destination or how "big" your adventure seems to be, but the question you are trying to unravel by heading out.

When you undertake a journey or a quest, the trick is to focus on your initial question while being open to the possibility that this question will evolve as you go along. The question you set out to answer might end up being entirely different from the more exciting question you discover as you travel. That's fine. In fact, that's great! You don't want to get swept away by every distraction or digression, but fostering your ability to recognize the signs of a promising new trail is an important mindset to cultivate when tackling this form. Donovan Hohn, the author of *Moby-Duck: The True Story of 28,800 Bath Toys Lost at Sea and of the Beachcombers, Oceanographers, Environmentalists, and Fools, Including the Author, Who Went in Search of Them* (the title speaks for itself), writes the following in the prologue of his book:

> But questions, I've learned since, can be like ocean currents. Wade in a little too far
> and they can carry you away. Follow one line of inquiry and it will lead you to another,
> and another. Spot a yellow duck dropped atop the seaweed at the tide line, ask yourself
> where it came from, and the next thing you know you're way out at sea, no land in sight.
> … You're wondering when and why yellow ducks became icons of childhood. You want
> to know what it's like inside toy factories in Guangdong. You're marveling at the scale of
> humanity's impact on this terraqueous globe and at the oceanic magnitude of your own
> ignorance. You're giving the plight of the Laysan Albatross many moments of thought.

What Hohn is pointing to here is the wonderful way in which questions can lead to more questions. So even if you have a fairly simple question when you start, each step of your journey may lead you to new and unexpected insights.

A GOAL BEYOND YOUR DESTINATION

Although an account of a journey is in some sense a reflective narrative, when you write a reflective narrative you are recalling something that happened in the past with the perspective of the present; when you undertake a journey or a quest, you are undertaking the experience for the explicit purpose of writing about your adventures. You travel with the intention of reporting on whatever noteworthy sights or sites you encounter along the way; you make a pilgrimage to pay homage to a person or a place you particularly revere; you set out on a quest to find something of value that only can be attained in a certain place or from a specific person. So your *stance* toward your material is altered by the intention of documenting what you experience. This naturally changes how you pay attention and what you are focusing on during your trip.

In other words, a destination is not enough. Without a reason to undertake your pilgrimage or quest, you might feel compelled to take notes about every single thing that happens along the way and then dump all these observations in an essay. You must find a way to interrogate your journey so that your experiences will gain significance, whether you carry out this interrogation while you are planning your trip, during the actual journey, or in a reflective state afterward. As with any essay, you must create meaning by analyzing, connecting, and reflecting on what is important. How does what you experienced on your journey connect to the larger culture? How do your discoveries plumb the human condition? How does your account of your journey give us a new way of seeing? Such meditations are what will lead you and your journey to significance.

THE SHAPE OF YOUR JOURNEY

As you read the essays in this section, you will find that some of the authors don't tell us anything about their preparations for their trip, while others offer brief explanations of their motives before they set out. (Consider Michael Paterniti's portrait of Leonid Sladnik in Chapter 8; Paterniti spends a good amount of time recounting how he came to learn of the giant and what was going through his mind before he bought that ticket to Ukraine.) Sometimes, the preparations, particularly the mental or philosophical ones, are just as important as the journey. In John Jeremiah Sullivan's essay about his trip to a Christian rock festival, his initial attitude toward his subject (sarcastic, satirical) and his lengthy preparations for his journey (hanging out in Christian chat-rooms with teenagers, riffing on the finer points of magazine writing, acquiring an enormous motorhome to make the drive across Pennsylvania) are crucial to his later experience at the festival. In particular, these preparations serve as a dramatic contrast to what he will reveal to the reader about the festival participants—and himself—in the essay's second half. Without the biting tone in the introduction and the author's stated mission of satirizing his experience in the glossy pages of GQ, what we come to find out about the author would lack the power of wonder and surprise.

This doesn't mean you will need to outline every step of the process that led up to your journey. Zadie Smith, in "One Week in Liberia," structures her essay according to the days of her trip: Monday to Saturday. She gives us no information about her preparation and, contrary to more standard practice, very little context about her reasons for going. We simply begin on the plane: "There are no flights from England to Liberia."

EVENTS AND OCCASIONS

One reason to carry out a journey or a quest is to travel somewhere with the goal of attending a particular event—a music festival such as South by Southwest in Austin, Texas, or the Bonnaroo Festival in Manchester, Tennessee, the Super Bowl, the annual Chicken Fling in your hometown, your cousin's 500-person wedding, or a comic-book convention. You might attend as someone who knows a lot about the event and its fans, or as someone who knows very little. If the latter, you will want to do research beforehand so you know which questions to ask, what elements of the event are not to be missed, and other details that might be logistically helpful. Often, your level of knowledge and experience will lie somewhere between novice and die-hard fan: after all, to carry out this sort of writing you must be intrigued enough to make the journey and to push your investigation and analysis to an interesting depth and complexity, but not so emotionally close to the event that you can't view the practices or the participants with the appropriate distance. In short, you want to find the balance between "insider" and "outsider." Think of Elwood Reid, who is both a part of his football team and not, or Jesmyn Ward, who spends her summers in her hometown in Mississippi but leaves each fall. Like Reid and Ward, most authors walk the fine line between belonging and not belonging. The former stance allows you access to your subject, while the latter arms you with objectivity and provides you with a question or a conflict that needs to be sorted out. After all, if you don't feel conflicted about your material, you won't have a reason to grapple with the complexities it presents.

That doesn't mean you can't write about something with which you've had no experience. You will gain the insider angle by undertaking the investigation, whether through library research, interviews, or feet-on-the-ground journalism. Just as your relationship to your material will grow more intimate as you carry out your investigation, so will your driving question become more specific or complicated as your journey continues. Or you might encounter something that makes your initial question moot, with a new one emerging in its place. For instance, attending a baseball game in your hometown's state-of-the-art, corporate-sponsored stadium could turn into an investigation of the fate of the neighborhood that surrounds the old, abandoned stadium.

John Jeremiah Sullivan, through his trip to a huge Christian rock festival, provides an incisive examination of the Christian rock phenomenon and a stirring exploration of faith and belief. As you read, note that Sullivan withholds some key information about himself until he hears the beginnings of a song by the Christian rock band Petra. This is not a deliberate attempt to keep information from his readers but instead a mimicking of his own emotional journey as he at last realizes something very powerful about himself and the people who surround him.

What is most powerful about each physical journey described in this chapter is the unexpected emotional journey that results. Each essay reminds us that our preconceived notions play a role in what we write, particularly if those notions are challenged, overturned, or completely changed in the course of our investigation.

By John Jeremiah Sullivan

UPON THIS ROCK

It is wrong to boast, but in the beginning, my plan was perfect.

I was assigned to cover the Cross-Over Festival in Lake of the Ozarks, Missouri, three days of the top Christian bands and their backers at an isolated midwestern fairground or something. I'd stand at the edge of the crowd and take notes on the scene, chat up the occasional audience member ("What's harder—homeschooling or regular schooling?"), then flash my pass to get backstage, where I'd rap with the artists themselves: "This Christian music—it's a phenomenon. What do you tell your fans when they ask you why God let Creed break up?" The singer could feed me his bit about how all music glorifies Him, when it's performed with a loving spirit, and I'd jot down every tenth word, inwardly smiling. Later that night, I might sneak some hooch in my rental car and invite myself to lie with a prayer group by their fire, for the fellowship of it. Fly home, stir in statistics. Paycheck.

But as my breakfast-time mantra says, I am a professional. And they don't give out awards for that sort of toe-tap, J-school foolishness. I wanted to know what these people are, who claim to love this music, who drive hundreds of miles, traversing states, to hear it live. Then it came, my epiphany: I would go with them. Or rather, they would go with me. I would rent a van, a plush one, and we would travel there together, I and three or four hard-core buffs, all the way from the East Coast to the implausibly named Lake of the Ozarks. We'd talk through the night, they'd proselytize at me, and I'd keep my little tape machine working all the while. Somehow I knew we'd grow to like and pity one another. What a story that would make—for future generations.

The only remaining question was: how to recruit the willing? But it was hardly even a question, because everyone knows that damaged types who are down for whatever's clever gather in "chat rooms" every night. And among the Jesusy, there's plenty who are super f'd up. He preferred it that way, evidently.

So I published my invitation, anonymously, at youthontherock.com, and on two Internet forums devoted to the good-looking Christian pop-punk band Relient K, which had been booked to appear at Cross-Over. I pictured that guy or girl out there who'd been dreaming in an attic room of seeing, with his or her own eyes, the men of Relient K perform their song "Gibberish" from *Two Lefts Don't Make a Right...But Three Do*. How could he or she get there, though? Gas prices won't drop, and Relient K never plays North Florida. Please, Lord, make it happen. Suddenly, here my posting came, like a great light. We could help each other. "I'm looking for a few serious fans of Christian rock to ride to the festival with me," I wrote. "Male/female doesn't matter, though you shouldn't be older than, say, 28, since I'm looking at this primarily as a youth phenomenon."

They seem like harmless words. Turns out, though, I had failed to grasp how "youth" the phenomenon is. Most of the people hanging out in these chat rooms were teens, and I don't mean 19, friends, I mean 14. Some of them, I was about to learn, were mere tweens. I had just traipsed out onto the World Wide Web and asked a bunch of 12-year-old Christians if they wanted to come for a ride in my van.

It wasn't long before the little fuckers rounded on me. "Nice job cutting off your email address," wrote "mathgeek29," in a tone that seemed not at all Christlike. "I doubt if anybody would give a full set of contact information to some complete stranger on the Internet.... Aren't there any Christian teens in Manhattan who would be willing to do this?"

"Oh, I should hope not," I blubbered.

A few of the children were credulous. "Riathamus" said, "i am 14 and live in indiana plus my parents might not let me considering it is a stranger over the Internet. but that would really be awsome." A girl by the name of "LilLoser" even tried to be a friend:

I doubt my parents would allow their baby girl to go with some guy they don't and I don't know
except through email, especially for the amount of time you're asking and like driving around
everywhere with ya.... I'm not saying you're a creepy petifile, lol, but i just don't think you'll get too
many people interested... cuz like i said, it spells out "creepy"... but hey—good luck to you in your
questy missiony thing. lol.

The luck that she wished me I sought in vain. The Christians stopped chatting with me and started chatting among themselves, warning one another about me. Finally one poster on the official Relient K site hissed at the others to stay away from my scheme, as I was in all likelihood "a 40 year old kidnapper." Soon I logged on and found that the moderators of the site had removed my post and its lengthening thread of accusations altogether, offering no explanation. Doubtless at that moment they were faxing alerts to a network of moms. I recoiled in dread. I called my lawyer, in Boston, who told me to "stop using computers."

In the end, the experience inspired in me a distaste for the whole Cross-Over Festival, and I resolved to refuse the assignment. I withdrew.

*****

The problem with a flash mag like the *Gentlemen's Quarterly* is that there's always some overachieving assistant, sometimes called Greg, whom the world hasn't beaten down yet and who, when you phone him, out of courtesy, just to let him know that "the Cross-Over thing fell through" and that you'll be in touch when you "figure out what to do next," hops on that mystical boon the Internet and finds out that the festival you were planning to attend was in fact not "the biggest one in the country," as you'd alleged. The biggest one in the country—indeed, in Christendom—is the Creation Festival, inaugurated in 1979, a regular Godstock. And it happens not in Missouri but in rural-most Pennsylvania, in a green valley, on a farm called Agape. This festival did not end a month ago; it starts the day after tomorrow. Already they are assembling, many tens of thousands strong. *But hey—good luck to you in your questy missiony thing. lol.*

I made one demand: that I not be forced to camp. I'd be given some sort of vehicle with a mattress in it, one of these pop-ups, maybe. "Right," said Greg. "Here's the deal.

I've called around. There are no vans left within a hundred miles of Philly. We got you an RV, though. It's a twenty-nine-footer." Once I reached the place, we agreed (for he led me to think he agreed), I would certainly be able to downgrade to something more manageable.

The reason twenty-nine feet is such a common length for RVs, I presume, is that once a vehicle gets much longer, you need a special permit to drive it. That would mean forms and fees, possibly even background checks. But show up at any RV joint with your thigh stumps lashed to a skateboard, crazily waving your hooks-for-hands, screaming you want that twenty-nine-footer out back for a trip to you *ain't sayin' where*, and all they want to know is: Credit or debit, tiny sir?

Two days later, I stood in a parking lot, suitcase at my feet. Debbie came toward me. She was a lot to love, with a face as sweet as a birthday cake beneath spray-hardened bangs. She raised a meaty arm and pointed, before either of us spoke. The thing she pointed at was the object about which I'd just been saying, "Not that one, Jesus, okay?" It was like something the ancient Egyptians might have left behind in the desert.

"Hi, there," I said, "Listen, all I need is, like, a camper van or whatever. It's just me, and I'm going 500 miles…"

She considered me. "Where ya headed?"

"To this thing called Creation. It's, like, a Christian-rock festival."

"You and everybody!" she chirped. "The people who got our vans are going to that same thing. There's a *bunch o' ya*."

Her coworker Jack emerged—tattooed, squat, gray-mulleted, spouting open contempt for MapQuest. He'd be giving me real directions. "But first let's check 'er out."

We toured the outskirts of my soon-to-be mausoleum. It took time. Every single thing Jack said, somehow, was the only thing I'd need to remember. White water, gray water, black water (drinking, showering, *le devoir*). Here's your this, never ever that. Grumbling about "weekend warriors." I couldn't listen, because listening would mean accepting it as real, though his casual mention of the vast blind spot in the passenger-side mirror squeaked through, as did his description of the "extra two feet on each side"—the bulge of my living quarters—which I wouldn't be able to see but would want to "be conscious of" out there. Debbie followed us with a video camera, for insurance purposes. I saw my loved ones gathered in a mahogany-paneled room to watch this footage; them being forced to hear me say, "What if I never use the toilet—do I still have to switch on the water?"

Mike pulled down the step and climbed aboard. It was really happening. The interior smelled of spoiled vacations and amateur porn shoots wrapped in motel shower curtains and left in the sun. I was physically halted at the threshold for a moment. Jesus had never been in this RV.

What should I tell you about my voyage to Creation? Do you want to know what it's like to drive a windmill with tires down the Pennsylvania Turnpike at rush hour by your lonesome, with darting bug-eyes and shaking hands; or about Greg's laughing phone call "to see how it's going"; about hearing yourself say "no No NO NO!" every time you try to merge; or about thinking you detect—beneath the mysteriously comforting blare of the radio—faint honking sounds, then checking your passenger-side mirror only to find you've been straddling the lanes for an unknown number of miles (those two extra feet!) and that the line of traffic you've kept pinned stretches back farther than you can see; or about stopping at Target to buy sheets and a pillow and peanut butter but then practicing your golf swing in the sporting-goods aisle for a solid twenty-five minutes, unable to stop, knowing that when you do, the twenty-nine-footer will be where you left her, alone in the side lot, hulking and malevolent, waiting for you to take her the rest of the way to your shared destiny?

She got me there, as Debbie and Jack had promised, not possibly believing it themselves. Seven miles from Mount Union, a sign read CREATION AHEAD. The sun was setting; it floated above the valley like a fiery gold balloon. I fell in with a long line of cars and trucks and vans—not many RVs. Here they were, all about me: the born again. On my right was a pickup truck, its bed full of teenage girls in matching powder blue T-shirts; they were screaming at a Mohawked kid who was walking beside the road. I took care not to meet their eyes—who knew but they weren't the same fillies I had solicited days before? Their line of traffic lurched ahead, and an old orange Datsun came up beside me. I watched as the driver rolled down her window, leaned halfway out, and blew a long, clear note on a ram's horn.

Oh, I understand where you are coming from. But that is what she did. I have it on tape. She blew a ram's horn. Quite capably. Twice. A yearly rite, perhaps, to announce her arrival at Creation.

My turn at the gate. The woman looked at me, then past me to the empty passenger seat, then down the whole length of the twenty-nine-footer. "How many people in your group?" she asked.

*****

I pulled away in awe, permitting the twenty-nine-footer to float. My path was thronged with excited Christians, most younger than 18. The adults looked like parents or pastors, not here on their own. Twilight was well along, and the still valley air was sharp with campfire smoke. A great roar shot up to my left—something had happened onstage. The sound bespoke a multitude. It filled the valley and lingered.

I thought I might enter unnoticed—that the RV might even offer a kind of cover—but I was already turning heads. Two separate kids said, "I feel sorry for him" as I passed. Another leaped up on the driver's-side step and said, "Jesus Christ, man," then fell away running. I kept braking—even idling was too fast. Whatever spectacle had provoked the roar was over now: The roads were choked. The youngsters were streaming around me in both directions, back to their campsites, like a line of ants around some petty obstruction. They had a disconcerting way of stepping aside for the RV only when its front fender was just about to graze their backs. From my elevated vantage, it looked as if they were waiting just a tenth of a second too long, and that I was gently, forcibly parting them in slow motion.

The Evangelical strata were more or less recognizable from my high school days, though everyone, I observed, had gotten better looking. Lots were dressed like skate punks or in last season's East Village couture (nondenominationals); others were fairly trailer (rural Baptists or Church of God); there were preps (Young Life, Fellowship of Christian Athletes—these were the ones who'd have the pot). You could spot the stricter sectarians right away, their unchanging antifashion and pale glum faces. When I asked one woman, later, how many she reckoned were white, she said, "Roughly 100 percent." I did see some Asians and three or four blacks. They gave the distinct impression of having been adopted.

I drove so far. You wouldn't have thought this thing could go on so far. Every other bend in the road opened onto a whole new cove full of tents and cars; the encampment had expanded to its physiographic limits, pushing right up to the feet of the ridges. It's hard to put across the sensory effect of that many people living and moving around in the open: part family reunion, part refugee camp. A tad militia, but cheerful.

The roads turned dirt and none too wide: Hallelujah Highway, Street Called Straight. I'd been told to go to "H," but when I reached H, two teenage kids in orange vests came out of the shadows and told me the spots were all reserved. "Help me out here, guys," I said, jerking my thumb, pitifully indicating my mobile home. They pulled out their walkie-talkies. Some time went by. It got darker. Then an even younger boy rode up on a bike and winked a flashlight at me, motioning I should follow.

It was such a comfort to yield up my will to this kid. All I had to do was not lose him. His vest radiated a warm, reassuring officialdom in my headlights. Which may be why I failed to comprehend in time that he was leading me up an almost vertical incline—"the Hill Above D."

I'm not sure which was first: the little bell in my spine warning me that the RV had reached a degree of tilt she was not engineered to handle, or the sickening knowledge that we had begun to slip back. I bowed up off the seat and crouched on the gas. I heard yelling. I kicked at the brake. With my left hand and foot I groped, like a person drowning, for the emergency brake (had Jack's comprehensive how-to sesh not touched on its whereabouts?). We were losing purchase; she started to shudder. My little guide's eyes looked scared.

I'd known this moment would come, of course, that the twenty-nine-footer would turn on me. We had both of us understood it from the start. But I must confess, I never imagined her hunger for death could prove so extreme. Laid out below and behind me was a literal field of Christians, toasting buns and playing guitars, fellowshipping. The aerial shot in the papers would show a long scar, a swath through their peaceful tent village. And that this gigantic psychopath had worked her vile design through the agency of a child—an innocent, albeit impossibly stupid, child...

My memory of the next five seconds is smeared, but logic tells me that a large and perfectly square male head appeared in the windshield. It was blond and wearing glasses. It had wide-open eyes and a Chaucerian West Virginia accent and said rapidly that I should "JACK THE WILL TO THE ROT" while applying the brakes. Some branch of my motor cortex obeyed. The RV skidded briefly and was still. Then the same voice said, "All right, hit the gas on three: one, two..."

She began to climb—slowly, as if on a pulley. Some freakishly powerful beings were pushing. Soon we had leveled out at the top of the hill.

There were five of them, all in their early twenties. I remained in the twenty-nine-footer; they gathered below.

"Thank you," I said.

"Aw, hey," shot back Darius, the one who'd given the orders. He talked very fast. "We've been doing this all day—I don't know why that kid keeps bringing people up here—we're from West Virginia—listen, he's retarded—there's an *empty field* right there."

I looked back and down at what he was pointing to: pastureland.

Jake stepped forward. He was also blond, but slender. And handsome in a feral way. His face was covered in stubble as pale as his hair. He said he was from West Virginia and wanted to know where I was from.

"I was born in Louisville," I said.

"Really?" said Jake. "Is that on the Ohio River?" Like Darius, he both responded and spoke very quickly. I said that in fact it was.

"Well, I know a dude that died who was from Ohio. I'm a volunteer fireman, see. Well, he flipped a Chevy Blazer nine times. He was spread out from here to that ridge over there. He was dead as four o'clock."

"Who are you guys?" I said.

Ritter answered. He was big, one of those fat men who don't really have any fat, a corrections officer—as I was soon to learn—and a former heavyweight wrestler. He could burst a pineapple in his armpit and chuckle about it (or so I assume). Haircut: military. Mustache: faint. "We're just a bunch of West Virginia guys on fire for Christ," he said. "I'm Ritter, and this is Darius, Jake, Bub, and that's Jake's brother, Josh. Pee Wee's around here somewhere."

"Chasin' tail," said Darius disdainfully.

"So you guys have just been hanging out here, saving lives?"

"We're from West Virginia," said Darius again, like maybe he thought I was thick. It was he who most often spoke for the group. The projection of his jaw from the lump of snuff he kept there made him come off a bit contentious, but I felt sure he was just high-strung.

"See," Jake said, "well, our campsite is right over there." With a cock of his head he identified a car, a truck, a tent, a fire, and a tall cross made of logs. And that other thing was...a PA system?

"We had this spot last year," Darius said. "I prayed about it. I said, 'God, I'd just really like to have that spot again—you know, if it's Your will.'"

I'd assumed that my days at Creation would be fairly lonely and end with my ritual murder. But these West Virginia guys had such warmth. It flowed out of them. They asked me what I did and whether I liked sassafras tea and how many others I'd brought with me in the RV. Plus they knew a dude who died horribly and was from a state with the same name as the river I grew up by, and I'm not the type who questions that sort of thing.

"What are you guys doing later?" I said.

Bub was short and solid; each of his hands looked as strong as a trash compactor. He had darker skin than the rest—an olive cast—with brown hair under a camouflage hat and brown eyes and a full-fledged dark mustache. Later he would share with me that friends often told him he must be "part N-word." He was shy and always looked like he must be thinking hard about something. "Me and Ritter's going to hear some music," he said.

"What band is it?"

Ritter said, "Jars of Clay."

I had read about them; they were big. "Why don't you guys stop by my trailer and get me on your way?" I said. "I'll be in that totally empty field."

Ritter said, "We just might do that." Then they all lined up to shake my hand.

*****

While I waited for Ritter and Bub, I lay in bed and read *The Silenced Times* by lantern light. This was a thin newsletter that had come with my festival packet. It wasn't really a newsletter; it was publisher's flackery for *Silenced*, a new novel by Jerry Jenkins, one of the minds behind the multi-hundred-million-dollar *Left Behind* series—twelve books so far, all about what happens after the Rapture, to people like me. His new book was a futuristic job, set in 2047. The dateline on the newsletter read: "March 2, 38." You get it? Thirty-seven years have passed since they wiped Jesus from history. *The Silenced Times* was laid out to look like a newspaper from that coming age.

It was pretty grim stuff. In the year 38, an ancient death cult has spread like a virus and taken over the "United Seven States of America." Adherents meet in "cell groups" (nice touch: a bit of old Commie lingo); they enlist the young and hunger for global hegemony while striving to hasten the end of the world. By the year 34—the time of the last census—44 percent of the population had professed membership in the group; by now the figure is closer to half. This dwarfs any other surviving religious movement in the land. Even the president (whom they mobilized to elect) has been converted. The most popular news channel in the country openly backs him and his policies; and the year's most talked-about film is naked propaganda for the cult, but in a darkly brilliant twist, much of the population has been convinced that the media are in fact controlled by...

I'm sorry! That's all happening now. That's Evangelicalism. *The Silenced Times* describes Christians being thrown into jail, driven underground, their pamphlets confiscated. A dude wins an award for ratting out his sister, who was leading a campus Bible study (you know how we do). Jerry Jenkins must blow his royalties on crack. I especially liked the part in *The Silenced Times* where it reports that antireligion forces have finally rounded up Jenkins himself—in a cave. He's 97 years old but has never stopped typing, and as they drag him away, he's bellowing Scripture.

Ritter beat on the door. He and Bub were ready to hear some Jars of Clay. Now that it was night, more fires were going; the whole valley was aromatic. And the sky looked like a tin punch lantern—thousands of stars were out. There were so many souls headed toward the stage, it was hard to walk, though I noticed the crowd tended to give Ritter a wider berth. He kind of leaned back, looking over people's heads, as if he expected to spot a friend. I asked about his church in West Virginia. He said he and the rest of the guys were Pentecostal, speaking in tongues and all that—except for Jake, who was a Baptist. But they all went to the same "sing"—a weekly Bible study at some-body's house with food and guitars. Did Ritter think everyone here was a Christian? "No, there's some who probably aren't saved. With this many people, there has to be." What were his feelings on that? "It just opens up opportunities for witnessing," he said.

Bub stopped suddenly—a signal that he wished to speak. The crowd flowed on around us for a minute while he chose his words. "There's Jewish people here," he said.

"Really?" I said. "You mean, Jew Jews?"

"Yeah," Bub said. "These girls Pee Wee brung around. I mean, they're Jewish. That's pretty awesome." He laughed without moving his face; Bub's laugh was a purely vocal phenomenon. Were his eyes moist?

We commenced walking.

I suspect that on some level—say, the conscious one—I didn't want to be noticing what I noticed as we went. But I've been to a lot of huge public events in this country during the past five years, writing about sports or whatever, and one thing they all had in common was this weird implicit enmity that American males, in particular, seem to carry around with them much of the time. Call it a laughable generalization, fine, but if you spend enough late afternoons in stadium concourses, you feel it, something darker than machismo. Something a little wounded, and a little sneering, and just plain ready for bad things to happen. It wasn't here. It was just...not. I looked for it, and I couldn't find it. In the three days I spent at Creation, I saw not one fight, heard not one word spoken in anger, felt at no time even mildly harassed, and in fact met many people who were exceptionally kind. I realize they were all of the same race, all believed the same stuff, and weren't drinking, but there were also 100,000 of them. What's that about?

We were walking past a row of portable toilets, by the food stands. As we came around the corner, I saw the stage, from off to the side. And the crowd on the hill that faced the stage. Their bodies rose till they merged with the dark. "Holy crap," I said.

Ritter waved his arm like an impresario. He said, "This, my friend, is Creation."

*****

For their encore, Jars of Clay did a cover of U2's "All I Want Is You." It was bluesy. That's the last thing I'll be saying about the bands.

Or, no, wait, there's this: The fact that I didn't think I heard a single interesting bar of music from the forty or so acts I caught or overheard at Creation shouldn't be read as a knock on the acts themselves, much less as contempt for the underlying notion of Christians playing rock. These were not Christian bands, you see; these were Christian-rock bands. The key to digging this scene lies in that one-syllable distinc-tion. Christian rock is a genre that exists to edify and make money off of evangelical Christians. It's message music for listeners who know the message cold, and, what's more, it operates under a perceived *responsibility*—one the artists embrace—to "reach people." As such, it rewards both obviousness and maximum palatability (the artists would say *clarity*), which in turn means *parasitism*. Remember those perfume dispensers they used to have in pharmacies—"If you like Drakkar Noir, you'll love Sexy Musk"? Well, Christian rock works like that. Every successful crappy secular group has its Christian off-brand, and that's proper, because culturally speaking, it's supposed to serve as a stand-in for, not an alternative to or an improvement on, those very groups. In this it succeeds wonderfully. If you think it profoundly sucks, that's because your priorities are not its priorities; you want to hear something cool and new, it needs to play something proven to please...while praising Jesus Christ. That's Christian rock. A Christian band, on the other hand, is just a band that has more than one Christian in it. U2 is the exemplar, held aloft by believers and nonbelievers alike, but there have been others through the years, bands about which people would say, "Did you know those guys were Christians? I know—it's freaky. They're still fuckin' good, though." The Call was like that; Lone Justice was like that. These days you hear it about indie acts like Pedro the Lion and Damien Jurado (or P.O.D. and Evanescence—de gustibus). In most cases, bands like these make a very, very careful effort not to be seen as playing "Christian rock." It's largely a matter of phrasing: Don't tell the interviewer you're born-again; say faith is a very important part of your life. And here, if I can drop the open-minded pretense real quick, is where the stickier problem of *actually being any good* comes in, because a question that must be asked is whether a hard-core Christian who turns 19 and finds he or she can write first-rate songs (someone like Damien Jurado) would ever have anything whatsoever to do with Christian rock. Talent tends to come hand in hand with a certain base level of subtlety. And believe it or not, the Christian-rock establishment sometimes expresses a kind of resigned *approval* of the way groups like U2 or Switchfoot (who played Creation while I was there and had a monster secular—radio hit at the time with "Meant to Live" but whose management wouldn't allow them to be photographed onstage) take quiet pains to distance themselves from any unambiguous Jesus-loving, recognizing that this is the surest way to connect with the world (you know that's how they refer to us, right? We're "of the world"). So it's possible—and indeed seems likely—that Christian rock is a musical genre, the only one I can think of, that has excellence-proofed itself.

*****

It was late, and the jews had sown discord. What Bub had said was true: There were Jews at Creation. These were Jews for Jesus, it emerged, two startlingly pretty high school girls from Richmond. They'd been sitting by the fire—one of them mingling fingers with Pee Wee—when Bub and Ritter and I returned from seeing Jars of Clay. Pee Wee was younger than the other guys, and cute, and he gazed at the girls admiringly when they spoke. At a certain point, they mentioned to Ritter that he would writhe in hell for having tattoos (he had a couple); it was what their people believed. Ritter had not taken the news all that well. He was fairly confident about his position among the elect. There was debate; Pee Wee was forced to escort the girls back to their tents, while Darius worked to calm Ritter. "They may have weird ideas," he said, "but we worship the same God."

The fire had burned to glowing coals, and now it was just we men, sitting on coolers, talking late-night hermeneutics blues. Bub didn't see how God could change His mind, how He could say all that crazy shit in the Old Testament—like don't get tattoos and don't look at your uncle naked—then take it back in the New.

"Think about it this way," I said. "If you do something that really makes Darius mad, and he's pissed at you, but then you do something to make it up to him, and he forgives you, that isn't him changing his mind. The situation has changed. It's the same with the old and new covenants, except Jesus did the making up."

Bub seemed pleased with this explanation. "I never heard anyone say it like that," he said. But Darius stared at me gimlet-eyed across the fire. He knew my gloss was theologically sound, and he wondered where I'd gotten it. The guys had been gracefully dancing around the question of what I believed—"where my walk was at," as they would have put it—all night.

We knew one another fairly well by now. Once Pee Wee had returned, they'd eagerly showed me around their camp. Most of their tents were back in the forest, where they weren't supposed to be; the air was cooler there. Darius had located a small stream about thirty yards away and, using his hands, dug out a basin. This was supplying their drinking water.

It came out that these guys spent much if not most of each year in the woods. They lived off game—as folks do, they said, in their section of Braxton County. They knew all the plants of the forest, which were edible, which cured what. Darius pulled out a large piece of cardboard folded in half. He opened it under my face: a mess of sassafras roots. He wafted their scent of black licorice into my face and made me eat one.

Then he remarked that he bet I liked weed. I allowed as how I might not *not* like it. "I used to love that stuff," he told me. Seeing that I was taken aback, he said, "Man, to tell you the truth, I wasn't even convicted about it. But it's socially unacceptable, and that was getting in the way of my Christian growth."

The guys had put together what I did for a living—though, to their credit, they didn't seem to take this as a reasonable explanation for my being there—and they gradually got the sense that I found them exotic (though it was more than that). Slowly, their talk became an ecstasy of self-definition. They were passionate to make me see *what kind of guys they were*. This might have grown tedious, had they been any old kind of guys. But they were the kind of guys who believed that God had personally interceded and made it possible for four of them to fit into Ritter's silver Chevrolet Cavalier for the trip to Creation.

"Look," Bub said, "I'm a pretty big boy, right? I mean, I'm stout. And Darius is a big boy"—here Darius broke in and made me look at his calves, which were muscled to a degree that hinted at deformity; "I'm a freak," he said; Bub sighed and went on without breaking eye contact—"and you *know* Ritter is a big boy. Plus we had two coolers, guitars, an electric piano, our tents and stuff, all"—he turned and pointed, turned back, paused—"in that Chevy." He had the same look in his eyes as earlier, when he'd told me there were Jews. "I think that might be a miracle," he said.

In their lives, they had known terrific violence. Ritter and Darius met, in fact, when each was beating the shit out of the other in middle-school math class. Who won? Ritter looked at Darius, as if to clear his answer, and said, "Nobody." Jake once took a fishing pole that Darius had accidentally stepped on and broken and beat him to the ground with it. "I told him, "Well, watch" where you're stepping," "Jake said. (This memory made Darius laugh so hard he removed his glasses.) Half of their childhood friends had been murdered—shot or stabbed over drugs or nothing. Others had killed themselves. Darius's grandfather, great-uncle, and onetime best friend had all committed suicide. When Darius was growing up, his father was in and out of jail; at least once, his father had done hard time. In Ohio he stabbed a man in the chest (the man had refused to stop "pounding on" Darius's grandfather). Darius caught a lot of grief—"Your daddy's a jailbird!"—during those years. He'd carried a chip on his shoulder from that.

"You came up pretty rough," I said.

"Not really," Darius said. "Some people ain't got hands and feet." He talked about how much he loved his father. "With all my heart—he's the best. He's brought me up the way that I am."

"And anyway," he added, "I gave all that to God—all that anger and stuff. He took it away."

God had left him enough to get by on. Earlier in the evening, the guys had roughed up Pee Wee a little and tied him to a tree with ratchet straps. Some other Christians must have reported his screams to the staff, because a guy in an orange vest came stomping up the hill. Pee Wee hadn't been hurt much, but he put on a show of tears, to be funny. "They always do me like that," he said. "Save me, mister!"

The guy was unamused. "It's not them you got to worry about," he said. "It's me."

Those were such foolish words! Darius came forward like some hideously fast-moving lizard on a nature show. "I'd watch it, man," he said. "You don't know who you're talking to. This'n here's as like to shoot you as shake your hand."

The guy somehow appeared to move back without actually taking a step. "You're not allowed to have weapons," he said.

"Is that right?" Darius said. "We got a conceal 'n' carry right there in the glove box. Mister, I'm from West Virginia—I know the law."

"I think you're lying," said the guy. His voice had gone a bit warbly.

Darius leaned forward, as if to hear better. His eyes were leaving his skull. "How would you know that?" he said. "Are you a prophet?"

"I'm Creation staff!" the guy said.

All of a sudden, Jake stood up—he'd been watching this scene from his seat by the fire. The fixed polite smile on his face was indistinguishable from a leer. "Well," he said, "why don't you go somewhere and *create* your own problems?"

I realize that these tales of the West Virginia guys' occasional truculence might appear to gainsay what I claimed earlier about "not one word spoken in anger," etc. But look, it was playful. Darius, at least, was performing a bit for me. And if you take into account what the guys have to be on guard for all the time back home, the notable thing becomes how effectively they checked their instincts at Creation.

In any case, we operated with more or less perfect impunity from then on.

This included a lot of very loud, live music between two and three o'clock in the morning. The guys were running their large PA off the battery in Jake's truck. Ritter and Darius had a band of their own back home, First Verse. They were responsible for the music at their church. Ritter had an angelic tenor that seemed to be coming out of a body other than his own. And Josh was a good guitar player; he had a Les Paul and an effects board. We passed around the acoustic. I had to dig to come up with Christian tunes. I did "Jesus," by Lou Reed, which they liked okay. But they really enjoyed "Redemption Song." When I finished, Bub said, "Man, that's really Christian. It really is." Darius made me teach it to him; he said he would take it home and "do it at worship."

Then he jumped up and jogged to the electric piano, which was on a stand ten feet away. He closed his eyes and began to play. I know enough piano to know what good technique sounds like, and Darius played very, very well. He improvised for an hour. At one point, Bub went and stood beside him with his hands in his pockets, facing the rest of us, as if guarding his friend while the latter was in this vulnerable trance state. Ritter whispered to me that Darius had been offered a music scholarship to a college in West Virginia; he went to visit a friend, and a professor heard him messing around on the school's piano. The dude offered him a full ride then and there. Ritter couldn't really explain why Darius had turned it down. "He's kind of our Rain Man," Ritter said.

At some juncture, I must have taken up my lantern and crept back down the hill, since I sat up straight the next morning, fully dressed in the twenty-nine-footer. The sound that woke me was a barbaric moan, like that of an army about to charge. Early mornings at Creation were about "Praise and Worship," a new form of Christian rock in which the band and the audience sing, all together, as loud as they can, directly to God. It gets rather intense.

*****

The guys had told me they meant to spend most of today at the main stage, checking out bands. But hey, fuck that. I'd already checked out a band. Mine was to stay in this trailer, jotting impressions.

It was hot, though. As it got hotter, the light brown carpet started to give off fumes from under its plastic hide. I tumbled out the side hatch and went after Darius, Ritter, and Bub. In the light of day, one could see there were pretty accomplished freaks at this thing: a guy in a skirt wearing lace on his arms; a strange little androgynous creature dressed in full cardboard armor, carrying a sword. They knew they were in a safe place, I guess.

The guys left me standing in line at a lemonade booth; they didn't want to miss Skillet, one of Ritter's favorite bands. I got my drink and drifted slowly toward where I thought they'd be standing. Lack of food, my filthiness, impending sunstroke: These were ganging up on me. Plus the air down here smelled faintly of poo. There were a lot of blazing-hot portable toilets wafting miasma whenever the doors were opened.

I stood in the center of a gravel patch between the food and the crowd, sort of gumming the straw, quadriplegically probing with it for stubborn pockets of meltwater.

I was a ways from the stage, but I could see well enough. Something started to happen to me. The guys in the band were middle-aged. They had blousy shirts and half-hearted arena-rock moves from the mid-'80s.

What was…this feeling? The singer kept grinning between lines, like if he didn't, he might collapse. I could just make out the words:

> There's a higher place to go
> (beyond belief, beyond belief),
> Where we reach the next plateau,
> (beyond belief, beyond belief)…

The straw slipped from my mouth.
"Oh, shit. It's Petra."

*****

It was 1988. The guy who brought me in we called Verm (I'll use people's nicknames here; they don't deserve to be dragooned into my memory-voyage). He was a short, good-looking guy with a dark ponytail and a devilish laugh, a skater and an ex-pot-head, which had got him kicked out of his house a year or so before we met. His folks belonged to this nondenominational church in Ohio, where I went to high school. It was a movement more than a church—thousands of members, even then. I hear it's bigger now. "Central meeting" took place in an empty warehouse, for reasons of space, but the smaller meetings were where it was at: home church (fifty people or so), cell group (maybe a dozen). Verm's dad said, Look, go with us once a week and you can move back in.

Verm got saved. And since he was brilliant (he became something of a legend at our school because whenever a new foreign student enrolled, he'd sit with her every day at lunch and make her give him language lessons till he was proficient), and since he was about the most artlessly gregarious human being I've ever known, and since he knew loads of lost souls from his druggie days, he became a champion evangelizer, a golden child.

I was new and nurturing a transcendent hatred of Ohio. Verm found out I liked the Smiths, and we started swapping tapes. Before long, we were hanging out after school. Then the moment came that always comes when you make friends with a born-again: "Listen, I go to this thing on Wednesday nights. It's like a Bible study—no, listen, it's cool. The people are actually really cool."

They were, that's the thing. In fifteen minutes, all my ideas about Christians were put to flight. They were smarter than any bunch I'd been exposed to (I didn't grow up in Cambridge or anything, but even so), they were accepting of every kind of weird-ness, and they had that light that people who are pursuing something higher give off. It's attractive, to say the least. I started asking questions, lots of questions. And they loved that, because they had answers. That's one of the ways Evangelicalism works. Your average agnostic doesn't go through life just *primed* to offer a clear, considered defense of, say, intratextual Scriptural inconsistency. But born-agains train for that chance encounter with the inquisitive stranger. And when you're a 14-year-old carting around some fairly undernourished intellectual ambitions, and a charismatic adult sits you down and explains that if you transpose this span of years onto the Hebrew calendar, and multiply that times seven, and plug in a date from the reign of King Howsomever, then you plainly see that this passage predicts the birth of Christ almost to the hour, despite the fact that the Gospel writers didn't have access to this information! I, for one, was dazzled.

But also powerfully stirred on a level that didn't depend on my naïveté. The sheer passionate engagement of it caught my imagination: Nobody had told me there were Christians like this. They went at the Bible with grad-seminar intensity, week after week. Mole was their leader (short for Moloch; he had started the whole thing, back in the '70s). He had a wiry, dark beard and a pair of nail-gun cobalt eyes. My Russian-novel fantasies of underground gatherings—shared subversive fervor—were flattered and, it seemed, embodied. Here was counterculture, without sad hippie trappings.

Verm hugged me when I said to him, in the hallway after a meeting, "I think I might believe." When it came time for me to go all the way—to "accept Jesus into my heart" (in that time-honored formulation)—we prayed the prayer together.

Three years passed. I waxed strong in spirit. Verm and I were sort of heading up the high school end of the operation now. Mole had discovered (I had discovered, too) that I was good with words, that I could talk in front of people; Verm and I started leading Bible study once a month. We were saving souls like mad, laying up treasure for ourselves in heaven. I was never the recruiter he was, but I grasped subtlety; Verm would get them there, and together we'd start on their heads. Witnessing, it's called. I had made some progress socially at school, which gave us access to the popular crowd; in this way, many were brought to the Lord. Verm and I went to conferences and on "study retreats"; we started taking classes in theology, which the group offered—free of charge—for promising young leaders. And always, underneath but suffusing it all, there were the cell-group meetings, every week, on Friday or Saturday nights, which meant I could stay out till morning. (My Episcopalian parents were thoroughly mortified by the whole business, but it's not easy telling your kid to *stop spending so much time at church.*)

Cell group was typically held in somebody's dining room, somebody pretty high up in the group. You have to understand what an honor it was to be in a cell with Mole. People would see me at central meeting and be like, "How is that, getting to rap with him every week?" It was awesome. He really got down with the Word (he had a wonderful old hippie way of talking; everything was something *action*: "time for some fellowship action...let's get some chips 'n' salsa action"). He carried a heavy "study Bible"—no King James for the nondenominationals; too many inaccuracies. When he cracked open its hand-tooled leather cover, you knew it was on. And no joke: The brother was gifted. Even handicapped by the relatively pedestrian style of the New American Standard version, he could twist a verse into your conscience like a bone screw, make you think Christ was standing there nodding approval. The prayer session alone would last an hour. Afterward, there was always a fire in the backyard.

Mole would sit and whack a machete into a chopping block. He smoked cheap cigars; he let us smoke cigarettes. The guitar went around. We'd talk about which brother was struggling with sin—did he need counsel? Or about the end of the world: It'd be soon. We had to save as many as we could.

I won't inflict on you all my reasons for drawing away from the fold. They were clichéd, anyway, and not altogether innocent. Enough to say I started reading books Mole hadn't recommended. Some of them seemed pretty smart—and didn't jibe with the Bible. The defensive theodicy he'd drilled into me during those nights of heady exegesis developed cracks. The hell stuff: I never made peace with it. Human beings were capable of forgiving those who'd done them terrible wrongs, and we all agreed that human beings were maggots compared with God, so what was His trouble, again? I looked around and saw people who'd never have a chance to come to Jesus; they were too badly crippled. Didn't they deserve—more than the rest of us, even—to find His succor, after this life?

Belief and nonbelief are two giant planets, the orbits of which don't touch. Everything about Christianity can be justified *within the context of Christian belief.* That is, if you accept its terms. Once you do, your belief starts modifying the data (in ways that are themselves defensible, see?), until eventually the data begin to reinforce belief. The precise moment of illogic can never be isolated and may not exist. Like holding a magnifying glass at arm's length and bringing it toward your eye: Things are upside down, they're upside down, they're right side up. What lay between? If there was something, it passed too quickly to be observed. This is why you can never reason true Christians out of the faith. It's not, as the adage has it, because they were never reasoned into it—many were—it's that faith is a logical door which locks behind you. What looks like a line of thought is steadily warping into a circle, one that closes with you inside. If this seems to imply that no apostate was ever a true Christian and that therefore, I was never one, I think I'd stand by both of those statements. Doesn't the fact that I can't write about my old friends without an apologetic tone just show that I never deserved to be one of them?

The break came during the winter of my junior year. I got a call from Verm late one afternoon. He'd promised Mole he would do this thing, and now he felt sick. Sinus infection (he always had sinus infections). Had I ever heard of Petra? Well, they're a Christian-rock band, and they're playing the arena downtown. After their shows, the singer invites anybody who wants to know more about Jesus to come backstage, and they have people, like, waiting to talk to them.

The promoter had called up Mole, and Mole had volunteered Verm, and now Verm wanted to know if I'd help him out. I couldn't say no.

The concert was upsetting from the start; it was one of my first encounters with the other kinds of Evangelicals, the hand-wavers and the weepers and all (we liked to keep things "sober" in the group). The girl in front of me was signing all the words to the songs, but she wasn't deaf. It was just horrifying.

Verm had read me, over the phone, the pamphlet he got. After the first encore, we were to head for the witnessing zone and wait there. I went. I sat on the ground.

Soon they came filing in, the seekers. I don't know what was up with the ones I got. I think they may have gone looking for the restroom and been swept up by the stampede. They were about my age and wearing hooded brown sweatshirts—mouths agape, eyes empty. I asked them the questions: What did they think about all they'd heard? Were they curious about anything Petra talked about? (There'd been lots of "talks" between songs.)

I couldn't get them to speak. They stared at me like they were waiting for me to slap them.

This was my opening. They were either rapt or retarded, and whichever it was, Christ called on me to lay down my testimony.

The sentences wouldn't form. I flipped though the list of dogmas, searching for one I didn't essentially think was crap, and came up with nothing.

There might have ensued a nauseating silence, but I acted with an odd decisiveness to end the whole experience. I asked them if they wanted to leave—it was an all but rhetorical question—and said I did, too. We walked out together.

I took Mole and Verm aside a few nights later and told them my doubts had overtaken me. If I kept showing up at meetings, I'd be faking it. That was an insult to them, to God, to the group. Verm was silent; he hugged me. Mole said he respected my reasons, that I'd have to explore my doubts before my walk could be strong again. He said he'd pray for me. Unless he's undergone some radical change in character, he's still praying.

*****

Statistically speaking, my bout with Evangelicalism was probably unremarkable. For white Americans with my socioeconomic background (middle to upper-middle class), it's an experience commonly linked to one's teens and moved beyond before one reaches 20. These kids around me at Creation—a lot of them were like that. How many even knew who Darwin was? They'd learn. At least once a year since college, I'll be getting to know someone, and it comes out that we have in common a high school "Jesus phase." That's always an excellent laugh. Except a phase is supposed to end—or at least give way to other phases—not simply expand into a long preoccupation.

Bless those who've been brainwashed by cults and sent off for deprogramming. That makes it simple: You put it behind you. But this group was no cult. They persuaded; they never pressured, much less threatened. Nor did they punish. A guy I brought into the group—we called him Goog—is still a close friend. He leads meetings now and spends part of each year doing pro bono dental work in Cambodia. He's never asked me when I'm coming back.

My problem is not that I dream I'm in hell or that Mole is at the window. It isn't that I feel psychologically harmed. It isn't even that I feel like a sucker for having bought it all. It's that I love Jesus Christ.

"The latchet of whose shoes I am not worthy to unloose." I can barely write that. He was the most beautiful dude. Forget the Epistles, forget all the bullying stuff that came later. Look at what He said. Read *The Jefferson Bible*. Or better yet, read *The Logia of Yeshua*, by Guy Davenport and Benjamin Urrutia, an unadorned translation of all the sayings ascribed to Jesus that modern scholars deem authentic. There's your man. His breakthrough was the aestheticization of weakness. Not in what conquers, not in glory, but in what's fragile and what suffers—there lies sanity. And salvation. "Let anyone who has power renounce it," he said. "Your father is compassionate to all, as you should be." That's how He talked, to those who knew Him.

Why should He vex me? Why is His ghost not friendlier? Why can't I just be a good Enlightenment child and see in His life a sustaining example of what we can be, as a species?

Because once you've known Him as God, it's hard to find comfort in the man. The sheer sensation of life that comes with a total, all-pervading notion of being—the pulse of consequence one projects onto even the humblest things—the pull of that won't slacken.

And one has doubts about one's doubts.

*****

"D'ye hear that mountain lion last night?"

It was dark, and Jake was standing over me, dressed in camouflage. I'd been hunched over on a cooler by the ashes for a number of hours, waiting on the guys to get back from wherever they'd gone.

I told him I hadn't heard anything. Bub came up from behind, also in camo. "In the middle of the night," he said. "It woke me up."

Jake said, "It sounded like a baby crying."

"Like a little bitty baby," Bub said.

Jake was messing with something at my feet, in the shadows, something that looked alive. Bub dropped a few logs onto the fire and went to the Chevy for matches.

I sat there trying to see what Jake was doing. "You got that lantern?" he said. It was by my feet; I switched it on.

He started pulling frogs out of a poke. One after another. They strained in his grip and lashed at the air.

"Where'd you get those?" I asked.

"About half a mile that way," he said. "It ain't private property if you're in the middle of the creek." Bub laughed his high expressionless laugh.

"These ain't too big," Jake said. "In West Virginia, well, we got ones the size of chickens."

Jake started chopping their bodies in half. He'd lean forward and center his weight on the hand that held the knife, to get a clean cut, tossing the legs into a frying pan. Then he'd stab each frog in the brain and flip the upper parts into a separate pile. They kept twitching, of course—their nerves. Some were a little less dead than that. One in particular stared up at me, gulping for air, though his lungs were beside him, in the grass.

"Could you do that one in the brain again?" I said. Jake spiked it, expertly, and grabbed for the next frog.

"Why don't you stab their brains before you take off the legs?" I asked.

He laughed. He said I cracked him up.

Darius, when he got back, made me a cup of hot sassafras tea. "Drink this, it'll make you feel better," he told me. I'd never said I felt bad. Jake lightly sautéed the legs in butter and served them to me warm. "Eat this," he said. The meat was so tender, it all but dissolved on my tongue.

Pee Wee came back with the Jews, who were forced to tell us a second time that we were damned. (Leviticus 11:12, "Whatsoever hath no fins nor scales in the waters, that shall be an abomination unto you.") Jake, when he heard this, put on a show, making the demi-frogs talk like puppets, chewing the legs with his mouth wide open so all could see the meat.

The girls ran off again. Pee Wee went after them, calling, "Come on, they're just playin'!"

Darius peered at Jake. He looked not angry but saddened. Jake said, "Well, if he wants to bring them girls around here, they oughtn't to be telling us what we can eat."

"Wherefore, if meat make my brother to offend," Darius said, "I will eat no flesh while the world standeth."

"First Corinthians," I said.

"8:13," Darius said.

*****

I woke without having slept—that evil feeling—and lay there steeling myself for the strains of Praise and Worship. When it became too much to wait, I boiled water and made instant coffee and drank it scalding from the lid of the peanutbutter jar. My body smelled like stale campfire. My hair had leaves and ash and things in it. I thought about taking a shower, but I'd made it two days without so much as acknowledging any of the twenty-nine-footer's systems; it would have been stupid to give in now.

I sat in the driver's seat and watched, through tinted glass, little clusters of Christians pass. They looked like people anywhere, only gladder, more self-contained. Or maybe they just looked like people anywhere. I don't know. I had no pseudo-anthropological moxie left. I got out and wandered. I sat with the crowd in front of the stage. There was a redheaded Christian speaker up there, pacing back and forth. Out of nowhere, he shrieked, "MAY YOU BE COVERED IN THE ASHES OF YOUR RABBI JESUS!" If I were to try to convey to you how loudly he shrieked this, you'd think I was playing wordy games.

I was staggering through the food stands when a man died at my feet. He was standing in front of the funnel-cake window. He was big, in his early sixties, wearing shorts and a short-sleeve button-down shirt. He just…died. Massive heart attack. I was standing there, and he fell, and I don't know whether there's some primitive zone in the brain that registers these things, but the second he landed, I knew he was gone. The paramedics jumped on him so fast, it was weird—it was like they'd been waiting. They pumped and pumped on his chest, blew into his mouth, ran IVs. The ambulance showed up, and more equipment appeared. The man's broad face had that slightly disgruntled look you see on the newly dead.

Others had gathered around; some thought it was all a show. A woman standing next to me said bitterly, "It's not a show. A man has died." She started crying. She took my hand. She was small with silver hair and black eyebrows. "He's fine, he's fine," she said. I looked at the side of her face. "Just pray for his family," she said. "He's fine."

*****

I went back to the trailer and had, as the ladies say where I'm from, a colossal fucking go-to-pieces. I kept starting to cry and then stopping myself, for some reason. I felt nonsensically raw and lonely. What a dickhead I'd been, thinking the trip would be a lark. There were too many ghosts here. Everyone seemed so strange and so familiar. Plus I suppose I was starving. The frog meat was superb but meager—even Jake had said as much.

In the midst of all this, I began to hear, through the shell of the twenty-nine-footer, Stephen Baldwin giving a talk on the Fringe Stage—that's where the "edgier" acts are put on at Creation. If you're shaky on your Baldwin brothers, he's the vaguely troglodytic one who used to comb his bangs straight down and wear dusters. He's come to the Lord—I don't know if you knew. I caught him on cable a few months ago, some religious talk show. Him and Gary Busey. I don't remember what Baldwin said, because Busey was saying shit so weird the host got nervous. Busey's into "generational curses." If you're wondering what those are, too bad. I was born-again, not raised on meth.

Baldwin said many things; the things he said got stranger and stranger. He said his Brazilian nanny, Augusta, had converted him and his wife in Tucson, thereby fulfilling a prophecy she'd been given by her preacher back home. He said, "God allowed 9/11 to happen," that it was "the wrath of God," and that Jesus had told him to share this with us. He also said the Devil did 9/11. He said God wanted him "to make gnarly cool Christian movies." He said that in November we should vote for "the man who has the greatest faith." The crowd lost it; it seemed like the trailer might shake.

When Jake and Bub beat on the door, I'd been in there for hours, rereading *The Silenced Times* and the festival program. In the program, it said the candle-lighting ceremony was tonight. The guys had told me about it—it was one of the coolest things about Creation. Everyone gathered in front of the stage, and the staff handed out a candle to every single person there. The media handlers said there was a lookout you could hike to, on the mountain above the stage. That was the way to see it, they said.

When I opened the door, Jake was waving a newspaper. Bub stood behind him, smiling big. "Look at this," Jake said. It was Wednesday's copy of *The Valley Log*, serving Southern Huntingdon County—"It is just a rumor until you've read it in *The Valley Log*."

The headline for the week read MOUNTAIN LION NOT BELIEVED TO BE THREAT TO CREATION FESTIVAL CAMPERS.

"Wha'd we tell you?" Bub said.

"At least it's not a threat," I said.

"Well, not to us it ain't," Jake said.

I climbed to their campsite with them in silence. Darius was sitting on a cooler, chin in hands, scanning the horizon. He seemed meditative. Josh and Ritter were playing songs. Pee Wee was listening, by himself; he'd blown it with the Jewish girls.

"Hey, Darius," I said.

He got up. "It's fixin' to shower here in about ten minutes," he said.

I went and stood beside him, tried to look where he was looking.

"You want to know how I know?" he said.

He explained it to me, the wind, the face of the sky, how the leaves on the tops of the sycamores would curl and go white when they felt the rain coming, how the light would turn a certain "dead" color. He read the landscape to me like a children's book. "See over there," he said, "how that valley's all misty? It hasn't poured there yet. But the one in back is clear—that means it's coming our way."

Ten minutes later, it started to rain, big, soaking, percussive drops. The guys started to scramble. I suggested we all get into the trailer. They looked at each other, like maybe it was a sketchy idea. Then Ritter hollered, "Get 'er done!" We all ran down the hillside, holding guitars and—in Josh's case—a skillet wherein the fried meat of some woodland creature lay ready to eat.

There was room for everyone. I set my lantern on the dining table. We slid back the panes in the windows to let the air in. Darius did card tricks. We drank spring water. Somebody farted; the conversation about who it had been lasted a good twenty minutes. The rain on the roof made a solid drumming. The guys were impressed with my place. They said I should fence it. With the money I'd get, I could buy a nice house in Braxton County.

We played guitars. The RV rocked back and forth. Jake wasn't into Christian rock, but as a good Baptist he loved old gospel tunes, and he called for a few, God love him. Ritter sang one that killed me. Also, I don't know what changed, but the guys were up for secular stuff. It turned out that Pee Wee really loved Neil Young; I mean, he'd never heard Neil Young before, but when I played "Powderfinger" for him, he sort of curled up like a kid, then made me play it again when I was done. He said I had a pretty voice.

We all told each other how good the other ones were, how everybody else should really think about a career in music. Josh played "Stairway to Heaven," and we got loud, singing along. Darius said, "Keep it down, man! We don't need everybody thinking this is the sin wagon."

The rain stopped. It was time to go. Two of the guys had to leave in the morning, and I needed to start walking if I meant to make the overlook in time for the candle-lighting. They went with me as far as the place where the main path split off toward the stage. They each embraced me. Jake said to call them if I ever had "a situation that needs clearing up." Darius said God bless me, with meaning eyes. Then he said, "Hey, man, if you write about us, can I just ask one thing?"

"Of course," I said.

"Put in there that we love God," he said. "You can say we're crazy, but say that we love God."

The climb was long and steep. At the top was a thing that looked like a backyard deck. It jutted out over the valley, commanding an unobstructed view. Kids hung all over it like lemurs or something.

I pardoned my way to the edge, where the cliff dropped away. It was dark and then suddenly darker—pitch. They had shut off the lights at the sides of the stage. Little pinpricks appeared, moving along the aisles. We used to do candles like this at church, when I was a kid, on Christmas Eve. You light the edges, and the edges spread inward. The rate of the spread increases exponentially, and the effect is so unexpected, when, at the end, you have half the group lighting the other half's candles, it always seems like somebody flipped a switch. That's how it seemed now.

The clouds had moved off—the bright stars were out again. There were fireflies in the trees all over, and spread before me, far below, was a carpet of burning candles, tiny flames, many ten thousands. I was suspended in a black sphere full of flickering light.

And sure, I thought about Nuremberg. But mostly I thought of Darius, Jake, Josh, Bub, Ritter, and Pee Wee, whom I doubted I'd ever see again, whom I'd come to love, and who loved God—for it's true, I would have said it even if Darius hadn't asked me to, it may be the truest thing I will have written here: They were crazy, and they loved God—and I thought about the unimpeachable dignity of that love, which I never was capable of. Because knowing it isn't true doesn't mean you would be strong enough to believe if it were. Six of those glowing specks in the valley were theirs.

I was shown, in a moment of time, the ring of their faces around the fire, each one separate, each one radiant with what Paul called, strangely, "assurance of hope." It seemed wrong of reality not to reward such souls.

These are lines from a Czeslaw Milosz poem:

And if they all, kneeling with poised palms,
millions, billions of them,
ended together with their illusion?
I shall never agree. I will give them the crown.
The human mind is splendid; lips powerful, and the
summons so great it must open Paradise.

That's so exquisite. If you could just mean it. If one could only say it and mean it.

They all blew out their candles at the same instant, and the valley—the actual geographical feature—filled with smoke, there were so many.

I left at dawn, while creation slept.

—2005

Learning from Other Writers (Sullivan)

1. This essay was originally published in *GQ,* a glossy magazine that carries articles on fashion, culture, and travel for a predominantly male readership. How does this audience affect how John Jeremiah Sullivan positions himself in the opening? What is the purpose of his tone? Is the tone potentially alienating for some readers? To whom is he appealing?

2. Although Sullivan's trip to Creation is clearly a journey, it is also a portrait of a subculture. What are the most telling details about Christian rock fans and how they view the world?

3. Why doesn't Sullivan tell us his about relationship to Christianity right at the beginning? What is the risk of withholding this information?

4. What role does luck play in Sullivan's journey? What events are out of his control, and how do these events affect both the narrative and the author's analysis of his subject?

5. As in George Orwell's "Shooting an Elephant," the conclusion of this essay takes place much earlier than the resolution. How does Sullivan's conclusion about his relationship to faith and belief change the way you understand the very end of this essay?

6. Sullivan writes: "My problem is not that I dream I'm in hell or that Mole is at the window. It isn't that I feel psychologically harmed. It isn't even that I feel like a sucker for having bought it all. It's that I love Jesus Christ." How does Sullivan use this last line of the paragraph to push his self-reflection to a deeper level? How does the last line illuminate the essay's ending? Would the ending work without this revelation?

7. What roles do Ritter, Darius, Bub, Josh, and Pee Wee play in the essay? How does their presence add to or complicate the driving question?

MORE ELABORATE OR AMBITIOUS JOURNEYS

In this section, George Saunders and Zadie Smith embark on even more elaborate and ambitious trips than Sullivan's. Most of you won't have the time or resources to take a trip to the Arabian Peninsula or West Africa for the purpose of writing about it for a class, but you will still gain insights into the journey form by studying these essays and examining how each author frames and carries out his or her quest. The techniques and methods for answering a driving question are still the same, whether you are returning to your former high school for the Homecoming game or working your way to Anchorage on a fishing boat. Similarly, you can make claims about the way in which we live and the influences that affect our lives whether you sail across an ocean or simply head across town.

In his funny yet poignant essay "The New Mecca," George Saunders travels to Dubai in the United Arab Emirates to explore a city with a reputation for being decadent, fake, and over-the-top opulent and expensive. Note the way he plays up his outsider status by admitting that he not only has never visited Dubai, he isn't sure where the city is. Almost immediately, Saunders pauses for some in-depth reflection, balancing the narrative of his journey with more insightful analysis and providing a serious contrast to his playful and sarcastic voice. When Saunders takes a break to drink a Coke in the Arabian Ice City, he uses this moment to pause the narrative so he can meditate on the relative sophistication of American and Arab cultures. (This is a common and useful technique: when you sit down to eat, when you find yourself driving from here to there or bobbing around an artificial lagoon in an inner tube, whenever the narrative pace drops to a lower gear, that's a good time to reflect, to analyze, to provide background information.) Here, Saunders realizes that as Americans, we often assume the same level of "sophistication/irony" in other people as we find in ourselves, and this can cause misunderstandings between Americans and the members of other cultures.

Saunders isn't stating this to sound superior or condescending; he is merely offering an observation he might never have made had he not taken this trip across the world. Looking at this passage in conjunction with the essay's final section, we see that Saunders realizes that hatred often arises not from inherent differences between cultures but from the gap between what we think we know about a place and its inhabitants and the reality of that place and the people who live there, the distance between the illusions we hold before we visit a place and the reality we experience once we travel far from home and try to connect with people seemingly unlike ourselves. Through his meditations on his journey to Dubai, Saunders hits on one of life's most basic truths, a truth that we must be reminded of again and again, generation after generation:

> In all things, we are the victims of The Misconception From Afar. There is the idea of a city, and the city itself, too great to be held in the mind. And it is in this gap (between the conceptual and the real) that aggression begins. No place works any different than any other place, really, beyond mere details. The universal human laws— need, love for the beloved, fear, hunger, periodic exaltation, the kindness that rises up naturally in the absence of hunger/fear/pain—are constant, predictable, reliable, universal, and are merely ornamented with the details of local culture.

In "One Week in Liberia," Zadie Smith travels from England to Liberia to try to understand the reasons for the Liberian civil war and, in a broader sense, to find an Africa beyond what exists in the Africa of popular imagination. Like Saunders, Smith begins her essay on a plane and allows her question to emerge slowly. But even in that first section, through the details Smith chooses to include—how the Africans and non-Africans are dressed ("only non-Africans are dressed for 'Africa'"); a girl whose T-shirt reads "The truth must be told"—we realize that Smith is traveling to Liberia to separate myth from reality. When she writes, "The truth about Liberia is disputed," her driving question begins to take shape. Smith wants to know what conditions are like in Liberia and in particular to investigate the reasons for the Liberian civil war, instigated by Charles Taylor. "In Europe and America," Smith tells us, "the Liberian civil war is described as a 'tribal conflict.' In Liberian classrooms children from half a dozen tribes sit together and do not seem to know what you mean when you ask if this causes a difficulty." Through the people she meets, from Oxfam workers to hotel guests to young girls to teachers, and the places she encounters (the road from the airport to the Mamba Point Hotel, the hotel itself, the NGOs along "UN Drive"), she uses the narrative of her journey to weave in facts and observations about Liberia's history and its present state of turmoil.

By George Saunders

THE NEW MECCA

PUT THAT STATELY PLEASURE PALACE THERE BETWEEN THOSE OTHER TWO

If you are like I was three weeks ago, before I went to Dubai, you may not know exactly where Dubai is. Near Venezuela? No, sorry, that is incorrect. Somewhere north of Pakistan, an idyllic mountain kingdom ruled by gentle goatherds? Well, no.

Dubai, actually, is in the United Arab Emirates, on the Arabian Peninsula, one hundred miles across the Gulf from Iran, about 600 miles from Basra, 1,100 from Kabul.

You might also not know, as I did not know, what Dubai is all about or why someone would want to send you there. You might wonder: Is it dangerous? Will I be beheaded? Will I need a translator? Will my translator be beheaded? Just before we're beheaded, will my translator try to get out of it by blaming everything on me?

No, no, not to worry. Dubai, turns out, is quite possibly the safest great city in the world. It is also the newest great city in the world. In the 1950s, before oil was discovered there, Dubai was just a cluster of mud huts and Bedouin tents along Dubai Creek: The entire city has basically been built in the last fifty years. And actually, the cool parts—the parts that have won Dubai its reputation as "the Vegas of the Middle East" or "the Venice of the Middle East" or "the Disney World of the Middle East, if Disney World were the size of San Francisco and out in a desert"—have been built in the last ten years. And the supercool parts—the parts that, when someone tells you about them, your attention drifts because these morons have to be lying (no one dreams this big or has that much available capital)—those parts are all going to be built in the next five years.

By 2010, if all goes according to plan, Dubai will have: the world's tallest skyscraper (2,300 feet), largest mall, biggest theme park, longest indoor ski run, most luxurious underwater hotel (accessible by submarine train); a huge (2,000-acre, 60,000-resident) development called International City, divided into nation-neighborhoods (England, China, France, Greece, etc.) within which all homes will be required to reflect the national architectural style; not to mention four artificially constructed island mega-archipelagoes (three shaped like giant palm trees, the fourth like a map of the world) built using a specially designed boat that dredges up tons of ocean-bottom sand each day and sprays it into place.

Before I saw Dubai for myself, I assumed this was bluster: Brag about ten upcoming projects, finally build one—smaller than you'd bragged—hope everyone forgets about the other nine.

But no.

I've been to Dubai, and I believe.

If America was looking for a pluralistic, tax-free, laissez-faire, diverse, inclusive, tolerant, no-holds-barred, daringly capitalist country to serve as a shining City on the Hill for the entire Middle East, we should have left Iraq alone and sponsored a National Peaceful Tourist Excursion to Dubai and spent our 90 quadrillion Iraq War dollars there.

Maybe.

*****

IN WHICH I FALL IN LOVE WITH A FAKE TOWN

From the air, Dubai looked something like Dallas circa 1985: a vast expanse of one- or two-story white boxes, punctuated by clusters of freakish skyscrapers. (An Indian kid shouted, "Dad, looks like a microchip!") Driving in from the airport, you're struck by the usual first-night-in-new-country exotica ("There's a *Harley-Davidson* dealership—right in the *Middle East!*"), and the skyscraper clusters were, okay, odd looking (like four or five architects had staged a weird-off, with unlimited funds)—but all in all, it was, you know, a city. And I wondered what all the fuss was about.

Then I got to my hotel.

The Madinat Jumeirah is, near as I can figure, a superresort consisting of three, or possibly six, luxury sub-hotels and two, or maybe three, clusters of luxury villas, spread out over about forty acres, or for all I know it was twelve sub-hotels and nine luxury-villa clusters—I really couldn't tell, so seamless and extravagant and confusing was all the luxury. The Madinat is themed to resemble an ancient Arabian village. But to say the Madinat is themed doesn't begin to express the intensity and opulence and areal extent of the theming. The site is crisscrossed by 2.3 miles of fake creeks, trolled night and day by dozens of fake Arabian water taxis (*abras*) piloted by what I can only describe as fake Arabs because, though dressed like old-timey Arabs, they are actually young, smiling, sweet-hearted guys from Nepal or Kenya or the Philippines, who speak terrific English as they pilot the soundless electrical *abras* through this lush, created Arabia, looking for someone to take back to the lobby, or to the largest outdoor pool in the Middle East, or over to Trader Vic's, which is also themed and looks something like a mysterious ancient Casbah inexplicably filled with beautiful contemporary people.

And so, though my first response to elaborate Theming is often irony (Who *did* this? And *why?* Look at that *modern exit sign* over that *eighteenth-century bedstead*. Haw!), what I found during my stay at the Madinat is that irony is actually my first response to tepid, lame Theming. In the belly of radical Theming, my first response was to want to stay forever, bring my family over, set up shop in my hut-evoking villa, and never go home again.

Because the truth is, it's beautiful. The air is perfumed, you hear fountains, the tinkling of bells, distant chanted prayers, and when the (real) Arabian moon comes up, yellow and attenuated, over a (fake) Arabian wind tower, you feel you are a resident of some ancient city—or rather, some ancient city if you had dreamed the ancient city, and the ancient city had been purged of all disease, death, and corruption, and you were a Founder/Elder of that city, much beloved by your Citizens, the Staff.

Wandering around one night, a little lost, I came to the realization that verisimilitude and pleasure are not causally related. How is this "fake"? This is real flowing water, the date and palm trees are real, the smell of incense and rose water is real. The staggering effect of the immense scale of one particular crosswalk—which joins two hotels together and is, if you can imagine this, a four-story ornate crosswalk that looks like it should have 10,000 cheering Imperial Troops clustered under it and an enigmatic young Princess waving from one of its arabesquey windows—that effect is *real*. You feel it in your gut and your legs. It makes you feel happy and heroic and a little breathless, in love anew with the world and its possibilities. You have somehow entered the landscape of a dream, the Platonic realization of the idea of Ancient Village—but there are real smells here, and when, a little dazzled, you mutter to yourself ("This is like a freaking dream, I love it, I, wow..."), you don't wake up, but instead a smiling Filipino kid comes up and asks if you'd like a drink.

On the flight over, I watched an interview with an employee of Jumeirah International, the company that manages the Madinat. Even though he saw it going up himself, he said, he feels it is an ancient place every time he enters and finds it hard to believe that, three years ago, it was all just sand.

*****

A WORD ABOUT THE HELP

UAE nationals comprise about 20 percent of the city's population. Until three years ago, only nationals were allowed to own property in Dubai, and they still own essentially all of it. Visually identifiable by their dress—the men wear the traditional white dishdashas; the women, long black gowns and abayas—these nationals occupy the top rung of a rigid social hierarchy: Imagine Hollywood, if everyone who'd been wildly successful in the movie business had to wear a distinctive costume.

A rung down from the Emiratis are some 200,000 expats (mostly Brits but also other Europeans, Russians, Lebanese, Indians) who comprise a kind of managerial class: the marketing people, the hotel managers, the human-resource gurus, the accountants, the lawyers, etc. But the vast majority of Dubai's expat population—roughly two-thirds of it—comes from poorer countries all around the world, mainly South Asia or Africa. They built Dubai, they run it with their labor but can't afford to own homes or raise their families here. They take their dirhams home and cash them in for local currency, in this way increasing their wealth by as much as tenfold. They live here for two years, five years, fifteen years; take home-leaves as often as every three months or as infrequently as never.

And even within this class there are stratifications. The hotel workers I met at the Madinat, for example, having been handpicked by Jumeirah scouts from the finest hotels in their native countries, are a class, or two, or three, above the scores of South Asian laborers who do the heavy construction work, who live in labor camps on the outskirts of town where they sleep ten to a room, and whose social life, according to one British expat I met, consists of "a thrilling evening once a month of sitting in a circle popping their bulbs out so some bloody Russian chickie can race around hand-jobbing them all in a mob."

You see these construction guys all over town: somewhat darker-complexioned, wearing blue jumpsuits, averting their eyes when you try to say hello, squatting outside a work site at three in the morning because Dubai construction crews work twenty-four hours a day, seven days a week.

There is much to be done.

*****

THE WILD WADI EPIPHANY

A short, complimentary golf-cart ride down the beach from the Madinat is Wild Wadi, a sprawling, themed water park whose theme is: A wadi is flooding! Once an hour, the sound of thunder/cracking trees/rushing waves blares through the facility-wide PA, and a waterfall begins dropping a thousand gallons of water a minute into an empty pond, which then violently overflows down the pedestrian walkways, past the gift shop.

Waiting in line, I'm part of a sort of United Nations of partial nudity: me, a couple of sunburned German women, three angry-looking Arab teens, kind of like the Marx Brothers if the Marx Brothers were Arabs in bathing suits with cigarettes behind their ears, who, I notice, are muttering to one another while glowering. Then I see what they're muttering/glowering about: several (like, fifteen) members of the United States Navy, on shore leave. You can tell they're Navy because they're huge and tattooed and innocently happy and keep bellowing things like, "Dude, fuck that, I am all *about* dancing!" while punching each other lovingly in the tattoos and shooting what I recognize as Rural Smiles of Shyness and Apprehension at all the people staring at them because they're so freaking loud.

Then the Navy Guys notice the Glowering Muttering Arabs, and it gets weirdly tense there in line. Luckily, it's my turn to awkwardly blop into a tube, and off I go.

This ride involves a series of tremendous water jets that blast you, on your tube, to the top of Wild Wadi, where, your recently purchased swim trunks having been driven up your rear by the jets, you pause, looking out over the entire city—the miles of stone-white villas, the Burj Al Arab (sail-shaped, iconic, the world's only seven-star hotel) out in the green-blue bay—just before you fly down so fast that you momentarily fear the next morning's headline will read MIDDLE-AGED AMERICAN DIES IN FREAK WATERSLIDE MISHAP; BATHING SUIT FOUND FAR UP ASS.

Afterward, I reconvene with my former line mates in a sort of faux river bend. Becalmed, traffic-jammed, we bob around in our tubes, trying to keep off one another via impotent little hand flips, bare feet accidentally touching ("Ha, wope, sorry, heh…"), legs splayed, belly-up in the blinding 112-degree Arabian sun, self-conscious and expectant, as in: "Are we, like, stuck here? Will we go soon? I hope I'm not the one who drifts under that dang *waterfall* over there!"

No one is glowering or muttering now. We're sated, enjoying that little dopey buzz of quasi accomplishment you feel after a surprisingly intense theme-park ride. One of the Arab kids, the one with the Chico hair, passes a drenched cigarette to me, to pass to his friend, and then a lighter, and suddenly everybody's smiling—me, the Arab Marxes, the sunburned German girls, the U.S. Navy.

A disclaimer: It may be that, when you're 46 and pearl white and wearing a new bathing suit at a theme park on your first full day in Arabia, you're especially prone to Big Naive Philosophical Realizations.

Be that as it may, in my tube at Wild Wadi, I have a mini epiphany: Given enough time, I realize, statistically, despite what it may look like at any given moment, we *will* all be brothers. All differences will be bred out. There will be no pure Arab, no pure Jew, no pure American-American. The old dividers—nation, race, religion—will be over-powered by crossbreeding and by our mass media, our world Culture o' Enjoyment.

Look what just happened here: Hatred and tension were defused by Sudden Fun.

Still bobbing around (three days before the resort bombings in Cairo, two weeks after the London bombings), I think-mumble a little prayer for the great homogeniz-ing effect of pop culture: Same us out, Lord MTV! Even if, in the process, we are left a little dumber, please proceed. Let us, brothers and sisters, leave the intolerant, the ideologues, the religious Islamist Bolsheviks, our own solvers-of-problems-with-troops behind, fully clothed, on the banks of Wild Wadi. We, the New People, desire Fun and the Good Things of Life, and through Fun, we will be saved.

Then the logjam breaks, and we surge forward, down a mini-waterfall.

Without exception, regardless of nationality, each of us makes the same sound as we disappear: a thrilled little self-forgetting Whoop.

*****

WE BUY, THEREFORE WE AM

After two full days of blissfully farting around inside the Madinat, I reluctantly venture forth out of the resort bubble, downtown, into the actual city, to the Deira souk. This is the real Middle East, the dark *Indiana Jones*—ish Middle East I'd pre-imagined: an exotic, cramped, hot, chaotic, labyrinthine, canopied street bazaar, crowded with room-size, even closet-size stalls, selling everything there is in the world to buy, and more than a few things you can't imagine anyone ever wanting to buy, or even accept for free.

Here is the stall of Plastic Flowers That Light Up; the stall of Tall Thin Blond Dolls in Miniskirts With Improbably Huge Eyes; the stall of Toy Semiautomatic Weapons; the stall of Every Spice Known to Man (SAFFRON BUKHOR, BAHRAT, MEDICAL HERBS, NATURAL VIAGRA); the stall of Coffee-Grinding Machines in Parts on the Floor; the stall of Hindi Prayer Cards; the stall of Spangled Kashmiri Slippers; of Air Rifles; Halloween Masks; Oversize Bright-Colored Toy Ships and Trucks; a stall whose walls and ceiling are completely covered with hundreds of cooking pots. There is a Pashtun-dominated section, a hidden Hindi temple, a section that suddenly goes Chinese, entire streets where nothing is sold but bolts of cloth. There's a mind-blowing gold section—two or three hundred gold shops on one street, with mysterious doors leading to four-story mini-malls holding still more gold shops, each overflowing with the yellow high-end gold that, in storybooks and Disney movies, comes pouring out of pirate chests.

As I walk through, a kind of amazed mantra starts running through my head: *There is no end to the making and selling of things there is no end to the making and selling of things there is no end...*

Man, it occurs to me, is a joyful, buying-and-selling piece of work. I have been wrong, dead wrong, when I've decried consumerism. Consumerism is what we are. It is, in a sense, a holy impulse. A human being is someone who joyfully goes in pursuit of things, brings them home, then immediately starts planning how to get more.

A human being is someone who wishes to improve his lot.

*****

SPEAKING OF IMPROVING ONE'S LOT: THE GREAT DUBAI QUANDARY

Dubai raises the questions raised by any apparent utopia: What's the downside? At whose expense has this nirvana been built, on whose backs are these pearly gates being raised?

Dubai is, in essence, capitalism on steroids: a small, insanely wealthy group of capital-controlling Haves supported by a huge group of overworked and underpaid Have-Nots, with, in Dubai's case, the gap between Haves and Have-Nots so wide as to indicate different species.

But any attempt to reduce this to some sort of sci-fi Masters and 'Droids scenario gets complicated. Relative to their brethren back home (working for next to nothing or not working at all), Dubai's South Asian workers have it great; likewise, relative to their brethren working in nearby Saudi Arabia. An American I met, who has spent the last fifteen years working in the Saudi oil industry, told me about seeing new South Indian workers getting off the plane in Riyadh, in their pathetic new clothes, clutching cardboard suitcases. On arrival, as in a scene out of *The Grapes of Wrath*, they are informed (for the first time) that they will have to pay for their flight over, their lodging, their food (which must be bought from the company), and, in advance, their flight home. In this way, they essentially work the first two years for free.

Dubai is not, in structure, much different: The workers surrender their passports to their employer; there are no labor unions, no organizing, no protests. And yet in Dubai, the workers tell you again and again how happy they are to be here. Even the poorest, most overworked laborer considers himself lucky—he is making more, much more, than he would be back home. In Saudi, the windfall profits from skyrocketing oil prices have shot directly upstairs, to the 5,000 or so members of the royal family, and from there to investments (new jets, real estate in London). In Dubai, the leaders have plowed the profits back into the national dream of the New Dubai—reliant not on oil revenue (the Dubai oil will be gone by 2010) but on global tourism. Whatever complaints you hear about the Emirati ruling class—they buy $250,000 falcons, squash all dissent, tolerate the financial presence of questionable organizations (Al Qaeda, various national Mafias)—they seem to be universally respected, even loved, because, unlike the Saudi rulers, they are perceived to put the interests of the people first.

On the other hand, relative to Western standards, Dubai is so antilabor as to seem medieval. In the local paper, I read about the following case: A group of foreign workers in Dubai quit their jobs in protest over millions of dirhams in unpaid wages. Since by law they weren't allowed to work for another company, these men couldn't afford plane tickets back home and were thus stuck in a kind of Kafka loop. After two years, the government finally stepped in and helped send the men home. This story indicates both the potential brutality of the system—so skewed toward the employer—and its flexibility relative to the Saudi system, its general right-heartedness, I think you could say, or at least its awareness of, and concern with, Western opinion: The situation was allowed to be reported and, once reported, was corrected.

Complicated.

Because you see these low-level foreign workers working two or three jobs, twelve, fourteen, sixteen hours a day, longing for home (a waiter shows me exactly how he likes to hold his 2-year-old, or did like to hold her, last time he was home, eight months ago), and think: Couldn't you Haves cut loose with just a little more?

But ask the workers, in your intrusive Western way, about their Possible Feelings of Oppression, and they model a level of stoic noble determination that makes the Ayn Rand in you think, Good, good for you, sir, best of luck in your professional endeavors!

Only later, back in your room, having waded in through a lobby full of high rollers—beautifully dressed European/Lebanese/Russian expats, conferring Emiratis, all smoking, chatting, the expats occasionally making a scene, berating a waitress—thinking of some cabdriver in the thirteenth hour of his fourteen-hour shift, worrying about his distant grandchild; thinking of some lonely young Kathmandu husband, sleeping fitfully in his sweltering rented room—do you get a sudden urge to move to Dubai and start a chapter of the Wobblies.

On the other hand:

A Kenyan security guard who works fourteen-hour days at Wild Wadi, euphoric about his new earning power, says to me: "I expect, in your writing, you will try to find the dark side of Dubai? Some positive, some negative? Isn't that the Western way? But I must say: I have found Dubai to be nearly perfect."

Complicated.

*****

THE UNIVERSITY OF THE BACK OF THE CAB

A partial list of wise things cabdrivers said to me in Dubai:

1. "If you good Muslim, you go straight, no talking talking, bomb blast! No. You go to mosque, to talk. You go straight!"

2. "This, all you see? So new! All new within! Within one year! Within within within! That building there? New within three year! All built within! Before, no! Only sand."

3. "You won't see any Dubai Arab man driving cab. Big boss only."

4. Re the Taliban: "If you put a man into a room with no way out, he will fight his way out. But if you leave him one way out, he will take it."

5. "The Cyclone Club? Please to not go there. It is a disco known for too many fuck-girls."

One night my driver is an elderly Iranian, a fan of George W. Bush who hates the Iranian government. He tells me the story of his spiritual life. When young, he says, he was a donkey: a donkey of Islam. Then a professor said to him: You are so religious, so sure of yourself, and yet you know absolutely nothing. And this professor gave him books to read, from his personal library. "I read one, then more, more," he says, nearly moving himself to tears with the memory. After two years, the driver had a revelation: All religious knowledge comes from the hand of man. God does not talk to us directly. One can trust only one's own mind, one's own intelligence. He has five kids, four grandkids, still works fourteen-hour days at 65 years old. But he stays in Dubai because in Iran, there are two classes: The Religious and The Not. And The Religious get all the privileges, all the money, all the best jobs. And if you, part of The Not Religious, say something against them, he says, they take you against a wall and...

He turns to me, shoots himself in the head with his finger.

As I get out, he says: "We are not different, all men are..." and struggles to remember the word.

"Brothers?" I say.

"No," he says.

"Unified?" I say.

"No," he says.

"Part of the same, uh...transcendent..."

"No," he says. He can't remember the word. He is old, very old, he says, sorry, sorry.

We say good-bye, promising to pray for our respective governments, and for each other.

*****

CLEANING AMONG THE MAYHEM

Dubai is a city of people who come from elsewhere and are going back there soon. To start a good conversation—with a fellow tourist, with the help, with just about any-body—simply ask: "Where are you from?" Everyone wants to tell you. If white, they are usually from England, South Africa, Ukraine. If not, they are from Sri Lanka, the Philippines, Kenya, Nepal, India.

One hotel seems to hire only Nepalese. One bar has only Ukrainians. You discover a pocket of Sri Lankan golf-cart drivers, all anxious to talk about the tsunami.

One day, inexplicably, everyone you meet, wherever you go, is from the Philippines.

"Where are you from?" you say all day, and all day people brightly answer: "Philippines!"

That night, at a club called Boudoir, I meet L, an employee of Ford in Dubai, a manic, funny, Stanley Tucci-looking guy from Detroit, who welcomes me into his party, gets me free champagne, mourns the circa-1990 state of inner-city Detroit: feral dogs roaming the streets, trees growing out of the upper stories of skyscrapers where "you know, formerly, commerce was being done, the real 1960s automobile fucking world-class commerce, man!" The night kind of explodes. This, I think, this is the repressive Arabian Peninsula? Apparently, anything is permitted, as long as it stays within the space within which it is permitted. Here is a Palestinian who lives in L.A. and whose T-shirt says LAPD—WHERE EVERYBODY IS KING. A couple of blond Russian girls dance on a rail, among balloons. On the dance floor, two other blonds dance alone. A guy comes up behind one and starts passionately grinding her. This goes on awhile. Then he stops, introduces himself, she shakes his hand, he goes back to grinding her. His friend comes up, starts grinding her friend. I don't get it. Prostitutes? Some new youthful social code? I am possibly too old to be in here? The dance floor is packed, the whole place *becomes* the dance floor, the rails are now packed with dancers, a Lebanese kid petulantly shouts that if this was *fucking Beirut*, the girls would be *stripped off* by now, then gives me a snotty look and stomps off, as if it's my fault the girls are still dressed. I drop my wallet, look down, and see the tiniest little woman imaginable, with whisk broom, struggling against the surge of the crowd like some kind of cursed Cleaning Fairy, trying to find a small swath of floor to sweep while being bashed by this teeming mass of gyrating International Hipsters. She's tiny—I mean *tiny*, like three feet tall, her head barely reaching all the gyrating waists—with thick glasses and bowl-cut hair.

Dear little person! It seems impossible she's trying to sweep the dance floor at a time like this, she seems uncommonly, heroically dedicated, like some kind of OCD janitor on the *Titanic*.

"Where are you from?" I shout.

"Philippines!" she shouts, and goes back to her sweeping.

*****

MY ARRIVAL IN HEAVEN

The Burj Al Arab is the only seven-star hotel in the world, even though the ratings system only goes up to five. The most expensive Burj suite goes for $12,000 a night. The atrium is 590 feet from floor to ceiling, the largest in the world. As you enter, the staff rushes over with cold towels, rosewater for the hands, dates, incense. The smell, the scale, the level of loving, fascinated attention you are receiving, makes you realize you have never really been in the lap of true luxury before. All the luxury you have previously had—in New York, L.A.—was stale, Burj-imitative crap! Your entire concept of *being inside a building* is being altered in real time. The lobby of the Burj is neither inside nor out. The roof is so far away as to seem like sky. The underbellies of the floors above you grade through countless shades of color from deep blue to, finally, up so high you can barely see it: pale green. Your Guest Services liaison, a humble, pretty Ukrainian, tells you that every gold-colored surface you see during your stay is actual twenty-four-karat gold. Even those four-story columns? Even so, she says. Even the thick fourth-story arcs the size of buses that span the columns? All gold, sir, is correct. I am so thrilled to be checking in! What a life! Where a kid from Chicago gets to fly halfway around the world and stay at the world's only seven-star hotel, and GQ pays for it!

But there was a difficulty.

*****

HELP, HELP, HEAVEN IS MAKING ME NERVOUS

Because, for complicated reasons, GQ couldn't pay from afar, and because my wife and I share a common hobby of maxing out all credit cards in sight, I had rather naively embarked on a trip halfway around the world without an operative credit card: the contemporary version of setting sail with no water in the casks. So I found myself in the odd position of having to pay the off-season rate of $1,500 a night, in cash. And because, turns out, to my chagrin, my ATM has a daily withdrawal limit (Surprise, dumb ass!), I found myself there in my two-floor suite (every Burj room is a two-story suite), wearing the new clothes I had bought back in Syracuse for the express purpose of "Arriving at the Burj," trying to explain, like some yokel hustler at a Motel 6 in Topeka, that I'd be happy to pay half in cash now, half on checkout, if that would be, ah, acceptable, would that be, you know, cool?

My God, if you could have bottled the tension there in my suite at the Burj! The absolute electricity of disappointment shooting back and forth between the lovely Ukrainian and my kindly Personal Butler, the pity, really...

Sorry, uh, sorry for the, you know, trouble... I say.

No, sir, the lovely Ukrainian says. We are sorry to make any difficulties for you.

Ha, I thought, God bless you, now *this* is service, this is freaking Seven-Star Service!

But over the next few hours, my bliss diminished. I was approached by the Lebanese Floor Butler, by several Mysterious Callers from Guest Services, all of whom, politely but edgily, informed me that it would be much appreciated if the balance of the payment could be made by me pronto. I kept explaining my situation (that darn bank!), they kept accepting my explanation, and then someone else would call, or come by, once again encouraging me to pay the remaining cash, if I didn't mind terribly, right away, as was proper.

So although the Burj is a wonder—a Themed evocation of a reality that has never existed, unless in somebody's hashish dream—a kind of externalized fantasy of Affluence, if that fantasy were being had in real time by a very rich Hedonistic Giant with unlimited access to some kind of Exaggeration Drug, a Giant fond of bright, mismatched colors, rounded, huge, inexplicable structures, dancing fountains, and two-story-tall wall-lining aquariums—I couldn't enjoy any of it. Not the electronic curtains that reveal infinite ocean; not the free-high-speed-Internet-accessing big-screen TV; not the Burj-shaped box of complimentary gourmet dates; not the shower with its six different Rube Goldbergian nozzles arranged so that one can wash certain body parts without having to demean oneself via bending or squatting; not the complimentary $300 bottle of wine; not the sweeping Liberace stairs or the remote-control front-door opener; not the distant view of The Palm, Jumeirah, and/or the tiny inconsequential boats far below, full of little people who couldn't afford to stay in the Burj even in their wildest dreams, the schmucks (although by the time of my third Admonitory Phone Call, I was feeling envious of them and their little completely-paid-for boats, out there wearing shorts, shorts with, possibly, some cash in the pockets)—couldn't enjoy any of it, because I was too cowed to leave my room. I resisted the urge to crawl under the bed. I experienced a sudden fear that a group of Disapproving Guest Services People would appear at my remote-controlled door and physically escort me down to the lobby ATM (an ATM about which I expect I'll be having anxiety nightmares the rest of my life), which would once again prominently display the words PROVIDER DECLINES TRANSACTION. It's true what the Buddhists say: Mind can convert Heaven into Hell. This was happening to me. A headline in one of the nine complimentary newspapers read, actually read: AMERICAN JAILED FOR NONPAYMENT OF HOTEL BILL.

Perhaps someone had put acid in the complimentary Evian?

*****

MON PETIT PATHETIC REBELLION

On one of my many unsuccessful missions to the ATM, I met an Indian couple from the UK who had saved up their money for this Dubai trip and were staying downtown, near the souk. They had paid $50 to come in and have a look around the Burj (although who they paid wasn't clear—the Burj says it discontinued its policy of charging for this privilege), and were regretting having paid this money while simultaneously trying to justify it. Although we must remember, said the husband to the wife, this is, after all, a once-in-a-lifetime experience! Yes, yes, of course, she said, I don't regret it for a minute! But there is a look, a certain look, about the eyes, that means: Oh God, I am gutsick with worry about money. And these intelligent, articulate people had that look. (As, I suspect, did I.) There wasn't, she said sadly, that much to see, really, was there? And one felt rather watched, didn't one, by the help? Was there a limit on how long they could stay? They had already toured the lobby twice, been out to the ocean-overlooking pool, and were sort of lingering, trying to get their fifty bucks' worth.

At this point, I was, I admit it, like anyone at someone else's financial mercy, a little angry at the Burj, which suddenly seemed like a rosewater-smelling museum run for, and by, wealthy oppressors-of-the-people, shills for the new global economy, membership in which requires the presence of A Wad, and your ability to get to it/ prove it exists.

Would you like to see my suite? I asked the couple.

Will there be a problem with the, ah…

Butler? I said. Personal butler?

With the personal butler? he said.

Well, I am a guest, after all, I said. And you are, after all, my old friends from college in the States. Right? Could we say that?

We said that. I snuck them up to my room, past the Personal Butler, and gave them my complimentary box of dates and the $300 bottle of wine. Fight the power! Then we all stood around, feeling that odd sense of shame/solidarity that people of limited means feel when their limitedness has somehow been underscored.

Later that night, a little drunk in a scurvy bar in another hotel (described by L, my friend from Detroit, as the place where "Arabs with a thing for brown sugar" go to procure "the most exquisite African girls on the planet" but which was actually full of African girls who, like all girls whose job it is to fuck anyone who asks them night after night, were weary and joyless and seemed on the brink of tears), I scrawled in my notebook: PAUCITY (ATM) = RAGE.

Then I imagined a whole world of people toiling in the shadow of approaching ruin, exhausting their strength and grace, while above them a whole other world of people puttered around, enjoying the good things of life, staying at the Burj just because they could.

And I left my ATM woes out of it and just wrote: PAUCITY = RAGE.

*****

LUCKILY, IT DIDN'T COME TO JAIL

Turns out, the ATM definition of *daily* is: After midnight in the United States. In the morning, as I marched the 2,500 dirhams I owed proudly upstairs, the cloud lifted. A citizen of the affluent world again, I went openly to have coffee in the miraculous lobby, where my waiter and I talked of many things—of previous guests (Bill Clinton, 50 Cent—a "loud-laughing man, having many energetic friends") and a current guest, supermodel Naomi Campbell.

Then I left the Burj, no hard feelings, and went somewhere even better, and more expensive.

*****

HEAVEN FOR REAL, PLUS IN THIS CASE IT WAS PAID FOR IN ADVANCE

The Al Maha resort is located inside a stunningly beautiful/bleak, rugged desert nature preserve an hour outside of Dubai. My Personal Butler was possibly the nicest man I've ever met, who proudly admitted it was he who designed the linens, as well as the special Kleenex dispensers. He had been at Al Maha since the beginning. He loved it here. This place was his life's work.

Each villa had its own private pool.

After check-in, we're given a Jeep tour of the desert by a friendly and intensely knowledgeable South African guide, of that distinct subspecies of large, handsome guys who love nature. I learn things. The oryx at Al Maha have adapted to the new water-sprinkler system in the following way: At dusk, rather than going down to the spring, they sit at the base of the trees, waiting for the system to engage. I see a bush called Spine of Christ; it was from one of these, some believe, that Christ's crown of thorns was made. I see camel bones, three types of gazelle. We pass a concrete hut the size of a one-car garage, in a spot so isolated and desolate you expect some Beckett characters to be sitting there. Who lives inside? A guy hired by the camel farmer, our guide says. He stays there day and night for months at a time. Who is he? Probably a Pakistani; often, these camel-feeding outposts are manned by former child camel-jockeys, sold by their families to sheiks when the kids were 4 or 5 years old.

For lunch, we have a killer buffet, with a chef's special of veal medallions.

I go back to my villa for a swim. Birds come down to drink from my private pool. As you lower yourself into the pool, water laps forward and out, into a holding rim, then down into the Lawrencian desert. You see a plane of blue water, then a plane of tan desert. Yellow bees—completely yellow, as if spray-painted—flit around on the surface of the water.

At dusk we ride camels out to the desert. A truck meets us with champagne and strawberries. We sit on a dune, sipping champagne, watching the sunset. Dorkily, I am the only single. Luckily, I am befriended by B and K, a beautiful, affluent Dubai-Indian couple right out of Hemingway. She is pretty and loopy: Angelina Jolie meets Lucille Ball. He is elegant, reserved, kind-eyed, always admiring her from a little ways off, then rushing over to get her something she needs. They are here for their one-and-a-half-year anniversary. Theirs was a big traditional Indian wedding, held in a tent in the desert, attended by 400 guests, who were transported in buses. In a traditional Indian wedding, the groom is supposed to enter on a white horse. White horses being in short supply in Dubai, her grandfather, a scion of old Dubai, called in a favor from a sheik, who flew in, from India, a beautiful white stallion. Her father then surprised the newlyweds with a thirty-minute fireworks show.

Fireworks, wow, I say, thinking of my wedding and our big surprise, which was, someone had strung a crapload of Bud cans to the bumper of our rented Taurus.

She is her father's most precious possession, he says.

Does her father like you? I say.

He has no choice, he says.

Back at my room, out of my private pool, comes the crazed Arabian moon, which has never, in my experience, looked more like a Ball of Rock in Space.

My cup runneth over. All irony vanishes. I am so happy to be alive. I am convinced of the essential goodness of the universe. I wish everyone I've ever loved could be here with me, in my private pool.

I wish *everyone* could be here with me, in my private pool: the blue-suited South Indians back in town, the camel farmer in his little stone box, the scared sad Molda-vian girls clutching their ostensibly sexy little purses at hotel bars—I wish they could all, before they die, have one night at Al Maha.

But they can't.

Because that's not the way the world works.

*****

"DUBAI IS WHAT IT IS BECAUSE ALL THE COUNTRIES AROUND IT ARE SO FUCKED UP"

In the middle of a harsh, repressive, backward, religiously excessive, physically terrifying region, sits Dubai. Among its Gulf neighbors: Iraq and Iran, war-torn and fanatic-ruled, respectively. Surrounding it, Saudi Arabia, where stealing will get your hand cut off, a repressive terrorist breeding ground where women's faces can't be seen in public, a country, my oil-industry friend says, on the brink of serious trouble.

The most worrisome thing in Saudi, he says, is the rural lower class. The urban middle class is doing all right, relatively affluent and satisfied. But look at a map of Saudi, he says: All that apparently empty space is not really empty. There are people there who are not middle-class and not happy. I say the Middle East seems something like Russia circa 1900—it's about trying to stave off revolution in a place where great wealth has been withheld from the masses by a greedy ruling class.

That's one way of saying it, he says.

Then he tells me how you get a date if you are a teenage girl in Saudi Arabia:

Go to the mall, wearing your required abaya. When a group of young guys walks by, if you see one you like, quickly find a secluded corner of the mall, take out your cell phone, lift your abaya, snap a picture of your face. Write your cell number on a piece of paper. When the boys walk by, drop the scrap at the feet of the one you like. When he calls, send him your photo. If he likes the photo, he will call again. Arrange a secret meeting.

The world must be peopled.

*****

THE TRUTH IS, I CAN'T DECIDE WHAT'S TRUE, HONESTLY

One night, at dinner with some People Who Know, I blurt out a question that's been bothering me: Why doesn't Al Qaeda bomb Dubai, since Dubai represents/tolerates decadent Western materialism, etc., and they could do it so easily? The Man Who Knows says, I'll tell you why: Dubai is like Switzerland during World War II—a place needed by everyone. The Swiss held Nazi money, Italian Fascist money. And in Dubai, according to this Person, Al Qaeda has millions of dollars in independent, Dubai-based banks, which don't always adhere to the international banking regulations that would require a bank to document the source of the income. A Woman Who Knows says she's seen it: A guy walks into a bank with a shitload of money, and they just take it, credit it, end of story. In this way, the People Who Know say, Dubai serves various illicit organizations from around the world: the Italian Mafia, the Spanish Mafia, etc., etc. Is this known about and blessed from the top down? Yes, it is. Al Qaeda needs Dubai, and Dubai tolerates Al Qaeda, making the periodic token arrest to keep the United States happy.

Later, the People Who Know are contradicted, in an elevator, by another Man Who Knows, a suave Luxembourgian who sells financial-services products to Dubai banks.

Dubai has greatly improved its banking procedures since 9/11. Why would a terrorist group want to bank here? he asks. Think about it logically: Would they not be better served in a country sympathetic to them? Iran, Syria, Lebanon?

Good point, I say, thanking God in my heart that I am not a real Investigative Journalist.

*****

IN WHICH SNOW IS MADE BY A KENYAN

Arabian Ice City is part of a larger, months-long festival called Dubai Summer Surprises, which takes place at a dozen venues around town and includes Funny Magic Mirrors, Snow Magician Show, Magic Academy Workshop, Magic Bubble Show, Balloon Man Show, and Ice Cave Workshop, not to mention Ice Fun Character Show. But Arabian Ice City is the jewel.

Because at Arabian Ice City, Arab kids see snow for the first time.

Arabian Ice City consists, physically, of: wall-length murals of stylized Swiss landscapes; two cardboard igloos labeled GENTS' MOSQUE and LADIES' MOSQUE, respectively (actual mosques, with shoes piled up inside the mock-ice doorways, through which people keep disappearing to pray); a huge ice cliff which, on closer inspection, is a huge Styrofoam cliff, being sculpted frantically to look more like ice by twenty Filipinos with steak knives; and a tremendous central cardboard castle, inside of which, it is rumored, will be the Snow.

This is a local event, attended almost exclusively by Emiratis, sponsored by the local utility company; an opportunity, a representative tells me, to teach children about water and power conservation via educational activities and "some encouraging gifts." Has he been to America? He makes a kind of scoffing sound, as in: Right, pal, I'm going to America.

"America does not like Arabs," he says. "They think we are...I will not even say the word."

"Terrorists," I say.

He shuts his eyes in offended agreement.

Then he has to go. There is continued concern about the safety of the Arabian Ice City. Yesterday, at the opening, they expected one hundred people in the first hour, and instead got 3,000. Soon the ice was melting, the children, who knew nothing of the hazards of Snow, were slipping, getting hurt, and they'd had to shut the whole thing down, to much disappointment.

Waiting in the rapidly growing line, I detect a sense of mounting communal worry, fierce concern. This is, after all, for the children. Men rush in and out of the Ice Palace, bearing pillows, shovels, clipboards. Several Characters arrive and are ushered inside: a red crescent with legs; what looks like a drop of toothpaste, or, more honestly, sperm, with horizontal blue stripes; the crankiest-looking goose imaginable, with a face like a velociraptor and a strangely solicitous Sri Lankan handler, who keeps affectionately swatting the goose-raptor's tail and whispering things to it and steering it away from the crowd so they can have a private talk. The handler seems, actually, a little in love with the goose. As the goose approaches, a doorman announces, robustly, "Give a way for the goose!" The goose and goose-tender rush past, the tender swatting in lusty wonderment at the goose's thick tail, as if amazed that he is so privileged to be allowed to freely swat at such a thick, realistic tail.

The door opens, and in we go.

Inside is a rectangle about the size of a tennis court, green-bordered, like one of the ice rinks Sears used to sell. Inside is basically a shitload of crushed ice and one Kenyan with a shovel, madly crushing. And it does look like snow, kind of, or at least ice; it looks, actually, like a Syracuse parking lot after a freezing night.

Then the Arab kids pour in: sweet, proud, scared, tentative, trying to be brave. Each is offered a coat, from a big pile of identical coats, black with a red racing stripe. Some stand outside the snow rink, watching. Some walk stiff-legged across it, beaming. For others the approach is: Bend down, touch with one finger. One affects nonchalance: Snow is nothing to him. But then he quickly stoops, palms the snow, yanks his hand back, grins to himself. Another boy makes a clunky snowball, hands it politely to the crescent-with-legs, who politely takes it, holds it awhile, discreetly drops it. The goose paces angrily around the room, as if trying to escape the handler, who is still swatting flirtatiously at its tail while constantly whispering asides up at its beak.

And the kids keep coming. On their faces: looks of bliss, the kind of look a person gets when he realizes he is in the midst of doing something rare, that might never be repeated, and is therefore of great value. They are seeing something from a world far away, where they will probably never go.

Women in abayas video. Families pose shyly, rearranging themselves to get more Snow in the frame. Mothers and fathers stand beaming at their kids, who are beaming at the Snow.

This is sweet, I scribble in my notebook.

And it is. My eyes well up with tears.

In the same way that reading the Bible, listening to radio preachers, would not clue the neophyte into the very active kindness of a true Christian home, reading the Koran, hearing about "moderate Islam," tells us nothing about the astonishing core warmth and familial sense of these Arab families.

I think: If everybody in America could see this, our foreign policy would change.

For my part, in the future, when I hear "Arab" or "Arab street" or those who "harbor, shelter, and sponsor" the terrorists, I am going to think of the Arabian Ice City, and that goose, moving among the cold-humbled kids, and the hundreds of videotapes now scattered around Arab homes in Dubai, showing beloved children reaching down to touch Snow.

*****

WHAT IS JED CLAMPETT DOING IN GITMO?

Having a Coke after Arabian Ice City, trying to get my crying situation sorted out, it occurred to me that the American sense of sophistication/irony—our cleverness, our glibness, our rapid-fire delivery, our rejection of gentility, our denial of tradition, our blunt realism—which can be a form of greatness when it manifests in a Gershwin, an Ellington, a Jackson Pollock—also causes us to (wrongly) assume a corresponding level of sophistication/irony/worldliness in the people of other nations.

Example One: I once spent some time with the mujahideen in Peshawar, Pakistan—the men who were at that time fighting the Russians and formed the core of the Taliban—big, scowling, bearded men who'd just walked across the Khyber Pass for a few weeks of rest. And the biggest, fiercest one of all asked me, in complete sincerity, to please convey a message to President Reagan, from him, and was kind of flabbergasted that I didn't know the president and couldn't just call him up for a chat, man-to-man.

Example Two: On the flight over to Dubai, the flight attendant announces that if we'd like to make a contribution to the Emirates Airline Foundation children's fund, we should do so in the provided envelope. The sickly Arab man next to me, whose teeth are rotten and who has, with some embarrassment, confessed to "a leg problem," responds by gently stuffing the envelope full of the sugar cookies he was about to eat. Then he pats the envelope, smiles to himself, folds his hands in his lap, goes off to sleep.

What one might be tempted to call *simplicity* could be more accurately called a *limited sphere of experience*. We round up "a suspected Taliban member" in Afghanistan and, assuming that Taliban means the same thing to him as it does to us (a mob of intransigent inconvertible Terrorists), whisk this sinister Taliban member—who grew up in, and has never once left, what is essentially the Appalachia of Afghanistan; who possibly joined the Taliban in response to the lawlessness of the post-Russian warlord state, in the name of bringing some order and morality to his life or in a misguided sense of religious fervor—off to Guantánamo, where he's treated as if he personally planned 9/11. Then this provincial, quite possibly not-guilty, certainly rube-like guy, whose view of the world is more limited than we can even imagine, is denied counsel and a possible release date, and subjected to all of the hardships and deprivations our modern military-prison system can muster. How must this look to him? How must *we* look to him?

My experience has been that the poor, simple people of the world admire us, are enamored of our boldness, are hopeful that the insanely positive values we espouse can be actualized in the world. They are, in other words, rooting for us. Which means that when we disappoint them—when we come in too big, kill innocents, when our powers of discernment are diminished by our frenzied, self-protective, fearful post-9/11 energy—we have the potential to disappoint them, bitterly, and drive them away.

*****

LOOK, DREAM, BUT STAY OUT THERE

My fourth and final hotel, the Emirates Towers, is grand and imperial, surrounded by gardens, palm trees, and an elaborate fountain/moat assembly that would look right at home on an outlying *Star Wars* planet.

One Thai prostitute I spoke with in a bar said she'd stayed at the Emirates Towers four or five times but didn't like it much. Why not? I wondered. Too business-oriented? Kind of formal, a bit stuffy? "Because every time, they come up in the night and t'row me out," she said.

Returning to the hotel at dusk, I find dozens of the low-level South Indian workers, on their weekly half-day off, making their way toward the Towers, like peasants to the gates of the castle, dressed in their finest clothes (cowboy-type shirts buttoned to the throat), holding clunky circa-1980s cameras.

What are they doing here? I ask. What's going on?

We are on holiday, one says.

What are their jobs? When can they go home? What will they do tonight? Go out and meet girls? Do they have girlfriends back home, wives?

Maybe someday, one guy says, smiling a smile of anticipatory domestic ecstasy, and what he means is: Sir, if you please, how can I marry when I have nothing? This is why I'm here: so someday I can have a family.

Are you going in there? I ask, meaning the hotel.

An awkward silence follows. In there? Them?

No, sir, one says. We are just wishing to take photos of ourselves in this beautiful place.

They go off. I watch them merrily photographing themselves in front of the futuristic fountain, in the groves of lush trees, photos they'll send home to Hyderabad, Bangalore. Entering the hotel is out of the question. They know the rules.

I decide to go in but can't locate the pedestrian entrance. The idea, I come to understand, after fifteen minutes of high-attentiveness searching, is to discourage foot traffic. Anybody who belongs in there will drive in and valet park.

Finally I locate the entrance: an unmarked, concealed, marble staircase with wide, stately steps fifty feet across. Going up, I pass a lone Indian guy hand-squeegeeing the thirty-three (I count them) steps.

How long will this take you? I ask. All afternoon?

I think so, he says sweetly.

Part of me wants to offer to help. But that would be, of course, ridiculous, melodramatic. He washes these stairs every day. It's not my job to hand-wash stairs. It's his job to hand-wash stairs. My job is to observe him hand-washing the stairs, then go inside the air-conditioned lobby and order a cold beer and take notes about his stair-washing so I can go home and write about it, making more for writing about it than he'll make in many, many years of doing it.

And of course, somewhere in India is a guy who'd kill to do some stair-washing in Dubai. He hasn't worked in three years, any chance of marriage is rapidly fading.

Does this stair washer have any inclination to return to India, surrender his job to this other guy, give up his hard-won lifestyle to help this fellow human being? Who knows? If he's like me, he probably does. But in the end, his answer, like mine, is: That would be ridiculous, melodramatic. It's not my job to give up my job, which I worked so hard these many years to get.

Am I not me? Is he not him?

He keeps washing. I jog up the stairs to the hotel. Two smiling Nepalese throw open the huge doors, greeting me warmly, and I go inside.

*****

GOOD-BYE, DUBAI, I'LL LOVE YOU FOREVER

Emirates airlines features unlimited free movies, music, and video games, as well as Downward-Looking and Forward-Looking live closed-circuit TV. I toggle back and forth between the Downward-Looking Camera (there are the Zagros Mountains, along the Iraq-Iran border) and *Meet the Fockers*. The mountains are green, rugged. The little dog is flushed down the toilet and comes out blue.

It's a big world, and I really like it.

In all things, we are the victims of The Misconception From Afar. There is the idea of a city, and the city itself, too great to be held in the mind. And it is in this gap (between the conceptual and the real) that aggression begins. No place works any different than any other place, really, beyond mere details. The universal human laws—need, love for the beloved, fear, hunger, periodic exaltation, the kindness that rises up naturally in the absence of hunger/fear/pain—are constant, predictable, reliable, universal, and are merely ornamented with the details of local culture. What a powerful thing to know: That one's own desires are mappable onto strangers; that what one finds in oneself will most certainly be found in The Other.

Just before I doze off, I counsel myself grandiosely: Fuck concepts. Don't be afraid to be confused. Try to remain permanently confused. Anything is possible. Stay open, forever, so open it hurts, and then open up some more, until the day you die, world without end, amen.

—2005

Learning from Other Writers (Saunders)

1. Saunders comments that anyone about to travel to Dubai might wonder: "Is it dangerous? Will I be beheaded? Will I need a translator? Will my translator be beheaded? Just before we're beheaded, will my translator try to get out of it by blaming everything on me?" What stereotype is Saunders engaging in here? What is the effect of such language on the essay's tone? Why is acknowledging stereotypes so important here?

2. Why is the comment by the Indian boy on the plane—he says that from the air, Dubai looks like a microchip—such a telling detail? What does this bit of dialogue tell us about Dubai? About the type of people who are traveling to Dubai? Examine the other bits of dialogue and the other telling details that Saunders chooses to include. What role do they play for both author and reader?

3. Why does Saunders spend so much time talking about the workers in Dubai, all of whom come from somewhere else? How does this line of inquiry relate to his analysis?

4. What does Saunders mean by his statement (after the scene with the snow): "If everybody in America could see this, our foreign policy would change"?

6. Saunders directly addresses his driving question at the end: "What a powerful thing to know: That one's own desires are mappable onto strangers; that what one finds in oneself will most certainly be found in The Other." Where in the essay has Saunders *shown* this? How does this statement relate to the other essays you have read in this book? In what ways might this conclusion be considered obvious or banal? In what ways might it be complex and profound?

By Zadie Smith

ONE WEEK IN LIBERIA

MONDAY

There are no direct flights from England to Liberia. Either you go to Brussels or you book with Astraeus, a specialist airline named after a Roman goddess of justice. It runs a service to Freetown, in neighboring Sierra Leone. The clientele are mostly Africans dressed as if for church. Formal hats, zirconias and Louis Vuitton holdalls are popular. A toddler waddles down the aisle in a three-piece suit and bow tie. Only non-Africans are dressed for "Africa," in khakis, sandals, wrinkled T-shirts. Their bags are ostentatiously simple: frayed rucksacks, battered cases. The luggage of a nomad people.

A cross section of travelers sit in a row. A glamorous African girl in a silky blouse, an English nun, an American aid worker and a Lebanese man, who describes himself as a "fixer": "I fix things in Freetown—electrical systems, buildings." He calls the well-dressed Africans soon-comes. "They come, they soon go. Their families assume they're rich—they try to live up to this idea." The plane prepares to land. The fixer looks out the window and murmurs, "White man's graveyard," in the same spirit that people feel compelled to say "the Big Apple" as their plane approaches JFK. This, like much else on the plane, accommodates the Africa of imagination.

In Sierra Leone everyone deplanes, taking the Africa of imagination with them, a story that has at least a familiar form. Who remains in the story of Liberia? Barely a dozen people, ushered to the front to stare at one another across the wide aisles of business class. The nun is traveling on: Sister Anne of the Corpus Christi Carmelites. Brown socks in brown sandals, brown wimple; a long, kindly face, mapped with wrinkles. She has worked in Liberia since the eighties, running a mission school in Greenville. "We left when the war became impossible—we're back now, teaching students. It's not easy. Our students have seen such terrible things. Beyond imagination, really." She looks troubled when asked to describe the Liberian character. "They are either very, very good people—or the opposite. It is very hard to be good in these conditions."

Flying low over Monrovia there are no lights visible, only flood rain and sheet lightning illuminating the branches of palm trees, the jungle in a bad movie. The airport is no bigger than a village school. The one-ring baggage carousel is open to the elements; through the aperture the lightning flashes. There are more baggage handlers than passengers. They mill without occupation, bored, soaking wet. It seems incredible that heat like this persists through rain. The only thing to see is the obligatory third-world Coke billboard, ironic in exact proportion to the distance from its proper American context. This one says COKE—MAKE IT REAL. Just after the Coke sign there is a contrary sign, an indication that irony is not a currency in Liberia. It is worn by a girl who leans against the exit in a T-shirt that says THE TRUTH MUST BE TOLD.

The truth about Liberia is disputed. It consists of simultaneously asserted, mutually exclusive "facts." The CIA World Factbook states that "in 1980, a military coup led by

Samuel Doe ushered in a decade of authoritarian rule," but not—as is widely believed in Liberia—that the CIA itself funded both the coup and the regime. Doe's successor, Charles Taylor, instigator of the 1989–97 Liberian civil war, in which an estimated three hundred thousand people died, is presently in the Hague awaiting trial for crimes against humanity, yet there are supportive hand-painted billboards across Monrovia (CHARLES TAYLOR IS INNOCENT!) and hagiographic collections of his speeches for sale in the airport. In Europe and America, the Liberian civil war is described as a "tribal conflict." In Liberian classrooms children from half a dozen different tribes sit together and do not seem to know what you mean when you ask if this causes a difficulty.

There is no real road network in Liberia. During the late-summer rainy season much of the country is inaccessible. Tonight the torrential rain is unseasonable (it is March), but the road is the best in the country, properly surfaced: one long, straight line from the airport to the Mamba Point Hotel in Monrovia. Lysbeth Holdaway, Oxfam's press officer, sits in the back of an all-weather 4×4 outlining Liberia's present situation. She has long chestnut hair, is in youthful middle age and dresses in loose linen; she looks like the actress Penelope Wilton. She "loves gardening and *most* of Radio 4" and worked for many years at the BBC. Four or five times a year she visits some of the more benighted countries of the world. Even by the standards with which she is familiar, Liberia is exceptional. "Three quarters of the population live below the poverty line— that's one U.S. dollar a day—half are on less than fifty cents a day. What infrastructure there was has been destroyed—roads, ports, municipal electricity, water, sanitation, schools, hospitals—all desperately lacking or nonexistent; eighty-six-percent unemployment, no street lights.…" Through the car window dead street lamps can be seen, stripped of their components during the war. Lightning continues to reveal the scene: small huts made of mud bricks; sheets of corrugated iron and refuse; more bored young men, sitting in groups, dully watching the cars go by. The cars are of two types: huge Toyota Land Cruiser pickups like this one, usually with "UN" stamped on their hoods, or taxis, dilapidated yellow Nissans, the back windows of which reveal six people squeezed into the backseats, four in the front. Our driver, John Flomo, is asked whether the essentials—a water and sanitation system, electricity, schools—existed prior to the war. "Some, yes. In towns. Less in the country." Even the electricity that lights the airport is not municipal. It comes from a hydro plant belonging to Firestone, the American rubber company famous for its tires. Firestone purchased one million acres of this country in 1926, a ninety-nine-year lease at the bargain rate of six cents an acre. It uses its hydro plant to power its operation. The airport electricity is a "gift" to the nation, although Firestone's business could not function without an airport. "All this is Firestone," says Flomo, pointing at the darkness.

TUESDAY

The Mamba Point Hotel is an unusual Liberian building. It is air-conditioned, with toilets and clean drinking water. In the parking lot a dozen UN trucks are parked. In the breakfast room the guests are uniform: button-down collars, light khakis,

MacBooks. "Here's the crazy thing," one man tells another over croissants. "Malaria isn't even a hard problem to solve." At a corner table, an older woman reels off blunt statistics to a newcomer, who notes them down: "Population, three point five million. Over a hundred thousand with HIV; male life expectancy, thirty-eight; female, forty-two. Sixty-five Liberian dollars to one U.S. Officially literacy is fifty-seven percent, but that figure is really prewar—there's this whole missing generation...." In the corner bar, a dozen male Liberian waiters rest against the counter, devotedly following *Baywatch*.

All trips by foreigners, however brief, are done in the NGO Land Cruisers. The two-minute journey to Oxfam headquarters passes an open rubbish dump through which people scavenge alongside skinny pigs. The NGO buildings are lined up on "UN Drive." Each has a thick boundary wall, stamped with its own logo, patrolled by Liberian security. The American embassy goes further, annexing an entire street. Oxfam shares its compound with UNICEF. These offices resemble an English sixth-form college, a white concrete block with swinging doors and stone stairwells. On each door there is a sticker: NO FIREARMS. Here Phil Samways, the country program manager, heads a small development team. He is fifty-four, sandy-haired, lanky, wearing the short-sleeved white shirt accountants favor in the summer months. Unusually, his is not a development background: for twenty years he worked at Anglian Water. He has an unsentimental, practical manner, speaking precisely and quickly: "We are moving out of the humanitarian disaster stage now—water and sanitation and so on. Now we're interested in long-term development. We choose schemes that concentrate on education and livelihoods, and the rehabilitation of ex-combatants, of which there are thousands, many of them children. We hope you'll talk to some of them. You'll see a few of our school projects while you're here, and our rural projects in Bong County, and also West Point, which is really our flagship project. West Point is a slum—half the population of Monrovia live in slums. And as you've seen, we have extreme weather—for eight months it rains like this and the country turns into a quagmire. Cholera is a massive problem. But you have to choose the area you're going to concentrate on, and we've chosen education. We found when we asked people what they needed most, people often said education first, over toilets, basic sanitation. Which should tell you something."

The atmosphere in the hallways is jovial and enthusiastic, like a school newspaper. The staff are mostly young Liberians, educated in the early eighties, before the school system collapsed, or schooled elsewhere in Africa. They are positive about the future, with much optimism focused upon Ellen Johnson-Sirleaf, the Harvard-educated economist and first female head of state in Africa. Johnson-Sirleaf won the presidency in 2005, narrowly defeating the Liberian footballer George Weah. At present she is abroad promoting foreign investment in her country. Liberia's expectations are on hold until her return. "We hope and pray," people say when her name comes up. For the moment, her real impact is conceptual rather than actual: Liberia is having its female moment. Everywhere the talk is of a new generation of girls who will "take Liberia into the future." The popular phrase among the NGO-ers is "gender strategy." The first visit of the day is to one of the "girls' clubs" Oxfam funds.

Abraham Paye Conneh, a thirty-seven-year-old Liberian who looks fifteen years younger, will accompany the visitors. He speaks a flamboyant, expressive English, peppered with the acronym-heavy language of NGOs. Prior to becoming Oxfam's education project officer, he held down three jobs simultaneously: lecturer at the University of Zion, teacher at the Liberia Baptist Theological Seminary and director of education at the West African Training Institute, a feat that netted him ten American dollars a day. He is the team's "character." He writes poetry. He is evangelical about Oxfam's work: "It's time for the women! We're understanding gender now in Liberia. We never educated our Liberian women before; we did not see their glorious potential! But we want the women of Liberia to rise up now! Oh, yes! Like Ellen rose up! We're saying, anything a man can do, a woman can do in the same superior fashion!"

Phil Samways, who enjoys Abraham's impromptu speeches but does not tend to encourage them, returns to practicalities. "Now, security is still an issue. There's a midnight curfew for everybody here—we ask that you comply with it. We get the odd riot—small, spontaneous riots. But you'll be fine with Abraham—you might even get a poem if you're lucky."

To Lysbeth and Abraham we now add the photographer, Aubrey Wade, a thirty-one-year-old Anglo-Dutchman. He is thin, dark blond. He wears a floppy sun hat beneath which a pert nose white with sunblock pecks. He rests his lens on the car window. Hand-painted billboards line the road. HAVE YOU BEEN RAPED? Also STOP RAPE IN LIBERIA. Lysbeth asks Abraham what other "particular problems women in Liberia face." The list is long: female circumcision, marriage from the age of eleven, polygamy, spousal ownership. Girls have "traditionally been discouraged from school." In some tribes, husbands covertly push their wives into sexual affairs so they may charge the offending man an "infidelity tax," paid in the form of unwaged labor. A culture of sexual favors predates the war. Further billboards warn girls not to offer their bodies in return for school grades, a common practice. The moral of Liberia might be "Where there is weakness, exploit it." This moral is not especially Liberian in character. In May 2006 a BBC investigation uncovered "systematic sexual abuse" in Liberia: UN peacekeepers offering food to teenage refugees in return for sex. In November of the same year a local anonymous NGO worker in Liberia told the corporation: "Peacekeepers are still taking advantage of the situation to sexually exploit young girls. The acts are still rampant despite pronouncements that they have been curbed."

In a school in Unification Town, fourteen girls from the girls' club are picked to sit with us in the new school "library." It is a small room, very hot. Lysbeth's cheeks bloom red, her hair sticks to her forehead. Our shirts are see-through with sweat. The small, random collection of textbooks on the shelves are a decade out of date. Next door is the typewriting pool, pride of the club. Here they learn to type on ten old-fashioned typewriters. It is not a "school" as that word is commonly understood. It is a building with a thousand children in it, waiting for a school to manifest itself. The preplanned questions—*Do you enjoy studying? What's your favorite subject?*—are rendered absurd. They answer quietly and sadly in a "Liberian English" that is difficult to understand. The teacher translates unclear answers. She is equally hard to understand. *What would you like to be when you grow up?* "Pilot" is a popular answer. Also "a sailor in the navy." By sea or by air, flight is on their minds. The remainder say "nurse" or "doctor" or "in government." The two escape routes visible in Liberia: aid and government. *What do your fathers do?* They are dead, or else they are rubber tappers. A girl sighs heavily. These are not the right questions. The exasperated teacher prompts: "Ask them how often they are able to come to school." Despair invades the room. A girl lays her head on the desk. No one speaks. "Ask me." It is the girl who sighed. She is fourteen; her name is Evelyn B. Momoh; she has a heart-shaped face, doll features. She practically vibrates with intelligence and impatience. "We have to work with our mothers in the market. We need to live and there's no money. It's very hard to stay in school. There's no money, do you understand? There's no money at all." We write this down. *Is the typing pool useful?* Evelyn squints. "Yes, yes, of course—it's a good thing; we are very thankful." There is the sense that she is trying hard not to scream. This is in contrast to the other girls, who only seem exhausted. *And the books?* Evelyn answers again. "I've read all of them now. I'm very good at math. I've read all the math books. We need more." *Are there books in your house?* Evelyn blinks slowly, gives up. We file out to the typing room. Aubrey takes pictures of Evelyn as she pretends to type. She submits to this as a politician might to a humiliating, necessary photo op. We file outside into the dry, maddening heat. Aubrey walks the perimeter looking for something to photograph. The school sits isolated on a dusty clearing bordered by monotonous rubber plantations. Evelyn and her girls arrange themselves under a tree to sing a close harmony song, typical, in its melody, of West Africa. "Fellow Liberians, the war is over! Tell your girls, fetch them to get them to school! Your war is over—they need education!" The voices are magnificent. The girls sing without facial affect; dead-eyed, unsmiling. Around us the bored schoolboys skulk. Nobody speaks to them or takes their picture. The teacher does not worry that boredom and disaffection may turn to resentment and violence: "Oh, no, they are very happy for the girls." As the visitors prepare to leave, Evelyn stops us at the steps. It is a strange look she has, so willful, so much in want, and yet so completely without expectation. The word *desperate* is often misused. This is what it means. "You will write the things we need. You have a pencil?" The list is as follows: books, math books, history books, science books, exercise books, copybooks, pens, pencils, more desks, a computer, electricity, a generator for electricity, teachers.

Driving back toward Monrovia:

"Abraham—isn't there a government education budget?"

"Oh, yes! Sure. Ms. Sirleaf has promised immediate action on essential services. But she has only a $120 million budget for the whole year. The UN budget alone in Liberia for one year is $875 million. And we have a $3.7 billion debt!"

"But how much did what we just saw cost?"

"Ten thousand. We built an extra section of the school, provided all the materials, et cetera. If it had not been done by us or another NGO, it would not be done at all."

"Do you pay teachers?"

"We are not *meant* to—we don't want a two-tier system. But we can *train* them, for example. Many of the teachers in Liberia have only been educated up to the age of twelve or thirteen themselves! We have the blind leading the blind!"

"But then you're acting like a government—you're doing *their* job. Is that what NGOs do?"

"[sigh] Look, there's no human resources, and there's no money. We all must fill in the gap: the UN, Oxfam, UNICEF, CCF, the NRC, the IRC, Medecins Sans Frontières, STC, PWJ—"

"?"

"Peace Wind Japan. Another NGO. I can make you a long list. But different aid has different obligations attached. With us, there are no obligations. The money goes directly."

"So people can send money to you earmarked for a particular project?"

"Oh, yes! [extended laughter] Please put that in your article."

WEDNESDAY

The street scene in Monrovia is postapocalyptic: people occupy the shell of a previous existence. The InterContinental Hotel is a slum, home to hundreds. The old executive mansion is broken open like a child's playhouse; young men sit on the skeletal spiral staircase, taking advantage of the shade. Abraham points out Liberia's state seal on the wall: a ship at anchor with the inscription "The Love of Liberty Brought Us Here." In 1822 freed American slaves (known as Americo-Liberians, or, colloquially, Congos) founded the colony at the instigation of the American Colonization Society, a coalition of slave owners and politicians whose motives are not hard to tease out. Even Liberia's roots are sunk in bad faith. Of the first wave of emigrants, half died of yellow fever. By the end of the 1820s, a small colony of three thousand souls survived. In Liberia they built a facsimile life: plantation-style homes, white-spired churches. Hostile local Malinke tribes resented their arrival and expansion; sporadic armed battle was common. When the ACS went bankrupt in the 1840s, it demanded the "country of Liberia" declare its independence. It was the first of many category errors: Liberia was not yet a country. Its agricultural exports were soon dwarfed by the price of imports. A pattern of European loans (and defaulting on same) began in the 1870s. The money was used to partially modernize the Black Americo-Liberian hinterlands while ignoring the impoverished indigenous interior. The relationship between the two communities is a lesson in the factitiousness of "race." To the Americo-Liberians, these were "natives"—an illicit slave trade in Malinke people continued until the 1850s. As late as 1931, the League of Nations uncovered the use of forced indigenous labor. Abraham, in the front seat, bends his head round to Lysbeth in the back: "You know what we say to that seal? *The Love of Liberty MET us here.*" This is a popular Liberian joke. He laughs immoderately. "So that's how it was. They came here, and they always kept the power away from us! They had their True Whig Party, and for 133 years we were a peaceful one-party state. But there was no justice. The indigenous are ninety-five percent of this country, but we had nothing. Oh, those Congos—they had every little bit of power. Everyone in the government was Congo. They did each other favors, gave each other money. We were not even allowed the vote until very late—the sixties!"

Lys asks a reasonable question: "But how would one *know* someone was a Congo?"

"Oh, you would *know*. They had a way of speaking, a way of dressing. They always called each other "Mister." Always the big man. And they lived *very well*. This," he says, waving at the devastation of Monrovia, "was all very nice."

The largest concrete structures—the old Ministry of Health, the old Ministry of Defense, the True Whig Party headquarters—are remnants of the peaceful, unjust regimes of President Tubman (1944–71) and President Tolbert (1971–80), for whom Liberians feel a perverse nostalgia. The university, the hospital, the schools, these were financed by a True Whig policy of massive international loans and deregulated foreign business concessions, typically given to agriculturally "extractive" companies, which ship resources directly out of the country without committing their companies to any value-added processing. For much of the twentieth century, Liberia had a nickname: Firestone Republic. The deals that condemned Liberians to poverty wages and inhumane living conditions were made in these old government buildings. The people who benefited most from these deals worked in these buildings. Now these buildings have rags hanging from their windows, bullet holes in their facades and thousands of squatters inside, without toilets, without running water. Naturally, new buildings are built, new deals are made. On January 28, 2005, while an interim "caretaker" government presided briefly over a ruined country (the elections were due later that year), Firestone rushed through a new concession: fifty cents an acre for the next thirty-seven years. A processing plant—for which Liberians have been asking since the 1970s—was not part of this deal. Ministers of finance and agriculture, who had no mandate from the people and would be out of office in a few months, negotiated the deal. It was signed in the Cabinet Room at the Executive Mansion in the presence of John Blaney, U.S. ambassador at the time. During the same period, Mittal Steel acquired the country's iron ore, giving the company virtual control of the vast Nimba concession area. The campaigning group Global Witness described the Mittal deal as a "case study in which multinational corporations seek to maximise profit by using an international regulatory void to gain concessions and contracts which strongly favour the corporation over the host nation."

It is a frustration for activists that Liberians have tended not to trace their trouble back to extractive foreign companies or their government lobbies. Liberians don't think that way. Most Liberians know how much a rubber tapper gets paid: thirty-five American dollars a month. Everyone knows how much a government minister is paid: two thousand American dollars a month—a Liberian fortune. No one can tell you Firestone's annual profit (in 2005, from its Liberia production alone: $81,242,190). In a country without a middle or working class, without *a functioning civic life*, government is all. It is all there is of money, of housing, of health care and schooling, of normal life.

It is the focus of all aspirations, all fury. One of the more reliable signs of weak democracy is the synonymity of the word *government* with government buildings. Storming Downing Street and killing the prime minister would not transfer executive power. In Liberia, as in Haiti, the opposite is true. The violence of the past quarter century has in part represented a battle over Congo real estate, in particular the second, infamous Executive Mansion. It is hard to find any Liberian entirely free of the mystique of this building. In the book *Liberia: The Heart of Darkness,* a gruesome account of the 1989–97 war, the author's descriptions of 1990's catastrophic battle for Monrovia are half war report, half property magazine:

> From the university campus, [Charles Taylor's] NPFL pounded the heavily fortified
> Executive Mansion: the huge magnificent structure built in 1964 by the Israelis at
> the cost of $20 million. With its back to the brilliant white beach of the Atlantic, the
> Executive Mansion is located at the point where West Africa comes closest to Brazil.

In 1990, that was President Samuel K. Doe inside, refusing to leave. Ten years earlier, in 1980, when the twenty-eight-year-old Doe, a semiliterate Krahn tribesman and master sergeant in the Liberian army, staged his coup d'état, his focus was also the executive mansion. He fought his way in, disemboweling President Tolbert in his bed.

We visit Red Light market. Aubrey: "Why is it called Red Light?"

Abraham: "Because a set of traffic lights used to be here."

It is a circular piece of land, surrounded by small shops and swarming with street traders. The shops have names like The Arun Brothers and Ziad's, all Lebanese owned, as is the Mamba Point Hotel. Almost all small business in Liberia is Lebanese owned. Abraham shrugs: "They simply had money at a time when we had no money." The bleak punch line is Liberia's citizenship laws: anyone not "of African descent" cannot be a citizen. Lebanese money goes straight back to Lebanon.

Women crouch around the market's perimeter, selling little polyethylene bags of soap powder. Some are from WOCDAL (Women and Children Development Association of Liberia), funded by Oxfam. WOCDAL lends them one hundred Liberian dollars (less than two American dollars) for a day. This gives the women a slight economic advantage in Red Light, analogous to the one the Lebanese had over the Liberians in the 1950s: money when others have none. No one else in Red Light can afford to buy a full box of soap powder. This the women then sell in pieces, keeping the profit and returning the one hundred dollars to WOCDAL. It is a curious fact that a box of soap powder, sold in many small parts, generates more money in the third world than in the first. A woman with five children tells us this enables her to send two of her three children to school. The other three work alongside her in the market. *How do you decide whom to send?* "I send the fourteen-and fifteen-year-olds to school, because they will be finished sooner. The five-, six-, and seven-year-olds work with me."

THURSDAY

From the 4x4, West Point does not look like a "flagship project." A narrow corridor of filth, lined on either side with small dwellings made of trash, mud, scrap metal.

Children with distended bellies, rotting food, men breaking rocks. It stretches for miles. The vehicle sticks in an alley too narrow to pass. The visitors must walk. Close up, the scene is different. It is not one corridor. There are many networks of alley. It is a city. Food is cooking. Small stalls, chicken skewers for sale. Children trail Aubrey, wanting their photograph taken. They pose boldly: big fists on knobby, twiggy arms. No one begs. We stop by a workshop stockpiled with wooden desks and chairs, solid, not unbeautiful. They are presently being varnished a caramel brown. A very tall young white man is here to show us around, Oxfam's program manager at West Point. "*This*," he says, placing both hands hard on the nearest desk for emphasis, "is great workmanship, no?" Lysbeth peers at the wood: "Um, you do know that's not quite dry?"

Patrick Alix is thirty years old. He is distinctly aristocratic looking, half French, and so unrelievedly serious the urge is to say stupid things in his presence. Before working in West Point, Patrick worked in Zambia doing emergency work, qualified as a chartered accountant, worked for the World Wildlife Fund in Indonesia ("I used to be an ecology militant"), performed a management evaluation of the French nuclear fusion reactor program, produced a Reggae album in Haiti and played violin in the Liverpool Philharmonic Orchestra. The above is not an exhaustive list. He has seen the situation in Liberia progress from the direst emergency to the beginnings of "development." "Basically, we've followed the returnees from the camps—many settled in this community. Sixty-five thousand people live here, thirty thousand of them children. Now, there are nineteen schools in the slum, yes? So—" *Wait. There are schools in a slum?* Patrick frowns, stops walking. He pinches his temples. "Sure," he says. "But we're going to the only government one. The rest are private, sharing space with churches, or mosques, with volunteer teachers. There's also a teacher's council here, a commissioner, the township council—you understand the slum is a township? It's organized into blocks and zones. The area representatives call meetings. Otherwise nothing would get done."

He sets off quickly through the chaotic little alleys, sure of his way. When we arrive, Patrick says: "You should have seen it before. This is the 'after' picture!" Aubrey takes a photograph of the long, low concrete building, its four large, bare rooms. Patrick says: "So Liberia has this unique freed-slave history.... What this means is the government structures were simply borrowed, lots of titles—minister for this, minister for that— but that was cosmetic.... Now, things have changed; they've pledged ten percent of their budget to education, which is enormous percentage-wise, but still only twelve million dollars *for the whole country*. There's too much to be done right now. NGOs fill the gap. What you saw back there was part of our livelihood project: fathers are taught how to make school furniture, which we, the school, buy from them at a fair price. They also sell this furniture to all the schools in West Point. And mothers make the uniforms—if that doesn't sound too traditionally gendered...."

Standing in front of the school are John Brownell, who manages the livelihood project, and Ella Coleman, who until recently was West Point's commissioner. Mr. Brownell is a celebrity in West Point: he played football for Liberia. This took him to the United States and Brazil. "Rio de Janeiro!" he says, and smiles fondly, as if speaking of heaven. He is crisp-shirted despite the heat, broad as a rugby player. Ms. Coleman is a kind of celebrity, too, well known throughout West Point. Hers is a hands-on approach to pastoral care. She will enter homes to check on suspected abuse. She keeps children at her own house if she fears for their safety. She is impassioned: "We have seven-year-old girls being raped by big men! I talk to parents—I educate people. People are so poor and desperate. They don't know. For example, if a mother is keeping her child home to earn fifty Liberian dollars at the market, I say to her: "That will keep you for a day! What about the future?" Another example: one of our very young boys here, he was always touching one of our girls—so I made him a friend. He was suspended—but sitting out there will not help. I went to his house. The whole family sleeps in one room. I said to his parents: you have exposed these children to these things too early. Anything that happens to this little girl, I will hold you responsible!"

And are some of your students ex-combatants? "Oh, my girl," says Ms. Coleman sadly, "there are ex-combatants everywhere. People live next to boys who killed their own families. We, as a people, we have so much healing to do."

Patrick explains logistics. The principal of the school is on thirty American dollars a month. To rent a shack in the slum for a month is four American dollars a week. Liberian teachers are easily bribed. You pay a little, you pass your exam. At the university level, the problem is endemic. Teaching qualifications are usually dubious. "It's dull to repeat, but this all stems from extreme poverty. If you're a teacher living in a shack on a pile of rubbish, you'd probably do the same." Mr. Brownell begins to speak hopefully of the Fast Track Initiative, to which Liberia has applied for money. He puffs out his wide chest proudly. One of the aims is to reduce class size from 344:1 to 130:1. Patrick nods quickly: "Yes, big man ... but that will take three years—while strategies are being made, these children need something now. Look at them. They're waiting."

"This is the sad truth," says Brownell.

In the shade, four girls are instructed to speak with us. The conversation is brief. They all want to be doctors. They kick the dust, refuse to make eye contact. We have only inanities to offer them anyway. *It's good that you all want to be doctors. The doctors will teach new doctors. There'll be so many doctors in Liberia soon!*

Lysbeth sighs, murmuring: "Except there's something like twenty-three Liberian doctors. And fourteen nurses. In the whole country."

The visitors wilt slightly; sit on a wall. The schoolgirls look on with pity—an unbearable reversal. They run off to help their mothers in the market. Meanwhile, Ms. Coleman is still talking; she is explaining that at some point the government will clear this slum, this school, everything and everyone in it. She does not think the situation impossible. She does not yet suffer from "charity fatigue." She is saying, "I trust it will be for the best. We made this community from the dirt, but we can't stay here."

FRIDAY

Bong country is beautiful. Lush green forest, a sweet breeze. There are pygmy hippopotamuses here and monkeys; a sense of Liberia's possibilities. Rich in natural resources, cool in the hills, hot on the beach. Nyan P. Zikeh is the Oxfam program manager for this region. He is compactly built, hand-some, boyish. He was educated during the last days of Tolbert's regime ("He was killed in my final year of high school"). Nyan helps rebuild the small village communities of Bong, a strategic area fought over by all the warring factions. People live in tiny traditional thatched huts arranged around a central ground. It is quiet and clean. The communities are close-knit and gather around the visitors to join the conversation. In one village a woman explains the food situation. She is "1-0-0," her children are (usually) "1-0-1"; there are many others who are "0-0-1." It is a binary system that describes meals per day. Still, things are improving: there are schools here now; there are latrines. Nyan's projects encourage the creation of rice paddies; the men work in them, and women take the rice to market. It is more than the subsistence farming that existed before the war. His dream is to connect all these villages in a trading ring that utilizes Bong's strategic centrality and sells produce on to Monrovia, Nyan: "You have to understand, in this area, everything was destroyed. The largest displaced camps were here. We helped people go back to where their villages formerly were; we helped them rebuild. All that you see here was done with DFID money—the Department for International Development. They are British. They funded us with £271,000 sterling—they gave us this twice. And I am happy to say we met a hundred percent of our targets. Creating infrastructure and training individuals. The money went a very long way. It helped to train Liberian staff. It helped provide assistance at the county level for the Ministry of Health. It was quite an enormous help."

"This is the good aid story," says Lysbeth. "People find that very boring."

As we leave the village, the gardener in Lysbeth looks around for signs of soil cultivation. Heavy, wet palms cascade over one another, but there are no fields. Nyan prides himself on his frankness: "We can't blame anyone else. The truth is we don't have the knowledge and skill about farming. It has always been slash, burn and plant. The only industrial farming our people have known here is the rubber plantations. That is the only major industry our people know. Everything else was not developed."

There are such things as third-world products. In the market where the women sell their rice, a boy's T-shirt reads DAVID BECKHAM, but the picture beneath is of Thierry Henry. The plastic buckets the women carry have bad ink jobs—the colors run like tie-dye. The products no one else wants come to Liberia. "And our meat is the same," explains Nyan, "chicken feet, pig feet. That's what people are sold. More tendon than flesh. No nutritional value."

Half a mile down the road, Mrs. Shaw, an eighty-year-old Liberian teacher, sits in front of her small home. She has taught three generations of Liberian children on a wage she describes as "less then the rubber tappers: twenty-five U.S. dollars a month." She says the children she teaches have changed over the years. Now they are "hot headed." *They are angry about their situation?* She frowns: "No, angry at each other." As we leave, Lysbeth spots three graves in the yard. "My sons—they were poisoned." Lysbeth assumes this is metaphorical, but Abraham shakes his head. He doesn't know what the poison is, exactly: maybe some kind of leaf extract. In the vehicle he explains: "Her sons, they were working in government, quite good jobs. It happens that when you're doing well, sometimes you are poisoned. They put something in your drink. I always watch my glass when I am out."

The visitors sit on the porch eating dinner at CooCoo's Nest, the best hotel in rural Liberia. Named after President Tubman's mistress, it is owned by his daughter; she lives in America now. In her absence it is run by Kamal E. Ghanam, a louche, chain-smoking Lebanese in a safari pantsuit, who asks you kindly not to switch on the light in your room until after 7 P.M. Kamal also manages the rubber plantation behind. He brings out the sangria as Abraham and Nyan bond. These two are members of a very small group in Liberia: the makeshift Liberian middle class, created in large part by the presence of the NGOs. "It's difficult," explains Abraham. "Even if I paint my house, people begin talking. *He is Congo now.* As soon as you have anything at all, you are isolated from the people." They show off their battle scars, knife wounds from street robberies. Aubrey, who has been photographing the plantations, arrives. He has news: he met a rubber worker in the field.

"His name is David. He doesn't know his age—but we worked out with various references to events during war that he's about thirty-five years old. He has three living children and three who died. He was born on the plantation and has worked there since he was ten or twelve, he thinks. He wants to be able to keep his own children in school, but at the current rate of pay he won't be able to afford to. He works seven days a week. He says workers on the plantation live in camps that were built in 1952. There are no schools or medical facilities nearby—anyway, he couldn't afford them. He taps about fifty pounds of raw latex per day. He said it's a long day, from sunrise until late. . . ."

Aubrey is breathless and excited: we have the feeling that we are intrepid journalists, uncovering an unknown iniquity. In fact, the conditions on Liberian rubber plantations are well documented. In a CNN report of 2005, Firestone president Dan Adomitis explained that each worker "only" taps 650–750 trees a day and that each tree takes two to three minutes. Taking the lower of these two estimates equals twenty-one hours a day of rubber tapping. In the past, parents have brought their children with them in order to help them meet the quota; when this was reported, Firestone banned the practice. Now people bring their children before dawn.

Kamal smokes, listens, sighs. He says, "Listen, this is how it is," as if talking of some unstoppable natural weather phenomenon. He pauses. Then, more strongly: "Now, be careful about this tapper. He is not from Firestone, I think. He is from a different place." Nyan smiles. "Kamal, we both know that plantation—it sells to a middleman who sells to Firestone. Everybody sells to Firestone." Kamal shrugs. Nyan turns back to the visitors: "Firestone is a taboo subject here. Everyone knows the conditions are terrible—their accommodation has no water, no electricity—but it is better paid than most work here. You would have to have a very strong lobby in the U.S. government to stop them. The whole reason Firestone came to Liberia in the first place was as a means of creating a permanent supply of rubber for the American military. The British had increased the taxes on Malaysian rubber—the Americans didn't want to pay that. They needed a permanent solution. So they planted the rubber—it's not native to Liberia. Really, they created a whole industry. It sounds strange, but these are some of the best jobs in Liberia."

Kamal goes inside to collect dessert. Abraham leans over the table.

"Do you know what people say? In 2003, when the war was at its worst, *the only places in Liberia that were safe* were the U.S. embassy and Firestone. Everywhere else there was looting and killing. The American Marines were offshore—we kept hoping they would come ashore. What were they waiting for? But we waited and then they sailed away. They did *nothing.* And that is when people got disappointed."

Everyone at the table is asked why they think the war happened. Nyan says: "Let me tell you first my candid feeling: every Liberian in one way or another took part in the war. Either spiritually, financially, psychologically or physically. And to answer your question: in a sense there was no reason. Brothers killed brothers, friends killed friends, only to come back the next day and regret they ever did it in the first place. For me the only real reason was greed. And poverty. All that the warlords wanted was property. When they stormed Monrovia, they did not even pretend to fight one another. They killed people in their homes and then painted their own names on the walls. When Ms. Sirleaf took over Guttridge's rubber plantation—2.8 million a month—it was still occupied by rebel forces, and they refused to leave for a year and a half. They wanted to be in the rubber business. But they destroyed the trees—didn't tap them properly. It will take another ten years to replant."

SATURDAY

Lunch in La Pointe, the "good restaurant" in Monrovia. The view is of sheer cliff dropping to marshland, and beyond this, blue green waters. During the war the beach was scattered with human skulls. Now it is simply empty. In Jamaica, tourists marry on beaches like these. They stand barefoot in wedding outfits in white sand owned by German hotel chains and hold up champagne flutes, recreating an image from a brochure. This outcome for Liberia—a normalized, if exploitative, "tourist economy"—seems almost too good to hope for. At present, La Pointe is patronized solely by NGO workers, government officials and foreign businessmen. A Liberian passes by in a reasonably nice suit. Abraham: "He's a Supreme Court judge." Another man in a tie: "Oh, he's Nigerian. He owns an airline." Everywhere in Liberia it is the same: there are only the very poor and the very powerful. In the missing middle, for now: the "international community." The monitoring agency GEMAP is in place. No government check over five hundred dollars can be signed without GEMAP's knowledge. *It is very hard to be good in these conditions.* President Johnson-Sirleaf has promised to review the 2005 Mittal Steel and Firestone concessions. *We hope and pray.*

Behind our table an Englishman, a Lebanese and a Liberian are having a lunch meeting:

Englishman: You see, I'm worried about management morale. The troops soon feel it if management is low. At the moment it's like a bloody sauna in there. Maybe we could just give them a few things... a nice bed, bedsheets, something so they won't be bitten to death at night.

They're so happy if you do that—you wouldn't believe it!

Liberian: My friend, *someone's* going to get malaria. It's inevitable.

Lebanese: This is true.

Liberian: I ask you please not to worry about malaria—we get it all the time in Liberia. I promise you we are used to it!

The history of Liberia consists of elegant variations on this conversation.

The Toyota rolls up in front of Paynesville School. Motto: *Helping our selve* [sic] *through Development.* Aubrey causes a riot in the playground: everyone wants their picture taken. Some are in uniform, others in NGO T-shirts. Fifty or so wear a shirt that says CHINA AND LIBERIA: FRIENDSHIP FOREVER. We are here only for one boy. We were given his name by Don Bosco Homes, a Catholic organization that specializes in the rehabilitation of child ex-combatants.

He is very small for fifteen, with a close-shaved, perfectly round head and long, pretty eyelashes. He has the transcendental air of a child lama. Three big men bring him to us in a corner of the yard and go to fetch a chair. He stays the wrist of one of the men with a finger and shakes his head. "It's too hot here to talk. We'll go inside."

In a small office at the back of the school, four nervous adults supervise the interview. Lysbeth, who has teenage children herself, looks as if she might cry even before Richard speaks. It's been a long week. Richard is determined to make it easy for us. He smiles gently at the Dictaphone: "It's okay. Are you sure that it's on?"

"My name is Richard S. Jack. I was twelve in 2003. I was living with my mother when the second civil war began. I was playing on a football field when men came and grabbed me. It was done by force—I had no desire to join that war. They called themselves the Marine Force. They took both teams of boys away. They threw us in a truck. I thought I wasn't going to see my parents anymore. They took me to Lofah Bridge. What happened there? We were taught to do certain things. We were taught to use AK-47s. I was with them for a year and a half. We were many different kinds of Liberians and Sierra Leoneans, many boys. The first one or two weeks I was so scared. After that it became a part of me. I went out of my proper and natural way. War makes people go out of their proper and natural way. It is a thing that destroys even your thoughts. People still don't know what the war was about. I know, It was a terrible misunderstanding. But it is not a part of me anymore. I don't want violence in me anymore. Whenever I sit and think about the past, I get this attitude: *I am going to raise myself up.* So I tell people about my past. They should know who I was. Sometimes it is hard. But it wasn't difficult to explain to my mother. She understood how everything was. She knew I was not a bad person in my heart. Now I want to be most wise. My dream is to become somebody good in this nation. I have a feeling that Liberia could be a great nation. But I also want to see the world. I love the study of geography. I want to become a pilot. You want me to fly you somewhere? Sure. Come and find me in ten years. I promise we will fly places."

—2007

Learning from Other Writers (Smith)

1. What is the effect of Smith's choice to begin her essay with "Day 1," without any introduction explaining the reason for her trip?

2. How does Smith's purpose in traveling to Liberia seem to shape the way she pays attention to details? The way she uncovers meaning?

3. Smith ends many of her sections with a line of dialogue without much commentary on what is said. Why do you think it is important for her to let the people she meets speak for themselves? What is the effect of ending with the words of a fifteen-year-old boy?

4. After overhearing the interchange about malaria between the Liberian and Lebanese men, Smith says: "The history of Liberia consists of elegant variations on this conversation." How so? Where else do we see such "elegant variations" in her essay?

5. How does the overall log of days reflect the experience of traveling? How does it allow her essays' driving question to develop and emerge?

Adding Your Voice

Interview someone you know about a vivid experience that you weren't present to witness. Better yet, try to interview two individuals about that same event. (As we will see in the next chapter when you read Charles Baxter's essay "The Chaos Machine," two individuals might recall the same events differently.) Collect these details and try to reconstruct the event as accurately and completely as possible. Remember: your goal is to reconstruct the experience—not to make things up.

CHAPTER 13

Meditations

The *meditative essay* is not a separate form but rather a stylistic variation on the forms we already have discussed. Any nonfiction structure can lend itself to a heavier or lighter dose of meditation, according to the writer's taste. Nonfiction minimalists such as John Hersey rely mostly on the objective presentation of scenes to get across their points, conveying meaning by selection and indirection rather than by overt thematic exposition, while maximalists such as George Saunders layer on trowelfuls of philosophical musings on the nature of time and familial responsibility and connection, the meaning of Dubai, or the ways in which Americans choose to view other cultures. At one end of the spectrum, the essay's meaning is created by selection or hinted at by indirection, with little if any analysis on the page. At the other end of the same spectrum, the formal seeds of the meditation may be compressed so tightly that the reader barely recognizes the structure's presence or the ways in which an experience or a journey, an experiment, an interview, or a visit to a museum might have served to generate the meditation; the writer compresses the essay's structure down to its barest kernel and allows his or her meditations to explode outward, popcorn-wise, from there.

The essays in this section examine broad topics such as fatherhood, communication, anxiety, catharsis, and grief. But in writing about these abstract concepts, the essayists rely on very specific, concrete language, detailed anecdotes, outside sources, and perceptive, precise analyses. Most likely, the authors did not sit down to write about the concept that eventually became the idea at their essay's core; rather, they started with a set of emotions, events, or states of being that seemed related. Often, when you write a meditative analysis, you find that specific events, images, or feelings start grouping themselves together in your mind, even if you don't yet know how or why these items are connected. Your role as you develop a meditative essay is to trust yourself to pursue and uncover the abstract idea that links the concrete elements that constitute your raw material.

If all of this seems pretty mystical, keep in mind that the interplay between your essay's driving question and a natural, organic form can help you to generate your meditation. As we discussed in Part I, you start with your question, then you move a step ahead in time or space as suggested by your form, which leads you to ponder your question in a more specific way, after which you move another step along the path.

THE NARRATIVE WITHIN

Many writers rely on a simple narrative to anchor a meditative essay, weaving in and out of the line of action as the events in the narrative inspire them to follow a certain line of reasoning. In "The Chaos Machine: An Essay on Postmodern Fatherhood," Charles Baxter uses the occasion of a journey in which he picked up his son, Daniel, from college to meditate on his improvised approach to raising a child. Baxter, who lost his father when he was eighteen months old, pauses the narrative again and again to meditate on Daniel's difficult infancy, childhood, and young adulthood, twentieth-century fatherhood in general, his own fears of fatherhood in particular, and his experiences growing up in the house of an emotionally distant, quasi-Victorian stepfather; as an extra twist, Baxter includes Daniel's footnotes to the narrative, as his son adds details, disagrees with his father's version of events, or provides a different perspective on their relationship.

by Charles Baxter, footnotes by Daniel Baxter

THE CHAOS MACHINE

AN ESSAY ON POSTMODERN FATHERHOOD

Late spring in southern Minnesota, 1998: the days build from deceptively clear mornings to damp, overheated afternoons. I have driven from Michigan to pick up my son at college and to take him home for summer break. As I enter Northfield, Minnesota—a sign announces the town, modestly boasting of its "Cows, Colleges, and Contentment"—I open the window and smell the faint receding scent of farm fields and the stronger cardboardish odor of the Malt-O-Meal plant just inside the city limits.

A strange mix, a pleasantly naive Midwestern smell. Our minivan, emptied of its benches and rear seat, should accommodate all my son's college paraphernalia, but the van, too, has an aroma—of Tasha, the family dog, a keeshond, and of the coffee I have been drinking mile after mile to stay awake. In fact, the van smells of all the Baxters. In Michigan the previous day I witnessed an accident near Albion, a woman driving suicidally into a bridge abutment; as a result, today I am shaky and still unnerved, and I am giving off a bad odor myself.

Daniel meets me in his dorm room. My spirit lifts when I see him. We hug. He is smiling but preoccupied and quiet, as he often is. Typical college kid? How would I know? He's the only son—the only child—I have. We arrange to go out to dinner at some air-conditioned Northfield bistro. Later, eating his pasta, a favorite food, he tells me that, yes, he will help me load up the van tomorrow, but, well, uh, he also needs to work with his friend Alex on a physics project the two of them have cooked up and have almost finished, a "Chaos Machine," as he calls it. He tries to explain to me what the Chaos Machine is, and I manage to figure out that it's some sort of computer randomizer. Much of the time when he explains anything technical to me—he has a brilliant mind for physics and engineering—I am simply baffled. I try to disguise my ignorance by nodding sagely and keeping my mouth shut. One's dignity should ideally stay intact in front of one's adult children.

So, OK, I will load the van tomorrow myself.[1]

I drop him off at his dorm and go back to the motel to get a night's sleep. All night—I suffer from insomnia, and the motel's pillow seems to be made out of recycled Styrofoam—I smell the production odors from the Malt-O-Meal plant, the smell of the hot cereal that I was served every winter when I myself was disguised as a child.

My own father died of a heart attack when I was

eighteen months old. I remember nothing of him, this smiling mythical figure, this insurance salesman, my dad (a word I have never been able to speak in its correct context to anyone). Said to have a great sense of humor, grace, and charm, John Baxter,

---

[1] I'm fairly certain that I had told my dad that we would both load the van after the Chaos Machine was complete My dad, however decided to load the van on his own before the machine was finished.

whoever he was, withdrew his model of fatherhood from me before I could get at it. It's not his fault, but there's a hole in me where he might have been. There's much that I don't know and have never known about parenthood and other male qualifiers, such as the handyman thing. I once tried to assemble a lawn mower by myself, and on its maiden voyage across the lawn, it sprayed screws and nuts and bolts in every direction, an entertaining spectacle for the onlookers, my wife and son.

Lying in the Northfield Country Inn, wide awake, I wonder if my father would have driven to my own college to help me move myself back home. Maybe yes. But somehow I doubt it. Growing up, I did not live in a universe in which such things ever happened.

In college, I was vaguely afraid of parenthood myself, as many young men are. Indeed, fatherhood, that form of parenthood specific to my gender, and which should be avoided at all costs, according to Donald Barthelme in *The Dead Father*, rose up before me during the early years of my marriage as a cloud of unknowing. What, past the conception stage, do fathers actually *do*? How should they behave? No usable models had presented themselves to me, though I had been given a good nonmodel, an intermittently generous, Yale-educated, martini-drinking, Shakespeare-quoting stepfather, a successful attorney, gardener, and quietly raucous anti-Semite who had loved me and taken care of me in a distant Victorian way. Stepfathering, however, is not identical to fathering, at least in my stepfather's case; for him, it was largely a peripheral occupation. It gave him the right to make pronouncements, his favorite being "Life is hard."

Recently, reading an account of Senator Jim Webb of Virginia, I note that he believes that a father's duty is to teach his sons to fight and to hunt. I haven't done either, nor will I. I am a traitor, it seems, to my gender. Once my wife said, "All you're teaching Daniel is irony."

Martha, my wife, always appeared to have a clear idea of what motherhood required right from the start and set to it with determination and alacrity. *Women don't need the manual*, I thought irritably at the time; *they just know how to do these things*. Me, I needed the manual. But the manual cannot be found in a book. So I was an ironic parent, a Chaos Machine myself.

Rules to live by:

1. *When the server brings the bill, always grab it before anyone else does.*

2. *Life isn't particularly serious until it becomes so.*

3. *Try to be kind to people. Be generous.*

4. *A god named Larry is the god of parking. Don't ask me how I know this. Pray to Larry for parking spaces when you need one, and you will be rewarded.*

The next day, Daniel and I have breakfast together. Then I begin loading the van. It's getting hot. Daniel's room is cluttered with clothes (a tropical-colored shirt[2] for his

---

[2] The shirt was red and shiny but was by no means a tropical shirt in the Jimmy Buffett sense of the term.

performances in his cult rock band, Grätüïtöüs Ümläüt,[3] for which he plays keyboards), amplifiers, CDs, books, including *Moby-Dick*, a VHS copy of *Repo Man*. Easy things first: I'll start with the blankets.

My son had a fearsomely difficult infancy. In those days, he had a different name: Nathaniel. He came out of the womb jaundiced and stayed jaundiced for longer than is usual. He could not breastfeed and lost weight following his birth. "Failure to thrive," the doctor said, darkly. When he was finally able to nurse, he proved, in time, to be colicky and irritable. The doctor prescribed phenobarbital, which helped, briefly. Then the house was filled, morning until night, with the sound of desperate crying from the nursery. This production of noise from babies is not unusual, and many parents get used to it. Martha did. I didn't. I would take Nathaniel outside under the crabapple tree, which sometimes calmed him down, but I was criticized for not letting him cry himself out.[4] We took Nathaniel off milk and supplemented his breastfeeding with soy, in the hopes that he would find it more digestible, then from soy to a manufactured protein called Nutramigen. Often when I hugged him, he bent backward away from me, as if in pain.

As Nathaniel lies in his crib, I watch him. I am afraid of him. I am afraid to pick him up; he looks so breakable. What if I drop him? What should I do, as his dad? On one occasion, I try to cut his baby fingernails and make a mistake, cutting into a bit of skin, and he begins to howl, and I am besieged with guilt over my carelessness. Martha comes upstairs. "What happened? What did you do?" she asks me, distraught.

On another occasion, I am feeding him with a baby bottle full of Nutramigen, and Martha comes upon me and is completely overcome with jealousy; she tries to talk it through but cannot defeat this emotion. She will feed Nathaniel from now on, she says. She cannot bear to see me feeding him. It does not occur to me to fight over this.

Heavier things now: I pack up Daniel's keyboard. *One* of his keyboards. He has several. Now his cello. The cello rests inside an enormous protective black case, lined inside with what looks like velvet.

More rules to live by:

5. *Music makes life easier and often just plain bearable.*

6. *Most good works require obsessive detail.*

7. *Losing your temper, though satisfying, usually doesn't get you anywhere, and it creates more trouble than it's worth.*

8. *Take long walks, especially on weekends. Nature restores the soul.*

Long after most children start speaking, Nathaniel continued to stay silent, or his words were so garbled that I could not understand them, though his mother usually

---

[3] GÜ was best known on campus for covers of "Psycho Killer" and "Jump," and the original mini-rock opera *Astronaughty*.

[4] My dad was often able to quiet me down by playing Brian Eno's *Music for Airports* while we drove around in his car.

could. She played with him, the blocks and the trains. But he was prone to sudden white-faced rages: once, carrying him into Lord & Taylor, I found myself, with Nathaniel in my arms, in front of the escalator, a device that seemed to frighten him, and he began to claw at my eyes. Around that same time, my wife's back had bite marks and scratch marks, where he had clawed at her. I carried my own wounds around, especially near my eyelids.

But I liked to carry him around anyway, anywhere, on my shoulders, a daddy thing to do. On Saturday night, we danced together to music on NPR and tumbled around on the living room floor, roughhousing. I *am inventing fatherhood,* I told myself. Like most grand concepts, fatherhood appeared to be made up of small, mosaiclike blocks of activities. In Hawaii, it means taking Nathaniel around to see the pop-up lawn sprinklers, which he adores.[5] Or forcing him to try chicken coated with honey. Or, back in Michigan, singing to him as he falls asleep, particularly "You Are My Sunshine." Or taking him to McDonald's, for the hamburgers (not the buns, which he will not eat). Trying to understand his speech, I give him a microphone attached to nothing and pretend to make him into a network correspondent, or a guest on a talk show.[6] I sit him on my lap so he can pound the keys on the typewriter, and I sit him on my lap again, downstairs, so he can pound the keys of the piano. This habit of playing the piano stays with him.

Nathaniel is obsessed with fountains, with elevator doors and escalators, and of gaps that divide and then close, such as screen doors that he can open and shut repetitively, all afternoon. He adores trains.

A young woman wearing a Carleton College T-shirt comes in asking for Daniel. I tell her that he's not here, that he's off with Alex working on the Chaos Machine. She nods, smiles, and disappears. She has a pleasantly absentminded expression freighted with intelligence, very much the norm at this college; I have rarely seen so many intelligent and physically awkward students in one place.[7] Seeing Carleton students playing Frisbee is like watching a convention of mathematicians out on a dance floor.[8] The sight is touching but laden with pathos.

I am physically clumsy. Daniel is physically clumsy, or was. Instead of shooting hoops, on almost every Sunday afternoon, winter and summer, he and his mother and I, along with Tasha, the dog, if she is up for it, go out walking in one of the Michigan parks. These walks constitute one of our family rituals—walking on a path in the woods affords both togetherness and privacy: you can be pensive, and in solitude, but you're being pensive and solitary in the company of your family, and you're being

---

[5] Unfortunately, this is true. I remember getting in trouble in Hawaii after I snuck out early one morning to watch the pop-up lawn sprinklers in action.

[6] My dad's short story "Talk Show" was based on this and the aforementioned Hawaii trip, although I don't remember there being anything about pop-up sprinklers in the story.

[7] None of my Carleton friends appeared physically awkward, at least to me anyway.

[8] In fairness to Carleton it should be noted that the women's and men's top-level ultimate Frisbee teams won the national championships in 2000 and 2001.

active, too. Families sometimes give the appearance of three or four solitudes living under the same roof. Ours certainly does. Did.[9]

Now I am carrying out Daniel's chair, purchased by us at ShopKo, and his computer, a giant, lumbering old Macintosh. Is it already afternoon? Sweat is pouring down my face and soaking my shirt.

Gertrude Stein, in *Everybody's Autobiography,* said that the twentieth century was the era of bad fathers. She noted that bad fathers would appear on the scene locally, within families, and nationally as bad political fathers—Hitler and Stalin—and that the appearance of these tyrants was an effort to reintroduce a dead God (He had died in the nineteenth century) and to put him in charge of the state apparatus. There has already been too much fathering in the twentieth century, Gertrude Stein said. My own parenting lacks a certain authority; I am a somewhat insincere and doubtful father, having never quite become accustomed to the role.

One morning when he was four years old, Nathaniel came downstairs, and when Martha called him "Nathaniel," he said, "Not Nathaniel. Daniel." And he became Daniel from then on.[10] He named himself. My brother Tom was frightened and appalled by our son's self-naming and worried about what would happen if he tried to do so again. What if he kept renaming himself? Chaos. Napoleon crowned himself—a blasphemy—and Daniel renamed himself, as hippies in my era did. So, OK. Why shouldn't children name themselves, particularly if they can't pronounce their given names? So we let him do it, and Martha went down to City Hall and had the birth certificate altered so that "Daniel" would appear on it instead of "Nathaniel."

Despite the normalization of his name, Daniel felt slightly different (to me, to others, maybe to himself) from other boys: obsessive, brilliantly intelligent—those shockingly intricate sentences! that diction level!—and physically at odds with himself. Other kids noticed, and eventually we took him out of public school and placed him in a Waldorf School, a Rudolf Steiner school, where many of the kids were oddballs (even his teacher called them "oddballs," and the teacher himself was no slouch, either, when it came to oddballdom), and where Daniel was accepted and loved by everybody.[11]

---

[9] The weekends followed a pleasant routine. My parents and I went out to dinner on Fridays. My dad, Tasha, and I would always go through the drive-through line at the nearby Taco Bell to get lunch on Saturday, where we (except for Tasha) would always order the same things we ordered every Saturday. After we ordered, she would start to growl if the drive-through line was slow, which it usually was at that particular Taco Bell. When we got home, Louis the parrot would squawk until he was given a nacho from my Nachos Supreme, and I would sneak a second nacho to Tasha. On Sunday afternoons we would go walking, as my dad mentioned, and we always had spaghetti for dinner afterward. My efforts at the time, however, to convince my parents to extend this system and have a different preset dinner for every night of the week were not successful.

[10] I'm not in a rush to let people know about the name switch, but I suppose this essay would be incomplete if this were omitted.

[11] My favorite years before Carleton were when I was at Steiner, from third through eighth grade.

I dismantle his desk and take it to the van. Or do I?[12] It's almost a decade later, now, as I write. The past is beginning to smear together, the years taking their kindly toll.

More rules to live by:

9. *When driving, respect the orderly flow of speeding traffic.*

10. *Use the left lane to pass. But don't stay there.*

11. *Life is really very simple; be open-hearted and try to live for others. Avoid pretense.*

Throughout his childhood and adolescence, we travel; we see the world, we view the United States (by car, by train), the three of us. Daniel and I both love Virgil Thomson's and Gertrude Stein's *Four Saints in Three Acts*, especially to drive to. An odd love for a father to pass down to a son, but it makes us both laugh.[13] Once, following a case of pneumonia, he says he wants to see New York City, and he and I take a slow train there and back, meeting in the dining car the lead singer for Herman's Hermits, who tells us about a "great novel," one of his favorites, *Atlas Shrugged*. As Daniel's father, I explain to my son after we have returned to our compartment why the famous singer in the dining car is full of shit. This, too, is a parental responsibility.

Daniel begins playing. He plays keyboards. From first grade onward, the house is full of music, morning and night. Mozart, Hummel, Beethoven, and then, later, Virgil Thomson's score for *Louisiana Story* and Ravel's Piano Concerto in G. Have I had anything to do with this? I played records and CDs constantly, but I can't play the piano, not really; classical music is simply one of the atmospheres Daniel has grown up in and breathed.

On short notice, I write lyrics for his rock band.

> You're from Banana Republic
> You look like J. Crew
> You're a victim of fashion
> I'm a victim of you.

Adolescence is supposed to be a scary time for parents. In America, at least, the norm is for boys to turn into sweaty, sticky, hostile monsters, full of rage against the world and their parents. They are full of alcohol and drugs; it is the time in life of

---

[12] Probably not. The desk was included with the furniture that came with the room.

[13] *Four Saints in Three Acts* is still funny and good driving music. Along with *Four Saints*, tapes of the NPR incarnation of *The Bob and Ray Radio Show* were a staple of my family's annual summer road trips to Minnesota's north shore. Growing up, I'm pretty sure I assumed that both *Four Saints* and *Bob and Ray* were also being listened to in many of the vehicles we passed on the freeway, but when I think about it now I can't remember the last time I've heard either of these mentioned in conversation or the media. I hope this is because I'm not talking to the right people or reading the right magazines, and that there are, in fact, plenty of people driving around with *Four Saints* and *Bob and Ray* in their CD-changers and iPods.

projectile vomiting. My wife and I await this change. We wait for yelling and slammed doors. It never happens. Daniel becomes a bit quieter but remains sweet and affable.

He did, however, along with a few of his adolescent chums, have a few other artistic ambitions, which included an intentionally ironic art video titled *Mr. Scary*. This feature, made in black and white, combined the moody expressionism of Bergman's middle period with the outsize silent-film theatrics of Eisenstein. Daniel, playing the eponymous Mr. Scary, accompanied by our dog, Tasha (who played herself [14]), walked through a forest, raised his eyebrows, answered the door speechlessly (Mr. Scary does not ever speak) when a salesman came to call, all these scenes shot in a pretentious, over-the-top High Art style. [15] A lighthouse served as a recurrent symbol of something. The tone of the film was jarring: think of *Aleksandr Nevskiy* in the suburbs. Like Orson Welles's *Don Quixote*, this work of cinematic artistry was never completed. It succumbed to its own irony.

I take his clock radio to the van. The vehicle is almost filled with the detritus of a young life.

When children are small, time often crawls. Then they grow, and time speeds up; once you couldn't get away from them, and then they're never around.

What do you mean, he's ready to apply to colleges? He was just born! He studies late, into the wee hours, and I cannot sleep myself until he turns his lights off and goes to bed. He struggles through the college applications, bitterly complaining every step of the way. One late afternoon, while he is laboring to complete the application for Northwestern University, which includes the demand that the prospective student write an essay explaining why he or she wants to go to Northwestern, I slip into my study and write a goof version of this essay for him, for laughs.

WHY I WANT TO GO TO NORTHWESTERN

by Daniel Baxter

Many is the time I have thought of the pleasing location of Northwestern University, situated on the shore of picturesque Lake Michigan. The campus, I have noted, is close enough to the rocky shore of this Great Lake so that students, carrying their heavy textbooks on the way to classes, can be pleasantly diverted by hearing the sounds of waves crashing on the rocks. These sounds are almost always mixed, in damp and rainy weather, with the sounds of muted foghorns, which make their way into the liberal arts classrooms where Shakespeare's plays are being taught by bearded and grizzled scholars. Foghorn sounds are like the lowing moos of anxious herds of cows, waiting to be milked. Certainly, from time to time, one must also be able to hear the muted clash and clang of freighters colliding. With the right kind of police scanner, you might also hear the radio distress calls. Perhaps, as Lucretius says in the second book of On the Nature of

---

[14] In the closing credits, Tasha is credited with the role of Cerberus.

[15] For example, the last scene featured close-ups of Mr. Scary's face, onto which 8 mm home movies were being projected, intercut with footage of imploding buildings from *Koyaanisqatsi*.

Things, *it is pleasant, even sublime, to see ships sinking in the distance if you yourself are on the shore, that is, at Northwestern, safe in a sort of "ivory tower" from danger. Lucretius calls this the sublime experience of beauty, and so it would be on the campus of this great institute of higher learning, home of the #1 Business School in the United States.*

But the beauties of Lake Michigan are not the only advantages of which Northwestern can boast, and there are many other reasons why I wish to attend this fine Big Ten center of erudition. The architecture of the buildings varies from Gothic Revival to 1950s Bauhaus to Frank Geary Las Vegas-style "postmodernism." This distinctive brand of eclectic architecture, so different from the bland brand of monomaniacal "Ivy League" architecture favored by our so-called "prestige" universities, gives to Northwestern a more democratic and populist "grab bag" appearance. Moving from one building to another on the Northwestern campus, from the threatening appearance of the Music Building to the turreted castlelike appearance of the Humanities Building (where many damsels are possibly in distress), the student hardly knows what to expect from one moment to the next. Call me an eclectic student, if you will, but I must say that Northwestern's unpredictable appearance, whether you approach it by bus, truck, train, or family car, is one of the particular sources of my interest in it.

On my two visits to Northwestern, I have noticed that most of the learnèd professors are quite mature. Their gray hairs and beards (not on the women, of course) are signs of learning and experience. Walking about on campus, one cannot but be impressed by their slow pace, their hands on their canes, as if they were thinking about "thoughts that lie too deep for tears." I was impressed by the colossal lecture halls and huge classes, and the Wildcats who were listening and dozing through the lectures, knowing that the professors would cover material that they had missed, their voices echoing in the immensity of the lecture chambers.

Northwestern has lately achieved a bit of a renaissance. I refer, of course, to the superlative record of the Northwestern football team. The school fight song (I have learned it) is the most memorable tune associated with any great public American university that I know of Any school worth its reputation must have a football team to keep up its manly institutional pride, and Northwestern has lately improved its athletic skills so that it is no longer known as the "whipping boy of the Big Ten." Now it is the Northwestern Wildcats that are doing the whipping!

In summary, Northwestern has much to offer me in its location next to Lake Michigan, in its surprisingly successful and bowl-headed football team, its always-surprising architectures, and its wise and aging faculty speaking to crowds of attentive youth. I can imagine myself dressed in the school's colors of purple and gold, waving a school banner displaying the word NORTH-WESTERN with pride. I hope you will agree.[16]

What kind of father would do such a thing? Write a mockery of such an essay? I would. That's the kind of father I am, the kind of father I have always been.

Daniel got into Northwestern, by the way (without ever visiting it), but did not go there. He went to Carleton instead, which is full of students like him.

---

[16] This essay still makes me laugh. Another Northwestern demand was to list my least favorite word, which was then, and still is, *potpourri*.

Here he is. The Chaos Machine is finished.[17] He's taller than I am, has longish brown hair, which used to be blond, widely spaced brown eyes that radiate interest and intelligence. He walks with his head slightly bent, as if he were ducking under a door frame. (Later, in his twenties, he begins to straighten up. But I am still trying to break him of the habit of walking with his hands clasped together in front of him.) He helps me finish loading the van, and we make it as far as Rochester, where we find a Mexican restaurant where we have dinner.[18] We drive that night as far as La Crosse, Wisconsin. He asks about Tasha, the dog, and Louis, the family bird, who also helped raise him.

These days, he works as a successful structural engineer, a bridge designer, in downtown Cleveland. He has published papers I cannot understand. He's a fine and wonderful young man.

The next morning, with Daniel sometimes driving (the person who does not drive is responsible for directions and what gets played on the van's audio system), we head toward Michigan. He instructs me on how to get onto the Chicago Skyway from the Dan Ryan. We both admire the sublimely sinister industrial magnificence of Gary, Indiana. I am proud of him. I love him. And he is a better driver than I am, much more alert, as the young should be, as they must be, to get where they're going.[19]

—2008

---

[17] The Chaos Machine, when completed, was an analog electrical-current waveform generator that consisted mostly of a small circuit board and several electronic instruments from the physics department attached to a metal rack and connected with cables. It was capable of generating waveforms with chaotic properties, the details of which I have since forgotten. The machine worked as planned, and Alex and I made a poster (which has either been thrown away or is gathering dust somewhere in the physics department) that explained its inner workings and reason for existence. Over the following summer, the machine was probably dismantled by members of the physics department who needed its parts back.

[18] I remember that we ate at the somewhat oddly named Mexican restaurant Carlos O'Kelly's.

[19] Except where I've noted previously, this essay is fairly accurate. It is worth mentioning that this is my first, and probably last, writing collaboration with my dad, unless my editing assistance for his last three novels counts. All in all, my dad is a nice guy. You'd like him.

Learning from Other Writers (Baxter)

1. Baxter notes that he was served Malt-O-Meal when he "was disguised as a child." What does he mean here? What do you think he is saying about children and adolescents? About adults?

2. Trace the way Baxter narrates the story of picking up Daniel from college. At what point in the essay does he diverge from the narrative to provide backstory and to meditate on fatherhood? What in the present narrative allows him to pause and reflect? How does he weave back to the central narrative?

3. What do you make of the list of life rules Baxter provides? Is he sincere? Ironic? A mixture of both? What about Daniel Baxter's footnoted comments—are those sincere? Ironic? Both?

4. When Daniel applies to Northwestern University, Baxter writes a mock admission-essay and gives it to his son as a joke. Why do you think he decided to include that mock essay, in its entirety, in this essay?

5. Baxter presents himself as confused about what it means to be a father and inept at his own attempts to be a father to his son. How do *you* judge his success as a father? How do you think Daniel views his father?

6. Baxter doesn't seem to think that he demonstrates typical parental or male behaviors. He also notes that as a child and an adolescent, Daniel did not exhibit the behaviors that children and adolescents are "supposed" to exhibit. How does this juxtaposition enhance the essay?

CULTURAL PHENOMENA

Often, an author's meditations are organized around a cultural phenomenon, and in our digital age, there is much to be said about the time we spend online. "Chathexis," which was written by the editors of the literary journal *n + 1*, provides perspective on the power of software to shape our lives, although in this case the result is argued not to be reductive but rather intensifying. The essay examines the concept of online chatting, specifically Gchat, the chat function used in Gmail, and its effects on our ability to converse. By starting with a brief history of furniture and the way the invention of the sofa and the padded chair allowed people to feel more comfortable as they engaged in long conversations, then moving on to delineate the evolution of online chatting from anonymous flirtation to on-the-job distraction to intimate, late-night conversation, the essay follows a fluid line of inquiry, with the authors using a progression of questions to move their analysis forward.

Whereas "Chathexis" examines the possible intimacy allowed by the chat tool, Natalie Bakopoulos's essay examines an absence of online intimacy as she explores her love-hate relationship to Facebook, addressing her mixed feelings about witnessing other people's online conversations and about interacting with her "friends" in such a public forum. By describing the anxiety she experiences in wanting a private life yet feeling left out without the public persona Facebook allows, Natalie provides an honest, often self-recriminating analysis of the ways in which she uses the network.

Finally, in "Games Are Not about Monsters," Christine Hartzler, a yoga-practicing poet pacifist, deconstructs her fascination with and love of video games, weaving in references to Buddhist philosophy, yoga, *Beowolf*, and the poetry of C.D. Wright. "Video games aren't about monsters, even when they are," Hartzler asserts; from there, she uses a loose structure based on a comparison of her favorite video games, which involve monster hunting and killing, to spin out a meditation on what exactly such games mean to her emotionally, intellectually, and artistically.

CHATHEXIS

Someone who wanted to know how we live might ask how we talk. Madame de Rambouillet talked in bed, stretched out on a mattress, draped in furs, while her visitors remained standing. Blue velvet lined the walls of the room, which became known as "the French Parnassus": a model for the 17th- and 18th-century salons, where aristocratic women led male *philosophes* in polite and lively discussion.

Talking, of course, is nothing new. But conversation, in the 17th century, was a novel ideal of speech: not utilitarian instructions or religious catechism, but an exchange of ideas, a free play of wit. Thus the hostesses of the Enlightenment received visitors in a new kind of furniture. In 1667, the Gobelins tapestry-weaving workshop became Louis XIV's official furniture supplier. Previously, fabric—like Madame de Rambouillet's velvet—had been confined to walls and clothing. The Gobelins were the first to apply it to chairs, which for many long, uncomfortable centuries had been small and hard. Now they were wide and soft—more like beds. The *fauteuil confessional*, for instance, had wraparound wings against which the listener might rest her cheek, as the priest had done behind his screen. Listening and talking became even easier in the 1680s, with the introduction of the sofa. Seating for two! For the first time in history, people could sit comfortably together indoors for long stretches—thereby making it easier for them to speak comfortably together for long stretches. Thus was conversation enshrined—en-couched—as a vehicle of Enlightenment, fundamental to the self-improvement of civilization.

Face-to-face exchanges continued in the exchange of letters. As the salon had the sofa, "written conversation"—as one style manual called it—had the desk, another invention of the 17th century. For men, there was the *bureau*—a big, heavy table for conducting official correspondence. (From *bureau* comes "bureaucracy.") For women, there was the *secrétaire*. Unlike the flat bureau, the light, portable secrétaire featured stacks of shelves and cubbyholes, which were kept locked. Some writing surfaces slid outward, like drawers. Others opened from the top, as if the desk were a jewelry box—or a laptop.

If talking is one thing, and conversation another, then what is chat?

In the early days of the internet, chatting was something that happened between strangers. "Wanna cyber?" millions of people asked, and millions answered: *Yes!* On AOL—as of 1994, the most popular internet service provider in the US—half the member-created chat rooms were for sex. AOL also launched the first mass IM interface, which was where the real action happened. Each conversation appeared as a flat, white square on your screen—it was like having sex on a tiled floor. But at least it was someone else's floor. Signing off was like walking out of a public bathroom. Nobody knew where anybody went: answers to "a/s/l?" were likely lies, screen names universally inscrutable. Because AOL permitted five screen names per account, it was possible to use one for strangers, another for friends. Before the introduction of the Buddy

List—in 1996, dubbed the "stalker feature" by AOL employees—you could come and go without any of them noticing.

Eventually, AOL's dominance waned as people signed up for free web-based email and downloaded desktop-based chat clients, like AOL's own Instant Messenger (1997). In AIM, all that remained of the original AOL was the AOL Buddy List, which hung in the corner of our screen. (Chat rooms were still out there, but mostly for terrorists and pedophiles.) Chatting now required constant tabbing between applications: browser for email, IM window, browser for search. Like hermit crabs outgrowing their shells, people kept shucking their old screen names for new ones.

Gmail changed all this. We signed up using our real name. So did our friends, and one day those names appeared in a column on the left side of our inbox. This was Gchat, and whenever we signed in, up came the gray, ghostly list of Gchattable names. And what names! Previously, we'd *decided* which screen names to include on our "Buddy Lists" (poor AOL: it came first and had to name the animals, and it named them in a corporate-Midwestern way that couldn't help but become comically creepy). Gmail made the choices for us, pulling names from our email contacts. It was like standing outside the door of a party that all your friends had been invited to. Maybe they had already arrived!

Gmail began "in beta" and by invitation only in 2004 and remained technically in beta for the next five years; it continued to feel exclusive long after everyone was using it. (Registration opened to the public in 2007.) Being new, it was also youthful: you could tell when a person signed up for email by the client they used—AOL between 1994 and 1999; Hotmail or Yahoo! between 1999 and 2004; after 2004, only Gmail. When Gmail automatically added Gchat to every user's inbox in 2006, it was like a conspiracy of the young against the old. We would chat while they thought we were working; they would grow old and die; we would inherit the earth and chat forever.

So what do we chat about? Not sex. Our real name is right there, and anyway the mood is all wrong. AOL was a series of semi-private suites; Gmail is an open loft, wallpapered with distractions. PROTEST HYDRO-FRACKING! says one email. Another is from our grandmother (grams31@aol.com): she misses us. Hard to picture anything less erotic than the inbox, that cluttered room whose door can never be locked. Imagine having sex and someone from the alumni association bursts in to ask for a donation. Everywhere the professional intrudes: a former coworker signs in; a friend's status message links to his latest article (Congrats, dude!). And as the virtual setting is all wrong for eros, so too is the actual one, because most of our Gchats happen at the office. We chat all day as we work, several windows open at once—windows into all the offices in all the cities where our friends spend their days Gchatting. Or we chat with coworkers, carrying on an endless conversation that sounds, to the half-aware ears of our superiors, like the soft tip-tapping clatter of real industry.

Our banalities are more shameful than any fantasy or confession. Gmail saves the histories of our chats, should we ever care to look. It turns out we use the internet to talk about what other people are talking about on the internet: "Oh god please look at what she just tweeted." "Hang on I'll find the link." And then there are the tactical chats—"I guess I am not that in the mood for Thai food?"—that would be harmless enough on their own. Mixed in with the rest, and preserved for all eternity, they assemble further evidence of our gross mortal wastefulness. Time is misspent twice: we talk about life as thoughtlessly as we live it. And the server farms know this.

In contrast to chat rooms, where we talked to many people in public, in Gchat we talk to many people *in private and simultaneously.* (We could gather our friends together—Group Chat has been around since 2007—but mostly we don't.) "As long as one is in society," said 18th-century salon hostess Suzanne Necker, "one must occupy oneself with others, never keeping silent out of laziness or from distraction." But distraction is endemic to daytime Gchatting, especially at work. The medium creates the illusion of intimacy—of giving and receiving undivided attention—when in fact our attention is quite literally divided, apportioned among up to six small boxes at a time. The boxes contain staccato, telegraphic exchanges, with which we are partially and intermittently engaged. Together the many chats divert us from work, speeding up time—yet look closely and you see time break down and stop. The clusters of text are followed by time-stamps, which Google inserts whenever the conversation lags. For David Hume, increased conversation between men and women corresponded to "an increase of humanity, from the very habit of conversing together." But Hume didn't know about Gchat, which offers us so many opportunities for conversation that conversation becomes impossible. We are distracted from chatting by chatting itself.

Eventually, we apologize for dropping the ball, invoking a more pressing technology: "Sorry, on the phone." But now it is our friend who doesn't respond! Is he really gone, or has the sneak downloaded that add-on that allows users to appear idle when they're chatting? Like a shield, the round orange icon affords protection—to the person behind it, who is permitted to ignore any unwanted chat, and to the sender of the unwanted chat, who can tell herself, *I guess he's not there.* The way we chat now—using plug-ins or hidden behind Gchat's own Invisibility feature—suggests that what we really want is a way out of chat. Consider chat's entry in the OED, which includes what must be the most melancholy example sentence in the history of example sentences: *"I keep getting messages popping up on my screen from people wanting to chat."* What anguish, when the definition of chat implies the desire not to chat! We, too, keep getting messages from people wanting to chat. And we keep being those people, too.

One good thing about work Gchats: they can't be videochats. The videochat is too eye-catching, too attention-getting—although the attention it gets would be other people's, not ours. For even when we maximize the video—when our friend's face swims into view, as large as our own, eclipsing our MacBook's starry default desktop—it still seems small and insignificant. Videochat—introduced to Gchat in 2008, and before that one of the major selling points of the popular chat client Skype—is a medium that, except for the way it allows you to display cats and babies to distant friends, is every bit as alienating as technophobes predicted. The built-in camera tends to cast everyone in the same gray pallor. Revealed to us in videochat, our friends are all nostril and no heart. Our interlocutor looks lonely, bored. Tired. We feel the same. Every relationship is reduced by videochat to two properties: 1) the inability to touch and 2) the lack of desire to.

There is something so *literal* about video. It reminds you of a world that can't imagine anything but itself. It's almost as bad as walking down the street. Our friends are made over into evasive strangers: just try making eye contact in videochat. You can't.[1] It's as bad as a first date, or a job interview—you sit there, face to face with another human being, and feel unseen. Videochat's promise of intimacy—friends on the other side of the world, looking at us in our homes!—makes us forget the conditions in which actual intimacy occurs. Where have we had our best conversations? When we were sharing a booth with someone in the back of a dark bar, or lying in bed, or walking somewhere, or nowhere at all, our faces turned in the same direction: outward, toward the world, into which we moved forward together. We arrive at a shared perspective when we do, actually, share a perspective—when we take, quite literally, the same view of things. Then, turning away from that view—and toward each other—can mark a moment of surpassing agreement or sympathy. There are no such moments in videochat.

No, there's nothing erotic about videochat, despite what the experts keep telling us. According to a study commissioned by the hotel chain Travelodge, in twenty years we will be having "virtual sex" with whoever is waiting for us back home. In the old days, the traveler might have seized the opportunity to sleep with someone else; or, more adventurously still, deployed the noble and fading, video-menaced art of phone sex. In the motels of the future, a guest will simply conjure her partner via Travelodge's "active skin electronics," which will be to sex what Gchat is to work: a way of making the dull endurable, a way to forget the fear that, stuck in the wrong office or the wrong relationship, *we are wasting our lives.*

It's already in our Gmail calendar: no Travelodge after 2030.

There is hope, but not for videochat. All we really need, to know love, is a plain old wireless connection and somewhere to lie down: the best Gchat conversations take place, like those of the salon, with one or both participants in repose, stretched out on a couch or in bed. Tucked beneath our covers, laptops propped on our knees—is this not the posture most conducive to meaningful Gchatting? In addition to being comfortable, our beds are private; on Gchat, we must be by ourselves to best be with others. Night affords another degree of solitude: like the lights in the apartment building across the street, Gchat's bright bulbs go out, one by one, until a single circle glows hopefully. Like Gatsby's green light, it is the promise of happiness.

---

[1] It's now possible not to make eye contact with up to ten people at once, thanks to Google's new social networking platform. Google+'s stated purpose is to make "sharing on the web more like sharing in real life," which is true only if "in real life" is understood to mean "on the rest of the internet." Instead of occurring in our inbox, group videochats—called Hangouts—open in separate windows, like pop-up ads. Each face moves inside its own rectangle, forming together a mosaic of talking heads. What sadist would take cable news as a model for conversation? It's like building a hotel using the blueprints for a prison.

For if, as Necker wrote, "the secret of conversation is continual attention," the enduring romance and appeal of Gchat can perhaps be explained by the way certain nighttime Gchats so effortlessly hold and reward our attention. Gchat returns philosophy to the bedroom as, late at night, we find ourselves in a state of rapturous focus. Which perhaps is why so many of us feel our best selves in Gchat. Silent, we are unable to talk over our friends, and so we become better and deeper listeners, as well as better speakers—or writers. (To be articulate—but not alone! To be with another person—but not inarticulate! When else does this happen?) We have time to express ourselves precisely, without breaking the rhythm. It's like the description of letter-writing in Françoise de Graffigny's 1747 novel *Lettres d'une Péruvienne*: "I feel myself being brought back to life by this tender occupation. Restored to myself, I feel as if I am beginning to live again." Chat's immediacy emphasizes response, reminding us that we do not simply create and express ourselves in writing, but create and express our relationships. Gmail—simultaneously salon sofa and locked secrétaire—stores the proof forever.

And who do we Gchat with, when it counts? Friends, past boyfriends, future boyfriends, other people's boyfriends. But rarely our actual boyfriend, who's next to us in bed, looking for something to watch on Hulu. (Unless he's out of town, in which case we chat with him, and are reminded why we fell for him in the first place.) Gchat is for friendship, and affairs. It's for allowing into the home everyone who isn't supposed to be there, who's supposed to be at home in their own bedroom. It offers a temporary escape from the prison of the family—a reversal of what Engels called "the great historical defeat of women"—and patriarchy, which depends on monogamy and its enforcement. When we sign into Gchat, we do not enter utopia, but sometimes we catch a glimpse of it. We initiate a conversation and, some nights later, resume it. Meanwhile we initiate another. These exchanges are not exactly casual, but they're not unique either. In Gchat, as in life, we are happiest when paying attention—when we belong completely to a conversation that continues. Might this be a model of commitment: truly felt on both sides, mutually desired, without exclusivity? These conversations don't occur at the exact same time—if we wanted threesomes, we'd be in Group Chat—but the long view is the one to be taken here, and the beginning of one chat does not mean the end of another.

At the very least, Gchat holds out the promise of "free commerce between the sexes" (Hume), which will surely be a feature of any utopia worth the name. Listen to people on first dates, old married couples, or anyone in transit between infatuation and resignation: mostly you hear the following of a tedious script. People say the things they always say, that they're supposed to say, that other people say. And we say these things, too! Yet Gchat has at times liberated us from this dialogue of the deaf, and provided us with a template for another way of talking. If, as Madame de Staël (Necker's daughter and the most famous salon hostess of all) put it, "the spoken word . . . is an instrument that is enjoyable to play," then chat—these broken lines, these misspelled words, this transliterated laughter, this long, unpunctuated scroll—has tempted us to compare it, at times, to the musical language that is poetry. But what it is, of course, is conversation. And that is compliment enough.

—2011

Learning from Other Writers (The Editors of n+1)

1. The essay begins with the idea of two people having a nice, long conversation on comfortable chairs or a sofa. How does this idea return, rather surprisingly, later in the essay?

2. About halfway through the essay the perspective changes, as if the authors have deliberately spent time knocking down Gchat only to build it back up. What is the effect of this strategy?

3. This essay was published in the literary journal *n + 1* by its editors. Who is their audience? What is the effect of comparing the green availability icon in Gchat to Gatsby's green light?

4. What other sources are brought into this essay? Why do these sources seem incongruous in an essay about online chatting and technology? Yet how do the sources enrich the authors' point?

5. The essay is attempting to define Gchat as its own type of conversation: not letter writing, not face-to-face conversation, not talking on the phone. How do the authors find Gchat to be a different form of communication from these other modes? How do they compare Gchat to much earlier forms of conversation? How do they argue for or against its intimacy?

By Natalie Bakopoulos

MY FACEBOOK ANGST

A few days ago, my friend Elizabeth posted an item to Facebook. I wanted to comment but held back, though not exactly because I had plenty of work to do. Instead I sent her a text: "Sometimes do you want to say something or post something or like something on FB, but then you think of all those unanswered emails and texts and silence yourself, so people won't see you 'wasting' time when you could be responding to them?"

"Sometimes?" she replied.

"It's called Twilt, that feeling," I answered, laughing, having coined the term on the spot.

Twilt *(n)*: the particular brand of guilt or self-reproach that results from posting, liking or commenting on items on Facebook or Twitter while simultaneously not responding to emails, text messages, phone calls or other types of personal communication with the knowledge or anxiety that the specific message senders will notice your public offerings and question your lack of private ones. Twilt, while related, is not the same as the guilt that results from general Internet-specific procrastination such as browsing blogs or online shopping, which, though it may result in its own brand of self-disgust, generally has no public shame component.

Adam Zagajewski, in his essay "The Shabby and Sublime," says that the poetry of recent years is "marked by a disproportion ... between powerful expressions of the inner life and the ceaseless chatter of self-satisfied craftsmen." The same could be said for Facebook updates, our contemporary confessional. *I have eaten the plums in the refrigerator, and they were yummy.* Facebook is bad for me because I not only embarrass myself, but I keenly feel the embarrassment of others whose lack of discretion, as I perceive it, I quietly judge and am embarrassed by all the same.

When someone starts a conversation with me on Facebook, in public, I'm mortified. There's a message function for that! I have email and a cellphone. Let me respond when I can, away from the watch of hundreds. Sometimes I disable my Wall so people can't write things there, until someone points it out and I feel guilty that I've done this so I change it back. I don't like to talk on the phone in public, and when a friend speaks too loudly in a cafe I am nervous that someone will overhear our conversation. At home I don't like the sensation of my husband overhearing me order pizza, let alone having more sensitive conversations with friends. I have never been one to kiss and tell, and I like to keep my private life private. Why I have a Facebook account at all still perplexes me. I like the idea of seeing what's going on, but I don't want to always be a part of it. I don't want to *not* be a part of it either. I want to swoop in and swoop out. But Facebook doesn't allow for inconsistency without amplifying it, a constant record of our obsessions and our contradictions to the point of caricature.

The conversations between couples embarrass me the most, whether they're sentimental or self-referential. It's not that you live with that person and somehow don't need electronic communication — I often text my husband across the table at a bar to make a snarky comment, or sometimes I send ridiculous things to the online printer in his office just to be impish. But it's done in private, between us. That's the point. It's something about the relationship having a public facade so contrived and self-aware that makes my eyes water with shame. We all have facades and personas, of course, that are not Internet confined. Game faces. Once, at a reading, a poet thanked his wife so gushingly that I whispered to my friend, *"That guy is totally having an affair."* I didn't know a thing about him. But it turns out, I was right. Maybe the wife requested the shout-out, but if I were his wife I would have smiled at the crowd and taken flight. Up, up and away.

Do you remember "This American Life's" 2001 episode about Superpowers, which poses the question: If you could have a superpower, would you choose Flight or Invisibility? My first reaction was and remains, flight. To fly! I'm petite and have spent a lifetime trying to fight invisibility, being intellectually overlooked, or feeling insignificant (this is not simply a result of my size but an entire slew of issues that would benefit from Lacanian psychoanalysis, which if I had I'd have to talk about in my status updates). I still have dreams where I'm flying, frequent dreams, and when I wake up I feel inexplicably happy. When I fly in my dreams, I don't sputter or start or anxiously hover. I soar, I glide, and it's fluid, like a manta ray moving through water. When I fly in my dreams I am all grace. My desire for flight would get me places faster, and in style.

But maybe my desire for flight is a sort of *conditional* invisibility; the idea of flight not only as the act of flying but the act of fleeing. I want to be part of the scene but to float somehow above it, to engage in the action but then be able to gracefully exit. I want to swoop on in and then glide away. But I want to be seen, for sure, and present. I just don't want to have to stay, and I certainly don't want anyone to comment on it.

It is also, of course, part of being a writer, to be part of a scene but also removed. Writing is about observation, but if I observe and immediately state then I've lost it, released it. The essay allows an expression of doubt but the Facebook update or conversation has a sort of self-satisfied glibness to it. It doesn't invite dialogue but somehow challenges it. There is also the lack of control. It could go anywhere. Someone could say something too revealing or racist or just plain idiotic, and there it is, linked to your name. It is not a place for the anxious, Facebook.

And there is the difference of stance. An essay is an attempt at dialogue, but a status update is a solicitation; the first is a meaningful hesitation or an assertive pronouncement, a languorous dip in a warm sea or a fast-paced race in a pool. But the essay swims all the same. A Facebook update is a haphazard nosedive into a near-empty watering hole. What if I break my neck? Will someone find me if my head is bleeding? If I post and no one comments, do I exist?

The comparison between the two forms needn't be made; we know the difference, yet it might explain my relative comfort, even ease, with the personal essay and my fear of any public sort of dialogue. Do I want to be invisible or do I want to fly? Although the personal is intimate, there is also the artifice of distance. When I fly in my dreams I can see myself flying while being aware of my place on the ground. Philip Lopate argues that a good essayist must see oneself from the ceiling, must turn oneself into a character. He is not advocating a "self-absorbed navel-gazing" but instead "a release from narcissism," an ability to "see yourself in the round."

I admit I am often self-amused by my status updates (what else are they for?), but I am rarely satisfied with them. In the rare case I am amused with myself when writing *anything,* that to me is a sure sign that it's going to need a very careful edit, or that it's garbage.

What I love best about that episode of "This American Life" is the moving analysis at the end, immediately after several of the show's guests comment on what it means to want invisibility or flight. John Hodgman reflects:

> Flight and invisibility touch a nerve. Actually, they touch two different nerves, speak to very different primal desires and unconscious fears … In the end, it's not a question of what kind of person flies and what kind of person fades. We all do both. … At the heart of this decision, the question I really don't want to face, is this: Who do you want to be, the person you hope to be, or the person you fear you actually are?

Am I becoming someone on Facebook or am I trying to escape her? I'm happy my partner is not on Facebook because I am spared that public embarrassment, of people wishing us happy anniversary or the pressure to comment, or not comment, on his witticisms or offerings: *J. just made fabulous butternut squash ravioli! From scratch!* Natalie likes this. And then he would like my liking, and another friend would find it cute, and like it too, and no one would know that we spent the last hour fighting because I overloaded the dryer and almost burned down the house.

I wouldn't mind if he joined Facebook, though, because he is the face man of our relationship and it would take some of the completely imagined but hugely felt pressure off me. ("Could you please like so-and-so's photos of her daughter's dance recital?") If we had a band, he'd be the lead singer and I'd be the bassist, hiding behind my hair. (No, not the drummer! No one sees the drummer!) The bassist can look up and make eye contact with the crowd for a moment and the crowd will go wild. They don't expect it, but they hope for it all the same. The face man: He has to be on all the time. It's his job to be on.

Do you remember the scene in "Sex in the City" where Carrie, upon receiving an email, ducks underneath her desk and shrieks, *Oh my god, can he see me?* A decade later it seems charming, like a text message from our grandmother. Yet the anxiety remains. Now, I suffer from what is surely a new psychological disorder: a DSM-IV classifiable paranoia that all my personal conversations are somehow being broadcast on Twitter. Is there a word for that?

—2012

Learning from Other Writers (Bakopoulos)

1. The essay is based on a contradiction: Bakopoulos wants to "keep [her] private life private," yet she still participates in social networking. Find other contradictions in this essay. How do they serve the essay's overall theme and analysis?

2. Phillip Lopate, whom the author quotes in her essay, writes (in the introduction to *The Art of the Personal Essay*) that we "forgive the essayist's self-absorption in return for the warmth of his or her candor." He also writes that we trust personal essayists "paradoxically, from the exposure of their betrayals, uncertainties, and self-mistrust." How do you see Lopate's ideas working in this essay?

3. What is Bakopoulos's driving question? How does her incorporation of outside sources help her to explore that question?

4. Where do you see moments of self-deprecation or self-mockery? What do they add to the essay?

5. One reaction to Bakopoulos's essay might be to say, "If you don't like Facebook, then don't use it." But the essay is about more than this decision. What other issues does the essay bring up, either directly or indirectly?

6. How does Bakopoulos's referencing ideas of flight and invisibility relate to ideas expressed in "Chathexis"?

7. How does the way Carr argues that the Internet reshapes our minds and even our personalities relate to this essay?

By Christine Hartzler

GAMES ARE NOT ABOUT MONSTERS

1. Video games aren't about monsters, even when they are.

In a role-play game, or RPG, gameplay consists largely of traveling and fighting battles. Traveling, like the "free and easy wandering" of the *Chang tzu*, isn't as easy as one might think—surviving monster attacks is usually the order of the day. Even so, traveling is one of my favorite things about RPGs because an RPG is a lengthy journey in a (hopefully) immersive world. My favorite game, *Shadow of the Colossus*, is difficult to place in a single game genre, but it's more RPG than anything else. You wander an expansive landscape, soaking up the aesthetic splendor, gathering information, and eventually, finding and fighting colossal monsters. Monster-killing is central to the game, and yet this game is no more about monster-killing than gardening is about slaughtering aphids or *Ender's Game* is about killing Buggers.

What sets *Shadow of the Colossus* apart from other RPGs is its successful elevation of monster-killing to near-spiritual levels. Monster-killing becomes, like Shiva's austerities in the mountain cave, complex and meaningful. Most games require frequent monster fights as you travel, which creates a constant low level of anxiety. *Shadow of the Colossus* compresses this anxiety into sixteen terrifying and epic boss battles. All monster-killing is inextricably linked to a game's quest, which gives that violence a feeling of greater purpose. A quest is a concept to which we, almost because of the archaic resonance of the word alone, attribute the capacity for meaning. So the tasks that make up a quest, such as monster-killing as you travel, can start to share in that aura of significance as you play. This is powerful in *Shadow of the Colossus* but also present in games jam-packed with minor monsters.

I've probably killed thousands of beasts. I'll spend 100 hours completing a game primarily consisting of monster fights. I'll do this, and if a game is good, I'm as clean as a whistle at the end, not drenched in psychic gore or remorse. Monster-killing is a practical reality of most games; it's best not to worry about or relish it too much. With monster-killing, as with practicing yoga postures, it helps to remember what it's all for. It's part of a quest for something meaningful, but monster-killing also relates to what, in RPGs, is often the main in-game activity: developing your character. Typically, higher levels of important characteristics, skills, etc. will accrue to your character as you complete battles. Your character (you) becomes a more multi-faceted, capable, and efficient being. Let's call this self-cultivation via monster-killing. In my experience, games that lack self-cultivation feel a bit one-dimensional; I recently played *Ms. Pac-Man* (the super-speed kind, of course) and felt once again the frustration of playing a character that does not evolve.

So, monster-killing has to mean more than survival and more than self-cultivation and more than entertainment. For a game story to have legs, monsters must be able to be seen as signifying something, and killing them must also signify something. Monster-killing does not have to be a hypersigil; it's more basic than that. The organizing moral principles of a game world often boil down to something desperately obvious: black-and-white, good and evil. This isn't bad in itself because a good game, like a good book, then takes the player into a more familiar ambiguity. Good and bad become less easily separated and less relevant, in fact, the longer you travel. It's sad when a game uses ambiguity itself to create interest, shifting the ground beneath our feet so frequently that we become bored and don't even care when the true enemy is revealed to be our best friend. The trick is to create, in the gamer, a commitment to a point of view, whatever its morality—dramatic plot twists are never quite as devastating as they're meant to be (unless the gamer or reader just hasn't paid attention, which I admit can happen—my failure to anticipate the ending of *Ender's Game* is a good example). No, I'd go for creating a creeping sense of doom, a teetering feeling, a worry—that's how to get people. Never is this more elegantly done than in *Shadow of the Colossus*. The narrative is only ever suggested, but the gamer is completely committed to the events, even as your understanding of what is really going on gradually shifts and grows.

2. Choices.

In *Shadow of the Colossus*, you play a man alone in the Cursed Lands. Only a hint of context is given, no explanation for his arrival there with a dead woman in his arms. The man is essentially nameless, since we don't learn his name until the end. There are decrepit buildings throughout the Cursed Lands, clearly built by people now absent. The present occupants of the area are mostly lizards, turtles, fish, birds, and sixteen Colossi, monsters that remain dormant until the man tracks them down and starts a fight. Each fight is absurd, terrifying in scale, a pesky fly of a man against a lumbering animated tower or a giant armored horse, until a glowing glyph is located somewhere on the Colossus and a sword thrust into it. Ribbons of black stream out of the monster and into the man after each kill.

They seem to replace the light in the man, and his skin takes on ever-darkening tattoos that suggest, as they do on the Colossi, that something's *in there*. What does all this mean? No official explanation has been made, but here's one idea: he doesn't realize it at first, but he doesn't hesitate once he does realize—he's sacrificing himself to bring his girl back to life. He's trading his soul bit by bit for monster souls. The monster souls are actually smaller pieces of one larger entity, which, fully reunited in the man's body at the end, ousts his soul.

So perhaps *Shadow of the Colossus* is, ultimately, a game about becoming a monster and setting evil free. All along, the man has been taking orders from a voice that emanates from a god-mouth in the roof of a crumbling temple filled with sixteen Colossi idols. It could be humiliating to be such a toady, to be used so, but if it is, then we're all a little pathetic, a bit tragic for our refusal to admit that we always serve something. In the end, the man appears to have agreed to trade his soul for his girl's. She opens her eyes as he is finally subsumed. The interesting question is, *At what point did the man agree to the trade? Did he just think all he had to do was take down a few monsters and he'd get his girl back? Did he know that he was reconstituting a force that would destroy him?* You never get the sense that the man is gleeful or macho or even confident as he battles the

Colossi; this is no *God of War*. If he isn't informed about the particulars of his task, at the very least I think his sobriety suggests that he knows something serious is at hand

Overall, *Shadow of the Colossus* is a remarkably neutral game, and I enjoy the freedom to speculate about the story and the man's state of mind. In *Cooling Time: An American Poetry Vigil*, C.D. Wright calls poetry a way of respecting the white space. That's exactly how I love poetry and how I love *Shadow of the Colossus*. I feel invited to participate in forming the meaning of this game. The game has room for my experience of it. Perhaps this is why the prospect of a film version of *Shadow of the Colossus* terrifies me. I dread being told with such emphatic finality what the game is "really" about. There is another writer who has already said what I mean here: in *Weight*, Jeanette Winterson calls herself a writer "who believes in the power of story telling for its mythic and not its explanatory qualities." The white space is where things are not explained and the reader or gamer is allowed in

Honestly, most games do a poor job of respecting the white space. RPGs often give you either a distinctly "good" or "evil" character to play. In some RPGs, however, such as *Oblivion: The Elder Scrolls* and *Fable 2*, you can cultivate yourself in either direction. Americans, it turns out, prefer to play good characters. I toyed with murder in both games and had no stomach for it. (I guess that makes me an exemplary American.) That killing in video games can become objectionable could be either a feature of the high realism of many of today's games or the possibility that we are now living in some kind of meta world, where everything is cleaner and less tangible than ever before and mostly originates in our minds. This is like living in a story. Today's tenet is that killing is bad even in games. This is because we live in our heads so much, everything we do and value sometimes seems more abstract than ever before. We do not live in a real world anymore and war is too real for our refined palates. Our moral context therefore lets us object to play killing. At least, this is one way of seeing it. I find it interesting that at some points in time, it appears that a taste or talent for killing did not automatically disqualify a person from society. Knights did the dirty work to protect the more refined aspects of civilization, as embodied by the Ladies. This is the story, anyway. But Knights weren't considered bad if they had to kill a beast or a beastly person—the Knights' work was in service of the good, and there was no moral quandary. But I think these stories live on and grab us today not because of their historical or literary merits but because we are fascinated by permitted murdering. Playing video games, then, becomes an exorcism of sorts—or a Tantric practice of excess meant to cure the obsession.

3. Hunting and not hunting.

Monster-killing is different, though. It's funny how you can know yourself to be mostly, if not just ethnically, a pacifist—being raised by Mennonite-raised parents—and you then find yourself *hunting*. It's digital hunting, but hunting nonetheless. There isn't any blood, but there are grunts and sighs and other intriguing sound effects (praises to the sound engineers) as the beasts give up the ghosts and whatever treasure they carry. I'd argue that the realism of many games is what makes it so easy for observing non-gamers to connect real-world violence with game-violence and skip right over the critical thinking part. Was this a problem in the era of *Jungle Pit* and *Space Invaders*? No, I don't recall anyone suggesting I not shoot at the alien-piloted ships encroaching on my personal space. (Now that was true exigency! That was do or die.) But just because I have to fight several vicious floating fish, mutated dinosaurs, and some Berserkers as I cross a desert in *Final Fantasy* 12 doesn't mean I'm a killer. Someone once asked me, "Don't you feel bad killing all those beautiful creatures?" It's my pleasure to inform you that not only do I not feel bad, I enjoy it. I'm getting paid and collecting mad loot.

Yet, monster killing isn't what any game or story is about. For me, *Halo 3* is not so much about hacking through an endless onslaught of aliens and Flood; it's almost entirely about the novelty, fun, and challenge of playing with a partner (I find the enemies' comments hilarious, too—something about their tone). *Shadow of the Colossus* is not so much about finding and fighting large beasts. While I did spend most of the game feeling terrified, I've got some sweet memories, too. The Cursed Lands are vast and still. A small breeze blows. Sun light is dappled under the trees, brilliant over the oceans, and it turns the crumbling stone shrines and plazas a soft platinum. A melancholy music plays during battles; otherwise, it's mostly environmental sounds: water, wind, Agro's hooves on the ground. I can hear these now. But what stays with me the most is the image of the woman's body lying in the temple, diffusing the sun with her white dress, the doves shifting around her, the man and his horse simply watching. A few feet from an aisle of menacing Colossus idols, the tender scene becomes sublime. Without the weight of words, it speaks of the frailty of the living, the uncertainty of our tasks, and the ache of love. It is mythic. It moves me.

4. The Path and the Glimpse.

But even in a gorgeous world, monsters are not just a distraction from these emotional treats. They are not just for killing either. Monsters could be the Path itself, the path to the end of suffering, a path worth walking on, that gives sense of direction and purpose to life. A holy man tries to walk toward God, away from the world. Other holy men try to help others find the path. Sometimes I wonder if I think by completing tasks I'll be enlightened. Sometimes I look at the end of my various efforts for a face shining behind the veil and I wonder if I'm conflating worship and task-completion. I'm knocking and knocking at the door, completing side-quests, collecting Nirnroots, rolling a katamari out of fireflies… Who waits on the other side of these doors? Does he even want what I am bringing to him? Is it even good?

I know a physicist who would chuckle at my dilemma. This man goes from A to B. Granted, his B is fusion energy, a true "creative sort" kind of vision, and the path between his A and B is far from dull. The important thing for him is to get there. Going from A to B—having a clear question and methodically answering it—in the rest of life oftentimes is dull. There is no room for wondering or wandering and asking what about C? When I think about what it is that makes playing RPGs interesting to me, it's not the A to B. That, in fact, is what makes them *boring*. There are no real stakes involved. If there were real stakes, a real possibility of closing an *Oblivion* gate and preserving humanity to flail poignantly another day, I might value basic A to B a bit more. I might reject my own formulation of monster-fighting as self-cultivation and call it critical training. But I prefer to live and play in worlds where self-cultivation, the cultivation of life, and the search for something divine are respected options. Consider: in our world, gardeners are usually respected and admired. They may cultivate the most arcane or common of life forms. They may grow things in apparent disarray or in the strictest regiments. In truth, they spend more time spreading silica to lacerate slugs' soft bodies, unleashing plagues of ladybugs upon the aphids, and drowning Japanese beetles in jars of soapy water than anyone ever knows. But no one would diminish gardeners' work as mere beetle-killing.

Ask why not and someone might say, "Because gardens are beautiful." Ah, beauty. The ultimate excuse and the ultimate end goal. The trump card. Beauty is God. Sometimes people will use God as a trump card, but that's just too obvious. God is unknowable. God is barely perceivable. Beauty is often attributed to God. What people who invoke either are really trying to do, I suspect, is indicate that something beyond us has been Glimpsed.

Can monster-killing cause a Glimpse? Perhaps. The figure of the Death-seeker is a warrior who does his warrior duty, but more than anything hopes to be killed himself one day, never is, battles on, and inadvertently becomes a better warrior, better than everyone else, his skills ascend beyond known levels, and to those who worship that sort of skill he gives the Glimpse. They call his killing beautiful, they call it God-given. For him, monster-killing was to be his path out of here, but like some kind of bitter Bodhisattva, his field of compassion is the field of blood and blade. The Death-seeker is like Arjuna. He does not want to fight, but God says Fighting is Your Duty, it is your duty to fight because that action keeps the world in balance. The hero Beowulf also has a duty to fight. The poem *Beowulf* is not about battling horrendous monsters—it's about keeping the world going, about following a code of behavior upon which life depends and derives its structure, its meaning, and its perpetuity. Without a hero to keep monsters away from the good people, all would be chaos and death. Power protects the people, and, as in Seamus Heaney's translation of *Beowulf*, "Behavior that's admired/is the path to power among people everywhere."

5. The qualities of a monster.

Which brings me to *Ender's Game*, by Orson Scott Card, and the question of what a monster really *is*. Like the monsters of *Beowulf*, the Buggers are known to be remorseless, inhuman outsiders with whom humans cannot communicate. When you can't communicate with something, the obvious course is to fight it, right? So humans and Buggers fight. The book is the story of Ender, a super-sensitive, super-intelligent child trained from age six to lead Earth's armies against the Buggers. Throughout the entire book, Ender is kept busy trying to survive against a wide range of more immediate threats to his survival—his violent brother, his unforgiving training program, his loneliness and isolation, his terror about becoming a monster himself. Always a new enemy for poor Ender. He is kept so busy trying keep his head on straight that he never has a minute to question the assumption driving everything—that the Buggers are monsters—and the first time I read the book I was so tangled in Ender's daily life that the story's denouement practically gutted me. To learn that the child-genius battle commander Ender has been tricked into wiping out the bugger race, and to witness his grief and remorse as he learns the truth about the Buggers—it was just too much. Turns out the Buggers were, more or less, everything a monster should be—hideous, aggressive, and incomprehensible—except an actual threat to humanity. From the beginning, Ender's reward for protecting humanity from the Buggers would be freedom from terror, as well as honor and glory, but in the end, in return for killing the Buggers, Ender is not free and is not honored. Ender is used, as the man in *Shadow of the Colossus* is, by a powerful and detail-withholding force.

Withholding details—in other words, failing to communicate well—is a sign of a monster. Those who use the child Ender are monstrous in their treatment of him, whatever their motivation. The Dormin, as the disembodied power in *Shadow of the Colossus* calls itself, speaks cryptically in a strange language; even without form, a more disturbing monster I've seldom encountered. I wish game designers would remember that giving monsters casual speech sort of neuters them. A monster is not for chitchat. A boss monster bloviating on its plans to kill you is comedic, not scary. Better to make the bosses unforthcoming, otherworldly, and alien. Especially since so many games promote the value of self-cultivation. In the game, your goal is to cultivate yourself into the ultimate of what you are (human, elf, whatever), the fullest expression of your potential, and why shouldn't this include communication skills? Sometimes it does: the Speechcraft skill in *Oblivion* perfectly fills this need. The more pleasantly and effectively you can communicate with townspeople, the higher your Speechcraft level. Among the many typical skills your character must develop, including weapon and armor skills, fighting skills, strength, endurance, magic, etc., Speechcraft is what truly separates you from thugs and monsters.

Self-cultivation is the process of becoming good at things. It is also the process of becoming "good" in the game's moral universe. All of us like being good, or at least knowing how to be bad. But let's put that aside. There are some terribly beautiful games out there, and they really aren't about good and bad, self-cultivation, or monster-killing. They offer a way to transcend necessity and ambition: deep appreciation, which is deep observation, a meditative state. A game can be played like this—*Shadow of the Colossus* allows it, but few others do, in my experience. I admit I indulge myself in this way of playing. I look for it. A game so perfectly rendered and self-contained, that requires so little compromise from my imagination—maybe it's just me, but just being *in* this kind of game world is itself the desired outcome. It's the good result, as the surgeons say. It's the end of yoga practice, as the yogis say, when you don't have to practice anymore because you have achieved enlightenment and now you can just lounge in the temple garden and leave the monster-killing to the noobs.

6. Postscript.

That, in part, is what monsters are for. Of course, monsters mostly just want to kill you. So there's great risk. But isn't there always? With great risk we are born. With great risk we love. With great risk we read books, listen to music, and play video games. It would seem that we cannot help but run around naked everywhere with our hearts hanging out. And then there are those monsters we fling ourselves against over and over until we get better, know more, can put our legs behind our head, or die. We need game monsters, since sometimes life's monsters are just too arbitrary, too, well, monstrous; it matters to be able to accomplish something, even if only in a game. That could be why we invent our gods, couldn't it? So we can suffer a little less.

—2009

Learning from Other Writers (Hartzler)

1. Early in the essay, Hartzler equates killing monsters in video games to practicing yoga postures. What is the effect of this comparison?

2. How does Hartzler develop this parallel between monster killing and yoga? How does she equate the experience of killing monsters in a game to something more philosophical and even spiritual?

3. Like Michael Rudin's "Writing the Great American ~~Novel~~ Video Game," this essay was first published on the Website of *Fiction Writers Review*. How might this essay have been different if Hartzler had written it for a trade video-game magazine instead of a literary journal focused on fiction?

4. Hartzler clearly notes that monster killing is not about the simple contrast between good and bad. She is careful to note that a good video game "takes the player into a more familiar ambiguity," but ambiguity alone is not enough to create interest. What do you make of this assertion? If you are video-game player, do you agree? If you are not, how might this apply to other forms of entertainment, from literature to films?

5. Hartzler realizes that she loves the game *Shadow of Colossus* because it is "neutral" and because she is not sure what the game is really *about*. She notes that all this "white space" allows the reader in. How can this be applied to Hartzler's other interests, from literature to yoga to beauty to religious faith?

FROM THE PERSONAL TO THE POLITICAL

V.V. (Sugi) Ganeshananthan does not use a straightforward reflective narrative to launch or structure her meditations but relies heavily on personal experience. In examining the nature of her grief ten years after the September 11 terrorist attacks, Ganeshananthan turns her gaze to Sri Lanka, where for more than twenty-five years the Sinhalese-dominated government waged war on the rebel Tamil Liberation Tigers, culminating in the civilian deaths of tens of thousands of Tamils (Ganeshananthan herself is ethnically Tamil, despite having been born and raised in the U.S.). She attempts to present the facts clearly before she brings in her own ideas, yet she doesn't hide her opinions about the war in Sri Lanka. When she notes that news organizations provided the world with little imagery of this war, especially as compared to the other atrocities in our collective memories, we understand that she is attempting to give voice to an event, to allow it to exist in our consciousness so we can properly mourn the loss. At first, we might not see the connection between the events of September 11 and this distant battle in Sri Lanka, but the linkage becomes resonant when Ganeshananthan writes, near the end of her essay:

> But in the two years after that battle, the Sri Lankan government consistently and strongly denied any civilian casualties as a result of their actions, referring to a zero-casualty policy and humanitarian rescue project, and insisting that Tamils who had died were members of the militancy. This victory, they declared, was part of their war on terror, and had been accomplished with admirable cleanliness and little cost.

Perhaps the author knew from the start that she was headed to this conclusion. After all, she knew that she was writing about grief, and she had experienced grief in response to September 11 as well as the conflict in Sri Lanka. But it also seems possible that she stumbled on this connection in the process of writing: two ideas presented themselves as linked in her mind, and she needed to write the essay to articulate the connection.

V. V. Ganeshananthan

THE POLITICS OF GRIEF

In the case of September 11 2001, communal loss is—comparatively, at least—well understood. Everyone saw or could see those deaths; they were on the news even as they happened; the broadcast was part of their lasting tragedy. Few perceived denial of the deaths as rational. Those responsible made sure there was plenty of physical evidence. No one fought the act of mourning and was taken seriously. Not so with what I saw from a great distance eight years later: the deaths of Tamil civilians at the end of Sri Lanka's civil war.

These deaths require, among other tasks, ongoing announcement and explanation—and because certain authorities have failed to fully acknowledge that the casualties occurred, saying *I grieve* means stating, repeatedly, *I believe that they did*. It is a kind of complicated voting. This recitation of the facts means a commitment not only to how definitively these people are gone, but also to hearing it over and over again as I am forced to argue for it. I resent this more than I could ever have thought possible, because in this country of grief, the best kind of shelter is to be understood, to have someone stop next to me and without asking anything, put their umbrella over us both, between us and the rain.

Before we ever came to this place, we heard reports of steady, gray fog—pale, opening clouds—late and sudden violent storms. Rumour has it that some people, surprised to stop here, never leave, while others, knowing another destination, are able to find slow but certain passage through. I myself am a wary traveler in this country. I can sense that groups of people move around me, but I am mostly alone: a stranger, feeling strange, on a rain-marked stone road, my umbrella blown inside out.

Grief is a country that looks different to each person entering it, to be sure. How does one find fellowship or shelter in loss? There is a hierarchy here; we measure the validity of grief in specific ways. And so before I talk about how death has touched me, I should say how it has not. I must acknowledge that some will see my grief as presumptuous, while others will find it inadequate: I did not know the people I am mourning, and I was not there. Still, I cannot imagine a road as smooth or a sky as blue as the ones I remember from the time before I came to this place and I cannot wish myself any happier. By any measure of reason, what happened to me was nothing— nothing more than watching and knowing and finally, imagining a terrible thing and how it might have happened. But although I was physically safe, the knowledge of that terrible thing became a shadow over everything I did and saw afterwards in a way I had not previously known was possible. Because the deaths involved were not only private, but also public and political, in their wake I found myself faced for the first time with both the desire for collective mourning and a complete inability to engage with it. All time and space was marked first and foremost by its relation to this disaster.

On the rare occasion that I stand under an umbrella, next to someone who already knows what happened, I feel a relief that I had never known before. This person understands how much I would give not to say this, or for anyone else not to ever have to say a sentence like this: You may never have heard of these deaths before, and you may never hear of them again, but in the spring of 2009, ten thousands of civilians who were ethnically Tamil, as I am ethnically Tamil, were killed in Sri Lanka, the country where my parents were born and I was not.

What a terrible sentence. Of course, these particular deaths did not happen in a vacuum, but in the context of nearly thirty years of war that cost many lives. Each of these deaths matters; the words of this history must be carefully negotiated, and even then, the ones I choose will fail in one way or another, because they cannot be exhaustive. The cause of the grief is necessarily politicized, and because I am electing some words and not others, from the moment I speak I open myself to attack. By grieving, I also automatically place myself in opposition to those who have denied that these deaths occurred. Some people may revel in my anguish; others will accuse me of inventing it; others still will use it to furnish the houses of their own causes. This grief, then, requires risk.

It also requires truthfulness. To talk about it in the most transparent and honest manner, I must retell not only the version of the story I consider the truest and the worst, but also the versions in which no one died, or in which those who died are unworthy of mourning. My words must reenact and contain not only the deaths and my grief, but also their negation.

The security forces of the Sinhalese-dominated government fought the rebel Liberation Tigers of Tamil Eelam for over a quarter of a century. The latter claimed sole representation of the country's minority Tamils, and aimed to establish a separate state for them following decades of discrimination by successive Sri Lankan governments. The Tigers' methods were brutal and included (but indeed, were not limited to) suicide bombings, child conscription, assassinations of elected Tamil officials and other Tamil dissenters, massacres of Sinhalese and Muslim civilians; extortion and coercion of Tamils in Sri Lanka and abroad. As the war escalated, the Sri Lankan government followed the decades of discrimination against its Tamil citizens with harassment, abduction, torture and murder by government-aligned forces, in government-controlled areas. Attacks on journalists, extrajudicial killings and disappearances rose. Criticism of the government was portrayed as support for terrorism, as the Tigers were banned in a number of places, including the US and the EU. They had long been thought undefeatable, but at long last, in the spring of 2009, the walls closed around them.

I had studied and watched this war for as long as I could remember, and still, the scale of the final battle, those last casualties, seemed different from any others. Never before had I seen such a catastrophe coming from so far away. It was avoidable. I spent much of that spring waiting or searching for news. The deaths were not widely broadcast as they happened, or even in their immediate aftermath; they happened on a small strip of beach and went mostly unseen. Press access by that point was severely curtailed, and there was little of the imagery that gets attention in modern war. After more than a quarter-century of fighting, Sri Lankan security forces had cornered the Tigers. With the Tigers: Tamil civilians. Reports from various authorities ranged wildly—300,000 civilians were trapped between the Tigers and the Sri Lankan Army; 40,000 civilians were trapped; certainly, tens of thousands of civilians were trapped. They counted; they didn't count; no one had counted them; they were counted incorrectly. The Tigers said the civilians were with them by choice; numerous accounts show otherwise—cadres shot some who tried to escape as security forces bore down, while still others found themselves forced into the Tigers' desperate ranks. The government, for its part, directed civilians to a no-fire zone, but subsequently shelled the same areas—and denied it. Calls for international intervention or a ceasefire yielded nothing.

And that spring, two Sri Lankan voices dominated the sphere of public conversation about that last battle: the pro-Tiger protestors of the Tamil diaspora, who waved their flags in cities around the world and failed to acknowledge that the rebels were complicit in civilian death, and the government and its supporters, who alleged that any grief for Tamil civilians was only a ploy to stop them from defeating the rebels. I had never felt so much and expressed so little, but what use were emotions? They would have made me prey. I recited facts instead, collecting them as a kind of armour. For weeks, I pored over the news, patching together information to learn as much as I could about what was happening. When the security forces finally defeated the Tigers, tens of thousands of civilians poured out of their prison. But in the days before that, tens of thousands of others surely died, their unseen bodies fallen on the fields of those battles.

Very little in the paragraphs above is uncontested or even complete—part of what makes this so wearying. As I watched what was happening, it seemed to me unbelievable that I could stand knowing about such a large atrocity in such depth. It seemed unbelievable that I had not died from this—that this level of grief was perhaps only a first circle. I, after all, lived in a place that pulsed with life; I had lost no one but myself.

That spring was my last in New York City, where I lived almost next door to Central Park. American analyses of the no-fire zone in Sri Lanka often compared the strip of land where the civilians were to the city's famous public space; at one point, they were the same size. The park had been my refuge for so long. Now it also seemed unbelievable that for the rest of my life, as a function of where I lived and how the news and war had unfolded, I would talk mostly to people who had no idea what had happened in the no-fire zone. I could walk down Central Park West and into the park itself, and once inside, I would pass people whose faces would show that they did not know. It was a collective loss, but on some level, it was private. My grief, too, had a political dimension; was I mourning because the people lost were Tamil, because they were Sri Lankan, because they were human? Were those all moral reasons to mourn? And how many of those faces in the park contained histories of loss that I would never know?

As the war ended, the government had the opportunity to promote reconciliation among the country's ethnic communities. There would be no minorities now, they said; everyone was Sri Lankan, and they wanted the Tamil diaspora, too, to help with the rebuilding. But in the two years after that battle, the Sri Lankan government consistently and strongly denied any civilian casualties as a result of their actions, referring to a zero-casualty policy and humanitarian rescue project, and insisting that Tamils who had died were members of the militancy. This victory, they declared, was part of their war on terror, and had been accomplished with admirable cleanliness and little cost.

It is a way of humiliating people, to say that their dead are not dead, to say that people are not even allowed to mourn. There was little room for the legitimate expression of grief during the war, and after it was over, what little was there dwindled. As the government said they were for reconciliation, they moved to shut down the spaces where Tamil civilians and loss could be remembered.

Tiger cemeteries were razed, even when families survived who might have wanted to visit the markers. In one instance, Army headquarters were built in the same space. When some Tamil civilians attempted to gather to remember their dead on the anniversary of the war's end, they had to face down officers of the Sri Lankan Army, as the north and east of the country remain heavily militarized. Indeed, in certain places civilian gatherings now require military approval. Innumerable people looking for missing loved ones filed cases and gave testimony, but many never found who they were looking for.

Pro-Tiger parties, too, used the deaths, making them into a way to move propaganda and implying that the slain civilians had willingly martyred themselves. Many called for investigations of war crimes, but named only the government as alleged perpetrators. Others, noting that much of the Tiger leadership had been killed, wondered how any accounting could be even-handed. The argument could carry on and on—but at what cost for the survivors? We must think of the living, some cautioned: the risks of our mourning were too high. At the same time, I wondered if any civilian had died on that beach with no survivors. Should that death go unlamented, I thought? Who would mourn and remember that person? Between all these arguments, there was little space left for grief—just as there had been little space for the people themselves.

As the years have passed, mounting evidence—various international reports, leaked video, eyewitness accounts—has made more and more public what those of us who followed it closely have known since the spring of 2009: large numbers of Tamil civilians did die while trapped between the government forces and the Tigers. Recently, in the face of increasing international pressure, the Sri Lankan government finally acknowledged—as a note in a much longer report praising their military and its action—that the war's end may have come at the expense of some civilian lives. They expressed no sorrow over these losses. Even as military losses are honoured in public ways, the civilians, who were also Sri Lankan citizens, remain unmourned. When the government issued this report, which was designed to counter a panel of experts who recommended to the UN Secretary General that he more thoroughly investigate the end of the war, I searched it for the word 'regret' and found nothing. *We're so sorry for your loss, which is our loss too; we wish it hadn't happened that way; they were our people too.* No, they did not say that. They said that it was unavoidable. Later, one official was quoted as saying any civilian casualties were collateral damage.

When I went to sleep the other night, I knew that about halfway around the world from me, the police were digging for the body of a man who had been missing for some time—a Sri Lankan human rights defender. I did not know this man, but I had been following his case. I knew that when I woke up, they would likely have found his body. I was right: by dawn in my time zone, they had discovered what seemed to be his remains. The case stood out because it was so rare for such a disappearance to be solved. Somehow, it was different this time perhaps because key people decided to push to find him—and there he was, his body under a half-built house. Someone had tried to erase him, to build something over his memory without acknowledging that he was there, and it had failed.

I do not want to be defined by disaster. I do not think this would help anyone, and it seems another way of letting disaster win. Still, it is important to me to keep the solidarity I feel not only for the living, but also for the dead, whose deaths were not necessary. So many people around the world must have this: a certain number of graves forming an angry abacus inside them. I may never again enter a large room without knowing how many it holds, and how many times again that number would have to be multiplied before it would equal the number of casualties most often repeated: forty thousand.

My heart still seizes, becomes that calculator, in any sizable space designed to contain a certain number of people. I remember this, and I remember how beautiful the city was that spring. I remember going to a concert and sitting there, noting how many seats were in front of me and how many behind. I had moved to New York many years after its great loss, and even in the stillness of that concert hall, with its soaring ceilings, it stunned me—the life of it. These things would always be true: on any night in New York City, even as an uncounted number of people had died, an uncounted number of people who lived would come to a concert hall to sit together, with strangers, and listen to music. My grief will not destroy me. In some times and places, we are given the space to build our memorials. Perhaps in others, we must learn to become them, even as we go on.

—2011

Learning from Other Writers (Ganeshananthan)

1. Ganeshananthan begins by evoking the terrorist attacks of September 11, 2001. Why do you think she begins this way?

2. Where in the essay does the author explain why both the September 11 deaths and the tens of thousands of Tamil civilian deaths are meaningful to her? Why is her connection to both events important?

3. How does Ganeshananthan use the motif of the umbrella throughout her essay?

4. Why do you think the author feels compelled to say, "And so before I talk about how death has touched me, I should say how it has not." How might she be anticipating her audience's resistance? What is the effect of such an admission?

5. The author is writing about something politically complicated. How does she make sure to address the complexity of her material? Find places in the language that show her attempt to be diplomatic while not watering down her stance. Why is this significant when you consider the theme of the essay? The title?

6. A good essay will illuminate something in a new light. Before this essay, had you considered the concept of mourning as a political act? How might mourning those lost in the terrorist attacks of 9/11 also be a political act?

Adding Your Voice

1. Think of a recent event in your life that was significant to you, even if that event was as personal as getting taken to or picked up from college by your parents. Freewrite about the experience. Then make a list of the abstract issues that arose from that experience and any specific questions that relate to those issues. Finally, let yourself freewrite as you meditate on any or all of those questions.

2. Think about the ways in which a specific form of technology has affected your life, whether positively, negatively, or both. Write an essay about how you first came to use this technology and the ways in which your relationship to the technology has changed over time.

3. What do you think defines the essence of a generation? What in the world of films, books, music, or other entertainment defines the essence of *your* generation? How? Why? Which movie, book, song, or video game gets this essence right? Which movies, books, songs, or video games get this essence wrong? Write an essay about how this cultural artifact is emblematic of your generation. You might want to start by describing your relationship to the work of art or form of entertainment, or you might start with a factual description of the phenomenon and move on from there.

4. Choose something you like to do that most people generally misunderstand or connect to an unfair stereotype. Like Hartzler, title your piece "X isn't about X"

and write a meditative essay wherein you try to figure out what X really *is* about, why X is important to you, and why your readers should overcome their misconceptions and understand the true nature of X.

5. Listen to the *This American Life* piece that Natalie cites in her essay. If you could choose between the powers of Flight or Invisibility, which would you choose? Write a short meditative essay examining why you would prefer one over the other and why you think you made the choice you made. (Link: http://www. thisamericanlife.org/radio-archives/episode/178/superpowers)

KEY FEATURES OF THE FORM

As you draft your essays, perhaps using the writing you have done in response to Adding Your Voice activities throughout this chapter, consider the common features of the investigation:

- Use a driving question to guide the inquiry beyond basic reporting on the subject;

- Go beyond presenting facts to uncover new information and lead your readers to an explicit or implicit claim about your material;

- Approach the material with a forensic state of mind;

- Develop a clear sense of the author's role in the investigation, whether central or peripheral;

- Anticipate and address the audience's possible resistance;

- Effectively introduce, contextualize, analyze, and cite outside sources;

- Effectively balance expository and scenic writing;

- Employ significant, concrete details;

- Employ an engaging voice and an appropriate tone;

- End with a conclusion that shows an intellectual or emotional distance traveled.

PART V

Alternative Structures

CHAPTER 14

Borrowed Forms

T *he writers in this section use alternative structures that adopt their shape from the essay's subject.* For example, Michelle Morano explores her relationship with her boyfriend, his depression, and their tenuous future by envisioning her essay as a lesson on the use of the subjunctive mood in Spanish. The essay, "Grammar Lessons," incorporates elements of the narrative, the portrait, and the investigation, but its organizing structure is a list of grammar rules.

As you will see from this chapter and the next ("Spatial Forms"), essays whose organizational schemes mimic the structures of objects, documents, buildings, or other discrete physical sites make up one of the most exciting segments of the genre. Although we refer to such structures as borrowed (or found) forms, we also like the term coined by Brenda Miller and Suzanne Paola in their textbook *Tell It Slant*. In honor of the hermit crab, which steals and inhabits the shells cast off by other creatures, Miller and Paola use the term "hermit-crab essay" to describe an "essay that appropriates the other forms as an outer covering to protect its soft, vulnerable underbelly. ... The 'shells' come from wherever you can find them, anywhere in the world. They may borrow from fiction and poetry, but they also don't hesitate to armor themselves in more mundane structures: the descriptions in a mail order catalog, for example, or the entries in a checkbook register." As Miller and Paola point out, such forms allow writers who might otherwise feel overwhelmed by the emotional intensity of their subject to gain not only structural but psychological mastery over their material.

OBJECTS

As we all know, certain objects can serve as repositories for our memories and emotions. Like Hamlet discoursing on vanity while cradling the skull of the jester Yorick, who once carried him on his back, sang to him, and told him jokes, any of us might pick up a basketball, a dancing shoe, or a yearbook and use it as a catalyst to contemplate our past. With a larger or more complex object, we might even structure our reminiscences according to its parts, moving from the glove compartment of a thirty-year-old refurbished Mustang to the monitors along its dash, to the back seat, to the trunk, to the hubcaps, to the fenders, to the ornament on the grill.

Illustrations of the object form are easiest to see in poetry. In Book Eighteen of *The Iliad* (an example we owe to John Hersey), Homer moves us around the scenes painted by Hephaistos on the five-folded shield of Achilles, using the images on the shield to spur his reflections on life in Greece and Troy. In a gesture that might have been inspired by these same Homeric lines, Keats holds in his hand that famous Grecian urn and uses the images along its sides—men pursuing women beneath an arbor of leafy trees, pipers piping timbrels, priests sacrificing a heifer at an altar—to structure his ruminations on beauty, youth, and art.

In a more contemporary example of this form, John McPhee, a master of creative nonfiction, organizes one of his essays according to the spaces on a Monopoly board and the moves generated by the roll of the dice during a Monopoly tournament, juxtaposed with a journey around the streets of the real Atlantic City in search of the fabled but hard-to-find Marvin Gardens. The essay, appropriately enough, is called "The Search for Marvin Gardens."

John Mcphee

THE SEARCH FOR MARVIN GARDENS

Go. I roll the dice—a six and a two. Through the air I move my token, the flatiron, to Vermont Avenue, where dog packs range.

The dogs are moving (some are limping) through ruins, rubble, fire damage, open garbage. Doorways are gone. Lath is visible in the crumbling walls of the buildings. The street sparkles with shattered glass. I have never seen, anywhere, so many broken windows. A sign—"Slow, Children at Play"—has been bent backward by an automobile. At the lighthouse, the dogs turn up Pacific and disappear. George Meade, Army engineer, built the lighthouse—brick upon brick, six hundred thousand bricks, to reach up high enough to throw a beam twenty miles over the sea. Meade, seven years later, saved the Union at Gettysburg.

I buy Vermont Avenue for $100. My opponent is a tall, shadowy figure, across from me, but I know him well, and I know his game like a favorite tune. If he can, he will always go for the quick kill. And when it is foolish to go for the quick kill he will be foolish. On the whole, though, he is a master assessor of percentages. It is a mistake to underestimate him. His eleven carries his top hat to St. Charles Place, which he buys for $140.

The sidewalks of St. Charles Place have been cracked to shards by through-growing weeds. There are no buildings. Mansions, hotels once stood here. A few street lamps now drop cones of light on broken glass and vacant space behind a chain-link fence that some great machine has in places bent to the ground. Five plane trees—in full summer leaf, flecking the light—are all that live on St. Charles Place.

Block upon block, gradually, we are cancelling each other out—in the blues, the lavenders, the oranges, the greens. My opponent follows a plan of his own devising. I use the Hornblower & Weeks opening and the Zuricher defense. The first game draws tight, will soon finish. In 1971, a group of people in Racine, Wisconsin, played for seven hundred and sixty-eight hours. A game begun a month later in Danville, California, lasted eight hundred and twenty hours. These are official records, and they stun us. We have been playing for eight minutes. It amazes us that Monopoly is thought of as a long game. It is possible to play to a complete, absolute, and final conclusion in less than fifteen minutes, all within the rules as written. My opponent and I have done so thousands of times. No wonder we are sitting across from each other now in this best-of-seven series for the international singles championship of the world.

On Illinois Avenue, three men lean out from second-story windows. A girl is coming down the street. She wears dungarees and a bright-red shirt, has ample breasts and a Hadendoan Afro, a black halo, two feet in diameter. Ice rattles in the glasses in the hands of the men.

"Hey, sister!"

"Come on up!"

She looks up, looks from one to another to the other, looks them flat in the eye.

"What for?" she says, and she walks on.

I buy Illinois for $240. It solidifies my chances, for I already own Kentucky and Indiana. My opponent pales. If he had landed first on Illinois, the game would have been over then and there, for he has houses built on Boardwalk and Park Place, we share the railroads equally, and we have cancelled each other everywhere else. We never trade.

In 1852, R. B. Osborne, an immigrant Englishman, civil engineer, surveyed the route of a railroad line that would run from Camden to Absecon Island, in New Jersey, traversing the state from the Delaware River to the barrier beaches of the sea. He then sketched in the plan of a "bathing village" that would surround the eastern terminus of the line. His pen flew glibly, framing and naming spacious avenues parallel to the shore—Mediterranean, Baltic, Oriental, Ventnor—and narrower transsecting avenues: North Carolina, Pennsylvania, Vermont, Connecticut, States, Virginia, Tennessee, New York, Kentucky, Indiana, Illinois. The place as a whole had no name, so when he had completed the plan Osborne wrote in large letters over the ocean, "Atlantic City." No one ever challenged the name, or the names of Osborne's streets. Monopoly was invented in the early nineteen-thirties by Charles B. Darrow, but Darrow was only transliterating what Osborne had created. The railroads, crucial to any player, were the making of Atlantic City. After the rails were down, houses and hotels burgeoned from Mediterranean and Baltic to New York and Kentucky. Properties—building lots—sold for as little as six dollars apiece and as much as a thousand dollars. The original investors in the railroads and the real estate called themselves the Camden & Atlantic Land Company. Reverently, I repeat their names: Dwight Bell, William Coffin, John DaCosta, Daniel Deal, William Fleming, Andrew Hay, Joseph Porter, Jonathan Pitney, Samuel Richards—founders, fathers, forerunners, archetypical masters of the quick kill.

My opponent and I are now in a deep situation of classical Monopoly. The torsion is almost perfect—Boardwalk and Park Place versus the brilliant reds. His cash position is weak, though, and if I escape him now he may fade. I land on Luxury Tax, contiguous to but in sanctuary from his power. I have four houses on Indiana. He lands there. He concedes.

Indiana Avenue was the address of the Brighton Hotel, gone now. The Brighton was exclusive—a word that no longer has retail value in the city. If you arrived by automobile and tried to register at the Brighton, you were sent away. Brighton-class people came in private railroad cars. Brighton-class people had other private railroad cars for their horses—dawn rides on the firm sand at water's edge, skirts flying. Colonel Anthony J. Drexel Biddle—the sort of name that would constrict throats in Philadelphia—lived, much of the year, in the Brighton.

Colonel Sanders' fried chicken is on Kentucky Avenue. So is Clifton's Club Harlem, with the Sepia Revue and the Sepia Follies, featuring the Honey Bees, the Fashions, and the Lords.

My opponent and I, many years ago, played 2,428 games of Monopoly in a single season. He was then a recent graduate of the Harvard Law School, and he was working for a downtown firm, looking up law. Two people we knew—one from Chase Manhattan, the other from Morgan, Stanley—tried to get into the game, but after a few rounds we found that they were not in the conversation and we sent them home. Monopoly should always be *mano a mano* anyway. My opponent won 1,199 games, and so did I. Thirty were ties. He was called into the Army, and we stopped just there. Now, in Game 2 of the series, I go immediately to jail, and again to jail while my opponent seines property. He is dumbfoundingly lucky. He wins in twelve minutes.

Visiting hours are daily, eleven to two; Sunday, eleven to one; evenings, six to nine. "NO MINORS, NO FOOD, Immediate Family Only Allowed in Jail." All this above a blue steel door in a blue cement wall in the windowless interior of the basement of the city hall. The desk sergeant sits opposite the door to the jail. In a cigar box in front of him are pills in every color, a banquet of fruit salad an inch and a half deep—leapers, co-pilots, footballs, truck drivers, peanuts, blue angels, yellow jackets, redbirds, rainbows. Near the desk are two soldiers, waiting to go through the blue door. They are about eighteen years old. One of them is trying hard to light a cigarette. His wrists are in steel cuffs. A military policeman waits, too. He is a year or so older than the soldiers, taller, studious in appearance, gentle, fat. On a bench against a wall sits a good-looking girl in slacks. The blue door rattles, swings heavily open. A turnkey stands in the doorway. "Don't you guys kill yourselves back there now," says the sergeant to the soldiers.

"One kid, he overdosed himself about ten and a half hours ago," says the M.P.

The M.P., the soldiers, the turnkey, and the girl on the bench are white. The sergeant is black. "If you take off the handcuffs, take off the belts," says the sergeant to the M.P. "I don't want them hanging themselves back there." The door shuts and its tumblers move. When it opens again, five minutes later, a young white man in sandals and dungarees and a blue polo shirt emerges. His hair is in a ponytail. He has no beard. He grins at the good-looking girl. She rises, joins him. The sergeant hands him a manila envelope. From it he removes his belt and a small notebook. He borrows a pencil, makes an entry in the notebook. He is out of jail, free. What did he do? He offended Atlantic City in some way. He spent a night in the jail. In the nineteen-thirties, men visiting Atlantic City went to jail, directly to jail, did not pass Go, for appearing in topless bathing suits on the beach. A city statute requiring all men to wear full-length bathing suits was not seriously challenged until 1937, and the first year in which a man could legally go bare-chested on the beach was 1940.

Game 3. After seventeen minutes, I am ready to begin construction on overpriced and sluggish Pacific, North Carolina, and Pennsylvania. Nothing else being open, opponent concedes.

The physical profile of streets perpendicular to the shore is something like a playground slide. It begins in the high skyline of Boardwalk hotels, plummets into warrens of "side-avenue" motels, crosses Pacific, slopes through church missions, convalescent homes, burlesque houses, rooming houses, and liquor stores, crosses Atlantic, and runs level through the bombed-out ghetto as far—Baltic, Mediterranean—as the eye can see. North Carolina Avenue, for example, is flanked at its beach end by the Chalfonte and the Haddon Hall (908 rooms, air-conditioned), where, according to one biographer, John Philip Sousa (1854–1932) first played when he was twenty-two, insisting, even then, that everyone call him by his entire name. Behind these big hotels, motels—Barbizon, Catalina—crouch. Between Pacific and Atlantic is an occasional house from 1910—wooden porch, wooden mullions, old yellow paint—and two churches, a package store, a strip show, a dealer in fruits and vegetables. Then, beyond Atlantic Avenue, North Carolina moves on into the vast ghetto, the bulk of the city, and it looks like Metz in 1919, Cologne in 1944. Nothing has actually exploded. It is not bomb damage. It is deep and complex decay. Roofs are off. Bricks are scattered in the street. People sit on porches, six deep, at nine on a Monday morning. When they go off to wait in unemployment lines, they wait sometimes two hours. Between Mediterranean and Baltic runs a chain-link fence, enclosing rubble. A patrol car sits idling by the curb. In the back seat is a German shepherd. A sign on the fence says, "Beware of Bad Dogs."

Mediterranean and Baltic are the principal avenues of the ghetto. Dogs are everywhere. A pack of seven passes me. Block after block, there are three-story brick row houses. Whole segments of them are abandoned, a thousand broken windows. Some parts are intact, occupied. A mattress lies in the street, soaking in a pool of water. Wet stuffing is coming out of the mattress. A postman is having a rye and a beer in the Plantation Bar at nine-fifteen in the morning. I ask him idly if he knows where Marvin Gardens is. He does not. "HOOKED AND NEED HELP?

CONTACT N.A.R.C.O." "REVIVAL NOW GOING ON, CONDUCTED BY REVER-
END H. HENDERSON OF TEXAS." These are signboards on Mediterranean and
Baltic. The second one is upside down and leans against a boarded-up window
of the Faith Temple Church of God in Christ. There is an old peeling poster on
a warehouse wall showing a figure in an electric chair. "The Black Panther Manifesto" is the title of the poster, and its message is, or was, that "the fascists have
already decided in advance to murder Chairman Bobby Seale in the electric chair."
I pass an old woman who carries a bucket. She wears blue sneakers, worn through.
Her feet spill out. She wears red socks, rolled at the knees. A white handkerchief,
spread over her head, is knotted at the corners. Does she know where Marvin Gardens is? "I sure don't know," she says, setting down the bucket. "I sure don't know.
I've heard of it somewhere, but I just can't say where." I walk on, through a block of
shattered glass. The glass crunches underfoot like coarse sand. I remember when
I first came here—a long train ride from Trenton, long ago, games of poker in
the train—to play basketball against Atlantic City. We were half black, they were
all black. We scored forty points, they scored eighty, or something like it. What I
remember most is that they had glass backboards—glittering, pendent, expensive
glass backboards, a rarity then in high schools, even in colleges, the only ones we
played on all year.

I turn on Pennsylvania, and start back toward the sea. The windows of the Hotel
Astoria, on Pennsylvania near Baltic, are boarded up. A sheet of unpainted plywood
is the door, and in it is a triangular peephole that now frames an eye. The plywood
door opens. A man answers my question. Rooms there are six, seven, and ten dollars a
week. I thank him for the information and move on, emerging from the ghetto at the
Catholic Daughters of America Women's Guest House, between Atlantic and Pacific.
Between Pacific and the Boardwalk are the blinking vacancy signs of the Aristocrat and
Colton Manor motels. Pennsylvania terminates at the Sheraton-Seaside—thirty-two
dollars a day, ocean corner. I take a walk on the Boardwalk and into the Holiday Inn
(twenty-three stories). A guest is registering. "You reserved for Wednesday, and this is
Monday," the clerk tells him. "But that's all right. We have *plenty* of rooms." The clerk is
very young, female, and has soft brown hair that hangs below her waist. Her superior
kicks her.

He is a middle-aged man with red spiderwebs in his face. He is jacketed and tied.
He takes her aside. "Don't say 'plenty,'" he says. "Say 'You are fortunate, sir. We have
rooms available.'"

The face of the young woman turns sour. "We have all the rooms you need," she
says to the customer, and, to her superior, "How's that?"

Game 4. My opponent's luck has become abrasive. He has Boardwalk and Park Place,
and has sealed the board.

Darrow was a plumber. He was, specifically, a radiator repairman who lived in Germantown, Pennsylvania. His first Monopoly board was a sheet of linoleum. On it he placed houses and hotels that he had carved from blocks of wood. The game he thus invented was brilliantly conceived, for it was an uncannily exact reflection of the business milieu at large. In its depth, range, and subtlety, in its luck-skill ratio, in its sense of infrastructure and socio-economic parameters, in its philosophical characteristics, it reached to the profundity of the financial community. It was as scientific as the stock market. It suggested the manner and means through which an underdeveloped world had been developed. It was chess at Wall Street level. "Advance token to the nearest Railroad and pay owner twice the rental to which he is otherwise entitled. If Railroad is unowned, you may buy it from the Bank. Get out of Jail, free. Advance token to nearest Utility. If unowned, you may buy it from Bank. If owned, throw dice and pay owner a total ten times the amount thrown. You are assessed for street repairs: $40 per house, $115 per hotel. Pay poor tax of $15. Go to Jail. Go directly to Jail. Do not pass Go. Do not collect $200."

The turnkey opens the blue door. The turnkey is known to the inmates as Sidney K. Above his desk are ten closed-circuit-TV screens—assorted viewpoints of the jail. There are three cellblocks—men, women, juvenile boys. Six days is the average stay. Showers twice a week. The steel doors and the equipment that operates them were made in San Antonio. The prisoners sleep on bunks of butcher block. There are no mattresses. There are three prisoners to a cell. In winter, it is cold in here. Prisoners burn newspapers to keep warm. Cell corners are black with smudge. The jail is three years old. The men's block echoes with chatter. The man in the cell nearest Sidney K. is pacing. His shirt is covered with broad stains of blood. The block for juvenile boys is, by contrast, utterly silent—empty corridor, empty cells. There is only one prisoner. He is small and black and appears to be thirteen. He says he is sixteen and that he has been alone in here for three days.

"Why are you here? What did you do?"

"I hit a jitney driver."

The series stands at three all. We have split the fifth and sixth games. We are scrambling for property. Around the board we fairly fly. We move so fast because we do our own banking and search our own deeds. My opponent grows tense.

Ventnor Avenue, a street of delicatessens and doctors' offices, is leafy with plane trees and hydrangeas, the city flower. Water Works is on the mainland. The water comes over in submarine pipes. Electric Company gets power from across the state, on the Delaware River, in Deepwater. States Avenue, now a wasteland like St. Charles, once had gardens running down the middle of the street, a horse-drawn trolley, private homes. States Avenue was as exclusive as the Brighton. Only an apartment house, a small motel, and the All Wars Memorial Building—monadnocks spaced widely apart—stand along States Avenue now. Pawnshops, convalescent homes, and the Paradise Soul Saving Station are on Virginia Avenue. The soul-saving station is pink, orange, and yellow. In the windows flanking the door of the Virginia Money Loan Office are Nikons, Polaroids, Yashicas, Sony TVs, Underwood typewriters, Singer sewing machines, and pictures of Christ. On the far side of town, beside a single track and locked up most of the time, is the new railroad station, a small hut made of glazed firebrick, all that is left of the lines that built the city. An authentic phrenologist works on New York Avenue close to Frank's Extra Dry Bar and a church where the sermon today is "Death in the Pot." The church is of pink brick, has blue and amber windows and two red doors. St. James Place, narrow and twisting, is lined with boarding houses that have wooden porches on each of three stories, suggesting a New Orleans made of salt-bleached pine. In a vacant lot on Tennessee is a white Ford station wagon stripped to the chassis. The windows are smashed. A plastic Clorox bottle sits on the driver's seat. The wind has pressed newspaper against the chain-link fence around the lot. Atlantic Avenue, the city's principal thoroughfare, could be seventeen American Main Streets placed end to end—discount vitamins and Vienna Corset shops, movie theatres, shoe stores, and funeral homes. The Boardwalk is made of yellow pine and Douglas fir, soaked in pentachlorophenol. Downbeach, it reaches far beyond the city. Signs everywhere—on windows, lampposts, trash baskets—proclaim "Bienvenue Canadiens!" The salt air is full of Canadian French. In the Claridge Hotel, on Park Place, I ask a clerk if she knows where Marvin Gardens is. She says, "Is it a floral shop?" I ask a cabdriver, parked outside. He says, "Never heard of it." Park Place is one block long, Pacific to Boardwalk. On the roof of the Claridge is the Solarium, the highest point in town—panoramic view of the ocean, the bay, the salt-water ghetto. I look down at the rooftops of the side-avenue motels and into swimming pools. There are hundreds of people around the rooftop pools, sunbathing, reading—many more people than are on the beach. Walls, windows, and a block of sky are all that is visible from these pools—no sand, no sea. The pools are craters, and with the people around them they are countersunk into the motels.

The seventh, and final, game is ten minutes old and I have hotels on Oriental, Vermont, and Connecticut. I have Tennessee and St. James. I have North Carolina and Pacific. I have Boardwalk, Atlantic, Ventnor, Illinois, Indiana. My fingers are forming a "V." I have mortgaged most of these properties in order to pay for others, and I have mortgaged the others to pay for the hotels. I have seven dollars. I will pay off the mortgages and build my reserves with income from the three hotels. My cash position may be low, but I feel like a rocket in an underground silo. Meanwhile, if I could just go to jail for a time I could pause there, wait there, until my opponent, in his inescapable rounds, pays the rates of my hotels. Jail, at times, is the strategic place to be. I roll boxcars from the Reading and move the flatiron to Community Chest. "Go to Jail. Go directly to Jail."

The prisoners, of course, have no pens and no pencils. They take paper napkins, roll them tight as crayons, char the ends with matches, and write on the walls. The things they write are not entirely idiomatic; for example, "In God We Trust." All is in carbon. Time is required in the writing. "Only humanity could know of such pain." "God So Loved the World." "There is no greater pain than life itself." In the women's block now, there are six blacks, giggling, and a white asleep in red shoes. She is drunk. The others are pushers, prostitutes, an auto thief, a burglar caught with pistol in purse. A sixteen-year-old accused of murder was in here last week. These words are written on the wall of a now empty cell: "Laying here I see two bunks about six inches thick, not counting the one I'm laying on, which is hard as brick. No cushion for my back. No pillow for my head. Just a couple scratchy blankets which is best to use it's said. I wake up in the morning so shivery and cold, waiting and waiting till I am told the food is coming. It's on its way. It's not worth waiting for, but I eat it anyway. I know one thing when they set me free I'm gonna be good if it kills me."

How many years must a game be played to produce an Anthony J. Drexel Biddle and chestnut geldings on the beach? About half a century was the original answer, from the first railroad to Biddle at his peak. Biddle, at his peak, hit an Atlantic City streetcar conductor with his fist, laid him out with one punch. This increased Biddle's legend. He did not go to jail. While John Philip Sousa led his band along the Boardwalk playing "The Stars and Stripes Forever" and Jack Dempsey ran up and down in training for his fight with Gene Tunney, the city crossed the high curve of its parabola. Al Capone held conventions here—upstairs with his sleeves rolled, apportioning among his lieutenant governors the states of the Eastern seaboard. The natural history of an American resort proceeds from Indians to French Canadians via Biddles and Capones. French Canadians, whatever they may be at home, are Visigoths here. Bienvenue Visigoths!

My opponent plods along incredibly well. He has got his fourth railroad, and patiently, unbelievably, he has picked up my potential winners until he has blocked me everywhere but Marvin Gardens. He has avoided, in the fifty-dollar zoning, my increasingly petty hotels. His cash flow swells. His railroads are costing me two hundred dollars a minute. He is building hotels on States, Virginia, and St. Charles. He has temporarily reversed the current. With the yellow monopolies and my blue monopolies, I could probably defeat his lavenders and his railroads. I have Atlantic and Ventnor. I need Marvin Gardens. My only hope is Marvin Gardens.

There is a plaque at Boardwalk and Park Place, and on it in relief is the leonine profile of a man who looks like an officer in a metropolitan bank—"Charles B. Darrow, 1889–1967, inventor of the game of Monopoly." "Darrow," I address him, aloud. "Where is Marvin Gardens?" There is, of course, no answer. Bronze, impassive, Darrow looks south down the Boardwalk. "Mr. Darrow, please, where is Marvin Gardens?" Nothing. Not a sign. He just looks south down the Boardwalk.

My opponent accepts the trophy with his natural ease, and I make, from notes, remarks that are even less graceful than his.

Marvin Gardens is the one color-block Monopoly property that is not in Atlantic City. It is a suburb within a suburb, secluded. It is a planned compound of seventy-two handsome houses set on curvilinear private streets under yews and cedars, poplars and willows. The compound was built around 1920, in Margate, New Jersey, and consists of solid buildings of stucco, brick, and wood, with slate roofs, tile roofs, multimullioned porches, Giraldic towers, and Spanish grilles. Marvin Gardens, the ultimate outwash of Monopoly, is a citadel and sanctuary of the middle class. "We're heavily patrolled by police here. We don't take no chances. Me? I'm living here nine years. I paid seventeen thousand dollars and I've been offered thirty. Number one, I don't want to move. Number two, I don't need the money. I have four bedrooms, two and a half baths, front den, back den. No basement. The Atlantic is down there. Six feet down and you float. A lot of people have a hard time finding this place. People that lived in Atlantic City all their life don't know how to find it. They don't know where the hell they're going. They just know it's south, down the Boardwalk."

—1972

Learning from Other Writers (McPhee)

1. How does McPhee weave together the two main threads of the essay? How does each strand influence the other?

2. How does the organization of McPhee's essay propel the essay forward?

3. What larger question about Monopoly, Atlantic City, or America is the author attempting to answer? How does that question lead McPhee to the central claim of the essay? What is that claim?

4. What would the essay lose if it were not structured around a game of Monopoly?

5. What is the role of the closing section about Marvin Gardens?

Adding Your Voice

A Singular Object:

Look around your dorm room, apartment, or parents' house for an object you find meaningful. As mentioned above, whether you choose a battered catcher's mitt or a yearbook or a car to analyze, the key is just that: analysis. And as is true of the examples presented earlier in this chapter (i.e., the poem about Achilles's shield or the essay based on a Monopoly game), you will want to structure your examination by moving *around* or *through* the object. As you do so, think about the way in which juxtaposing and comparing various elements of the object might cause some deeper significance to emerge. A pointe shoe for ballet dancers is not simply a shoe—it is comprised of several important parts: the toe box, which dancers will intentionally scuff up so as not to slip when they're on pointe; the elaborate ribbon, which must be tied in a specific way to bind the shoe to the foot; the various types of toe pads that are inserted into the toe box once it is broken in; and so on. (A complex object such as a car or a desk or a toy box might contain or be comprised of smaller objects. That's fine. You can still use the larger object as the organizing scheme for your essay and then analyze the individual parts as you get to them.)

A Collection of Objects:

1. The contents of bookshelves, closets, and drawers can hold objects that mimic a person's psyche. Purses, wallets, and backpacks can similarly reveal significant aspects of their owner's character. Think of a container or storage space whose contents reveal something about your own psyche or about someone else's psyche or character. What question does this collection of objects raise about your subject? Using the objects you have chosen as evidence or clues, play detective (or forensic psychiatrist) and try to answer your central question about your subject.

2. Choose a period of your life that strikes you as important (seventh grade, a parent's illness, a semester abroad). List five objects that pop into your mind

as important to that period. Describe each object on an index card, then lay the cards on a table so all five can be seen at once. Freewrite to figure out what question connects all five descriptions. After moving the index cards around on the table, settle on an order that makes sense to you. Try to articulate *why* this relationship makes sense to you—i.e., try to trace the hidden or unconscious connections. Then, using the five descriptions on the cards and the meditations suggested by the freewriting part of the assignment, write a collage essay. If you need to add or subtract objects or meditations, feel free to do so. What anecdotes or stories go with the objects? What feelings? Now think of a sixth object from that same period of your life that seems completely *un*related to the original five. Freewrite a meditation about the ways in which this object doesn't fit. Then write a segment about how, despite everything, this object *does* fit with the other five. Add this segment to your essay.

DOCUMENTS

Just as you can structure an essay by moving your readers around an object or a collection of objects, so, too, can you organize your material by following the images or words on a painting, map, photograph, or other document (this form has grown more familiar as we have become accustomed to the layout of a Web page). The authors of the regular Annotation feature in *Harper's* magazine create visual essays by commenting on the parts of noteworthy objects. "Conduct Unbecoming," by Anthony Lydgate, is arranged around a document called Form 2910, the Victim Reporting Preference Statement, which soldiers use to report sexual harassment or assault. Lydgate comments on various sections of the form to highlight the procedure that victims of such mistreatment must follow, from acknowledging that they have discussed their options with a counselor (who often discourages them from filing a report) to deciding, if they do report the sexual assault, whether to file a restricted or an unrestricted report, and so on.

But the essay doesn't just *explain* Form 2910; it explores the form's implications, analyzing the effects of the required counseling (the Defense Department estimates that only one-fifth of all sexual assault cases are officially reported), the consequences of filing this report, and the typical proceedings of a court martial. By explicating all that is really entailed or implied by each section of the form, Lydgate argues that the Victim Reporting Preference Statement, though it purportedly exists to protect the sexual assault victim, "serves as little more than a series of implied threats that effectively coerce victims into silence."

CONDUCT UNI

The military's sexual-assault probl

On January 11, 2008, a North Carolina county sheriff found the charred remains of Lance Corporal Maria Lauterbach buried beneath a backyard fire pit. Her murderer, Cesar Laurean, was a fellow Marine, whom she had accused eight months earlier of rape. Prior to her death, Lauterbach had endured a drawn-out sexual-assault investigation and confronted a command hierarchy that failed to protect her from further harassment. During a press conference, four days after her body was discovered, a military spokesman praised her attacker, describing him as a "stellar Marine." (The same spokesman called Lauterbach a "solid Marine.") Though her ordeal had a singularly grim ending, experiences like Lauterbach's are commonplace, as became clear last February when a group of soldiers and veterans launched a class action alleging serious problems with the military's handling of sexual-assault cases. Even in its bureaucratic paperwork, the Defense Department values obedience and decorum over justice for victims. Soldiers who want to report abuse must use Form 2910, the Victim Reporting Preference Statement, which serves as little more than a series of implied threats that effectively coerce victims into silence.

The cornerstone of the military's response to sexual assault is a network of coordinators and advocates who help survivors obtain medical assistance and file official reports. A lawyer for Maria Lauterbach's family called these advocates "victim listeners," people good at expressing concern but "not proactive" and "not independent." Drawn primarily from the ranks, response coordinators are torn between advocacy and self-preservation—between prodding commanders and placating them. When Jessica Kenyon, a former Army private and a plaintiff in February's lawsuit, reported her rape, the coordinator advised her to put her sexual-assault accusation "on the back burner" out of consideration for her career. It's not surprising, then, that overall reporting rates are low. The Defense Department estimates that the 3,158 sexual assaults involving service members recorded last year account for only a fifth of the actual number that took place.

Should a survivor choose to report a sexual assault, Form 2910 gives her the option of filing a restricted report, which grants her access to medical and counseling services without opening an investigation—protecting her career while allowing her assailant to go unpunished. Restricted reporting also sets a statute of limitations. If a victim fails to derestrict her report within a year, all evidence of the rape is destroyed, leaving it "no longer available for any future investigation or prosecution efforts." The majority of the military's sexual-assault victims are under twenty-five and come from the bottom of the enlisted ranks. They are new to military life, devoid of power, and susceptible to intimidation. Restricted reporting does little to help them. Sergeant Rebekah Havrilla, whose rape during a deployment to Afghanistan was photographed by her attacker, filed a restricted report. When she later sought help from a military chaplain, one of the few confidants Form 2910 permits, he told her that the assault "must have been God's will."

UNBECOMING

…sault problem, *by Anthony Lydgate*

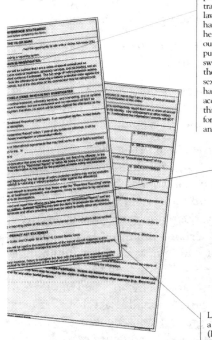

If a victim files an unrestricted report, military law enforcement launches an inquiry, promising survivors both the distant prospect of justice and the more immediate trauma of an investigation. Sergeant Myla Haider, another plaintiff from February's lawsuit, was raped while serving with the Army's Criminal Investigative Command; having seen her colleagues' routine mishandling of sex crimes, she chose not to report her assault at all. Even a competently managed investigation does not guarantee a fair outcome. Military law gives commanders wide latitude to dole out so-called nonjudicial punishments—verbal reprimands, docked pay, diminished rations—as a way of dealing swiftly with "minor" offenses while avoiding what the Manual for Courts-Martial calls the "stigma" of a federal conviction. Over the past several years, fewer than half of sexual-assault cases deemed viable by command have actually gone to trial. A third have ended in nonjudicial punishments, which are sometimes levied not just against accused rapists but against their victims as well. According to the lawsuit, commanders threatened to charge Corporal Sarah Albertson with "inappropriate barracks conduct" for drinking alcohol at the time of her rape. Later, after forcing Albertson to work in an office with her assailant, they reprimanded her for having a panic attack.

In the event of a court martial, enlisted service members are customarily tried and sentenced by juries of their superiors—the same kinds of superiors who are alleged to have asked a woman soldier whether she "liked it in the ass," spit on another for failing a knot-tying quiz, and told a third, after watching a video of her gang rape, that she "did not struggle enough." Juries are constrained in the sentences they can impose on officers, a standard colloquially known as "different spanks for different ranks." Perhaps the greatest problem in the prosecution of rape, however, is the prosecutors themselves. Former Defense Secretary Robert Gates has described a pattern wherein defendants hire seasoned attorneys while the military assigns inexperienced prosecutors. A Defense Department task force found that most prosecutors had "little or no experience" with sexual assault. One military lawyer told investigators, "In the civilian world, you would not have a one-year-out-of-law-school person working on a rape case."

Last fall, the Air Force released a dramatized public-service announcement in which a gallant airman (known in the credits as Bystander) rescues a drunken airwoman (Potential Victim) from a pack of would-be rapists (Guys 1, 2, and 3). After Bystander plucks Potential Victim from the jaws of danger, she leans her head on his shoulder and swoons, "I'm so glad there are good guys out there," to which he manfully responds, "Be safe, sweetie." The video is emblematic of how the military views sexual assault—as an offense invited by alcohol, perpetrated by a few hooligans, and corrected by heroic intervention. The 2012 defense budget, which will likely pass Congress this fall, promises some improvements to the military's sexual-assault policy: more consistent training for victim advocates, better privacy protection, and legal counseling for victims. Unaddressed by these reforms is military culture itself, which views rape and harassment as anomalies rather than by-products of an institution built on submission to authority. As Clifford Stanley, who oversees the Defense Department's sexual-assault prevention initiative, admits, there are "some real dopes out there" in the armed forces. Everyone else, he says, is stellar. ∎

Learning from Other Writers (Lydgate)

1. Although Lydgate is using a nontraditional form, his argument is expressed in a traditional way. What is his claim? Where is it stated in the essay? How is its placement similar to the placement of the writer's argument in a more conventional essay?

2. How does centering the essay on the physical document and highlighting certain sections help the writer to focus and develop the complexity of his analysis?

3. How does the author bring in outside sources? Where? How do these sources serve as evidence to support and inform his argument?

4. The essay's last section references a public-service announcement. How does the analysis here correlate with the section of the document to which it is matched? How does this final image highlight the argument's development?

Although Anthony Lydgate exposes the subtle argument and persuasive power of Form 2910, the Victim Reporting Preference Statement, many documents are meaningless without the context of a personal or historical connection. A photograph of your great-grandfather from the early 1900s, for example, would mean nothing to someone who found it in a junk shop. Yet to you and your family, the photo is an invaluable part of your personal history. And because you possess a certain amount of inside information about this individual and his life, you have the unique opportunity to decipher the picture at hand—the significance of the oak table your great-grandfather is standing beside, which was brought from Massachusetts to Michigan when your great-grandparents settled there and was their only real possession; the fact that your great grandfather's suit had been borrowed for the photograph, a document that was staged for the sole purpose of being sent back east as "evidence" to convince extended family members that he and his new family were thriving on the new homestead, which wasn't necessarily the case yet; and so on.

By annotating this photograph and exposing what would be hidden from the general public, you can use the document as a lens to examine larger social issues, related to immigration or suffrage or early medicine. Conversely, lacking that knowledge, you might find yourself with a motive to dig deeper and *figure out* the significance of this person's life, interviewing your grandparents and parents and turning to records at the local historical society to see what you can uncover about your ancestors' migration to Michigan. Either way, what matters is that by juxtaposing the dynamic but fleeting and elusive realities of a human life with the factual but silent evidence of a static, impersonal document such as a photograph, a will, or a map, you will create for yourself a unique and compelling opportunity for analysis.

Adding Your Voice

Find a painting, map, photograph, or similar document that you can annotate and analyze for meaning. Imagine zooming in on parts of the document as Lydgate does in order to interpret, decipher, and extract significance from what would be invisible or meaningless to anyone else. You might choose a school planner, your birth certificate, your family's mass-mailed holiday newspaper, your parents' divorce decree, your best friend's hand-drawn map of his secret trout-fishing streams—any document that you can maneuver through and use to structure and guide your examination will serve your purposes.

LISTS AND REPETITION

Though we don't include them here, some of the most successful contemporary short stories borrow their structures from lists and create order through repetition. "Girl" by Jamaica Kincaid is structured according to a list of rules and admonitions from a mother to a daughter; "Lust" by Susan Minot recounts the young narrator's sexual encounters with boys and men; and "The Things They Carried" by Tim O'Brien lists the tangible and intangible burdens carried by a group of soldiers in Vietnam. Poets also use repetition. Walt Whitman's "I Hear America Singing" (which can be found in any edition of *Leaves of Grass* or on the Web) is one of the most famous examples of a list poem.

So, too, many essayists have taken to ordering their meditations according to lists. We already have seen one of our authors use repetition as an organizing element of his work. In "The Master of Machines" (Chapter 8), Daniel Rivas subtly uses the phrase "This was my father" to focus and structure his portrait of his father, eventually manipulating his final use of the phrase by casting it in the present tense: "This is my father." Repetition, then, serves as structural glue for the author's meditations and pushes both writer and reader toward reflective analysis.

As discussed earlier, Michelle Morano structures her essay "Grammar Lessons" around the rules of the subjunctive mood in Spanish. Each rule on the list provides an opportunity for her to narrate sections of her story about her depressed boyfriend and her recent move to Spain. In addition to providing a nontraditional framework for her essay, the rules for using the subjunctive mood in Spanish (to express uncertainty, doubt, hope, feeling, etc.) imbue the essay with thematic significance. The rules for the subjunctive become intertwined with the emotional heart of the story, because, as we all know, little about love, or human relationships, is ever really certain.

GRAMMAR LESSONS: THE SUBJUNCTIVE MOOD

THINK OF IT THIS WAY: learning to use the subjunctive mood is like learning to drive a stick shift. It's like failing in love with a car that isn't new or sporty but has a tilt steering wheel and a price you can afford. It's like being so in love with the possibilities, with the places you might go and the experiences you might have, that you pick up your new used car without quite knowing how to drive it, sputtering and stalling and rolling backward at every light. Then you drive the car each day for months, until the stalling stops and you figure out how to downshift, until you can hear the engine's registers and move through them with grace. And later, after you've gained control over the driving and lost control over so much else, you sell the car and most of your possessions and move yourself to Spain, to a place where language and circumstance will help you understand the subjunctive.

Remember that the subjunctive is a mood, not a tense. Verb tenses tell *when* something happens; moods tell *how true*. It's easy to skim over moods in a new language, to translate the words and think you've understood, which is why your first months in Spain will lack nuance. But eventually, after enough conversations have passed, enough hours of talking with your students at the University of Oviedo and your housemate, Lola, and the friends you make when you wander the streets looking like a foreigner, you'll discover that you need the subjunctive in order to finish a question, or an answer, or a thought you couldn't have had without it.

In language, as in life, moods are complicated, but at least in language there are only two. The indicative mood is for knowledge, facts, absolutes, for describing what's real or definite. You'd use the indicative to say, for example:

> *I was in love.*
> Or, *The man I loved tried to kill himself.*
> Or, *I moved to Spain because the man I loved, the man who*
> *tried to kill himself, was driving me insane.*

The indicative helps you tell what happened or is happening or will happen in the future (when you believe you know for sure what the future will bring).

The subjunctive mood, on the other hand, is uncertain. It helps you tell what could have been or might be or what you want but may not get. You'd use the subjunctive to say:

> *I thought he'd improve without me.*
> Or, *I left so that he'd begin to take care of himself.*

Or later, after your perspective has been altered, by time and distance and a couple of *cervezas* in a brightly lit bar, you might say:

> *I deserted him* (indicative).
> *I left him alone with his crazy self for a year* (indicative).
> *Because I hoped* (after which begins the subjunctive) *that being apart might allow us to*
> *come together again.*

English is losing the subjunctive mood. It lingers in some constructions ("If he *were* dead . . . ," for example), but it's no longer pervasive. That's the beauty and also the danger of English — that the definite and the might-be often look so much alike. And it's the reason why, during a period in your life when everything feels hypothetical, Spain will be a very seductive place to live.

In Spanish, verbs change to accommodate the subjunctive in every tense, and the rules, which are many and varied, have exceptions. In the beginning you may feel defeated by this, even hopeless and angry sometimes. But eventually, in spite of your frustration with trying to explain, you'll know in the part of your mind that holds your stories, the part where grammar is felt before it's understood, that the uses of the subjunctive matter.

1. *With* Ojalá

Ojalá means "I hope" or, more literally, "that Allah is willing." It's one of the many words left over from the Moorish occupation of Spain, one that's followed by the subjunctive mood because, of course, you never know for sure what Allah has in mind.

During the first months in Spain, you'll use the word by itself, a kind of dangling wish. "It's supposed to rain," Lola will say, and you'll respond, *"Ojalá."* You'll know you're confusing her, leaving her to figure out whether you want the rain or not, but sometimes the mistakes are too hard to bear. "That Allah is willing it wouldn't have raining," you might accidentally say. And besides, so early into this year of living freely, you're not quite sure what to hope for.

Each time you say *ojalá*, it will feel like a prayer, the *ja* and *la* like breaths, like faith woven right into the language. It will remind you of La Mezquita, the enormous, graceful mosque in Córdoba. Of being eighteen years old and visiting Spain for the first time, how you stood in the courtyard filled with orange trees, trying to admire the building before you. You had a fever then, a summer virus you hadn't yet recognized because it was so hot outside. Too hot to lift a hand to fan your face. Too hot to wonder why your head throbbed and the world spun slowly around you.

Inside, the darkness felt like cool water covering your eyes, such contrast, such relief. And then the pillars began to emerge, rows and rows of pillars supporting red-and-white brick arches, a massive stone ceiling balanced above them like a thought. You swam behind the guide, not even trying to understand his words but soothed by the vastness, by the shadows. Each time you felt dizzy you looked up toward the arches, the floating stone. Toward something that felt, you realized uncomfortably, like God. Or Allah. Or whatever force inspired people to defy gravity this way.

Ten years later, after you've moved to Oviedo, the man you left behind in New York will come to visit. You'll travel south with him, returning to La Mezquita on a January afternoon when the air is mild and the orange trees wave tiny green fruit. He'll carry the guidebook, checking it periodically to get the history straight, while you try to reconcile the place before you with the place in your memory, comparing the shadows of this low sun with the light of another season.

You'll be here because you want this man to see La Mezquita. You want him to feel the mystery of a darkness that amazes and consoles, that makes you feel the presence in empty spaces of something you can't explain. Approaching the shadow of the door, you'll both untie the sweaters from around your waists, slipping your arms into them and then into each other's. He will squint and you will hold your breath. *Ojalá*, you'll think, glimpsing in the shadows the subjunctive mood at work.

2. *After Words of Suasion and Negation*

In Oviedo, you'll become a swimmer. Can you imagine? Two or three times a week you'll pack a bag and walk for thirty-five minutes to the university pool, where you'll place clothes and contact lenses in a locker, then sink into a crowded lane. The pool is a mass of blurry heads and arms, some of which know what they're doing and most of which, like you, are flailing. You keep bumping into people as you make your way from one end of the pool to the other, but no one gets upset, and you reason that any form of motion equals exercise.

Then one day a miracle happens. You notice the guy in the next lane swimming like a pro, his long arms cutting ahead as he glides rhythmically, stroke-stroke-breath. You see and hear and feel the rhythm, and before long you're following him, stroking when he strokes, breathing when he breathes. He keeps getting away, swimming three laps to your every one, so you wait at the edge of the pool for him to come back, then follow again, practicing. At the end of an hour, you realize that this man you don't know, a man you wouldn't recognize clothed, has taught you to swim. To breathe. To use the water instead of fighting against it. For this alone, you'll later say, it was worth moving to Spain.

Stroke-stroke-breath becomes the rhythm of your days, the rhythm of your life in Oviedo. All through the fall months, missing him the way you'd miss a limb, your muscles strain to create distance. Shallow end to deep end and back, you're swimming away.

From memories of abrupt mood shifts. From the way a question, a comment, a person walking past a restaurant window could transform him into a hunched-over man wearing anger like a shawl. From the echo of your own voice trying to be patient and calm, saying, "Listen to me. I want you to call the doctor." In English you said "listen" and "call," and they were the same words you'd use to relate a fact instead of make a plea. But in Spanish, in the language that fills your mind as you swim continually away, the moment you try to persuade someone, or dissuade, you enter the realm of the subjunctive. The verb ends differently so there can be no mistake: requesting is not at all the same as getting.

3. With Si *or* Como Si

Si means "if." *Como si* means "as if." A clause that begins with *si* or *como si* is followed by the subjunctive when the meaning is hypothetical or contrary to fact. For example:

If I'd known he would harm himself, I wouldn't have left him alone.

But here we have to think about whether the if-clause really is contrary to fact. Two days before, you'd asked him what he felt like doing that night, and he'd responded, "I feel like jumping off the Mid-Hudson Bridge." He'd looked serious when he said it, and even so, you'd replied, "Really? Would you like me to drive you there?" *As if* "it were a joke.

If you had known he was serious, that he was thinking of taking his life, would you have replied with such sarcasm? In retrospect it seems impossible not to have known — the classic signs were there. For weeks he'd been sad, self-pitying. He'd been sleeping too much, getting up to teach his freshman composition class in the morning, then going home some days and staying in bed until evening. His sense of humor had waned. He'd begun asking the people around him to cheer him up, make him feel better, please.

And yet he'd been funny. Ironic, self-deprecating, hyperbolic. So no one's saying you should have known, just that maybe you felt a hint of threat in his statement about the river. And maybe that angered you because it meant you were failing to be enough for him. Maybe you were tired too, in need of cheering up yourself because suddenly your perfect guy had turned inside out. Or maybe that realization came later, after you'd had the time and space to develop theories.

The truth is, only you know what you know. And what you know takes the indicative, remember?

For example: You knew he was hurting himself. The moment you saw the note on his office door, in the campus building where you were supposed to meet him on a Sunday afternoon, you knew. The note said, "I'm not feeling well. I'm going home. I guess I'll see you tomorrow." He didn't use your name.

You tried calling him several times, but there was no answer, so you drove to the apartment he shared with another graduate student. The front door was unlocked, but his bedroom door wouldn't budge. You knocked steadily but not too loudly, because his housemate's bedroom door was also closed and you assumed he was inside taking a nap. *If* you'd known that his housemate was not actually home, you would have broken down the door. That scenario is hypothetical, so it takes the subjunctive — even though you're quite sure.

The human mind can reason its way around anything. On the drive to your own apartment, you told yourself, He's angry with me. That's why the door was locked, why he wouldn't answer the phone. You thought, If he weren't so close to his family, I'd really be worried. If today weren't Mother's Day. If he didn't talk so affectionately about his parents. About his brother and sisters. About our future. If, if, if.

When the phone rang and there was silence on the other end, you began to shout, "What have you done?"

In Spain, late at night over *chupitos* of bourbon or brandy, you and Lola will trade stories. Early on, you won't understand a lot of what she says, and she'll understand what you say but not what you mean. You won't know how to say what you mean in Spanish; sometimes you won't even know how to say it in English. But as time goes on, the stories you tell will become more complicated. More subtle. More grammatically daring. You'll begin to feel more at ease in the unreal.

For example: *If* you hadn't gone straight home from his apartment. *If* you hadn't answered the phone. *If* you hadn't jumped back into your car to drive nine miles in record time, hoping the whole way to be stopped by the police. *If* you hadn't met him on the porch, where he had staggered in blood-soaked clothes. *If* you hadn't rushed upstairs for a towel and discovered a flooded bedroom floor, the blood separating into water and rust-colored clumps. *If* you hadn't been available for this emergency.

As the months pass in Spain, you'll begin to risk the *then*. His housemate would have come home and found him the way you found him: deep gashes in his arm, but the wounds clotting enough to keep him alive, enough to narrowly avoid a transfusion. His housemate would have called the paramedics, ridden to the hospital in the ambulance, notified his parents from the emergency room, and greeted them after their three-hour drive. His housemate would have done all the things you did, and he would have cleaned the mess by himself instead of with your help, the two of you borrowing a neighbor's wet-dry vac and working diligently until you — or he — or both of you — burst into hysterical laughter. Later this housemate would have moved to a new apartment, just as he has done, and would probably be no worse off than he is right now.

You, on the other hand, would have felt ashamed, guilty, remiss for not being available in a time of crisis. But you wouldn't have found yourself leaning over a stretcher in the emergency room, a promise slipping from your mouth before you could think it through: "I won't leave you. Don't worry, I won't leave you." As *if* it were true.

4. *After Impersonal Expressions*

Such as *it is possible, it is a shame, it is absurd*.

"*It's possible* that I'm making things worse in some ways," you told the counselor you saw on Thursday afternoons. He'd been out of the hospital for a few months by then and had a habit of missing his therapy appointments, to which you could respond only by signing up for your own.

She asked how you were making things worse, and you explained that when you told him you needed to be alone for a night and he showed up anyway at eleven, pleading to stay over, you couldn't turn him away. She said, "*It's a shame* he won't honor your request," and you pressed your fingernails into the flesh of your palm to keep your eyes from filling. She asked why you didn't want him to stay over, and you said that sometimes you just wanted to sleep, without waking up when he went to the bathroom and listening to make sure he came back to bed instead of taking all the Tylenol in the medicine cabinet. Or sticking his head in the gas oven. Or diving from the balcony onto the hillside three stories below. There is nothing, you told her, nothing I haven't thought of.

She said, "Do you think he's manipulating you?" and you answered in the mood of certainty, "Yes. Absolutely." Then you asked, "*Isn't it absurd* that I let him manipulate me?" and what you wanted, of course, was some reassurance that it wasn't absurd. That you were a normal person, reacting in a normal way to a crazy situation.

Instead she said, "Let's talk about why you let him. Let's talk about what's in this for you."

5. After Verbs of Doubt or Emotion

You didn't think he was much of a prospect at first. Because he seemed arrogant. Because in the initial meetings for new instructors, he talked as if he were doing it the right way and the rest of you were pushovers. Because he looked at you with one eye squinted, as if he couldn't quite decide.

You liked that he was funny, a little theatrical, and a great fan of supermarkets. At ten, after evening classes ended, he'd say, "Are you going home?" Sometimes you'd offer to drop him off at his place. Sometimes you'd agree to go out for a beer. And sometimes you'd say, "Yeah, but I have to go to the store first," and his eyes would light up. In the supermarket he'd push the cart and you'd pick items off the shelf. Maybe you'd turn around and there would be a whole rack of frozen ribs in your cart, or after you put them back, three boxes of Lucky Charms. Maybe he'd be holding a package of pfeffernusse and telling a story about his German grandmother. Maybe it would take two hours to run your errand because he was courting you in ShopRite.

You doubted that you'd sleep with him a second time. After the first time, you both lay very still for a while, flat on your backs, not touching. He seemed to be asleep. You watched the digital clock hit two-thirty a.m. and thought about finding your turtleneck and sweater and wool socks, lacing up your boots, and heading out into the snow. And then out of the blue he rolled toward you, pulled the blanket up around your shoulders, and said, "Is there anything I can get you? A cup of tea? A sandwich?"

You were thrilled at the breaks in his depression, breaks that felt like new beginnings, every time. Days, sometimes even weeks, when he seemed more like himself than ever before. Friends would ask how he was doing, and he'd offer a genuine smile. "Much better," he'd say, putting his arm around you. "She's pulling me through the death-wish phase." Everyone would laugh with relief, and at those moments you'd feel luckier than ever before, because of the contrast.

Do you see the pattern?

6. To Express Good Wishes

Que tengas muy buen viaje, Lola will say, kissing each of your cheeks before leaving you off at the bus station. *May you have a good trip.* A hope, a wish, a prayer of sorts, even without the *ojalá*.

The bus ride from Oviedo to Madrid is nearly six hours, so you have a lot of time for imagining. It's two days after Christmas, and you know he spent the holiday at his parents' house, that he's there right now, maybe eating breakfast, maybe packing. Tonight his father will drive him to Kennedy Airport, and tomorrow morning, very early, you'll meet him at Barajas in Madrid. You try to envision what he'll look like, the expression on his face when he sees you, but you're having trouble recalling what it's like to be in his presence.

You try not to hope too much, although now, four months into your life in Spain, you want to move toward instead of away. Toward long drives on winding mountain roads, toward the cathedral of Toledo, the mosque at Córdoba, the Alhambra in Granada. Toward romantic dinners along the Mediterranean. Toward a new place from which to view the increasingly distant past. You want this trip to create a separation, in your mind and in his, between your first relationship and your real relationship, the one that will be so wonderful, so stable, you'll never leave him again.

Once you've reached Madrid and found the *pensión* where you've reserved a room, you'll get the innkeeper to help you make an international call. His father will say, "My God, he can't sit still today," and then there will be his voice, asking how your bus ride was, where you are, how far from the airport. You'll say, "I'll see you in the morning." He'll reply, "In seventeen hours."

The next morning, the taxi driver is chatty. He wants to know why you're going to the airport without luggage, and your voice is happy and excited when you explain. He asks whether this boyfriend writes you letters, and you smile and nod at the reflection in the rearview mirror. "Many letters?" he continues. "Do you enjoy receiving the letters?" In Spain you're always having odd conversations with strangers, so you hesitate only a moment, wondering why he cares, and then you say, "Yes. Very much." He nods emphatically, "*Muy bien.*" At the terminal he drops you off with a broad smile. "*Que lo pases bien con tu novio,*" he says. *Have a good time with your boyfriend.* In his words you hear the requisite subjunctive mood.

7. In Adverbial Clauses Denoting Purpose, Provision, Exception

How different to walk down the street in Madrid, Toledo, Córdoba, to notice an elaborate fountain or a tiny car parked half on the sidewalk, and comment aloud. You've loved being alone in Spain, and now, even more, you love being paired.

On the fifth day you reach Granada, find lodging in someone's home. Down the hallway you can hear the family watching TV, cooking, preparing to celebrate New Year's Eve.

In the afternoon you climb the long, slow hill leading to the Alhambra and spend hours touring the complex. You marvel at the elaborate irrigation system, the indoor baths with running water, the stunning mosaic tiles and views of the Sierra Nevada. Here is the room where Boabdil signed the city's surrender to Ferdinand and Isabella; here is where Washington Irving lived while writing *Tales of the Alhambra*. Occasionally you separate, as he inspects a mural and you follow a hallway into a lush courtyard, each of your imaginations working to restore this place to its original splendor. When you come together again, every time, there's a thrill.

He looks rested, relaxed, strolling through the gardens with his hands tucked into the front pockets of his pants. When you enter the Patio of the Lions — the famous courtyard where a circle of marble lions projects water into a reflecting pool — he turns to you wide-eyed, his face as open as a boy's.

"Isn't it pretty?" you keep asking, feeling shy because what you mean is "Are you glad to be here?"

"*So* pretty," he responds, taking hold of your arm, touching his lips to your hair.

The day is perfect, you think. The trip is perfect. You allow yourself a moment of triumph: I left him *so that* he would get better without me, and he did. I worked hard and saved money and invited him on this trip *in case* there's still hope for us. And there is.

Unless. In language, as in experience, we have purpose, provision, exception. None of which necessarily matches reality, and all of which take the subjunctive.

On the long walk back down the hill toward your room, he turns quiet. You find yourself talking more than usual, trying to fill the empty space with cheerful commentary, but it doesn't help. The shape of his face begins to change until there it is again, that landscape of furrows and crags. The jaw thrusts slightly, lips pucker, eyebrows arch as if to say, "I don't care. About anything."

Back in the room, you ask him what's wrong, plead with him to tell you. You can talk about anything, you assure him, anything at all. And yet you're stunned when his brooding turns accusatory. He says it isn't fair. You don't understand how difficult it is to be him. Your life is easy, so easy that even moving to a new country, taking up a new language, is effortless. While every day is a struggle for him. Don't you see that? Every day is a struggle.

He lowers the window shade and gets into bed, his back turned toward you.

What to do? You want to go back outside into the mild air and sunshine, walk until you remember what it feels like to be completely alone. But you're afraid to leave him. For the duration of his ninety-minute nap, you sit paralyzed. Everything feels unreal: the darkened room, the squeals of children in another part of the house, the burning sensation in your stomach. You tremble, first with sadness and fear, then with anger. Part of you wants to wake him, tell him to collect his things, then drive him back to the airport in Madrid. You want to send him home again, away from your new country, the place where you live unencumbered — but with a good deal of effort, thank you. The other part of you wants to wail, to beat your fists against the wall and howl, *Give him back to me.*

Remember: purpose, provision, exception. The subjunctive runs parallel to reality.

8. After Certain Indications of Time, If the Action Has Not Occurred

While is a subjunctive state of mind. So are *until, as soon as, before,* and *after.* By now you understand why, right? Because until something *has happened,* you can't be sure.

In Tarifa, the wind blows and blows. You learn this even before arriving, as you drive down Route 15 past Gibraltar. You're heading toward the southernmost point in Spain, toward warm sea breezes and a small town off the beaten path. You drive confidently, shifting quickly through the gears to keep pace with the traffic around you. He reclines in the passenger's seat, one foot propped against the dashboard, reading from *The Real Guide*, open against his thigh. "Spreading out beyond its Moorish walls, Tarifa is known in Spain for its abnormally high suicide rate — a result of the unremitting winds that blow across the town and its environs."

You say, "Tell me you're joking." He says, "How's that for luck?" Three days before, you'd stood in Granada's crowded city square at midnight, each eating a grape for every stroke of the New Year. If you eat all twelve grapes in time, tradition says, you'll have plenty of luck in the coming year. It sounds wonderful — such an easy way to secure good fortune — until you start eating and time gets ahead, so far ahead that no matter how fast you chew and swallow, midnight sounds with three grapes left.

In Tarifa, you come down with the flu. It hits hard and fast — one minute you're strolling through a whitewashed coastal town, and the next you're huddled in bed in a stupor. He goes to the pharmacy and, with a handful of Spanish words and many gestures, procures the right medicine. You sleep all day, through the midday meal, through the time of siesta, past sundown, and into the evening. When you wake the room is fuzzy and you're alone, with a vague memory of him rubbing your back, saying something about a movie.

Carefully you rise and make your way to the bathroom — holding on to the bed, the doorway, the sink — then stand on your toes and look out the window into the blackness. By day there's a thin line of blue mountains across the strait, and you imagine catching the ferry at dawn and watching that sliver of Morocco rise up from the shadows to become a whole continent. You imagine standing on the other side and looking back toward the tip of Spain, this tiny town where the winds blow and blow. That's how easy it is to keep traveling once you start, putting distance between the various parts of your life, imagining yourself over and over again into entirely new places.

Chilly and sweating, you make your way back to bed, your stomach fluttering nervously. You think back to Granada, how he'd woken from a nap on that dark afternoon and apologized. "I don't know what got into me today," he'd said. "This hasn't been happening." You believe it's true; it hasn't been happening. But you don't know *how true.*

You think: He's fine now. There's no need to worry. He's been fine for days, happy and calm. I'm overreacting. But overreaction is a slippery slope. With the wind howling continuously outside, the room feels small and isolated. You don't know that he's happy and calm right now, do you? You don't know how he is today at all, because you've slept and slept and barely talked to him.

You think: If the movie started on time — but movies never start on time in Spain, so you add, subtract, try to play it safe, and determine that by ten forty-five your fretting will be justified. At eleven you'll get dressed and go looking, and if you can't find him, what will you do? Wait until midnight for extra measure? And then call the police? And tell them what? That he isn't back yet and you're afraid because you're sick and he's alone and the wind here blows and blows, enough to make people crazy, the book says, make them suicidal? This is the *when*, the *while*, the *until*. The *before* and *after*. The real and the unreal in precarious balance. This is what you moved to Spain to escape from, and here it is again, following you.

The next time you wake, the room seems brighter, more familiar. You sit up and squint against the light. His cheeks are flushed, hair mussed from the wind. His eyes are clear as a morning sky. "Hi, sweetie," he says, putting a hand on your forehead. "You still have a fever. How do you feel?" He smells a little musty, like the inside of a community theater where not many people go on a Sunday night in early January. He says, "The movie was hilarious." You ask whether he understood it, and he shrugs. Then he acts out a scene using random Spanish words as a voice-over, and you laugh and cough until he flops down on his stomach beside you.

Here it comes again, the contrast between what was, just a little while ago, and what is now. After all this time and all these miles, you're both here, in a Spanish town with a view of Africa. You feel amazed, dizzy, as if swimming outside yourself. You're talking with him, but you're also watching yourself talk with him. And then you're sleeping and watching yourself sleep, dreaming and dunking about the dreams. Throughout the night you move back and forth, here and there, between what is and what might be, tossed by language and possibility and the constantly shifting wind.

9. In Certain Independent Clauses

There's something extraordinary — isn't there? — about learning to speak Spanish as an adult, about coming to see grammar as a set of guidelines not just for saying what you mean but for understanding the way you live. There's something extraordinary about thinking in a language that insists on marking the limited power of desire.

For example: At Barajas Airport in Madrid, you walk him to the boarding gate. He turns to face you, hands on your arms, eyes green as the sea. He says, "Only a few more months and we'll be together for good. Right, sweetie?" He watches your face, waiting for a response, but you know this isn't a decision, something you can say yes to. So you smile, eyes burning, and give a slight nod. What you mean is, *I hope so*. What you think is, *Ojalá*. And what you know is this: The subjunctive is the mood of mystery. Of luck. Of faith interwoven with doubt. It's a held breath, a hand reaching out, carefully touching wood. It's humility, deference, the opposite of hubris. And it's going to take a long time to master.

But at least the final rule of usage is simple, self-contained, one you can commit to memory: Certain independent clauses exist only in the subjunctive mood, lacing optimism with resignation, hope with heartache. *Be that as it may*, for example. Or the phrase one says at parting, eyes closed as if in prayer: *May all go well with you*.

—2005

Learning from Other Writers (Morano)

1. This essay is written in the second person ("you"). What is the effect of this rhetorical strategy?

2. Morano begins with an analogy between learning to use the subjunctive mood and learning to drive a stick shift car. What is the subtext of this analogy? That is, what do learning to drive a manual transmission and learning to use the subjunctive mood have in common? What do they stand for metaphorically?

3. Morano uses an alternative structure to shape her essay, which means that (within her list of rules) she reveals her story in a non-chronological fashion. Why do you think she makes this choice? How does she pace the revelation of new pieces of information without manipulating or confusing the reader? How do the rules of the subjunctive and the way she describes these rules allow her to give us, or hint at, more crucial information?

4. Following the fifth rule, "After Doubt or Emotion," Morano provides details of her initial courtship. Why are these details important? Why do you think she chooses not to place these details in the opening section of the essay? At the end of this section, when she asks, "Do you see a pattern?," whom is she addressing? Is there both an implied and direct "you" here?

5. Note the arrangement of these rules. Why do you think Morano begins with the rule "With *Ojala*" and ends with "In Certain Independent Clauses"?

6. Morano concludes by saying that "certain independent clauses exist only in the subjunctive mood, lacing optimism with resignation, hope with heartache." How does this conclusion relate to her relationship with her boyfriend and the essay as a whole? Why is the word "independent" significant?

Adding Your Voice

In the 2011 romantic comedy *No Strings Attached*, the character played by Ashton Kutcher makes Natalie Portman's character—an emotionally detached young doctor—a "period" mix. Yes. All the songs have to do with, you guessed it, menstruation: bleeding, flow, the color red, etc. The effect is humorously deplorable. But the mix represents a blundered attempt by Kutcher's character to gain more emotional intimacy with the woman with whom he is having sex. The ups and downs typical of all romantic comedies ensue, and after the Portman character has realized what she has lost, we see her driving around in the middle of the night, listening to one of the songs, singing and crying: "Keep bleeding, I keep, keep bleeding." The mix provides a physical touchstone for the emotional undercurrents of the story.

Movie soundtracks often provide signposts for a movie, and a playlist can do the same for an essay. Make a music mix or a playlist of songs organized with a specific person, place, or theme in mind, and then freewrite on what each song might represent or what images it brings to mind. Try not to be too literal: you don't want to spend too much time discussing the song and its lyrics, but rather use the playlist as a scaffolding device. You might include a song you heard on your first date, or the band you went to see the night before you broke up. Think of what *story* your musical arrangement of songs might be telling about that time in your life, that relationship, that place, or the theme around which you have arranged your mix. The list of songs might provide a structure to your essay in the same way that the rules of the subjunctive mood provide a structure to Michelle Morano's "Grammar Lessons."

Another way to try this is to work *backward* from an existing mix. Find an old mix that you made (two of the authors of this textbook, Natalie and Jeremiah, at one time in their lives created many mix tapes, though you probably burned your mixes on CDs or created playlists on your iPod) and think about what was going on in your life at the time. Was the mix created for a specific person? A specific event, such as your eighteenth birthday or an after-prom party? Mood music to drive to? Freewrite on the memory each song conjures. Is a story emerging? A driving question about that time in your life? A claim you can articulate about how and why certain songs *needed* to be back-to-back, or how the pacing of the mix functioned to convey meaning?

CHAPTER 15

Spatial Forms

We have seen the way authors use narrative to organize and present their material, but some of the most original and effective essays rely more heavily on movements through space than movements through time. To understand what this means, imagine walking down Main Street of the small town where you grew up. What memories would emerge as you pass this store or that restaurant? Maybe you worked behind the counter at the local pharmacy one summer and waited tables at the pizza place on weekends during your senior year. Maybe you visited certain restaurants and stores only with your mother or father. Likewise, imagine the bus route that you took each day to elementary school. Think of the memories embedded at each stop along the way. Any site that you can map—your backyard, a roller-skating rink, a gymnastics center—has the potential to serve as the organizing principle for a spatial essay.

You might find it helpful to think of a spatial essay as resembling a tour, which differs from a journey or a quest only in that the writer is already *there* when the essay starts (i.e., a tour usually realizes a movement from place to place or object to object within a house, museum, or park). Joan Didion's iconic and melancholy reflections on why she can't stop thinking about the Hoover Dam constitute a perfect example of the analysis that can develop when a writer tours a site she finds rich in meaning.

In "Ranch House," Eileen uses the rooms of her parents' 1950s ranch-style house in upstate New York to paint an eerie portrait of her childhood. By cataloging the carefully organized contents of her parents' closets, the remedies stocked in the family's medicine cabinets, the utensils and cleaning supplies on the shelves and in the drawers of her mother's avocado-green kitchen, the scary (though perfectly ordinary) items in the basement, and the sparse, sad furnishings of her grandmother's attic apartment, Eileen tries to convey how determined her parents were to shelter her and her siblings from the realities of their not-so-distant immigrant past.

While the house serves as the structuring device for the author's meditations, moving as it does from closet to closet and room to room, the essay's significance arises from the precise, deadpan language she uses to catalogue and describe the items in those closets and rooms and the way in which the house and all the objects in it represent a microcosm of a larger truth about what it means to grow up the middle-class child or grandchild of immigrants. This is the key to a successful spatial essay: the significance of the subject must extend beyond the scaffolding used to frame or build the essay's contents.

Although not included here, there are many wonderful examples of this model. Lawrence Weschler, in his bizarre and brilliant book *Mr. Wilson's Cabinet of Wonders*, takes his readers on a tour of the exhibits they would encounter if they were fortunate enough to visit the mind-bending Museum of Jurassic Technology in Los Angeles. And in his frequently anthologized essay "Where Worlds Collide," Pico Iyer ponders the ironies and complexities of our multiracial nation while wandering the vast interior spaces of the weirdly outdated LAX airport in Los Angeles.

Joan Didion

AT THE DAM

Since the afternoon in 1967 when I first saw Hoover Dam, its image has never been entirely absent from my inner eye. I will be talking to someone in Los Angeles, say, or New York, and suddenly the dam will materialize, its pristine concave face gleaming white against the harsh rusts and taupes and mauves of that rock canyon hundreds or thousands of miles from where I am. I will be driving down Sunset Boulevard, or about to enter a freeway, and abruptly those power transmission towers will appear before me, canted vertiginously over the tailrace. Sometimes I am confronted by the intakes and sometimes by the shadow of the heavy cable that spans the canyon and sometimes by the ominous outlets to unused spillways, black in the lunar clarity of the desert light. Quite often I hear the turbines. Frequently I wonder what is happening at the dam this instant, at this precise intersection of time and space, how much water is being released to fill downstream orders and what lights are flashing and which generators are in full use and which just spinning free.

I used to wonder what it was about the dam that made me think of it at times and in places where I once thought of the Mindanao Trench, or of the stars wheeling in their courses, or of the words *As it was in the beginning, is now and ever shall be, world without end, amen.* Dams, after all, are commonplace: we have all seen one. This particular dam had existed as an idea in the world's mind for almost forty years before I saw it. Hoover Dam, showpiece of the Boulder Canyon project, the several million tons of concrete that made the Southwest plausible, the *fait accompli* that was to convey, in the innocent time of its construction, the notion that mankind's brightest promise lay in American engineering.

Of course the dam derives some of its emotional effect from precisely that aspect, that sense of being a monument to a faith since misplaced. "They died to make the desert bloom," reads a plaque dedicated to the 96 men who died building this first of the great high dams, and in context the worn phrase touches, suggests all of that trust in harnessing resources, in the melliorative power of the dynamo, so central to the early Thirties. Boulder City, built in 1931 as the construction town for the dam, retains the ambience of a model city, a new town, a toy triangular grid of green lawns and trim bungalows, all fanning out from the Reclamation building. The bronze sculptures at the dam itself evoke muscular citizens of a tomorrow that never came, sheaves of wheat clutched heavenward, thunderbolts defied. Winged Victories guard the flagpole. The flag whips in the canyon wind. An empty Pepsi-Cola can clatters across the terrazzo. The place is perfectly frozen in time.

But history does not explain it all, does not entirely suggest what makes that dam so affecting. Nor, even, does energy, the massive involvement with power and pressure and the transparent sexual overtones to that involvement. Once when I revisited the dam I walked through it with a man from the Bureau of Reclamation. For a while we trailed behind a guided tour, and then we went on, went into parts of the dam where visitors do not generally go. Once in a while he would explain something, usually in that recondite language having to do with "peaking power," with "outages" and "dewatering," but on the whole we spent the afternoon in a world so alien, so complete and so beautiful unto itself that it was scarcely necessary to speak at all. We saw almost no one. Cranes moved above us as if under their own volition. Generators roared. Transformers hummed. The gratings on which we stood vibrated. We watched a hundred-ton steel shaft plunging down to that place where the water was. And finally we got down to that place where the water was, where the water sucked out of Lake Mead roared through thirty-foot penstocks and then into thirteen-foot penstocks and finally into the turbines themselves. "Touch it," the Reclamation said, and I did, and for a long time I just stood there with my hands on the turbine. It was a peculiar moment, but so explicit as to suggest nothing beyond itself.

There was something beyond all that, something beyond energy, beyond history, something I could not fix in my mind. When I came up from the dam that day the wind was blowing harder, through the canyon and all across the Mojave. Later, toward Henderson and Las Vegas, there would be dust blowing, blowing past the Country-Western Casino FRI & SAT NITES and blowing past the Shrine of Our Lady of Safe Journey STOP & PRAY, but out at the dam there was no dust, only the rock and the dam and a little greasewood and a few garbage cans, their tops chained, banging against a fence. I walked across the marble star map that traces a sidereal revolution of the equinox and fixes forever, the Reclamation man had told me, for all time and for all people who can read the stars, the date the dam was dedicated. The star map was, he had said, for when we were all gone and the dam was left. I had not thought much of it when he said it, but I thought of it then, with the wind whining and the sun dropping behind a mesa with the finality of a sunset in space. Of course that was the image I had seen always, seen it without quite realizing what I saw, a dynamo finally free of man, splendid at last in its absolute isolation, transmitting power and releasing water to a world where no one is.

—1970

Learning from Other Writers (Didion)

1. What is Didion's driving question about the Hoover Dam? Why does she expect her readers to care about her question?

2. What is the source of the quote in paragraph two ("As it was in the beginning, is now and ever shall be, world without end, amen")? What is the function of this quote in the essay as a whole?

3. How does each part of the Hoover Dam contribute to the author's meditation on her driving question?

4. In the first section of the essay, Didion presents an image of the Hoover Dam as reflected in her mind's eye. In the second section, she takes us on a tour of the actual dam. What is her strategy in the final paragraph (i.e., from what perspective is she viewing the dam)? What is the effect of this strategy on your understanding of the essay's driving question?

5. Locate a copy of the poem "Ozymandias" by Percy Bysshe Shelley (it's readily available on the Web). Discuss the ways in which Didion's essay alludes to or borrows from Shelley's poem in terms of style, tone, theme, and/or structure. Should Didion have made her allusions and borrowings more explicit?

Eileen Pollack

RANCH HOUSE

In 1954, my parents drove around Long Island until they found a house they liked. They wrote away to get the plans, then built a similar house in the town we lived in. Bad enough to grow up in a cookie-cutter ranch house on Long Island; how much worse to grow up in upstate New York, in a cookie-cutter copy of a cookie-cutter ranch house on Long Island.

But my parents liked the way the ranch house looked, and the rooms were considered large ("although they wouldn't be anything now," my mother says). The house was completely new—no one had ever died there, no one had been poor or sick. Although my father worried how he could afford the mortgage of a hundred and five a month, my mother assured him that his dental practice would only grow and the house would cost less to maintain and heat than an older, cheaper dwelling.

If you are like me and grew up comfortably middle class, you find it hard to credit the poverty and despair that drove your parents to strive to become middle class in the first place. My parents' parents all were immigrants. My mother's father died when she was young; her mother went to work selling hats at Macy's, and my mother took a job as secretary for a man who kept trying to pinch her bottom. My father grew up at his parents' shabby hotel in the Catskills, where the family spent the summer hustling to please the guests and the rest of the year huddling to keep warm in the bungalow across the street and living off whatever groceries remained in the pantry at season's end.

My father and the other Jewish men who survived the war used their GI loans to build ranch houses on two streets carved from a pasture that until then had been owned by a farmer named Champlain. Like most fifties parents, mine viewed their role as providing their children with an orderly, hygienic home, the best medical care money could buy, and a college education. I didn't spend much time with either parent, and, when I did, we didn't discuss our inner lives. One of my few opportunities to feel close to my mother came when I sat outside her bathroom and watched her shave. Her body hair seemed erotic. And I coveted her electric razor, with its sleek turquoise body and the stainless steel blades you popped up with a button and cleaned with a tiny brush.

My most intimate moments with my father revolved around shaving, too. He would lean back and close his eyes while I patted his cheeks with cream, then shaved him with his double-edged chrome Gillette. I was only five, so the razor didn't contain a blade, but I enjoyed the nearness to my father's flesh, the Vitalis he allowed me to smooth through his hair, and the way, when I was done, he would snap his fingers and chant:"Shave and a haircut [snap snap] two bits," then hand me a quarter, which I didn't realize at the time was "two bits."

Then I came upon him finishing a real shave, after which he ejected something shiny and thin into a slot at the back of his medicine cabinet. "What was that?" I asked.

"What was what? The blade? You can't shave without a blade, pussycat. That's what cuts off the beard."

I might have felt cheated, except that when my father showed me how sharp a blade could be, I grew dizzy and nearly fainted. I asked where the used blades went, and my father said they fell to the basement through a space in the wall, leaving me to think about the walls of our house filling up with razor blades.

I think about them still.

Whenever my parents left the house, I would open my mother's drawers and rifle through the sachet-scented slips, underpants, brassieres, and scarves. In her closet hung immaculately laundered blouses and skirts; upside down on a rack along the floor were her impossibly narrow shoes, as if dozens of Rockettes lay buried beneath the boards.

The same infuriating order reigned in my father's closet. His suit coats hung on shoulder-shaped wooden hangers; each carefully polished shoe lay impaled on a wooden shoetree as jointed and realistic as the ankle and foot of a marionette. This bothered me more than the rifle that leaned in the corner. I wasn't any more afraid of my father's guns than I feared the ammunition belts and canteens he had brought home from the war—I loved to strap these on when I played soldier with my brother.

What I found scarier was the label gun in that closet. Why did everything need a label? Was anything so unusual in our house that we didn't know what it was? I would sneak the gun from its shelf and dial each letter of my name, pulling the trigger as a blue plastic tape poked from the mouth like a lettered tongue.

Until one time the tape got stuck. Panicked, I loosened the screw that held the halves together, at which point the insides came flying out. I spirited the pieces to my room, then spent a wretched hour jamming them back inside, until, in despair, I fit the label gun in its box and replaced it in the closet, not revealing what I had done until forty years later, when my father lay dying in Florida. "So *that's* what happened to that label gun!" he said, relief washing across his face.

Perhaps the incident with the label gun haunted me because I was so uneasy about my own insides coming out. My parents were obsessed with our bowel movements, the one aspect of our health they felt able to control. And every fifties parent lived in fear of the polio epidemic that had crippled so many kids; even now, my mother thinks I will be stricken by paralysis if I sit around for more than a few minutes in a damp bathing suit.

My parents were so preoccupied with our bodies that I became hypervigilant as well. It was as if they had erected an electrified fence around our house, and instead of this making me feel secure, I wandered the perimeter, peering out to see what had frightened them. Nothing gave me greater pleasure than going through my father's drawers and coming upon the heavy red pen-light whose beam I loved to shine down my mirrored throat; or the blood pressure cuff I wrapped around my arm and pumped with a rubber bulb until I felt as musclebound as Popeye; or my father's stethoscope, with its deliriously creepy yellow tubes, valentine-shaped earpieces that fit neatly inside my ears, and shiny, cold head that I pressed against my chest to hear my own heart beat (*but-but, but-but, but-BUT*), unless it was thumbing through my mother's gilt-edged

Merck Manual hoping to find a symptom I might have. (I am probably the last child in America who was able to convince a doctor she had St. Vitus's Dance.)

In the bathroom I shared with my older siblings, I took perverse delight in handling the rubber bulbs my father used to remove wax from our ears and both kinds of thermometers, oral and rectal. Despite my terror of the latter, I longed to play with the mercury inside the bulb, an activity I had been introduced to by my dad, who brought home mercury from his dental office so we children could play with the shimmery quicksilver blobs, which would skitter across a mirror, break into ever-smaller blobs, and then, if we coaxed them back, re-cohere in a single blob that slithered inside the vial, except for the remaining particles that adhered to our skin and lungs.

But the scariest aspect of that bathroom was my parents' insistence that at all times there be a roll of toilet paper on the spindle, with the tissue coming from the bottom, and on the tank a spare roll, its true appearance disguised beneath the dress of a plastic doll, said dress having been crocheted in hot-pink yarn by my grandmother down in Florida. Whoever used the last sheet of toilet paper on the roll on the spindle was obliged to replace that roll with the spare from the top of the toilet, then retrieve a fresh roll from the closet, jam the doll's legs down the center, pull down her skirt, and place that roll on the tank. Once, my father scolded me so excessively for failing to perform that obligatory final step that I took five rolls from the closet, piled them on the tank, and stuffed the doll's legs in the uppermost roll, but purposely neglected to pull down her skirt. Instead, I yanked down the bodice of her dress, dabbed nail-polish nipples on her breasts, and smeared a sensuous leer on her dollish lips. To which my father—no tyrant he—responded by holding up his hands and telling me that I had won.

Although this didn't relieve me from having to obey the rules the next time.

In addition to the rolls of toilet tissue my mother hoarded, the hall closet held towels and sheets she had hung outside to dry, which meant that even on the darkest, coldest winter night you could bury your face in the linens and smell a sky-blue summer's day. However, to do so was to run a risk. Beneath those linens lurked the laundry chute, into which my brother threatened to stuff me. I was afraid of getting stuck, and equally afraid of *not* getting stuck and plunging to the concrete floor below. I was the messy child, the wild child, always tearing my clothes or staining them, and at some level I feared I would someday get washed and bleached and ironed like everything else that went down that chute.

I still dream about that closet. It was the nexus where time and space converged and did magical, nightmarish things. No one in my family ever talked about the Holocaust, but I had picked up enough to know that if Nazis banged down our door, I could hide by lowering myself down the chute and hanging on there with my fingers. So central was that laundry chute to my imagination that I tried to write a book in which it served as a passage from one realm to the next—the wardrobe to Narnia, the rabbit hole to Wonderland—except that I couldn't envision the enchanted world into which my heroine would emerge on the other side.

Perhaps what I craved wasn't an escape from reality so much as a way to burrow from the present to the past and learn what the shiny veneers in my family's ranch house were meant to hide. On nights when my father deigned to show home movies, he would remove the portable screen from the closet and set it up in the living room—the contraption reminded me of a stiff-backed butler who would lean to one side and remove from his pocket a giant handkerchief, which he unfurled before his chest and held patiently while we watched the show. Since I was the youngest, by the time I arrived on the scene my parents had grown tired of taking movies and I felt cheated not to see myself growing up on the screen as my siblings had done. Still, everyone else's lives formed the Old Testament to my New. No wonder my siblings wished I never had come along. How much happier they seemed twirling around the living room at the center of my parents' gaze before their lives were ruined by my late arrival.

In one bit of film, my brother, disguised in an oversized nose, mustache, and Captain Spalding hat, sneaks around the living room waving a wood machete. (On the wall in his room hung an actual steel machete that my father had brought home from India, where he had been stationed during the war, as well as a sword with a three-foot-long triangular blade inscribed with foreign lettering. Sometimes, my brother would take down the steel machete, slide it from its leather scabbard, and describe the damage it might inflict on a human limb; or he would show me the grooves that ran along the sides of my father's triangular sword. "These are the blood gutters," he would say. "You can still make out the stains.") In the home movie, my sister puts her hands to her mouth and screams a silent scream before allowing herself to be tied to a chair, at which point my brother pulls out a magic wand and makes her vanish. He looks around for a second victim and makes my toddler self vanish, too. As much as I enjoyed seeing myself assume this starring role, I couldn't figure out how I had been made to disappear and was troubled by the possibility that my brother truly did have this power and might use it again if I disobeyed him.

So much for the private part of our house. On the way to the public spaces, you passed the two closets in the hall—not only the closet with the chute, but its identical and opposing twin, in which we kept our coats, along with the card table on which my mother and her friends played mahjongg (the mahjongg set was a thing of beauty, with its richly colored racks and hand-painted ivory tiles), the bridge chairs, and the accordion-pleated covers my dad hefted down to protect the mahogany table in the dining room. There was nothing worth exploring in that closet. Our public selves were beyond reproach.[1]

---

[1] The only scary story about that closet concerns my father's hat. Once, my father came down with the flu, and our neighbor stopped by to see him. Mr. Rothblatt put his fedora beside my dad's, then took my father's hat by accident. The next day, when my father dragged himself out of bed to go to work, he put on what he thought was his fedora and started screaming, "Will! Will!" (My mother's name is Wilma, which is frightening in itself.) "The virus must have gone to my brain and swelled my head!"

Nor was there anything scary about our living room, just the usual French provincial furniture, the tinny piano most of us could play with various degrees of lack of talent, the black-and-white television set whose cloth-covered speakers I jabbed with a pencil simply for the satisfaction of watching the point go through—a set replaced much later by a color console that had a stereo, although we owned few records besides *Fiddler on the Roof,* a comedy routine by Myron Cohen, and that album by the guy who could imitate all the Kennedys.

Back when my father still made fires, he might bring up firewood from the basement, then get down on his knees and look up the chimney to make *absolutely sure* the flue was open, after which he lit the kindling and drew the metallic curtains shut. I loved everything about those fires—the poker my brother used for stirring up the flames, the chenille rug my mother spread across the hearth, the long-handled fork she brought in from the kitchen so we could jab marshmallows into the flames until they lit up like sugary torches. But my father stopped building fires, his excuse being that if there was a fire in the fireplace, the thermostat, which was situated in the living room, thought the whole house was warm and didn't heat the other rooms, an excuse that made no sense since the only time this happened we were gathered comfortably around the fire and didn't mind the other rooms being cold. I think his edict had more to do with the absurdity of devoting so much care to maintaining a house, only to build a fire that threatened to burn it down. My mother put a plastic fern on the andirons, and, decade after decade, the wood in the basement grew so dry it might have burst into flames of its own accord, not to mention that it was stacked inches from the furnace.

In the kitchen, every item glowed with the pride and care my mother had bestowed on acquiring and maintaining it. Among the objects I loved were the heavy steel garlic-press, which crushed the soft white bulbs and riced them through its grid in delectable creamy threads; the egg slicer, on whose curved plastic bed you placed the egg before bringing down the wires; the Waring Blendor, which sat like a Siamese cat with its cord wrapped around its base; the potato peeler; the melon bailer; the nested measuring cups and spoons; the cookie press; and the flour sifter.

Like every fifties kitchen, ours could boast a plethora of specially designed cabinets and drawers, multiplied by my family's need to keep two sets of everything, one for dairy and one for meat. Every few months, my mother would hold the door while the delivery man stomped inside in his bloodstained smock and deposited crates of freshly slaughtered chickens and cuts of lamb and beef, after which she and my grandmother devoted the day to koshering the meat in brine, reaching inside the chickens and yanking out the liver, the heart, the lungs, scraping the pin feathers off the feet, cutting apart the breasts, snipping off the wings with giant shears, then wrapping each portion in wax paper, labeling the packet with a pen, and ferrying it downstairs to the freezer.

We ate parts of the cows and chickens regular Americans never ate. An enormous grainy tongue might boil on the stove all day. My grandmother stuffed intestines with breadcrumbs and sautéed these in a pan. One of my favorite delicacies was chicken skin fried in fat, but I also loved to suck the feet and necks. That is, until I figured out these were *animals* we were eating. After that, I cringed whenever I saw my father use the electric knife to slice a breast, felt sick when I saw the taste buds on the tongue, couldn't bear the vertebrae in a can of salmon. I would sit there with a slab of liver on my plate, crying to be excused, while all across America the children of parents who had grown up in the Depression sat in their own ranch houses spurning the meat their parents had worked so hard to put on their own Formica tables.

Not only did everything in our kitchen have its place, the place for it had its place. There were special racks for spices, special drawers for waxed paper, Saran wrap, and aluminum foil, and in a special corner-shaped cupboard, a lazy Susan for our pots and pans (the name struck me as an insult—who was this Susan and didn't she mind?). The refrigerator came with special compartments for vegetables, fruit, butter, milk, and eggs, but that didn't satisfy my mother, who bought Tupperware in every shape—most notably, a container in which to keep a head of iceberg lettuce fresh (you impaled the core on a plastic spike, then set the head in a lettuce-shaped plastic tub). Often I got in trouble for failing to close all four corners of the container designed to hold a block of American cheese, the necessity for which eluded me since each slice was already extremely well protected in its own hermetically sealed plastic sleeve.

Of course, the main feature of any fifties ranch was the front-facing picture window. When I think of our house, I see my grandmother sitting sideways in a chair, arms resting on the sill as she gazes out at the street, waiting for the occasional car to pass. When my brother and sister and I were young, she helped to cook and to care for us, but after we got older there was little for her to do. The few things she owned she kept upstairs, the exception being a brass mortar the size of a man's top hat (the date on the bottom, 5-3-1829, made that mortar older than anything else in the house by 120 years), and the barbell-shaped pestle I used for crushing nuts, although I couldn't imagine why anyone would have shlepped such a cumbersome object all the way from Europe. It was a wonder the steamship hadn't sunk from all that weight.[2]

Like most fifties families, ours changed radically in the sixties. My mother enrolled at SUNY New Paltz, where she majored in English but also enjoyed biology, with its revelations as to how her children had grown inside her and the opportunities it provided for her to demonstrate her facility at dissection, a talent she attributed to all the years she had spent reaching inside those chickens and yanking out their guts. As a result of her being preoccupied with these courses, my father finally learned where we kept the silverware and how to open a can of soup.

---

[2] I recently learned that the ship that carried my grandmother to America in 1903 had, four years earlier, nearly gone down in frigid seas. The ship was presumed to have sunk, only to limp into harbor a few weeks later with all forty-seven passengers alive and well, the captain having lost only one crewmember and 107 horses, which he had ordered thrown overboard to save the human cargo.

Then my mother redid our kitchen. Before, the cabinets were plain pink wood, the appliances white, the floor yellow-and-gray linoleum. After, the cabinets were those heavy dark wood monstrosities every kitchen in America now seems to come equipped with; the appliances were avocado green, with an elaborately curved and fluted gilt-edged vent above the stove; and the floor was a spongy vinyl in a darker shade of green to complement the avocado. The only fixture that didn't get updated was my grandmother, who remained staring out the window as before.

I had mixed feelings about the basement. That was where the razor blades went to die. On the other hand, I loved tagging along when my brother and his friends played ping-pong, darts, or pool. The pool table was an expensive full-size model that I wasn't allowed to play on for fear I would rip the felt. Instead, I hung around and watched and tried not to mind when the older kids twirled the blue chalk cube on my nose.

The coffin-shaped freezer held not only those packets of kosher meat, but the salamis my father had been given as a gift by the butcher, whose son he had helped get into dental school. Later, the butcher accidentally electrocuted himself by walking into his own freezer, stepping in a puddle, and touching an electric cord, after which the salamis seemed as eerie and repulsive as his severed limbs would have been.

The shelves above the freezer held harmless odds and ends, or so I thought, until my brother asked me to take down a bag and I opened it and saw a human skull, although this turned out to be not the severed head of a murder victim, as my brother claimed, but my father's teaching aid from dental school.

The roaring, whooshing furnace kept us warm . . . until the day the needle on the gauge shot up into the red and we managed to get outside only moments before the whole tiling blew up, covering everything in the house with soot.

I never went near my father's table saw, whose shrill whine set my teeth on edge. But I loved to keep my mother company while she sorted and washed our clothes, then stretched my father's trousers on wire frames, or stood ironing his handkerchiefs, shirts, and underwear.

To one side of the laundry area, above the bright blue bottles the Seltzer Man delivered to our house, hung a coconut that my grandmother down in Florida had turned into a hideously leering head, with seashells for eyes, a feather for the nose, and (don't ask me why) a shoe-tree beneath its jaw. That coconut head scared us all, but it was like some powerful evil idol we were too superstitious to get rid of.

The door to the garage wasn't powered by an opener; someone had to get out of the car and pull it up, a job I hated because I feared the driver might—accidentally or on purpose—gun the gas while I was standing between the bumper and the door.

Beside the car hung our shovels, rakes, picks, and hoes, as well as a lethal-looking axe and a pair of pruning shears with the wingspan of a condor. My terror of insects made me shirk most outdoor chores, but I begged to be allowed to ride the mower (a request my father vetoed because I might cut off my hands or feet), and I couldn't get enough of the blood-red plastic tube with the three-inch spring-loaded needle that my father would fill with poison and pay me to use to kill dandelions by stabbing them at the heart of their pointy, saw-toothed whirls and injecting the poison home.

The exterior of our house was as fastidiously maintained as the interior. The grass was perfectly mowed and raked, and each willow's branches hung as neat as a starlet's bangs. If one of the maples needed to have a limb sawed off, my father painted the socket black. We also owned a plum tree, whose enticing purple fruit my parents forbade us to eat because the plums, they said, were poison. You can imagine our horror when our uncle from New Jersey, who had driven up to see my grandmother, walked over and picked a plum. "Uncle James!" we cried. "No! Those plums are poison!" At which he laughed and said, "Poison? Who ever heard of a poison plum?" and took a bite. Later, when he suffered no ill effects, we ran outside and ate a few plums ourselves.

The attic was divided into a single long playroom for us kids and a bedroom for my grandmother. The floors were made of some waxy brown substance that reminded me of melted crayons (this provided the perfect surface on which to slide on stocking feet, though you had to be careful not to slam headfirst into the radiators at either end), and the walls were a mottled fake-wood pasteboard I could have punched through with my fist. On either side of the playroom you could open a dwarfish door and step inside the eaves, which we were forbidden to do because we might fall through to the rooms below.

In the closet nearest the stairs, my parents kept albums of crumbling photos, woolens protected by icy nuggets of paradichlorobenzene (the camphoraceous scent, like gasoline, skunk, or farts, begged to be inhaled), and the blond Shirley Temple curls that had been clipped from my mother's head when she was a child and saved, as if she might yet someday pursue the acting career she had wanted to pursue in high school, before her father and brothers laughed her out of it.

Beside the closet stood a bookcase in which my parents kept the requisite ranch-house set of Reader's Digest condensed novels, along with my father's anatomy texts (from which I learned what a syphilitic chancre on a penis looks like), and a history of World War Two that I must have read twenty times (had the world really gone so mad only a few years before?).

In the playroom, we kept the Monopoly and Scrabble boards, along with newer games like Operation, in which you tried to remove the patient's funny bone or appendix without setting off an alarm and killing him. Someone had given my brother a chemistry set and, despite my fear of what he would do to me if he discovered this violation, I couldn't resist weighing out and mixing the bilious yellow powders, filling the burner with alcohol and lighting the flame, and peering through the black plastic funnel that contained a lump of radium, which I held to my eye to see the atomic sparks (no doubt starting a chain reaction that one day will manifest itself as a tumor in my optic nerve).

My grandmother's windowless bathroom was scarcely bigger than a telephone booth—it didn't contain a shower or a bath, but in all the years she shared our house, I don't recall seeing her carry her towel down the stairs to use either of the first-floor bathrooms. The room's only furnishings were a vinyl-covered stool, a bright pink enema-bag, and a canister filled with chocolaty grains of a laxative called Senekot.

Despite everywhere I had to play, I brought my friends here, because where else did it get so dark? One person would hide an object, then the rest of us would shut the lights and go in and find it. Or I ordered my friends to play Concentration Camp, in which the loser had to do whatever the winner ordered.

Growing up—and for most of my adult life—I assumed that my grandparents' families hadn't left anyone behind when they emigrated to the United States prior to World War I. I didn't find out until recently, when I was doing some genealogical research on the web, that my grandmother lost her brother, his wife, their son, and the son's entire young family to the Nazis. I don't know exactly how they died, but given the accounts I unearthed of the butchery inflicted on the sixteen thousand Jews who were living in Czortkow when the Germans took the city in July 1941, my grandmother's relatives might have been burned alive in their houses by their Ukrainian neighbors, with the Germans looking on in approval, or shot in the streets by the Gestapo, or marched into the woods and executed and buried in a mass grave somewhere on the road to Jagielnica, or worked to death in any of a number of forced labor camps, or herded into a ghetto where they fell victim to typhus or starvation or the final *Aktion* against the Jews in October of that year, or, if they managed to join the underground and escape to the forest, betrayed by the Ukrainians and wiped out by German soldiers in the spring of '43. I knew none of this until last year; nor, it seems, did my mother. Most likely, my grandmother knew only that her brother and his family had perished in the war. And yet something prompted me to play that game of Concentration Camp in her bathroom. That is, until the only Christian girl in the neighborhood objected to being ordered to wear her underpants on her head and went home and told her mother.

Other than the items in that bathroom, my grandmother owned a container for her dentures, as well as her passport and citizenship papers, a photo of her mother, her father's Sweeney Toddish razor—which she used to trim her corns, a procedure that terrified me since the razor was so sharp and my grandmother's eyesight so bad—and a yellow dish she kept filled with Hershey kisses in case anyone came upstairs. Once, my friend Wendy and I dressed up like Eskimos to fool my grandmother into thinking we weren't the same children to whom she had just given two chocolate kisses, and lo, the disguises worked!

Somehow, this scarcity of possessions meant that my grandmother's only real role was to shower her love on me. I would wake before dawn and trundle upstairs with a book, then stare at her until she opened her eyes and saw me. Without her glasses, her eyes were watery, deep, and dark, like the water in the pond behind our house. "*Mameleh!*" she would cry, then grope for the glasses and put them on, a moment as thrilling as my father's declaration that the ice on the pond had frozen and was now thick enough to skate on. "Come," she would say, then pull me up and read the book.

I am not saying my grandmother loved me more than anyone else, but I was the youngest and by far the neediest, and I gave her more opportunities to show her love than anyone else did. "The Old Country?" she would say. "Mud, mud, and more mud. That's what I remember about the Old Country." Nor were her early years in America all that great. Not knowing she needed glasses, her teachers smacked her face for not being able to read what was written on the board. At thirteen, she got pulled out of school and sent to work sewing buttons on ladies' coats.

No, the good days were now, living in the attic of the ranch house that her daughter and dentist son-in-law had invited her to live in. Her only complaint was that whenever we had a storm, the thunder sounded loudest in the attic, a complaint my family laughed at. How could thunder sound louder on the second floor than on the first? I laughed along with them, but the thunder in the attic sounded louder to me as well.

Then my grandmother began to ask the same questions over and over. She forgot to shut off the stove, or she wandered away, only to be found in a neighbor's yard. My mother was teaching school by then, and I was rarely home. We couldn't find anyone to stay with her and watch her. And so, one afternoon, my mother and I drove my grandmother to a nursing home. "I know where you're taking me," she said. "I would rather you just left me beside the road to die." It was a beautiful nursing home, but my grandmother kept saying, "I know where I am. I would rather you give me poison." When the time came for my mother and me to take our leave, my grandmother flung herself against the elevator doors, yelling, "Take me home! Take me home!" I had nightmares about that for years.

Like me, most of the young people in my neighborhood went to college and moved away. We bought Cape Cods in Boston, Colonials in Atlanta, condos in Manhattan, fake adobe townhouses in Arizona. In the past few years, my gay friends have started to buy ranch houses and redecorate them in such an inviting way that I might consider moving in, if not for my fear that I would drive up and see my grandmother's face framed in the picture window.

Not long ago, I went back to my hometown and took a walk around my neighborhood, ticking off the misfortunes of the families who used to live there. There was the neighbor who was agoraphobic (how had we failed to notice that she never left her house?). The neighbor who was bipolar. The neighbor whose father ran off with a girl my age. The mentally ill neighbor my age who came back to live with her mother, then picked up a pair of scissors and stabbed her in the neck and killed her. The neighbor whose son joined the Marines, sustained an injury, contracted AIDS from his transfusion, and died. And the neighborhood cleaning lady, Helen, who was found dead in her apartment down the street, possibly the victim of abuse by her husband and/or their daughter. The secrets in my own family turned out to be minor—an unusually high incidence of gay uncles, aunts, and cousins, and one or two relatives who served brief stints in jail. There were only those razor blades in the wall, the rolls of toilet tissue in the closet, and all that Tupperware in the fridge.

Our neighborhood, like our town, has gone downhill since I lived there. My house seems to be the only property that looks better instead of worse. The family that lives there now is Indian; the father is an executive at the bank. The yard is even more fastidiously maintained than when my father was in charge. When I explained to the owner that I used to live there, he took me on a tour, although his children and wife and in-laws kept retreating as we advanced. In the living room, the decor was a combination of American bourgeois and Indian, everything in its place, the house as obsessively neat as it used to be. The kitchen had been redone in white. I didn't ask to see the attic, but the father ushered me to the basement, which he had finished to provide a playroom for his kids, a laundry room for his wife, an office for himself, and a shrine to the family gods at which he and his wife and in-laws no doubt prayed that the walls of their lovely ranch house would keep their children safe from the poverty and disease, madness, despair, and death that their ancestors must have suffered. The temple roof looked familiar, but it took me a while to realize that he must have salvaged it from the kitchen when his wife tore out and replaced the elaborately curved and fluted avocado-green vent from above our stove.

—2011

Learning from Other Writers (Pollack)

1. Pollack writes of the fires in the fireplace: "I loved everything about those fires—the poker my brother used for stirring up the flames, the chenille rug my mother spread across the hearth, the long-handed fork she brought in from the kitchen so we could jab marshmallows in the flames until they lit up like sugary torches." What else about the fires gave her so much pleasure? Why did her father stop building fires in the fireplace? How is this a telling detail both about her theme, her driving question, and her upbringing? Where in the essay does the image of fire come up in a far darker way?

2. Though Pollack examines in great detail the intricacies of her childhood home, the essay reads as a portrait of her parents. By carefully chronicling the neatness and order of the house in which she grew up, what is she exposing about her parents? Their generation? Her own generation? An era? Where in the essay do you see this larger-scale significance developing?

3. The essay shifts in tone when Pollack takes us to explore the basement. Why do you think she chooses to navigate through the basement at this point in the essay? What has come right before this section? What information comes after it?

4. Where does the description of the exterior of the house fall in the essay? Why do you think Pollack chooses to position this section where she does?

5. Early in the essay, Pollack writes: "Perhaps what I craved wasn't an escape from reality so much as a way to burrow from the present to the past and learn what the shiny veneers in my family's ranch house were meant to hide." Later in the essay, we see some of what those "shiny veneers" might have been hiding. How is this as much Pollack's discovery as it is ours?

Adding Your Voice

Think of a building or some other physical setting (i.e., a playground, an empty lot, a soccer stadium) in the neighborhood or town in which you grew up. Take your readers on an actual or remembered tour of that building or site while meditating on a question related to your childhood or to the history, economy, or sociology of your neighborhood or hometown.

Process, Craft, and Revision

CHAPTER 16

Process and Craft

The materials in Part VI of Creative Composition *are designed to serve as a companion to the earlier parts of the book.* So feel free to use these chapters early and often. We hope that the materials here will serve as a useful supplement to your development as a writer, just as they have helped us craft and revise our own work.

In this section, we offer four essays that tackle important aspects of the writing process: close reading, drafting, characterization, and argumentation. As we noted in Chapter 5, the key to good writing is good reading. Mike Bunn's essay "How to Read Like a Writer" not only exemplifies this practice, but also takes readers through the step-by-step process of developing close-reading skills and discovering how reading essays in this manner can help you to improve your writing.

In her now-famous essay "Shitty First Drafts," Anne Lamott stresses the importance of multiple drafts and asserts that "[a]lmost all good writing begins with terrible first efforts." As Lamott so rightly advises, we must get our ideas down on paper, any way we can, before we can even begin to polish them.

Phillip Lopate's "Writing Personal Essays: On the Importance of Turning Yourself into a Character" discusses the importance of characterization in general and, in particular, turning ourselves into characters in our own work. "You need to be able to see yourself from the ceiling," Lopate writes. Only through an accurate, objective assessment of the past are we able to analyze and extract meaning from our experience.

Finally, in "Argumentation in a Culture of Discord," Frank L. Cioffi's eloquent claim that the best arguments "present no irrefutable proofs, no indelible answers" and succeed by "approaching understanding" is right in line with our own argument that a good essay always stems from a genuine driving question. Although Cioffi's explicit audience here is fellow teachers of writing (the essay was originally published in *The Chronicle of Higher Education*), the implied audience includes anyone who writes. His essay on argumentation is itself an elegant argument, drawing a cause-and-effect relationship between the way argumentation is usually approached in our popular media and in the classroom and most students' reluctance to engage in such argumentative discourse themselves.

Mike Bunn

HOW TO READ LIKE A WRITER

In 1997, I was a recent college graduate living in London for six months and working at the Palace Theatre owned by Andrew Lloyd Webber. The Palace was a beautiful red brick, four-story theatre in the heart of London's famous West End, and eight times a week it housed a three-hour performance of the musical *Les Miserables*. Because of antiquated fire-safety laws, every theatre in the city was required to have a certain number of staff members inside watching the performance in case of an emergency.

My job (in addition to wearing a red tuxedo jacket) was to sit inside the dark theater with the patrons and make sure nothing went wrong. It didn't seem to matter to my supervisor that I had no training in security and no idea where we kept the fire extinguishers. I was pretty sure that if there *was* any trouble I'd be running down the back stairs, leaving the patrons to fend for themselves. I had no intention of dying in a bright red tuxedo.

There was a Red Coat stationed on each of the theater's four floors, and we all passed the time by sitting quietly in the back, reading books with tiny flashlights. It's not easy trying to read in the dim light of a theatre—flashlight or no flashlight—and it's even tougher with shrieks and shouts and gunshots coming from the stage. I had to focus intently on each and every word, often rereading a single sentence several times. Sometimes I got distracted and had to reread entire paragraphs. As I struggled to read in this environment, I began to realize that the way I was reading—one word at a time—was exactly the same way that the author had written the text. I realized writing is a word-by-word, sentence-by-sentence process. The intense concentration required to read in the theater helped me recognize some of the interesting ways that authors string words into phrases into paragraphs into entire books.

I came to realize that all writing consists of a series of choices.

I was an English major in college, but I don't think I ever thought much about reading. I read all the time. I read for my classes and on the computer and sometimes for fun, but I never really thought about the important connections between reading and writing, and how reading in a particular way could also make me a better writer.

What Does It Mean to Read Like a Writer?

When you Read Like a Writer (RLW) you work to identify some of the choices the author made so that you can better understand how such choices might arise in your own writing. The idea is to carefully examine the things you read, looking at the writerly techniques in the text in order to decide if you might want to adopt similar (or the same) techniques in your writing.

You are reading to learn about writing.

Instead of reading for content or to better understand the ideas in the writing (which you will automatically do to some degree anyway), you are trying to understand how the piece of writing was put together by the author and what you can learn about writing by reading a particular text. As you read in this way, you think about how the choices the author made and the techniques that he/she used are influencing your own responses as a reader. What is it about the way this text is written that makes you feel and respond the way you do?

The goal as you read like a writer is to locate what you believe are the most important writerly choices represented in the text—choices as large as the overall structure or as small as a single word used only once—to consider the effect of those choices on potential readers (including yourself). Then you can go one step further and imagine what *different* choices the author *might* have made instead, and what effect those different choices would have on readers.

Say you're reading an essay in class that begins with a short quote from President Barack Obama about the war in Iraq. As a writer, what do you think of this technique? Do you think it is effective to begin the essay with a quote? What if the essay began with a quote from someone else? What if it was a much *longer* quote from President Obama, or a quote from the President about something other than the war?

And here is where we get to the most important part: *Would you want to try this technique in your own writing?*

Would you want to start your own essay with a quote? Do you think it would be effective to begin your essay with a quote from President Obama? What about a quote from someone else?

You could make yourself a list. What are the advantages and disadvantages of starting with a quote? What about the advantages and disadvantages of starting with a quote from the President? How would other readers respond to this technique? Would certain readers (say Democrats or liberals) appreciate an essay that started with a quote from President Obama better than other readers (say Republicans or conservatives)? What would be the advantages and disadvantages of starting with a quote from a *less* divisive person? What about starting with a quote from someone *more* divisive?

The goal is to carefully consider the choices the author made and the techniques that he or she used, and then decide whether you want to make those same choices or use those same techniques in your own writing. Author and professor Wendy Bishop explains how her reading process changed when she began to read like a writer:

> It wasn't until I claimed the sentence as my area of desire, interest, and expertise—until I wanted to be a writer writing better—that I had to look underneath my initial readings. ... I started asking, *how*—*how* did the writer get me to feel, *how* did the writer say something so that it remains in my memory when many other things too easily fall out, *how* did the writer communicate his/her intentions about genre, about irony? (119–20)

Bishop moved from simply reporting her personal reactions to the things she read to attempting to uncover *how* the author led her (and other readers) to have those reactions. This effort to uncover how authors build texts is what makes Reading Like a Writer so useful for student writers.

How is RLW Different from "Normal" Reading?

Most of the time we read for information. We read a recipe to learn how to bake lasagna. We read the sports page to see if our school won the game, Facebook to see who has commented on our status update, a history book to learn about the Vietnam War, and the syllabus to see when the next writing assignment is due. Reading Like a Writer asks for something very different.

In 1940, a famous poet and critic named Allen Tate discussed two different ways of reading:

> There are many ways to read, but generally speaking there are two ways. They correspond to the two ways in which we may be interested in a piece of architecture. If the building has Corinthian columns, we can trace the origin and development of Corinthian columns; we are interested as historians. But if we are interested as architects, we may or may not know about the history of the Corinthian style; we must, however, know all about the construction of the building, down to the last nail or peg in the beams. We have got to know this if we are going to put up buildings ourselves. (506)

While I don't know anything about Corinthian columns (and doubt that I will ever *want* to know anything about Corinthian columns), Allen Tate's metaphor of reading as if you were an architect is a great way to think about RLW. When you read like a writer, you are trying to figure out how the text you are reading was constructed so that you learn how to "build" one for yourself. Author David Jauss makes a similar comparison when he writes that "reading won't help you much unless you learn to read like a writer. You must look at a book the way a carpenter looks at a house someone else built, examining the details in order to see how it was made" (64).

Perhaps I should change the name and call this Reading Like an Architect, or Reading Like a Carpenter. In a way those names make perfect sense. You are reading to see how something was constructed so that you can construct something similar yourself.

Why Learn to Read Like a Writer?

For most college students RLW is a new way to read, and it can be difficult to learn at first. Making things even *more* difficult is that your college writing instructor may expect you to read this way for class but never actually teach you how to do it. He or she may not even tell you that you're supposed to read this way. This is because most writing instructors are so focused on teaching writing that they forget to show students how they want them to read.

That's what this essay is for.

In addition to the fact that your college writing instructor may expect you to read like a writer, this kind of reading is also one of the very best ways to learn how to write well. Reading like a writer can help you understand how the process of writing is a series of making choices, and in doing so, can help you recognize important decisions you might face and techniques you might want to use when working on your own writing. Reading this way becomes an opportunity to think and learn about writing.

Charles Moran, a professor of English at the University of Massachusetts, urges us to read like writers because:

> [when] we read like writers we understand and participate in the writing. We see the choices the writer has made, and we see how the writer has coped with the consequences of those choices. ... We "see" what the writer is doing because we read as writers; we see because we have written ourselves and know the territory, know the feel of it, know some of the moves ourselves. (61)

You are already an author, and that means you have a built-in advantage when reading like a writer. All of your previous writing experiences—inside the classroom and out—can contribute to your success with RLW. Because you "have written" things yourself, just as Moran suggests, you are better able to "see" the choices that the author is making in the texts that you read. This in turn helps you to think about whether you want to make some of those same choices in your own writing, and what the consequences might be for your readers if you do.

What Are Some Questions to Ask Before You Start Reading?

As I sat down to work on this essay, I contacted a few of my former students to ask what advice they would give to college students regarding how to read effectively in the writing classroom and also to get their thoughts on RLW. Throughout the rest of the essay I'd like to share some of their insights and suggestions; after all, who is better qualified to help you learn what you need to know about reading in college writing courses than students who recently took those courses themselves?

One of the things that several students mentioned to do first, before you even start reading, is to consider the *context* surrounding both the assignment and the text you're reading. As one former student, Alison, states: "The reading I did in college asked me to go above and beyond, not only in breadth of subject matter, but in depth, with regards to informed analysis and background information on *context*." Alison was asked to think about some of the factors that went into the creation of the text, as well as some of the factors influencing her own experience of reading—taken together these constitute the *context* of reading. Another former student, Jamie, suggests that students "learn about the historical context of the writings" they will read for class. Writing professor Richard Straub puts it this way: "You're not going to just read a text. You're going to read a text within a certain context, a set of circumstances. ... It's one kind of writing or another, designed for one audience and purpose or another" (138).

Among the contextual factors you'll want to consider before you even start reading are:

- Do you know the author's purpose for this piece of writing?
- Do you know who the intended audience is for this piece of writing?

It may be that you need to start reading before you can answer these first two questions, but it's worth trying to answer them before you start. For example, if you know at the outset that the author is trying to reach a very specific group of readers, then his or her writerly techniques may seem more or less effective than if he/she were trying to reach a more general audience. Similarly—returning to our earlier example of beginning an essay with a quote from President Obama about the war in Iraq—if you know that the author's purpose is to address some of the dangers and drawbacks of warfare, this may be a very effective opening. If the purpose is to encourage Americans to wear sunscreen while at the beach this opening makes no sense at all. One former student, Lola, explained that most of her reading assignments in college writing classes were designed "to provoke analysis and criticisms into the style, structure, and *purpose* of the writing itself."

In What Genre Is This Written?

Another important thing to consider before reading is the genre of the text. Genre means a few different things in college English classes, but it's most often used to indicate the *type* of writing: a poem, a newspaper article, an essay, a short story, a novel, a legal brief, an instruction manual, etc. Because the conventions for each genre can be very different (who ever heard of a 900-page newspaper article?), techniques that are effective for one genre may not work well in another. Many readers expect poems and pop songs to rhyme, for example, but might react negatively to a legal brief or instruction manual that did so.

Another former student, Mike, comments on how important the genre of the text can be for reading:

> I think a lot of the way I read, of course, depends on the type of text I'm reading. If I'm reading philosophy, I always look for signaling words (however, therefore, furthermore, despite) indicating the direction of the argument . . . when I read fiction or creative nonfiction, I look for how the author inserts dialogue or character sketches within narration or environmental observation. After reading To the Lighthouse [sic] last semester, I have noticed how much more attentive I've become to the types of narration (omniscient, impersonal, psychological, realistic, etc.), and how these different approaches are utilized to achieve an author's overall effect.

Although Mike specifically mentions what he looked for while reading a published novel, one of the great things about RLW is that it can be used equally well with either published or student-produced writing.

Is This a Published or a Student-Produced Piece of Writing?

As you read both kinds of texts you can locate the choices the author made and imagine the different decisions that he/she might have made. While it might seem a little weird at first to imagine how published texts could be written differently—after all, they were good enough to be published—remember that all writing can be improved.

Scholar Nancy Walker believes that it's important for students to read published work using RLW because "the work ceases to be a mere artifact, a stone tablet, and becomes instead a living utterance with immediacy and texture. It could have been better or worse than it is had the author made different choices" (36). As Walker suggests, it's worth thinking about how the published text would be different—maybe even *better*—if the author had made different choices in the writing because you may be faced with similar choices in your own work.

Is This the Kind of Writing You Will Be Assigned to Write Yourself?

Knowing ahead of time what kind of writing assignments you will be asked to complete can really help you to read like a writer. It's probably impossible (and definitely too time consuming) to identify *all* of the choices the author made and *all* techniques an author used, so it's important to prioritize while reading. Knowing what you'll be writing yourself can help you prioritize. It may be the case that your instructor has assigned the text you're reading to serve as model for the kind of writing you'll be doing later. Jessie, a former student, writes, "In college writing classes, we knew we were reading for a purpose—to influence or inspire our own work. The reading that I have done in college writing courses has always been really specific to a certain type of writing, and it allows me to focus and experiment on that specific style in depth and without distraction."

If the text you're reading is a model of a particular style of writing—for example, highly emotional or humorous—RLW is particularly helpful because you can look at a piece you're reading and think about whether you want to adopt a similar style in your own writing. You might realize that the author is trying to arouse sympathy in readers and examine what techniques he/she uses to do this; then you can decide whether these techniques might work well in your own writing. You might notice that the author keeps including jokes or funny stories and think about whether you want to include them in your writing—what would the impact be on your potential readers?

What Are Questions to Ask As You Are Reading?

It is helpful to continue to ask yourself questions *as* you read like a writer. As you're first learning to read in this new way, you may want to have a set of questions written or typed out in front of you that you can refer to while reading. Eventually—after plenty of practice—you will start to ask certain questions and locate certain things in the text almost automatically. Remember, for most students this is a new way of reading, and you'll have to train yourself to do it well. Also keep in mind that you're reading to understand how the text was *written*— how the house was built—more than you're trying to determine the meaning of the things you read or assess whether the texts are good or bad.

First, return to two of the same questions I suggested that you consider *before* reading:

- What is the author's purpose for this piece of writing?
- Who is the intended audience?

Think about these two questions again as you read. It may be that you couldn't really answer them before, or that your ideas will change while reading. Knowing *why* the piece was written and *who* it's for can help explain why the author might have made certain choices or used particular techniques in the writing, and you can assess those choices and techniques based in part on how effective they are in fulfilling that purpose and/or reaching the intended audience.

Beyond these initial two questions, there is an almost endless list of questions you might ask regarding writing choices and techniques. Here are some of the questions that one former student, Clare, asks herself:

> When reading I tend to be asking myself a million questions. If I were writing this, where would I go with the story? If the author goes in a different direction (as they so often do) from what I am thinking, I will ask myself, why did they do this? What are they telling me?

Clare tries to figure out why the author might have made a move in the writing that she hadn't anticipated, but even more important, she asks herself what *she* would do if she were the author. Reading the text becomes an opportunity for Clare to think about her own role as an author.

Here are some additional examples of the kinds of questions you might ask yourself as you read:

- How effective is the language the author uses? Is it too formal? Too informal? Perfectly appropriate?

Depending on the subject matter and the intended audience, it may make sense to be more or less formal in terms of language. As you begin reading, you can ask yourself whether the word choice and tone/ language of the writing seem appropriate.

- What kinds of evidence does the author use to support his/her claims? Does he/ she use statistics? Quotes from famous people? Personal anecdotes or personal stories? Does he/she cite books or articles?

- How appropriate or effective is this evidence? Would a different type of evidence, or some combination of evidence, be more effective?

To some extent the kinds of questions you ask should be determined by the genre of writing you are reading. For example, it's probably worth examining the evidence that the author uses to support his/her claims if you're reading an opinion column, but less important if you're reading a short story. An opinion column is often intended to convince readers of something, so the kinds of evidence used are often very important.

A short story *may* be intended to convince readers of something, sometimes, but probably not in the same way. A short story rarely includes claims or evidence in the way that we usually think about them.

- Are there places in the writing that you find confusing? What about the writing in those places makes it unclear or confusing?

It's pretty normal to get confused in places while reading, especially while reading for class, so it can be helpful to look closely at the writing to try and get a sense of exactly what tripped you up. This way you can learn to avoid those same problems in your own writing.

- How does the author move from one idea to another in the writing? Are the transitions between the ideas effective? How else might he/she have transitioned between ideas instead?

Notice that in these questions I am encouraging you to question whether aspects of the writing are *appropriate* and *effective* in addition to deciding whether you liked or disliked them. You want to imagine how other readers might respond to the writing and the techniques you've identified. Deciding whether you liked or disliked something is only about you; considering whether a technique is appropriate or effective lets you contemplate what the author might have been trying to do and to decide whether a majority of readers would find the move successful. This is important because it's the same thing you should be thinking about while you are writing: how will readers respond to this technique I am using, to this sentence, to this word? As you read, ask yourself what the author is doing at each step of the way, and then consider whether the same choice or technique might work in your own writing.

What Should You Be Writing As You Are Reading?

The most common suggestion made by former students—mentioned by every single one of them—was to mark up the text, make comments in the margins, and write yourself notes and summaries both during and after reading. Often the notes students took while reading became ideas or material for the students to use in their own papers. It's important to read with a pen or highlighter in your hand so that you can mark—right on the text—all those spots where you identify an interesting choice the author has made or a writerly technique you might want to use. One thing that I like to do is to highlight and underline the passage in the text itself, and then try to answer the following three questions on my notepad:

- What is the technique the author is using here?
- Is this technique effective?
- What would be the advantages and disadvantages if I tried this same technique in my writing?

By utilizing this same process of highlighting and note taking, you'll end up with a useful list of specific techniques to have at your disposal when it comes time to begin your own writing.

What Does RLW Look Like in Action?

Let's go back to the opening paragraph of *this* essay and spend some time reading like writers as a way to get more comfortable with the process:

> In 1997, I was a recent college graduate living in London for six months and working at the Palace Theatre owned by Andrew Lloyd Webber. The Palace was a beautiful red brick, four-story theatre in the heart of London's famous West End, and eight times a week it housed a three-hour performance of the musical Les Miserables. Because of antiquated fire-safety laws, every theatre in the city was required to have a certain number of staff members inside watching the performance in case of an emergency.

Let's begin with those questions I encouraged you to try to answer *before* you start reading. (I realize we're cheating a little bit in this case since you've already read most of this essay, but this is just practice. When doing this on your own, you should attempt to answer these questions before reading, and then return to them as you read to further develop your answers.)

- Do you know the author's purpose for this piece of writing? I hope the purpose is clear by now; if it isn't, I'm doing a pretty lousy job of explaining how and why you might read like a writer.
- Do you know who the intended audience is? Again, I hope that you know this one by now.
- What about the genre? Is this an essay? An article? What would *you* call it?
- You know that it's published and not student writing. How does this influence your expectations for what you will read?
- Are you going to be asked to write something like this yourself? Probably not in your college writing class, but you can still use RLW to learn about writerly techniques that you might want to use in whatever you do end up writing.

Now ask yourself questions *as* you read,

> In 1997, I was a recent college graduate living in London for six months and working at the Palace Theatre owned by Andrew Lloyd Webber. The Palace was a beautiful red brick, four-story theatre in the heart of London's famous West End, and eight times a week it housed a three-hour performance of the musical Les Miserables. Because of antiquated fire-safety laws, every theatre in the city was required to have a certain number of staff members inside watching the performance in case of an emergency,

Since this paragraph is the very first one, it makes sense to think about how it introduces readers to the essay. What technique(s) does the author use to begin the text? This is a personal story about his time working in London. What else do you notice as you read over this passage? Is the passage vague or specific about where he worked? You know that the author worked in a famous part of London in a beautiful theater owned by a well-known composer. Are these details important? How different would this opening be if instead I had written:

In 1997, I was living in London and working at a theatre that showed Les Miserables.

This is certainly shorter, and some of you may prefer this version. It's quick. To the point. But what (if anything) is lost by eliminating so much of the detail? I *chose* to include each of the details that the revised sentence omits, so it's worth considering why. Why did I mention where the theater was located? Why did I explain that I was living in London right after finishing college? Does it matter that it was after college? What effect might I have hoped the inclusion of these details would have on readers? Is this reference to college an attempt to connect with my audience of college students? Am I trying to establish my credibility as an author by announcing that I went to college? Why might I want the readers to know that this was a theater owned by Andrew Lloyd Weber? Do you think I am just trying to mention a famous name that readers will recognize? Will Andrew Lloyd Weber figure prominently in the rest of the essay?

These are all reasonable questions to ask. They are not necessarily the *right* questions to ask because there are no right questions. They certainly aren't the only questions you could ask, either. The goal is to train yourself to formulate questions as you read based on whatever you notice in the text. Your own reactions to what you're reading will help determine the kinds of questions to ask.

Now take a broader perspective. I begin this essay—an essay about *reading*—by talking about my job in a theater in London. Why? Doesn't this seem like an odd way to begin an essay about reading? If you read on a little further (feel free to scan back up at the top of this essay) you learn in the third full paragraph what the connection is between working in the theater and reading like a writer, but why include this information at all? What does this story add to the essay? Is it worth the space it takes up?

Think about what effect presenting this personal information might have on readers. Does it make it feel like a real person, some "ordinary guy," is talking to you? Does it draw you into the essay and make you want to keep reading?

What about the language I use? Is it formal or more informal? This is a time when you can really narrow your focus and look at particular words:

Because of antiquated fire-safety laws, every theatre in the city was required to have a certain number of staff members inside watching the performance in case of an emergency.

What is the effect of using the word "antiquated" to describe the fire-safety laws? It certainly projects a negative impression; if the laws are described as antiquated it means I view them as old-fashioned or obsolete. This is a fairly uncommon word, so it stands out, drawing attention to my choice in using it. The word also sounds quite formal. Am I formal in the rest of this sentence?

I use the word "performance" when I just as easily could have written "show." For that matter, I could have written "old" instead of "antiquated." You can proceed like this throughout the sentence, thinking about alternative choices I could have made and what the effect would be. Instead of "staff members" I could have written "employees" or just "workers." Notice the difference if the sentence had been written:

> Because of old fire-safety laws, every theatre in the city was required to have a certain number of workers inside watching the show in case of an emergency.

Which version is more likely to appeal to readers? You can try to answer this question by thinking about the advantages and disadvantages of using rormal language. When would you want to use formal language in your writing and when would it make more sense to be more conversational?

As you can see from discussing just this one paragraph, you could ask questions about the text forever. Luckily, you don't have to. As you continue reading like a writer, you'll learn to notice techniques that seem new and pay less attention to the ones you've thought about before. The more you practice, the quicker the process becomes, until you're reading like a writer almost automatically.

I want to end this essay by sharing one more set of comments by my former student, Lola, this time about what it means to her to read like a writer:

> Reading as a writer would compel me to question what might have brought the author to make these decisions, and then decide what worked and what didn't. What could have made that chapter better or easier to understand? How can I make sure I include some of the good attributes of this writing style into my own? How can I take aspects that I feel the writer failed at and make sure not to make the same mistakes in my writing?

Questioning why the author made certain decisions. Considering what techniques could have made the text better. Deciding how to include the best attributes of what you read in your own writing. This is what Reading Like a Writer is all about. Are you ready to start reading?

Works Cited

Bishop, Wendy. "Reading, Stealing, and Writing Like a Writer." *Elements of Alternate Style: Essays on Writing and Revision.* Ed. Wendy Bishop. Portsmouth, NH: Boynton/Cook, 1997. Print.

Jauss, David. "Articles of Faith." *Creative Writing in America: Theory and Pedagogy.* Ed. Joseph Moxley. Urbana, IL: NCTE, 1989. Print.

Moran, Charles. "Reading Like a Writer." *Vital Signs I.* Ed. James L. Collins. Portsmouth, NH: Boynton/Cook, 1990. Print.

Straub, Richard. "Responding—Really Responding—to Other Students' Writing." *The Subject Is Reading.* Ed. Wendy Bishop. Portsmouth, NH: Boynton/Cook, 2000. Print.

Tate, Allen. "We Read as Writers." *Princeton Alumni Weekly* 40 (March 8, 1940): 505–506. Print.

Walker, Nancy. "The Student Reader as Writer." *ADE Bulletin* 106 (1993) 35–37. Print.

Anne Lamott

SHITTY FIRST DRAFTS

Now, practically even better news than that of short assignments is the idea of shitty first drafts. All good writers write them. This is how they end up with good second drafts and terrific third drafts. People tend to look at successful writers, writers who are getting their books published and maybe even doing well financially, and think that they sit down at their desks every morning feeling like a million dollars, feeling great about who they are and how much talent they have and what a great story they have to tell; that they take in a few deep breaths, push back their sleeves, roll their necks a few times to get all the cricks out, and dive in, typing fully formed passages as fast as a court reporter. But this is just the fantasy of the uninitiated. I know some very great writers, writers you love who write beautifully and have made a great deal of money, and not one of them sits down routinely feeling wildly enthusiastic and confident. Not one of them writes elegant first drafts. All right, one of them does, but we do not like her very much. We do not think that she has a rich inner life or that God likes her or can even stand her. (Although when I mentioned this to my priest friend Tom, he said you can safely assume you've created God in your own image when it turns out that God hates all the same people you do.)

Very few writers really know what they are doing until they've done it. Nor do they go about their business feeling dewy and thrilled. They do not type a few stiff warm-up sentences and then find themselves bounding along like huskies across the snow. One writer I know tells me that he sits down every morning and says to himself nicely, "It's not like you don't have a choice, because you do — you can either type or kill yourself." We all often feel as if we are pulling teeth, even those writers whose prose ends up being the most natural and fluid. The right words and sentences just do not come pouring out like ticker tape most of the time. Now, Muriel Spark is said to have felt that she was taking dictation from God every morning — sitting there, one supposes, plugged into a Dictaphone, typing away, humming. But this is a very hostile and aggressive position. One might hope for bad things to rain down on a person like this.

For me and most of the other writers I know, writing is not rapturous. In fact, the only way I can get anything written at all is to write really, really shitty first drafts.

The first draft is the child's draft, where you let it all pour out and then let it romp all over the place, knowing that no one is going to see it and that you can shape it later. You just let this childlike part of you channel whatever voices and visions come through and onto the page. If one of the characters wants to say, "Well, so what, Mr. Poopy Pants?," you let her. No one is going to see it. If the kid wants to get into really sentimental, weepy, emotional territory, you let him. Just get it all down on paper, because there may be something great in those six crazy pages that you would never have gotten to by more rational, grown-up means. There may be something in the very last line of the very last paragraph on page six that you just love, that is so beautiful or wild that you now know what you're supposed to be writing about, more or less, or in what direction you might go — but there was no way to get to this without first getting through the first five and a half pages.

I used to write food reviews for *California* magazine before it folded. (My writing food reviews had nothing to do with the magazine folding, although every single review did cause a couple of canceled subscriptions. Some readers took umbrage at my comparing mounds of vegetable puree with various ex-presidents' brains.) These reviews always took two days to write. First I'd go to a restaurant several times with a few opinionated, articulate friends in tow. I'd sit there writing down everything anyone said that was at all interesting or funny. Then on the following Monday I'd sit down at my desk with my notes and try to write the review. Even after I'd been doing this for years, panic would set in. I'd try to write a lead, but instead I'd write a couple of dreadful sentences, xx them out, try again, xx everything out, and then feel despair and worry settle on my chest like an x-ray apron. It's over, I'd think, calmly. I'm not going to be able to get the magic to work this time. I'm ruined. I'm through. I'm toast. Maybe, I'd think, I can get my old job back as a clerk-typist. But probably not. I'd get up and study my teeth in the mirror for a while. Then I'd stop, remember to breathe, make a few phone calls, hit the kitchen and chow down. Eventually I'd go back and sit down at my desk and *sigh* for the next ten minutes. Finally I would pick up my one-inch picture frame, stare into it as if for the answer, and every time the answer would come: all I had to do was to write a really shitty first draft of, say, the opening paragraph. And no one was going to see it.

So I'd start writing without reining myself in. It was almost just typing, just making my fingers move. And the writing would be terrible. I'd write a lead paragraph that was a whole page, even though the entire review could only be three pages long, and then I'd start writing up descriptions of the food, one dish at a time, bird by bird, and the critics would be sitting on my shoulders, commenting like cartoon characters. They'd be pretending to snore, or rolling their eyes at my overwrought descriptions, no matter how hard I tried to tone those descriptions down, no matter how conscious I was of what a friend said to me gently in my early days of restaurant reviewing. "Annie," she said, "it is just a piece of *chicken*. It is just a bit of *cake*."

But because by then I had been writing for so long, I would eventually let myself trust the process — sort of, more or less. I'd write a first draft that was maybe twice as long as it should be, with a self-indulgent and boring beginning, stupefying descriptions of the meal, lots of quotes from my black-humored friends that made them sound more like the Manson girls than food lovers, and no ending to speak of. The whole thing would be so long and incoherent and hideous that for the rest of the day I'd obsess about getting creamed by a car before I could write a decent second draft. I'd worry that people would read what I'd written and believe that the accident had really been a suicide, that I had panicked because my talent was waning and my mind was shot.

The next day, though, I'd sit down, go through it all with a colored pen, take out everything I possibly could, find a new lead somewhere on the second page, figure out a kicky place to end it, and then write a second draft. It always turned out fine, sometimes even funny and weird and helpful. I'd go over it one more time and mail it in.

Then, a month later, when it was time for another review, the whole process would start again, complete with the fears that people would find my first draft before I could rewrite it.

Phillip Lopate

WRITING PERSONAL ESSAYS: ON THE NECESSITY OF TURNING ONESELF INTO A CHARACTER

In personal essays, nothing is more commonly met than the letter *I*. I think it a perfectly good word, one no writer should be ashamed to use. Especially is first person legitimate for this form, so drawn to the particulars of character and voice. The problem with "I" is not that it is in bad taste, but that fledgling personal essayists may think they've said or conveyed more than they actually have with that one syllable. In their minds, that "I" is swarming with background and a lush, sticky past, and an almost too fatal specificity, whereas the reader, encountering it for the first time in a new piece, sees only a slender telephone pole standing in the sentence, trying to catch a few signals to send on. In truth, even the barest "I" holds a whisper of promised engagement and can suggest a caress in the midst of more stolid language. What it doesn't do, however, is give us a clear picture of who is speaking.

To do that, the writer needs to build herself into a character. And I use the word *character* much the same way the fiction writer does. E.M. Forster, in *Aspects of the Novel*, drew a famous distinction between "flat" and "round" characters—between those fictional personages seen from the outside who acted with the predicable consistency of caricatures, and those whose complexities or teeming inner lives we came to know. But whether the writer chooses to present characters as flat or round, or a combination, the people on the page—it scarcely matters whether they appear in fiction or nonfiction—will need to become knowable enough in their broad outlines to behave "believably," at the same time as free willed enough to intrigue us with surprises. The art of characterization comes down to establishing a pattern of habits and actions for the person you are writing about and introducing variations into the system. In this respect, building a character is a pedagogic model, because you are teaching the reader what to expect.

So how do you turn *yourself* into a character? First of all, you need to have—or acquire—some distance from yourself. If you are so panicked by any examination of your flaws that all you can do is sputter defensively when you feel yourself attacked, you are not going to get very far in the writing of personal essays. You need to be able to see yourself from the ceiling: to know, for instance, how you are coming across in social situations, and to assess accurately when you are charming, and when you seem pushy, mousy, or ridiculous. From the viewpoint of honest essay writing, it is just as unsatisfactorily distorting to underrate yourself all the time, and think you are far less effective than you actually are, than to give yourself too much credit. The point is to begin to take inventory of yourself so that you can present that self to the reader as a specific, legible character.

A good place to start is your quirks. These are the idiosyncracies, stubborn tics, antisocial mannerisms, and so on that set you apart from the majority of your fellowmen. There will be more than enough time later to assert your common humanity, or better yet, to let the reader make the mental bridge between your oddities and those of everyone else. But to establish credibility, you would do well to resist coming across at first as absolutely average. Who wants to read about that bland creature, the regular Joe? The mistake many beginning essayists make is to try so hard to be likable and nice, to fit in, that the reader, craving stronger stuff (at the very least, a tone of authority), gets bored. Literature is not a place for conformists, organization men. The skills of the kaffeeklatsch—restraining one's expressiveness, rounding out one's edges, sparing everyone's feelings—will not work as well on the page.

The irony is that most of us suspect—no, we *know*—that underneath it all we *are* common as dirt. But we may still need to maximize that pitiful set of quirks, those small differences that seem to set us apart from others, and project them theatrically, the way actors work with singularities in their physical appearances or vocal textures. In order to turn ourselves into characters, we need to *dramatize* ourselves. I don't mean inventing or adding colorful traits that aren't true; I mean positioning those that are already in us under the most clearly focused, sharply defined light. It's a subtractive process: You need to cut away the inessentials and highlight just those features in your personality that lead to the most intense contradictions or ambivalence.

An essay needs conflict, just as a short story does. Without conflict, your essay will drift into static mode, repeating your initial observation in a self-satisfied way. What gives an essay dynamism is the need to work out some problem, especially a problem that is not easily resolved. Fortunately, human beings are conflicted animals, so there is no shortage of tensions that won't go away. Good essayists know how to select a topic in advance that will generate enough spark in itself, and how to frame the topic so that it will neither be too ambitious nor too slight—so that its scale will be appropriate for satisfying exploration. If you are serenely unconflicted when you first sit down to write an essay, you may find yourself running out of steam. If you take on a problem that is too philosophically large or historically convoluted, you may choke on the details and give up.

Still, these are technical issues, and I am inclined to think that what stands in the way of most personal essays is not technique but psychology. The emotional preparedness, if you will, to be honest and open to exposure.

The student essayist is torn between two contrasting extremes:

A. "I am so weird that I could never tell on the page what is really, secretly going on in my mind."

B. "I am so boring, nothing ever happens to me out of the ordinary, so who would want to read about me?"

Both extremes are rooted in shame, and both reflect a lack of worldliness. The first response ("I am so weird") exaggerates how isolated one is in one's "wicked" thoughts, instead of recognizing that everyone has strange, surreal, immoral notions. The second response ("My life is so boring and I'm so boring") requires a reeducation so that the student essayists can be brought to acknowledge just those moments in the day, in their loves and friendships, in their family dynamics, in their historical moments, in their interactions with the natural world, that remain genuinely perplexing, vexing, luminous, unresolved. In short, they must be nudged to recognize that life remains a mystery—even one's own so-called boring life. They must also be taught to recognize the charm of the ordinary: that daily life that has nourished some of the most enduring essays.

The use of literary or other models can be a great help in invoking life's mystery. I like to remind myself, as well as my students, of the tonal extremes available to us. It is useful to know we can rant as much as Dostoyevsky's Underground Man or Céline's narrators, that we can speak—as the poet Mayakovski says—"At the Top of My Voice." That we can be passionate as Hazlitt and Baldwin, or even whine, the way Joan Didion sometimes does, albeit with self-aware humor. It is useful to remind students, enamored of David Lynch or Quentin Tarantino movies, that some of that bizarre sensibility can find a place in their essays—that "outlaw" culture does not have to be left outside the schoolhouse. At the same time, it is necessary to introduce them to the sane, thoughtful, considered, responsible essayists like George Orwell or E.B. White. From both sets of models we can then choose how reasonable or hysterical we want to come across at any time: in one piece, seem the soul of reason; in another, a step away from the loony bin.

Mining our quirks is only the beginning of turning ourselves into characters. We are distinguished one from another as much by our pasts, the set of circumstances we are born into, as by the challenges we have encountered along the way, and how we choose to resolve them, given our initial stations in life. It means something very different to have been born the second-oldest boy in an upper-middle-class Korean family that emigrated from Seoul to Los Angeles than to have been born the youngest female in a poor Southern Baptist household of nine.

Ethnicity, gender, religion, class, geography, politics: These are all strong determinants in the development of character. Sometimes they can be made too much of, as in the worst sort of "identity politics," which seeks to explain away all the intangibles of a human being's destiny by this or that social oppression. But we must be bold in working with these categories as starting points: be not afraid to meditate on our membership in this or that community, and the degree to which it has or has not formed us.

When you are writing a memoir, you can set up these categories and assess their importance one by one, and go on from there. When you write personal essays, however, you can never assume that your readers will know a thing about your background, regardless of how many times you have explained it in previous essays. So you must become deft at inserting that information swiftly and casually—"I was born in Brooklyn, New York, of working-class parents"—and not worry about the fact that it may be redundant to your regular readers, if you're lucky enough to have any. In one essay, you may decide to make a big thing of your religious training and very little of your family background; in another, just the opposite; but in each new essay, it would be a good idea to tell the reader both, simply because this sort of information will help to build you into a character.

In this sense, the personal essayist must be like a journalist, who respects the obligation to get in the basic orienting facts—the who, what, where, when, and why—as close to the top of every story as possible.

So now you have sketched yourself to the reader as a person of a certain age, sex, ethnic and religious background, class, and region, possessing a set of quirks, foibles, strengths, and peculiarities. Are you yet a character? Maybe not: not until you have soldered your relationship with the reader, by springing vividly into his mind, so that everything your "I" says and does on the page seems somehow—oddly, piquantly— characteristic. The reader must find you amusing (there, I've said it). Amusing enough to follow you, no matter what essay topic you propose. Whether you are writing this time on world peace or a bar of soap, readers must sense quickly from the first paragraph that you are going to keep them engaged. The trouble is that you cannot amuse the reader unless you are already self-amused. And here we come to one of the main stumbling blocks placed before the writing of personal essays: self-hatred.

It is an observable fact that most people don't like themselves, in spite of being, for the most part, decent enough human beings—certainly not war criminals—and in spite of the many self-help books urging us to befriend and think positively about ourselves. Why this self-dislike should be so prevalent is a matter that would require the best sociological and psychoanalytic minds to elucidate; all I can say, from my vantage point as a teacher and anthologist of the personal essay, is that an odor of self-disgust mars many performances in this genre and keeps many would-be practitioners from developing into full-fledged professionals. They exhibit a form of stuttering, of never being able to get past the initial, superficial self-presentation and diving into the wreck of one's personality with gusto.

The proper alternative to self-dislike is not being pleased with oneself—a smugness equally distasteful to the reader—but being *curious about* oneself. Such self-curiosity (of which Montaigne, the father of the essay, was the greatest exemplar) can only grow out of that detachment or distance from oneself about which I spoke earlier.

I am convinced that self-amusement is a discipline that can be learned; it can be practiced even by people (such as myself) who have at times a strong self-dislike or at least self-mistrust. I may be tired of myself in everyday life, but once I start narrating a situation or set of ideas on the page, I begin to see my "I" in a comic light, and I maneuver him so that he will best amuse the reader. My "I" is not me, entirely, but a character drawn from aspects of myself, in somewhat the same way (less stylized or bold, perhaps) that Chaplin drew the Little Fellow or Jerry Lewis modeled the arrested-development goofball from their experiences. I am willing to let my "I" take his pratfalls; maintaining one's dignity should not be a paramount issue in personal essays. But first must come the urge to entertain the reader. From that impulse everything else follows.

There is also considerable character development in expressing your opinions, prejudices, half-baked ideas, etc., etc., provided you are willing to analyze the flaws in your thinking and to entertain arguments against your hobbyhorses and not be too solemn about it all. The essay thrives on daring, darting flights of thought. You must get in the habit of inviting, not censoring, your most far-fetched, mischievous notions, because even if they prove cockeyed, they may point to an element of truth that would otherwise be inaccessible. When, for instance, I wrote my essay "Against Joie de Vivre,"

I knew on some level that it was an indefensible position, but I wanted to see how far I could get in taking a curmudgeonly stance against the pursuit of happiness. And indeed, it struck a chord of recognition in many readers, because lots of us are "so glad to be unhappy," at least as much as we "want to be happy." (To quote two old songs.)

Finally, it would do well for personal essayists to follow another rule of fiction writers, who tell you that if you want to reveal someone's character, actions speak louder than words. Give your "I" something to do. It's fine to be privy to all of "I's" ruminations and cerebral nuances, but consciousness can only take us so far in the illumination of character. Particularly if you are writing a memoir essay, with chronology and narrative, it is often liberating to have the "I" step beyond the observer role and be implicated crucially in the overall action. How many memoir pieces suffer from a self-righteous setup: the writer telling a story in which Mr. or Ms. "I" is the passive recipient of the world's cruelty, the character's first exposure to racism or betrayal, say. There is something off-putting about a nonfiction story in which the "I" character is right and all the others wrong, the "I" infinitely more sinned against than sinning. By showing our complicity in the world's stock of sorrow, we convince the reader of our reality and even gain his sympathy.

How much more complicated and alive is George Orwell's younger self, the "I" in "Such, Such Were the Joys," for having admitted he snitched on his classmates, or James Baldwin's "I" in "Notes of a Native Son," for acknowledging how close he came to the edge with his rages about racism in restaurants. Character is not just a question of sensibility: There are hard choices to be made when a person is put under pressure. And it's in having made the wrong choice, curiously enough, that we are made all the more aware of our freedom and potential for humanity. So it is that remorse is often the starting point for good personal essays, whose working-out brings the necessary self-forgiveness (not to mention self-amusement) to outgrow shame.

I have not touched on some other requirements of the personal essay, such as the need to go beyond the self's quandaries, through research or contextualization, to bring back news of the larger world. Nor have I spoken of the grandeur of the so-called formal essay. Yet even when "I" plays no part in the language of an essay, a firm sense of personality can warm the voice of the impersonal essay narrator. When we read Dr. Johnson and Edmund Wilson and Lionel Trilling, for instance, we feel that we know them as fully developed characters in their own essays, regardless of their not referring personally to themselves.

The need thus exists to make oneself into a character, whether the essay uses a first- or third-person narrative voice. I would further maintain that this process of turning oneself into a character is not self-absorbed navel gazing, but rather a potential release from narcissism. It means you have achieved sufficient distance to begin to see yourself in the round: a necessary precondition to transcending the ego—or at least writing personal essays that can touch other people.

by Frank L. Cioffi

ARGUMENTATION IN A CULTURE OF DISCORD

Last October, the comedian-philosopher Jon Stewart did writing teachers a great service. Accosting the hosts of CNN's *Crossfire*, Stewart accused them of shortchanging the American public by failing to offer a forum for genuine debate and by reducing issues to black/ white, right/wrong dichotomies. CNN apparently agreed, as it canceled the show after a twenty-three-year run. And while I certainly admit that Stewart himself argued unfairly, his point nonetheless stands: Our media do not provide a forum for actual debate. Instead they're a venue for self-promotion and squabbling, for hawking goods, for infomercials masquerading as news or serious commentary. In terms of discussing issues, they offer two sides, pick one: Either you are for gay marriage or against it, either for abortion or for life, either for pulling the feeding tube or for "life."

This failure to provide a forum for argumentative discourse has steadily eroded students' understanding of "argument" as a concept. For decades, my college writing classes have stressed the need to write papers with an argumentative edge. Yet students don't get it. Either they don't understand what I mean, or they reject the whole enterprise. A few years ago, one of them—"G.M."—wrote me an e-mail message that exemplifies many students' position:

> In reading your ideas over the difficulty of [getting] students to accept an argumentative thesis, I wonder … how much one could say that it [has been] caused by the pre-millennial movement of pacificism? In my lifetime I have not seen something so polarizing as war and thus I have not felt the amount of momentary certainty that past generations have. … Violence is on another level entirely, for I do not believe in war, but confrontation's very redeemable qualities are normally overlooked. …

G.M. seemed to think I was advocating a verbal violence that he—his whole generation—was loath to undertake. While I responded that written argument was by its nature nonviolent, I nonetheless understood from whence he drew his conclusions: He saw "argument" in media-defined terms.

Part of the problem of teaching argumentative writing is that "argument" means "heated, contentious verbal dispute" as well as "argumentation." Some writing texts make this confusion worse: One in front of me uses a handsome cover illustration by Julia Talcott that shows two people from whose open mouths issue, respectively, a red triangle and a blue circle. I don't think this kind of visual is likely to help matters. Like the figures in "Laughing Stock," the media feature arguers who have entrenched, diametrically opposed positions.

Students typically don't want to attempt "argument" or take a controversial position to defend, probably because they've seen or heard enough of the media's models—Bill O'Reilly, Ann Coulter, or Al Franken, to name a few—and are sick of them. If I were an eighteen-year-old college freshman assigned an argumentative essay, I'd groan in despair, either because I found the food-fight-journalism model repulsive or because, like G.M., I didn't feel strongly enough about anything to engage in the furious invective that I had all too often witnessed. Maybe the unanticipated consequence of the culture of contentious argument—and this, I think, was Stewart's larger point—is the decline in the general dissemination of intellectual, argumentative discourse more broadly construed.

I propose that we teach students more about how intellectual discourse works, about how it offers something exciting—yet how when it succeeds, it succeeds in only approaching understanding. The philosopher Frank Plumpton Ramsey puts it bluntly but eloquently: "Meaning is mainly potential." Philosophical and, more generally, argumentative discourse presents no irrefutable proofs, no indelible answers. In fact, the best writing of this kind tends not to answer but to raise questions, ones that perhaps the audience hadn't previously considered. Or to put it in terms my college-age nephew uses, when you're writing argument, don't go for the slam-dunk.

At the same time, we should make students aware that they're not alone on the court. We need, that is, to emphasize more the need for counter arguments, which inevitably force writers to place themselves in the audience's position and to attempt to imagine what that audience values and feels—what objections it might intelligently raise. In *On Liberty*, John Stuart Mill asserts that 75 percent of an argument should consist of counter arguments. And, further, writers should not merely parrot these, but must "know them in their most plausible and persuasive form ... must feel the whole force of the difficulty which the true view of the subject has to encounter and dispose of." Presenting and empathizing with counter arguments forces an author to go somewhere new, to modify her initial position into one more nuanced, more complex, more problematic—perhaps to one of greater potential, to use Ramsey's formulation.

Now this might be very well for philosophical or literary-critical discourse, but what of scientific discourse? What of historical or legal discourse? I suggest that all these fields require an argumentative stance, if not in the papers that students write at the freshman or even undergraduate level, then in professional journals and monographs, and that stance should be the model for student writing. While these models differ some from field to field, all academic writing starts with a problem, a hypothesis, or a question. And the idea is not to solve this problem or answer that question with previously extant notions. This kind of writing should offer something original, imaginative, something the audience would not have thought of before and might even initially reject. Yet it invites that rejection, seeks out disconfirmatory material, naysaying positions. Working against the initial rejection, it logically persuades the audience how a proposed solution betters other current solutions, covers a wider range of data, or undermines previous notions. In short, this kind of writing looks at other answers and engages them, proving them in need of some rethinking, recontextualizing, or reimagining. And though its answer might not be perfect, it's closer—it asymptotically approaches a truth.

Yet can every student be an Einstein? Should we urge every student to come up with writing that resembles the professional writing of one's discipline, when many students have difficulty constructing paragraphs, constructing sentences, or construing meaning of central texts? Probably not at every level. I know that much writing instruction and many writing programs (such as, for example, the one I direct) are often expected to "help students learn how to punctuate." And I know that's an important tool. I sympathize with professors who must wade through mounds of hastily composed, unproofread, usage-dull essays that bring only a fixed glaze to their readers' eyes.

But if we focus on defining our genre and discourse, showing students what it is that we do, we might just get students excited about discovering new ideas, about reimagining old problems, about writing something that somehow matters. Then they will often realize the need to present their ideas in a more "correct," formal English. They will work on their papers, putting them through multiple drafts, consulting with tutors, with us. They might even start perusing usage texts. In short, we need to work toward providing students fulfillment in the very process of writing, rather than in only the grade we give to the product.

Not surprisingly, that kind of thought and writing process is difficult to teach. It's easier to give "evaluative" writing assignments for which there are more or less clear-cut answers: Summarize this. Give a precis of that. Answer this question. Give us an outline. Fill in the blank. True or false?

Using writing only as an evaluative tool, these assignments invoke the consumer-like currency-exchange model. Think of how in the course of a semester so much of a discipline's dialectical ambiguity emerges, yet how often we will use "evaluative" writing assignments such as the aforementioned, with the expressed purpose of see-ing if students "got" the "material," which even for us is slippery and elusive. And the transitive verb really matters here: I "got" a new iPod; I "got" a pair of Gap jeans; I "got" John Rawls's "veil of ignorance" concept; I "got" an A. This pedagogy resembles the consumer myth: There is an answer (a product, an idea, a methodology, a theory, a grade); it's this. Like consumerism, this pedagogy reduces enormously complex issues to simplistic solutions: canned answers qua canned soup. Or as one of my colleagues puts it, "Human beings, pork and beans, they're all the same!"

By offering such assignments, we unwittingly embrace what the media have led people to believe that intellectual debate and discourse consist of. People on shows such as *Crossfire* stake out a position, and they iterate and reiterate that position. They give examples of what they mean and "defend" themselves by ignoring or deliber-ately misconstruing vicious attacks from the opposing side. But this is not intellectual discourse; it's discourse packaged as product. Academic, intellectual discourse—true debate, the attempt to genuinely advance knowledge, the use of imaginative arguments in general—cannot be easily captured in a half-hour television program. Such dis-course requires time and labor. It requires sustained analysis and construction of an intended audience. It requires careful marshaling of evidence, organization of ideas, rewriting, rethinking. It may seem a little boring to listen to, and is often too dense to grasp at first hearing.

How is this "exciting" or at all attractive? Why would anyone want to engage in "academic" discourse, except for some deferred reward, such as, well, a college degree? Why, in a larger sense, do we do what we do? (It isn't for the money.) I think there are larger rewards to scholarship, to argumentative writing. We have a curiosity about how things work (or fail to), and the writing we do attempts to satisfy that curiosity, to explain problems to ourselves, to others. Though Richard D. Altick's book *The Scholar Adventurers* might be a hard sell to the general public, his fundamental idea still stands: There are risk and danger to scholarship; it takes some courage to undertake it. For example, we might figure out more how the universe operates, but that discovery might well undermine our previously held conceptions. So while our writing might not serve to amuse, and it might not gather miscellaneous thumbprints in the waiting room of a car-repair shop, it might just advance human knowledge. Lofty, perhaps, but I think true.

Most people never encounter such discourse. And most students, on entering college, have no idea of what it's like. They've come from a culture that wants answers, not nuanced problematizations, not philosophy. They've been conditioned, as have most Americans, to seek out a position where a simple choice will solve the problem. They've been conditioned to see ideas as being part of a marketplace, just like sweat-shirts, snowboards, or songs, and when they are asked to produce ideas, they look to that marketplace for a model. And students do this with their research papers as much as with their arguments. How often, in fact, does a student's research paper look like an amateur journalist's report of multiple facts and views, a superficial survey of x number of sources, with no argument even implied?

I don't want to disparage consumer culture too much, since I often define myself against its dazzling and dreamy backdrop, but consumer culture (and the media, which are a part of it) often works against us in higher education. It makes arguments all the time, but they're not sound, intellectual arguments. It manufactures a need, it contrives a teleology. For example, now there's an even better TV or home gym or soap to buy; now you can improve your looks, your skin, your mood, your erectile capacity. In short, the consumer myth suggests that some consumer products can end, even satisfy, our hydra-headed desire. So the culture offers the beauteous product with one tentacle, but if you take it, two new beckoning heads pop up. More insidiously, consumer discourse, by concretizing satisfactions for the desires it creates, implies that any desires not satisfiable by culture—i.e., not purchasable—can only be perverse or bizarre; any complicated solutions, absurd.

Student writing resembles in microcosm the consumer-product myth insofar as it offers contrived problems for which there are equally contrived, predictable, pre-packaged solutions. Indeed, this writing too often offers ideas that can be supported relatively easily, with abundant, even overwhelming, evidence. Consider, for example, the "five-paragraph essay" so often taught in high schools around the country and further abetted by the new SAT exam. Paragraph one offers an introduction, including a thesis at the end of the introduction. It's best if this thesis has three points. The subsequent three paragraphs develop and explain these thesis- supporting points. The last paragraph, the conclusion, sums up the paper and restates the thesis.

Nothing wrong with that, is there? Well, there is. It resembles the script for commercials. It inhibits, even prohibits freedom of thought. It's static—more noise than signal. There's no real inquiry going on, no grappling with complexities. It seeks only support, and readily available support at that. It can appear to be heated, resembling the screaming-heads model. But it's one-sided, and it goes nowhere, except to its inevitable end, which resembles or reproduces its beginning.

When we try to teach argument in the classroom, we have to fight a model of discourse that, zombielike, still stalks many classrooms. At the same time, we're pressed to provide a better model for students than the reasoned, calm approach, the one that engages and responds to counter arguments, that strives only to approach an understanding. The model for this in public discourse is as hard to find as the genre is to explain or justify. It's no surprise that we can't stick an ice pick through the five-paragraph monster's gelid heart.

The best argumentative writing expands and transforms the ideas of the writer. It questions itself, actively seeking out emergent problems along the way. And it ends not with a definitive, an in-your-face "So there!" (or a "You should just read the Bible!"), but probably with more complex questions, ones that push the continuum of the subject matter. Of course students don't initially like this model: It's not very tidy. It doesn't offer an easy answer or position. It seems to waver, or to embody a predetermined "flip- flop" mentality. (This is the kind of thing that weakened John Kerry's credibility with voters.) But at the same time, students know that the model is better than the five-paragraph essay. One student told me writing in the argumentative mode was "scary." It's just not something they've been taught to do—yet its being tantamount to a transgressive act can make it much more attractive.

Why so? I think this might stem from a very simple human emotion that both the culture—and many writing assignments, too—seems desperate to eradicate: longing. Frederick Exley, in *A Fan's Notes*, talks about this issue. After college, his protagonist plans to get a certain kind of apartment in New York, a certain kind of job, and a certain kind of girlfriend. He even plans to be a "Genius." He has all these longings that need to be fulfilled. But in fact, what he hadn't really learned in college was that longings are better left unfulfilled: "Literature is born out of the very longing I was so seeking to suppress," he writes. Writing argument is all about longing—a longing for the truth. And this longing is inherently unsatisfiable.

Emerson frequently argued for the value of "conation," that is, the perpetual striving for something. We don't want to perpetually strive—or long—for anything, much less the truth. We want more immediate gratification: Get there, solve it, and get out. Consider Iraq—a war in which our desire for a "that's that" resolution has smashed up against a problem defying easy solution. It's a war that has challenged our American notion of who we are—are we people who use torture, for example?—at the same time that it's thrown into relief our "can do" notion of ourselves. And what do people think about this war? I don't think they want to think about it. But it's not that they're lazy or craven. Nor am I implying that the desire for immediate gratification is wicked—it's just not something provided by intellectual discourse or argument. People simply haven't been given the right models of how to think. That's our job; that's what academic argument's about. Jon Stewart was right to have attacked *Crossfire* and its brand of discourse. Now it's up to us to create an intellectual alternative—not just for our students, but for the public as well.

CHAPTER 17

Revision

evision is a process of seeing again. Literally, "re-visioning." The first draft of an essay helps us to figure out what we want to say; subsequent revisions help us to say what we mean to say in the most effective and polished manner.

When you are drafting an essay, try not to censor yourself. Getting words on the page is messy but exciting. However, once you have completed that initial effort—what Donald Murray refers to in "The Maker's Eye" as "the zero draft"—it's time to step back and assess your work from a more objective point of view, pushing yourself toward clarifying and refining your driving question, pursuing at least a partial answer to that question, deepening your analysis, improving your execution. Later in this chapter, we will discuss the peer-review workshop, which is a useful means to develop objectivity about your own writing and to see your essay from another reader's point of view. But before you submit your essay for workshop, you will want to be sure that you have pushed your work as far as you can go on your own.

THE STAGES OF REVISION

Revision takes place in stages. At the global level, you will be considering the structure of your paper as a whole; at the level of the paragraph, you might be re-examining the formation and development of your ideas and themes; at the sentence level, you will be sharpening your language and honing the specificity of your details. The best advice we can give is that you don't try to tackle all these different components at once. Instead of struggling to make each sentence or paragraph or page "perfect" before going on to the next sentence or paragraph or page, choose a single global element to focus on and go through the entire paper with this one task in mind. Once you have completed that round of improvement, choose another global component of the paper to reconsider. Making many passes over the paper like this will save you a lot of time in the long run. Also, be sure that you start with the big issues such as structure before working your way down to smaller issues such as language. After all, it's a waste of time to polish a paragraph that you might end up deleting after you have revised the structure.

Speaking of what to keep and what to get rid of, before the invention of computers, writers would often cut apart the sections of a rough draft, rearrange them on a table or on the floor, and then paste or tape the sections to the pages of a legal pad in a new or better order. They would cut out the salvageable parts of an early draft, tape them to a pad, then write the new version of the essay in and around those sections. Although cumbersome, this method allowed the writer to see the entire essay at a glance and try this or that structural possibility without losing track of large chunks of text drifting through hyperspace. As retro as this sounds, don't be afraid to take a pair of scissors and cut a hard copy of your essay into sections, then rearrange those sections and tape them to a pad before returning to your computer and keying in the changes.

That said, what follows are some useful questions to ask yourself during the revision process. We fully expect that you will adapt the strategies we present here to fit your own methods; after all, there is no "right" way to revise a paper.

Global Level

- **Who is the audience for your essay?** What would that audience know or not know about you and your subject? What expectations, prejudices, or preconceived notions would your audience bring to your material? What would be the appropriate vocabulary and tone to use when speaking to this audience? Would your readers need any background information to clarify or contextualize what you are telling them? Might your essay cause some readers to become squeamish? Combative? Despairing? Do you want to address any of these reactions?

- **Why does this essay matter to anyone besides you?** Where do you tap into broader social concerns? How might your experience translate to a reader, even if indirectly? For example, most of us will never face shooting an elephant, as George Orwell describes in his essay. Yet we can identify with his experience because the majority of us have acted in a way we knew was wrong because of the influence of others. So ask yourself: How is my situation a *microcosm* of something larger? How is my situation an example of a *phenomenon*?

- **What's at stake?** The reader needs to know the driving question of your essay almost immediately. If the reader is still struggling after a few pages to figure out what you are trying to understand or uncover, you probably are in trouble. This doesn't mean that you have to spell out everything right at the start, but the reader should be able to identify the question with which you are grappling.

- **Where does the story truly begin?** At what moment does your material heat up and get exciting? Is that where you actually start your essay? Reflective narratives usually fall into one of two categories: they are either "build-up" or "fall-out" essays. George Orwell and Elwood Reid focus on the build-up of rising conflict and action, creating tension for the reader. We wonder: *Will Orwell shoot the elephant? Will Reid drop out of football or get injured too badly to continue playing?*

Fall-out essays chronicle the aftermath or consequences of a powerful incident. Lucy Grealy writes about the fall-out that occurs following her cancer surgery—and how that fall-out affects the next twenty years of her life. Ask yourself: "Is my story about what happened *prior* to an important event, or is it about what happened *afterward*?"

- **The struggle is the story.** One of the hardest parts of writing creative nonfiction is balancing *scene* and *exposition*. A rule of thumb when making the choice between the two modes of writing: Use a scene when you want the reader to *experience* the moment, particularly a moment that reveals something about someone's character or is crucial to the development of the story; use exposition when you are *delivering information* (backstory, someone's biography, a definition, technical explanations, statistics) or when you are transitioning from one scene and/or time period to another.

- **Is there enough reflection?** Analysis is fundamental to any successful essay. Without analysis, your narrative is little more than an anecdote. One way to think of your job as a writer is as an "interpreter"—someone who makes sense of or meaning from a specific occurrence. By connecting and synthesizing ideas in a unique or thoughtful way, you will be giving readers a new way of seeing your topic. Go over what you have written and highlight the passages in which you meditate on your driving question. Are there places in your essay where additional analysis seems called for by the importance of what just happened, what is about to happen, or what you have discovered in your research?

- **Have you built enough analysis into the body of your essay?** The central analysis can, and probably will, come near the end of your narrative. But just as the structure of your essay needs to grow and build, so should your analysis. Think of how Lucy Grealy weaves notions of gender, sexuality, and identity throughout her essay "Mirrorings" to lead up to and support her final analysis. (Note: In argumentative terms, she uses her experience as evidence to support her final claim.) Similarly, Orwell's final analysis on the powerlessness inherent in the practice of imperialism emerges from his development of themes of power and authority throughout earlier portions of his essay.

- **Do you have strong evidence?** Even when you are writing about your own life, you will need to back up your assertions with evidence. As you look at your first draft, ask yourself if there is anything you need to add to support your claims. Who might disagree with your interpretation of events or the evidence you use to support your claims? How might you convince such skeptics that you are right?

- **What have you discovered?** Is your conclusion obvious (i.e., "Don't disobey your parents," or "Don't start off on a wilderness hike without a compass")? Have you simply re-proved a moral your readers already accept as true (i.e., "Don't judge a book by its cover," or "What doesn't kill you makes you stronger")? Is there some less obvious discovery you might make based on your actual experience, your research, or your discussions with other people? Might your experience *disprove* an adage or proverb or other accepted form of conventional wisdom?

Paragraph Level

- **Take your essay one step at a time.** Each paragraph needs to build on the ideas introduced in the previous paragraph. An easy way to determine whether a paragraph is doing its job is to ask the following: What is the goal or purpose of this paragraph? What is it doing to help develop my essay's analysis or argument? If the answers aren't clear, you need to question the paragraph's necessity, its placement, and/or its role in your paper. Similarly, don't try to cram too many ideas in a paragraph or your analysis will get lost. One paragraph = one idea.

- **Use in-scene writing where appropriate.** Good in-scene writing is made up of the following four components: description, action, dialogue, and interiority. But an essay can't be made up *only* of scenes. You also need exposition and reflection. Strong writing exhibits a balance among all three major elements. Ask yourself if your essay exhibits such a balance. If it doesn't, which mode is being underused? Overused?

- **Avoid filler.** Once you have decided which sections of your essay should be written in scene and which should be presented as summary or exposition, take a look at the summary or exposition and see if any of the information you have included is just filler. Ask yourself: "Do I absolutely need this information for the story to make sense? If I get rid of it, what might be lost?" The reader doesn't need to see *every* step in the process or hear *every* detail and anecdote, just the ones that are crucial to developing the narrative.

- **Give the reader insider details.** Remember that most readers aren't familiar with your world. The reader needs to feel as if he or she is learning not only about you, but also your subject. Insider details help to establish authority. Be sure that your details are doing real work—helping you to answer your essay's driving question, underscoring your essay's theme, strengthening our understanding of your characters, bringing alive your setting—and that the details are *significant*.

- **Contextualize your outside sources.** If you have incorporated outside sources, what is the purpose of engaging these other thinkers? How does the work of experts inform or support your own work? Have you introduced and explained the relevance of your sources' ideas, or merely dropped them in like nuts and cherries in a fruitcake? Have you properly cited all quotations and ideas that belong to other people? Have you appropriately interpreted your research in the context of your driving question?

Sentence Level

- **Cut anything that's not essential.** Go through your essay and ask yourself if there are sections or scenes that don't relate to your driving question. If there are, force yourself to cut them. Next, go through and ask yourself whether each paragraph is vital to your essay. If it isn't, force yourself to cut it. If you consider a given paragraph vital to your essay, go through it sentence by sentence and ask yourself whether each sentence is vital to that paragraph, and if it isn't, force yourself to cut it. Once you have gotten your essay down to its essential sentences, go through each sentence word by word and ask yourself if each word is vital to that sentence, and if it isn't, force yourself to cut it. Rather than seeing this as a chore, you can see it as a game—you want your essay to be as concise and lean as possible.

- **Avoid empty nouns.** An empty noun is a noun that is so vague or abstract it doesn't ignite any of your readers' five senses (especially the sense of sight) or lead your readers to experience any emotion. The most common examples of vague nouns tend to be "it" and "thing," but "situation," "problem," "process," "type," "sort," and "kind" are ubiquitous as well. You would be surprised how powerful and vivid a passage can become simply by changing most of the empty nouns and pronouns to concrete nouns and names. (And don't be worried about repeating nouns. Readers would rather see the word "dog" three times than see "it" three times).

- **Beware of vague phrases.** Remember in the beginning of this book, when we tried to guess what various writers meant when they talked about "dealing with their parents' problems with alcohol" or the "situations in their homes"? If a parent has "a problem with alcohol," he or she is an alcoholic (or, in milder cases, a drinker, or, still yet, someone who disapproves of consuming even a drop of alcohol!). A "domestic violence situation" is a case of wife beating or child abuse. And if someone is "engaged in a decision-making process to determine whether to absent himself from a dysfunctional football-type situation," he is deciding whether to quit a team because the coach forces kids to play even when they are injured.

- **Steer clear of empty verbs.** As you might guess, an empty verb is a verb that doesn't convey a concrete action. At this point in your writing life, you probably have heard teachers warn you not to use the passive voice, so we will just offer a brief reminder that "The ball was hit" is always less vivid than "The toddler hit the ball," while "The pie was eaten" leaves out the vital information that "The old lady ate the pie." But even experienced writers need frequent nagging to prod them to purge their sentences of "is/was" verbs. "There was blood on the floor" rarely can compete with "Blood pooled on the floor."

- **Root out "Engfish."** As we mentioned in Chapter 10, you want to avoid what Ken Macrorie calls "fishy English," or verbiage that comes from students' attempts to mimic jargon or diction they don't normally use. If you don't tend to say "thereupon" or "whereby" or "veritable plethora of deconstructed, postmodern, postcolonial, hermeneutic strategies" in your everyday life, why would you write such pretentious phrases in an essay? Erudition and elegance are often to be admired, but if your prose strikes you as unnecessarily verbose, convoluted, or pretentious, ask yourself: "If I were explaining this to my best friend from home, or to my mother or little brother, what wording would I use?" You want to sound like the best version of yourself, but yourself all the same.

- **Hunt out redundancies.** All of us write drafts that contain sentences such as: "After my father divorced my mother, he left the marriage and went to live in an utterly dingy, completely empty apartment that wasn't furnished on the outskirts of town." The trick is to catch such a sentence before the final draft and compress it to: "My father divorced my mother and went to live in a dingy, unfurnished apartment on the outskirts of town." Other redundancies require that you believe your verbs are actually doing their jobs. Consider these examples: "I thought to myself"; "I shrugged my shoulders"; "I whispered softly"; "I staggered in a jerky motion"; "I ran quickly."

- **Let your draft sit for a few days.** At the very least, sleep on it. Then reread what you have written with fresh eyes and revise as needed.

FEEDBACK AND PEER WORKSHOPS

When writers have done everything they can do on their own, most show their work to at least one other person, or to the members of a peer-critique group, to solicit feedback (Jeremiah's essay "Workshop Is Not for You," included in this section, outlines the benefits of reading and critiquing the work of your peers, in addition to having your essays read by your fellow writers). The goal of a good critic is to act as an honest respondent to the work. Thoughtful questions can be just as helpful to an author as criticisms or suggestions for improvement.

Speaking of suggestions, when you are reading someone else's work, remember this is not *your* paper; it's the writer's. Try to understand what the writer is going for, regardless of whether you identify with the subject. Tailor your comments with your classmate's goals and style of execution in mind. This is not to say that you can't identify aspects of the text that don't work for you, but be sure that your suggestions are directed toward helping the writer achieve his or her vision and voice rather than *your* vision and voice.

Finally, be aware that someone in your peer-critique group might write a paper illuminating a topic on which you hold the opposite position. If your classmate's essay doesn't support his analysis or conclusion, if you don't find her arguments convincing, by all means speak up. But you also must remain open to your classmate's point of view—and open to having your perceptions of the world changed. Our mantras for a good peer-critique: (1) Do No Harm; and (2) Meet the Writer Halfway.

Guidelines for Peer Review

In addition to allowing you the time to develop a coherent response to your classmates' work, written critiques guarantee that each individual's suggestions are given a voice, ensuring that the writer hears each and every opinion, not simply those opinions that are the most popular or stated in the loudest or most eloquent terms.

This is not to say that you won't write a critique and then, after hearing some of your classmates' opinions, wish you could change your interpretation or your suggestions. That's fine. But it is still instructive for the writer to see your initial reaction to his or her work. After all, if you read an essay in a particular way, other students probably did as well. And the cause of your misinterpretation might be something the writer will want to address.

As Jeremiah notes in his essay, writing critiques and trying to figure out constructive suggestions to help your classmates improve their work ultimately will be just as valuable for you as for them. Criticism is a reflective art, and you will naturally find yourself more aware of missteps or achievements in your own work when you see them in the work of others.

We recommend reading the essay you are responding to twice. The first time, you should read simply for comprehension—to understand the subject, the driving question, and the basic structure of the essay. Don't bother with line-edits at this stage. The second time, you should read with a pen or pencil in hand, making a minimum of three or four notes per page. These can be initial responses, such as "Great example!" or "I love this line!" Or you can point the writer toward places where he or she might need to do more work ("You're rushing this scene" or "Missed opportunity for analysis here"). Regardless, your reactions will give the writer real-time feedback on how his or her work is being interpreted. A good respondent will offer a variety of responses, from the global to the sentence level, as we discussed in the revision section.

Once you have offered suggestions in the margins of the manuscript, you should compose a typed or handwritten critique of the essay as a whole. What follows is a list of possible topics, approaches, and questions that you can integrate into your feedback. Just as it's productive to approach revision in stages, it's often helpful to vary the *type* of feedback that you are offering a writer. Here, we have tried to categorize the sorts of questions you might draw upon as you respond to a classmate's essay. Depending on the form of the essay or the goal of the assignment, you might find yourself focusing on one category more than another. Not all of these items will apply to every essay; the idea here is to get you thinking about the approach you might take when assessing another writer's work.

Unlike the responses you scribble in the margins of the manuscript, the goal of a written or typed critique is to give more holistic feedback to the writer. Together, these two elements comprise a complete critique. You won't always have the time or opportunity to do both, but be aware that each method offers the writer a different way of seeing his or her essay.

What's Working

- First, a writer needs to know what is working well, so pinpoint the most vivid or interesting scenes, the most engaging characters, and the details, lines of dialogue, or passages of reflection or analysis that add the most to the essay. This will help the writer continue to develop those strengths in each subsequent draft and/or essay.

- It's also helpful to let a writer know what you would like to see *more* of.

Question or Claim

- Restate the driving question the writer is exploring. If the question isn't coming through clearly, this will be the most important element of the essay for the writer to clarify, as the driving question frames the way a reader will approach the essay as a whole.

- Similarly, you might articulate the argument or claim at which the essay ultimately arrives. Is it debatable? Is it original?

Style and Clarity

- Is the voice unique and natural? Is the tone appropriate?

- Is there thoughtful attention to language? Are the sentences clear and concise, as well as structurally varied?

- Do you feel you need more backstory or context to understand the essay?

- Does the writer overuse details, or use too few? Are the details significant?

Structure

- Is the manuscript's structure clear? Different forms require different technical elements and different approaches to the material.

- Does the essay begin in an interesting, compelling way and build to a strong conclusion?

- Does each paragraph or section introduce new ideas and/or analysis so that the essay *develops* in a complex way?

- Is the pacing too fast or too slow? Is there too much "build-up"? Not enough "fall-out"?

- Is there careful attention to transitions from one idea to the next? Between sentences, paragraphs, and sections?

- What suggestions do you have for the writer to expand the essay? To condense it? Be specific (and tactful) in locating specific moments in the text for expansion or contraction.

- Similarly, are there missed opportunities for a scene? Are there scenes that could be rendered more efficiently and effectively in summary or exposition?

- Does the writer use all four elements of in-scene writing? Is there too much **dialogue**, or not enough? Is the **description** vivid? Are there revealing gestures or **actions**? Are the inner workings of the author's mind (his or her "**interiority**") helping to illuminate or translate the scene for the reader?

- Does the writer develop characters (including himself or herself) fully?

Evidence and Support

- Can you trace the process by which the writer develops at least a partial answer to his or her driving question? Has the writer proven his or her discovery or argument to be valid?

- Does the essay incorporate appropriate evidence and a thorough analysis of the evidence, regardless of whether that evidence is based on personal experience or traditional research?

- Is an appropriate amount of resistance to the author's argument included in the essay? Has the author considered viewpoints other than his or her own?

- Is the author's research integrated effectively into the main body of the essay?

- Has the writer used an appropriate amount and range of sources? Are those sources used as evidence to back up the writer's claim, or are they simply talking *for* the writer?

- Has each source been effectively introduced, or are the quotes simply "dropped in"? Are sources correctly cited and attributed?

Analysis, Significance, and Originality

- Has the essay answered the "So What?" question? That is, does the essay's topic matter to anyone beyond the writer?

- Does the essay probe below the surface, giving the subject meaning by analyzing what it represents or signifies or how it is part of a larger phenomenon?

- Is the writer's discovery interesting? Are the essay's conclusions obvious, or are they surprising? Does the essay illuminate the topic in a new and interesting way? Does it give the reader a new way of seeing the topic, text, or issue?

Responding to Feedback

You can't address every comment you will hear about your work. Just as there is an art to writing critiques, so, too, is there an art to synthesizing criticism. You will need to learn when to listen to suggestions and when to ignore advice that—while no doubt well intentioned—doesn't line up with what you were going for in your essay. The tricky part is identifying which is which! Most of your peers have honestly and intelligently offered the best feedback on your work that they were able to provide. And the best reader for one of your essays might not be the best reader for the next. So try to be as honest with yourself as possible. Don't discount a suggestion just because you don't like it or don't want to hear it, but at the same time make your peace with not taking every suggestion offered. Ultimately, you can't write by committee.

As before, here are a few tips to bear in mind as you synthesize feedback on your work.

- Try not to get defensive. If your class meets as a group to discuss your essay, write down everything you hear, whether praise or constructive criticism. Sitting through a workshop is like listening to a doctor talk about an upcoming operation: you think you are taking in everything the doctor says, but you tend to forget most of what you hear because your heart is pounding too loudly. In the case of workshop, surprisingly, most people tend to forget their readers' praise!

- Ask yourself which suggestions ring true or echo your own fears about your essay. Which suggestions make you excited about returning to your computer? Which suggestions seem beside the point or wrongheaded? Which suggestions would turn your essay into an essay you never intended to write? Might these new intentions be better than your old ones? Might you want to change your intentions and start over? Why or why not?

- Once you have identified the most helpful criticism, go back to your essay and make the improvements that ring true or seem helpful. If feedback from your readers has significantly changed your understanding of your essay's driving question or the form that will best allow you to explore it, then you will probably find it easiest to start over from scratch. Otherwise, make a list of all the changes you want to make, categorize them as (1) global, (2) paragraph level, or (3) sentence level, and then set yourself the goal of accomplishing the improvements one by one rather than trying to make all the improvements at the same time, in one huge revision.

- Try not to feel overwhelmed. Know that everyone gets lost at some point in the revision of an essay. If you do get lost, try to freewrite until you have found your way past your confusion. In particular, freewrite about *why* you are stuck. Often, by articulating the roadblock you are facing, you will find a way through, around, or over it.

For further reading about the process of revision, please refer to "The Maker's Eye" by Donald M. Murray, included in this section. Also in this chapter, you will find Jeremiah's essay about the benefits of workshop.

Donald M. Murray

THE MAKER'S EYE: REVISING YOUR OWN MANUSCRIPTS

When students complete a first draft, they consider the job of writing done — and their teachers too often agree. When professional writers complete a first draft, they usually feel that they are at the start of the writing process. When a draft is completed, the job of writing can begin.

That difference in attitude is the difference between amateur and professional, inexperience and experience, journeyman and craftsman. Peter F. Drucker, the prolific business writer, calls his first draft "the zero draft" — after that he can start counting. Most writers share the feeling that the first draft, and all. of those which follow, are opportunities to discover what they have to say and how best they can say it.

To produce a progression of drafts, each of which says more and says it more clearly, the writer has to develop a special kind of reading skill. In school we are taught to decode what appears on the page as finished writing. Writers, however, face a different category of possibility and responsibility when they read their own drafts. To them the words on the page are never finished. Each can be changed and rearranged, can set off a chain reaction of confusion or clarified meaning. This is a different kind of reading which is possibly more difficult and certainly more exciting.

Writers must learn to be their own best enemy. They must accept the criticism of others and be suspicious of it; they must accept the praise of others and be even more suspicious of it. Writers cannot depend on others. They must detach themselves from their own pages so that they can apply both their caring and their craft to their own work.

Such detachment is not easy. Science-fiction writer Ray Bradbury supposedly puts each manuscript away for a year to the day and then rereads it as a stranger. Not many writers have the discipline or the time to do this. We must read when our judgment may be at its worst, when we are close to the euphoric moment of creation.

Then the writer, counsels novelist Nancy Hale, "should be critical of everything that seems to him most delightful in his style. He should excise what he most admires, because he wouldn't thus admire it if he weren't ... in a sense protecting it from criticism." John Ciardi, the poet, adds, "The last act of the writing must be to become one's own reader. It is, I suppose, a schizophrenic process, to begin passionately and to end critically, to begin hot and to end cold; and, more important, to be passion-hot and critic-cold at the same time."

Most people think that the principal problem is that writers are too proud of what they have written. Actually, a greater problem for most professional writers is one shared by the majority of students. They are overly critical, think everything is dreadful, tear up page after page, never complete a draft, see the task as hopeless.

The writer must learn to read critically but constructively, to cut what is bad, to reveal what is good. Eleanor Estes, the children's book author, explains: "The writer must survey his work critically, coolly, as though he were a stranger to it. He must be willing to prune, expertly and hard-heartedly. At the end of each revision, a manuscript may look . . . worked over, torn apart, pinned together, added to, deleted from, words changed and words changed back. Yet the book must maintain its original freshness and spontaneity."

Most readers underestimate the amount of rewriting it usually takes to produce spontaneous reading. This is a great disadvantage to the student writer, who sees only a finished product and never watches the craftsman who takes the necessary step back, studies the work carefully, returns to the task, steps back, returns, steps back, again and again. Anthony Burgess, one of the most prolific writers in the English-speaking world, admits, "I might revise a page twenty times." Roald Dahl, the popular children's writer, states, "By the time I'm nearing the end of a story, the first part will have been reread and altered and corrected at least 150 times. . . . Good writing is essentially rewriting. I am positive of this."

Rewriting isn't virtuous. It isn't something that ought to be done. It is simply something that most writers find they have to do to discover what they have to say and how to say it. It is a condition of the writer's life.

There are, however, a few writers who do little formal rewriting, primarily because they have the capacity and experience to create and review a large number of invisible drafts in their minds before they approach the page. And some writers slowly produce finished pages, performing all the tasks of revision simultaneously, page by page, rather than draft by draft. But it is still possible to see the sequence followed by most writers most of the time in rereading their own work.

Most writers scan their drafts first, reading as quickly as possible to catch the larger problems of subject and form, and then move in closer and closer as they read and write, reread and rewrite.

The first thing writers look for in their drafts is *information*. They know that a good piece of writing is built from specific, accurate, and interesting information. The writer must have an abundance of information from which to construct a readable piece of writing.

Next writers look for *meaning* in the information. The specifics must build to a pattern of significance. Each piece of specific information must carry the reader toward meaning.

Writers reading their own drafts are aware of *audience*. They put themselves in the reader's situation and make sure that they deliver information which a reader wants to know or needs to know in a manner which is easily digested. Writers try to be sure that they anticipate and answer the questions a critical reader will ask when reading the piece of writing.

Writers make sure that the *form* is appropriate to the subject and the audience. Form, or genre, is the vehicle which carries meaning to the reader, but form cannot be selected until the writer has adequate information to discover its significance and an audience which needs or wants that meaning.

Once writers are sure the form is appropriate, they must then look at the *structure*, the order of what they have written. Good writing is built on a solid framework of logic, argument, narrative, or motivation which runs through the entire piece of writing and holds it together. This is the time when many writers find it most effective to outline as a way of visualizing the hidden spine by which the piece of writing is supported.

The element on which writers may spend a majority of their time is *development*. Each section of a piece of writing must be adequately developed. It must give readers enough information so that they are satisfied. How much information is enough? That's as difficult as asking how much garlic belongs in a salad. It must be done to taste, but most beginning writers underdevelop, underestimating the reader's hunger for information.

As writers solve development problems, they often have to consider questions of *dimension*. There must be a pleasing and effective proportion among all the parts of the piece of writing. There is a continual process of subtracting and adding to keep the piece of writing in balance.

Finally, writers have to listen to their own voices. *Voice* is the force which drives a piece of writing forward. It is an expression of the writer's authority and concern. It is what is between the words on the page, what glues the piece of writing together. A good piece of writing is always marked by a consistent, individual voice.

As writers read and reread, write and rewrite, they move closer and closer to the page until they are doing line-by-line editing. Writers read their own pages with infinite care. Each sentence, each line, each clause, each phrase, each word, each mark of punctuation, each section of white space between the type has to contribute to the clarification of meaning.

Slowly the writer moves from word to word, looking through language to see the subject. As a word is changed, cut, or added, as a construction is rearranged, all the words used before that moment and all those that follow that moment must be considered and reconsidered.

Writers often read aloud at this stage of the editing process, muttering or whispering to themselves, calling on the ear's experience with language. Does this sound right — or that? Writers edit, shifting back and forth from eye to page to ear to page. I find I must do this careful editing in short runs, no more than fifteen or twenty minutes at a stretch, or I become too kind with myself. I begin to see what I hope is on the page, not what actually is on the page.

This sounds tedious if you haven't done it, but actually it is fun. Making something right is immensely satisfying, for writers begin to learn what they are writing about by writing. Language leads them to meaning, and there is the joy of discovery, of understanding, of making meaning clear as the writer employs the technical skills of language.

Words have double meanings, even triple and quadruple meanings. Each word has its own potential of connotation and denotation. And when writers rub one word against the other, they are often rewarded with a sudden insight, an unexpected clarification.

The maker's eye moves back and forth from word to phrase to sentence to paragraph to sentence to phrase to word. The maker's eye sees the need for variety and balance, for a firmer structure, for a more appropriate form. It peers into the interior of the paragraph, looking for coherence, unity, and emphasis, which make meaning clear.

I learned something about this process when my first bifocals were prescribed. I had ordered a larger section of the reading portion of the glass because of my work, but even so, I could not contain my eyes within this new limit of vision. And I still find myself taking off my glasses and bending my nose toward the page, for my eyes unconsciously flick back and forth across the page, back to another page, forward to still another, as I try to see each evolving line in relation to every other line.

When does this process end? Most writers agree with the great Russian writer Tolstoy, who said, "I scarcely ever reread my published writings, if by chance I come across a page. It always strikes me: all this must be rewritten; this is how I should have written it."

The maker's eye is never satisfied, for each word has the potential to ignite new meaning. This article has been twice written all the way through the writing process. ... Now it is to be republished in a book. The editors made a few small suggestions, and then I read it with my maker's eye. Now it has been re-edited, re-revised, re-read, and re-re-edited, for each piece of writing to the writer is full of potential and alternatives.

A piece of writing is never finished. It is delivered to a deadline, torn out of the typewriter on demand, sent off with a sense of accomplishment and shame and pride and frustration. If only there were a couple more days, time for just another run at it, perhaps then. ...

By Jeremiah Chamberlin

WORKSHOP IS NOT FOR YOU

Whenever my students complain about workshop, their gripes invariably have to do with issues of reciprocity. Or, rather, the lack thereof—they have spent a great deal of time carefully reading and writing thoughtful comments on the work of their peers, only to receive the vaguest feedback in return. They are angry because they feel that workshop is a social contract. Specifically, one predicated on The Golden Rule: *Do Unto Others As You Would Have Them Do Unto You.* They've spent months "putting in their time" writing critiques and commentary with the understanding that the "payoff" for this diligence would be receiving the same level of attention to and suggestions for their work. Sometimes they are so angry about this violation of community trust that they can barely resist naming names. And even if they are mature enough to look past the issues of betrayal and fairness, there is still the practical matter of lacking direction for their revisions. So they come to me seeking retribution. Justice.

Needless to say, they aren't pleased when I tell them it doesn't matter. "Workshop isn't about your work, " I say. "In fact, in a perfect workshop you might never have your writing read by your peers."

Now their anger has turned to confusion. "Then what's the point?" they ask. To them, this is the whole bargain—you read someone else's work so they'll read yours.

"The point of workshop is to make you a better writer."

"That's what I mean," they reply. (They think I've misunderstood them.) "How am I supposed to get better if I don't know what's wrong with my writing?"

"You become a strong writer by *writing* critiques, not reading them, " I say. Being forced to analyze the effectiveness of other writers' stories and to then provide them with clear, concise, specific suggestions for improvement will do more to develop a writer's craft than almost anything else. Through this process writers develop a stronger objectivity about their own work, sharpen their critical thinking skills, and hone their language. A writer can't always recognize flat dialogue or abrupt scenes or uneven pacing in her own work, but she can sure as hell see it in someone else's. And the more adept she becomes at identifying it elsewhere, the more easily that skill becomes adapted into her own writing—it becomes second nature.

At this point in the conversation, most students will begrudgingly admit that commenting on the work of others has benefits for their own writing. But they will still grumble that writing critiques feels like busywork, that the same task could be accomplished by reading the work of their peers and then simply discussing it in the open forum of the class (after all, part of their complaint—whether voiced or not—has to do with the amount of time they spent on the other person's writing). What I try to explain, however, is that the effort required to articulate *why* and *how* the components of a story are working will not only force them to think more deeply about their understanding of the story's central concerns, but might also challenge their initial reading of the piece. This takes time.

Now, I know it's not much of a consolation to tell ourselves "They're only hurting themselves" when we don't receive the thoughtful feedback we'd hoped for on our work. Nor am I arguing that constructive criticism isn't helpful; there are real benefits to having our stories read closely by our peers. After all, simply understanding the physics of force, inertia, and angle of impact that govern the game of pool doesn't necessarily mean I'll be able to sink the ball when I lean over the felt with my cue; it takes years of practice before these skills become engrained, and even then it still takes a mixture of focus, concentration, and luck to pull off a difficult bank shot. So having someone who can comment on our form, our follow-through, even our choice of shots as we learn can be tremendously helpful and instructive.

But at the same time, by mistakenly believing that the most beneficial aspect of the workshop experience in terms of our artistic development is what takes place when it's "our day" to have our writing critiqued, we do ourselves—and our work—an enormous disservice. Understanding, instead, that one of the best opportunities for personal growth as an author comes from the sustained, close reading and articulate analysis of someone else's writing will have the effect of shifting the workshop model from one of social contracts, fairness, and duty to that of true learning and mutual respect. More important, we might come to realize that the most selfish thing we can do for our own work is to be altruistic. Perhaps *that's* the point.

GETTING FROM FIRST TO FINAL DRAFT

Here we include the first and final drafts of two student essays, both of which were written by recent students of ours in introductory writing courses at the University of Michigan. By examining the similarities and differences between these two revisions, you will begin to see how individual the revision process is—for different writers and for different types of essays.

The first essay we are including, a reflective narrative by Caitlin Fey entitled "Cover-a-Girl," has a straightforward driving question: "Why do I wear make-up?" As the writer traces the origins of her obsession with make-up, what this fascination says about her as a young woman, and how it has shaped her identity, her driving question eventually becomes: "Why do I *still* wear make-up?" What makes this essay a thoughtful meditation on standards of beauty and self-worth is the honesty of the author's inquiry, along with the sharpness of her analysis and the complexity of her response to a complicated question. Instead of blaming "the media," which would have been an easy target, she teases out the myriad factors that collectively influence the way we think about ourselves—our friends, our parents, our classmates, and, yes, the articles and photographs in *Seventeen* magazine.

Read the first draft of Fey's essay and make notes in the margins as if you were responding to the work of one of your peers, as described earlier in this section. Then read the revision. What has been changed? What are the effects of those changes? How has the essay been improved? Is there a clearer narrative development? How has the analysis deepened? And so on.

Title

In sixth grade, I was invited to Cayla Hart's sleepover birthday party. Cayla and her BFF, Chelsea, were the queen bees of all 11-year-old girls in my town. I was lucky enough to be one of the chosen ones who had been invited to the exclusive birthday party. Only about 10 girls had the opportunity to sit down on Cayla's plush suede sofas to watch Finding Nemo that night. All of us gasped in unison when Nemo's family was attacked, and all of us laughed together when Dory sang "just keep swimming." After the movie, we sang "Happy Birthday" and devoured a red velvet cake. We were having fun, but I wondered why Katelyn, another one of the popular girls, wasn't there.

Then Chelsea came out of the bathroom wearing nothing but booty-shorts and a bra. "Guess who I am, guys," she said as she strutted across the room with her high heels clacking on the hard-wood floor. Her gaudy red lipstick covered some of her face like she had deliberately colored outside of the lines in a coloring book. All of the other girls couldn't control their giggles. I let out a nervous laugh; it was not as funny to me as Dory had been. I knew that she was making fun of Katelyn, who I thought was one of her best friends.

"Katelyn is such a slut!" Cayla laughed, "I'm so glad I didn't invite her!" She flipped back her platinum blonde hair with a dainty hand. What was going on? I squirmed in my place on the sofa. I began to brush the material of the sofa in one direction making it darker, then in the opposite direction, making it lighten up again. "She should at least learn how to put on make-up!" Cayla said. Everyone else agreed. I looked up from the sofa to examine each face in the room: everyone was wearing mascara, eye-shadow, and blush, and everyone's hair was straightened or curled. How had I not noticed before? The rest of the night, there was a huge effort to reveal every one of Katelyn's flaws. I had to leave before they noticed my appearance. I called my Mom to pick me up early, saying that I had a stomachache. Then I wondered if they would talk about me after I left. I shouldn't have cared.

When I got home that night, I examined myself in my previously unused full-length mirror. My hair was wavy in places it shouldn't be. My face was so plain. My eyes looked tired, and my cheeks were pale. How had I never known that I looked this way before? I asked my Mom for make-up and a hair-straightener. At first, she was reluctant saying that I was too young to wear make-up and that she hadn't worn it until she was in high school. But I guilted her into allowing me to paint my face with cosmetics by seventh grade.

For three years of middle school, I drifted away from Cayla and Chelsea. I became friends with a slightly less popular crowd of girls. We were Hollister-jeans-and-polo-shirt preppy, but, most of the time, we were nice girls. In class, though, I would notice Cayla and Chelsea passing notes back and forth under the table. I would wonder if I was ever the subject of those notes. Were they talking about me? Had my make-up worn off after gym class?

1

I began to notice the mistakes that other girls made with their make-up. Some would wear too much eyeliner. Some would not notice that their face and neck were different colors. Some would have clumpy eyelashes. But worst of all, some wouldn't wear any make-up at all. I felt bad that the poor girls didn't realize what they looked like. Seventeen Magazine told me that guys were more attracted to girls when they wear less makeup, but that was a little blurb on the page before a giant picture of an airbrushed face of a model advertising CoverGirl.

Picture day of Freshman year, I was getting ready to go to the high school. I was satisfied with the practice smile that my mirror had been forced to endure all morning. I was wearing a new shirt that I had picked out specifically for my first high school picture. It was a cerulean blue scoop-neck that complemented my light blue eyes. I had thought this out; this picture was important. It was going to be in the yearbook for eternity. Everyone would look through the rows of pictures and decide which 1" by 1.5" rectangles held the prettiest faces in the school. I thought I was ready. My Mom walked into my room, which smelt of burning hair because she had bought me a cheap hair-straightener. She asked, "Are you wearing make-up?"

"Yeah, I'm ready to go."

"Maybe you should put some more make-up on before the picture," she said before leaving my room. I looked back at my reflection and applied another layer of make-up with a trembling hand.

In High school, I used to glance at myself in every reilective surface that I passed: darkened windows, glass display cases in the hallways, computer and TV screens. People probably thought that I was admiring myself, but I was doing the opposite. I had to make sure my hair wasn't flat, and that my make-up hadn't smudged.

I started to run Cross Country in high school. My friend, Meris, picked me up in the mornings for summer practices. One day in the summer before Junior year, I was woken up by my generic Latin-dance-music ringtone. "Hey, I'm here," Meris said.

"Ahh! Okay, give me a minute!" I said, my voice cracking. I threw off my pink covers and plopped myself down on the floor in front of the mirror, the carpet was stained black in spots where I had wiped my mascara-stained fingers numerous times before. My legs were perfectly placed in the indents that I had created in the carpet, I looked at my face; I had work to do. "'I don't need a lot of make-up. I'm only going to Cross Country practice," I thought to myself.

I applied my nude-colored Neutrogena foundation. Even skin tone just like that. Then my hands subconsciously reached for my rose blush. Suddenly, I had life in my cheeks. I couldn't resist my eyeliner. My eyes magically looked bigger. It just took two more seconds, so I put on water-proof mascara too. I threw my hair up in a ponytail. No, that didn't look right. I took it down and put it back up, more carefully this time. Better.

The Latin-dance-music ringtone played again. I told Meris I'd be right outside. I threw on some shoes and ran from the air-conditioned house into the summer heat. When I got into her car, Meris asked, "Caitie, why the hell are you wearing make-up to practice?"

2

"I don't know. I just felt like it," I replied. I know I wore it because people would see me while I was running on the public bike path. I liked getting honked at by cars passing by; it made me feel good. I know I should've felt uncomfortable that strangers were objectifying me while I ran, but that was actually when I felt most comfortable. After running in the intense humidity for a few miles, I would wipe the sweat off my face with my shirt. Then there would be a beige smudge on my shirt, and my make-up would be gone.

Later that year, I woke up late one morning. I put on my face of powders because I had gotten my routine down to a few minutes, but I would be late for school if I straightened my hair, so I left it the way it fell naturally. I opened the door of the school wishing that the day would be over as soon as possible. Then I walked by a friend that said, "I really like your hair today." I received so many complements, so I started wearing my hair that way every day. I thrived off of their attention.

"Why do you even bother getting ready for school?" my friend, Andrew, inquired of Libby and me at the lunch table one day. Our peanut-butter-and-jelly-sandwich conversation had shifted to the topic of aesthetics. "Hannah probably wakes up three hours before school starts to get ready, but she just looks terrible," he said, kicking me under the table with his Vans shoes to get me to look over at her in the lunch line. Hannah was a friend of ours that used to be a chubby, brunette girl that wore no make-up. In ninth grade, she died her hair blonde and discovered cosmetics. Every year her hair became more blonde, her skin became more orange, and her eyes became more outlined with black. As I looked at her, I noticed that she looked like a Barbie doll: fake. Libby answered Andrew, but I honestly don't remember what she said. I just needed to get to a mirror to make sure that my face didn't look like Hannah's.

After that, I tried to make my face look more natural. I wore less make-up, but I couldn't bring myself to go to school with a naked face. I attempted to rock the "I don't care what I look like" look that Cayla and Chelsea had recently taken up. That didn't work out. I felt that I looked like a completely different person without the help of cosmetics. I didn't recognize myself after I washed my face at night. The truth is though, that no one would've cared if I didn't wear make-up for a day. They might not have even noticed.

Of course in Senior year, like every other girl, I dreamt about becoming Homecoming Queen: the way the plastic tiara would feel when it was placed on my head, the smell of buttered popcorn and football-players' sweat in the fall night breeze, the cheers and jealousy of everyone sitting on the cold, hard bleachers as they announce my name. That moment wasn't mine. It was Chelsea's, and I was sitting on the cold, hard bleachers when it happened. Chelsea, the girl who had mocked Katelyn with red lipstick in sixth grade. The girl who had caused my addiction to make-up. The girl who didn't wear make-up anymore. She had expected to win; she was still one of the queen bees, and she was the prettiest Senior girl, especially without make-up on. As the tiara was placed on her head, I wondered if she was ever self-conscious. Probably not.

Even today, I put on blush and mascara to go to the library, It wasn't a lot, but it made me feel comfortable. My roommate walked into the bathroom as I was putting it on, and she gave me a look that said, "You're crazy. It's just the library." But I just never want to be the 11-year-old girl on that suede sofa again, so I'm always prepared with my weapons: brushes and powders. I try to be secretive about my love affair with make-up, but it's obvious.

I walk through the library with confidence, attracting glances from guys who must think I'm pretty, or maybe they just happened to look up at the wrong moment. I wish I could feel pretty without my make-up and their glances, but I just can't. The image of the 11-year-old ChelseaHannah has followed me through middle school, high school, and now college. She struts along behind me in her high heels as I walk, and all I hope is that I can at least outshine this little girl. Wearing make-up is like smoking for me. I've done it for seven years, and I'm probably never going to quit.

4

Caitlin Fey

Professor Chamberlin

English 125

16 March 2012

Cover-a-Girl

I attempted to lean casually against the faded blue lockers while I mindlessly stared at the stains in the carpet. Six minutes until class started. I didn't dare enter the classroom until it was one minute before the bell rang. I didn't want to seem too eager, but I was. This was the class that I had with Cayla and Chelsea. They were the queen bees of all eleven-year-old girls in my town: the pretty girls who wore nice clothes and had cute boys draped around their shoulders at all times. I was lucky to be one of the chosen ones whom they condescended to speak to in Social Studies class. "Caitie," I heard a silky voice sound. I looked up from a blackened piece of gum on the floor, which must have seen the bottoms of thousands of shoes, and saw Cayla and Chelsea approach smiling. "This is for you," Cayla said as she held out a small white envelope sealed with a flower sticker. I couldn't take my eyes off the sticker as I lifted my heavy hand to take the invitation. They walked into class giggling as I stood frozen with joy, still staring at the tiny flower; it was much prettier than the gum on the floor. I was invited to Cayla's birthday party.

Only about ten girls had the opportunity to sit down on Cayla's plush suede sofas to watch *Finding Nemo* that night. All of us gasped in unison when Nemo's family was attacked, and all of us laughed together when Dory sang "just keep swimming." After the movie, we sang "Happy Birthday" obnoxiously and devoured a red velvet cake. *Maybe I am going to be one of them,* I thought. We were having innocent fun, but I wondered why Katelyn, another one of the popular girls, wasn't there.

Then Chelsea came out of the bathroom wearing nothing but booty-shorts and a bra. "Guess who I am, guys," she said as she strutted across the room with high heels clacking on the hard-wood floor. Her gaudy red lipstick covered some of her face as if she had deliberately colored outside of the lines in a coloring book. All of the other girls couldn't control their giggles. I let out a nervous laugh; it was not as funny to me as Dory had been. I knew that she was making fun of Katelyn, who I thought was one of her best friends.

"Katelyn is such a slut!" Cayla laughed, saying, "I'm so glad I didn't invite her!" She flipped back her platinum blonde hair with a dainty hand. *What*

continued

is going on? I thought. I squirmed in my place on the sofa. I drew my legs in closer to my body and began to brush the material of the sofa in one direction, making it darker, then in the opposite direction, making it lighten up again. "She should at least learn how to put on make-up!" Cayla exclaimed. Everyone else agreed. I looked up from the sofa to frantically examine each face in the room: everyone was wearing mascara, eye shadow, and blush, and everyone's hair was either straightened or curled. How had I not noticed before? My face was bare.

The rest of the night, there was a huge effort to reveal every one of Katelyn's flaws. With each accusation of her social misconduct, my vision of myself grew clearer. I had to leave before they noticed my appearance. I used the kitchen phone to call my mom and asked her to pick me up early, saying that I had a stomach ache. Then I wondered if they would talk about me after I left. I shouldn't have cared, but I did.

When I got home, I examined myself in my previously unused full-length mirror. My hair was wavy in places it shouldn't have been. My face was plain. My eyes looked tired, and my cheeks were so pale that I looked sickly. *How did I not notice I looked this way before tonight?* I thought. I had been walking through the halls at school thinking that I was normal, but now I knew better. I was thankful. I asked my mom for make-up and a hair-straightener. At first, she reluctantly said that I was too young to wear make-up and that she hadn't worn it until she was in high school. I thought that my constant complaints finally made her cave in, but she probably took me to the Rite Aid cosmetics section because she saw my desperation in wanting to fit in. She allowed me to paint my face with cosmetics by seventh grade because she didn't want her daughter to feel ugly. She knew insecurity; all girls know it at some point.

During the next few years of middle school, I became friends with a slightly less popular crowd of girls. We were Hollister-jeans-and-polo-shirt preppy, but, most of the time, we were nice girls. We never mocked one another. I always felt comfortable around them because I thought that I was just as pretty as most of them. I drifted away from Cayla and Chelsea, but in Social Studies class, I would see them passing notes back and forth under the wooden table when the teacher was turned around scribbling something on the white board. My attention would sway away from the teacher and be solely focused on Chelsea's fluffy pink pen as it moved across the page, writing what were sure to be harmful words. I wondered if I was ever the subject of those notes. *Were they talking about me? Had my make-up worn off after gym class?*

I began to notice the mistakes that other girls made with their make-up. Some wore too much eyeliner. Some didn't notice that their face and neck were different colors. Some had clumpy eyelashes. But worst of all, some wore no make-up at all. I felt bad that these poor girls didn't realize what they looked like. *That used to be me.* In reality, I was probably the only one who noticed these tiny details. My eyes were especially tuned to notice any wrongdoing in the realm of appearance, but what seemed like a social infraction to me was *just* make-up to others.

Picture day of Freshman year, I was getting ready to go to the high school for that moment of fate when the flash would blind my eyes. I was satisfied with the practice smile that my mirror had been forced to endure all morning. My new shirt was a cerulean blue scoop-neck that complemented my light blue eyes. This picture was important; it was going to be in the yearbook for eternity. Everyone would look through the rows of pictures and decide which 1" by 1.5" rectangles held the prettiest faces. I thought I was ready. My mom walked into my room, which smelled of burning hair because she had bought me a cheap hair-straightener years before. She asked, "Are you wearing make-up?"

"Yeah, I'm ready to go."

"Maybe you should put some more make-up on before the picture," she said before leaving my room. Her words left a lasting sting as I looked back at my reflection and applied another layer of make-up with a trembling hand. I had to be a face that she could be proud of. I knew that she just wanted to have a nice picture of me to hang on the wall, but I forced myself to hold back tears of anger so that my mascara wouldn't run. I had moved up to the next level of make-up wearing; it wasn't kids' stuff anymore. My mother had stopped seeing me as a little girl that needed to be protected from make-up. Mothers have to think that their children are beautiful, but one day the veil of love that obscures their vision is lifted to reveal the truth: zitty, gangly, and awkward teenagers complete with braces and frizzy hair.

In high school, I used to glance at myself in every reflective surface that I passed. I would even pretend to admire student artwork in glass display cases in the hallways so that I could check how I looked. People probably thought that I was admiring myself, but I was doing the opposite. I had to make sure my hair wasn't flat and that my make-up hadn't smudged.

One day in the summer before Junior year, I was woken up by my generic Latin-dance-music ringtone. "Hey, I'm here," Meris said through the speaker of my LG flip phone. She was waiting outside my house to pick me up for our summer Cross Country practice.

"Ahh! Okay, give me a minute!" I said, my voice cracking. I threw off my pink covers and plopped myself down on the floor in front of the mirror, the

continued

carpet stained black in spots where I had wiped my mascara-stained fingers numerous times before. My legs were perfectly placed in the indents that I had created in the carpet. I looked at my face. *I don't need a lot of make-up. I'm only going to Cross Country practice*, I tried to convince myself.

I applied my nude-colored Neutrogena foundation. Even skin tone just like that. Then my hands subconsciously reached for my rose blush. Suddenly, I had life in my cheeks. I tried, but I couldn't resist my eyeliner. My eyes magically looked bigger. It just took two more seconds, so I put on waterproof mascara too. I threw my hair up in a ponytail. No, that didn't look right. I took it down and put it back up, more carefully this time. Better.

The Latin-dance-music ringtone played again. I told Meris I'd be right outside. I threw on some shoes and ran from the air-conditioned house into the summer heat. When I got into her car, Meris looked at my face and asked, "Caitie, why the hell are you wearing make-up to practice?"

"I don't know. I just felt like it," I replied.

But I wore it because people would see me while I was running on the public bike-path. I liked getting honked at by cars passing by; it made me feel good. I should've felt uncomfortable that strangers were objectifying me while I ran, but that was actually when I felt most comfortable. This anony-mous attention from a friendly or perverted (however you want to look at it) male stranger with a car horn was all I needed to feel attractive for a minute. He could have been listening to music or focusing on the road, but instead he was looking at me and gracing me with the kind acknowledgment of a honk or two. The honks meant that I was worth looking at, and that someone thought I was pretty, even if it wasn't me.

After running in the intense humidity for a few miles, I would wipe the sweat off my face with my shirt. Then there would be a beige smudge on my shirt, and my make-up would be gone. I would let down my hair after prac-tice to try to hide my face.

Later in the year, I woke up late one morning. The groggy morning feel-ing was stabbed by a jolt of panic when I looked at my failure of an alarm clock. The first thing I did was put on my face of powders, but I would be late for school if I straightened my hair, so I left it the way it fell naturally. I opened the door of the school wishing that the day would be over as soon as possible so that no one would notice my hair. Then I walked by a friend who said, "I really like your hair today." I received so many compliments that I started wearing my hair that way every day. I thrived off their attention. Every compliment helped wipe away the sheet of fog that covered my mirror of self-perception.

Fey 5

"Why do you even bother getting ready for school?" my friend Andrew inquired of Libby and me at the lunch table one day. Our peanut-butter-and-jelly-sandwich conversation had shifted to the topic of aesthetics. "Hannah probably wakes up three hours before school starts to get ready, but she just looks terrible," he said, kicking me under the table with his Vans shoes to get me to look over at her in the lunch line. Hannah was a friend of ours who used to be a chubby, brunette girl who wore no make-up. In ninth grade, she had dyed her hair blonde and discovered cosmetics. Every year her hair became more blonde, her skin became more orange, and her eyes became more outlined with black. As I looked at her, I noticed that she looked like a Barbie doll: fake. Libby answered Andrew, but I didn't hear what she said. I just needed to get to a mirror to make sure that my face didn't look like Hannah's.

Later, in senior year, Hannah became the running joke of our school. Everyone talked about her behind her back, including me. But I only agreed with what others said because I knew that she was just another girl who had a misperception of herself. Hannah lived on ignorantly in her blissful world of bronzer and bleach as nasty jokes and comments were created in her trails. If she could've been so wrong about being beautiful and not even know it, then I could've been wrong too. I was never sure of what other people were thinking. What if they were saying the same things behind my back? Did I have good enough friends who would tell me the truth about my face?

After the lunch with Andrew, I tried to make my face look more natural. I wore less make-up, but I couldn't bring myself to go to school with a naked face. I was confused because *Seventeen* magazine told me that guys were more attracted to girls when they wore less make-up, but that was a little blurb on the page before a giant picture of an airbrushed face advertising CoverGirl cosmetics. There were never models or actresses that didn't wear make-up, and they were who I looked up to. Everyone loved them, and I wanted every-one to love me. I failed to rock the "I don't care what I look like" look that Chelsea had recently taken up. She had grown into her athletically toned body and was now a star basketball player, so she didn't seem to have time to put on make-up. She had perfectly clear skin that glowed with a natural tan; her hazel eyes seemed to shine without eyeliner, and she got a flush in her cheeks just from laughing at the jokes that the popular guys whispered into her ears. Her confidence shined through and wasn't blocked by any powders or liquid foundations. She didn't need make-up to be beautiful and confi-dent, and that just made me even more jealous of her. I felt that I looked like

continued

a completely different person without the help of cosmetics. I didn't recognize myself after I washed my face at night. I wanted to be the better version of myself, the prettier version, and that version went down the drain of the sink every night to be reborn in the morning.

Of course at the beginning of Senior year, like every other girl, I dreamt about becoming Homecoming Queen: the way the plastic tiara would feel when it was placed on my head, the smell of buttered popcorn and football-players' sweat in the fall night breeze, the cheers and jealousy of everyone sitting on the cold, hard bleachers as they announced my name. That moment wasn't mine. It was Chelsea's, and I was sitting on the cold, hard bleachers when it happened. Chelsea, the girl who had mocked Katelyn with red lipstick in sixth grade. The girl who had caused my addiction to make-up. The girl who didn't wear make-up anymore. She had expected to win; she was still one of the queen bees, and she was the prettiest Senior girl, even without make-up. As the tiara was gently placed on her head, I wondered if she was ever self-conscious. Her smug smile told me she probably wasn't.

Chelsea was never a real person to me. She was an unrealistic ideal that I would never be able to reach. I never made an effort to find out if she listened to the same radio station that I did, or if she read the same books that I did. I kept her in a glass box; I only looked, but did not hear or touch. I was scared that if I found out that she was anything other than a bitch, I would have to stop hating her. But I don't hate her now; she's not the bratty eleven-year-old girl that I remember, or the homecoming queen that I was jealous of. She is just a girl that had confidence in herself and her beauty at a time when I did not.

Even today, though, I was putting on blush and mascara to go to the library. It wasn't a lot, but it made me feel comfortable. My roommate walked into the bathroom as I was putting it on, and she gave me a look that said, "You're crazy. It's just the library." But I just never want to be the eleven-year-old girl on that suede sofa again, so I am always prepared with my weapons: brushes and powders. I try to be secretive about my love affair with make-up, but it's obvious.

I walk through the library with confidence, attracting glances from guys who must think I'm pretty, or maybe they just happen to look up at the wrong moment. I wish I could feel pretty without my make-up and their glances, but I just can't. The shadow of the eleven-year-old Chelsea has followed me through middle school, high school, and now to college. She struts along behind me in her high heels as I walk, and all I hope is that I can at least outshine this little girl.

Learning from other Writers (Fey)

1. On first glance, what do you notice about Fey's revision? Freewrite on why the final draft feels more complete and fully realized than the first. Are there weaknesses in Fey's first draft that you notice in your own early drafts?

2. Examine the new opening. Why do you think Fey chose to make this change?

3. Find three new details that were not in the original. What is their effect on the essay as a whole? On the development of the essay's theme?

4. Find three new passages of analysis or meditation. Describe why each passage is significant to the essay and why each is necessary.

5. Discuss the balance between exposition and scene in the first and final drafts. When does the writer use exposition? When does she use scene? What are the effects of these decisions on the success of the revision?

6. The ending has not completely changed, though the way we arrive at it is slightly different in the final draft than it was in the initial draft. How has the writer better *earned* her ending?

Carlina Duan opens her research examination "If You're Happy and You Know It, LOL" with a scene that generations of college students can identify with—being late for class. What is new here for Duan and her "Facebook-friending, Internet-surfing generation" is the role that technology now plays in this familiar narrative of being late for school. Trained by social networking platforms such as Facebook and Twitter to seek acceptance via "Likes" and "Retweets," Duan argues that she and her peers have "become increasingly conditioned to understand—and to feel—happiness based on the approval of others." She concludes this analysis with a provocative claim about herself and her peers, writing: "In short, we've lost the ability to know when we're happy on our own."

Throughout her examination of the nature of happiness and the ways in which the definition of happiness has changed for Generation Y, Duan builds complexity into her work, weaving outside sources and personal experience into a probing investigation. Her essay is multi-layered and nuanced, yet it is guided from start to finish by a simple driving question: What is happiness, and how has the definition of happiness changed from my grandparents' or parents' generation to my own?

Notice, too, how Duan draws on elements from each of the forms we have studied to structure her essay. She begins with narrative to frame and contextualize her argument, later using elements of scene to capture a Black Friday trip to the mall with her cousin and to illustrate the extent to which this phenomenon is affecting her peers. Duan is also profiling her generation through the lens of technology, capturing its essence via social networking and communication. And she is investigating the way in which technology may be affecting a generation's understanding of happiness, drawing on multi-disciplinary research from diverse fields such as psychology, statistics, neurology, and social science. What should be admired here is the way in which Duan has synthesized all she has learned about each of these forms (i.e., reflective narrative, profile, research investigation) to create a compelling and complex essay.

As with Fey's essay, read the first draft of "If You're Happy And You Know It, LOL" and make notes in the margins as if you were responding to an essay by one of your peers. Next, read the revision. How has the essay been changed? What are the effects of those changes? Is the analysis deeper in the second version than in the first? Where and how so? Are the details more specific? Is there a clearer development of ideas? And so on.

If You're Happy And You Know It, LOL: An Examination of the Evolution of Happiness Across Generations *(Rough Draft)*

In September 1988, reggae musician Bobby McFerrin released a spunky new track that quickly surged in popularity. Titled: "Don't Worry, Be Happy" the song featured whistle-filled acoustics and an amiable, buttery melody. It was the sort of song that could be chanted during a game of hopscotch, blasted throughout a supermarket, or belted off-key during a family reunion. *Don't worry!* Americans became fond of exclaiming, *be happy!* The song helped shape a new American theory of happiness – happiness as denial of one's troubles; a concept of leisurely contentment; gratitude for everything at hand. Generation X became coined as the generation born into the lyrics and ideology of Bobby McFerin; a generation who viewed joy in simple, colloquial terms of acceptance. Predated by the slightly-older Baby Boomer crowd, who recognized happiness in large-scale events like Woodstock and Beatlemania; Generation X contrarily found happiness slumped on the couch, after a long day of work. Yet in today's society, this kind of happiness - sparked by relaxed refusal to examine stress - is rare, unbridled. Instead, happiness today is portrayed as the comically strong superhero; almost always accompanied by its trusty sidekick: technology.

So how - and why - did happiness change?

Over the past few decades, the United States has splashed its way through trends - evolving from a land in bell-bottom jeans to a country bundled in wireless networks and touch-screen characters. Upon attained, each trend has been closely shadowed by a burst of satisfaction from its cultural followers. More importantly, as each generation loses its step to a new one, new perceptions of joy are created. The expiration dates of each trend stem from their generational influence; happiness leaking out only when something old is replaced by a newer, fresher concept. In this way, the evolution of happiness has trickled its way through the United States; all old perceptions of joy replaced almost instantaneously by the arrival of technology.

The 21st century unveils an American society churning with reasons to chitchat. At the height of this social atmosphere is the Millennial Generation - primarily those born in the 1980s to 1990s - also called Generation Y. To our neighbors, we continually gush over the latest technological trends, styles, and appliances. We sift through online catalogues. Comment on news blogs. We smile, shop, question, and learn with gadgets. Our fingers kiss buttons in a rapid-fire stream of clacking. Our eyes glaze over and spin like glinting CD discs. Like author Dr. Andrew Weil describes: "Many people today spend much of their waking time surfing the Internet, texting and talking on mobile phones, attending to email, watching television, and being stimulated by other new media—experiences never available until now" (10). Needless to say, we live in a world peppered with distractions. Around us, the chirp of computers, cell phones, and iPods never pauses to shut up. The generation raised in this society has grown up with a philosophy: to be heard, accepted, and a flourishing member of society, you must talk back. In short, the equation to happiness for Generation Y rides

1

alongside chatter. In this way, the need for constant communication has sparked a unique happy-state mentality in our generation. In order to be happy, we must be in near-continuous contact with our environment; prompting a need for self-validation in a world that increasingly highlights our individual insignificance.

Now, more than ever, we are enveloped in a global society; a world that continues to grow in awareness of surrounding countries, cultures, and people. For many, the world "increasingly exists as a cultural horizon within which we (to varying degrees) frame our existence" (Tomlinson 30). Teens and children are the most influenced by globalization, as they grow up with "the intensification of consciousness of the world as a whole" (Robertson 8). This broadening global awareness has created a sharp insecurity among members of Generation Y; as we are forced to contemplate our own self-worth in an exponentially growing world. Due largely to technology, we are able to connect with new countries in more direct and assertive methods; modes of communication in which our GenX and Baby Boomer predecessors never had. We create snippets of many cultures to form a diverse cloak of information. "A young person living in Britain today can access hip hop in South Africa and a young person in India enjoy the latest American soap operas. Cultures from across the world are fragmented, appropriated and reinterpreted in other contexts to form new hybrid cultures..." (Cray, Collins-Mayo, Mayo and Savage 7). The media has further contributed to this sense of smallness. As we focus more on the colossal size of the Earth, our self-view shrinks. With TV channels blaring 24-hour news, magazine articles touting the effects of the Chinese economy upon American goods, and newspapers highlighting celebrity red carpet events, we feel even tinier. "The images, values, and opportunities [adolescents] perceive as being part of the global culture undermine their belief in the value their local cultural practices. At the same time, the ways of the global culture seem out of reach to them, too foreign to everything they know from their direct experience" (Arnett 778). This sense of cultural exclusion creates a natural human instinct - flocking towards a source of comfort; something that will amplify our own meaning. We fear losing our importance within all the information we're being fed. In this case, meaning is enhanced by social networking sites.

My Twitter home page refreshes itself every thirty seconds, as the lives of others pop up on my screen in clipped, 160-character phrases. Rarely do I take the time to read each one. Instead, I skim; scanning statuses for the laughable, the cringe-worthy, the shame. There's something therapeutic about inking your own state-of-being onto the Internet, where you know countless others are sitting at their screens, watching. On the Web, you can edit to satisfaction. You can make mistakes and erase them. You have the pleasure of perfecting yourself; of presenting yourself in the most attractive light. As New York Times essayist and author William Deresiewicz puts it, "...when we speak in our own names, on Facebook and so forth, we're strenuously cheerful, conciliatory, well-groomed." (7) Best of all, we have a guaranteed audience. According to the Facebook Company Statistics page, Facebook currently has more than 800 million active users; the average user having about 130 Facebook friends, with "more than 900 million objects that people interact with (pages, groups, events and community pages)".

It seems my fellow Americans and I all feel the urge to insert ourselves into a list of Facebook notifications. And why not? Facebook makes us feel temporarily wanted. We receive a certain sense of delight at being important enough to merit a Twitter Retweet. When the red notification button on Facebook pops up, we may internally squeal. A Facebook notification prompts curiosity, longing, and thrill. Clicking the notification produces the same feeling of eagerness we get when peeling open a neatly wrapped birthday present - wondering, what's inside the box? Who's it from? Is it the dream gift I've always wanted? Or is it something even better? We ponder our Facebook notifications with a mixture of hopeful anticipation and greed. And when we discover somebody comments favorably upon our photos, "likes" our statuses, or "Friends" our account, we feel a strong sense of achievement at having "done" something to earn others' approval. We know that through a hubbub of other online users, *we* were the ones important enough not to be skimmed over or ignored.

In fact, the design of Facebook and other social media sites only serve to enhance our satisfaction. On Facebook, the existence of the "Like" thumbs-up button - opposed to a "Dislike" button - amplifies our quest for positivity. Whether we make a conscious effort to or not, we beam at the amount of "likes" our Facebook selves accumulate. It's simple: to be liked creates happiness. The popular blogging site Tumblr utilizes a similar "like" system, where users can click a heart-shaped button for posts they find enjoyable. The more hearts somebody gets, the more loved their blog is; and thus, it can be assumed the more happier they become. Our thirst for such notifications, and other forms of communication like it (text messaging, emails, blog posts) reflect our strong need for attention, and the happiness that comes when we receive this attention. Just as we'd act if given a compliment, we glow when something online is directed at *us*. Social networking sites like Facebook, Twitter, and Tumblr are kings at feeding our own self-confidence. As Deresiewicz comments, "We're all selling something today, because even if we aren't literally selling something [...] we're always selling ourselves. We use social media to create a product—to create a brand—and the product is us" (7). When we're bought by others, we earn our profits in happiness. In Generation Y, our joy stems from public scrutiny.

Unlike previous generations, Generation Y has easier, quicker and more accessible tools to magnify our value with - tools that can relieve us of our self-worth with a click of the button. Meanwhile, letter-writing Is seen as conventional. In fact, I almost never write letters unless they are thank you cards to an older group of family friends. "Sending greeting cards has declined by about 15-20 percent among both married and single people over the last decade or two" (Putnam 105). In classrooms today, technology is being implemented through Powerpoint slides, Youtube videos, and iMovie projects. In the fifth grade, I took a Type-To-Learn computing class; and since then, find that the letters on the keyboard are more familiar to me than my own pen.

3

Technology has consumed our lives, and in a sense, it acts as a strong validation of our characters, re-assuring us of our worth to others.

Coupled with the media, technology enhances Generation Y's perception of happiness even further. Downtown metropolitan cities are prime examples. In New York City, billboards sweat through layers of ads, each one bursting with daily swagger: "Buy this fat-free protein bar to improve your health!"; "Take a new gorgeous wardrobe home with you!" Television sets invite us to purchase even wider screens. Our mailboxes - both digital and real - swamp with coupon books and offers. On Facebook, I log on to meet clothing retailers and textbook stores. And seated deep within all these advertisement pleas is longing. Instead of finding contentment with what we currently have, today's media floods our minds with objects we don't own - but feel we should attain. In this way, happiness is an assertion of our claim to material goods. Generation Y has grown up with the media instructing us we *need* material goods in order to gain fulfillment in our lives. A cycle thus forms: The media creates a swirl of pressure upon our shoulders, demanding us, again and again, to give into cravings. Media tells us we are happy when we satisfy those cravings, and then successively shoves us with newer and cooler objects to try and obtain. Thus, Generation Y derives happiness from an information-surfeit. We need material objects to, as a society, be happy.

Yet how does the United States, as a one nation, define happiness? Our founding fathers must've agreed that the concept was important. After all, joy is a prime part of our Declaration to Independence: "…[citizens] are endowed by their Creator with certain unalienable Rights, that among these are Life, Liberty and the pursuit of Happiness." Happiness in itself was viewed as an achievable goal in early America. But how exactly is happiness monitored in our nation?

The answer is it's not. At least, not clearly.

In Bhutan, a small country in the Himalayas, prosperity is measured by the government in "gross national happiness (GNH)". The country emphasizes psychological wellbeing over economy; arguing that happiness, rather than economic growth, is a better indicator of national success. (Arora) To effectively assess happiness, Bhutan implements a series of annual surveys, whereupon the Gross National Happiness Commission then evaluates and bases its national policies off of. Great Britain has also adapted a similar policy, creating a Happiness Index to measure its citizens' levels of contentment. Other countries across the globe, like France and Canada, are currently considering adopting similar proposals. Yet despite its rise across the world, our government has yet to measure our own happiness. It can be argued that this is a good thing. After all, do we really need another governmental invasion of our personal affairs? Besides, it's hard to weigh happiness when it's such an individual, subjective term.

But what Generation Y has yet to realize is that in the United States, happiness is portrayed as an *impersonal* abstraction. As a generation, we are happy when we're the furthest away from our flesh identities - when we're purchasing goods, on the

4

computer, on the phone, or being told virtually of our assets. Instead of acknowledging fulfillment in our own actions, we root our joy in others' perceptions: eagerly trying to see ourselves from their eyes. For us, happiness is weighed too heavily upon material objects, money, and the social acceptance of others rather than what happiness, at its core, *should* be: pure, unrestrained bliss - "no worries" about anything, especially the words of others.

Recent Stanford University studies show that the current generation of college-age students do not know how to read happiness in their peers: "In another study, the researchers found a sample of 140 Stanford students unable to accurately gauge others' happiness even when they were evaluating the moods of people they were close to—friends, roommates and people they were dating." (Copeland 1) So does happiness still exist in our society? It can be said that by seeking happiness in public recognition. Generation Y is diminishing its own definition of joy to shreds; re-shaping "happiness" to mean "self-validation". Perhaps our lack of a government-monitored ideal of happiness is that we don't take happiness into consideration when regarding our success. Instead, we associate happiness with attention-grabbing networks like Facebook, text messaging, and material goods. Today's generation of Generation Y, the children *of* the baby boomers, has an even more difficult time deciphering happiness than other generations. Happiness, for us, has become masked in a series of self-validations and fierce longing to be recognized as important. We are caught in the collision of constant communication and material goods; leading us to question whether or not we'll ever return to the days of Bobby McFerrin, a state of "not worrying" about others, or technology ... simply being happy with ourselves and our surroundings.

Works Cited

Arnett, Jeffrey Jensen, "The Psychology Of Globalization." *American Psychologist* 57.10
   (2002):774–783, *PycARTICLES*. Web. 21 Nov. 2011.

Arora, Vishal. "Would Bhutan's Happiness Index Work in Britain?" *The Guardian*, 14 Apr. 2011.
   Web. 21 Nov. 2011. <http://www. guardian, co. uk/commentisfree/belief/2011 /apr/14/
   david-cameron-bhutan-happiness-index>.

Copeland, Libby. "The Anti-Social Network." *Slate Magazine - Politics, Business, Technology, and
   the Arts - Slate Magazine.* 26 Jan. 2011. Web. 21 Nov. 2011. <http://www.slate.com/articles/
   double_x/doublex/2011/01/the_antisocial_network.html>.

Deresiewicz, William. "Generation Sell." *The New York Times: Sunday Review* [New York City] 12
   Nov. 2011: SR1+. Print.

Giddens, Anthony. *Modernity and Self-indentity: Self and Society in the Late Modern Age.* Stanford,
   CA: Stanford UP, 1991. Print.

Putnam, Robert D. *Bowling Alone: the Collapse and Revival of American Community.* New York:
   Simon & Schuster, 2000. Print.

Robertson, Roland. *Globalization: Social Theory and Global Culture.* London: Sage Publications,
   2000. Print.

Savage, Sara B., Sylvia Collins-Mayo, Bob Mayo, and Graham Clay. *Making Sense of Generation Y: the
   World View of 15-25-year-olds.* London: Church House, 2006. Print.

Tomlinson, John. *Globalization and Culture.* Chicago: University of Chicago, 1999. Print.

Walther, J. B., Van Der Heide, B., Kim, S.-Y., Westerman, D. and Tong, S. T. (2008), The Role of
   Friends' Appearance and Behavior on Evaluations of Individuals on Facebook: Are We Known
   by the Company We Keep?. Human Communication Research, 34: 28–49.

Weil, Andrew, "Don't Let Chaos Get You Down." *Newsweek* 10 Nov, 2011: 9–10. Print.

Duan 1

Carlina Duan

Professor Chamberlin

English 125.012

8 December 2011

If You're Happy and You Know It, LOL:
An Examination of the Evolution of Happiness Across Generations

I'm late.

Class started ten minutes ago, and I'm a scramble of legs and arms as I hurl feet into sneakers, dash from bed to table, stuff Cheerios into mouth, and curse myself for staying up late again. But as I grab the doorknob, I pause. My laptop sits angelically on my desk. If I squint from this distance, I can make out the Firefox Internet icon, pulsing like an invitation.

The day before, I had put up a new Facebook profile picture, taken by the Chinese seaside during a trip to visit my extended family in Qingdao. The photograph featured me posing barefooted by the shore of the Yellow Sea, peeking at bouncing sailboats on the waves. One hour after posting, four of my Facebook friends had "Liked" my picture, and three had commented their praise. I felt good.

Which is to say, I felt beautiful—radiant in a sort of self-relieving glow. People "Liked" my face! People thought I was worth looking at! Their admiration marked the approval I needed to keep living my life as me. I didn't need to cut my hair. Didn't need to wear more make-up. According to my Facebook friends, I was golden, gorgeous.

Plopping my backpack on the floor, I inch towards my desk. In a flurry of familiar clicks, I open a new Firefox window, type Facebook into the address bar, and eagerly wait for my home page to load.

- 36 new Facebook notifications lie before me, brilliantly outlined in red.
- 36 more people have "Liked" and commented on my profile picture.
- 36 reasons to blush, caught in a warm cloud of flattery.

Joy rushes in. I'm happy at being "Liked," happy at being noticed, happy at having somebody tell me I resemble an America's Next-Top Model contestant.

I'm now twenty minutes late for class, yeah, but I'm in for a beautiful day. And the rest of my Facebook-friending, Internet-surfing generation is with me.

~

continued

Duan 2

In September 1988, Bobby McFerrin released a spunky new track that surged in popularity. Titled "Don't Worry, Be Happy," the song featured whistle-filled acoustics and an amiable, buttery melody. *"Don't worry!"* Americans became fond of exclaiming, *"Be happy!"* The song promoted happiness as denial of one's troubles and gratitude for what was at hand. Generation X, personified in Douglas Coupland's books and in films like *Reality Bites*, might have found happiness singing along with McFerrin. But in modern society, this leisurely contentment is rare. Instead, happiness in the twenty-first century is accompanied by an urgent self-absorption.

So how—and why—did the perception of happiness change?

Today, our world loves to chitchat. To our friends, we continually gush over the latest technological trends, styles, and appliances. Our fingers kiss buttons in a rapid-fire stream of clacking. Our eyes glaze over and spin like glinting CD discs. And around us, the chirp of computers, cell phones, and iPods never ceases. At the height of this social atmosphere lies my generation, Generation Y: the babies of the 1980s and 1990s. In a recent *Newsweek* article, Dr. Andrew Weil, author, physician, and the founder of the Spontaneous Happiness program, scorns our easy accessibility to the media: "Many people today spend much of their waking time surfing the Internet, texting and talking on mobile phones, attending to email, watching television, and being stimulated by other new media—experiences never available until now" (10). Needless to say, we live in a world peppered with distractions. As a result, Generation Y has grown up with a philosophy: to be heard and accepted in society, we must talk back. This need for constant communication has sparked a unique happy-state mentality in our generation. In order to be happy, we must be in near-continuous contact with our environment. Consequently, we become increasingly conditioned to understand—and to feel—happiness based on the approval of others. In short, we've lost the ability to know when we're happy on our own.

As our global awareness expands through technology and increasing travel, my generation experiences insecurity. Suddenly, not everything revolves around us. The world is *also* about Canada. And Germany. And India and Spain and France. We're forced to view society through a universal lens. We begin to question our own self-worth in such a huge world.

The media has further contributed to this sense of smallness. As we focus more on the colossal size of the Earth, our self-view shrinks. With TV channels blaring 24-hour news, magazine articles touting the effects of the Chinese economy upon American goods, and newspapers highlighting celebrity red carpet events, we feel even tinier.

Duan 3

Jeffrey Arnett, a research professor and psychologist at Clark University, examines the discordant effects of globalization on teenagers. He notes: "The images, values, and opportunities [adolescents] perceive as being part of the global culture undermine their belief in the value their local cultural practices. At the same time, the ways of the global culture seem out of reach to them, too foreign to everything they know from their direct experience" (778). We're disoriented at the amount of cultural information available to us. When we glimpse the larger world, the task of fitting in suddenly seems overwhelming. We fear losing our importance within all the facts we're being fed. This sense of cultural exclusion guides us towards a natural human instinct: comfort. In our insecurity, we flock towards a support system to amplify our own meaning. We turn to social networking sites.

My Twitter home page refreshes itself every second, as the lives of others pop up on my screen in clipped, 140-character blurbs. Each day, I add my own blurb to the mix. There's something therapeutic about inking your own state-of-being onto the Internet, where you know countless others are sitting at their screens, watching. On the Web, you can edit to satisfaction. You can make mistakes and erase them. You have the pleasure of perfecting yourself. As William Deresiewicz, a *New York Times* essayist and author, puts it, "When we speak in our own names, on Facebook and so forth, we're strenuously cheerful, conciliatory, well-groomed" (7). Best of all, we have a guaranteed audience. According to the Facebook Company Statistics page, Facebook currently has more than 800 million active users; the average user having about 130 Facebook friends, with "more than 900 million objects that people interact with (pages, groups, events and community pages)."

It seems my fellow Americans and I all feel the urge to insert ourselves into a list of Facebook notifications. And why not? Facebook makes us feel wanted. We're delighted at being important enough to merit a friend request. When the red notification button pops up, we may internally squeal. Clicking the notification produces the same feeling of eagerness we get when peeling open a neatly wrapped birthday present—wondering, is it the dream gift I've always wanted? Or is it something even better? We ponder our Facebook notifications with a mixture of hopeful anticipation and greed.

In fact, our brains are wired for this. Scientific evidence tells us dopamine—the neurotransmitter responsible for feelings of pleasure—plays a role in our never-ending enthusiasm for Facebook notifications. Susan Weinschenk, a psychologist, argues that the brain is attached to these notifications:

continued

> With the Internet, Twitter, and texting we now have almost instant gratification of
> our desire to seek. [...] We get into a dopamine induced loop ... dopamine starts
> us seeking, then we get rewarded for the seeking which makes us seek more. It
> becomes harder and harder to stop looking at email, stop texting, stop checking
> our cell phones to see if we have a message or a new text. (1)

In short, self-validation becomes an addiction. When we discover that somebody comments favorably upon our photos, "Likes" our statuses, or "Friends" our account, we feel a strong sense of achievement at having "done" something to earn others' approval. We know that through a hubbub of other online users, *we* were the ones important enough not to be skimmed over or ignored. And we always want more.

The design of Facebook and other social media sites only serves to enhance our satisfaction. On Facebook, the existence of the "Like" thumbs-up button—opposed to a "Dislike" button—amplifies our quest for smiles. Whether we make a conscious effort to or not, we beam at the amount of "Likes" our Facebook selves accumulate. It's simple: to be liked creates happiness. The popular blogging site Tumblr utilizes a similar "Like" system, where users can click a heart-shaped button for posts they find enjoyable. The more hearts somebody gets, the more loved their blog is; and thus, it can be assumed the happier they become.

In a 2009 scientific study of 596 online blogs, researchers Ko and Kuo discovered a correlation between happiness and blogging. Instead of promoting loneliness, they demonstrated, blogging actually has psychological benefits (75). This makes sense. On the Internet, we're suddenly not so alone. We look towards the Web for intimate conversations, good company, and attention. As a generation, isolation seems to be our greatest fear.

Blogging, chatting online, and Tweeting calm our worries of obscurity. Just as we'd act if given a compliment, we glow when something online is directed at *us*. Social networking sites like Facebook, Twitter, and Tumblr are kings at feeding our own self-confidence. As Deresiewicz comments, "We're all selling something today, because even if we aren't literally selling something ... we're always selling ourselves. We use social media to create a product—to create a brand—and the product is us" (7). When we're "bought" by others through their acceptance of us, we earn our profits in happiness. Thus, Twitter Retweets and Facebook comments act as forms of currency propelling our joy. We're glad to make the cash, because it means we were objects of desire, and being desired makes us happy.

Yet it's clear that this longing for social acceptance has been stamped within us for centuries. After all, isn't the classic fairytale *The Ugly Duckling* all about fulfilling the wish to belong? His happily-ever-after moment—finding a family with the swans—loosens

Duan 5

a visceral yearning in everyone, not just Generation Y. But while the human race has preserved this hunger to belong up until modern-day, twenty-first-century inventions such as Facebook have piqued our appetites by providing visual, concrete mediums for us to experience our joy. Facebook acts as our physical certificate of acceptance within a community, outlining our achievements on "walls." We actively watch our happiness grow on the screen in ways that the Ugly Duckling never could; and we can return to the exact moment of this joy, over and over again.

Furthermore, our virtual Facebook walls present us with physical archives of our likeability—evidence that is preserved to the exact date and from the exact people. In our modern era, "Likes," statuses, and comments are documented and saved on the page. This provides a historical contrast. In the past, acceptance and its accompanying happy ending have only included those directly involved. But now, Facebook and other technologies provide a visual symbol of happiness, a happiness that can be relived by everyone who sees the source. We can point straight to our Facebook pages to *anyone* and smugly show off how Joe the football player accepted our Friend request. Each individual has an equal chance to fit in, achieve joy, and consequently witness how others fit in. In this way, happiness becomes all about proving our own acceptance to our community.

And it's an urgent sense of happiness. Our joy today is quick, fleeting. Armed with our cell phones, we are pushed towards what Rockefeller University's Bruce McEwen, a professor of Neuropsychiatry, coins "a wholly artificial sense of urgency" (Michaud 146). Faced with speedy communication networks, we falsely believe that there's always somebody waiting for us to reply. This seemingly pressing duty results in a short-term mindset—a mindset that freakishly resembles our conversations. We're engrained to live our lives based on actions that only just preceded the present, mirroring our habit to reply immediately to what's just been said. Thus, twenty-first-century interactions reflect qualities of the Facebook Newsfeed. We behave dependent upon Facebook time stamps of "a few seconds ago," "a minute ago," "2 hours ago" ... the point being we operate with a perception of only the near future.

Moreover, our emotional spectrum itself becomes trimmed to the emoticons of a computer keyboard. Happiness—along with sadness, confusion, fear, even seduction—are imprinted into digital faces sent rapidly by hitting the "Return" key. The instant-message era has transformed Generation Y into an instant-emotion era. Abbreviated phrases such as "LOL," "WTF," and "FML" might have caused our ancestors to scratch

continued

their heads, yet conversely, these phrases have allowed us to expand upon our functions as fast-moving, "live in the moment" human beings.

Our urgency is further illuminated through our constant need to upgrade our digital technology. A few days ago, I ordered a new iPhone from the Sprint company. On the store's glinting walls hung an advertisement. The poster featured an iPhone bathed in glowing light, beaming underneath bold lettering: "Our greatest reward is making our customers happy." Like the majority of its customers, I wanted to believe that Sprint didn't care about my money, that it only cared about my smile. As the salesman touted the voice-recognition features of the iPhone 4S, a grin slid across my face. Sprint's ad was working. I was irrepressibly happy. I felt the weight of my old phone within my pocket. It was eco-friendly, unbroken, easy to use. Its only problem was its aching familiarity. I feared boredom – not only with my old phone, but with myself. I relished the iPhone 4S because of its possibility: touch-screen, music, Internet. ... I wanted the swift, cursory pleasure that tagged along with a new cell phone, because I hungered for the magic that this attainment promised. I wanted to belong in the hip, trend-setting group of iPhone users, instead of remaining dully alone with my old cell phone. But I also knew, unconsciously, how rapidly everyone's invigoration with the iPhone 4S would fade once Apple released the iPhone 5, the iPhone 6, and onward. ...

I'm not alone in my current enchantment. In November 2011, *Newsweek* magazine predicted 30 million iPhones to sell within this year's holiday season (Streib 25). The release of the iPhone 4S has prompted a dash to phone retailers to purchase the latest, hottest gadget. This sales pattern is described by psychologists as "hedonic adaption," a phenomenon where people quickly embrace changes—for example, in the marketplace— "in order to maintain a stable level of happiness" (Rosenbloom 1). Basically, we shop geared towards a happy "buzz," and upon its disappearance, we buy newer material goods to reclaim the feeling. Instead of finding contentment with what we currently have, our minds flood with objects we don't own—but feel we should attain to belong.

While the advertisement industry has always planted this insatiability in consumers, modern-day advertisements seem to be even more pressing and omnipresent. Our dependence upon the Internet in schools, in the workplace, and at home creates an information-surfeit. When we seek information on websites like Twitter and Facebook, we also receive pleas to purchase. Generation Y has grown up with the media instructing us we *need* material goods in order to gain fulfillment in our lives. As a result, happiness becomes all about indulging our need to belong, and publicizing our belonging to others.

On Black Friday this year, I accompanied my eager sixteen-year-old cousin to the Briarwood Mall at midnight. Armed with a purse full of coupons and cash, she dove through the doors of Macy's like a frenzied truck driver, barreling through the aisles. When we returned home, laden with shopping bags, my cousin darted straight to the computer. She immediately logged into Twitter. "I'm just so happy!" she hooted, and typed: "Black Friday success! #forthewin."

My cousin wasn't the only one who broadcasted her delight. I logged onto Facebook that night to greet numerous statuses boasting grand deals. One of my high school classmates bragged: "Got a buncha cute stuff, hell yeah :) :)!" with fifteen different people "liking" her new investments.

Of course, material happiness isn't new to us. What *is* new is the way we enhance our happiness by broadcasting it to others. I wasn't sure if my cousin's true happiness stemmed from her great deals, or from *telling* others so she could receive their public praise.

Yet a happy status is simply that: a status—a current standing that disappears with the passage of time. It can be said that Generation Y has no concept of sustained, long-lasting happiness. Instead, our happiness is status-like in its brevity. And as soon as it disappears, we run back seeking more.

More important, our happiness doesn't stop at the individual level. It encompasses our contentment at a societal level as well. Our Founding Fathers plugged joy into our Declaration of Independence, emphasizing the concept's communal importance: "... [citizens] are endowed by their Creator with certain unalienable Rights, that among these are Life, Liberty and the pursuit of Happiness." The objective was for each individual to chase after his own happiness, which would heighten the country's overall wellbeing.

In Bhutan, a small country in the Himalayas, this idea is portrayed quite literally. The government measures Bhutan's prosperity in terms of Gross National Happiness (GNH). The country emphasizes psychological wellbeing over economy, arguing that happiness, rather than economic growth, is a better indicator of national success (Arora). To effectively assess happiness, Bhutan implements a series of annual surveys. The surveys ask citizens to rank their degree of happiness on a numerical scale, in areas such as "health, time use, education, culture, good governance, ecology, community vitality, and living standards" (Centre for Bhutan Studies). The results of these surveys create national policies geared towards those specific areas. Great Britain has also

continued

embraced a similar policy, creating a Happiness Index to measure its citizens' levels of contentment. Other countries across the globe, such as France and Canada, are currently considering adopting similar proposals (Stratton). Yet despite the program's rise across the world, our nation has yet to measure our own happiness. It can be argued that this is a good thing. After all, do we really need another governmental invasion of our personal affairs? Besides, it's hard to weigh happiness when it's such an individual, subjective term. But perhaps the deeper reason behind our reluctance is that we know an American Gross National Happiness would be impossible.

In the United States, Generation Y's happiness is portrayed as an *impersonal* abstraction. As an age group, we are happiest when we're the furthest away from our physical, "real" identities. We gain joy when we're purchasing goods, on the computer, or being told virtually of our assets. Instead of acknowledging our own virtues, we base our happiness upon what others think of us, eagerly trying to see ourselves from their eyes. In the guise of Facebook "Likes" and Twitter Retweets, our happiness is calculated by the social acceptance of others. We don't know how to measure our own happiness, because we've become so accustomed to having others measure it out for us.

~

Current research reveals that as a generation, our view of happiness differs drastically from that of our parents and, certainly, our grandparents. A 2010 psychological experiment, carried out by researchers at the University of Pennsylvania, investigated the shifting types of happiness that occur over a lifespan. The experiment, which analyzed more than 12 million personal blogs, surveys, and laboratory results, demonstrates that the meaning of happiness differs across generations:

> When a 20-year-old and a 60-year-old express feeling "happy," they are likely feeling different things. When individuals are young, they primarily experience happiness as feeling excited; however, as they get older, they come to experience happiness more as feeling peaceful. Furthermore, an age-related increase in focus on the present moment appears to drive this shift. (Mogilner 396)

Perhaps this has always been the case, and shouldn't be surprising—as people age, we can assume that what matters to them and makes them happy will invariably shift. And, as such, perhaps we shouldn't worry that Generation Y's definition of happiness seems to be connected to the fleeting excitement associated with quantifying the number of "friends" or "Likes" we have. Yet what *is* troublesome is how Generation Y recognizes (or doesn't) recognize happiness in others. A new research study executed

Duan 9

at Stanford University shows that current college-age students do not know how to read happiness in their peers. Alex Jordan, the psychology graduate student who conducted the experiment, recorded his participants' miscalculations of happiness in others. He discovered: "...a sample of 140 Stanford students [were] unable to accurately gauge others' happiness even when they were evaluating the moods of people they were close to—friends, roommates and people they were dating" (Copeland 1). Jordan's study only surveyed college students, leaving us to question whether an older population would achieve the same outcome. Still, the results are disconcerting. Why can't we figure out when people of our own age—people who we should connect the *easiest* with—are happy? Perhaps this effect is due to our lack of physical interactions with one another. By sending one another smiley faces and Facebook Friend requests online, we've developed a lack of awareness about tangible friendships, forgetting what a true LOL really looks like outside the computer screen. Instead, our focus has adjusted to view happiness *online*, through belonging in a technology-dependent community.

It can be said that by seeking happiness in public recognition, Generation Y is diminishing its own definition of joy, re-shaping "happiness" to mean "self-validation." But is this ultimately as gloomy of an ending as it appears to be? After all, as we grow with our gadgets, so does the rest of the world. Our dependence upon technology has molded an evolving society—one that communicates more than ever before, one that has multiple networks and access points, one that isn't limited by geography. While we fix ourselves inside online commentary, we also create new modes and models for expression. The Internet makes room for more voices to be deemed significant, and heard. At its core, our desire to belong within a community can be seen as a worthwhile one, not just a desperate need to fit in. Groups can enhance our own value, giving us the support networks that we need, and allowing us to learn more about those around us—and ourselves. For as we update our Twitter statuses, we are essentially giving others more opportunities to better understand us, and vice-versa.

So, yes, there are very real risks inherent in how we interact with our new technology. And maybe Generation Y needs to break out of its technology bubble from time to time to find *other* ways of feeling happy. But perhaps we can also view our relationship and use of technology as an opportunity—an opportunity to reflect our joy as a complex, dynamic element of our lives, not something that can be mapped out on a flat scale. Perhaps we might even find ways to be happier than our predecessors have ever been, because we are unafraid and more aware of our own growth on the screen.

continued

Works Cited

Arnett, Jeffrey Jensen. "The Psychology Of Globalization." *American Psychologist* 57.10 (2002): 774-83. *PsycARTICLES*. Web. 21 Nov. 2011.

Arora, Vishal. "Would Bhutan's Happiness Index Work in Britain?" *The Guardian*. 14 Apr. 2011. Web. 21 Nov. 2011.

Centre for Bhutan Studies. "Results of the Second Nationwide 2010 Survey on Gross National Happiness." *Gross National Happiness*. The Centre for Bhutan Studies, 25 Jan. 2011. Web. 4 Dec. 2011. <http://www.grossnationalhappiness.com/>.

Copeland, Libby. "The Anti-Social Network." *Slate Magazine*. Slate Magazine. 26 Jan. 2011. Web. 21 Nov. 2011.

Deresiewicz, William. "Generation Sell." *New York Times: Sunday Review* 12 Nov. 2011: SR1+. Print.

Ko, H-C, and F-Y Kuo. "Can Blogging Enhance Subjective Well-being through Self-disclosure?" *CyberPsychology & Behavior* 12.1 (2008): 75-79. Print.

Michaud, Ellen. "Sleep To Be Sexy, Smart, and Slim." *Reader's Digest* Apr. 2008: 140-49.

Mogilner, Cassie, Sepandar D. Kamvar, and Jennifer Aaker. "The Shifting Meaning of Happiness." *Social Psychological and Personality Science* 2.4 (2011): 395-402. Print.

Rosenbloom, Stephanie. "But Will It Make You Happy?" *New York Times* 8 Aug. 2010: B1. Print.

Stratton, Allegra. "Happiness Index to Gauge Britain's National Mood." *The Guardian* 14 Nov. 2010. Web. 27 Nov. 2011.

Streib, Lauren. "Black Friday Breakdown." *Newsweek* 26 Nov. 2011: 25. Print.

Tomlinson, John. *Globalization and Culture*. Chicago: University of Chicago, 1999. Print.

Twenge, Jean M. *Generation Me: Why Today's Young Americans Are More Confident, Assertive, Entitled–and More Miserable than Ever before*. New York: Free Press, 2006. Print.

Weil, Andrew. "Don't Let Chaos Get You Down." *Newsweek* 10 Nov. 2011: 9-10. Print.

Weinschenk, Susan. "100 Things You Should Know About People: #8 — Dopamine Makes You Addicted To Seeking Information." *What Makes Them Click*. N.p., 7 Nov. 2009. Web. 4 Dec. 2011. <http://www.whatmakesthemclick.net/2009/11/07/100-things-you-should-know-about-people-8-dopamine-makes-us-addicted-to-seeking-information/>.

U.S. Travel and Tourism Industries. Office of Travel and Tourism Industries, 1 Jan. 2011. Web. 03 Dec. 2011. <http://tinet.ita.doc.gov/> .

Learning from other Writers (Duan)

1. Duan opens the revision of her essay with a personal anecdote about being late for class. How does this new beginning change the way a reader approaches her essay? How does the introductory anecdote frame the subsequent analysis? What does the essay gain from this addition?

2. How would you describe the tone of Duan's essay? Has the tone changed from one draft to the next? If so, how? Where?

3. In the revision, Duan divides her investigation into three sections. What is the function of each section? How are the sections distinct from one another? How do they work together?

4. Duan adds several scenes to the revision of her essay. How do her scenes serve as evidence to support her argument?

5. Compare the Works Cited pages of both drafts of this essay. What new sources have been added? Where and how have these new sources been incorporated into the revision?

6. How has the writer changed the ending of her essay? In what way do you see an evolution in Duan's thinking about her subject, as evidenced by this conclusion? Is she simply putting a happy face on what otherwise might seem like a depressing analysis of her generation's dependence on new technologies, or is she illuminating the often-overlooked benefits of social networking? In short: what is the *significance* of Duan's conclusion?

AUTHOR BIOGRAPHIES

Tamar Adler (1977 –) grew up in suburban New York in the one house on her block heated by a wood stove instead of central heat. She cared more about books than food so was startled to learn, as a 26-year-old editor at *Harper's Magazine*, that she was meant to be a chef. Her younger brother was, too, which laid the groundwork for the long feud she documents in her award-winning essay "Sibling Rivalry at the Stove." After running a restaurant attached to an organic farm in Athens, Georgia, then cooking at Chez Panisse in Berkeley, California, Adler returned to the northeast to write *An Everlasting Meal*, published by Scribner in 2011. She now reads and writes and cooks, and speaks about reading and writing and cooking.

Sherman Alexie (1966 –) is an acclaimed novelist, poet, filmmaker, and writer of short fiction. Two of his most recent books are *Face*, poetry from Hanging Loose Press, and *War Dances*, poems and stories from Grove Press. Together with Chris Eyre, he wrote the screenplay for the movie *Smoke Signals*, which was based on his short story "This is What it Means to Say Phoenix, Arizona." The movie won two awards at the 1998 Sundance Film Festival and was released internationally by Miramax Films. He grew up on the Spokane Indian reservation and now lives in Seattle.

Steve Amick (1964 –) is the author of *The Lake, the River & the Other Lake* and *Nothing But a Smile*, both Michigan Notable Books. He received a BA from St. Lawrence University and an MFA in creative writing from George Mason University. His short stories have appeared in *Playboy, The Southern Review, Michigan Quarterly Review, Story*, and *McSweeney's*, as well as in various anthologies and on National Public Radio. He lives in Ann Arbor, where he was born, with his wife and son, and teaches in the Northwestern MFA writing workshop.

Christopher Bakken (1967 –) is the author of two books of poetry: *Goat Funeral*, which was awarded the Helen C. Smith Memorial Prize by the Texas Institute of Letters for the best book of poetry published in 2006; and *After Greece*, for which he was awarded the 2001 T.S. Eliot Prize in Poetry. He is also co-translator of *The Lions' Gate: Selected*

Poems of Titos Patrikios. His poems, essays, and translations have appeared in *The Paris Review, Ploughshares, Gettysburg Review, Parnassus: Poetry in Review,* and *Odyssey Magazine*. His recipe for Greek island lamb burgers with feta won *Food and Wine*'s August burger competition. He is an Associate Professor of English at Allegheny College, and his book *Honey, Olives, Octopus: Adventures at the Greek Table* will be published by University of California Press in 2013.

Charles Baxter (1947 –) is the author of five novels, five collections of short stories, three collections of poetry, and two collections of essays on fiction: *Burning Down the House* and *The Art of Subtext: Beyond Plot*. He has also edited several anthologies on the craft of writing. "The Chaos Machine" originally appeared in *The Believer*. His novel *The Feast of Love* was a fiction finalist for the 2001 National Book Award and became a major motion picture in 2007. From 1989 to 2002, he was a member of the MFA faculty at the University of Michigan. He is a regular contributor to *The New York Review of Books* and now teaches at the University of Minnesota in Minneapolis, his hometown.

Eula Biss (1977 –) received a BA in nonfiction writing from Hampshire College and an MFA in nonfiction writing from the University of Iowa. She has published two books: *The Balloonists* (2002) and *Notes from No Man's Land* (2009), which received the Graywolf Press Nonfiction Prize and the National Book Critics Circle Award for criticism. Her work has been recognized by a Pushcart Prize, a Rona Jaffe Writers' Award, and a 21st Century Award from the Chicago Public Library, and she has received a Guggenheim Fellowship and a Howard Foundation Fellowship. Her essays have appeared in *The Believer, Gulf Coast, Columbia, Ninth Letter, North American Review, Bellingham Review, Seneca Review,* and *Harper's*. She teaches writing at Northwestern University.

Mike Bunn (1974 –) was born and raised in McMinnville, Oregon, then left home for college in California. After moving to London, England, and working in the West End's famous Palace Theater for six months, he relocated to Austin, Texas, where he spent two years writing and working odd jobs. He holds an MFA in creative writing from the University of Pittsburgh and a PhD from the Joint Program in English & Education at the University of Michigan. He is a full-time faculty member of the Writing Program at the University of Southern California.

Nicholas Carr (1959 –) is most recently the author of *The Shallows: What the Internet Is Doing to Our Brains,* which was a Pulitzer Prize nominee and a *New York Times* bestseller. He has written for *The Guardian, The Atlantic, The New York Times, The Wall Street Journal, Wired, The Times of London, The New Republic,* and *The Financial Times*. His essay "Is Google Making Us Stupid?" has also appeared in *The Best American Science and Nature Writing 2009, The Best Spiritual Writing 2010,* and *The Best Technology Writing 2009*. He writes the popular blog Rough Type (http://www.roughtype.com/) and holds a BA from Dartmouth College and an MA in English and American Literature and Language from Harvard University.

Frank L. Cioffi (1951 –) is the author of *Formula Fiction?: An Anatomy of American Science Fiction, 1930-39* (1982) and *The Imaginative Argument: A Practical Manifesto for Writers* (2005). His work also has appeared in various journals, including *Narrative, The Chronicle of Higher Education, and The Journal of English Teaching Techniques.* He has received awards from the National Endowment for the Humanities and from the Council for the International Exchange of Scholars and has taught at Indiana University, Eastern New Mexico University, The University of Gdansk, Central Washington University, Princeton University, Bard College, and Scripps College. Currently, he is Writing Director at Baruch College in New York.

Bernard Cooper (1951 –) is an O. Henry Prize–winning fiction writer, also known for his memoirs: *Maps to Anywhere* (1990), which won the PEN/Ernest Hemingway Award; *Truth Serum* (1996); and *The Bill from My Father: A Memoir* (2006). His work has appeared in *Harper's Magazine, GQ,* and *The Paris Review,* and in several volumes of *The Best American Essays.* He has taught at Antioch/Los Angeles and at the UCLA Writer's Program. Currently, he is an art critic for *Los Angeles Magazine.*

Meghan Daum (1970 –) is the author of a novel, *The Quality of Life Report* (a *New York Times* Notable book of 2003), and a collection of essays, *My Misspent Youth* (2001), in which "Music Is My Bag" (originally published in *Harper's*) appears. She was born in California but grew up on the East Coast, earning her undergraduate degree from Vassar and an MFA in creative writing from Columbia. She is a columnist for the *Los Angeles Times* and has published nonfiction in *The New Yorker, The Believer, GQ,* and *Vogue.* She can also be heard on National Public Radio's *Morning Edition* and *This American Life.*

Joan Didion (1934 –) is the mother of the personal, political essay. She appeared on the literary scene in the 1960s and ever since then has been a nonfiction powerhouse, pumping out precise, elegant prose on everything from 1960s counterculture to Central American politics to her own private grief. As of 2006, all of Didion's nonfiction books, including the National Book Award winner *The Year of Magical Thinking,* are available in the single volume *We Tell Ourselves Stories in Order to Live.* Her memoir *Blue Nights,* about the death of her daughter, was published in 2011. A sixth-generation Californian, she now lives in New York.

Carlina Duan (1993 –) is currently a student at the University of Michigan, where she balances schoolwork and poetry slams with Frisbee playing and baking. She is one of the founding editors of Ann Arbor's Red Beard Press, a youth-driven publishing company. Duan was a recipient of the 2012 University of Michigan Hopwood Underclassmen Poetry and Non-Fiction Awards. Her essay "If You're Happy And You Know It, LOL" was awarded the University of Michigan English Department's 2012 Feinberg Family First-Year Writing Prize.

Andre Dubus III (1959 –) began school at Bradford College, where his father, the late author Andre Dubus II, taught. After dropping out of a PhD program at the University of Wisconsin, he worked as an actor, a carpenter, a private investigator, a bartender, and a bounty hunter while he wrote on the side. Now a successful novelist and short story writer, Dubus teaches at the University of Massachusetts Lowell. His novel *House of Sand and Fog* was a 1999 National Book Award Finalist and is now a motion picture. His most recent book is *Townie: A Memoir* (2011).

Barbara Ehrenreich (1941 –) sees no conflict between her roles as journalist and activist. In addition to being a full-time journalist and author, she fights for peace, women's rights, fair health-care, and economic justice. You can find her essays and opinion pieces in *The New York Times, Harper's,* and *Time* (where she is a contributing writer), and at her blog, www.barbaraehrenreich.com. The essay in this anthology began as a feature for *Harper's* on the effects of the 1996 Welfare Reform Act and became the bestselling book *Nickel-and-Dimed: On (Not) Getting by in America* (2001). She is also the author of several other books—most recently, *Bright-sided: How Positive Thinking is Undermining America* (2009).

Nora Ephron (1941 – 2012) received Academy Award nominations for Best Original Screenplay for the movies *When Harry Met Sally, Silkwood,* and *Sleepless in Seattle,* which she directed. She also was nominated for Best Adapted Screenplay for *Julie and Julia,* which contrasts the life of Julia Child and a young New Yorker named Julie who attempted to cook all the recipes in Julia Child's *Mastering the Art of French Cooking.* Her final book, *I Remember Nothing,* contains her humorous and poignant reflections on aging. Her strategy for forgetfulness was to keep lists of things she refused to know anything about in the first place, such as the Kardashians, Twitter, and all Housewives.

Beth Ann Fennelly (1971 –) lives in Oxford, MS, with her husband, the novelist Tom Franklin, with whom she has collaborated on one novel and three children. Fennelly's previous publications include three books of poetry and a book of essays on motherhood called *Great with Child.* She has been awarded a Pushcart, a grant from the National Endowment for the Arts, a United States Artists Grant, and a Fulbright to Brazil. She directs the MFA Program at the University of Mississippi, where she was the 2011 Liberal Arts Teacher of the Year.

Caitlin Fey (1992 –) is a student at the University of Michigan studying Environmental Science and Anthropology. In her first year at Michigan she received the William J. Brantrom Freshman Prize for being in the top 5% of her class. She plans on graduating in 2014.

Caitlin Flanagan (1961 –) is a contributing editor at *The Atlantic* and a former staff writer at *The New Yorker.* She was born and raised in Berkeley, California, and studied Art History at the University of Virginia, where she received her BA and MA. She is the author of *To Hell with All That: Loving and Loathing Our Inner Housewife* (2006) and, most recently, *Girl Land* (2012), which explores the lives of adolescent girls.

V.V. Ganeshananthan (1980 –) teaches fiction and non-fiction writing in the MFA program at the University of Michigan, where she is the Zell Visiting Professor of Creative Writing. Her debut novel, *Love Marriage,* was long-listed for the Orange Prize. Much of her work is set in or relates to Sri Lanka and its diaspora communities. Her full name has 24 letters and ten syllables. Her last name is pronounced Gun-ay-SHAN-an-than.

Atul Gawande (1965 –) is a surgeon and public health researcher who practices general and endocrine surgery at Brigham and Women's Hospital in Boston and teaches surgery at the Harvard Medical School. He has been a staff writer for *The New Yorker* since 1998 and has written three bestselling nonfiction books, including *Complications,* which was a finalist for the National Book Award.

Malcolm Gladwell (1963 –) is a prolific journalist, cultural critic, and the author of four *New York Times* bestselling books, including *The Tipping Point: How Little Things Make a Big Difference* (2000); *Blink: The Power of Thinking Without Thinking* (2005); and *Outliers: The Story of Success* (2008). His fourth book, *What the Dog Saw* (2009), is a compilation of essays published in *The New Yorker.* He graduated from the University of Toronto, Trinity College, with a degree in history. He lives in New York City.

Lucy Grealy (1963 – 2002) attended Sarah Lawrence College and received her MFA in creative writing from the Iowa Writers' Workshop, where she met fellow writer Ann Patchett. Their friendship is the subject of Patchett's memoir *Truth & Beauty* (2005). Grealy struggled with facial disfigurement due to cancer for most of her life, as chronicled in her 1994 memoir *Autobiography of a Face.* She died in 2002.

Christine Hartzler (1975 –) holds an MFA in Poetry from the University of Michigan. She has worked for Oxford University Press, both here and across the pond, since 1998, editing and writing elementary ESL materials. She has two cats, a toddler, and a husband. Her HP (that's "hit points," for the uninitiated) is really, really high: she hasn't slept much since October 2010, but she's still alive.

John Hersey (1914 – 1993) was born in China and moved to the United States when he was ten. After graduating from Yale and Cambridge, he became the Far East correspondent for *Time,* and during WWII he also wrote for *Life* and *The New Yorker.* As a war journalist, Hersey accompanied the U.S. Army on the invasions of Italy and Sicily, and the novel inspired by his experiences there, *A Bell for Adano* (1944), won a Pulitzer Prize. After the U.S. dropped the atomic bomb on Hiroshima, Hersey was commissioned by *The New Yorker* to write a series of articles about the decimated city. He chose to demonstrate the effects of the atomic explosion by following six survivors, and the resulting pieces were so powerful that *The New Yorker* dedicated an entire issue to printing them (August 31, 1946). The material was published as the book *Hiroshima* later that year.

Ann Hodgman (1956 –) is the author of humor books, cookbooks, and more than forty children's books. Her work has also appeared in *The Atlantic Monthly, The New Yorker,* and *Salon.* "No Wonder They Call Me a Bitch" did not appear in her regular food column but was first published in *Spy* Magazine, where Hodgman was a Contributing Editor; later it was selected for *The Best American Essays of 1990.* A graduate of Harvard College, she lives and writes in Connecticut with her husband, two children, and many pets.

Anne Lamott (1954 –) is the bestselling author of *Bird by Bird* (1995), a book on the writing life, from which "Shitty First Drafts" is taken. She also has written seven novels, including *Crooked Little Heart* (1998), *Blue Shoe* (2003), and *Imperfect Birds* (2011), and five works of nonfiction, including *Operating Instructions* (2005). Her most recent book, *Some Assembly Required* (2012), is about her son becoming a father at the age of 19. She is a frequent contributor to the online magazine Salon.com.

Phillip Lopate (1943 –) has written novels, collections of poetry, and book-length works of film criticism, but his forte arguably is the personal essay, as evinced by the following collections: *Bachelorhood* (1981), *Against Joie de Vivre* (1989), and *Portrait of My Body* (1996). Lopate is also the editor of the anthology *The Art of the Personal Essay* (1994) and the author of the Phillip Lopate reader, *Getting Personal* (2003). He holds the John Cranford Adams Chair at Hofstra University and teaches in the MFA programs at Columbia, The New School, and Bennington.

Michael Lowenthal (1969 –) is the author of the novels *Charity Girl* (2007), *Avoidance* (2002), and *The Same Embrace* (1998), and his short stories have been published in *Tin House, Southern Review, Kenyon Review,* and Esquire.com. His nonfiction has appeared in *The New York Times Magazine, Boston Magazine, The Washington Post,* the *Boston Globe,* and *Out,* and he has received fellowships from the Bread Loaf and Wesleyan writers' conferences, the MacDowell Colony, and the Massachusetts Cultural Council. He is also the winner of the James Duggins Outstanding Mid-Career Novelists' Prize. He studied English and comparative religion at Dartmouth College and now lives in Boston and teaches creative writing in the low-residency MFA program at Lesley University.

James McBride (1957 –) is a writer and musician. His debut novel, *Miracle at St. Anna,* was translated into a movie directed by Spike Lee, and McBride wrote the script for the film. He is a former staff writer for the *Boston Globe, People,* and *The Washington Post,* and his work has appeared in *Essence, Rolling Stone,* and *The New York Times.* In addition to being a well-published writer, he is a saxophonist and has written music and lyrics for Anita Baker, Grover Washington, Jr., Gary Burton, and the PBS television character "Barney." He is a native New Yorker and is currently a Distinguished Writer in Residence at New York University.

John McPhee (1931 –) has been a staff writer at *The New Yorker* since 1965 and has published 28 books of nonfiction. One of the founding fathers of the New Journalism, he is famous for rendering complex, specialized material in readable and literary ways. *Annals of the Former World*, McPhee's tetralogy on geology, was published in a single volume in 1998 and awarded the Pulitzer Prize in 1999. Today, he teaches nonfiction at Princeton University, his alma mater.

Michele Morano (1964 –) has received awards from the Rona Jaffe Foundation, the MacDowell Colony, the American Association of University Women, the Magazine Association of the Southeast, the *Crab Orchard Review*, and the Illinois Arts Council. Her essays have appeared in *Georgia Review, Missouri Review, Under the Sun*, and *Fourth Genre: Contemporary Writers of/on Creative Nonfiction*. "Grammar Lessons: In the Subjunctive Mood" was originally published in *Crab Orchard Review* and then reprinted in *Best American Essays 2006*; it also was included in her book of essays, *Grammar Lessons: Translating a Life in Spain* (2007). She received her PhD in English and her MFA in nonfiction writing from the University of Iowa. She is Associate Professor of English at DePaul University in Chicago.

Donald M. Murray (1924 – 2006) was a Pulitzer prize-winning journalist and Professor Emeritus of English at the University of New Hampshire, where he taught for 26 years and helped establish a graduate program in Composition Studies. He wrote several books on the art of writing and teaching, such as *The Craft of Revision*, recently released as an Anniversary Edition (2012). For 20 years he wrote the "Over 60" column for the *Boston Globe*. He died in 2006.

Judith Ortiz Cofer (1952 –) was born in Hormigueros in Puerto Rico, but soon after her birth, her father, who was in the U.S. Navy, was transferred to New Jersey. Though her family often traveled back and forth to Puerto Rico, Ortiz Cofer attended school in Paterson and later in Augusta, Georgia. She holds a BA in English from Augusta College and an MA from Floridan Atlantic University. A poet and fiction writer as well as an essayist, she has been honored with a long list of awards, including a nomination for the Pulitzer Prize for her early novel *The Line of the Sun*. Her work has appeared in magazines such as the *Georgia Review, Kenyon Review, Southern Review, and Glamour* and has been anthologized in *Best American Essays 1991, The Pushcart Prize*, and the *O. Henry Prize Stories*. She is currently the Regents' and Franklin Professor of English and Creative Writing at the University of Georgia. Her most recent novel is *If I Could Fly* (2011).

George Orwell (1903 – 1950), christened Eric Arthur Blair, was born in British India and then moved to England in 1904. When it came time to attend university, Blair was unable to pay or to win a scholarship, so he joined the Indian Imperial Police in Burma, where he learned to hate imperialism. Blair returned to England, resigned from the service, and struggled for many years to support himself before changing his name and earning a reputation as a journalist. Today, we remember Orwell as one of the finest essayists of the twentieth century and as the author of the acclaimed novels *Animal Farm* (1945) and *1984* (1949).

Michael Paterniti (1974 –) is a contributing editor for *GQ*, where, in addition to the essay about Leonid the giant included here, he has written about such far-ranging topics as Olympic medalists, the Al-Jazeera network, Guantanamo Bay, and the sartorial style of Italian gentlemen. He also writes for *The New York Times Magazine*. His most recent book is *Driving Mr. Albert: A Trip Across America With Einstein's Brain* (2000). He lives in Portland, Maine.

Elwood Reid (1966 –) played football for the Michigan Wolverines as an undergraduate, then went on to earn his MFA from the University of Michigan in 1996. His first novel, *If I Don't Six* (1998), describes the daily life of a Big Ten football player in scandalizing detail. Reid is also the author of the story collection *What Salmon Know* (1999) and the novels *Midnight Sun* (2000) and *D.B.* (2004). He and his wife and their five children divide their time between Montana and California, where Reid works as a scriptwriter.

Daniel Rivas (1978 –) grew up in the state of Washington and graduated with an MFA in creative writing from the University of Michigan. He won a Hopwood Award for his essay "The Master of Machines," and the piece later appeared in the literary journal *Brick*. Rivas now eats at food carts, wanders through bookstores, and writes in Portland, Oregon.

Michael Rudin (1984 –) lives a double life, juggling his writing between mercenary missions and literary ones. As the founder of Armed Mind, an advertising consultancy specializing in product narratives, his writing won gold in the 2012 Game Marketing Awards. When not penning for the man, he's crafting fiction that has been recognized with a Hopwood Award and a recent publication in the literary journal *The Collagist*. He's also written essays for *The Journal of Electronic Publishing* and *Fiction Writers Review*, where he lends a hand as director of marketing and development.

George Saunders (1958 –) is a bestselling writer of short stories, essays, novellas and children's books. His writing has appeared in *The New Yorker*, *Harper's*, *McSweeney's*, and *GQ*, among many other publications. Writing for *GQ*, he traveled to Africa with Bill Clinton. He has won the National Magazine Award for fiction several times and is the recipient of an O. Henry Prize. Both of his story collections, *CivilWarLand in Bad Decline* (1997) and *Pastoralia* (2001), were *New York Times* Notable Books. In 2006 he received a "genius grant" given by the MacArthur Foundation. He teaches in the creative writing program at Syracuse University.

David Sedaris (1956 –) has been famously funny since 1992, when National Public Radio broadcast his "Santaland Diaries" about working as a Macy's Christmas elf. Since then, Sedaris's humorous essays have appeared regularly in *The New Yorker* and frequently been presented on NPR. Four of his essay collections have been *New York Times* Bestsellers: *Naked* (1997); *Holidays on Ice* (1997); *Me Talk Pretty One Day* (2000); and *Dress Your Family in Corduroy and Denim* (2004). His most recent collection is *Squirrel Seeks Chipmunk: A Wicked Bestiary* (2012). He lives and works in Paris with his partner, Huge Hamrick.

Naomi Shihab Nye (1952 –) is a Palestinian-American poet who has lived in St. Louis and Jerusalem and now makes her home in San Antonio. Known for her poetry, lyric essays, and anthologies on the Middle East, she is the winner of four Pushcart Prizes, a Guggenheim Fellowship, and the Lavan Award from the National Academy of Poets. Her poetry collection 19 *Varieties of Gazelle* (2005) was a finalist for the 2002 National Book Award. Nye is also an award-winning writer of poetry and essays for young adults.

Zadie Smith (1975 –) is the author of three novels—*White Teeth* (2000), *Autograph Man* (2002), and *On Beauty* (2005)—and a collection of essays called *Changing My Mind: Occasional Essays* (2009). One of her pieces of advice on writing is to "try to read your own work as a stranger would read it, or even better, as an enemy would." She is widely published in such publications as *The Guardian, The New York Review of Books,* and *The New Yorker,* and she writes the "New Books" column for *Harper's.* She is a professor in the creative writing program at New York University.

John Jeremiah Sullivan (1974 –) is a contributing writer for *The New York Times Magazine* and is an editor of *The Paris Review.* He also writes for *Harper's Magazine* and the *Oxford American* and was a longtime GQ correspondent. He has twice received a National Magazine Award, as well as a Whiting Writers' Award and a Pushcart Prize. He is the author of the *Blood Horses* (2004), partly memoir, partly investigation into the history of the thoroughbred racehorse, and *Pulphead* (2011), a collection of essays. He lives in Wilmington, North Carolina.

Margaret Talbot (1961 –) has been a staff writer at *The New Yorker* since 2003. Previously, she was a contributing writer at *The New York Times Magazine* and an editor at *The New Republic.* She is the recipient of the Whiting Writers' Award and was one of the founding editors of *Lingua Franca,* a magazine that covered academic, intellectual, and literary life. In her most recent book, *The Entertainer: Magic, Movies, and My Father's Twentieth Century,* Talbot examines the rise of American popular culture through the lens of her father's career in Hollywood.

Jesmyn Ward (1977 –) is the author of the novels *Where the Line Bleeds* and *Salvage the Bones,* which won the 2011 National Book Award. Her work has appeared in *A Public Space, Oxford American,* and *The New York Times Book Review.* She received her BA from Stanford University and her MFA in Creative Writing from the University of Michigan. She is currently working on a memoir.

Philip Weiss (1956 –) is a New York journalist and essayist who has written extensively on the Clinton Administration, American Jewish life, and American-Israeli relations. He is also the author of *American Taboo: A Murder in the Peace Corps* (2004) and the blog "Mondoweiss," which covers American policy in the Middle East (at www.philipweiss. org). He co-edited *The Goldstone Report: The Legacy of the Landmark Investigation of the Gaza Conflict* (2011) with Adam Horowitz and Lizzy Ratner.

E. B. White (1899 – 1985) once said of Thoreau's *Walden*: "Every man, I think, reads one book in his life, and this one is mine." White's commemorative essay "Walden" (August 1939) first appeared in "One Man's Meat," the regular column he wrote for *Harper's Magazine* from 1938 to 1943. "Once More to the Lake" appeared there in 1941. Throughout his career, While also wrote for *The New Yorker* and *The Atlantic Monthly*. He was one of America's greatest literary stylists, a master of the essay form, and also the author of the children's classics *Stuart Little* (1945) and *Charlotte's Web* (1952). His 1959 revision of William Strunk's writing guide, *The Elements of Style*, is still widely used in composition courses. In 1978, White received a special Pulitzer citation for his letters, essays, and his body of work as a whole.

Meaghan Winter (1982 –) holds an MFA from Columbia University and is currently working on a book about people who buy and sell human hair. She lives in Manhattan.